ALTERNATIVE TRAVEL DIRECTORY

The Complete Guide to Traveling, Studying & Living Overseas

GENERAL EDITORS

Nicole Rosenleaf Ritter
Clayton A. Hubbs

CONTRIBUTING EDITORS

Gina Doggett, Susan Griffith, Cynthia Harriman, Deborah McLaren,
William Nolting, Susan Sygall, Kathy Widing, Arline K. Wills

Transitions Abroad Publishing
Amherst, Massachusetts
http://www.TransitionsAbroad.com/

CONTRIBUTING EDITORS
William E. J. Doane (Internet Resources), Gina Doggett (Chapter 16),
Susan Griffith (Chapter 9), Cynthia Harriman (Chapter 5),
Deborah McLaren (Chapter 7), William Nolting (Chapter 10),
Susan Sygall (Chapter 6), Kathy Widing (Chapter 1), Arline K. Wills (Chapter 3)

TYPESETTING
Janis G. Sokol

Content Engineer
William E. J. Doane

COVER DESIGN
Rick Schneider

COVER PHOTO
Ingrid Marn Wood

PREFACE TO THE SIXTH EDITION

The *Alternative Travel Directory,* produced by the editors of *Transitions Abroad* magazine annually since 1993, is a one-volume selection of the most essential practical information on the overseas alternatives to "packaged" tourism: independent travel, ecotravel, educational travel and study, and living overseas. Opportunities for working overseas, along with a selection of placement and training programs, are collected separately in the biannual *Work Abroad: The Complete Guide to Finding a Job Overseas.* Ordering information is on page 65.

The growth in the number and variety of listings in each new volume of the *Alternative Travel Directory* indicates a burgeoning interest in avoiding the international tourist trails and traps that tend to isolate travelers from the people and culture of the host country. Readers of *Transitions Abroad* magazine are among the growing number of visitors to other countries who recognize the enormous rewards that come from seeing the world up close and from the hosts' perspective.

For a variety of reasons, our readers are spending longer periods of time abroad. Some go as "working travelers," who pay for their extended journeys with short-term jobs. Others go abroad to find more permanent positions in the new global economy. Everyone from diplomats to students preparing to spend a year in Europe will benefit from the wealth of tools for overseas travel, study, and living found in the *Alternative Travel Directory.*

To stay up to date on all the latest practical information on work, study, independent travel, and living abroad subscribe to *Transitions Abroad* magazine. For an examination copy call 800-293-0373 or visit our continuously updated web site, [www.TransitionsAbroad.com], where you can also sign-up for our free email newsletter, *TA eNews.*

Medical Insurance & Assistance

HealthCare Global

provides $100,000 medical coverage for Americans **traveling or studying** abroad for up to six months.

MedHelp Worldwide

provides $500,000 medical coverage for Americans **living or studying** overseas for up to one year.

Both MedHelp Worldwide and HealthCare Global provide coverage for hospitalization expenses, doctor's office visits, prescription medicines, etc. and medical evacuation to a better hospital or back to a hospital near your home in the U.S.A.

The policies also include the services of a worldwide network of assistance centers. A toll-free or collect telephone call puts you in contact with an English speaking assistance specialist, a service that will be a tremendous comfort in any kind of emergency!

Wallach & COMPANY, INC.

(800) 237-6615 or (540) 687-3166

107 West Federal Street, Post Office Box 480
Middleburg, Virginia 20118-0480 U.S.A.

Fax: (540) 687-3172   E-mail: info@wallach.com   www.wallach.com

In 1977 I launched *Transitions Abroad*, a magazine of practical information for independent travelers who go abroad to live, work, study, or travel for reasons other than those connected with mass tourism. The title "Transitions" was meant to suggest the changes that occur when travelers leave home behind and truly immerse themselves in a new environment.

Many of the first writers for *Transitions Abroad* were students, just back from a semester or year of travel and study abroad. Writing in the first issue, Gary Langer, then a student at the Univ. of New Hampshire, described staying at the Jerusalem guesthouse of an elderly Armenian called Mr. A. Those who sought out Mr. A were travelers, not tourists:

"Travelers and tourists, the distinction is simple: Tourists are those who bring their homes with them wherever they go, and apply them to whatever they see. They are closed to experience outside of the superficial. Travelers left home at home, bringing only themselves and a desire to see and hear and feel and take in and grow and learn. Tourists do not go to Mr. A's. They would not appreciate him, nor he them. And the main reason travelers go to Mr. A's is for Mr. A."

Taken out of context, Langer's contrast between travelers and tourists may sound a bit exaggerated and smug (after all, we are all in one sense tourists when we travel to another country). But the distinction has long been made between those who seem to travel more to confirm what they already know than to gain new understanding of themselves and of others. One thinks of Mark Twain's 1860s satirical novel, *Innocents Abroad*, on American travelers who brought so much cultural (and other) baggage with them that they were only "In-a-Sense" Abroad.

The stereotypical tourist—whether of Twain's time or ours—doesn't so much abandon his own familiar environment for the sake of engaging with a new one as have himself transported to a foreign place, taking with him as much of his familiar environment as possible. He views the unfamiliar people, places, and culture through the windows or walls of the familiar and pretends that he is still at home. If he must speak to the natives he does so loudly, thereby giving them every opportunity to understand him.

The modern traveler, on the other hand, is increasingly interested in experiencing new people, places, and cultures on their own terms and precisely because they are unfamiliar. The transition is not simply a passage from one place to another; it is a change in perspective and perception.

Interest in alternative travel, or travel for enrichment, grew rapidly in the 1970s and 1980s, in part a result of international air travel becoming affordable to a much larger group of people. In 1989 *Travel & Leisure* magazine commissioned Louis Harris Associates, Inc. to survey thousands of traveling Americans to find out why they traveled. To their surprise, the interviewers found that three travelers out of four took their last trip to improve their minds, to gain new perspectives, and to meet new people. Asked to name their dream vacation, only 10 percent named a place in the U.S. The conclusion of the pollsters was that international travel for personal growth was increasing more rapidly than any other form of nonbusiness travel.

In 1991 Arthur Frommer wrote: "After 30 years of writing standard guidebooks, I began to see that most of the vacation journeys undertaken by Americans were trivial and bland. . . . Travel in all price ranges is scarcely worth the effort unless it is associated with people, with learning and ideas. To have meaning at all, travel must involve an encounter with new and different outlooks and beliefs. . . . At its best, travel should challenge our preconceptions and most cherished views, cause us to rethink our assumptions, shake us a bit, make us broader-minded and more understanding."

"Not to have met the people of other cultures in a nontouristic setting," Frommer concludes in *The New World of Travel,* "is not to have lived in this century."

Detailing the ways to meet people of other cultures in a nontourist setting has been the major purpose of *Transitions Abroad* since its beginning 23 years ago. In each issue of the magazine we select and publish the most important sources of information on alternative travel—including work abroad—along with a selection of programs and other opportunities for the curious and independent-minded.

We revise and update this information continuously. At the end of each year we bring it all together in one volume: the *Alternative Travel Directory.* The three sections— Independent Travel, Study Abroad, and Living Abroad—contain our selection of the major alternatives to mass tourism. (A volume on work abroad is published separately.)

The experience of travel involves a continuum or a progression from the familiar to the new. On the one extreme are the unadventurous packaged tourists or mass tourists described above who spend a good portion of their trip in a literal bubble being whisked along on a guided tour, usually in an air-conditioned bus. They make virtually no decisions on their own and are taken, on a fixed schedule, from one attraction (often man-made for their benefit) to another. They observe and photograph but rarely actively experience their surroundings.

On the other extreme are those relatively few travelers who avoid the tourist scene altogether and strike out on their own. They are on no fixed schedule or itinerary and settle where they like for as long as they like, finding casual work when necessary to cover their modest expenses or to pay for moving on.

Between these two extremes are those of us in that growing group of travelers who like to go on our own, often to pursue a particular interest, but only after enough planning and preparation to insure that our limited time and money will be well spent. We don't want to be bound to a group or have our experience spoiled by hordes of tourists; on the other hand, we want to be comfortable and feel sufficiently secure to accomplish our goals.

In recent years the most rapid area of growth in alternative travel has been ecotourism. As contributing editors Deborah McLaren writes in the introduction to Responsible Travel Resources (Chapter 7), "As people around the planet become more concerned about their environment, more curious about people of different cultures, and more willing to think differently, travel is changing."

Are we traveling responsibly? Or do we, by the very act of flying to a faraway place, contribute to the destruction of its environment and culture? The editors of *Transitions Abroad* and of this volume are proud that for more than 20 years we have provided readers with the best and most comprehensive information on ways to travel responsibly, that is on ways to preserve the world's natural and human environment.

Independent Travel Abroad. The travel resources and programs in the first nine chapters are grouped under the heading of independent or "life-seeing travel." The latter term comes from the concept of the Scandinavian School for Life (adult continuing education schools to enrich the mind, sometimes but not always to teach a vocational skill) which we described in the first issue of *Transitions Abroad* in 1977. Axel Dessau, director of the Danish Tourist Office, is credited with applying the concept to tourism. Visitors to Denmark are able to engage in activities that match their particular interests—for example, educators may visit schools and stay in the homes of teachers.

The fact that similar home and hospitality exchanges are proliferating throughout the world–as more of us travel from one foreign host's home to another rather than to tourist hotels–is just one indication of the increasing desire on the part of international travelers for an authentic engagement with the local people. For more and more travelers, including the readers of *Transitions Abroad*, life-seeing has replaced sightseeing.

Chapter 1 is a country-by-country guide to the best guidebooks and background reading to consult as you begin to make your overseas travel plans. Chapter 2 lists the best opportunities and resources for combining a trip overseas with your interest or hobby, say by taking Italian cooking classes in Tuscany or birdwatching in the Amazon. Chapters 3 through 6 cover the best travel information resources and selected programs for seniors, for families traveling with children, and for persons with disabilities. Chapters 7 and 8 cover the major resources and programs exemplifying culturally and environmentally responsible travel, the fastest growing of all forms of alternative travel. Chapter 9 lists volunteer programs around the world for travelers who want to work and live with local people while contributing to the host community.

Study Abroad. In Chapter 10 we list the most useful resources for learning opportunities abroad. Whereas all travel is at least potentially educational, the programs and resources for people of all ages described in chapters 12 through 15 are structured learning experiences. Those organized for undergraduates carry academic credit. Older adults are welcome to take part in most academic programs for no credit, usually at a reduced price.

Living Abroad. In Chapter 16 Gina Doggett, herself an expatriate American living in Paris, has helped put together an incredibly comprehensive list of where to find everything you need to know about living abroad: organizations for Americans abroad (Democrats, Republicans, women, etc.), guides for individual countries, books on cross-cultural adjustment and health and safety and language learning, home and hospitality exchange organizations, and other publications on living abroad and reentry and retirement abroad. As in the earlier chapters, we include up-to-date email addresses and web sites where available.

Whatever your age, whatever your reason for travel, we think you'll find the overseas travel alternative you're looking for here. If not, let us know and we'll try to include it in the next issue of *Transitions Abroad* and next year's edition of the *Alternative Travel Directory*. Our address is Transitions Abroad, P.O. Box 1300, Amherst, MA 01004-1300; info@TransitionsAbroad.com; [http://www.TransitionsAbroad.com/].

Clay Hubbs
Amherst, MA
December 1999

INDEPENDENT TRAVEL

More people are traveling with a purpose other than sightseeing—whether it be teaching English in Korea, volunteering in Guatemala, cooking in Tuscany, or learning French in Provence. Another trend is the desire of travelers to see "real life," break down barriers, and get closer to the people.

Kathy Widing, Abroad in Books Editor

One

Independent Travel
The Best Resources

Whether you intend to go abroad for a week or a month, every trip requires planning. The more you learn about your destination, the better equipped you are to embark on your adventure. We hope the extensive resources below will help you choose which road to follow. Those marked with an asterisk are particularly recommended. Happy travels!

Guidebook Series

*Access Guides (Harper Collins). Well-organized guides with informative walking routes.

*Blue Guides (W. W. Norton and Co.). Incredibly detailed British series covering history, culture, walks, driving tours, etc. New this year: Prague, Provence, Cote d'Azur.

*Cadogan Guides (Globe Pequot Press). Excellent, all-purpose guidebooks at moderate prices. New this year: Venetia and The Dolomites.

*Culture Shock! Series (Graphic Arts). Guides to customs and etiquette of various cultures. New this year: Jakarta, Ukraine, Italy, Succeed in Business: Japan, Succeed in Business: Britain, Paris at Your Door.

*Footprints Handbooks (U.S. distributor, NTC/Contemporary). The original book in the series is the old reliable *South American Handbook.* New this year: Singapore.

*Insight Guides (APA Publications). In-depth background, historical, cultural discussion with good destination information. Over 150 guides to most international destinations. Insight Pocket Guides include a fold-out map and cover over 100 locales. Insight Compact Guides have expanded beyond Europe. New this year: Kenya, Jerusalem, Shakespeare Country. New this year: Ibiza, Athens, Belfast, Bermuda, Cuba.

*Interlink, an important independent publishing house, specializes in world literature, history and politics, music, ethnic cooking, and crafts as well as world travel. Wild Guides series: Illustrated guides to the wild places in the modern world. New this year: Spain, Britain. Travellers History series: Concise historical background on cities and countries. New this year: Australia, India. In Focus Guides: Lively and thought-provoking introduction to the country's people, politics, and culture. New this year: Nicaragua, Brazil. Spectrum Guides: Lavishly illustrated guides with detailed country descriptions. New this year: Jordan. Independent Walker series: New this year: Ireland, Italy. Traveler's Wine Guides: New edition this year: Italy. Cities of the Imagination (new series): In-depth cultural, historical, and literary guides to the great cities of the world: Buenos Aires, Oxford, Mexico City.

*Let's Go Guides (St. Martin's Press). Still the best all-purpose budget guides around. Thoroughly updated annually. New this year: South Africa, Ireland, Turkey.

*Lonely Planet Guides (Lonely Planet Publications). **On a Shoestring Guides:** Ultra-low-budget guides of considerable reputation. New this year: *Europe on a Shoestring.* **Lonely Planet Country and Regional Guides:** Excellent guides for the adventurous traveler. All-purpose, all price ranges with plenty of low-cost choices. New this year: Dominican Republic and Haiti, Provence and Cote d'Azur, Corsica, Croatia. **City Guides** New this year: Rome, Barcelona, Edinburgh. **Walking/Trekking Guides** new this year: *Walking in Britain.* **Journeys:** New line of travel literature with titles on Australia, Japan, New Guinea, Syria, Jordan, Africa, Central America. **Pisces: Diving and Snorkeling Guides:** Destinations such as the Great Barrier Reef, Belize, Fiji, Cuba, Honduras, etc.

*Michelin Green Guides (Michelin Travel Publications). Comprehensive travel guides with sightseeing and trip planning information for countries, cities, and regions of Europe and beyond. New this year: Mexico/Guatemala/Belize, Alsace/Lorraine/Champagne, Amsterdam. *Michelin Red Guides are comprehensive guides to restaurants and hotels throughout Europe. **Michelin in Your Pocket Guides** are pocket-sized travel guides full of helpful information for short trips.

*Moon Travel Handbooks (Moon Publications). Provide thorough cultural, historical, and political coverage, as well as exhaustive practical information aimed at getting travelers the best value for money. New this year: Canadian Rockies.

*Rick Steves' Country Guides (John Muir). Annually updated budget travel insights by *Transitions Abroad* contributing editor on the cities and regions of Europe. Also tips on transport, lodging, and dining. New this year: Paris, London.

*Rough Guides (Penguin). Written for independent budget travelers, with a political awareness and a social and cultural sensitivity that makes them unique. New this year: Japan, Jordan, Maya world, Sydney (in mini series).

*Time Out (Penguin) From the editors of *Time Out* in London, these guides detail the practical facts of lodging and eating out as well as arts and entertainment, plus sections for students, gays, lesbians, business travelers. New this year: Moscow/St. Petersburg, Lisbon, Venice.

Around the World Program (McDonald and Woodward). Sponsored by the American Geographical Society, provides substantive introductions by authorities to single countries.

Berlitz Travel Guides (Berlitz Publishing). **Discover Series:** Good background and pre-trip information.

Bradt Guides (Globe Pequot Press). Reliable guides originating in the U.K. covering less traveled destinations for the adventurous traveler. New this year: Cape Verde Islands, Haiti, Dominican Republic.

Day Trips Series by Earl Steinbecker (Hastings House). Oriented to public transportation.

Exploring Rural Europe Series (Passport Books). Driving tours of 1 day to 1 week acquaint the traveler with the history, character, and cuisine of the region. Titles for Austria, France, England, Germany, Ireland, Greece, Portugal, Spain.

Eyewitness Guides (Dorling Kindersley Publishing). Well-designed with lots of color and illustrations, many in 3-D. Good for art and architecture. New this year: Budapest, Dublin, Australia.

Fielding's Guides (Fielding Worldwide). Good general guidebooks for all budget levels.

Fodor's Guides (Fodor's Travel Publications/Random House). **Fodor's Gold Guides** and **Pocket Guides:** The largest all-purpose series with over 100 titles covering countries, cities, and regions all over the world. **Fodor's Exploring Guides:** Well-organized guides with good maps, color photos, detailed information on sights, and lots of interesting facts. **Fodor's Citypacks:** pocket-sized guides with fold-out maps. **Up CLOSE** guides: For budget and adventurous travelers oriented to getting off the beaten path. New this year: Central America.

Frommer's Guides (Macmillan). Solid, all-purpose favorite of many travelers. Frommer's comprehensive series covers all price ranges from deluxe to inexpensive for several countries and regions. The **Dollar-a-Day** series is more budget oriented. City guides available for many major cities. New this year: Denmark, Sweden, Southeast Asia. **Walking Tour** series includes Paris, London, Berlin, Venice, Tokyo, Spain's Favorite Cities. **Food Lover's Companion** series includes: France, Italy. **Frommer's Irreverent Guides** include: Amsterdam, London, Paris, Virgin Islands. **Frommer's Driving Tours** present interesting regional driving routes with lots of tips and sightseeing information.

Karen Brown's Country Inns and Itineraries Series (Random House). Offers some great choices throughout Western Europe. Primary selections, organized as part of an itinerary, can be quite expensive but there are usually moderate and sometimes low-cost alternatives as well.

Knopf Guides (Knopf). Heavy focus on art and architecture with lots of photos, drawings, and plans. New this year: Rome, Rio de Janeiro.

Let's Go Map Guides (St. Martin's Press). Combined guidebook and folding laminated maps from the budget travel leaders. Maps for Amsterdam, Berlin, Florence, London, Madrid, Paris, Prague, Rome.

Maverick Guides (Pelican Publishing). General guidebooks covering accommodations, sights, background, etc.

National Geographic Traveler (National Geographic Books). Beautifully presented with good background. Well-written articles with excellent maps and photographs. Great Britain, France, Canada, London, Paris. New series.

Nelles Guides (Seven Hills Books). Cover culture and history plus basics on lodgings, sights, and getting around. Good maps. New this year: Canary Islands, Greek Islands, Costa Rica, Sweden, Poland.

Passport Regional Guides (Passport Books). This series divides countries and continents into areas and provides detailed information: Africa, China, France, Italy, Indonesia, India, Great Britain, Malaysia, Portugal, Russia.

Sierra Club Adventure Guides (Sierra Club Books). Fine guides to every adventure under the sun.

Travelers' Tales (O'Reilly and Assoc.). Not regular guidebooks with sights and lodgings but a collection of travelers' tales from experienced travelers. New this year: Japan.

Treasures and Pleasures of. . .Best of the Best (Impact Publications). Designed for people who want to appreciate local cultures by shopping from local artists and craftspeople.

Ulysses Travel Guides (Ulysses Travel Publications). Thorough guides for the independent traveler, complemented by a well-researched cultural perspective. New this year: Montreal, Oaxaca, Puerto Escondido.

Best Planning Guides

*A Journey of One's Own: Uncommon Advice for the Independent Woman Traveler** by Thalia Zepatos (The Eighth Mountain Press). 2nd ed. Detailed advice on practical matters for women traveling abroad alone.

*Alternative Travel Directory.** Annual. $19.95 plus $4 s/h (Transitions Abroad Publishing, 800-293-0373, fax 413-256-0373). The most comprehensive 1-volume guide to independent travel, living, and study abroad. By the editors of *Transitions Abroad* magazine.

*Create Your Own European Adventure: Leave the Guidebooks at Home** by Clive Shearer (Newjoy Press, orders only 800-876-1373). Remarkably detailed planning and preparation guide.

*The Globetrotter's Guide** by Wayne Smits and Carol E. Dolinko. Essential skills for the budget traveler.

*Shawguides (www.shawguides.com).** Shaw Guides' educational travel guides are now available on the Internet: descriptions of more than 3,400 cooking schools, photo workshops, writers' conferences, art and craft workshops, learning and language vacations, and golf, tennis, and water sports schools and camps worldwide. Searchable by keyword, name, state, country, region, month, and specialty. Site also lists organizations and publications relating to each subject.

*Travel Companion Exchange,** P.O. Box 833, Amityville, NY 11701; 516-454-0880 or 800-392-1256. $6 sample newsletter. Widely recommended listings for travelers seeking companions and outstandingly useful newsletter for all travelers.

*Work Your Way Around the World** by Susan Griffith (Peterson's Guides). 7th ed. Excellent firsthand information, by country, on short-term jobs to keep you going by **Transitions Abroad** contributing editor.

Adventures in Good Company: The Complete Guide to Women's Tours and Outdoor Trips by Thalia Zepatos (The Eighth Mountain Press). Profiles more than 100 companies worldwide that offer trips for women.

Air Courier Bargains: How to Travel Worldwide for Next to Nothing by Kelly Monaghan (Intrepid Traveler). Complete guide to courier travel in U.S. and around the world.

Amateur's Guide to the Planet by Jeannette Belliveau (Beau Monde Press). Reports on 12 adventure journeys reflect author's responses to diverse cultures and how people live. Good background reading for responsible travelers.

Archaeology Abroad, 31-34 Gordon Sq., London WC1H 0PY, England. Three annual bulletins list worldwide archaeological digs with details of staffing needs and costs; 011- 44-171-

504-4750, fax 011-44-171-383-2572; arch.abroad@ucl.ac.uk, [www.britarch.ac.uk/archabroad].

The Archaeology Handbook: A Field Manual and Resource Guide by Bill McMillon (John Wiley & Sons). How-to and where-to guide for volunteers.

The Art of Pilgrimmage: The Seeker's Guide to Making Travel Sacred by Phil Cousineau (Conari Press, orders only 800-685-9595). Travel for personal meaningfullness.

Auto Europe Wallet Card. Toll-free telephone access codes to reach AT&T, MCI, and Sprint in 20 countries; 800-223-5555; [www.autoeurope.com]. Also the *Auto Europe Free CD Rom Travel Planner,* an interactive guide to planning your trip to Europe.

Big Book of Adventure Travel by James Simmons (John Muir Publications). A source book of worldwide guided adventure tours.

Bugs, Bites and Bowels by Dr. J. Howarth (Cadogan). A guide on healthy travel covering prevention, diagnosis, and cure.

Campus Lodging Guide (B & J Publications). 19th ed. Details on hundreds of inexpensive accommodations on university campuses throughout the world.

Consolidators: Air Travel's Bargain Basement (Intrepid Traveler). A 73-page list of U.S. and Canadian companies that buy blocks of seats from the airlines at discounts and pass savings on to the consumer.

Damron Address Book by Ian Phillips (Damron Co., annual). The original gay travel guide lists over 10,000 gay-friendly B and Bs, bars, cafes, and more in North America and major European cities.

Do's and Taboos Around the World: A Guide to International Behavior by Roger Axtell (John Wiley & Sons). Advice for the business and pleasure traveler on what to do and not to do in other cultures.

Fly Cheap by Kelly Monaghan (Intrepid Traveler). Everything you need to know to save on airfares, including specific strategies, tactics, and contacts.

Fly for Less by Gary E. Schmidt (Travel Publishing, Inc.; 800-241-9299, fax 651-501-9230). Detailed coverage of how to find reduced price airfare, including the 25 best consolidators selling international and domestic bargains.

Foiling Pickpockets and Bag Snatchers and Other Travel Related Crimes or Scams. Order Jens Jurgen's 24-page booklet from: Travel Companion Exchange, Inc., P.O. Box 833, Amityville, NY 11701-0833. One copy $4, two copies $6.

Ford's Freighter Travel Guide (Ford's Travel Guides). Very informative. Updated semi-annually.

The Gift of Travel: The Best of Travelers' Tales by Larry Habegger, James O'Reilly, and Sean O'Reilly (Travelers' Tales). These stories from all over the world confirm in simple ways that travel is one of the best teachers.

Going Abroad? Superintendent of Documents, U.S. Government Printing Office, Washington, DC 20420; 202-512-1800. Free pamphlet with safety tips; includes order form for other U.S. government publications on foreign travel and residency.

Hostelling Directory, P.O. Box 37613, Washington, DC 20013-7613; 202-783-6161, fax 202-783-6171; hiayhserv@hiayh.org, [www.hiayh.org] (Hostelling International—International Youth Hostel Federation). Two annual volumes: Europe and Africa/Americas/Asia/Pacific. Lists nearly 5,000 hostels in over 70 countries for all ages.

Hostelling International, P.O. Box 37613, Washington, DC 20013-7613; 202-783-6161, fax 202-783-6171; hiayhserv@hiagh-org, [www.iiayh.org]. Nearly 5,000 hostels in over 70 countries for all ages. Two annual volumes: Europe and Africa/Americas/Asia/Pacific.

Hot Spots (Fielding Worldwide). Compendium of stories complementing World's Most Dangerous Places (see below).

In Search of Adventure: A Wild Travel Anthology by Bruce Northam and Brad Olsen (CCC Publishing). Lively new collection of traveler's tales.

Jewish Travel Guide by Michael Zaidner (ISBS). Lists Jewish organizations throughout the world.

More Women Travel (Penguin). From Rough Guide series.

Ordnance Survey Maps, Atlases and Guides Catalogue. 1999. Ordnance Survey Customer Information: 011-44-1703-792755, fax 011-44-1703-792602; psharp@ordsvy.gov.uk, [www.ordsvy.gov.uk]. Detailed maps and atlases for U.K. and Commonwealth countries as well as specialty guides—cycling, motoring, etc.

THE BACKDOOR INTERNET

A WIDE WORLD OF ADVICE AND TRAVEL SECRETS ON THE WEB

By Rick Steves

Cyberspace is filled with online travel talk offering global news, visa information, flight and hotel reservations, and travel advice, plus forums where vagabonds hang out between trips. If you have a particular travel concern or need, you can get a world of advice through your modem. Novices might consider the book Net Travel: How Travelers Use the Internet by Michael Shapiro, which covers excellent online travel resources and tips on how to stay online while on the road. Newcomers to Transitions Abroad may want to consult this magazine's selection of the useful travel web sites at [www.TransitionsAbroad.com].

Tourist Information. The Tourism Offices Worldwide Directory is a searchable directory of the locations, phone numbers, and web sites of tourist information offices [www.towd.com]. For travel tips, city and subway maps, and information on cultural sites for most European destinations, consult City.Net [www.city.net] and Mapquest [www.mapquest.com].

Events. Musi-Cal [http://concerts.calendar.com] and Events Worldwide [www.eventsworldwide.com] make it easy to find live concerts, sporting events, and cultural happenings.

Visas, Warnings, Shots. For the latest on visa requirements, visit [http://travel.state.gov/foreignentryreqs.html]. For more warnings than your mom could think up, tiptoe through the U.S. Department of State's Travel Warnings [http://travel.state.gov/travel_warnings.html]. For country-by-country information on staying healthy, check out the Centers for Disease Control [www.cdc.gov/travel/index.htm].

News. Browse through AJR Newslink [www.newslink.org].

Communication. For translations of key words and sound clips, try Travlang's Foreign Language for Travelers [www.travlang.com]. For a fun look at non-verbal communication, visit Gestures Around the World [http://webofculture.com/edu/gestures.html]. Their quest is to "examine the proper body etiquette in the nations of the world on a per continent basis."

Changing Money. Get the latest exchange rates with the Universal Currency Converter [www.xe.net/currency]. Visa [www.visa.com] and MasterCard [www.mastercard.com/atm] have ATM locators that will help you pinpoint Cirrus and Plus machines.

Photography. For tips on taking better pictures, focus on Photosecrets and its online gallery [www.photosecrets.com].

Flights. For links to air travel, consider the Air Traveler's Handbook [www.cs.cmu.edu/afs/cs/user/mkant/Public/Travel/airfare.html]. For a circumnavigatory trip, try Around the World Traveler [www.atwTraveler.com]. If you think courier flights are worth the hassle, check out the Air Courier Assn. at [www.courier.to] or the International Assn. of Air Travel Couriers at [www.courier.org].

Train and Car Travel. Plan your train travel with the help of Deutsche Bahn's online timetable search service [http://bahn.hafas.de]. The European Railway Server [http://mercurio.iet.unipi.it] and Dan Youra's Ferry Guide [www.youra.com/ferry/intlferries.html] will lead you to the web sites of the European railway and ferry systems. Those traveling by car find Motoeuropa helpful [www.ideamerge.com/motoeuropa].

Accommodations. The Hotel Guide lists over 60,000 hotels, inns, and bed and breakfasts in Europe [www.hotelguide.com]. You can search a destination, choose a hotel, and book your reservation online. For the traveler on a shoestring budget, Eurotrip [www.eurotrip.com] and the Internet Guide to Hostelling [www.hostels.com] offer cheap accommodations and transportation resources on the Internet. Servas, a worldwide organization, connects travelers with host families for the noble goal of building world peace through international understanding. Stay in homes of other members around the world—plan to hang around to talk and share and learn [http://servas.org].

Moving Overseas. Expatriates, job seekers, tax dodgers, and adventurers visit Escape Artist [www.escapeartist.com].

Off the Beaten Track. Looking for a cultural site, hotel, or restaurant that is off the beaten track? Use the many email discussion lists and Usenet newsgroups to contact a European living in the area or a traveler who has just returned. Often travelers find a place to stay with European residents through these forums. DejaNews is a searchable directory that will help you find the right forum [www.dejanews.com]. Use the keywords "travel" or "culture" and the name of your destination in your search.

Travel Zines, Newsletters, and Travel Tales. The Connected Traveler offers travel tales, humor, sounds, photos, and video from around the world [www.travelmedia.com/connected]. Travel Mag highlights exotic locations— remote parts of Africa or the Far East—with monthly features, news, health issues, and an intriguing Crime of the Month section [www5.red.net/travelmag]. My Europe Through the Back Door web site offers a monthly newsletter, a Graffiti Wall for you to share your travel tips, a continually-updated railpass guide, and plenty more [www.ricksteves.com]. A good site for backpackers is How to See the World: The Art of European and World Travel Backpacking [http://artoftravel.com], written by an independent traveler. For stories of personal journeys to almost anywhere, try Virtex [www.coil.com/~jhegenbe/virtex.htm]. Journeywoman, just for women, has tips, tales, and classifieds [www.journeywoman.com]. Mobility International USA provides a monthly newsletter and a huge directory of resources for disabled travelers [www.miusa.org]. If you're looking to publish your own work, visit Adventures Great and Small [www.great-adventures.com/plan/publish.html], or [www.TransitionsAbroad.com].

On the Road

To send and receive email in Europe, those without a laptop can use Hotmail.com at any place with web access. This free service allows you to access your current email account via the web. If you're traveling with a laptop, see if your Internet service offers global roaming services in Europe to access the Internet with a local phone call. TeleAdapt provides the know-how and adapters you need to connect your modem to the various telephone plugs throughout Europe [www.teleadapt.com].

Also try Roadnews [www.roadnews.com], which has everything you need to stay connected to the cyberworld while traveling in the real one.

Drop by cybercafes to stay in touch while traveling. Check the Internet Café Guide [www.netcafeguide.com] for a listing of these plugged-in places.

Passport to World Band Radio (International Broadcasting Services). Hour-by-hour, country-by-country listings for world band radio programming; hq@passport.com.

The Pocket Doctor: A Passport to Healthy Travel by Stephen Bezruchka, M.D. (Mountaineers). 23rd ed. A compact health guide for the traveler.

The Practical Nomad: How to Travel Around the World by Edward Hasbrouck (Moon Travel Handbooks). Essential information on airfare strategies, travel documents, information sources, and more.

Rough Guide to the Internet and World Wide Web (**Rough Guides**). Listings and web sites on many topics, including much travel-related information.

Rough Guide: First Time Europe and Rough Guide: First Time Asia (Rough Guides). Practical information, tips, and advice for the novice traveling in these two areas.

Safety and Security for Women Who Travel by Sheila Suan and Peter Laufer (Travelers' Tales). Authors and world travelers help lay to rest fears and provide guidance.

SCOPE Quarterly Newsletter (International SOS Assistance, 800-523-8662, fax 215-244-0165; scholastic@intsos.com, [www.intsos]). Informational newsletter providing travel tips, news, and articles to independent travelers.

Single-Friendly Travel Directory edited by Diane Redfern. Frequently updated listing of hundreds of tour companies, cruise lines, lodges, spas, resorts, and travel clubs whose functions and pricing are attractive to single and solo travelers. Included with subscription to *Connecting: Solo Travel Network*. Connecting, P.O. Box 29088, 1996 W. Broadway, Vancouver, BC V6J 5C2, Canada; 800-557-1757; [www.cstn.org].

Speaking Vegetarian. The Globetrotter's Guide to Ordering Meatless in 197 Countries by Bryan Geon (Pilot Books). An overview of what to expect—from the vegetarian perspective—in over 197 foreign countries, with phonetic pronunciation table.

Specialty Travel Index. Biannual directory/magazine of special interest and adventure travel listing over 600 tour operators worldwide. $10 per year for 2 issues from Specialty Travel Index, 305 San Anselmo Ave., Suite 313, San Anselmo, CA 94960; 415-459-4900, fax 415-459-4974; [www.specialtytravel.com].

Staying Healthy in Asia, Africa, and Latin America (Moon Publications).

There's No Toilet Paper on the Road Less Traveled: The Best of Travel Humor and Misadventure by Doug Lansey (Travelers' Tales, [www.travelerstales.com]). Proving once again that a sense of humor is the one travel tool you shouldn't leave home without.

The Thrifty Traveler, P.O. Box 8168, Clearwater, Fl 33758; 800-532-5731, fax 727-447-0829; editor@thriftytraveler.com, [www.thriftytraveler.com]. Twelve-page monthly newsletter includes a special section for over-50 travelers and a section on Internet travel news.

Tips for the Savvy Traveler by Deborah Burns and Sarah May Clarkson (Storie Publishing). Hundreds of valuable tips from planning to coming home.

Tips on Renting a Car. Council of Better Business Bureau, 4200 Wilson Blvd., Arlington, VA 22209; 703-276-0100. $2 with long SASE. Guide to getting the most service for your money from car rental companies. Ask for their other "Tips On" publications.

Transformative Adventures, Vacations and Retreats by John Benson (New Millennium). Worldwide organizations offering programs for personal change—meditation retreats, health spas, etc.

Travel Alone & Love It—A Flight Attendant's Guide to Solo Travel by Sharon B. Wingler (Chicago Spectrum Press, $14.95). Instructions on how to plan your own successful solo journey.

Travel and Learn by Evelyn Kaye (Blue Panda). Describes more than 2,000 vacations in arts, archaeology, language, music, nature, and wildlife.

Travel by Cargo Ship (Cadogon).

Travel with Others without Wishing They'd Stayed Home by Nadine Nardi Davidson (Prince Publishing). A survival guide to traveling with your spouse, lover, boss, friends, kids, someone else's kids, relatives, pet, and yourself.

Travel with Peace of Mind (International SOS Assistance). Brochure informing individual travelers about medical, personal, and travel assistance when needed while overseas.

The Traveler's Atlas (Barron's Educational Series, 800-645-3476; [www.barronseduc.com]). A beautiful coffee table book plus a planning guide with regional background information.

Traveler's Handbook: Essential Guide for Every Traveler (WEXAS/Globe Peqout). Good resource.

Volunteer Vacations by Bill McMillon (Chicago Review Press). 5th ed. More than 500 opportunities worldwide.

Wild Planet! 1,001 Extraordinary Events for the Inspired Traveler by Tom Clynes (Visible Ink). Thorough compendium of festivals, cultural events, and holidays spanning the globe.

Women's Traveller '99 by Gina M. Gatta, Ian Philips. (Damron Company).

The World Awaits: Comprehensive Guide to Extended Backpack Travel by Paul Otteson (John Muir Publications). Practical book with details for life on the road.

World Music from the Rough Guides Series (Penguin). References and information on music spanning the globe.

World's Most Dangerous Places by Robert Young Pelton and Coskun Aral (Fielding Worldwide). Firsthand experiences, advice on protecting yourself, etc.

You Can Travel Free by Robert W. Kirk (Pelican). Author tells how he has traveled a half-million miles for free.

Best Travel Web Sites

*Arthur Frommer's Outspoken Encyclopedia of Travel, [www.frommers.com]. Information on budget and alternative travel.

*The Cybercafé Search Engine, [http://cybercaptive.com]. Lists over 2,000 cybercafés in 125 countries which offer a multitude of services for the international traveler.

*Deutsche Bahn AG, [http://bahn.hafas.de/english.html]. Up-to-date timetables for train service in Europe. Well-designed site has options for text-only browsers and English or German language.

*European Hostels.com, [www.europeanhostels.com]. Well-organized site lists over 1,550 hostels throughout Europe and rates the top 50.

*iAgora, [www.iagora.com]. A good place to network with other international travelers; offers a good selection of links.

*Roadnews, [www.roadnews.com]. Traveling with your computer? This site has everything you need to stay connected to the "cyberworld" while traveling in the real one.

*Transitions Abroad, [www.TransitionsAbroad.com]. The central hub of alternative travel online with links to the web sites of everyone listed in our resource and program directories. You can purchase books reviewed in our resource directories and read articles and features from recent editions of Transitions Abroad magazine.

1travel.com, [www.1travel.com]. Helps cost-conscious consumers find the best rates for airfares and accommodations worldwide. They take airline and/or hotel requests and deliver them to travel agents who, in turn, email the best itinerary options back to the consumer.

Accommodation Search Engine, [www.ase.com]. An online database of hotels, bed and breakfasts, inns, etc. worldwide.

Airhitch®, [www.airhitch.org]. Get to Europe cheaply by taking advantage of seats left empty on commercial flights.

American Society of Travel Agents, [www.astanet.com/pub]. Includes a directory of travel agents who specialize in particular types of trips, as well as a great deal of international travel information and resources.

Backpack Europe on a Budget, [www.backpackeurope.com]. Backpacking and hostelling information, tips, and links for student and budget travelers planning a trip to Europe.

Budget Travel, [www.budgettravel.com]. Geographically indexed contact information for travelers who "don't want to pay 5-star prices."

City Rail Transit, [http://pavel.physics.sunysb.edu/RR/metro.html]. Information and links for train and subway travel just about everywhere on the globe: maps, timetables, etc.

CNN Travel Guide, [www.cnn.com/TRAVEL]. Travel news, destination information, booking information.

Currency Converter, [www.oanda.com/converter/travel]. This site features a program that will do conversions for almost 200 different currencies.

Ecola Newsstand, [www.ecola.com]. Links to more than 6,600 English language newspapers and magazines worldwide.

Electronic Embassy Page, [www.embassy.org/embassies]. A list of all of the foreign embassies in the U.S.

Epicurious Traveler, [http://travel.epicurious.com]. Conde Nast's site has budget travel info and discussion forums as well as other resources for travelers.

EUnet Traveller, [www.traveller.eu.net]. Excellent information and resources for global Internet access.

European Travel Network, [www.discountairfares.com]. This nonprofit site is a good place to find budget travel information such as cheap fares and hotels.

Everything's Travel, [http://members.aol.com/trvlevery]. Possibly the largest collection of travel links available. Also has bookstore.

EXES Travel Search Engine, [www.exes.com]. Only indexes travel related pages.

Global On-line Travel, [www.got.com]. An all-purpose information/service site for world travelers. One can book a flight or hotel room, get information on a travel destination, or browse their web links.

Globetrotters Club, [www.bigfoot.com/~globetrotters]. This 50+-year-old club is a great place for independent travel enthusiasts of all ages to network.

GoAbroad Home Page, [www.goabroad.com]. A site for alternative travel including information on study abroad, living abroad, alternative travel, and more. Offers a searchable database of overseas travel programs.

Hostelling International, [www.iyhf.org]. The "Worldwide Hostels" section lists hostels in 75 countries.

Hostels of Europe, [www.hostelseurope.com]. Lists Europe's finest youth hostels and hotels; also offers budget travel links, a travel bookstore, a free electronic newsletter, and more.

InfoHub Specialty Travel Guide, [www.infohub.com]. Comprehensive, easily searchable database of special interest travel programs.

Internet Guide to Hostelling, [www.hostels.com]. Among the largest directories of hostels in the world, also a bulletin board and travel links.

Izon's Backpacker Journal, [www.izon.com]. An extensive list of links and a modest list of free youth/budget travel guides.

Journeywoman Online, [www.journeywoman.com] is for women who love to travel; a free email newsletter is delivered to you in minutes.

Kasbah Travel Information, [www.kasbah.com]. A travel search engine with over 100,000 sites listed.

Le Travel Store, [www.letravelstore.com]. Travel gear, accessories, publications. Their San Diego storefront has been in business since 1976.

Lonely Planet, [www.lonelyplanet.com]. The site for a premier travel book publisher has great content and a sense of humor.

Maiden Voyages, [www.maiden-voyages.com]. *Maiden Voyages* is a literary consumer magazine for women; web site contains a large directory of tour operators who cater to women.

Net News for the Thrifty Traveler, [www.thriftytraveler.com]. Information on web sites that are helpful to budget travelers.

No Shitting in the Toilet, [www.noshit.com.au]. "A celebration of everything that is perverse about travel."

Online Tourist Information, [www.efn.org/~rick/tour]. Links to web pages and tourist boards in over 150 countries.

Places to Stay, [www.placestostay.com]. An extensive online reservation service for hotels, bed and breakfasts, inns, and resorts worldwide with up-to-the-minute information on prices and availability.

Preview Travel, [www.previewtravel.com]. This well-known ticket-booking site features a destination guide section which offers free information (provided by Fodor's Guides) on over 200 regions worldwide.

RailServe, [www.railserve.com]. Their "Passenger and Urban Transit" links have information and links for rail travel worldwide.

Rec.Travel Library, [www.travel-library.com]. Personal travelogues and worldwide travel and independent travel information.

Shoestring Travel, [www.stratpub.com]. An e-zine with lots of links and an emphasis on the exchange of information among budget travelers.

Third World Traveler, [www.thirdworldtraveler.com]. Provides alternative travel information and opportunities for travelers to act on behalf of social and economic justice in the Third World.

Travel Document Services, [www.traveldocs.com]. Provides visa services for U.S. citizens for most countries for which an entry visa is required; also has up-to-date information on most countries. You can browse their travel resources and purchase relevant books.

Travel Source, [www.travelsource.com]. A decent selection of adventure travel links.

TravelBids, [www.travelbids.com]. An online auction that allows travelers to save money by getting bids from many travel agents. You name the flight and travel agents bid to offer you the lowest price.

TravelPage.com, [www.travelpage.com]. Where to go, how to get there, and what to expect.

Travlang, [www.travlang.com]. Provides useful tools for the traveler and those interested in learning a foreign language; also links to other places on the net providing related services.

Universal Currency Converter, [www.xe.net/currency]. See how many yen your dollar will fetch.

www.worldwide.edu. Travel planning information broken down into 25 categories, plus an impressive list of educational travel programs.

Africa

Africa's Top Wildlife Countries by Mark W. Nolting (Global Travel Publishers). Excellent reference by an authority on African wildlife.

Africa: Literary Companion by Oona Strathern (Passport Books). Compilation of literature, background, and cultural information.

African Customs and Manners by E. Devine and N. Braganti (St. Martin's Press). Dos and taboos on the African continent.

Beyond Safaris by Kevin Danaher (Africa World Press). A guide to building people-to-people ties with Africans.

Bicycling in Africa by David Mozer (International Bicycle Fund, 4887 Columbia Dr. S., Apt. T-8, Seattle, WA 98108-1919; Tel./fax 206-767-0848; ibike@ibike.org, [www.ibike.org]). How to do it, with supplements on 17 separate countries.

Guide to South Africa by Philip Briggs (Bradt Publishing). Comprehensive guide to the new South Africa.

Kilimanjaro and Mount Kenya: A Climbing and Trekking Guide by Cameron M. Burns (Mountaineers).

Namibia: Independent Traveler's Guide by Scott and Lucinda Bradshaw (Hippocrene). Essential for anyone making their way across the country's vast expanse.

The Safari Companion: A Guide to Watching African Mammals by Richard Estes (Chelsea Green Publishing). Good reference.

Touring Southern Africa (Thomas Cook) Independent holidays in South Africa, Botswana, Namibia, Lesotho, Swaziland, Mozambique, Zimbabwe.

Albania

Series: *Blue Guides, Bradt.

Antarctica

Series: Bradt, *Cadogan, *Lonely Planet.

Asia

Asia Overland by Mark Elliott and Will Klass (Trailblazer). Routes and planning for overland options across Asia.

Southeast Asia : Literary Companion by Alistair Dingwell (Passport Books). Compilation of literature, background, and cultural information.

Thailand, Malaysia, Singapore by Rail by Brian McPhee (Bradt).

Tibet by Elizabeth B. Booz (Seven Hills). Comprehensive. Includes bibliography and language guide.

Tibet Guide by Stephen Batchelor (Wisdom Publications). Its people and culture.

The Traveler's Guide to Asian Customs and Manners by Elizabeth Devine and Nancy Braganti (St. Martin's Press).

Series: *Blue Guides, *Cadogan, *Culture Shock!, Customs and Etiquette, Fielding, Fodor, *Footprints, Frommer, *Insight Guides, *Interlink, *Let's Go, *Lonely Planet (Pisces), *Moon Handbooks, Passport Regional Guides, Sierra Club, *Rough Guides, Travelers' Tales, Treasures and Pleasures of. . .

Australia

A Traveler's Literary Companion edited by Robert Ross (Whereabouts Press). Modern short stories by Australian authors.

Australia and New Zealand by Campervan and/or Car with Stopovers in the Cook Islands, Fiji, Hawaii, and Tahiti by Richard W. and LeeOna S. Hostrop (ETC Publications). Provides complete

Volunteer Abroad!

A World Of Opportunities Is Yours!

How long do you want to volunteer?

For 3 – 6 weeks
contact Cross-Cultural Solutions
at 1-800-380-4777 or www.crossculturalsolutions.org

For 3 months
contact Global Routes
at 1-510-848-4800 or www.globalroutes.org

For 1 year
Community Development Projects: contact Visions In Action
at 1-202-625-7403 or www.visionsinaction.org

English Teaching: contact WorldTeach
at 1-800-4-TEACH-0 or www.worldteach.org

information on how to reserve campervan/car in U.S. and on camps and scenic sights in "Down Under."

Australia and New Zealand by Rail by Colin Taylor (Bradt Publishing).

The Australian Bed and Breakfast Book by J. and J. Thomas (Pelican). Stay in private homes, on farms, and in guest houses with friendly hosts.

Bushwalking in Australia by John and Monica Chapman (Lonely Planet Publications).

Cycling Australia by Ian Duckworth (Bicycle Books).

Stepping Lightly on Australia by Shirley LaPlanche (Globe Pequot). Traveler's guide to ecotourism in this land of diverse flora and fauna.

Series: Berlitz, *Culture Shock!, Driving Tours, Eyewitness, Fielding, Fodor, Frommer, *Insight Guides, Let's Go, *Lonely Planet, Maverick, *Moon, Nelles, *Rough Guides, Sierra Club, Time Out, Treasures and Pleasures of... (Lonely Planet also covers each state plus regions.).

Austria

Austria: Charming Small Hotels by Paul Wade (Hunter). A selection of small hotels with character.

Walking Easy in the Austrian Alps (Globe Pequot). Hiking guide for active adults.

Series: Berlitz, *Blue Guides, Driving Tours, Exploring Rural Europe, Eyewitness, Fodor, Frommer, Insight Guides, Karen Brown, Knopf, *Let's Go, *Lonely Planet, *Michelin, Off the Beaten Track, *Rick Steves, *Rough Guides.

Baltic Countries

Series: Bradt, *Insight Guides, *Lonely Planet, *Rick Steves.

Bulgaria

Essential Bulgaria by David Ash (Passport Books). Pocket size guide.

Series: *Rough Guides.

Canada

Canada Campground Directory (Woodalls/Globe Pequot). Complete guide to campgrounds and RV parks.

Canadian Bed & Breakfast Guide by Gerda Pantel (Penguin, 14th ed.). Over 1,250 entries.

Eastern Canada Travel Smart by Felicity Munn (John Muir Publications). Do-it-yourself practical guide with itineraries.

Guide to Eastern Canada and **Guide to Western Canada** by Frederick Pratson (Globe Pequot). Both guides provide thorough information on all aspects of travel in Canada.

Hostels Canada by Paul Karr (Globe Pequot Press). At-a-glance ratings of 200 hostels.

Inside/Out British Columbia by Jack Christie (Sasquatch Books). A guide to camping, hiking, biking, and skiing in B.C., as well as restaurant and lodging suggestions.

Nova Scotia & The Maritimes by Bike: 21 Tours Geared for Discovery by Walter Sienko (Mountaineers).

Vancouver Best Places by K. Wilson (Sasquatch Books). 2nd ed.

Series: *Access, Berlitz, *Culture Shock!, Fodor, Frommer, *Insight Guides, *Let's Go, *Lonely Planet, *Michelin, *Moon, National Geographic, Nelles, *Rough Guides, Sierra Club, Ulysses.

Caribbean/West Indies

*Caribbean Islands Handbook by Sarah Cameron (Footprints Handbooks). Best single guide.

Adventure Guide to ... Barbados, Bermuda, Dominican Republic, Jamaica, Puerto Rico Trinidad/Tobago, and the Virgin Islands (Hunter Publications). Practical guides for the adventurous traveler.

Best Dives in the Caribbean by J. and J. Huber (Hunter Publications). 2nd ed. Covers 24 islands.

Caribbean Adventures in Nature by Michel de Freitos (John Muir). Outdoor adventuring.

Caribbean Literary Companion by James Ferguson (Passport Books). Compilation of literature, background and cultural information.

Caribbean Ports of Call by Kay Showker (Globe Pequot). A guide to the ports of the Caribbean.

Diving Bermuda by Jesse Cancelmo and Mike Strohofer (Aqua Quest Publications). Diving sites, information on marine life, shipwrecks, and travel in Bermuda.

Diving Off the Beaten Track by Bob Burgess (Aqua Quest Publications). Diving in various Caribbean destinations.

Series: *Access, Berlitz, *Cadogan, Fielding, Fodor, *Footprints, Frommer, *Insight Guides, *Interlink, *Lonely Planet (Pisces), *Moon, Nelles, *Rough Guides, Sierra Club, Treasures and Pleasures of..., Ulysses.

Central America

*Costa Rica: The Ecotraveller's Wildlife Guide by Les Beletsky (Academic Press). Detailed similar titles for Belize and Northern Guatemala.

*Guatemala Guide, Belize Guide, Costa Rica Guide by Paul Glassman and Travel Line Press (Open Road). Comprehensive.

*Guatemala: Adventures in Nature by Richard Mahler (John Muir Publications). Comprehensive.

Adventures in Nature Series... (John Muir) Available for Guatemala, Belize, and Honduras. Focus on adventure and outdoor travel.

The Costa Rica Traveler (Getting Around in Costa Rica) by Ellen Searby (Windham Bay Press). 4th ed. Good background notes. Nature travel.

Costa Rica Traveler's Literary Companion by B. Ras (Whereabouts Press). Compilation of short stories by Costa Rican authors.

Costa Rica's National Parks and Preserves: A Visitor's Guide by Joseph Franke (Mountaineers).

Diving Belize by Ned Middleton (Aqua Quest Publications). Diving sites, information on marine life and travel in Belize.

Explore Belize by Harry S. Pariser (Hunter Publications). 4th ed. Practical guide for the adventurous traveler.

Hidden Baja by Richard Harris (Ulysses Press). Tourist spots and out-of-the-way locales.

Hidden Belize by Stacy Ritz (Ulysses). Good detailed information on Belize.

Hidden Cancun and the Yucatan by Richard Harris (Ulysses Press). Covers Cancun as well as more remote areas of the Yucatan peninsula, including listings of sights, lodging, and outdoor adventures.

Honduras and Bay Islands Guide by J. Panet (Open Road). Good all-around guide.

Latin America by Bike: A Complete Touring Guide by W. Siekno (Mountaineers). From Mexico through Central America to the tip of Argentina.

The New Key to Costa Rica by Beatrice Blake and Anne Becher. 1998. $17.95 (Ulysses Press). Good all-around guide to Costa Rica with an ecology focus. Also available: *The New Key to Cancun and the Yucatan* by Richard Harris (2nd ed., $14.95); *The New Key to Ecuador and the Galapagos* by David L. Pearson and David W. Middleton (3rd ed., $17.95); and *Hidden Belize* by Stacy Ritz ($15.95), *Hidden Guatemala* by Richard Harris ($16.95).

The New Key to Ecuador and the Galapagos by David L. Pearson and David W. Middleton (Ulysses Press). An emphasis on the outdoors and ecotourism.

On Your Own in El Salvador by Jeff Brauer. New. Comprehensive.

Pura Vida by Sam Mitchell (Menasha Ridge Press). The waterfalls and hot springs of Costa Rica.

Traveller's Survival Kit: Central America by Emily Hatchwell and Simon Calder (Vacation Work). Extensive practical information and town-by-town guide to the 7 countries of this region. £8.95.

Series: Bradt, *Culture Shock!, Fodor, *Footprints, Frommer, *Insight Guides, Knopf, *Let's Go, *Lonely Planet (Pisces), *Moon, *New Key, *Rough Guides, Sierra Club, Ulysses.

China/Hong Kong

China by Bike: Taiwan, Hong Kong, China's East Coast by Roger Grigsby (Mountaineers).

China by Rail by Douglas Streatfeild-James (Trailblazer).

China Regional Guides (Passport Books). Includes Fujian, Xian, Beijing, Yunnan.

Essential Chinese for Travelers by Fan Zhilong (China Books). Basic phrasebook, dictionary, and cassette, includes sections on hotels, transportation, money, food, and business. Rev. 1996.

Silk Route by Rail by Dominic Streatfeild-James (Trailblazer).

Trekking in Russia and Central Asia: A Traveler's Guide by Frith Maier (Mountaineers).

Series: Berlitz, *Blue Guides, *Culture Shock!, Customs and Etiquette, Fodor, Frommer, *Insight, *Interlink, *Lonely Planet, Maverick, *Moon Handbooks, Nelles, *Rough Guides.

Cuba

Guide to Cuba by Stephen Fallon (Bradt Publishing).

Reader's Companion to Cuba edited by Alan Ryan (Harcourt Brace). Selection of travel writing about the island.

Series: Berlitz, Bradt, *Footprints, *Insight Guides, *Lonely Planet (Pisces), *Moon, Passport, Ulysses.

Czech and Slovak Republics

Prague Traveler's Literary Companion by P. Wilson (Whereabouts Press). Compilation of short stories by Prague writers.

Series: Berlitz, *Blue Guides, *Culture Shock!, Customs & Etiquette, Eyewitness, Fodor, Frommer, *Insight Guides, Knopf, *Let's Go, *Lonely Planet, *Michelin, Nelles, *Rough Guides, Time Out.

Europe

***Europe** (Michelin). Thirty-five countries of Europe, from Albania to Yugoslavia, between the familiar green covers.

***Europe 101: History and Art for the Traveler** by Rick Steves and Gene Openshaw (John Muir Publications). Wonderful.

***Europe Through the Back Door** by Rick Steves (John Muir Publications). The best "how-to" and preparation book for Europe with lots of useful hints and information.

***Europe Through the Back Door Travel Newsletter,** Rick Steves, ed. Quarterly. Free from Europe Through the Back Door, Inc., 120 4th Ave. N., Edmonds, WA 98020. Our favorite travel newsletter.

***Mona Winks: A Guide to Enjoying Europe's Top Museums** by Rick Steves and Gene Openshaw (John Muir Publications).

Central & Eastern Europe: Literary Companion by James Naughton (Passport Books). Compilation of literature, background, and cultural information.

Cheap Sleeps Europe 1999 by Katie Wood (Ebury Press, Trafalgar Square). Budget accommodations.

Eastern Europe by Rail by Rob Dodson (Bradt Publications). Practical guide.

Euroad: Complete Guide to Motoring in Europe by Bert Lief (VLE Ltd.). Maps include driving times and distances in miles.

Europe by Bike: 18 Tours Geared for Discovery by Karen and Terry Whitehill (Mountaineers). 2nd ed.

Europe by Eurail, 1999-2000 by Laverne Ferguson (Globe Pequot). How to tour Europe by train.

Europe by Train 1999 by Katie Wood (Ebury Press/Trafalgar Square). A budget travel guide.

Europe for Free: Hundreds of Free Things to Do in Europe by Brian Butler (Mustang Publishing).

Europe's Wonderful Little Hotels & Inns: The Continent by Hilary Rubinstein and Carolyn Raphael (St. Martin's Press).

First-Time Europe: Everything You Need to Know Before You Go by Louis CasaBianca (Rough Guides). Trip planning for low-budget travelers.

Garden Lover's Guides to: Britain/France/Germany/Italy by Wayne Smits and Carol E. Dolinko (Chronicle). Essential skills for the budget traveler.

Moto Europa by Eric Bredesen (Seren Publishing). Details on renting, driving, buying, and selling a car.

On the Rails Europe edited by Melissa Shales (Passport Books). Routes, maps, transport information.

Planning Your Trip to Europe. European Travel Commission. Free from European Planner, P.O. Box 1754, New York, NY 10185.

Postcards from Europe by Rick Steves (John Muir Publications). Collection of 25 years of travel tales from veteran European traveler and writer.

Thomas Cook European Timetable. $27.95 plus $4.50 shipping from Forsyth Travel; 816-942-9050, 800-367-7984; [www.forsyth.com]. Rail schedules for trains on every European and British main line.

Travel Guide to Jewish Europe by Ben Frank (Pelican). Jewish historical sites, Holocaust memorials, neighborhoods, restaurants, etc.

Traveler's Guide to European Camping by Mike and Teri Church (Rolling Homes Press, call 425-822-7846.) Lots of campground listings.

Traveling Europe's Trains by Jay Brunhouse (Pelican). Detailed itineraries.

Understanding Europeans by Stuart Miller (John Muir Publications). Insights into European behavior, history and cultural heritage.

Walking Europe from Top to Bottom by Susan Margolis and Ginger Harmon (Sierra Club Books). Follows the Grande Randonnée Cinque on a 107-day journey (you can do smaller portions).

Walks Through Paris, London, Rome, Amsterdam, etc (VLE Ltd.). Street-by-street walking maps through 13 principal European cities.

Series: *Access, Berlitz, *Blue Guides, Bradt, *Cadogan, Fielding, Fodor, Frommer, *Insight Guides, *Let's Go, *Lonely Planet, *Michelin, Nelles, *Rick Steves, *Rough Guides.

France

Alastair Sawday's Special Paris Hotels/Alastair Sawday's French Bed & Breakfast (Alastair Sawday Publishing). Accommodations with character, comfort, and value.

An Insider's Guide to French Hotels: $50-$90 a Night for Two by Margo Classé (Wilson Publishing). Covers centrally located hotels in many French cities.

Art Sites France: Contemporary Art and Architecture Handbook by Sidra Stitch (Art Sites; orders 800-888-4741). First in a new series of travel guides on contemporary art and architecture.

Bed and Breakfasts of Character and Charm in France (Rivages Guides).

Camping and Caravaning France (Michelin Publications). Campgrounds, town plans, location information, plus facilities.

Cheap Sleeps in Paris and **Cheap Eats in Paris** by Sandra A. Gustafson (Chronicle). Guides to inexpensive lodgings, restaurants, bistros, and brasseries.

France by Bike: 14 Tours Geared for Discovery by Karen and Terry Whitehall. (Mountaineers).

France on Foot, Village to Village, Hotel to Hotel: How to Walk the French Trail System On Your Own by Bruce LeFavour (Attis Press; 707-963-3723, fax 707 963-6089; attis@napanet.net).

France: Literary Companion by John Edmondson (Passport Books). Compilation of literature, background, and cultural information.

Hotels & Restos de France by Philippe Gloaguen (Rough Guides). First-time translation of France's popular *Guide du Routard*.

Hotels and Country Inns of Charm and Character in France (Rivages Guides).

Literary Cafés of Paris by Noel Riley Fitch (Starrhill Press). Sit in Parisian cafes and read about the writers who made them famous.

No More Hotels in Paris by Cynthia Lynn (Newjoy Press; orders only 800-876-1373). Finding rentals and other accommodations.

On the Rails Around France, Belgium, Netherlands and Luxembourg by Roger Thomas (Passport Books). Routes, maps, transport information.

Paris for Free (Or Extremely Cheap) by Mark Beffart (Mustang Publishing).

Paris Inside Out by Anglophone S.A. An insider's guide for resident students and discriminating visitors on living in the French capital.

Paris-Anglophone by David Applefield. Print and online directory of essential contacts for English speakers in Paris.

Rick Steves' Paris by Rick Steves (John Muir Publications). New Rick Steves guide that will help travelers get the most for their time and money while in Paris.

The Unknown South of France: A History Buff's Guide by Henry and Margaret Reuss (Harvard Common Press). A guide to the history and culture of the south of France.

Walking Easy in the French Alps (Globe Pequot). Hiking guide.

Series: *Access, Berlitz, *Blue Guides, *Cadogan, *Culture Shock!, Customs and Etiquette, Driving Tours, Daytrips, Exploring Rural Europe, Eyewitness, Fielding, Fodor, Frommer, *Insight Guides, *Interlink, Karen Brown, Knopf, *Let's Go, *Lonely Planet, *Michelin, National Geographic, Nelles, Off the Beaten Track, Passport Regional Handbooks, *Rick Steves, *Rough Guides, Time Out, Ulysses.

Germany

Germany by Bike: 20 Tours Geared for Discovery by Nadine Slavinski (Mountaineers).

Traveler's Guide to Jewish Germany by Hirsch and Lopez (Pelican). Sites, synagogues, memorials, and exhibitions.

Series: Berlitz, *Blue Guides, *Cadogan, Customs and Etiquette, Daytrips, Driving Tours, Exploring Rural Europe, Fodor,

Frommer, Insight Guides, *Interlink, Karen Brown, *Let's Go, *Michelin, *Rick Steves, *Rough Guides.

Greece

Greece: A Traveler's Literary Companion edited by Artemis Leontis (Whereabouts Press). Modern short stories by Greek authors.

Series: Berlitz, *Blue Guides, *Cadogan, Customs and Etiquette, Exploring Rural Europe, Eyewitness, Fodor, Frommer, *Insight Guides, *Interlink, Knopf, *Let's Go, *Lonely Planet, *Michelin, Nelles, *Rough Guides.

Hungary

Cheap Eats Prague, Vienna, Budapest/Cheap Sleeps Prague, Vienna, Budapest by Sandra Gustafson (Chronicle). Inexpensive places to eat and sleep.

Series: Berlitz, *Blue Guides, Customs and Etiquette, Fodor, Frommer, *Insight Guides, *Lonely Planet, Nelles, *Rough Guides, Time Out.

Indian Subcontinent

Bhutan: Himalayan Kingdom by Booz (Passport Books). Focuses on background, history, etc.

From Here to Nirvana: The Yoga Journal Guide to Spiritual India by Anne Cushman and Jerry Jones (Berkley Publishing Group, 375 Hudson St., New York, NY 10014). Details on everything from yogis and gurus to ashrams and temples.

India by Stanley Wolpert (Univ. of California Press). A concise and comprehensive guide to Indian history and culture by an authority.

India by Rail by Royston Ellis (Bradt).

OVERSEAS HEALTH AND SAFETY ONLINE

By Rebecca W. Acosta

American Society of Tropical Medicine and Hygene (ASTMH), [www.astmh.org]. Site includes a list of international exchange opportunities, including organizations, links, and information on accredited programs in tropical medicine and travelers' health. Publishes *Health Hints for the Tropics.*

Centers for Disease Control and Prevention (CDC), 888-232-3228; [www.cdc.gov]. The CDC is the first place you should look before you travel to find out about specific disease outbreaks and general travel health information.

International Assn. for Medical Assistance to Travelers (IAMAT), iamat@sentex.net, [www.sentex.net/~iamat]. Provides a directory of English-speaking doctors in 500 cities in 120 countries. Also information on health risks and immunizations worldwide, detailed information on tropical disease, climatic, and sanitary conditions.

International Aviation Safety Assessment, [www.faa.gov/avr/iasa.htm] An online list of the FAA's ratings of foreign contries' ability to adhere to the international airline safety standards.

International Society of Travel Medicine, [www.istm.org]. The largest organization of professionals dedicated to the advancement of the specialty of travel medicine; online directory of travel clinics.

International Travel and Health 1999 (World Health Organization, 49 Sheridan Ave., Albany, NY 12210; 518-436-9686; [www.who.org]). Vaccination requirements and health advice.

MCW International Traveler's Clinic, [www.intmed.mcw.edu/travel.html]. The Medical College of Wisconsin has a list of links to information on traveler's health and safety.

Shoreland's Travel Health Online, [www.tripprep.com]. An excellent site for travelers' health and safety information, including a planning guide and country information.

Traveler's Medical and Vaccination Center, [www.tmvc.com.au]. Worldwide information on traveling healthy and a good selection of links to other organizations.

U.S. State Department: Travel Warnings and Consular Info, 202-647-5225; [http://travel.state.gov/travel_warnings.html]. Advisories to travelers about destinations and dangers to avoid. Consular Information Sheets include U.S. embassy or consulate locations, health conditions, political disturbances, currency and entry regulations, crime and security information, etc.

India: Literary Companion by Simon Weightman (Passport Books). Compilation of literature, background, and cultural information.

Silk Route by Rail by Dominic Streatfeild-James (Trailblazer).

Tibet: Roof of the World (Passport Books). 3rd ed. Focuses on background, history.

Trekking in Indian Himalayas by G. Weare (Lonely Planet).

Trekking in Nepal: A Traveler's Guide by Stephen Bezruchka (Mountaineers, 7th ed.).

Trekking in the Annapurna Region by Bryn Thomas (Trailblazer).

Trekking in the Everest Region by Jamie McGuinness (Trailblazer).

Trekking in Tibet: A Traveler's Guide by Gary McCue (Mountaineers).

Series: Berlitz, *Cadogan, *Culture Shock!, Customs and Etiquette, Fodor, *Footprints, Frommer, *Insight, *Interlink, *Let's Go, *Lonely Planet, *Moon Handbooks, Nelles, Passport Regional Guides, *Rough Guides, Travelers' Tale.

Indonesia, Malaysia, Singapore

Eat Smart In Indonesia by Joan and David Peterson (Ginkgo Press). Cuisine, menu guide, market foods, and more.

Passport Regional Indonesia Guides (NTC/Contemporary Publishing). Excellent coverage of the islands of the Indonesian Archipelago. Titles include Bali, Java, Spice Islands, Sumatra, Underwater Indonesia, and more.

Thailand, Malaysia, Singapore by Rail by Brian McPhee (Bradt).

Series: Berlitz, Bradt, *Culture Shock!, Customs and Etiquette, Fielding, *Footprints, *Insight Guides, Knopf, *Lonely Planet, Maverick, *Moon Handbooks, Nelles, Passport Regional Guides, *Rough Guides.

Italy

An Insider's Guide to Italian Hotels: $40-$75 a Night for Two by Margo Classé (Wilson Publishing). Covers centrally located hotels in many Italian cities.

Cento Citta: A Guide to the "Hundred Cities and Towns" of Italy by Paul Hofmann (Henry Holt). Beyond the major tourist cities.

Cheap Eats Italy/Cheap Sleeps Italy by Sandra Gustafson (Chronicle). Inexpensive places to eat and sleep.

Hotels and Country Inns of Character and Charm in Italy (Rivages Guides).

Independent Walker's Guide Italy by Frank Booth (Interlink). Planning and preparation for 35 great walks throughout Italy.

Touring Club of Italy Guides (Abbeville). Established series of Italian guidebooks recently translated into English. Excellent maps. New this year: Sicily, Naples, Milan.

Walking and Eating in Tuscany and Umbria by James Lasdun and Pia Davis (Penguin).

Walking Easy in the Italian Alps (Globe Pequot). Hiking guide.

Series: *Access, Berlitz, *Blue Guides, *Cadogan, Citywalks, Customs and Etiquette, Daytrips, Driving Tours, Exploring Rural, Eyewitness, Fielding, Fodor, Frommer, *Insight Guides, *Interlink, Karen Brown, Knopf, *Let's Go, *Lonely Planet, *Michelin, Nelles, Off the Beaten Track, Passport Regional Guides, *Rick Steves, *Rough Guides, Time Out, Travelers' Tales.

Japan

Cycling Japan by B. Harrell (Kodansha).

Hiking in Japan by Paul Hunt (Kodansha). Mountain trails, maps, great geological notes.

Japan Traveler's Tales: True Stories of Life on the Road by Donald W. George and Amy G. Carlson (Travelers' Tales, [www.travelerstales.com]).

Japan-Think, Ameri-Think by Robert J. Collins (Penguin). An irreverent guide to understanding the cultural differences.

Japan: A Literary Companion by Harry Guest (Passport Books). Compilation of literature, background, and culture.

Ski Japan! by T.R. Reid (Kodansha).

Series: Berlitz, *Cadogan, *Culture Shock!, Customs and Etiquette, Fodor, Frommer, *Insight Guides, *Interlink, *Lonely Planet, *Moon Handbooks, Travelers' Tales.

Korea

Series: *Culture Shock!, Fodor, *Insight Guides, *Lonely Planet, *Moon Handbooks.

Malta

Series: Berlitz, *Blue Guides, *Cadogan, *Insight Guides, *Michelin.

Mexico

*The People's Guide to Mexico by Carl Franz (John Muir Publications). A wonderful read—full of wisdom, too.

Diving Cozumel by Steve Rosenberg (Aqua Quest Publications). Diving sites, information on marine life, archaeological sites, and travel.

Eat Smart In Mexico: How to Decipher the Menu, Know the Market Foods, and Embark on a Tasting Adventure by Joan and David Peterson (Ginkgo Press). A travel guidebook to Mexico for food lovers who want to get to the heart of the culture through the cuisine.

Mexico Spas and Hot Springs by Mike Nelson (Roads Scholar Press). World-class spas to simple hot springs.

Mexico: A Hiker's Guide to Mexico's Natural History by Jim Conrad (Mountaineers). Steers hikers through Mexico's natural landscape while illuminating its natural history.

Mexico: Adventures in Nature by Ron Mader (John Muir Publications). Focuses on adventure and outdoor travel.

Traveler's Guide to Camping in Mexico by Mike and Terri Church (Rolling Homes Press). Explore Mexico with RV or tent.

The Yucatan: A Guide to the Land of Maya Mysteries by Antoinette May (Wide World Publishing). A respected guide focusing on cultural considerations, history, Mayan legends. Includes photographs.

Series: *Access, Berlitz, Bradt, *Cadogan, *Culture Shock!, Daytrips, Fielding, Fodor, Footprints, Frommer, *Insight Guides, Knopf, *Let's Go, *Lonely Planet (Pisces), *Michelin, *Moon Handbooks, Nelles, *New Key, *Rough Guides, Travelers' Tales, Ulysses.

Middle East

Guide to Lebanon by Lynda Keen (Bradt Publishing).

Israel on Your Own by Harriet Greenberg (Passport Books). 2nd ed. All-purpose guide to independent travel.

Israel: Traveler's Literary Companion edited by M. Gluzman and N. Seidman (Whereabouts Press). Short stories by Israeli authors.

Lebanon: A Travel Guide by Reid, Leigh and Kennedy (Pelican Publishing). General guide.

Petra: A Traveller's Guide by Rosalyn Maqsood (Garnet Publications) Guide to Jordan's most famous historical attraction.

Spectrum Guides (Interlink Publishing). Beautifully photographed, good cultural and background information. Available for: Jordan, United Arab Emirates.

Series: Bradt, Berlitz, *Blue Guides, *Cadogan, *Culture Shock!, Customs and Etiquette, Fodor, *Footprints, Frommer, Knopf, Insight, *Interlink, *Let's Go, *Lonely Planet (Pisces), Maverick, *Michelin, Nelles, *Rough Guides.

Myanmar (Burma)

Series: Bradt, *Culture Shock!, Fielding, *Footprints, *Insight Guides, *Lonely Planet, *Moon Handbooks, Nelles. (Transitions Abroad urges you not to visit Burma.)

Netherlands, Belgium, Luxembourg

Cycling the Netherlands, Belgium & Luxembourg by Katherine and Jerry Widing (Bicycle Books). Planning, preparation, touring information, and routes through the three most bicycle-friendly countries in Europe.

On the Rails Around France, Belgium, Netherlands, and Luxembourg by Roger Thomas (Passport Books). Routes, maps, transport information.

Series: Berlitz, *Blue Guides, *Cadogan, *Culture Shock!, Customs and Etiquette, Daytrips, Eyewitness, Fodor, Frommer, *Insight Guides, Knopf, *Lonely Planet, *Michelin, *Rick Steves, *Rough Guides, Time Out.

New Guinea

Bushwalking in Papua New Guinea by Riall Nolan (Lonely Planet Publications).

Series: *Lonely Planet , Passport Regional Guides.

New Zealand

Australia and New Zealand by Campervan and/or Car with Stopovers in the Cook Islands, Fiji, Hawaii, and Tahiti by Richard W. and LeeOna S. Hostrop (ETC Publications). Complete information on how to reserve campervan/car from U.S. and camps and scenic sights "Down Under."

Australia and New Zealand by Rail (Bradt Publishing).

By Kathy Hoke

Traveling alone does not mean being alone. For mostly good reasons people are more likely to engage in conversation with a solo traveler than a couple or group of travelers. As a woman who often travels alone, I've appreciated these encounters far more than I've been bothered by them.

Here are some tips to make your solo journey fun and safe:

Plan ahead. Armed with knowledge about your destination's attractions, local transportation, and housing, you will arrive more confident of your ability to navigate. Consult your local library, maps, the Internet, and the wisdom of those who've been where you want to go.

Assume people are eager to meet you and give you a hand. Guidebooks usually skip this point and instead tell you how to watch out for your safety and money. Precautions are important, but only a tiny minority of any population preys on travelers. You can miss out on some wonderful encounters if you allow fear to guide you. Learn to size people up quickly.

Use public transportation. Study the subway map and train routes and take advantage of passes that suit your travel needs. You never know when a stranger on a train will become your newest friend.

Stay at a youth hostel. Despite their name, youth hostels attract many travelers over age 30. Like younger people, older adults choose hostels to stretch their budgets and to meet interesting travelers from around the world. Hostel managers and guests can offer useful travel tips.

Have a flexible plan. Pick your destination ahead of time, but take advantage of opportunities that arise as you meet interesting strangers.

Use common sense. You can dodge most of the creepy people in the usual ways by making your money hard to get, leaving your valuable jewelry at home, and avoiding travel at night, especially in isolated places. Look confident, even if you're not. You might discover you have more confidence than you ever realized.

The New Zealand Bed and Breakfast Book by J. and J. Thomas (Pelican). Lists over 300 private homes and hotels.

New Zealand by Bike: 14 Tours Geared for Discovery by Bruce Ringer (Mountaineers, 2nd ed.).

Series: Berlitz, Fielding, Fodor, Frommer, *Insight Guides, Let's Go, *Lonely Planet, Maverick, *Moon, Nelles, Sierra Club.

Pacific

Adventuring in the Pacific (Sierra Club). For the adventurous traveler.

Hidden Tahiti and French Polynesia by Robert Kay. (Ulysses). Practical guide emphasizing highlights off the beaten track.

Series: *Lonely Planet, Pisces, *Moon Handbooks, Sierra Club. Lonely Planet, and Moon Handbooks have many titles that focus on this area by island groups and individual islands.

Philippines

Series: *Culture Shock!, *Insight Guides, *Lonely Planet, *Moon Handbooks, Nelles.

Poland

Eat Smart In Poland by Joan and David Peterson (Ginkgo Press). Cuisine and menu guide plus more.

Hiking Guide to Poland and Ukraine by Tim Burford (Bradt).

People to People Poland by Jim Haynes (Zephyr Press). One of a series of books on Central Europe for travelers who want to experience life as the locals live it. Lists over 1,000 locals to contact.

Polish Cities (Pelican). A guide to Warsaw, Krakow, and Gdansk.

Series: Bradt, Customs and Etiquette, Eyewitness, *Insight Guides, *Lonely Planet, *Rough Guides.

Portugal

Special Places to Stay in Spain and Portugal by Guy Hunter-Watts (Alastair Sawday Publishing). Accommodations with character, comfort, and value.

Series: Berlitz, *Blue Guides, *Cadogan, Daytrips, Exploring Rural Europe, Fielding, Fodor, Frommer, *Insight Guides, Karen Brown, *Let's Go, *Lonely Planet, *Michelin, Passport Regional Guides, *Rick Steves, *Rough Guides, Ulysses.

Romania

Hiking Guide to Romania (Bradt).

Russia and the NIS

Georgian Republic by Roger Rosen (Passport Books). First comprehensive guide in English.

Hiking Guide to Poland and Ukraine by Tim Burford (Bradt).

Language and Travel Guide to Ukraine by L. Hodges (Hippocrene). Revised edition.

Russia Survival Guide by Paul Richardson (Russian Information Services). Comprehensive guide with practical information.

Siberian Bam Rail Guide by Athol Yates (Trailblazer). The second Trans-Siberian Railway.

Trans-Siberian Handbook by Bryn Thomas (Trailblazer). Solid information.

Trekking in Russia and Central Asia: A Traveler's Guide by Frith Maier (Mountaineers).

Where in St. Petersburg by Scott McDonald (Russian Information Services). Practical information, maps, and information on the city.

Series: Berlitz, *Blue Guides, *Cadogan, *Culture Shock, Customs and Etiquette, Fodor, Frommer, *Insight Guides, *Interlink, Knopf, *Lonely Planet, *Rough Guides. Distributors: Russian Information Services, 89 Main St., Montpelier, VT 05602; 800-639-4301. Free Access Russia and Central Europe catalog, Russian Life magazine.

Scandinavia

Series: Berlitz, *Blue Guides, Bradt, *Culture Shock!, Fodor, Frommer, *Insight Guides, *Lonely Planet, Nelles, *Rick Steves, *Rough Guides.

Singapore

Thailand, Malaysia, Singapore by Rail by Brian McPhee (Bradt).

South America

Backpacking and Trekking in Peru and Bolivia by Hilary Bradt (Bradt).

Eat Smart In Brazil by Joan and David Peterson (Ginkgo Press). Cuisine, menu guide, market foods and more.

Inca Trail: Cuzco and Machu Picchu by Richard Danbury (Trailblazer). Trekking information.

Latin America by Bike: A Complete Touring Guide by W. Sienko (Mountaineers). From Mexico through Central America all the way to the tip of Argentina.

South America's National Parks: A Visitor's Guide by William Leitch (Mountaineers). A long-needed introduction to South America's great ecological treasures.

South and Central America: Literary Companion by Jason Wilson (Passport Books). Compilation of literature, background, and cultural information.

Traveler's Guide to Latin America Customs & Manners by N. Braganti and E. Devine (St. Martin's Press). An important aid in understanding Latin American culture.

Trekking in Bolivia: A Traveler's Guide by Yossi Brain (Mountaineers).

Series: Berlitz, Bradt, *Cadogan, Fielding, Fodor, *Footprints, Frommer, *Insight Guides, *Let's Go, *Lonely Planet, *Moon, *New Key, *Rough Guides, Travelers' Tales, Ulysses.

Spain

An Insider's Guide to Spain Hotels: $40-$80 a Night for Two by Margo Classé (Wilson Publishing). Covers centrally located hotels in many Spanish cities.

Series: Berlitz, *Blue Guides, *Cadogan, *Culture Shock!, Daytrips, Driving Tours, Exploring Rural Europe, Eyewitness, Fielding, Fodor, *Footprints, Frommer, *Insight Guides, *Interlink, Karen Brown, *Let's Go, Maverick, *Michelin, Nelles, *Rick Steves, *Rough Guides, Time Out, Travelers' Tales.

Special Places to Stay in Spain and Portugal by Guy Hunter-Watts. (Alastair Sawday Publishing). Accommodations with character, comfort, and value.

Trekking in Spain by Marc Dubin (Lonely Planet Publications). Both day hikes and overnight treks.

Switzerland

Switzerland by Rail by Anthony Lambert (Bradt Publishing).

Switzerland: The Smart Traveler's Guide to Zurich, Basel and Geneva by Paul Hofmann (Henry Holt).

Walking Easy in the Swiss Alps by C. and C. Lipton (Globe Pequot). Hiking guide for active adults.

Walking in Switzerland (Lonely Planet). From long hikes to day walks.

Walking Switzerland the Swiss Way: From Vacation Apartments, Hotels, Mountain Inns, and Huts by Marcia and Philip Lieberman. (Mountaineers, 2nd ed).

Series: Berlitz, *Blue Guides, Bradt, *Culture Shock!, Daytrips, Driving Tours, Fodor, Frommer, *Insight Guides, Karen Brown, *Let's Go, *Lonely Planet, *Michelin, *Rick Steves.

Taiwan

Series: *Culture Shock!, *Insight Guides, *Lonely Planet.

Thailand

Chiang Mai: Thailand's Northern Rose (Passport Books). Good planning information.

Diving in Thailand by Collin Piprell (Hippocrene). Best diving sites with information on preparation, facilities, etc.

Thailand, Malaysia, Singapore by Rail by Brian McPhee (Bradt).

Series: Berlitz, Bradt, *Culture Shock!, Customs and Etiquette, Fielding, *Footprints, *Insight Guides, Knopf, *Lonely Planet, Maverick, *Moon Handbooks, Nelles, Passport Regional Guides, *Rough Guides, Treasures and Pleasures of...

Turkey

Series: Berlitz, *Blue Guides, *Cadogan, *Culture Shock!, Fodor, Frommer, *Insight Guides, *Interlink, Knopf, *Let's Go, *Lonely Planet, *Michelin, Nelles, *Rough Guides.

United Kingdom and Ireland

*Rick Steves' London** by Rick Steves (John Muir Publications). New Rick Steves guide that will help travelers get the most for their time and money while in London.

*The Visitor's Guide to Northern Ireland** by Rosemary Evans (Dufour Editions). A new edition of the only book-length travel guide to Northern Ireland.

Bed & Breakfast Directory by Ken Platt (Seven Hills). Over 3,000 B and Bs in all price ranges.

Bed and Breakfast Ireland by Elsie Dillard and Susan Causin (Chronicle). Guide to over 300 of Ireland's best B and Bs.

Best Bed and Breakfasts: England, Scotland, Wales 1999-2000 by Sigourney Wells (Globe Pequot). Alphabetical by county.

Brit-Think, Ameri-Think by Jane Walmsley (Penguin). An irreverent guide to understanding the cultural differences.

Britain Bed & Breakfast, Ireland Bed & Breakfast, Scotland Bed & Breakfast by Tim Stiwell (Seven Hills). Easy to use, good maps, up to date.

Cheap Eats in London and Cheap Sleeps in London (Chronicle Books). 100 inexpensive places to eat and sleep.

Cycle Tours in the U.K. (Ordnance Survey). Sixteen different guides, each describing around 24 different one-day trips in the U.K.

Cycling Great Britain by Tim Hughes (Bicycle Books).

Cycling Ireland by Philip Routledge (Bicycle Books).

Dublin on a Shoestring by Matthew Magee, et al. (Irish Books & Media). Handy pocket-sized treasure trove of useful contemporary facts, figures, and useful information.

England by Bike: 18 Tours Geared for Discovery by Les Woodland (Mountaineers).

English and Scottish Tourist Board Publications (Seven Hills). Selection includes titles on Hotels, B and Bs, Self-Catering, Staying on a Farm, Activity Breaks.

Europe's Wonderful Little Hotels & Inns: Great Britain and Ireland by Hilary Rubinstein and Carolyn Raphael (St. Martin's Press).

Great British Bed & Breakfast by Ken Platt (Seven Hills). 600 of Britain's finest B and Bs.

Holidays at British Universities. Free brochure from British Universities Accommodation Consortium, Ltd., Box 1732, University Park, Nottingham, England NG7 2RD; fax 011-44-115-942-2505; buac@nottingham.ac.uk, [www.buac.co.uk]. Lists universities that offer accommodations during vacation periods and those that offer noncredit summer classes for visitors.

Hotels and Restaurants of Britain, 1999 by British Hospitality Association (Globe Pequot).

Independent Walker's Guide to Britain and **Independent Walker's Guide to Ireland** by Frank Booth (Interlink). Scenic walks through the countryside.

Ireland by Bike: 21 Tours Geared for Discovery by Robyn Krause (Mountaineers, 2nd ed).

Ireland: Complete Guide and Road Atlas (Globe Pequot). Comprehensive guide, organized by regions.

Irish Bed & Breakfast Book by Frank and Fran Sullivan (Pelican).

Literary Villages of London by Luree Miller (Starrhill Press). The author's favorite walks past the London homes and haunts of celebrated writers.

London for Free by Brian Butler (Mustang Publishing).

National Trust Handbook (Trafalgar Square). Lists National Trust properties including homes, gardens, castles, lighthouses.

On the Rails Around Britain and Ireland edited by Neil Wenborn (Passport Books). Routes, maps, transport information.

Passport Guide to Ethnic London by Ian McAuley (Passport Books). A guide to history, food, culture—neighborhood by neighborhood.

Scotland Bed and Breakfast (British Tourist Authority). Over 2,000 B and Bs listed.

Special Places to Stay in Britain by Alastair Sawday (Alastair Sawday Publishing). Accommodations with character, comfort, and value.

Walking in Britain by David Else (Lonely Planet).

Series: *Access, Berlitz, *Blue Guides, *Cadogan, Customs and Etiquette, Daytrips, Driving Tours, Exploring Rural Europe, Eyewitness, Fielding, Fodor, Frommer, *Insight Guides, *Interlink, Karen Brown, Knopf, *Let's Go, *Lonely Planet, *Michelin, National Geographic, Nelles, Passport Regional Guides, *Rick Steves, *Rough Guides, Time Out, Treasures and Pleasures of…

Vietnam, Laos, Cambodia

Guide to Vietnam by John R. Jones (Bradt). Every province and area of interest is described in detail, along with fascinating cultural information.

Vietnam: Traveler's Literary Companion edited by J. Balaban and N. Qui Duc (Whereabouts Press). Compilation of short stories by Vietnamese writers.

Series: Bradt, *Culture Shock!, Customs and Etiquette, Fielding, *Footprints, *Insight Guides, *Lonely Planet, Maverick, *Moon, Nelles, *Rough Guides.

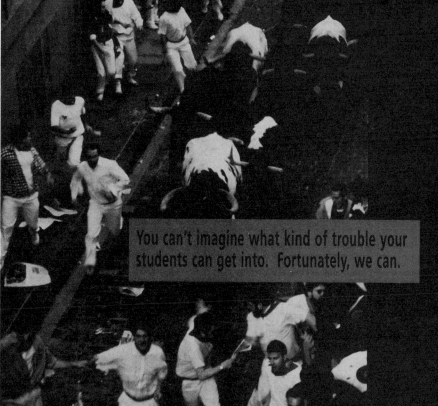

You can't imagine what kind of trouble your students can get into. Fortunately, we can.

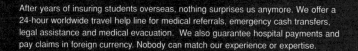

Hemingway, the Spanish Years. (Unauthorized field trip.)

After years of insuring students overseas, nothing surprises us anymore. We offer a 24-hour worldwide travel help line for medical referrals, emergency cash transfers, legal assistance and medical evacuation. We also guarantee hospital payments and pay claims in foreign currency. Nobody can match our experience or expertise.

For more information on World Class Coverage plans, call 1-800-303-8120, ext 5430 or visit www.culturalinsurance.com

CULTURAL
INSURANCE
SERVICES
INTERNATIONAL

THE EXPERIENCE TO INSURE YOUR CULTURAL EXPERIENCE.

CISI

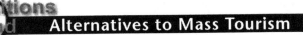

TWO

The following listing of specialty travel vacations was supplied by the organizers. Contact the program directors to confirm costs, dates, and other details. Please tell them you read about their program in this book! Programs based in more than one country or region are listed under "Worldwide."

Africa

Tanzania/Zanzibar Circuits. We specialize in wildlife safari and nature trails in Tanzania/Zanzibar and mountain trekking, photography safaris on the northern and southern circuit of Tanzania, beach holidays to the islands of Zanzibar, Pemba, Mafya. For incentive and FITS group and students both camping and lodge hotels.
   Dates: Year round. **Cost:** Student discount rates: Lodge/hotel $150 per day. Camping $90 per day all inclusive. Valid till Nov 99 (min. 5 people). **Contact:** R.S. Chuwa, Managing Director, Equatorial Safaris Ltd, P.O. Box 2156, Arusha, Tanzania; Tel./fax 011-255-57-3302; equatorial@yako.habari.co.tz, [whiteyellow.com/equatorialsafaris].

Argentina

Instituto de Lengua Española (ILEE). Located downtown in the most European-like city in Latin America, Buenos Aires. Dedicated exclusively to teaching Spanish to foreigners. Small groups and private classes year round. All teachers hold Master's degrees in Education or Literature and have been full-time Spanish professors for years. Method is intensive,

conversation-based. Student body is international. Highly recommended worldwide. Ask for individual references in U.S.
   Dates: Year round. **Cost:** Four-week intensive program (20 hours per week) including homestay $1,400; 2 weeks $700. Private classes $19 per hour. Registration fee (includes books) $100. **Contact:** Daniel Korman, I.L.E.E., Director, Av. Callao 339, 3 fl. (1048), Buenos Aires, Argentina; Tel./fax 011-54-1-375-0730. In U.S.: David Babbitz; 415-431-8219, fax 415-431-5306; ilee@overnet.com.ar, [www.studyabroad.com/ilee].

Asia

Ancient Arts Abroad. Create your own independent study. Based on your goals we'll design an itinerary including personalized instruction in: alternative healing methods, martial arts fengshui, yoga, ethnic arts/cuisine…introduction to kihapsool acupressure/cheonjisool martial art techniques in Korea; Chinese studies in Singapore. On-site representatives' follow-up workshops arranged internationally.
   Dates: Flexible scheduling to coincide with your travel plans. **Cost:** Vary depending on program/options selected. **Contact:** B. Sherbo,

Director, Scholarly Pursuits International, Inc., 11 Joslin Rd., Exeter, NH 03833; awdn@yahoo.com.

Asian Medicine and Culture in Nepal. As featured in *USA Today*, an extraordinary opportunity to learn from experts the many varieties of Asian healing systems while you experience the Himalayas with their breathtaking vistas, encounter a variety of cultures and their rituals, visit Chitwan Wildlife Sanctuary, and explore the wondrous city of Kathmandu. Free brochure: 800-833-2444.

Dates: Mar 14-31; Apr 2-27; Sep 3-21; Oct 4-19; Nov 5-23. **Cost:** $2,800-$3,624 plus airfare depending on 14- or 19-day tour and season. Includes breakfast, 3 banquets, lodging, air and land transportation in Nepal, guides and fees. Optional low-cost 2-night stay in Bangkok **Contact:** Explorations, 3515 Woodland Rd., Ann Arbor, MI 48104; 734-971-4754, fax 734-971-0042; emcnepal@worldnet.att.net, [www.explorations-alt-med.com].

Cultural Adventure. Millennium treks and safaris and other special interest tours. Filming, scuba diving, fishing, mountain expeditions, yoga and health. Custom-designed programs.

Dates: Apr-Sep. **Cost:** From $40-$120 per day per person. **Contact:** Rajeev Chadha, Quest Tours Pvt., Ltd., 108, Antriksh Bhawan, 22, K.G. Marg, Connaught Pl., New Delhi 110 001, India; 011-91-11-3317738, 3721612, 91-129-260257 (24 hrs.), fax 011-91-11-3357489; questour@del2.vsnl.net.in, paroaj@usa.net, [www.inetindia.com/travel/t_agents/quest].

The Silk Road to Samarkand. A cultural tour of Uzbekistan, the major trading center of the Silk Road, including stops in Khiva, Bukhara, Shakrisabz, and Samarkand. Travel along a historically flourishing trade route, rich in silk, textiles and spices, beautiful mosques and medreses in the exotic landscape of Central Asia.

Dates: Aug 20-Sep 5. **Cost:** $4,175 includes land, airfare, and all meals. **Contact:** Samy Rabinovic, New Horizons, P.O. Box 187, Newton, PA 18940; 215-860-8869, fax 215-860-7779; nhiint@aol.com, [www.indigoturizm.com.tr/newhorizons.htm].

Australia

The Adventure Company. The Adventure Company, Australia specializes in top quality adventure and nature tours for individuals and groups. We run a variety of scheduled trips, all of which involve a strong nature element. Many of the tours take place in World Heritage listed national parks. Hike along ancient Aboriginal rainforest trails, sea kayak along pristine coastline and deserted islands, mountain bike through small country villages on the Atherton Tablelands or visit Aboriginal art sites dating back 40,000 years.

Dates: Call program for information. Join 1- to 12-day trips. **Cost:** $50-$1,500, including all trips departing from Cairns. **Contact:** Gary Hill, The Adventure Company, Australia, P.O. Box 5740, Cairns, Queensland 4870, Australia; 011-61-7-4051-4777, fax 011-61-7-4051-4888; adventures@adventures.com.au, [www.adventures.com.au]. In U.S.: 800-388-7333.

WWOOFING (Willing Workers on Organic Farms). Learn organic growing while living with a host family. Twelve hundred hosts in Australia or travel the world with over 600 hosts on all continent where you work in exchange for food and board.

Dates: Year round. **Cost:** AUS$40 single, AUS$45 double. **Contact:** WWOOF Australia, Buchan, Victoria 3885, Australia; 011-61-3-5155-0218, fax 011-61-3-5155-0342; wwoof@net-tech.com.au, [www.wwoof.com.au].

Austria

Aquarelle and Music. Landscape painting and chamber music at the Koenigsee (Bavaria). Historic setting (1711). Organized by St. Rupert's Order of Salzburg. Tutors: Frana Buear and Walter Hermann Sallagar, CSRO.

Dates: Sep 7-17. **Cost:** EUR900 inclusive price. **Contact:** W.H. Sallagar, Neulinggasse 42/10, Vienna, A-1030, Austria; Tel./fax 011-43-1-7141710.

Canada

Edphy International. A French international sports camp offering language courses, sports specialization, and a tour program.

Dates: Jun-Aug. **Cost:** Starts at CAN$470 per week plus $75 registration fees (1999). **Contact:** Luc Dubois, President, Edphy International, Inc., 4582 Couturier St., Laval, Quebec H7T 2T1, Canada; 888-463-3749, 450-687-5662, fax 450-687-6304.

West Coast Rail Tours. Active group of railway enthusiasts who run railway oriented tours throughout British Columbia. One day to 9 days. Remote areas, photo ops, wildlife—all inclusive packages.

Dates: Year round. **Cost:** Contact sponsor. **Contact:** West Coast Rail Tours, Box 2790, Stn. Main, Vancouver, BC, V6B 3X2, Canada; 800-722-1233; tours@wcra.org.

Wilderness Guide Training. Licensed guide outfitting business conducts 1- and 2-week training programs in guiding and outdoor adventure tourism. Programs include: horsehandling, western mountain riding, guiding, horse packing/shoeing/logging, back country living, and operational procedures. Acquire skills for pack horse trips, guest ranch adventures, alpine fishing, ecotourism, big game viewing, and photo safaris.

Dates: Two-week guide training: May 2-14, May 16-28, May 30-Jun 11; 1-week guide training: Jul 4-10, Aug 15-21. **Cost:** All inclusive packages: 2-week guide training CAN$2,056; 1-week guide training CAN$1,067. **Contact:** Sylvia Waterer or Kevan Bracewell, Chilcotin Holidays Guest Ranch, Gun Creek Road, Gold Bridge, BC, V0K 1P0, Canada; Tel./fax 250-238-2274; chilcotin_holidays@bc.sympatico.ca, [www.chilcotinholidays.com].

Wilderness Lodging. Purcell Lodge is Canada's finest remote mountain lodge. It sets a new environmental standard in sustainable tourism development. A few miles beyond the crowds of Banff and Lake Louise lies true solitude. A spectacular helicopter flight leaves the familiar far behind. Inside, the comfort of a fine country manor. Outside, your own natural paradise. Peaceful walks in alpine meadows, guided ski tours in stunning surroundings.

Dates: Late Jun-early Oct, Dec-Apr. **Cost:** All-inclusive American plan $85-$140 per night. **Contact:** Paul Larson, Manager, Purcell Lodge, Places Less Travelled Ltd., P.O. Box 1829, Golden, BC, Canada V0A 1H0; 250-344-2639, fax 250-344-5520; places@rockies.net, [www.purcell.com].

Caribbean

Sailing on Sir Francis Drake. Experience the romance of sail aboard the historic, 3-masted schooner, Sir Francis Drake. Share your vacation with only 28 sun and fun-loving sailmates. The most relaxing vacation afloat. Swim, snorkel, and dance to the Caribbean beat beneath the stars.

Dates: Winter: through Apr; summer: May-Nov. **Cost:** $995-$1,395 for 7 nights includes all food on board. **Contact:** Gaye L. Torrey, Director of Marketing, Tall Ship Adventures, Inc., 1389 S. Havana St., Aurora, CO 80012; 800-

662-0090, 303-755-7983, fax 303-755-9007; info@tallshipadventures.com, [www.tallshipadventures.com].

Chile

Rafting Bio Bio and Futaleufu. Bio Bio: Rafting 60 km of some of the world's most spectacular class IV-V rapids. Pass lava-rock canyons, rare Araucaria Pine forest, hot springs, and smoking volcanoes. Futaleufu (Patagonia): Ultimate rafting for the paddler looking for challenging rivers with huge, clear, warm water in the most amazing setting.

Dates: Jan, Feb, Mar, Apr. **Cost:** Bio Bio $475, Futaleufu $1,310. **Contact:** Cascada Expediciones, Orrego Luco 040, Providencia, Santiago, Chile; 011-56-2-234-2274, 232-7214, fax 011-56-2-233-97-68; info@cascada-expediciones.com.

Costa Rica

Costa Rican Language Academy. Costa Rican-owned and operated language school offers first-rate Spanish instruction in a warm and friendly environment. Teachers with university degrees. Small groups or private classes. Included free in the programs are airport transportation, coffee and natural refreshments, excursions, Latin dance, Costa Rican cooking, music, and conversation classes to provide students with complete cultural immersion.

Dates: Year round (start anytime). **Cost:** $135 per week or $220 per week for program with homestay. All other activities and services included at no additional cost. **Contact:** Costa Rican Language Academy, P.O. Box 336-2070, San José, Costa Rica; 011-506-221-1624 or 011-506-233-8914 or 011-233-8938, fax 011-506-233-8670. In the U.S.: 800-854-6057; crlang@sol.racsa.co.cr, [www.crlang.co.cr/index.html].

Horizontes Nature Tours. For more than 15 years, Horizontes has operated quality, personalized travel programs for people interested in nature observation, conservation, education, soft adventure, and meaningful interaction with local people. We operate custom-designed group and individual itineraries for renowned international tour companies, universities, and nonprofit organizations worldwide. Plus a wide selection of package tours.

Dates: Custom trips, 1-day, and multi-day package tours available year round. **Cost:** Call for details. **Contact:** Terry Pratt, Marketing Director, Horizontes Nature Tours, P.O. Box

1780-1002 P.E., San José, Costa Rica; 011-506-222-2022, fax 011-506-255-4513; horizont@sol.racsa.co.cr.

Intensive Spanish Training. The Institute for Central American Development Studies (ICADS) offers 4-week progressive programs in intensive Spanish language—4 1/2 hours daily, 5 days a week. Small classes (4 or fewer students). Activities and optional afternoon internships emphasize environmental issues, women's issues, development, human rights, and public health. Supportive learning environment. Homestays and field trips. Great alternative for the socially conscious.

Dates: Programs begin first Monday of each month. **Cost:** $1,400 includes airport pick-up, classes, books, homestay, meals, laundry, lectures, activities, field trips, and internship placements. **Contact:** ICADS, Dept. 826, P.O. Box 025216, Miami, FL 33102-5216; 011-506-225-0508, fax 011-506-234-1337; icads@netbox.com, [www.icadscr.com].

Learn Spanish While Volunteering. Assist with the training of Costa Rican public school teachers in ESL and computers. Assist local health clinic, social service agencies, and environmental projects. Enjoy learning Spanish in the morning, volunteer work in the after-noon/evening. Spanish classes of 2-5 students plus group learning activities; conversations with middle class homestay families (1 student per family). Homestays and most volunteer projects are within walking distance of school in small town near the capital, San José.

Dates: Year round, all levels. Classes begin every Monday (except Apr 17-21 and Dec 18-29), volunteer program is continuous. **Cost:** $345 per week for 28 hours of classes and group activities plus Costa Rican dance and cooking classes. Includes tuition, 3 meals per day, 7 days per week, homestay, laundry, all materials, weekly 3-hour cultural tour, and airport transportation. $25 one-time registration fee. **Contact:** Susan Shores, Registrar, Latin American Language Center, PMB 123, 7485 Rush River Dr., Suite 710, Sacramento, CA 95831-5260; 916-447-0938, fax 916-428-9542; lalc@madre.com.

Live Among the Giant Grasses. Work with an learn about Tropical Bamboos from bamboo furniture maker, sculptor, and gardener, Brian Erickson. This program offers a general orientation on the subject of bamboo, including opportunities to work in a botanical garden, participate in the development of a small bamboo plantation and assume workshop tasks utilizing bamboos.

Dates: Year round, 1 month sessions, beginning the 1st of each month. **Cost:** $750 for 1st month, $600 additional months. Includes private sleeping space, shared bath, meals. Airfare and insurance not included. **Contact:** Patricia Erickson, Apdo. 295-7210 Guapiles, Costa Rica; fax 011-506-710-6161; brieri99@yahoo.com.

Europe

¿?don Quijote In-Country Spanish Language Schools. Offers Spanish language courses in our 6 schools in Spain and 5 partner schools in Latinoamerica. Our courses (standard, intensive, business, D.E.L.E., tourism, flight attendants and refresher for teachers) are all year round, from 2 weeks on. Students can combine different cities and schools. Academic credit is available.

Dates: Year round—fall, spring, winter, and summer, 2 weeks to a full year of study. **Cost:** Email or check web site for details. **Contact:** ¿?don Quijote In-Country Spanish Language Schools, calle/Placentinos n°2, Salamanca 37008, Spain; 011-34-923-268860, fax 011-34-923-268815; amusa@donquijote.org, [www.donquijote.org].

Archaeology Summer School. Introduces participants to the theory and practice of archaeology in general and to Mediterranean and Maltese archaeology in particular. Two-week course is followed by 4 weeks of excava-tion and finds processing experience. Partici-pants may register for a range of 2-6 week options.

Dates: Jun 12-Jul 21. **Cost:** From $625-$2,000 includes accommodations. **Contact:** Jean Killick, International Office, Foundation for International Studies, Old Univ. Bldg., St. Paul St., Valletta VLT 07, Malta; 011-356-234121/2, fax 011-356-230538; jkil@um.edu.mt, [www.um.edu.mt/shortcourses/].

Best of Europe/Footloose. Highest quality escorted and independent walking holidays in Europe. Small, compatible groups and great service.

Dates: Year round but particularly May-Oct. **Cost:** From £247-£1,800. **Contact:** Aline Kellroghlian, Alternative Travel Group, 69-71 Banbury Rd., Oxford OX2 6PE, England; 011-44-1865-315-665, fax 011-44-1865-315-697; info@alternative-travel.co.uk.

Coopersmith's Garden Tours. One-of-a-Kind Tours of gardens, manor houses, palaces, castles and museums in Britain, Europe, and New Zealand. Upscale tours of 6-20 people, spending 3 and 4 nights at each country inn or manor house hotel. Large, comfortable coaches, superb escorts, gourmet cuisine. Since 1984.
Dates: May-Feb. **Cost:** $2,900-$4,900. **Contact:** Paul Coopersmith, Coopersmith's England, Box 900, Inverness, CA 94937; 415-669-1914, fax 415-669-1942; paul@coopersmiths.com, [www.coopersmiths.com].

The Essential Cookery Course. Four-week intensive residential cookery course taking students through methods and principles more frequently covered in a longer course. Progress from basic skills to complex techniques, with the emphasis on practical hands-on cookery.
Dates: Jan, Feb, May, Jul-Aug, Sep, Oct, Nov. **Cost:** £1,990. **Contact:** Cookery at the Grange, Whatley, Frome, Somerset, BA11 3JU, England; Tel./fax 011-44-1373-836579; cookery.grange@clara.net, [www.hi-media.co.uk/grange-cookery].

Euro-Bike and Walking Tours. Twenty-sixth year of providing luxury tours to 15 countries in Europe. Beginner and experienced. See why our customers return year after year. Free brochure.
Dates: May-Oct, 6-15 day tours. **Cost:** Starting at $1,645. **Contact:** Euro-Bike and Walking Tours, P.O. Box 990, Dekalb, IL 60115; 800-321-6060; info@eurobike.com, [www.eurobike.com].

Inniemore School of Painting. Painting courses run at Highland Lodge, set in stunning location. Full board or self-catering. All standards taught, on Isle of Mull, Scotland. Est. 1967.
Dates: May-Sep. **Cost:** Course from £400 all inclusive (1999). **Contact:** Andrew Mazur, Inniemore Lodge, Pennyghael, Isle of Mull, Scotland, PA70 6HD; 011-44-1681-704201.

Issue-Specific Travel Courses. Visit 1 to 4 cities. Topics include International Business and Economics, Comparative Education, Historical Literature, Social Service Systems, and other crosscultural studies. Emphasis on personal interaction between students and European professionals and providing a holistic cultural experience. Two- to 5-week programs. Three to 6 credit hours—undergraduate, graduate, or audit basis—through the Univ. of Missouri-Kansas City.

Dates: Early summer. **Cost:** Approx. $2,000 (does not include airfare). **Contact:** People to People International, Collegiate and Professional Studies Abroad, 501 E. Armour Blvd., Kansas City, MO 64109-2200; 816-531-4701, fax 816-561-7502; collegiate@ptpi.org, [www.ptpi.org/studyabroad].

Language, Arts, and Sports. Active learning vacations: French, Spanish, Italian, Portuguese; cooking, painting, drawing, photography workshops. Combine eduVacational interests. French and sailing or skiing; Spanish and golf; bicycle tours—more countries, more ideas. We match individual needs and interests with programs and options: family stay, apartment, hotel; intensive to total immersion; small groups or study and live in your teacher's home.
Dates: Programs run from 1 week to months. **Cost:** Includes room and board, tuition. **Contact:** Mary Ann Puglisi, eduVacations[sm], 1431 21st St. NW, Suite 302, Washington, DC 20036; 202-857-8384, fax 202-463-8091.

Mozart's Europe Tour. A European tour featuring attendance at 9-10 major music/opera festivals, extensive sightseeing (included in tour), special visits, and interviews related to the life of Mozart and other composes in central Europe. Accommodations are 50 percent deluxe, 50 percent superior first class.
Dates: Jun-Sep. **Cost:** Approx. $3,800-$4,000, depending on length of tour. **Contact:** Dr. Norman Eagle, 2037 Majorca Dr., Canard, CA 93035; Tel./fax 805-382-0969; eagle@goldenwave.com.

Nonreciprocal Homestay Arrangement. Any age student, any date for language learning. International Links arranges homestays in France, Spain, Germany for language students. We guarantee that there will be a young person or similar age as visiting student. No other foreign student in family. Local organizer.
Dates: Year round. **Cost:** £245 per week excluding travel. Full board arrangement and living as a member of the family. **Contact:** International Links, 145 Manygate Ln., Shepperton Middlesex TW17 9EP, England; 011-44-1932-222294, fax 011-44-1932-229300.

Stone Sculpture Workshops. Since 1985 Marble & Art Workshops has offered marble sculpture workshops in the international center of sculpture, Pietrasanta, Italy. Created, organized, and assisted by American sculptor Lynne Streeter, these courses offer the chance to learn classical stone carving techniques in an inspirational and creative environment. Also: Spain, alabaster, and moldmaking.

Dates: Pietrasanta, Italy: Session I Jun; session II Jul; session III Sep. Barcelona, Spain: Aug. **Cost:** Call for details. **Contact:** Lynne Streeter, P.O. Box 7371, Oakland, CA 94601; 510-533-8893, fax 510-436-0630.

Yoga for Everyone. Yoga is for everyone. Ruth White has the ability to enable people to see through their limitations and experience a sense of freedom and well-being. As seen on her TV series, she endeavors to adapt her instruction to the needs of her students. Her workshops are popular in Europe, Australia, India, and Greece and are suitable for everyone.

Dates: Year round. **Cost:** Approx. £100 per weekend. **Contact:** Ruth White, Ruth White Yoga Centre, Church Farm House, Spring Close Ln., Cheam, Surrey SM3 8PU, U.K.; 011-44-181-644-0309, fax 011-44-181-287-5318; [www.ruthwhiteyoga.com].

France

"Le Marmiton" Cooking School. Le Marmiton cookery school offers its clients the chance to learn about French cuisine. Lessons are given in a 19th century kitchen, and we invite only the best chefs from around the region to teach. The pupils prepare a delightful meal which is then enjoyed by the whole class and any friends they might wish to invite. Internships for professionals for 1 month or more are available.

Dates: Five classes per month except in Jan, Jul, and Aug (1999). **Cost:** From FF400 per person per class to FF490 for a 6-night, 5-day package with lodging. **Contact:** Martin Stein, Hotel de la Mirande, 4, place de La Mirande, F-84000 Avignon, France; 011-33-4-90-85-93-93, fax 011-33-4-90-86-26-85; [www.la-mirande.fr].

Arts in a French Country House. "La Maison Verte" in the south of France offers weekly workshops throughout the summer. Examples include pottery, yoga, singing, Alexander technique, painting, wine tasting, and cooking. Very French, very rural.

Dates: Jun-Sep. **Cost:** £350 includes accommodations, tuition, some meals. **Contact:** Linda Garnett, 55 High St., Hemingford Grey, Huntingdon PE18 9BN, U.K.; Tel./fax 011-44-1480-495364.

Atelier de Calvisson. Painting courses (oil, watercolor, pastel, drawing). Outdoors. Beginners to advanced. Individual tuition. Full board in the artist's house, private room with bath and wc.

Dates: Apr-Oct. **Cost:** FF2,850 per week. **Contact:** Corinne Burckel de Tell, 30420 Calvisson, France; 011-33-4-66-01-23-91, fax 011-33-4-01-42-19.

Français General et de Specialité. Courses for adults who need to express themselves with the greatest possible fluency, whether for leisure or professional purposes. General French, commercial and business French, language and culture courses are available. One to 14 weeks, 4 lessons or more per day in small groups. Extracurricular activities: cooking, wine tasting, painting, golf, tennis, excursions.

Dates: Every second Monday from Jan 3. **Cost:** From FF3,500 for 2 weeks. **Contact:** Astrid Giorgetta, IS, Aix-en-Provence, 9 Cours des Arts et Mètiers, Aix-en-Provence 13100, France; 011-33-4-42-93-47-90, fax 011-33-4-42-26-31-80; is.aix@pacwan.fr, [www.is-aix.com].

French Language and Cooking. Live and study in 18th century Château de Mâtel. Adult residential courses in French language and French country cooking in a relaxed, convivial atmosphere. Small classes and quality teaching. Reasonable prices. Comfortable single, twin rooms. Good food and wine taken with teachers. Heart of Burgundy, Beaujolais, and Lyons area. Access to the world via Internet and computer.

Dates: Every Sunday May-Nov. **Cost:** From $820 full board and classes in château. **Contact:** Michael Giammarella in U.S.: 800-484-1234 ext 0096 or Ecole des Trois Ponts, Château de Mâtel, 42300 Roanne, France; 011-33-477-70-80-01, fax 011-33-477-71-5300; info@3ponts.edu, [www.3ponts.edu].

French Language Learning Vacations. Learn French while discovering the chateaux of the Loire Valley, the secrets of Provence, or the sandy beaches of the Mediterranean. Our programs are designed for independent travelers sharing a passion for the French culture and lifestyle. We offer a choice of locations in Tours, Aix-en-Provence, Montpellier, Paris, or Nice.

Dates: Two or more weeks year round. **Cost:** Two-week packages range from $825-$1,265. Includes classes, housing and fees. **Contact:** Jim Pondolfino, French-American Exchange, 111 Roberts Court, Box 7, Alexandria, VA 22314; 800-995-5087, fax 703-549-2865; faetours@erols.com, [www.faetours.com].

French Painting Holidays. We are based in Les Pays de la Loire at Le Petit Bois Gleu and welcome painters, from beginners to profes-

By Kent St. John

At one time or another while traveling abroad, you're bound to get that throat-tightening fear when you reach for your travel essentials and something is missing. Countless times a day on a trip I reach for my passport, credit cards, tickets, and cash for the security that comes when "you know your papers are in order."

Travel Insurance Kit

Before departing, construct your personal "travel insurance kit" by doing pre-trip research. I usually start with embassy and consulate information. The State Department (see sidebar) can be accessed by phone, fax, or Internet for important addresses and phone numbers you will need in an emergency. The U.S. consul's number and address in the areas you will be traveling to can be a great help. One of the consular section's primary functions is to provide emergency services to travelers—such as replacing a passport, locating medical assistance, arranging the transfer of funds, and locating you if a family crisis occurs.

A photocopy of the first two pages of your passport can speed up the issuance of a temporary or replacement passport. I also carry two extra passport photos in case a visa is required for an unplanned destination. It's also a good idea to leave copies of important information stateside with family or a trusted friend. If your passport is lost or stolen, the first step is to notify the local police, then the consul section. With a photocopy, there's a good chance a new passport can be issued within 24 hours. If you are traveling in a country that has no U.S. foreign post, it's a wise to register with a consular office in an adjacent country.

Money Emergencies

One of the biggest traveler's worries is the loss of funds. What to do if an unexpected cash crisis does develop depends on your individual situation. If the country you're in has ATM machines, a simple call to family or a trusted friend can get a deposit into your account and you're back on the road. If not, or if a larger amount is needed for an emergency, the Overseas Citizen Services (see sidebar) is a great option. For a $20 processing fee, the Department of State trust establishes a local account in your name so that funds can be forwarded abroad. The fastest way to get money is to send a money order via Western Union, payable to the Department of State. Send it to the Overseas Citizens Services, Department of State, Washington, DC 20520. The accompanying message must include the sender's name, address, and telephone number, as well as the name and overseas address of the recipient. Upon receipt, OSC will send a telegram to the U.S. embassy or consulate authorizing next day disbursement.

You can also mail a certified check (with the $20 fee included) to Overseas Citizen Services, CA/OSC, Room 4811, Department of State, 2201 C St. NW, Washington, DC 20520. But keep in mind that even overnight mail may take several days to arrive. Both the sender's and receiver's names and the location of the receiver must be included in an accompanying letter.

A bank wire is a one- to three-day solution for transferring funds to financially ailing travelers. Nations Bank will handle a wire transfer from a stateside bank for a $32 fee. Send it to: Nations Bank, Department of State Branch, 2201 C St., NW, Washington, DC 20520; 202-624-4750 at ABA #114000653, Account #7476363838. Account name: PUPID State Department, Special instructions: "OCS/Trust for benefit of [recipient's name]" U.S. Embassy/Consulate [city, country]. Be sure the sender includes his or her name and telephone number.

In all of the above transfers the funds are usually received in the foreign country's currency and not in U.S. dollars. American Express, 800-543-4080, also provides a money transfer service with fees that depend on where and what amount is being transferred.

Leave an Itinerary

If you're traveling for more than two weeks or to an area that is somewhat remote, leave an itinerary with someone back home and register with the closest embassy or consulate. When you do, you must provide a Privacy Act waiver before information can be released to third parties. This is called a Welfare/ Whereabouts check and essentially aids those back home to notify you of any emergency. Along with your itinerary, leave your family this OCS number: 202-647-5225. If they need to contact you they should have the following information handy: your passport number, date and place of birth, and your itinerary. This service can ease the minds of those at home about your well-being.

Medical Services

Medical emergencies seem to be the one area most often left to chance. The consul has a list of medical services available, but arrangements must be made by you or a traveling companion who can also notify family or friends.

A travel health insurance policy is an option to consider, especially if you are going abroad for a long period or have some pre-trip health concerns. The average policy coverage is about $10,000. In the May/June 1998 issue of *Transitions Abroad* Leslie Pappas explains the different types of coverage, especially long-term stays. Rick Steves' column in the May/June 1999 issue contains good tips for staying healthy on your journey. And, as explained in the July/August issue, the Center for Disease Control has a site devoted to information on the diseases to guard against worldwide at [www.cdg.gov/travel/ blusheet.htm]. Travel Medicine Inc., 800-872-8633 has a catalog of products that can help prevent health problems abroad.

The biggest nightmare for any American citizen abroad is to be arrested. Rules one through 10: know the country's laws and do not break them. You are subject to the laws of the countries you visit. A U.S. consular officer cannot demand your release, represent you at trial, or pay legal fees with U.S. government funds. Much of what the officer can do is controlled by the country you are arrested in. He or she can provide a list of attorneys, notify family, and monitor your health and welfare as permitted. Depending on what country you're in, the ongoing support provided includes arranging dietary supplements and examinations by an independent physician. The funding for ongoing support must be provided by family or, if destitute, by a loan from the U.S. government's EMDA program. Since many countries follow the Napoleonic code of "guilty until proven innocent," it is best to be a law-abiding traveler.

Contact Information

State Department Consular Affairs: 202-647-3000, fax 202-647-3000; [www.state.gov/wwwservices.html].

Overseas Citizens Services, Department of State, Room 4811, Washington, DC 20520; 24-hour Traveler's Hot Line 202-647-5225. Emergencies after OCS working hours: 202-647-4000 (ask for the OCS duty officer).

Centers for Disease Control, 1600 Clifton Rd. NE, Atlanta, GA 30333; [www.cdg.gov/travel/travel2.htm].

American Express: 800-543-4080.

Travel Medicine Inc.: 800-872-8633.

sional artists and nonpainting partners. Also sculpture courses. Special painting courses in a chateau in the Lot valley.

Dates: Apr-Oct inclusive. **Cost:** From £340 full board and tuition. **Contact:** S. Goodchild, Le Petit Bois Gleu, 53800, Renazé, France; Tel./fax 011-33-243-068-386.

Horizons in Provence: Artistic Travel. Provence evokes images of vineyards, olives, sun-filled landscapes, and a profusion of antique monuments. It is all this and more. A week in the stunning hilltop village of Venasque, ringed by Roman monuments, sleepy wine villages, red ocher cliffs and mountains. Lodging in a charming bed and breakfast. Workshops include Painting, Photography, Fabric Printing and Design, Language Arts: Conversational French.

Dates: Apr 7-14; Sep 9-16. **Cost:** $1,455 (lodging, all meals except 1 lunch, tuition, and field trips). **Contact:** Karen Totman-Gale, Horizons, 108 N. Main St.-T, Sunderland, MA 01375; 413-665-0300, fax 413-665-4141; horizons@horizons-art.org, [www.horizons-art.org].

REMPART—Preserving the Past. REMPART aims to preserve the French cultural heritage through the restoration of threatened buildings and monuments. It consists of a grouping of more than 140 autonomous associations organizing workcamps providing a wide variety of work projects involving the restoration of medieval towns, castles, churches, ancient walls, wind/watermills, and industrial sites. Work includes masonry, excavations, woodwork, stone cutting, interior decorating, and clearance work. Opportunities for sports, exploring the region, and taking part in local festivities. Minimum age is 13. Previous experience is not necessary. Some knowledge of French required.

Dates: Workcamps last from 2 to 3 weeks. Most of them are open during Easter holidays and from Jul to Sep. A few camps are open throughout the year. **Cost:** FF220 for insurance, FF40-FF50 per day for food and accommodations. Volunteers help with camp duties, pay their own fares, and should bring a sleeping bag. **Contact:** Sabine Guilbert, Union Rempart, 1 rue des Guillemites, 75004 Paris, France; 011-33-1-42-71-9655, fax 011-33-1-42-71-7300; contact@rempart.com.

Ways of Seeing. Independent cultural center in southwest France founded by British artist (international reputation) and experienced teacher (ex-Univ. of London). Options include: retreats (bed and breakfasts); personal study programs (creative writing, design, drawing, painting, photography, sculpture, interdisciplinary studies); cultural tours (from Lascaux to Lautrec). For personal interest or careers. All custom designed.

Dates: Determined by client, any time of year. **Cost:** From FF680 (3 nights bed and breakfast, double-bedded room); FF200 per hour (personal tuition in English or French); from FF1,500 (1-day tour, transport and guide, entry fees). **Contact:** Sally Gosheron, Atelier de la Rose, 46700 Montcabrier, France; 011-33-565-246636, fax 011-33-565-365997; sallygosheron@wanadoo.fr, [www.franceguides.net/rose.htm].

Ghana

The Art and Culture of Ghana. This is a special opportunity to interact with Africans in their homes and workplaces. We offer village stays, traditional crafts, drumming, and dance lessons. Photo shoots, visits to historic sites, museums, galleries, schools, and healers. If it's in Ghana we can take you to it.

Dates: Vary. **Cost:** $2,500 for 14 days (1999). **Contact:** Ellie Schimelman, ABA Tours, 45 Auburn St., Brookline, MA 02446; Tel./fax 617-277-0482; abatours@ultranet.com, [www.ultranet.com/~abatours].

Greece

Art School of the Aegean. Art classes and Greek studies in a small seaside village on the island of Samos. Classes: Pinhole Camera, Mosaic/Tile Making, Landscape Painting, Paper Making and Installation Project, Multimedia Sculpture. Evening program: Classical Greek Studies, Art History, and an informal introduction to the Greek language and Contemporary Greek culture. For adult and college students.

Dates: Tour: Jun 15; art classes: Jun 20. Payment due by Apr 1. **Cost:** $1,970 includes double occupancy accommodations, 1 art class, evening lectures and Greek studies. Tour: Approx. $600 for 4-day guided tour which includes visits to archaeological sites as well as art galleries and Athens. **Contact:** Susan Trovas, Director, Art School of the Aegean, P.O. Box 1375, Sarasota, FL 34230-1375; 941-351-5597; greece3@gte.net, [www.studyabroad.com/aegean].

Goddess Tour Crete/Lesbos. Educational tours for women led by well-known author and feminist theologian Carol P. Christ. Goddess pilgrimage to Crete and Women's Quest in

Lesbos. Academic credit available. Walk on ancient stones; nourish your soul with healing images.

Dates: Crete: May 27-Jun 10, Sep 30-Oct 14; Lesbos: Jun 25-Jul 9. **Cost:** Crete $2,275 includes airfare from NYC; Lesbos $2,150 includes airfare from NYC. **Contact:** Ariadne Institute, 1306 Crestview Dr., Blacksburg, VA 24060; Tel./fax 540-951-3070.

Guatemala

Art Workshops in Guatemala. We provide 10-day art classes in a wide variety of arts including backstrap weaving; photography; beading; papermaking; creative writing; visual, fiber, book arts, and much more. All classes are held in Antigua, Guatemala.

Dates: Classes held during Jan, Feb, Mar, Apr, and Nov. **Cost:** Approx. $1,700 including airfare from U.S., lodging, tuition, field trips, and all ground transportation. **Contact:** Liza Fourre, Director, Art Workshops in Guatemala, 4758 Lyndale Ave. S, Minneapolis, MN 55409-2304; 612-825-0747, fax 612-825-6637; info@artguat.org, [www.artguat.org].

Eco-Escuela de Español and Bio Itza Programs. You want to learn Spanish, we want volunteers for conservation and community development projects in El Petén, Guatemala. The town is located close to Tikal and adjacent to the Maya Biosphere Reserve (the largest protected area in Central America) so you will be surrounded by natural and archaeological wonders and immersed in Mayan culture. This is a community owned project and participation in it will support local communities.

Dates: Year round. Arrive on weekend, start classes on Monday. **Cost:** A fee of $200 covers tuition with 20 hours per week of one-on-one Spanish language instruction, airport pick-up, transfer to the town by boat, homestay, and 3 meals per day. **Contact:** Sandra at G.A.P. Adventures, 266 Dupont St., Toronto, ON, M5R 1V7, Canada; 800-465-5600; adventure@gap.ca.

India (Nepal)

Spiritual India: A Yoga Journey. A 21-day tour through diverse sections of India both geographically and spiritually. Visit the important pilgrimage sites of Sikhs, Buddhists, Jains, Muslims, and Hindus. Optional yoga and meditation practice during the tour with various master teachers. The group size is limited to 16.

Dates: Sep, Oct, Nov. **Cost:** $2,550 includes accommodations, meals, guide, transport by private bus, entrances (1999). **Contact:** Spirit of India, 888-367-6147; inquire@spirit-of-india.com, [www.spirit-of-india.com].

Israel

Tel Dor Excavation Project. The Tel Dor Excavation Project is devoted to investigating one of the largest coastal cities in ancient Israel. Volunteers will be engaged in all facets of field archaeology, and in some of the preliminary work of artifact analysis.

Dates: May 30-Aug 11. **Cost:** $28 per day and $65 participation fee per week. **Contact:** Dr. I. Sharon, Tel Dor Excavation Project, Institute of Archaeology, Hebrew Univ., Jerusalem, Israel.

Italy

Adventure, Art, and Bill Gennaro. Instruction in the principles and elements of composition, perspective, color, technique, painting, drawing, art mnemonics. All levels in oil, acrylic, watercolor. Customized workshops to suit already-formed groups of 15 (minimum) to 25 (maximum). Almost anywhere in Italy.

Dates: Workshops held May-Oct. **Cost:** Group selects dates, accommodations, and location for guaranteed quotes. **Contact:** Bill Gennaro, 41 Lincoln Terr., Harrington Park, NJ 07640; 201-768-5606.

Art and Design in Florence. The Accademia Italiana is an international, university-level institute of art and design. The Accademia offers courses in art, fashion, interior, industrial and textile design during the autumn and spring semesters and fashion design, fashion illustration, drawing and painting, window display design and Italian language during the months of June and July.

Dates: Jan 14-May 22, Jun, Jul, Sep 9-Dec 22. **Cost:** Depends on course chosen. **Contact:** Barbara McHugh, Accademia Italiana, Piazza Pitti n. 15, 50125 Florence, Italy; 011-390-55-284616/211619, fax 011-390-55-284486; modaita@tin.it, [www accademic.italiana.com].

Biking and Walking Tours. Specializing in Italy for over 10 years, Ciclismo Classico distills the "Best of Italy," offering more unique Italian destinations than any other active vacation company. Educational, full-service tours for all abilities in Umbria, Tuscany, Piedmont, the Dolomites, Puglia, Sicily, the Amalfi Coast, Cinque Terre, Sardegna, Abruzzo, Campania, Corsica, and Elba. Charming accommodations, expert bilingual guides, cooking demonstrations, wine tastings, support vehicle, detailed route instructions, visits to local festivals, countryside picnics—an unforgettable cultural indulgence.

Dates: Apr-Nov (70 departures). Call for specific dates. **Cost:** $1,700-$3,500. **Contact:** Lauren Hefferon, Director, Ciclismo Classico, 30 Marathon St., Arlington, MA 02474; 800-866-7314 or 781-646-3377; info@ciclismoclassico.com, [www.ciclismoclassico.com].

Glorious Tuscany: Artistic Travel. Tuscany is studded with panoramic landscapes, ancient walled villages, olive groves, and vineyards...and capped by the gorgeous cities of Florence and Siena. Lodging in a charming country inn/villa in the heart of Chianti country, perfectly situated to see the sites of the region. Workshops include Painting, Lampworking/Glass Beads, Mosaics, Silversmithing and Jewelry, Photography, Cooking, Conversational Italian.

Dates: Apr 20-May 6; Oct 14-21. **Cost:** $1,455 (lodging, all meals except 1 lunch, tuition, and field trips). **Contact:** Karen Totman-Gale, Horizons, 108 N. Main St.-T, Sunderland, MA 01375; 413-665-0300, fax 413-665-4141; horizons@horizons-art.org, [www.horizons-art.org].

Hilltowns of Umbria and Tuscany. Crafts, culture, and cuisine—an exploration of 2 regions in Italy to visit small, quaint hidden villages in the remote countryside, sample regional foods and wines. Small group travel. Art instruction and critiques.

Dates: Jun. **Cost:** $2,995 accommodations, private bus transportation, 8 meals, all breakfasts, full-time bilingual tour director. (1999). **Contact:** Personalized Travel for Artists, Roberta Kritzia, 5455 Sylmar Ave., #902, Sherman Oaks, CA 91401; 888-994-2404, 818-994-2402, fax 818-994-5529.

Italiaidea. We offer every level and format of Italian study from intensive short-term "survival Italian" courses to advanced, semester-long courses; on-site lectures and visits to historic sites in Italy, conversation, and flexible scheduling. For over 10 years we have been offering college credit courses at numerous U.S. college and university programs in Italy; we now offer both academic assistance and travel/study assistance to our client institutions. Homestays are offered as well as accommodations in shared apartments.

Dates: Year round. **Cost:** Sixty-hour group course LIT780,000; 25-hour one-on-one program LIT1,200,000; 15 hour-specific purposes or culture LIT1,330,000 (taxes not included). **Contact:** Carolina Ciampaglia, Co-Director, Piazza della Cancelleria 5, 00186 Roma, Italy; 011- 390-6-68307620, fax 011-390-6-6892997; italiaidea@italiaidea.com, [www.italiaidea.com].

Italian in Florence or by the Sea. Study Italian in a 16th century Renaissance palace in the center of Florence, or in a classic Tuscan town just 30 minutes from the sea. Koiné Center's professional language teachers and small class sizes encourage active participation by each student. Cultural program, guided excursions, choice of accommodations including host families.

Dates: Year round; starting dates each month. **Cost:** Two-week intensive program from $350; 3 weeks from $455; 4 weeks from $570. Call for prices of longer stays. **Contact:** In Italy: Dr. Andrea Moradei, Koiné Center, Via Pandolfini 27, 50122 Firenze, Italy; 011-390-55-213881. In North America: 800-274-6007; homestay@teleport.com, koine@firenze.net, [www.koinecenter.com].

Italian Language Courses. Italian Language Institute offers the possibility of studying the Italian language (2-, 3-, or 4-week courses) in the beautiful Italian hill country of central Italy. Housing available in private apartment, with families, hotel. Courses offered year round at 6 language levels. Special summer session on the Amalfi coast.

Dates: Twelve 4-week sessions starting in mid-Jan and ending in mid-Dec. **Cost:** From 250 Euros, housing from 197 Euros. **Contact:** Atrium, P.za Papa Giovanni XXIII, 3-61043 Cagli (PS), Italy; Tel./fax 011-390-721-790321; atrium@info-net.it, [www.info-net.it/atrium].

Myth and Movement. Jeanne Bresciana, renowned dancer, educator, and director of the Isadora Duncan International Institute, combines movement with history, art, music and poetry in a sensory odyssey through locales rich in myth and beauty. Using movement, you will explore the creative forces within yourself and the Tuscan landscape, lush with vineyards awaiting harvest.

Dates: Sep 20-26. **Cost:** $2,045 includes meals and local ground transportation. Airfare not included. **Contact:** Tuscany Institute for Advanced Studies, c/o Ellen Bastio, 4626 Knoy Rd., #7, College Park, MD 20740; 800-943-8070.

Tuscany: Ango-Italian Study Tours. Vallicorte, a 17th century converted farmhouse with stunning views in the hills near Lucca, provides the base for art history tours and landscape painting and cookery classes. Small groups are led by recognized professionals in their fields. A houseparty atmosphere, excellent food and wines, and carefully planned itineraries make these 1-week holidays a memorable experience.

Dates: Every spring and fall (May-Jun, Sep-Oct). **Cost:** $1,765, $1,680, $1,765 respectively. Includes 7 nights' accommodations, all meals at Vallicorte with wine at dinner, accompanied excursions and tuition. Airfare not included. **Contact:** Margery Rutherford, Kirriemuir Tours, P.O. Box 67, N. Ferrisburg, VT 05473; 802-425-3100, fax 802-425-2305; kirrie@together.net, [www.Vallicorte.demon.co.uk].

Latin America

Explorama Lodge Special. One night at the Iquitos Hotel plus 2 nights at each of the 3 Explorama lodges, including visits to the longest canopy walkway in the world, ethnobotanical plant garden, primary rainforest reserve of over 250,000 acres. Meals, lodging, excursions, guides, 200 miles total boat excursions on Amazon and Napo rivers.

Dates: Starts every Tuesday year round. **Cost:** 2000-2001: $899 per person in twin bedded room. **Contact:** Peter Jenson, Explorama Lodges, Box 446, Iquitos, Peru; 800-707-5275. In Peru: 011-51-94-25-2530, fax 011-51-94-25-2533; amazon@explorama.com, [www.explorama.com].

Language and Cultural Studies. Which school is best for you? Let us help you choose the Spanish language school in Mexico or Costa Rica that best suits your needs. Whether you want college credit, special vocabulary for your job, or just a fabulous language learning vacation, we can guide you in your selection because we've been there ourselves.

Dates: Flexible starting dates throughout the year. **Cost:** Depends on location, options, length of stay. Tuition prices start at $125 per week. **Contact:** Talking Traveler, 620 SW 5th, #400, Portland, OR 97204; 800-274-6007, fax 503-274-9004; homestay@teleport.com, [www.talkingtraveler.org].

Mexico

Intensive Spanish in Cuernavaca. Cuauhnahuac, founded in 1972, offers a variety of intensive and flexible programs geared to individual needs. Six hours of classes daily with no more than 4 students to a class. Housing with Mexican families who really care about

you. Cultural conferences, excursions, and special classes for professionals. College credit available.

Dates: Year round. New classes begin every Monday. **Cost:** $70 registration fee; $680 for 4 weeks tuition; housing $18 per night. **Contact:** Marcia Snell, 519 Park Dr., Kenilworth, IL 60043; 800-245-9335, fax 847-256-9475; lankysam@aol.com.

Language and Culture in Guanajuato. Improve your Spanish in the most beautiful colonial city in Mexico. We teach one-on-one or in small groups for up to 8 hours daily. Spanish, Mexican history, cooking, literature, business, folk dancing, and politics. Students of all ages and many nationalities. Homestays with families, field trips, movies, hikes, theater, dance performances.

Dates: Year round. New classes begin every Monday. Semester programs begin in Jan and Aug. **Cost:** $925. Includes 4 weeks of classes and homestay with 3 meals daily. **Contact:** Director Jorge Barroso, Instituto Falcon, Mora 158, Guanajuato, Gto. 36000 Mexico; 011-52-473-1-0745; infalcon@redes.int.com.mx, [http://institutofalcon.com].

Mar de Jade Ocean-Front Resort. Tropical ocean-front retreat center in a small fishing village on a beautiful half-mile beach north of Puerto Vallarta. Surrounded by lush jungle with the warm, clear sea at our door, enjoy swimming, hiking, horseback riding, massage, and meditation. Study Spanish in small groups. Gain insight into local culture by optional volunteer work in community projects, such as rural community clinic, our local library, or a model home garden. Mar de Jade also has meeting facilities and provides a serene and intimate setting for group events.

Dates: Year round. **Cost:** Twenty-one day volunteer/Spanish program May-Nov 15 $1,000 (student discount available); Nov 15-Apr $1,080. Includes room and board in a shared occupancy room and 15 hours per week of volunteer work. Vacation: May-Nov 15 room and board $50 per night; Nov 16-Apr $55 per night. Spanish $80 per week with minimum 1 week (6 nights) stay. **Contact:** In Mexico: Tel./fax 011-52-322-2-3524; info@mardejade.com, [www.mardejade.com]. U.S. mailing address: 9051 Siempre Viva Rd., Suite 78-344, San Diego, CA 92173-3628.

New Zealand

Albatross Encounters. Tours to view the albatross and other species of ocean-going birds off the coast of Kaikoura, NZ. Forty out of 92 species of New Zealand's sea birds are commonly sighted here. We provide a unique opportunity for "close up" views of these magnificent sea birds.

Dates: Year round. Weather permitting. **Cost:** NZ$60 adult, NZ$35 per child under 15 years (1999). **Contact:** Lynette Buurman, Manager, OceanWings, 58 West End, Kaikoura 8280, New Zealand; 011-64-3-319-6777, fax 011-64-3-319-6534; info@oceanwings.co.nz, [www.oceanwings.co.nz].

New Zealand Immersion Tour. Experiential tour combining the beauty, wildlife, culture, and unique activities of New Zealand with fine dining and cozy accommodations.

Dates: Jan-Apr, Sep-Dec. **Cost:** $2,250 for 1 week, $4,950 for 3 weeks (1999). **Contact:** Stacey Bean, 800-206-8322; blksheep@aa.net.

Pacific

Custom Made Individual and Small Group Tours. Travel for the environmentally concerned and intellectually curious.

Dates: Call for details. **Cost:** Call for details. **Contact:** Billie Foreman, Ecotours International, P.O. Box 1853, Pebble Beach, Ca 93953; Tel./fax 831-625-3135; bforeman@redshift.com.

Papua New Guinea

Trans Niugini Tours. Nature and culture programs are offered in 3 areas: the Highlands, the Sepik Area, and a marine environment on the North Coast. Each area has its own distinct culture and environment, with comfortable wilderness lodges.

Dates: Weekly departures. **Cost:** $889-$3,570 per person (land cost). **Contact:** Bob Bates, Trans Niugini Tours, P.O. Box 371, Mt. Hagen, Papua New Guinea; 800-521-7242 or 011-675-542-1438, fax 011-675-542-2470; travel@pngtours.com, [www.pngtours.com].

Peru

Willka T'ika Garden Guest House. This is the only healing retreat and yoga center in Peru's Sacred Valley. Located between Machu Picchu and Cusco, Willka T'ika is just minutes away from Inca ruins and sacred sites and is open to special interest groups of 5-30 people.

Dates: Monthly special interest programs. Sacred tours: Apr, May-Jun, Sep, Dec-Jan. **Cost:** $2,650 starting and ending in Cusco. Includes Cusco, Machu Picchu, and Amazon (Amazon flight included). **Contact:** Terry Cumes, Magical Journey/Willka T'ika, 915 Cole St., Suite 236, San Francisco, CA 94117; Tel./fax 888-PERU-070; info@travelperu.com, [www.travelperu.com].

Romania

Transylvanian Traditions. Tour Bucharest and see a Romanian Orthodox church, outdoor village museum, and Ceaucescue's former palace. Stop at Lazarea Castle and Bicaz George. Travel to Csango villages, Sighisoara, Korund, Cluj, and villages where people still live by treasured traditional customs. End in Budapest with a sunset dinner cruise on the Danube.

Dates: Jun 1-15. **Cost:** $3,190. **Contact:** Cross-Culture, Inc., 52 High Point Dr., Amherst, MA 01002-1224; 800-491-1148, 413-256-6303, fax 413-253-2303; travel@crosscultureinc.com, [www.crossculture.com].

Spain

Cortijo Romero. Year round alternative holidays in Andalucia, Spain. Each week includes a 20-hour personal development course.

Dates: Begins every Saturday, year round. **Cost:** £335-£375 includes full board, course, full day excursion. **Contact:** Janice Gray, Cortijo Romero, Little Grove, Grove Lane, Chesham HP5 3QQ, U.K.; 011-44-1494-782720, fax 011-44-1494-776066; bookings@cortijo-romero.co.uk, [www.cortijo-romero.co.uk].

Intensive Spanish Courses, Seville. CLIC IH, one of Spain's leading language schools, is located in the heart of Seville, the vibrant capital of Andalucia. With year-round intensive Spanish language courses, business Spanish, and official exam preparation taught by highly qualified and motivated native teachers, CLIC IH combines professionalism with a friendly atmosphere. Academic credits available. Accommodations are carefully selected and we offer a varied cultural program as well as exchanges with local students.

Dates: Year round. **Cost:** Approx. $930 for a 4-week Spanish course and homestay, individual room, 2 meals per day. **Contact:** Bernhard Roters, CLIC International House Seville, Calle Albareda 19, 41001 Sevilla, Spain; 011-34-95-450-2131, fax 011-34-95-456-1696; clic@clic.es, [www.clic.es].

Sweden

Backroad Travel in Sweden. Bicycling and walking vacations in the unspoiled and beautiful countryside of Sweden. Follow Viking trails. Experience the rich Swedish culture with a native guide. Vacations include charming accommodations, breakfast and dinners, support vehicle, bilingual guides, and guided tours. New for this year: tours to Iceland.
  Dates: Jul 1-Aug 31. **Cost:** Call for details. **Contact:** Backroad Travel in Sweden, 18 Lake Shore Dr., Arlington, MA 02474; 888-648-3522 or 781-646-2955, fax 781-648-3522; cfranzel@aol.com, [http://members.aol.com/cfranzel/backroad.htm].

Uppsala Int'l. Summer Session. Sweden's oldest academic summer program focuses on learning the Swedish language. All levels from beginners to advanced. Additional courses in Swedish history, social institutions, arts in Sweden, Swedish film. Excursions every Friday. Extensive evening program includes both lectures and entertainment. Single rooms in dormitories. Apartments at extra cost. Open to both students and adults. Credit possible.
  Dates: Jun 18-Aug 11; Jun 18-Jul 14; Jul 16-Aug 11, Jul 2-Aug 11. **Cost:** SEK22,200 (approx. $2,620) for the 8-week session, SEK12,000 (approx. $1,420) for the 4-week session. Includes room, some meals, all classes, evening and excursion program. **Contact:** Dr. Nelleke van Oevelen-Dorrestijn, Uppsala Int'l. Summer Session, Box 1972, 751 47 Uppsala, Sweden; 011-31-13-521-23-88 or 011-46-18-10-23-70, fax 011-31-13-521-2389; nduiss@wxs.nl or nelleke.vanoevelen@uiss.org, [www.uiss.org].

Tanzania

Wildlife Safaris. We organize wildlife safaris to Lake Manjara, Ngorongoro Crater, Tarangire (lodge and camping safaris), Mt. Kilimanjaro-Mt. Meru climb with professional guides. Cultural tourism and walking safaris. Agent for precious stones. Budget student safari program.
  Dates: Advance booking program. **Cost:** Available on request. **Contact:** Mr. Herman Kimaro, Polly Adventure and Safaris, Ltd., P.O. Box 8008, Arusha, Tanzania, Africa; fax 011-255-57-8360/4454; polly@whiteyellow.com, [www.whiteyellow.com/polly].

Turkey

Central and Eastern Anatolia. Enjoy the spectacular scenery and magnificent historical sites and experience the art, culture, and people that are the "magic" of Anatolia. Discover the fascination of this region with expert commentaries and highlighted visits to: Ebru Marbellers, textile museums, ceramic artists, carpet weaving villages, local artisans, and nomadic encampments.
  Dates: Jun 11-27; Oct 8-24. **Cost:** $3,450 includes land, airfare, and all meals. **Contact:** Samy Rabinovic, New Horizons, P.O. Box 187, Newton, PA 18940; 215-860-8869, fax 215-860-7779; nhiint@aol.com, [www.indigoturizm.com.tr/newhorizons.html].

United Kingdom and Ireland

An Irish Idyll—From Dublin to Bantry Bay: Artistic Travel. From historic Dublin to mountain landscapes, fields of green to quaint villages and dramatic ocean views...this evocative country has a beauty all its own. Lodging in a charming bed and breakfast in the gorgeous seaside village of Kinsale—perfectly situated to see the diversity of the Irish panorama. Workshops include Painting, Silversmithing and Jewelry Design, Photography, Flameworking/Glass Beads.
  Dates: May 6-13, Sep 16-23. **Cost:** $1,465 (lodging, meals, tuition, and field trips). **Contact:** Karen Totman-Gale, Horizons, 108 N. Main St.-T, Sunderland, MA 01375; 413-665-0300, fax 413-665-4141; horizons@horizons-art.org, [www.horizons-art.org].

Annual Readers Theatre Workshop. A 2-week program that covers all aspects of Readers Theatre and related fields with a large faculty, morning classes, out-of-class activities. Up to 12 credits available from the Univ. of Southern Maine. No previous experience required for this unique hands-on study.
  Dates: Jul. **Cost:** $1,395 (1999). **Contact:** Dr. Bill Adams, Director, P.O. Box 17193, San Diego, CA 92177; 619-276-1948, fax 619-576-7369; [www.readers-theatre.com].

Art and Design Courses in London. Attend Camberwell College of Arts and Chelsea College of Art and Design, London's most important art schools. Short courses available in ceramics, computer design, conservation, drawing and painting, graphic design, history of art, illustration, interior design, metalwork, mosaic, papermaking, photography, printmaking, sculpture, stained glass, textiles, and video.
  Dates: Year round. **Cost:** From £65-£650 per course. **Contact:** Jane Coyle, Camberwell and Chelsea Short Course Unit, Camberwell College of Arts, Peckham Rd., London SE5 8UF, U.K.; 011-44-171-5146311, fax 011-44-171-5146315.

SELF-GUIDED NATURE TOURS IN HONDURAS

By Jon Kohl

Few tourists visit Honduras. However, that will soon change. Hurricane Mitch dealt a big blow to export crops such as bananas and coffee. As a result of the storm, the government has declared tourism and maquilas (American clothing factories located in developing countries to take advantage of low labor costs) to be the principal sources of foreign currency until other industries recover.

By visiting those working in grassroots community ecotourism you can directly contribute to the conservation effort and see how the military has gone from defending Honduras' political borders to protecting its parks.

Local conservation groups hope soon to offer regionwide tours, but for now they can help you organize your own. Starting in Tela, about an hour from the San Pedro Sula airport, you can take a boat tour to Jeannette Kawas National Park. While there, you'll want to stop off at a Garifuna community. The Garifuna originated from a slave ship that capsized about 200 years ago. The slaves swam ashore on St. Vincent Island and mixed with Arawak Indians. Their descendents live along the coast from Belize to Nicaragua. If you go with the local conservation group there, PROLANSATE, ask for guide Juan Pablo Lino, a Garifuna from the area and a graduate of our training course for bilingual guides.

While in Tela don't miss the Lancetilla Botanical Garden, one of the best gardens in Latin America (see Transitions Abroad, September/October 1998). Look for Victor, a Lenca Indian, another bilingual graduate, and an excellent birder. You can take a comfortable bus ride east to La Ceiba, the third largest city in Honduras. Catch the bus on the highway, not at the Tela bus station. Any cab driver will know where to drop you off. As you drive along the highway through pineapple and citrus fields, Pico Bonito National Park, the largest national park in the country, towers over your right shoulder. Ask for German, a former park guard and a highly charismatic graduate of our course who is the only person to have hiked to the peak of Pico Bonito four times.

To your left along the coast, the rivers of Pico Bonito drain into the Cuero y Salado Wildlife Refuge, a mangrove forest with interconnecting channels and a population of manatees. Nery is the guide to go with to see the mangroves and waterborne communities surrounding it.

If you continue east along the highway in a bus or rented car, you will reach Trujillo, one of the deepest undeveloped ports in the world. There is also a national park, a wildlife refuge, an old Spanish fort, and the grave of William Walker, an American soldier of fortune who tried to conquer Central America. Both Sammy and Adner (also a Garifuna) are excellent bilingual guides.

No matter which guide accompanies you, be sure to ask about the problems their organization faces—problems such as illegal timbering, the capture of parrots for the pet trade, and the draining of wetlands to plant African palms. In addition to fighting for the protected areas, these guides promote the development of ecotourism and offer interpretive programs to foreigners.

A visit to Honduras is an educational experience not to be found in Costa Rica or Ecuador. But visit now. In five years the Caribbean coast will likely be another place entirely.

Travel Information

Background can be found in the environmental travel guide by *Transitions Abroad* columnist Ron Mader: *Honduras: Adventures in Nature* (John Muir, 1998).

In Tela visit:
- the PROLANSATE office (fprocans@hondutel.hn; Tel. 011-504-448-2042);
- Garifuna Tours (garifuna@hondutel.hn; Tel. 011-504-448-2904).

In La Ceiba visit:
- FUCSA, the NGO that manages Cuero y Salado Wildlife Refuge (fucsa@laceiba.com; Tel. 011-504-443-3029);
- FUPNAPIB (fupnapib@laceiba.com; Tel. 011-504-443-3824);
- Eurohonduras (eurohonduras@caribe.hn; Tel. 011-504-443-0933);
- Moskitia Ecoaventuras (moskitia@laceiba.com; Tel. 011-504-442-0104);
- Tourist Options (touristoptions@caribe.hn; Tel. 011-504-440-0265).

In Trujillo visit:
- FUCAGUA (011-504-434-4294);
- Turtle Tours (011-504-434-4431; ttours@hondutel.hn).

On Roatan visit the Bay Island Conservation Association (Tel. 011-504-445-1424). They can recommend tour operators and dive shops.

British Culture and Institutions. On-site examination of British ideas and culture, media, political and legal institutions, and featured year 2000 attractions. London-based, with trips to Oxford, Stratford-upon-Avon, Salisbury, Stonehenge, and Bath. Retracing steps of Jack the Ripper, Sherlock Holmes, Dickens, Rumpole, Beckett, Hobbes, More, Mill, Churchill, etc.

Dates: Jul 22-Aug 12. **Cost:** $2,900 all-inclusive, includes airfare. **Contact:** Dr. Walter Mead, International Studies Program, Campus Box 6120, Illinois State Univ., Normal, IL 61790-6120; 309-829-7009 or 309-438-5365, fax 309-438-3987; wbmead@ilstu.edu

British Studies at Oxford. This program of study in one of the world's most prestigious universities offers undergraduate and graduate credit in art history, business, communication, drama, education, English literature, history, and political science taught by Oxford Univ. professors. The participants live in private rooms tidied daily by the college staff, who also serve 3 bountiful and tasty meals a day in the Great Hall. Field trips are an integral part of each course as well as group trips to the theater in Stratford-upon-Avon and London.

Dates: Summer: Jul 4-Jul 24; Jul 25-Aug 14; or Jul 4-Aug 14. **Cost:** $3,100 for 3 weeks; $5,750 for 6 weeks. Includes 4 or 8 credits, travel in Britain for course related events, theater, entrance to museums, dinners in country inns, and many field trips. Overseas travel not included. **Contact:** Dr. M.B. Pigott, Director, British Studies at Oxford, 322 Wilson Hall, Oakland Univ., Rochester, MI 48309-4401; 248-652-3405 or 248-370-4131, fax 248-650-9107; pigott@oakland.edu, [www.oakland.edu/oxford].

Homestay U.K. Experience life in an English family as a homestay guest, all ages, from 12-75 years old. Individual tours can be arranged and small groups can be catered to. The holiday program is prepared according to individual requests.

Dates: Any dates throughout the year to suit individual requirements. **Cost:** From £95 per person per week. **Contact:** Belaf Holidays, Banner Lodge, Cherhill, Calne, Wiltshire SN11 8XR, U.K.; 011-44-1249-812551, 011-44-1249-821533; belaf@aol.com.

Island Horizons. Specialist in Northwest Scotland highlands and islands (especially Isle of Skye). Guided ecowalks and historical tours. Also audio guides. Share the magic of changing light on water and mountains, the elusive glimpse of wild stag, eagle, otter. Small groups, qualified and insured leaders.

Dates: Apr-Oct. **Cost:** £545-£695 for 6 days. Includes local travel, accommodations, and meals. **Contact:** Jean Stewart, 'Sundown' Croft Rd., Lochcarron, Wester Ross, Scotland IV54 8YA, U.K.; Tel./fax 011-44-1520-722-238; jeannie@dial.pipex.com.

The Joe Mooney Summer School. Traditional Irish Music, Song, and Dance and daily workshops in fiddle, flute, tin whistle, killeann pipes, button accordion, piano accordion, harp, banjo, concertina, bodhran, traditional singing, and set dancing. Evening lectures, recitals, concerts and céilthe.

Dates: Jul. **Cost:** £35 (1999). **Contact:** Nancy Woods, Joe Mooney Summer School, Drumshanbo, Co. Leitrim, Ireland; 011-353-78-41213; nwoods@ie.

Kiltartan Hedge School. An informal but detailed exploration of the Coole Park and Ballylee writings of W.B. Yeats in their natural habitat. The group is friendly in spirit and limited in size. For all who enjoy good poetry.

Dates: Jul. **Cost:** £50, tuition only (1999). **Contact:** Louis Muinzer, 33 Jameson St., Belfast BT7 2GU, Northern Ireland; Tel./fax 011-44-353-1232-649010.

Landscape Painting in the Burren. Professional art tutors take painters outdoors on location for sketching and painting in the famous Burren country of North Clare: rockscapes, seascapes, streetscapes. Media include oils, watercolors, pastel, gouache, acrylics. Accommodations in Irish Tourist Board approved B and B. Studio, materials, and equipment available.

Dates: May-Sep weekly and weekends. **Cost:** From $450 per week. Includes tuition, accommodations, and full breakfast. **Contact:** Christine O'Neill, The Burren Painting Centre, Lisdoonvarna, Co. Clare, Ireland; 011-353-65-74208, fax 011-353-65-74435; isclo@indigo.ie, [http://indigo.ie/~isclo].

Lower Shaw Farm. Day, weekend, and weeklong courses and holidays for all ages including circle dancing, fungus foray, singing weekend, weaving with willow, rag rugs. Autumn activities: family weekend, living willow structures, Christmas crafts. Working weekends: organic gardening, good food, convivial atmosphere.

Dates: Vary. **Cost:** Free-£100. **Contact:** Lower Shaw Farm, Old Shaw Ln., Shaw, Swindon, Wiltshire SN5 9PJ, U.K.; Tel./fax 011-44-1-793-771080.

Old Barn Bed and Breakfast. Bed and breakfast in a converted 200-year-old Kentish barn. New Ashford, Tenterden, Sissinghurst Castle. Good touring base. Excellent English/vegetarian breakfast.

Dates: Year round. **Cost:** Contact sponsor. **Contact:** The Old Barn, Bridge Farm, Bethersden, Kent TN26 3LE, U.K.; 011-44-870-740-1180, fax 011-44-1233-820-547; atd@ukpages.net, [www.ukpages.net/b-b1.htm].

Residential Music Summer Schools. The U.K.'s unique center for the study and practice of music. We provide expert tuition from many distinguished professional figures from the major educational establishments. Harp, flute orchestra, London brass, "wind plus," wind quartet, banjo, big band, international viola summer schools. Full program available.

Dates: Year round. **Cost:** Contact organizations for details. **Contact:** Helen Marshall, Benslow Music Trust, Benslow Ln., Hitchin, Hertfordshire SG4 7AA, U.K.; 011-44-462-459446, fax 011-44-462-440171.

Residential Pottery Courses. A rich broad choice pottery experience is offered at an English country workshop 1 hour from London.

Dates: Every week of the summer. **Cost:** £310 all inclusive (workshop and residence). **Contact:** Alan Baxter Pottery Workshop, The White House, Somersham, Ipswich, Suffolk IP8 4QA, U.K.; Tel./fax 011-44-1473-831256; abaxter@netcomuk.co.uk, [www.ecn.co.uk/alanbaxter/index.htm].

Sail and Paint the Suffolk Coast. Using water-based media, join artist Angela Dammery. Accommodated 5 nights on board the 100-year-old Thames sailing barge Wyuenhoe. A unique tutored painting holiday sailing to unspoiled locations along the East Anglian coast. Cruise begins and ends at Ipswich, Suffolk.

Dates: Contact sponsor. **Cost:** Contact sponsor. **Contact:** Angela Dammery, Broadland Arts Centre, 43 The Crossways, Westcliff on Sea, Essex SS0 8PU, U.K.

Summer Studies in London. An exceptional opportunity to study alongside U.K. students and enjoy a taste of British academic life. The summer program offers more than 80 credit-bearing courses across a broad range of subject areas including computing, drama, criminology, the environment, and business.

Dates: Early Jul-mid-Aug. **Cost:** Approx. $3,440 includes tuition, orientation, meal plan, accommodations, social programs. **Contact:** Anita Mascarenhas, Summer School Office,

Middlesex Univ., Trent Park Campus, Bramley Rd., London N14 4Y2, U.K.; 011-44-181-362-5782, fax 011-44-181-362-6697; a.mascarenhas@mdx.ac.uk.

Univ. of Cambridge International Summer Schools. Largest and longest established program of summer schools in the U.K. Intensive study in Cambridge as part of an international community. Term I (4 weeks) and Term II (2 weeks) of the International Summer School offer over 60 different courses. Three-week specialist programs: Art History, Medieval Studies, History, English Literature, Shakespeare, Science. Wide range of classes on all programs. U.S. and other overseas institutions grant credit. Guidelines available.

Dates: Jul-Aug. **Cost:** Tuition from £475-£690 (2 to 4 weeks), accommodations from £250-£950 (2 to 4 weeks). Six-week period of study also possible by combining 2 summer schools. **Contact:** Ali James, Development as Publicity Officer, International Division, Univ. of Cambridge, Madingley Hall, Cambridge CB3 8AQ, U.K.; 011-44-1954-280398, fax 011-44-1954-280200; acj28@cam.ac.uk, [www.cam.ac.uk/cambuniv/conted/intsummer].

University Stays. Standard and en suite accommodations available throughout the U.K. during summer, Easter, and Christmas vacations to suit all budgets (no single supplements). Excellent range of dining, sports, and leisure facilities and activity and study holidays. Some accommodations available year round.

Dates: See above. **Cost:** Contact sponsor. **Contact:** Carole Formon, BUAC, Box 1732, University Park, Nottingham NG7 2RD, U.K.; 011-44-115-950-4571, fax 011-44-115-942-2505; buac@nottingham.ac.uk, [www.buac.co.uk].

Walking Tours in England and Scotland. Walking and hiking tours with sightseeing in the beautiful countrysides of England and Scotland. Local guides and talks by experts. Lodging at splendid country hotels and inns with sumptuous food. All meals and all sightseeing included. Since 1985.

Dates: Apr-Oct, weekly. **Cost:** $1,700-$1,900, 7 to 8 days, all inclusive (1999). **Contact:** Seth Steiner, English Lakeland Ramblers; 800-724-8801, fax 212-979-5342; Britwalks@aol.com; [www.ramblers.com].

Weaving, Spinning, and Dyeing. Residential courses in weaving, spinning, and dyeing. Weekly according to demand. Small groups (max. 6). Qualified expert tuition. Rugs, hangings, fabric, tapestry, tablet, inkle, ikat.

Dates: Apr-Oct. **Cost:** Contact sponsor. **Contact:** Martin Weatherhead, Snail Trail Handweavers, Penwenallt Farm, Cilgerran, Cardigan SA43 2TP, United Kingdom; 011-44-239-841-228; snailtrail97@hotmail.com.

Women's Magical Tour. Visit ancient goddess and pagan sites, celebrate Beltain in Padstow in traditional village celebration, enjoy the beauty of Cornwall with Cheryl Stratton, author of *Pagan Cornwall, Land of the Goddess.*
Dates: Late Apr-early May. **Cost:** Approx. $1,300-$1,700. **Contact:** Pat Hogan, Sounds & Furies Productions, P.O. Box 21510, 1850 Commerial Dr., Vancouver, BC, V5N 4AO, Canada; 604-253-7189.

United States

Internship, Seminar Programs. Internship program in Washington, DC with Middle East organizations, dealing with such issues as Palestine, U.S.-Arab relations, and trade. Supplementing the internship are lectures from scholars and government employees familiar with the issues facing the Arab world.
Dates: Jun-Aug. **Cost:** Call for information. **Contact:** National Council on U.S.-Arab Relations, 202-293-0801; internship@ncusar.org.

Kansas Archaeology Training Program. Dates: May, Jun. **Cost:** $15 registration fee and all expenses. **Contact:** Virginia A. Wulfkuhle, Kansas State Historical Society, Archaeology Office, 6425 SW 6th Ave., Topeka, KS 66615-1099; 785-272-8681 ext 268, fax 785-272-8682; vwulfkuhle@hspo.wpo.state.ks.us.

Worldwide

American-Int'l Homestays. Stay in English-speaking foreign homes. Explore foreign cultures responsibly. Learn foreign languages. Perfect for families or seniors. Learn how other people live by living with them in their homes.
Dates: Year round. **Cost:** From $100 per night. **Contact:** Joe Kinczel, American-Int'l Homestays, P.O. Box 1754, Nederland, CO 80466; 303-642-3088 or 800-876-2048, fax 303-642-3365; ash@igc.apc.org.

California Academy of Sciences Travel Program. Academy-led tours place participants in the context of specifically chosen natural environments. Teaching, understanding, and conservation are our goals.
Dates: Programs vary in length from 5 days to 3 weeks. **Cost:** Approx. $2,000-$10,000. **Contact:** Bonnie Frey, Travel Dept., California Academy of Sciences, Golden Gate Park, San Francisco, CA 94118; 415-750-7348, fax 45-750-7346; bfrey@calacademy.org.

CHI World Travel/Study Programs for All Ages. CHI was established in 1980 as a nonprofit organization to encourage people to reach out and explore the world. Call us or visit our website. We have worldwide highschool academic programs, cultural and/or language immersions with homestays; group tours personalized for schools or for the general public. Internships, au pair and teaching positions also available.
Dates: Vary. **Cost:** Vary according to destination and length of program. **Contact:** Cultural Homestay International, 2455 Bennett Valley Rd., #210B, Santa Rosa, CA 95404; 800-395-2726, fax 707-523-3704; chigaylep@msn.com, [www.chinet.org/outbound.html].

Custom Group Tours. Student, adventure, vacation, senior, and theme group travel arrangements worldwide. Interesting and exciting destinations are easy with our custom itineraries and careful planning.
Dates: Year round. **Cost:** Vary. **Contact:** Ralph Joksch, Cruise Tours, 2201 Pillsbury Rd., B-1A, Chico, CA 95926; 800-248-6542, fax 530-895-8255; cruise-tours@pobox.com.

Customized Groups. Offers customized groups to anywhere in the world with specialization in Australia and New Zealand.
Dates: Year round. **Cost:** From $699. **Contact:** Worldwide Tours and Travel, Inc., 393 W. State, Suite B, Eagle, ID 83616; 888-697-0911, fax 208-938-0913; wwtourtrvl@aol.com.

Earthwatch Institute. Unique opportunities to work with leading scientists on 1- to 3-week field research projects worldwide. Earthwatch sponsors 160 expeditions in over 30 U.S. states and in 60 countries. Project disciplines include archaeology, wildlife management, ecology, ornithology and marine mammalogy. No special skills needed—all training is done in the field.
Dates: Year round. **Cost:** Tax deductible contributions ranging from $695-$3,995 support the research and cover food and lodging expenses. Airfare not included. **Contact:** Earthwatch, 680 Mt. Auburn St., P.O. Box 9104-MA, Watertown, MA 02472; 800-776-0188, 617-926.8200; info@earthwatch.org, [www.earthwatch.org].

Field Expeditions. Field Expeditions are year round, hands-on workshops that take participants to places that inspire them through contact with other cultures, landscapes, and disciplines. Regular expeditions include trips to Nepal, Scotland, India, Jamaica, France, the Grand Canyon, and the American Southwest.

Dates: Jamaica (painting) Apr 21-29, (photography and painting) Nov 3-11; Nepal (ceramics) Jan 30-Feb 20. **Cost:** Contact organization for details. **Contact:** Anderson Ranch Arts Center, PO Box 5598, Snowmass Village, CO 81615; 970-923-3181, fax 970-923-3871; info@andersonranch.org; [www.andersonranch.org].

First Choice for Home Exchange. Vacation Homes Unlimited offers the ideal travel alternative for people who want not only to see an area but to experience it. Cut your travel costs dramatically and join the thousands who have found home exchange to be comfortable, convenient, and earth friendly. Directory and Internet memberships available.

Dates: Year round. **Cost:** $65 per year directory membership, $65 per year Internet membership, $95 per year directory and Internet. **Contact:** Anne Pottinger, Vacation Homes Unlimited, P.O. Box 1562, Santa Clarita, CA 91386; 800-VHU-SWAP, 661-298-0376, fax 661-298-0576; vhuswap@scv.net, [www.vacation-homes.com].

From Farmhouse to Teahouse. Unique cultural advnetures in Japan and Scotland with emphasis on arts, architecture, and interaction with local culture.

Dates: May, Oct, and Jul (2-week trips) (1999). **Cost:** $3,685-$4,085. **Contact:** Journey East, P.O. Box 1161, Middletown, CA 95461; 800-527-2612, fax 707-987-4831.

Global Volunteers. The nation's premier short-term service programs for people of all ages and backgrounds. Assist mutual international understanding through ongoing development projects throughout Africa, Asia, the Caribbean, Europe, the Pacific, North and South America. Programs of 1, 2, and 3 weeks range from natural resource preservation, light construction, and painting to teaching English, assisting with health care, and nurturing at-risk children. No special skills or foreign languages are required. Ask about the Millennium Service Project.

Dates: Over 150 teams year round. **Cost:** Tax-deductible program fees range from $450 to $2,395. Airfare not included. **Contact:** Global Volunteers, 375 E. Little Canada Rd., St. Paul, MN 55117; 800-487-1074, fax 651-407-5163; email@globalvolunteers.org, [www.globalvolunteers.org].

Language Immersion Programs. Learn a language in the country where it's spoken. Intensive foreign language training offered in Costa Rica, Russia, Spain, France, Italy, Germany, and Ecuador for students aged 16 and older. Classes are taught in up to 8 different proficiency levels and are suitable for beginners as well as people with advanced linguistic skills. All courses include accommodations and meals. Lots of extracurricular activities available. Students can earn college credit through Providence College.

Dates: Courses start every second Monday year round. Year programs commence in Sep, semester programs in Jan, May, and Sep. **Cost:** Varies with program, approx. $950 per 2-week course. **Contact:** Stephanie Greco, Director of, Admissions, EF International Language Schools, EF Center, 1 Education St., Cambridge, MA 02142; 800-992-1892, fax 617-619-1701; ils@ef.com.

Nature Expeditions International. Educational soft adventure programs since 1973. Trips to over 20 countries in Africa, Asia, Australia, and Latin America. Full range of adventure cruising programs. Each expedition offers upscale accommodations, unique cultural activities, and 3-4 different soft adventures. Specializing in creating distinctive itineraries led by expert guides. Flexible, guaranteed departure dates.

Dates: Year round. **Cost:** Call for details. **Contact:** Nature Expeditions, International, 7860 Peters Rd., Suite F-103, Plantation, FL 33324; 800-869-0639 or 954-693-8852, fax 954-693-8854; naturexp@aol.com, [www.naturexp.com].

Off the Beaten Path. Unique, flexible, and affordable travel opportunities for individuals and small groups. MIR is a 13-year veteran specialty tour operator with representation in Moscow, St. Petersburg, Kiev, Irkutsk, Ulan Ude, and Tashkent. Homestays, Trans-Siberian rail journeys, Silk route expeditions, Mongolian adventures, China voyages, Trans-Caucasus discoveries. Customized independent and group travel.

Dates: Year round; scheduled departures for tours. **Cost:** Homestays from $40 a night; full packaged tours from $1,895. Contact organization for a catalog. **Contact:** MIR Crporation, 85 S. Washington St., Suite 210, Seattle, WA 98104; 800-424-7289 or 206-624-7289, fax 206-624-7360; mir@igc.apc.org, [www.mircorp.com].

Outer Edge Expeditions. Specializes in small group, remote adventures to all 5 continents outside the U.S. Activities include kayaking, rafting, dogsledding, trekking, cultural exploration, caving, biking, and more.

Dates: Year round. **Cost:** From $995-$4,200. **Contact:** Outer Edge Expeditions, 45500 Pontiac Trail, Walled Lake, MI 48390; 800-322-5235 or 248-624-5140, fax 248-624-6744; adventure@outer-edge.com, [www.outer-edge.com].

Santa Barbara Museum of Art. Twenty tours a year include domestic and foreign destinations around the world. Emphasis is on culture: art, architecture, gardens, archaeology, cultural history. Ranges from small groups with private visits to larger, more economical, opportunities.

Dates: Year round. **Cost:** $800-$28,000 (1999). **Contact:** Shelley Ruston; 805-884-6435, fax 805-966-6840; sruston@sbmuseart.org.

Travel Art Workshops. Come and make art with us this summer. Explore your creativity in a group setting with enthusiastic, experienced teachers. This summer ARTE|VITA offers inspiring, down-to-earth, and reasonably priced art workshops for adults in Tuscany, Italy, and Antigua, Guatemala. Check out our web site or call for brochure.

Dates: Italy: May-Jun, Guatemala: Jul-Aug. **Cost:** Italy $2,150, Guatemala $1,900. Includes homemade meals, studio space, ground transportation, museum admission fees, and reading materials. Airfare and art supplies not included. **Contact:** ARTE|VITA, 1081 High Falls Rd., Catskill, NY 12414; 212-726-1379; [www.artevita.net].

UC Research Expeditions (UREP). Adventure with a purpose. Join research expeditions in archaeology, anthropology, environmental studies, and more. Get off the beaten track, help in research that benefits local communities. No special experience necessary. Free brochure.

Dates: May-Sep (2 weeks). **Cost:** From $700-$1,700 (tax deductible). **Contact:** Univ. of California Research Expeditions Program (UREP); 530-752-0692, fax 530-752-0681; urep@ucdavis.edu, [http://urep.ucdavis.edu].

Women's Travel Club. Largest women's travel club in the U.S., room share guarantees, small groups, cultural and spa vacations.

Dates: Year round. **Cost:** $325-$4,500. **Contact:** Phyllis Stoller, The Women's Travel Club 21401 NE 38 Ave., Adventura, FL 33180; 800-480-4448; womantrip@aol.com, [www.womenstravelclub.com].

WorldTeach. WorldTeach is a nonprofit, nongovernmental organization which provides opportunities for individuals to make a meaningful contribution to international education by living and working as volunteer teachers in developing countries.

Dates: Year round. **Cost:** $4,800-$5,950. Includes international airfare, health insurance, extensive training, and in-country support. **Contact:** WorldTeach, Harvard Institute for International Development, 14 Story St., Cambridge, MA 02138; 800-4-TEACH-0 or 617-495-5527, fax 617-495-1599; info@worldteach.org, [www.worldteach.org].

ALTERNATIVES TO MASS TOURISM

For over 20 years, *Transitions Abroad* magazine has helped independent travelers have the overseas experiences they desire. Each issue is packed with the information travelers need to journey overseas their *own* way.

SHORT-TERM JOBS (JAN/FEB)

• Pick up short-term jobs as you go along or volunteer your services for room and board. The most mobile skill is teaching English. This issue provides a country-by-country directory of schools and programs where you can get training and placement programs.

SPECIAL INTEREST (MAR/APR)

• Whether it's hiking, sailing, or cooking, following your *own* interest is much more satisfying than fighting the crowds. Our worldwide directory of credit-bearing summer as well as semester and year courses worldwide will give you choices around the world.

LANGUAGE VACATIONS (MAY/JUN)

• In Central America, $125 a week buys full room and board plus four hours a day of private tutoring. Our May/June directory features overseas language programs.

OVERSEAS TRAVEL PLANNER (JUL/AUG)

• This most information-packed issue of the year will help you map out an affordable strategy for your next trip abroad. A small encyclopedia of what you need to plan your journey.

WORK ABROAD (SEP/OCT)

• This issue brings together all the sources of information you need to find work overseas. Includes a directory of worldwide volunteer opportunities.

RESPONSIBLE TRAVEL (NOV/DEC)

• One of *Transitions Abroad*'s principal objectives is to promote travel that respects the culture and environment of the host country. Our special directory describes responsible adventure travel programs by region and country, with the emphasis on locally organized tourism.

THREE

The dynamics of travel have changed in the last several years—for seniors as well as for the general population. Older travelers once wanted a comfortable tour of castles and churches in familiar territory; foreign travel meant a tour of the Continent. Today they are heading for exotic destinations like Sulawesi and Zimbabwe.

Senior Publications

Britain on Your Own: A Guide for Single Mature Travelers by Dorothy Maroncelli. West Wind Books. 1997. $12.95.

Dept. of State Publications. *Travel Tips for Older Americans,* and *A Safe Trip Abroad* are $1.50 each from Superintendent of Documents, U.S. Government Printing Office, Washington, DC 20402; 202-512-1800, fax on demand 202-512-2250; http://travel.state.gov/travel_pubs.html.

Doctor's Guide to Protecting Your Health Before, During and After International Travel by Dr. W. Robert Lange. 1997. Addresses travelers' health issues with particular emphasis on seniors; includes a special section on retiring or relocating abroad, as well as tips and precautions for travelers with chronic health problems, disabilities and handicaps. $9.95 plus $3.50 s/h from Pilot Books, 127 Sterling Ave., P.O. Box 2102, Greenport, NY 11944; 800-79PILOT; fax 516-477-0978; pilotmail@hamptons.com, [www.pilotbooks.com].

How to Retire Abroad by Roger Jones. 1993. £8.99. Written by an English specialist in expatriate matters. How to Books Ltd., Plymbridge House, Estover Rd., Plymouth, PL6

7PZ, U.K.; 011-44-1-752-202301, fax 752-202331; orders@plymbridge.com, [www.howtobooks.co.uk].

Marco Polo. A quarterly magazine for adventurous travelers over 50. $10 for 4 issues from Marco Polo Publications, 520 Hickory Ave., Oldsmar, FL 34677.

The Mature Traveler's Book of Deals. More than 140 pages of discounts especially for the mature traveler throughout the world. $7.95 plus $1.95 s/h. Call 800-466-6676 for credit card purchases or send check to The Mature Traveler, P.O. Box 15791, Sacramento, CA 95852-0791.

The Mature Traveler. Monthly 12-page newsletter listing discounts and destinations for the mature traveler. Send $2 for a random sample copy or $29.95 for a 12-month subscription. P.O. Box 50400, Reno, NV 89513-0400.

Season of Adventure: Traveling Tales and Outdoor Journeys of Women Over 50 (Adventura Series, No. 10) edited by Jean Gould. 1996. $15.95 from Seal Press Feminist Publishers.

The Story of Elderhostel by Eugene S. Mills (Univ. Press of New England, 1993, $25).

The Thrifty Traveler, P.O. Box 8168, Clearwater, Fl 33758; 800-532-5731, fax 727-447-0829; editor@thriftytraveler.com, [www.thriftytraveler.com]. Twelve-page monthly newsletter filled with resources, tips, and budget travel strategies. Includes a special section for over-50 travelers. $29 per year; sample issue $4.

Travel Tips for Older American, Tips for Americans Residing Abroad, etc. (U.S. Dept. of State, Consular Affairs, Public Affairs Office, Rm. 6831, Washington, DC 20520-4818). These booklets provide general information on passports, visas, health, currency, and other travel tidbits for U.S. citizen planning to travel overseas.

Unbelievably Good Deals and Great Adventures That You Absolutely Can't Get Unless You're Over 50 by Joan Rattner Heilman. Contemporary Books (11th ed., 1999, $11.95).

Senior Tour Sponsors

Accessible Kiwi Tours New Zealand, Ltd. Adventure or leisure tours for all, including disabled or elderly. Group or individual tours New Zealand-wide. Accessible Kiwi Tours New Zealand, Ltd., P.O. Box 550, Opotiki, New Zealand; 011- 64-7-315-7867, fax 011- 64-7-315-5056; kiwitour@wave.co.nz, [www.accessible-tours.co.nz].

Alaska Snail Trails. P.O. Box 210894, Anchorage, AK 99521. Ten-day, 5-day, and 1-day Alaskan tours; 800-348-4532, 907-337-7517, fax 907-337-7517.

Gadabout Tours, 700 E. Tahquitz Canyon Way, Palm Springs, CA 92262; 800-952-5068, fax 760-325-5127.

Golden Age Travelers, Pier 27, The Embarcadero, San Francisco, CA 94111; 800-258-8880, fax 415-776-0753.

Golden Escapes, Inc., a Canadian travel company, produces a brochure, "Golden Escapes for the 50+ Traveller," 75 The Donway West, Suite 710, Toronto, ON M3C 2E9, Canada.

Grand Circle Travel, 347 Congress St., Boston, MA 02210; 800-597-3644, [www.gct.com]. More than 200 programs worldwide. Free booklet: "101 Tips for Mature Travelers."

Over the Hill Gang, 1820 W. Colorado Ave., Colorado Springs, CO 80904; 719-389-0022. Skiing, hiking, and biking for those over 50.

Photo Explorer Tours. Five programs annually include: China, Tibet, Myanmar (Burma), Turkey, India, Nepal, Central Asia, Iran, South Africa. Prices range from $1,995 (Explore Turkey) to $5,395 (Silk Road from China to Persia), plus air. Photo Explorer Tours, 2506 Country Village, Ann Arbor, MI 48103; 800-315-4462, fax 734-996-1481; decoxphoto@aol.com, [www.denniscox.com/tours.htm].

Senior Travel Tips. is published 8 times a year with a focus on travel opportunities close to home and around the world. Principal audience is group travel planners for clubs and organizations and tour operators. Contact them at 5281 Scotts Valley Dr., Scotts Valley, CA 95066; 408-438-6085, fax 408-438-4705; elana@seniortraveltips.com, linneasj@aol.com.

Sterling Tours. offers an 11-day performing arts tour featuring theater and music in London and the Edinburgh festival. $2,353 plus airfare. Sterling Tours, 2707 Congress St., Suite 2-G, San Diego, CA 92110; 800-727-4359, fax 619-299-5728.

Senior Transportation

Senior Fare Bargain Report by Jens Jurgen (Travel Companion Exchange, Inc., P.O. Box 833, Amityville, NY 11701; 516-454-0880 or 800-392-1256. $3). This 8-page booklet, revised monthly, covers all details of the various senior airfares offered by most airlines for domestic and some international travel.

Senior Fare Bargain Report, by Jens Jurgen. Revised monthly. (Travel Companion Exchange, Inc.), P.O. Box 833, Amityville, NY 11701; 516-454-0880 or 800-392-1256. $3 (2 copies $4 postpaid). This eight-page booklet covers all details of the various senior airfares offered by most airlines for domestic and some international travel.

TravLtips Association. Unusual cruises: freighters, yachts, expeditions. Membership includes magazine and free reference book. $20 a year. P.O. Box 580218, Flushing, NY 11358; 800-872-8584; [www.travltips.com].

Senior Web Sites

Access-Able Travel Source, [www.access-able.com]. A free Internet information service for mature and disabled travelers: accessibility guide for countries, states and provinces, and cities; also accommodations, transportation, attractions, adventures, doctors and equipment rental and repair, specialty travel agents, and a comprehensive list of disability links and publications. Pages include discussion forums and *What's News,* an online newsletter. Contact: 303-232-2979, fax 303-239-8486.

Adult Living Channel, [www.adultlivingchannel.com/travel/travelframe.htm]. Has a good selection of links for destinations and travel discounts for seniors.

Airlines.com Senior Travel Information, [www.airlines.com/rc-senior.html]. A list of links to some great discounts and deals for senior air travelers.

Senior Women Web Travel Section, http://seniorwomen.com/travel.htm. Links of use to senior women travelers.

SeniorCom, [www.senior.com/travel], is an online community for senior citizens. Their travel section has tips, ideas, destinations, and more. You can also join their travel club to meet and travel with seniors with similar travel interests.

Seniors-Site Travel Information, http://seniors-site.com/travel/index.html. Links and information of interest to senior citizen travelers.

SeniorsSearch.com Travel Section, [www.seniorssearch.com/stravel.htm]. A search directory exclusively for the over 50 age group, it has links to web sites with information and resources for senior travelers.

Educational Travel Programs

Archaeology Abroad, 31-34 Gordon Sq., London WC1H OPY, England; 011-44-171-504-4750; fax 011-44-171-383-2572; arch.abroad@ucl.ac.uk, [www.britarch.ac.uk/archabroad]. Three annual bulletins list worldwide archaeological digs with details of staffing needs and costs.

Earthwatch Expeditions, 680 Mt. Auburn St., P.O. Box 9104, Watertown, MA 02472; 800-776-0188. Help scientists on worldwide expeditions. No experience necessary. Completely tax deductible.

Elderhostel, 75 Federal St., Boston, MA 02110; 877-426-8056; [www.elderhostel.org]. Educational adventures for older adults. Sponsors over 2,000 nonprofit, short-term programs in 70 countries. Must be 55 or over; younger companions are allowed.

Golden Opportunities: A Volunteer Guide for Americans over 50 by Andrew Carroll. Peterson's Guides, 1994, $14.95.

Interhostel, 6 Garrison Ave., Durham, NH 03824; 800-733-9753, [www.learn.unh.edu]. Over 50 educational travel programs per year worldwide for mature travelers age 50 and up.

Saga Holidays, "Road Scholar" Educational Travel Programs, 222 Berkeley St., Boston, MA 02116; 617-262-2262 or 800-621-2151, [www.sagaholidays.com].

Senior Summer School offers active seniors 55+ an affordable opportunity to enhance their summer through education, leisure, and discovery at campus locations across the U.S. and Canada. P.O. Box 4424, Deerfield Beach, FL 33442-4424; 800-847-2466; [www.seniorsummerschool.com].

Travelearn. Ten-day to 3-week programs for adults in 17 countries on 6 continents. On-site lectures and field experiences by local resource specialists. Travelearn, P.O. Box 315, Lakeville, PA 18438; 800-235-9114; travelearn@aol.com, [www.travelearn.com].

Volunteer Vacations by Bill McMillon. Chicago Review Press, 6th ed., 1997, $16.95. Includes 2,000 opportunities worldwide plus personal stories.

Four

The following listing of senior travel programs was supplied by the organizers. Contact the program directors to confirm costs, dates, and other details. Please tell them you read about their program in this book! Programs based in more than one country or region are listed under "Worldwide."

Africa

Cross-Cultural Solutions in Ghana. Experience the vibrant, colorful culture of West Africa and make a difference at the same time. This unique short-term volunteer program enables volunteers to work with local social service organizations in fields as diverse as health care, education, skills training, and arts/recreation. Volunteers receive continual professional support from our U.S. and Ghana-based staff. No skills or experience required—only a desire to help and learn.

Dates: Three-week programs run year round. Longer term placements can be arranged. **Cost:** $1,850 covers all Ghana-based expenses. International airfare, insurance, and visa not included. Program fee is tax deductible for U.S. residents. **Contact:** Cross-Cultural Solutions, 47 Potter Ave., New Rochelle, NY 10801; 914-632-0022 or 800-380-4777, fax 914-632-8494; info@crossculturalsolutions.org, [www.crossculturalsolutions.org].

Austria

Aquarelle and Music. Landscape painting and chamber music at the Koenigsee (Bavaria). Historic setting (1711). Organized by St. Rupert's Order of Salzburg. Tutors: Frana Buear and Walter Hermann Sallagar, CSRO.

Dates: Sep 7-17. **Cost:** EUR900 inclusive price. Contact: W.H. Sallagar, Neulinggasse 42/10, Vienna, A-1030, Austria; Tel./fax 011-43-1-7141710.

Costa Rica

COSI (Costa Rica Spanish Institute). COSI offers high quality instruction at reasonable prices. We offer Spanish classes in San José and at a beautiful national park (beach and rainforest). Homestay is also available. Volunteer work opportunities and special discounts in tours.

Dates: Year round. **Cost:** Prices start at $280 per week including classes in groups of maximum 5 students, homestay, cultural activities, books, access to email, airport pickup. **Contact:** COSI, P.O. Box 1366-2050, San Pedro, San José, Costa Rica; 011-506-234-1001, fax 011-506-253-2117. From U.S. 800-771-5184; cosicr@sol.racsa.co.cr, [www.cosi.co.cr].

Learn Spanish While Volunteering. Assist with the training of Costa Rican public school teachers in ESL and computers. Assist local health clinic, social service agencies, and environmental projects. Enjoy learning Spanish in the morning, volunteer work in the afternoon/evening. Spanish classes of 2-5 students plus group learning activities; conversations with middle class homestay families (1 student per family). Homestays and most volunteer projects are within walking distance of school in small town near the capital, San José.

Dates: Year round, all levels. Classes begin every Monday (except Apr 17-21 and Dec 18-29), volunteer program is continuous. **Cost:** $345 per week for 28 hours of classes and group activities plus Costa Rican dance and cooking classes. Includes tuition, 3 meals per day, 7 days per week, homestay, laundry, all materials, weekly 3-hour cultural tour, and airport transportation. $25 one-time registration fee. **Contact:** Susan Shores, Registrar, Latin American Language Center, PMB 123, 7485 Rush River Dr., Suite 710, Sacramento, CA 95831-5260; 916-447-0938, fax 916-428-9542; lalc@madre.com.

Europe

Heart of Europe Tour. Fully escorted 15-day tour of Holland, Belgium, Germany, Austria, Italy, Switzerland, and France. Includes all breakfasts, all but 4 dinners, sightseeing, accommodations, taxes, tips, and service charges. Air and land inclusive prices available from over 200 departure cities.

Dates: Mar-Dec. **Cost:** $1,685 land only (1999). **Contact:** Image Tours, Inc., 5011 28th Street SE, Grand Rapids, MI 49512-2096; 800-968-9161, fax 616-957-0103.

Self-Guided Vacations for Independent Travelers: Walking, biking, cross-country skiing in France, Italy, England, Ireland, and Switzerland. Travel at your own pace, with support behind the scenes. No group to slow you down or rush you. Route instructions, accommodations, luggage transfers, emergency support provided. Bike included on cycling tours. Flexible itineraries. Stay in B and Bs, family-run hotels, country manors. Safe, affordable, enriching.

Dates: Year round. **Cost:** Vary per tour and number of days. **Contact:** Randonnée Tours, 249 Bell Ave., Winnipeg, MB, Canada; 204-475-6939, fax 204-474-1888; info@randonneetours.com, [wwww.randonneetours.com].

France

Discover Provence. A 2-week program intended for seniors and all those who wish to combine a language course with a guided discovery of our wonderful region and its culture. Includes French classes every morning, 3 excursions, a cooking class, wine tasting, cultural lectures and social activities. Other courses also available.

Dates: Feb 14, May 8, Sep 11, Nov 6. (All year for other courses.) **Cost:** FF4,400 including course and all activities. **Contact:** Astrid Giorgetta, IS, Aix-en-Provence, 9 Cours des Arts et Mètiers, Aix-en-Provence 13100, France; 011-33-4-42-93-47-90, fax 011-33-4-42-26-31-80; is.aix@pacwan.fr, [www.is-aix.com].

French in France. Among the ways to learn French, total immersion is the most enjoyable and the most effective. We have been doing it for 20 years in a small historical city located in Normandy (west of Paris, close to the seaside). We welcome people at any age and any level in 1- to 10-week programs, intensive or vacation type, from mid-Mar to mid-Nov.

Dates: Spring: Mar 20-May 27; summer: Jun 12-Aug 26; fall: Sep 4-Nov 11. **Cost:** From $525 per week (tuition, room and board, and excursions). **Contact:** Dr. Alméras, Chairman, French American Study Center, 12, 14, Blvd. Carnot, B.P. 4176, 14104 Lisieux Cedex, France; 011-33-2-31-31-22-01, fax 011-33-2-31-31-22-21; centre.normandie@wanadoo.fr, [http://perso.wanadoo.fr/centre.normandie/].

French Language and Cooking. Live and study in 18th century Château de Mâtel. Adult residential courses in French language and French country cooking in a relaxed, convivial atmosphere. Small classes and quality teaching. Reasonable prices. Comfortable single, twin rooms. Good food and wine taken with teachers. Heart of Burgundy, Beaujolais, and Lyons area. Access to the world via Internet and computer.

Dates: Every Sunday May-Nov. **Cost:** From $820 full board and classes in château. **Contact:** Michael Giammarella in U.S.: 800-484-1234 ext 0096 or Ecole des Trois Ponts, Château de Mâtel, 42300 Roanne, France; 011-33-477-70-80-01, fax 011-33-477-71-5300; info@3ponts.edu, [www.3ponts.edu].

Immersion Course in French. Intensive 2-4 week course for professional adults in Villefranche (next to Nice) overlooking the French Riviera's most beautiful bay; 8 hours a day with 2 meals. Audiovisual classes, language lab, practice sessions, discussion-lunch. Evening film showings, evening outings with teachers, excursions to cultural landmarks. Accommodations in comfortable private apartments.

Dates: Courses start Jan, Feb, Mar, May, Jun, Aug, Sep, Oct, Nov, Dec. **Cost:** Tuition fees: Dec-Apr FF14,100/4 weeks; May-Nov FF16,700/4

By Kent St. John

Nothing can upset your traveling plans more than an unexpected problem with an airline. To many people, the Warsaw Convention— the international treaty governing international air travel liability—sounds like a 1960s Cold War movie. The other agreement on air travel, the Conditions of Carriage or Tariff Rules, is the contract with the airline you make when you buy your ticket. Some knowledge of the stipulations of both can go a long way toward securing your airline rights.

Much of the Conditions of Carriage agreement is on the ticket and ticket jacket, but not all. You have a right to know all the terms, such as boarding priorities and compensation if a flight is delayed or cancelled. Conditions of Carriage vary from airline to airline, and the hidden terms can make a difference.

A copy of your airline's conditions is available upon request at all ticket counters. If you have a problem, demand to see it. I have found several times that just asking for a copy when a boarding problem appears helps far more than ranting at the boarding gate personnel.

A summary of most of the airlines' conditions can be obtained from the Air Transportation Association (see sidebar) for a fee. Another great place to obtain different airlines' conditions is a web site run by Terry Trippler, an authority on airline carriage rules (see sidebar).

Major problems can be avoided by taking some simple precautions, the most important of which is checking in for the flight within the time required.

Bumping. If you are bumped because of overbooking, the carrier should arrange to get you to your destination within four hours of your original scheduled arrival. If it does not, you should be compensated $400 or double the one-way fare, whichever is greater. You do not have to accept vouchers, you can insist on cash or check. If the bump is because of a change of craft or weather, no compensation is due.

If a flight is overbooked, the airlines will almost always try to find volunteers who will accept a later flight for vouchers. Before you agree, make sure you are guaranteed a seat and not put on standby status. If a seat cannot be guaranteed, make sure you are covered under Rule 240, which allows you to fly on another carrier. If the new flight is more than two hours away, ask for a meal voucher and free phone call. By volunteering, I have traveled free to Europe several times on money vouchers.

If a different class is offered, take it. While being moved to coach from first or business is not a happy proposition, you will be refunded the difference in fares. Far worse is a delayed or cancelled flight.

Delays. The airlines do not guarantee their schedules, especially if the reasons are outside the company's control. If you are delayed, the first step is to see if other airlines are being affected. If not, ask to be covered under Rule 240. The airline would obviously prefer that you wait for their own scheduled flight, so you must ask. Make sure the alternate is a confirmed flight.

For delayed or canceled flights, vouchers usually go to those who make their discomfort best understood. Try to enlist the gate agent's support politely. Remember they have the power to upgrade, compensate, waive fees, and provide preferred seating.

Lost or Stolen Tickets. Another flyer's nightmare is a lost or stolen ticket. The first rule is to treat your ticket as cash. Photocopy each ticket. If a ticket is lost, contact the carrier immediately. Replacement or credit is faster when a police report is filed.

Lost Baggage. Valuables and necessities in your carry-on bag are not covered by any airline, so treat them with care. Even if an airline employee assures you that your luggage is on the next flight, make sure a claim is filed. There is a time limit to file a claim, so do it quickly. The limit of compensation, $1,250 ($640 on an international flight), is governed by the Warsaw Convention Agreement and the Tariff Rules.

If the contents of your bags are worth more than $1,250 (or $640), additional coverage can be purchased at the rate of $2 per $100 value, up to $5,000. Know the contents of your bags; this will make it easier to claim compensation.

If you cannot get satisfaction from the airlines, the first place to contact is the U.S. Department of Transportation (see below), which tracks and investigates consumer complaints. The DOT also compiles statistics on delayed and cancelled flights, overbooking, and baggage problems. The Air Travel Consumers Report is available from the Consumer Information Center, Department 124D, Pueblo, CO 81009. A nonprofit group called Aviation Consumer Action Project (see below) also assists with complaints and publishes Facts and Advice for Airline Passengers.

Who to Contact

Department of Transportation, Office of Consumer Affairs, 400 7th St., SW, Washington, DC 20590; 202-366-2220. **Aviation Consumer Action Project,** Box 19029, Washington, DC 20036; 202-638-4000. **Air Transportation Association**, 1301 Pennsylvania Ave., Suite 1100, Washington, DC 20004; 800-497-3326; [www.air-transport.org]. **Terry Tippler's site on airline rules**: [www.rulesoftheair.com].

weeks. Accommdations: Dec-Apr FF2,000-FF5,200/4 week; May-Nov FF2,300-FF5,800/4 weeks. **Contact:** Frédéric Latty, Institut de Francais, 23, avenue General Leclerc, 06230 Villefranche Sur Mer, France; 011-33-493-01-88-44, fax 011-33-493-76-92-17; instfran@aol.com, [www.institutdefrancais.com].

Italy

Italian in Florence or by the Sea. Study Italian in a 16th century Renaissance palace in the center of Florence, or in a classic Tuscan town just 30 minutes from the sea. Koiné Center's professional language teachers and small class sizes encourage active participation by each student. Cultural program, guided excursions, choice of accommodations including host families.

Dates: Year round; starting dates each month. **Cost:** Two-week intensive program from $350; 3 weeks from $455; 4 weeks from $570. Call for prices of longer stays. **Contact:** In Italy: Dr. Andrea Moradei, Koiné Center, Via Pandolfini 27, 50122 Firenze, Italy; 011-390-55-213881. In North America: 800-274-6007; homestay@teleport.com, koine@firenze.net, [www.koinecenter.com].

Latin America

Explorama Lodge Special. One night at the Iquitos Hotel plus 2 nights at each of the 3 Explorama lodges, including visits to the longest canopy walkway in the world, ethnobotanical plant garden, primary rainforest reserve of over 250,000 acres. Meals, lodging, excursions, guides, 200 miles total boat excursions on Amazon and Napo rivers.

Dates: Starts every Tuesday year round. **Cost:** 2000-2001: $899 per person in twin bedded room. **Contact:** Peter Jenson, Explorama Lodges, Box 446, Iquitos, Peru; 800-707-5275. In Peru: 011-51-94-25-2530, fax 011-51-94-25-2533; amazon@explorama.com, [www.explorama.com].

Language and Cultural Studies. Which school is best for you? Let us help you choose the Spanish language school in Mexico or Costa Rica that best suits your needs. Whether you want college credit, special vocabulary for your job, or just a fabulous language learning vacation, we can guide you in your selection because we've been there ourselves.

Dates: Flexible starting dates throughout the year. **Cost:** Depends on location, options, length of stay. Tuition prices start at $125 per week.

Contact: Talking Traveler, 620 SW 5th, #400, Portland, OR 97204; 800-274-6007, fax 503-274-9004; homestay@teleport.com, [www.talkingtraveler.org].

Mexico

Spanish Language Institute. A program designed to provide students with ideal learning environment which is conducive to thinking, writing and speaking naturally in Spanish within the context or real-life situations. Discover the Mexican culture with a university group, organization, professionals, travelers and special program of individualized needs for executives.

Dates: Year round. Classes begin every Monday. **Cost:** $150 per week. **Contact:** María Ramos, Academic Spanish Language Institute, Bajada de la Pradera #208, Colonia Pradera, Cuernavaca, Morelos 62191, Mexico; jessram@mor1.telmex.net.mx, [http://Cuernavaca.infosel.com.mx/sli/sli-page.htm].

Papua New Guinea

Trans Niugini Tours. Nature and culture programs are offered in 3 areas: the Highlands, the Sepik Area, and a marine environment on the North Coast. Each area has its own distinct culture and environment, with comfortable wilderness lodges.

Dates: Weekly departures. **Cost:** $889-$3,570 per person (land cost). **Contact:** Bob Bates, Trans Niugini Tours, P.O. Box 371, Mt. Hagen, Papua New Guinea; 800-521-7242 or 011-675-542-1438, fax 011-675-542-2470; travel@pngtours.com, [www.pngtours.com].

Spain

Seniors Spanish in Malaga. Widely recognized to be one of Spain's leading language schools, Malaca Instituto offers a program specially designed to help seniors learn the Spanish they need to enjoy traveling in Spanish-speaking countries. Our senior students love the international atmosphere and being among people of all ages.

Dates: Starting Feb 7, 21; Mar 6, 20; Apr 3, 17; May 1, 15, 29; Oct 2, 16, 30; Nov 13. **Cost:** PTS66,500 for 2-week course and activities. **Contact:** Bob Burger, Malaca Instituto, c/Cortada 6, 29018 Malaga, Spain; 011-34-95-229-3242, fax 011-34-95-229-6316; espanol@malacainst-ch.es, [www.malacainst-ch.es].

Worldwide

Cross-Cultural Solutions. Experience the vibrant, colorful culture of India, Ghana, or Peru and make a difference at the same time. This unique short-term volunteer program enables volunteers to work with local social service organizations in fields as diverse as health care, education, skills training, and arts/recreation. Volunteers receive continual professional support from our U.S. and India-based staff. No skills or experience required—only a desire to help and learn.
Dates: Contact organization for details. **Cost:** $1,850 covers in-country transportation, accommodations, board, and support. International airfare, insurance, and visa not included. Program fee is tax deductible. **Contact:** Cross-Cultural Solutions, 47 Potter Ave., New Rochelle, NY 10801; 800-380-4777 or 914-632-0022, fax 914-632-8494; info@crossculturalsolutions.org, [www.crossculturalsolutions.org].

Independent Homestay Abroad. Independent Homestay Programs focus on the homestay experience. These programs are ideal for independent teen and adult travelers desiring full immersion in another culture and language for a short period of time.
Dates: One to 4 weeks, year round. **Cost:** Varies. **Contact:** Outbound Department, Center for Cultural Interchange, 17 N. 2nd Ave., St. Charles, IL 60174; 888-ABROAD1, fax 630-377-2307; karen@cci-exchange.com, [www.cci-exchange.com].

Interhostel. Interhostel, now in its 19th year, offers study/travel programs for adults 50 years and older to locations in the U.S. and all over the world. One- and 2-week programs include lectures, presentations, field trips, sightseeing, cultural and social activities. Call for a free catalog or visit our website.
Dates: Over 75 programs throughout the year. **Cost:** U.S. programs: $600-$800; foreign programs: $2,800-$3,500. Includes meals, accommodations, activities, and foreign airfare. **Contact:** Interhostel, Univ. of New Hampshire Continuing Education, 6 Garrison Ave., Durham, NH 03824; 800-733-9753, fax 603-862-1113; learn.dce@unh.edu, [www.learn.unh.edu/interhostel].

Language Travel Programs for All Ages. For all ages and all Spanish levels. Spanish classes, excursions, cultural activities. One week to 6 months. Various settings: beaches, mountains, small towns, large cities, etc. Countries: Mexico, Costa Rica, Guatemala, Honduras, Panamá, El Salvador, Argentina, Chile, Ecuador, Peru, Uruguay, Venezuela, Puerto Rico, Dominican Republic, Bolivia, Spain.
Dates: Programs start every week or every month. **Cost:** Depends on location. Prices start at $175 per week and include classes, homestay, travel insurance, most meals, some cultural activities. **Contact:** AmeriSpan Unlimited, P.O. Box 40007, Philadelphia, PA 19106; 800-879-6640, fax 215-751-1100; info@amerispan.com, [www.amerispan.com].

Leisure Language Learning. Language Liaison sends people all over the world! This is the best in leisure language learning. Programs for seniors, families, executives, teens, leisure travelers and connoisseurs. Combine activities and cultural excursions with language learning and special interests. Learn something meaningful on your vacation and come back with more than just pictures.
Dates: Every week year round. **Cost:** Varies with program. **Contact:** Nancy Forman, Language Liaison Inc., 1610 Woodstead Ct., Suite 130, The Woodlands, TX 77380; 800-284-4448 or 281-367-7302, fax 281-367-4498, learn@languageliaison.com, [www.languageliaison.com].

Travel-Study Seminars. Learn from people of diverse backgrounds about their economic, political, and social realities. Emphasis on the views of the poor and oppressed. Programming in Mexico, Central America, South Africa, and Cuba. Call for a free listing of upcoming seminars.
Dates: Ongoing. **Cost:** $1,000-$4,500 depending on destination and length of trip. **Contact:** Center for Global Education, Augsburg College, 2211 Riverside Ave., Box TR, Minneapolis, MN 55454; 800-299-8889, fax 612-330-1695; globaled@augsburg.edu, [www.augsburg.edu/global].

WorldTeach. WorldTeach is a nonprofit, nongovernmental organization which provides opportunities for individuals to make a meaningful contribution to international education by living and working as volunteer teachers in developing countries.
Dates: Year round. **Cost:** $4,800-$5,950. Includes international airfare, health insurance, extensive training, and in-country support. **Contact:** WorldTeach, Harvard Institute for International Development, 14 Story St., Cambridge, MA 02138; 800-4-TEACH-0 or 617-495-5527, fax 617-495-1599; info@worldteach.org, [www.worldteach.org].

FIVE

FAMILY TRAVEL RESOURCES

*Parents approach overseas travel with obvious trepidation.
"We're thinking of going to Switzerland with our two-year-old.
Are we nuts?" Or, "Our 14-year-old barely speaks to us. Will
two weeks in Mexico help or will we end up hating each other?"*

Camping Resources

Country-by-Country Booklets, Many national
tourist offices in Europe provide excellent free
camping guides or maps. Austria offers
Camping/Caravaning; **Belgium** *Camping;*
Britain: a free 150-page book *Camping and
Caravan Parks;* **France:** *Guide Officiel Camping/
Caravaning* available from the Fedération
Française de Camping et de Caravaning, 78 rue
de Rivoli, 75004 Paris; 011-33-1-42-72-84-08,
fax 011-33-1-42-72-70-21; **Germany:** Ask
regional tourist offices for great free camping
guides; **Italy:** *Campeggiare in Italia* that includes
a free map and list of sites from NTO or from
Federcampeggio, via V. Emanuele 11, Casella
Postale 23, 50041 Calenzano, Firenze, Italy (fax
011-390-55-882-59-18); **Norway:** *Camping-OG
Bobilturisme;* Portugal offers *Roteiro Campista,*
available from larger local tourist offices or
from Federaçáp Portuguesa de Campismo, Av. 5
Outubro, Lisboa Codex, Portugal; **Spain:** *Guía
de Campings;* **Switzerland:** *Camping.*

**Cultural Misunderstanding: The French-
American Experience** by Raymonde Caroll.
Translated by Carol Volk. Univ. of Chicago
Press. $11.95. A fascinating exploration of the
differences in social interaction in France and
the U.S. For adults.

Eurocamp, Hartford Manor, Norwich, Cheshire,
England CW8 1HW; 011-44-1606-787870;
[www.eurocamp.com]. All the best of hotel life
(even separate bedrooms) with the interaction
and low prices of a campground. The clientele
at most sites is very international, so chances are
your kids will be playing with kids from all over
Europe.

Europa Camping and Caravaning. Stuttgart,
Germany: Drei-Brunnen. Available from
[www.amazon.de] (the German version of
Amazon.com) or from REI, P.O. Box C-88126,
Seattle, WA 98188; 800-426-4840. $19.95. The
only good European guide to campgrounds
available in the U.S., with maps, ferry information and currency-exchange tips.In English,
German or France.

Europe by Van and Motorhome by David Shore
and Patty Campbell from Shore/Campbell
Publications ($13.95 plus $1 s/h). A comprehensive resource to everything involved with
buying, renting, or simply surviving in an RV or
camper in Europe.

Family Campers and RVers, 4804 Transit Rd.,
Bldg. 2, Dewpew, NY 14043-4704; 800-245-
0755; [www3.pgh.net/~dscott/ferv.html].
Family memberships in this camping organiza-

THE TRACKING GAME

SEARCHING FOR ROOTS ABROAD IS CHALLENGING AND FUN

By Marian Behan Hammer

As a family vacation activity, discovering the towns and villages of immigrant ancestors has become a popular and fun thing to do—a fascinating detective project that can lead to unexpected pleasures. Most countries encourage and help travelers play the game, inviting us to come and dig among musty records. Trouble is, few of us know where or how to begin our search.

"My interest in ancestors began while my family and I were visiting my brother in Detroit," said Jim Dolan of Yacolt, Washington. "It was Memorial Day and we all went to the cemetery to place a flag on the grave of my paternal grandfather. My children asked a lot of questions about their great grandfather, questions neither my brother nor I could answer. We weren't even sure in which war he had fought. Since then I've visited older relatives who supplied me with all sorts of needed information, and next summer my family and I will travel to Cork, Ireland where grandfather lived as a boy. Hopefully, I'll be able to absorb some of my grandfather's culture and maybe even find a cousin or two."

Dolan took the right steps before flying off to Ireland—first interviewing his parents and other older family members. Frequently, older relatives have photographs, house records, wills, and family letters they are willing to share. They may know of church records where baptismal, confirmation, marriage, and death records were kept with scrupulous care in 18th and 19th century family Bibles.

Don't overlook cemeteries where family members are buried. Some old tombstones have an entire family history engraved on them. Books are available in most Genealogical Society libraries that list cemetery locations, along with quadrants and lot numbers.

If you can't get information from older relatives, there are other ways to start your search. Perhaps the best organized aid to amateur and professional genealogists alike is the Genealogical Society of Salt Lake City, established by the Mormon Church. There you can search nearly 1.5 million rolls of microfilmed records from archives from every state and most foreign countries, more than 195,000 books and eight million family group record forms. Floors of the huge complex are organized geographically. Family history centers, at Mormon churches in most cities, can arrange loans of the Salt Lake City records.

Among the most helpful information in Salt Lake City and in the U.S. National Archives are census records and steamship passenger arrival records. Census records from 1790 onwards are available to the public. They reveal birthplaces, and, after 1900, immigration dates. Passenger records tell not only when and where an immigrant arrived in this country but from which foreign port he departed and sometimes his birthplace. Other sources to research are U.S. military records, social security records, places of employment, school records, fraternities, deeds, and obituaries—and don't forget the Internet.

However, according to Jack Decker, a member of the Genealogical Society of Oregon, you should keep in mind while reading old documents that meanings of words and the spelling of many surnames change over the years. "Letters may have been added or dropped," he says, "and it is not uncommon to find family names spelled several different ways."

For example, Margaret Floto Meyer discovered that in her ancestor search her maiden name had once been spelled Floteau. When her great-great-grandfather entered the U.S. an immigration officer dropped the French spelling of his name in favor of a more phonetic sounding one, and the family has continued to use the shorter spelling every since.

Not all searches for family records are successful. The fun is in the hunt: putting everything together is like working on a giant jigsaw puzzle. Eventually, data, facts, names, and dates fit together and fall into place to give you a picture of your family. The reward is worth the effort. Just walking the paths our ancestors once trod, experiencing life in their town, perhaps visiting the house where they lived or having a drink in the same pub in which they drank, helps us to imagine life in their times and gives us a strong sense of continuity and belonging.

Ancestor Searches

U.S. National Archives and Records Service, 8th and Pennsylvania Ave., NW, Washington, DC 20408; **U.S. Immigration and Naturalization Service**, Washington, DC; **The Genealogical Society of Salt Lake City**, 35 NW Temple, Salt Lake City, UT 84115. **International Vital Records Handbook** by Thomas Jay Kemp lists addresses of most foreign genealogical archival services including: Register General, Joyce House, 8-11 Lombard St. E., Dublin 2, Ireland; Director General, 2nd Division, Civil Affairs Bureau, Ministry of Justice, 1-1-1 Kasumigaseki, Chiyoda-ku, Tokyo 100, Japan; Standesant, Germany; Le Marie, France; **Russian-American Genealogical Archival Service (RAGAS)**, P.O. Box 236, Glen Echo, MD 20812.

tion are $25 and include children under 18. For an additional $10 members can purchase an International Camping Carnet.

Family Travel Organizations

Abercrombie & Kent, 1520 Kensington Rd., Suite 212, Oak Brook, IL 60523, 800-323-7308. fax 630-954-3324, [www.abercrombiekent.com]. A wide range of itineraries tailored to families traveling during summer and school vacation.

AmeriSpan Unlimited, P.O. Box 40007, Philadelphia, PA 19106; 800-879-6640; info@AmeriSpan.com, [www.AmeriSpan.com]. Family, teen, senior, and adult language programs in 12 countries in Mexico, Spain, Central and South America. Housing with a host family.

Backroads, 801 Cedar St., Berkeley, CA 94710-1800; 800-462-2848. Family biking and walking trips in the U.S., Canada, Costa Rica, Czech Republic, France, and Switzerland. Children of all ages welcome.

Butterfield & Robinson, 70 Bond St., Suite 300, Toronto, ON M5B 1X3, Canada; 800-678-1147; [www.butterfield.com]. Pricey deluxe family walking and biking trips in Italy, Holland, Morocco, Canada, and Belize for families with teenagers.

Experience Plus!, 415 Mason Court, Unit 1, Ft. Collins, CO 80524; 800-685-4565, fax 970-493-0377; tours@experienceplus.com, [www.xplus.com]. Walking and cycling tours in Europe for families with teens.

Family Travel Forum. Membership organization ($48 per year) publishes newsletter and web site on global family travel including destinations, health and parenting tips, travel deals, family tour operators, and provides customized travel information. FTF Membership Dept., Cathedral Station, P.O. Box 1585, New York, NY 10025-1585; 888-FT-FORUM, fax 212-665-6136; [www.familytravelforum.com].

Family Travel Made Easy, 424 Bridge St., Ashland OR 97520; 800-826-7165, fax 541-488-3067; [www.about-family-travel.com/company.htm]. A service that specializes in tailor-made vacations that suit your family's needs in Europe, Israel, and the Mediterranean.

Familyhostel, 6 Garrison Ave., Durham, NH 03824; 800-733-9753; [www.learn.unh.edu]. Offers 10-day trips to Austria, Wales, France, Switzerland, and England (destinations vary

yearly) to adults traveling with school-age kids 8-15. Trips mix education and recreation plus a chance to meet local families.

Grand Travel, 6900 Wisconsin Ave., Suite 706, Chevy Chase, MD 20815; 800-247-7651, fax 301-913-0166; [www.grandtrvl.com]. Tour company specializing in outings to Europe, Africa, and Australia for grandparents and grandkids.

Hostelling International (AYH), 733 15th St., NW, Suite 840, Washington, DC 20005; 202-783-6161; [www.iyhf.org] or [www.hiayh.org]. Many hostels have private family rooms. Advance reservations are required.

Idyll, Ltd., P.O. Box 405, Media, PA 19063; 888-868-6871, fax 610-565-5142; info@untours.com, [www.untours.com]. Arranges apartment rentals for families and includes low-key orientation at your destination.

Journeys International, 107 Aprill Dr., Suite 3, Ann Arbor, MI 48103; 734-665-4407 or 800-255-8735; [www.journeys-intl.com]. Specially-designed socially responsible family trips include Himalayan trekking, African safaris, trips to Australia, the Galapagos, Panama, and Costa Rica.

Overseas Adventure Travel, 625 Mt. Auburn St., Cambridge, MA 02138; 800-221-0814. Intercultural adventure trips for families and individuals. Families can choose a Galapagos Wildlife Adventure, a Serengeti Safari, a Costa Rica natural history trip, plus many other adventures.

Sister Cities International, Suite 250, 1300 Pennsylvania Ave., NW, Washington, DC 20004; 202-312-1200, fax 202-312-1201; [www.sister-cities.org]. Check the web site directory of existing city pairs, or to find out how to set up a sister city program.

Society for the Protection of Nature in Israel, 28 Arrandale Ave., Great Neck, NY 11024; 212-398-6750, fax 212-398-1665. Operates 1-14-day hikes and nature explorations—even a camel tour—in different parts of Israel. Expert environmental guides and low costs. Accommodations are in the group's field study centers or hostels. Children age 10 and up welcome.

Special Expeditions, 720 5th Ave., 6th Fl., New York, NY 10019; 800-762-0003; [www.expeditions.com]. A variety of itineraries, including the Galapagos, made more interesting with special scavenger hunts and educational puzzles for the kids.

Travelling with Children, Dan and Wendy Hallinan, 2313 Valley St., Berkeley, CA 94702; 510-848-0929, fax 510-848-0935; twc87@aol.com. An experienced traveling family arranges home rentals, airfares, and special itineraries for other traveling families, especially in Europe.

Wildland Adventures, 3516 NE 155th St., Seattle, WA 98155; 800-345-4453, fax 206-363-6615. Family trips to Costa Rica, Honduras, Belize, Peru, the Galapagos, Turkey, Africa, Alaska, and Panama. Some trips include homestays and other intercultural opportunities.

World Pen Pals, P.O. Box 337, Saugerties, NY 12477; Tel./fax 914-246-7828. Promotes international friendship and cultural understanding through correspondence between young people under age 23. Pen friends offered by gender and continent but for specific countries phone first to verify availability. Send $3 and SASE for each pen pal desired.

Zephyr Press, 50 Kenwood St., Brookline, MA 02446; Tel./fax 617-713-2813; zephyr@world.std.com. Zephyr publishes the *Explorers Guide to Russia,* and an *Explorers Guide to Moscow,* and a series of "People to People" guides for Russia, Poland, Romania, Czech Republic/Slovak Republic, Hungary/Bulgaria, Baltic Republics. Prices vary. While not geared specifically to family travelers, the guides are a good source for family contacts.

Family Travel Publications

Adventuring with Children: An Inspirational Guide to World Travel and the Outdoors by Nan Jeffrey. Excellent overseas and domestic advice for active families who want to backpack, sail, bicycle, or canoe. $14.95 from Menasha Ridge Press, 700 S. 28th St., Suite 206, Birmingham, AL 35233; 800-247-9437.

Best Places to Go: A Family Destination Guide by Nan Jeffrey. Recommendations and specifics on budget, culturally-aware family visits to Europe and Central and South America. $14.95 from Menasha Ridge Press (above).

Children's Book of London, Children's Book of Britain (Usborne Guides). Available through BritRail, 551 5th Ave., Suite 702, New York, NY 10176; 212-490-6688.

Children's Books in Print (R.R. Bowker, annual). Your public library should have this. Look up the countries you'll be visiting in the subject index. Then read as many books as you can with your kids before you go.

Continental Sites Guide. Available from The Caravan Club, East Grinstead House, East Grinstead, W. Sussex RH19 1UA, U.K.; 011-44-1342-32-69-44, fax 011-44-1342-41-02-58. Excellent annual 2-volume campground guide covers sites in Europe, with readers' reports, good directions.

Dream Sleeps: Castle and Palace Hotels of Europe by Pamela L. Barrus. Fairytale hotels that are open to the public for lodging and dining. Order from Amazon.com or $25 from Carousel Press (below).

The Family Travel Guides Catalog. Carousel Press, P.O. Box 6038, Berkeley, CA 94706-0038. 510-527-5849; info@carousel-press.com; [www.carousel-press.com]. Most of the books mentioned in this list—and dozens of others—are available through Carousel Press. Send $1 or 33¢ long SASE for catalog.

Family Travel Times, 40 5th Ave., New York, NY 10011; 888-822-4FTT, 212-477-5524; [www.familytraveltimes.com]. $39 per year. Bimonthly online newsletter of worldwide family travel news. Lots of tips for traveling with infants to teens.

Family Travel: Terrific New Vacations for Today's Families by Evelyn Kaye (Blue Panda). Parent-tested trips—where to find them and what they cost. Includes houseswaps, educational trips with universities, nature trips, and dinosaur digs.

France for Families. A Touch of France, 660 King George Rd., Fords, NJ 08863; 800-738-5240, fax 732-738-0917; [www.atouchoffrance.com]. Neat program arranges family tours or "a la carte" activities—from art to cooking to perfume making—for kids in Paris and elsewhere in France.

Guide de la France des Enfants by Marylène Bellenger. Editions Rouge & Or, 11 rue de Javel, 75015 Paris, France. If you can read French, pick this one up in Paris. Exhaustive guide to sites all over France for kids up to 15.

Gutsy Mamas: Travel Tips and Wisdom for Mothers on the Road by Marybeth Bond. Traveler's Tales, San Francisco, CA. $7.95. Small volume of tips and first-person anecdotes that should help families and single mothers gather the courage to take unconventional trips with the kids.

Have Children Will Travel, P.O. Box 152, Lake Oswego, OR 97034; toll-free 877-699-5869, fax 503-636-0895. $29 per year. Quarterly family

FAMILIES MEETING FAMILIES

MAKING VITAL CONNECTIONS OVERSEAS HINGES ON TRIP PLANNING

By Cynthia Harriman

If you're a *Transitions Abroad* reader, it's a fair assumption that you think travel is about *people* rather than *places*: When you visit another country you want to meet its inhabitants and learn about their lives, not simply wander through a series of cathedrals and museums. For families traveling with children, then, the challenge is to figure out how to meet other families.

We first took our kids overseas when they were 10 and 13. We had visions of meeting people at the grocery store or on the street and making new friends all over Europe. But this rarely happened. In general, the only connections we made were the ones we planned before we left home.

When planning a trip abroad, stop and think about how you make friends at home. It's almost exclusively through people you already know at work, at your health club, at the PTA. When was the last time you made a friend in the checkout line at Kmart? Have you picked up anybody at the beach since you turned 19?

Even when you do make these chance encounters, they're more likely when you're alone. Family togetherness on a trip eliminates a lot of the need to reach out. So how do you give your kids the rich experience of meeting other kids their own age in another country? The best solutions hinge on how you plan your trip and where you stay.

Planning to Meet Other Families

Start planning long before you travel. One good way to start is by finding a pen pal in the area where you're going. Kids in other countries start learning English in elementary school, so language shouldn't be a barrier. Several kid-centered web sites will lead you to a pen pal. If you're wary of cyberspace strangers, traditional pen pal clearinghouses will match your child with someone in your selected country. Months or even years later, it's a huge pleasure for these pen pals to actually meet in person.

Look to any organizations to which you already belong. Are you a member of Rotary or some other worldwide service club? Write to the Rotary in your vacation area and say you'd like to meet local families with kids of similar age to yours. Or write to a local church of your denomination and say you'd like to meet congregation members.

Professional interests work well, too. If you're a teacher, a nurse, or a plumber, write to the tourist office in a town you'd like to visit and ask for information about organizations that cater to your peers locally. As a computer consultant, I made contacts with computer dealers in Spain and England. But I waited until after I arrived instead of writing ahead, and it was almost time to leave by the time I felt really connected and comfortable with my new friends.

Personal connections are best of all. Does your mail carrier know someone in Portugal? Isn't this year's high school exchange with Greece? Didn't your neighbor's sister marry someone from Hong Kong? Ask them all if they would be willing to pass the word that you're interested in meeting other families.

Before our first trip, my husband wrote to a half-dozen men he had met briefly on a business trip three years earlier. Two wrote back and arranged Dads-only business lunches. Several didn't reply. But the last one invited us to his country home in Spain for a long weekend. This shocked us: Lew had met Señor Ramos only once. But Pedro and his wife Juana had kids the same age as ours and were eager to exchange ideas. Sam learned that Spanish 10-year-olds like computer games as much as he does. Gema Ramos was surprised to learn that Libby, her same age, got *paid* for babysitting the neighbors' kids. Without a word of common language, Juana taught me how to slice up a whole fish and peel potatoes really fast, while the men discussed common business interests. The obvious lesson: don't dismiss the smallest possible connection overseas.

Picking Where You Stay

The other big factor that greatly affects whom you meet is where you stay. Park your clan at a Best Western in Paris and you'll meet some nice folks from Cleveland or Tucson—if they venture out of their rooms. Stay in a youth hostel with family rooms, and you'll hook up with folks from all over the world.

Youth hostel family rooms are one of the best-kept secrets in budget travel. Of the approximately 2,100 youth hostels in Europe, over 1,500 of them offer family rooms. You don't have to split up and sleep in gender-segregated dorms; you can have your own room that sleeps four to six family members. Best of all, hostels are designed for mingling, much more so than hotels. There are game rooms, common dining areas, playgrounds and yards—all places where it's easy to meet other people.

Campgrounds are another great place to meet other families. In Europe, camping does *not* mean perching on a lonely mountaintop in a cramped, leaky tent. European campgrounds are usually near cities. Many locals rent the same site every year and set up elaborate RVs or huge tents.

You can join in the campground spirit by renting a bungalow or a luxury tent at these same campgrounds, many of which have laundries, discos, chic stores, and movie theaters. One *Transitions Abroad* reader raved to us about a British organization called Eurocamp, which offers tents with separate bedrooms, air conditioning, and gas grills at campsites all over Europe.

Many families decide to stay put when traveling with kids. In that case a home exchange turns out to be a great way to meet other families. You'll be in a residential area surrounded by other families, and your host family will be glad to hook you up with the neighbors. Many home exchanges start with a one-day overlap, when your hosts will welcome you to their home and throw a neighborhood cookout to help you meet their friends. (Or maybe the overlap is on your side and you'll do the same for them.) Your kids will have bikes and basketballs and will head for the local playground, which multiplies the opportunities for meeting kindred souls.

newsletter of travel resources and tips; deb@havechildrenwilltravel.com, [http://havechildrenwilltravel.com].

The History of Art for Young People by Anthony Abrams and H.W. Janson. Try your library before you go, and let your kids "shop" for masterpieces they'd like to see in Europe.

How To Fly—For Kids! (Corkscrew Press, $10.95). Activities to keep children busy during long, boring plane flights.

How to Take Great Trips with Your Kids by Sanford Portno and Joan Flynn Portnoy. (Harvard Common Press, $9.95).

Japan for Kids: The Ultimate Guide for Parents and their Children by Jeanne Huey Erickson and Diane Wiltshire Kanagawa. Kodansha International, 114 5th Ave., New York, NY 10011. 1992. $15. Not just a tour guide: includes everything from playgrounds and museums to how to have a baby in Japan. Comprehensive and well-written.

Kids Love Israel; Israel Loves Kids by Barbara Sofer. New 2nd ed. includes lodging, camps, language, food, plus over 300 sightseeing ideas for the whole country. $17.95 from Kar-Ben Copies, 6800 Tildenwood Ln., Rockville, MD 20852; 301-984-8733. Kept current on publishers web site: [www.karben.com].

Kids' Trips in Tokyo: A Family Guide to One-Day Outings by Ivy Maeda, Kitty Kobe, Cynthia Ozeki, and Lyn Sato. Kodansha International. Organized by 1-day itineraries, with info for infants and older kids. Excellent resource.

Le Guide de la Science en France. Hachette Guides, 79 Boulevard Saint-Germain, 5006 Paris. A wonderful guide to factory visits, nature parks, aquariums, and all things scientific in France. Includes editors' top picks.Buy it on arrival.

Le Guide du Routard Junior…Paris et ses environs avec vos enfants. Hachette Livre. 1999. Widely available in Paris. Includes activities, restaurants and shops recommended for kids.

Take Your Kids to Europe by Cynthia Harriman. 3rd ed. Globe Pequot Press, P.O. Box 833, Old Saybrook, CT 06475; 800-243-0495. Not simply a list of places to go, but a good intercultural guide for how and why to travel in Europe with children.

Travel with Children by Maureen Wheeler (Lonely Planet). 3rd ed. The definitive guide to third world travel with kids, covering both logistics and cultural interchange; first-person stories from other travelers.

The Traveler's Toolkit: How to Travel Absolutely Anywhere. Not specifically for families, but a great "attitude" book to help new travelers feel comfortable taking on the world. Menasha Ridge Press (see first entry above).

Usborne Children's Book of Europe by Rebecca Treays. Usborne. 1993. Available online from W.H. Smith at [www.bookshops.co.uk]. Comprehensive enough for parents, but written for kids to read, too.

Family Travel Web Sites

About Family Travel, [www.about-family-travel.com]. A travel service web site that specializes in tailor-made vacations to suit your family's needs.

Family Travel Forum, [www.familytravelforum.com]. The Family Travel Forum (FTF) is dedicated to the ideals, promotion, and support of travel with children (see their listing). Their web site includes a selection of family travel titles available through amazon.com.

The Family Travel Network, [www.usacontact.com]. Connect with other families who take traveling with children seriously.

Have Children Will Travel, [http://havechildrenwilltravel.com]. Web site for their newsletter (see their listing). Not only can you preview and get information about their printed publication, but they'll answer your family travel questions by email.

http://family.go.com/categories/travel. This commercial site has resources for family travel in the U.S. and abroad.

About.com, [travelwithkids.about.com]. About.com's family travel site (with Teresa Plowright as the guide) is billed as "a guide to the many ways you can use the web to plan and even purchase your family holidays: discount airfares, vacation ideas, trip reports, info about destinations, and more."

Quinwell Travel, [www.quinwell.com]; 800-339-8892. Information and booking services for traveling with children on cruise ships and family travel in general.

Six

Disability Travel
Resources & Programs

More and more people with disabilities are looking to get off the tourist track, get to know the local people and culture, and still stay within a budget. For travelers with disabilities, these are not easy tasks. Yet more and more people with limited mobility are becoming independent, nontraditional travelers.

Disability Organizations

Barrier Free Travel, Ian J. Cooper, 36 Wheatley St., North Bellingen, NSW 2454, Australia; 011-61-0266551-733. Provides information on travel for persons with disabilities in Australia and the world's major cities. One-time fee of AUS$75. *Access Guide to Sydney,* $10 plus s/h.

Calvert Trust Exmoor, Wistlandpound, Kentisbury, Barnstaple, Devon, EX31 4SJ, U.K. Offers holidays for people of all abilities. Both self-catering and catered accommodations. Outdoor activities and indoor pool; calvert.exmoor@btinternet.com, [www.calvert-trust.org.uk].

Disability Rights Education and Defense Fund. 800-466-4232 (TDD and voice).

Full Data Ltd., 808 Malabanas Rd., 2009 Angeles City, The Philippines; 011-63-2-81-24277, fax 011-63-2-81-50756. Provides publications and information on travel in Thailand, Taiwan, Macao, China, India, Nepal, Singapore, Vietnam, Laos, and Cambodia.

The Guided Tour, Inc., 7900 Old York Rd., Suite 114B, Elkins Park, PA 19027-2339; 800-783-5841 or 215-782-1370, fax 215-635-2637; [www.guidedtour.com]. Programs for persons with developmental and physical challenges. Free brochure.

Handicapped Scuba Association International, 1104 El Prado, San Clemente, CA 92692; Tel./fax 949-498-6128; [http://ourworld.compuserve.com/homepages/hsahdq]. Offers information on dive trips and where you can learn to dive.

Hidden Treasures Travel, 501 Florence Dr., Vacaville, CA 95688; 888-5-HIDDEN, fax 707-447-0681. This organization specializes in assisting travelers with brain injuries, but serves people of all abilities.

IAMAT, 417 Center St., Lewistown, NY 14092; 716-754-4883 or 519-836-0102; iamat@sentex.net, [www.sentex.net/~iamat]. Lists English-speaking doctors in foreign countries who agree to their standards and fee structure.

Mobility International USA (MIUSA). P.O. Box 10767, Eugene, OR 97440; 541-343-1284, fax 541-343-6812; miusa@igc, [www.miusa.org]. A national, nonprofit organization dedicated to expanding equal opportunities for people with disabilities in international exchange, leadership development, disability rights training, and community service. The **National Clearing-**

house on Disability and Exchange (NCDE), a joint venture by MIUSA and United States Information Agency, strives to increase the participation of people with disabilities in the full range of international exchange opportunities by providing free information and referrals to individuals, disability organizations and exchange.

Moss Rehab Hospital Referral Service, 1200 W. Tabor Rd., Philadelphia, PA 19144; 215-456-9600 or 9603; [www.mossresourcenet.org]. A telephone referral center for international travel accessibility.

Society for the Advancement of Travel for the Handicapped, 347 5th Ave., Suite 610, New York, NY 10016; 212-447-7284; [www.sath.org]. Publishes newsletter and information booklets on trip planning for persons with disabilities. Their web site has a good selection of links and information.

Winged Fellowship Trust. offers holidays and short-term residential respite care in the U.K. Winged Fellowship Trust, Angel House, 20-32 Pentonville Rd., London N1 9XD, U.K.; 011-44-171-833-2594, fax 011-44-171-278-0370; admin@wft.org.uk, [www.wft.org.uk/index2.htm].

Disability Publications

A World Awaits You (Away), A periodical journal devoted to disability travel and exchange. For a free examination copy send your mailing address to Mobility International USA (see Organizations above).

Access First News, Access First Travel, 239 Commercial St., Malden, MA 02148; 800-557-2047, 781-322-1610, fax 781-322-4842. Newsletter contains destination descriptions, calendar of events, other accessibility information.

Access to the Skies, Paralyzed Veterans Assn., 801 18th St., NW, Washington, DC 20006; 202-872-1300 ext. 790. Quarterly newsletter provides information on accessible airline travel.

Accessible Holidays in the British Isles 1999: A Guide for Disabled People by Royal Association for Disability and Rehabilitation (RADAR), 12 City Forum, 250 City Rd., London EC1V 8AF, U.K.; 011-44-71-250-3222. Over 1,000 places to stay in all parts of the U.K. and Republic of Ireland. £13 postpaid.

The Air Carriers Act: Make It Work for You. Free from the Paralyzed Veterans of America 888-860-7244.

Building Bridges edited by Julie Ann Cheshire (Mobility International USA, 3rd ed., 1998). More than 200 pages of suggestions and creative ideas for including, recruiting, and accommodating people with disabilities in international programs. Includes information on volunteer service programs and legal issues for international advisers. $20.

The Diabetic Traveler, P.O. Box 8223, Stamford, CT 06905. $18.95 per year. A newsletter with articles and information of particular interest to travelers with diabetes.

Directory of Travel Agencies for the Disabled by Helen Hecker (Twin Peaks Press.) $19.99 plus $5 s/h from Twin Peaks Press, P.O. Box 129, Vancouver, WA 98666-0129; 800-637-2256 (credit card orders), 360-694-2462, fax 360-696-3210; twinpeak@pacifier.com. Lists more than 370 travel agencies and tour operators in U.S. and worldwide.

Emerging Horizons, a newsletter which provides unbiased views of accessible travel options. Sample copies from: P.O. Box 278, Ripon, CA 95366; 209-599-9409; [www.candy-charles.com/Horizons].

Home Is in the Heart. Accommodating People with Disabilities in the Homestay Experience. Video provides information and ideas for exchange organizations. Discusses how to recruit homestay families, meet accessibility needs, and accommodate international participants with disabilities. Available in English, open captioned. Order from MIUSA (above). $49.

Hostelling International Directories. indicate with a symbol those hostels that are accessible. Available from Hostelling International, P.O. Box 37613, Washington, DC 20013-7613; fax 202-783-6171; hiayhserv@hiayh.org, [www.hiayh.org]. International guides are $13.95 and North American Guide is free to members, nonmembers $3.

Loud, Proud & Passionate: Including Women with Disabilities in International Development Programs by MIUSA. Contact MIUSA (above) for ordering information, $18 (members), $25 (nonmembers), international orders add $10 s/h. Includes guidelines to ensure inclusion of women with disabilities in the development process, as well as personal experience stories and resources. Alternate formats available upon request. Available in English and Spanish.

Mobility International Newsletter is a quarterly magazine featuring information on projects and events worldwide aimed at disabled people. Available from Mobility International (above).

Mobility International Tourists Guides for European Union Countries offer information for travelers with disabilities. Available from Mobility International, 18, Boulevard Baudoiun, B-1000 Brussels, Belgium; 011-32-2-201-56-08, fax 011-32-2-201-57-63; mobint@arcadis.be.

Ports of Call, 522 E. Broadway, Princeton, IN 47670. Quarterly newsletter covering topics of interest to the disabled traveler. Subscription: $5 donation suggested.

TDI National Directory and Guide. Annual directory of TTY accessible residences, businesses, government agencies, and interest groups in all 50 states plus special listings of nationwide toll-free numbers and relay services. Resource guide $25 for 1 year, $45 for 2 years from Telecommunications for the Deaf, Inc., 8630 Fenton St., Suite 603, Silver Springs, MD 20910-3803; 301-589-3786, TTY 800-935-2258, then say, 301-589-3006, fax 301-589-3797; caroltdi@aol.com.

Travel for the Disabled by Helen Hecker (Twin Peaks Press, address above). $19.99 plus $5 s/h. How and where to find information, travel tips, and access guides for travelers with disabilities.

Wheelchair Through Europe. Graphic Language Press, P.O. Box 270, Cardiff by the Sea, CA 92007; 760-944-9594. $13. Resources on accessible sites in Europe, including hotels, transportation, and resources.

The Wheelchair Traveler, 123 Ball Hill Rd., Milford, NH 03055; 603-673-4539. Information on hotels, motels, restaurants, and sightseeing for wheelchair users.

Disability Tour Programs

Able to Travel/Partnership Travel, Inc., 239 Commercial St., Malden, MA 02148; 800-559-2047, fax 617-986-4225).

Accessible Journeys, Howard J. McCoy, 35 W. Sellers Ave., Ridley Park, PA 19078; 800-846-4537, fax 610-521-6959; sales@disabilitytravel.com, [www.disabilitytravel.com]. Slow walkers, wheelchair travelers, friends and family.

Accessible Kiwi Tours New Zealand, Ltd. Adventure or leisure tours for all, including disabled or elderly. Group or individual tours New Zealand-wide. Accessible Kiwi Tours New Zealand, Ltd., P.O. Box 550, Opotiki, New Zealand; 011-64-7-315-7867, fax 011-64-7-315-5056; kiwitour@wave.co.nz, [www.accessible-tours.co.nz].

Associated Travel Service, Ltd. P.O. Box 09027, Milwaukee, WI 53209; 800-535-2045. Arranges individual and group travel for people with disabilities.

Bare Cove Travel, 16 North St., Hingham, MA 02043; 781-749-7750, fax 781-749-1022; apeter6203@aol.com. Arranges travel for people with disabilities.

Cruisin' With Carol (Higgins), P.O. Box 1923, Lake Oswego, OR 97035; 503-246-0706.

Directions Unlimited, 123 Green Ln., Bedford Hills, NY 10507; 800-533-5343 or 914-241-1700, fax 914-241-0243; cruiseusa@aol.com. Specializes in arranging vacations and tours for persons with disabilities.

Enable Travel Services, New Frontiers, 7545 S. Univ. Blvd., Littleton, CO 80122. Plans trips for travelers with disabilities, as well as working with groups and individuals.

Flying Wheels Travel, 143 W. Bridge, P.O. Box 382, Owatonna, MN 55060; 800-535-6790, fax 507-451-1685; thq@ll.net. A tour operator and travel agency with an international client base.

Holiday Care Service, Imperial Buildings, 2nd Floor, Victoria Rd., Horley, Surrey, RH6 7PZ, U.K.; 011-44-1293-774-535, fax 011-44-1293-784-647. The U.K.'s central source of holiday information for disabled and disadvantaged persons.

Keli Tours, 19 Hacharoshet St., Keidar-Center, Raanana, Israel; 011-972-9-740-9490, fax 011-972-9-740-9408. Offers tours of the Middle East and Israel for people with and without disabilities; eli_meiri@keli-tours.co.il.

NeverLand Adventures, 800-817-8226 or outside the U.S. 619-696-6068; neverland@home.com. A disabled owned and operated Australian tour/travel agency offering unique and diverse itineraries and accessibility without compromise: Outback experience, Aboriginal culture, Sydney Opera, much more.

Over The Rainbow Accessible Travel, Inc. David McKown, 186 Mehani Circle, Kihei, HI 96753; 808-879-5521.

Search Beyond Adventures. Specializes in international and domestic tours for people with disabilities. Free catalog with 200 tours available. Call 800-800-9979.

FIRSTHAND LESSONS

By Susan Sygall

I've been traveling in my wheelchair for more than 25 years and would like to share some of my best tips:

I use a light-weight manual wheelchair with pop-off tires. I have a net bag under my wheelchair where I store my daypack. A backpack fits on the back of my chair; if I can't carry it myself (since I usually travel alone), I don't take it.

I keep a bungee cord with me for when I can't get my chair in a car or to secure it on a train, and I always insist on using my own wheelchair to the airline gate. When I transfer planes I again insist that I get my own chair rather than use the wheelchairs provided by the airlines.

Bathrooms are always a hassle, so I have learned to use creative ways to transfer into narrow bathrooms (or use a belt to narrow my wheelchair width). To be honest, when there are no accessible bathrooms in sight I have found ways to relieve myself discreetly just about anywhere—from outside the Eiffel Tower to a glacier in a national park. You gotta do what you gotta do. Hopefully, one day the access will improve. But in the meantime there is a world out there to be discovered. Bring along an extra pair of pants and a great sense of humor.

I always try to learn some of the local language because it cuts through the barriers when people stare (and they do) and also comes in handy when I need assistance in going up a curb or a flight of steps.

Don't accept other people's notions of what is possible—I have climbed Masada in Israel and made it to the top of the Acropolis in Greece.

When I go to a museum I'm sure to ask about freight elevators because almost all have them.

I always get information about disability groups where I am going: they will have the best access information and many times they will become your new traveling partners and friends. Remember, you are part of a global family of disabled people.

Don't confuse being flexible and having a positive attitude with settling for less than your rights. I expect equal access and constantly let people know about the possibility of providing access through ramps or other modifications. When I believe my rights have been violated I do whatever is necessary to remedy the situation so the next traveler or disabled person in that country won't have the same frustrations.

See The World Travel. Agent organizes travel for disabled. See the World Travel, 1903 Brandonview Ave., c/o Summint Travel, Richmond, VA 23231; world2c@bellatlantic.net.

Trips, Jim Peterson, 960 E. 19th St., Eugene, OR 97403; 541-686-1013, fax 541-465-9355; trips@tripsinc.com, [www.tripsinc.com].

Wheelchair Travel, Ltd., Trevor Pollitt, 1 Johnston Green, Guildford, Surrey, GU2 6XS, England; 011-44-1483-233640, fax 011-44-1483-23772; [www.wheelchair-travel.co.uk]. A self-drive rental, taxi, and tour service specifically for disabled people, especially the wheelchair-user.

Wheels Up!. 888-389-4335. A travel agency specializing in planning and arranging travel for people who use wheelchairs.

Disability Travel Programs

The following listing of responsible travel tours and programs was supplied by the organizers. Contact the program directors to confirm costs, dates, and other details. Please tell them you read about their program in this book! Programs based in more than one country or region are listed under "Worldwide."

Canada

Discover Accessible Canada and Québec. Special tours for special needs in summer, fall, or winter through cultural and panoramic areas of the Belle Province or eastern Canada. Our guide, *Québec accessible,* is also available for self-planned tours.
Dates: May-Oct. Cost: Guide CAN$15, tours from CAN$129. Contact: Chantal Roy, Kéroul in Montreal; 514-252-3104, fax 514-254-0766; info@keroul.qc.ca, [www.keroul.qc.ca].

Costa Rica

COSI (Costa Rica Spanish Institute). COSI offers high quality instruction at reasonable prices. We offer Spanish classes in San José and at a beautiful national park (beach and rainforest). Homestay is also available. Volunteer work opportunities and special discounts in tours.
Dates: Year round. Cost: Prices start at $280 per week including classes in groups of maximum 5 students, homestay, cultural activities, books, access to email, airport pickup. Contact: COSI, P.O. Box 1366-2050, San Pedro, San José, Costa Rica; 011-506-234-1001, fax 011-506-253-2117. From U.S. 800-771-5184; cosicr@sol.racsa.co.cr, [www.cosi.co.cr].

Europe

Accessible Italy. Accessible tourist services all over Italy for people with disabilities.
Dates: Call for details. Cost: Call for details. Contact: Massimo Micotti, Accessible Italy, Piazza Pitagora 9, 10137 Turin, Italy; 011-39-0113096363, fax 011-39-0113091201; m.micotti@agora.stm.it, [www.tour-web.com/accessibleitaly].

Worldwide

Disability Rights/Leadership Development. Mobility International USA (MIUSA) coordinates programs for people with and without disabilities focused on disability rights, leadership development and cross-cultural learning. Through the National Clearinghouse on Disability and Exchange, MIUSA also provides information and referrals for other international exchange requests.
Dates: Summers, 2-4 weeks. Cost: $500-$1,000 program fees. Contact: Melissa Mueller, Exchange Coordinator, Mobility International USA, P.O. Box 10767, Eugene, OR 97440; 541-343-1284 (V/TTY), fax 541-343-6812; info@miusa.org, [www.miusa.org].

IES and Access Abroad. Access Abroad is a project that seeks to enhance study abroad opportunities for students with disabilities. This project is funded by FIPSE, U.S. Department of Education Project #P116B70598. IES is involved in this grant with the Univ. of Minnesota and Pennsylvania State Univ. All IES centers, particularly IES Paris and IES Vienna, are working to counsel and assist students with disabilities who wish to study abroad.
Dates: IES offers full year, semester, or 6-week summer sessions. Cost: For more information about costs and financial aid, please contact IES directly. Contact: IES (Institute for the International Education of Students), 33 N. LaSalle, 15th Fl., Chicago, IL 60602; 800-995-2300, fax 312-944-1448; info@iesabroad.org, [www.iesabroad.org].

Wine Tours/Cruises. Help you tour the Sonoma County wine country and cruises that are best for disabled guests. Sonoma County is located 60 miles north of San Francisco. Familiar with champagne cellars and private wineries that are accessible.

Dates: No set dates. FITS to the area. Cost: $35 initial research fee and wine tours custom designed. Contact: Linda Reitzell, Sunset Travel; 707-887-7905, fax 707-887-7920.

Disability Web Sites

Access-Able Travel Source, 303-232-2979 (Voice), fax 303-239-8486; [www.access-able.com]. A free Internet information service for mature and disabled travelers: accessibility guide for countries, states and provinces, and cities; also accommodations, transportation, attractions, adventures, doctors, and equipment rental and repair, specialty travel agents, and a comprehensive list of disability links and publications. Pages include discussion forums and What's News, an online newsletter.

Arthur Frommer's Outspoken Encyclopedia of Travel, [www.frommers.com/specialpeople/dis]. Offers a section on resources for travelers with disabilities.

Disability Net: Travel, [www.disabilitynet.co.uk/info/holidays/index.html]. Links, news, and informaton for disabled travelers.

Dtour: A Disabled Visitors Guide to Ireland, [http://ireland.iol.ie/infograf/dtour]. Lists facilities in Ireland for travelers who have movement or sensory disabilities.

Everything's Travel, Disability Travel Section, [http://members.aol.com/Atlases/special/disab.htm]. A good selection of links to sites of interests.

EWABLEnet, [www.dpa.org.sg]. The Disabled People's Association of Singapore's web site includes attractions, hotels, and other resources.

Global Access, a Network for Disabled Travelers, [www.geocities.com/paris/1502]. Includes an extensive archive of disabled travelers' reports on worldwide destinations, as well as travel tips, and links to disabled travel sites.

New Horizons, [www.faa.gov/acr/dat.htm]. A wealth of information for the disabled air traveler. Sections include: Planning Your Trip, and Compliance Procedures.

New Mobility, [www.newmobility.com]. An extension of the print magazine, New Mobility. Includes many links to other sites, as well as some information on travel for persons with disabilities.

Tourism for All, [http://andi.casaccia.enea.it/hometur.htm]. Database information on accessible sites includes Italy, Sweden, Berlin, Germany, Spain, and soon more countries.

Winged Fellowship Trust, [www.wft.org.uk]. Offers worldwide tours with one-to-one care to people with disabilities.

SEVEN

RESPONSIBLE TRAVEL RESOURCES

As people around the planet become more concerned about their environment, more curious about people of different cultures, and more willing to think differently, travel is changing. Travelers are planning their own itineraries, often combining some time for relaxation with more active and meaningful experiences that contribute to the preservation of local environments. The following selection of resources will help you in these efforts.

Ecotourism Organizations

Aboriginal Tourism Authority, Inc., P.O. Box 1240, Station "M," Calgary, AB T2P 2L2, Canada; 780-261-3022, fax 780-261-5676; tourism@istar.ca, [www.aboriginalnet.com/ata.html]. Western Canada's most up-to-date databank, meeting the needs of tour operators and the growing aboriginal tourism market.

Alaska Wilderness Recreation and Tourism Assn (AWRTA), P.O. Box 22827-TA, Juneau, AK 99802; 907-463-3038, fax 907-463-3280; awrta@alaska.net, [www.alaska.net/~awrta]. Membership organization of small, locally-owned ecotour operators and native-owned ecotourism programs. Promotes the protection of Alaska's wild places.

Alternative Tour Thailand, 14/1 Soi Rajatapan, Rajaprarop Rd., Tayathai, Bangkok 10400, Thailand; 011-66-2-245-2963. Supports environmental efforts of small communities throughout Thailand by organizing low-impact tours and homestays.

Annapurna Conservation Area Project (ACAP), ACAP Headquarters Ghandruk, Ghandruk Panchayat, Kaski District, Nepal. An international project that uses trekkers' fees to protect the environment and culture of the Gurung people in north central Nepal.

Baikal Reflections, Inc., P.O. Box 310, Mesa, CO 81643-0310; 970-268-5885, fax 970-268-5884; baikal@ITI2.net. Offers programs to Siberia.

Belize Ecotourism Association, 195A Vista Del Mar, Ladyville 025-2806, Belize. Organization of ecotourism groups, provides information.

Bhutan Tourism Authority, Bhutan Tourism Corporation Ltd., P.O. Box 159, Thimphu, Bhutan; 011-975-2-22854/24045/22647; [www.kingdomofbhutan.com/travel.html]. The Bhutanese government is implementing a new ecotourism management program in the Jigme Dorji National Park.

Bina Swadaya Tours, Jln. Gunung Sahari III/7, Jakarta 10610, P.O. Box 1456, Jakarta, 10014, Indonesia; 011-62-21-420-44-02, fax 011-62-21-425-65-40; bst@cbn.net.id. Operating since 1987 under the ownership of NGO Bina Swadaya, BST specializes in a community-based ecotourism to support economic betterment of local people and nature conservation. For cultural interaction, travelers visit rural community to learn about Indonesia's daily life and ethnic tribes, and experience village stays to observe community's income generating development projects. Destinations include Java, Bali, Sumatra, and Kalimantan (Borneo).

Conservation International/Ecomaya International, 2501 M St., NW, Suite 200, Washington, DC 20037; 800-429-5660 ext. 264, fax 202-887-5188; s.vigilante@conservation.org, [www.ecomaya.com]. Ecomaya International was established by Conservation International Guatemala to serve as a marketing arm to a number of small community development projects (Spanish language schools, jungle trails, rainforest products) in the Peten region of Guatemala. These community-owned businesses provide the residents of the Peten with economic alternatives to hunting, logging, and other environmentally destructive activities.

COOPRENA (National Eco-Agricultural Cooperative Network of Costa Rica), Apdo. 6939-1000 San Jose, Costa Rica; 011-506-259-3605/259-3401; cooprena@sol.racsa.co.cr. Consortium of cooperatives developing eco-agro tourism and small farms.

Cousteau Society, Project Ocean Search, 870 Greenbriar Cir., #402, Chesapeake, VA 23320; 757-523-9335; cousteau@infl.net. Good marine guidelines and information about threats to the world's oceans.

Earth Island Institute, 300 Broadway, Suite 28, San Francisco, CA 94133; 415-788-3666; [www.earthisland.org/abouteii/abouteii.html]. Provides organizational support to individuals in developing projects for the conservation and restoration of the global enviornment. Thirty projects worldwide including Baikal Watch and ecotours to eastern Russia, [www.earthisland.org/baikal/ecotours.html].

Earthstewards Network, PeaceTrees Vietnam. P.O. Box 10697, Bainbridge Island, WA 98110; 206-842-7986, fax 206-842-8918. For PeaceTrees projects contact Martha Hathaway; vizage@aol.com.

Eco-Source, P.O. Box 4694, Annapolis, MD 21403-4694; ecosource@podi.com, [www.podi.com/ecosource]. Information on tour operators, consultants, lodges, resorts, travel agencies, destinations and jobs, all related to sustainable tourism. Also contains educational material on sustainable tourism, plus interactive games and informational activities.

Eco-Tour Samoa, Funealii Lumaava Sooaemalelagi and Steve Brown, Managers Rainforest Ecolodge, P.O. Box 4609, Matautu-uta, Samoa; Tel./fax 011-685-22144; mobile phone 71414, 71415; info@ecotoursamoa.com, ecotour@samoa.net, [www.ecotourssamoa.com]. Offering professionally-guided 7-day ecotours as well as Eco-Researcher and Eco-Volunteer programs all designed to support community-based tourism and sustainable tourism.

Eco-Travel Services, 1212 Broadway, Suite 910, Oakland, CA 94612; 800-655-4053, 510-655-4054; ecotravel@wonderlink.com. Nationwide individual and corporate travel arrangements; supports local economies and environmentally conscious operations instead of quick profits; publishes newsletter, *eXito Travel,* to help the adventurous independent traveler find low-cost airfare to anywhere in Latin America.

Ecotourism Association of Australia, P.O. Box 3839, Alice Springs, Northern Territory 0871, Australia; 011-61-89-528-308.

Ecotourism Society, P.O. Box 755, North Bennington, VT 05257; 802-447-2121, fax 802-447-2122; ecomail@ecotourism.org, [www.ecotourism.org]. A membership organization of ecotour operations around the world.

Ecoventure, Ronald Ziegler, Washington State Univ. Libraries, Pullman, WA 99164-5610; fax 509-335-6721; ziegler@wsu.edu. Ecoventure is helping develop a database, BaseCamp, to provide travelers with information on ecotourism.

Europe Conservation, Via Fusetti, 14-20143 Milano, Italy; 011-390-2-5810-3135.

European Center for Eco Agro Tourism, P.O. Box 10899, Amsterdam 1001 EW, The Netherlands. Promotes eco-agro tourism, a sustainable tour option for people with green thumbs.

Euroter, 82, rue Francois Rolland, F 94130 Nogent-sur-Marne, France; 011-331-4514-6421. Publishes principles for developing green tourism in European villages.

Friends of Malae Kahana, P.O. Box 305, Laie, HI 96762; 808-293-1736. Native Hawaiian civic group operates ecotourism and low-impact tourism along historic beach.

Friends of PRONATURA, 240 East Limberlost Dr., Tucson, AZ 85705; 520-887-1188; closfree@aol.com. Network of ecological groups working in Mexico.

Golondrinas Cloudforest Conservation Project, Calle Isabel La Catolica 1559, Quito, Ecuador; 011-593-2-226-602, fax 011-593-2-222-390. A conservation organization conserving 25,000 hectares of cloudforests on the northwest slopes of the Andes. They have volunteer and educational programs, including a 4-day trek through the Cerro Golondrinas area.

Hawaii Ecotourism Association, P.O. Box 61435, Honolulu, HI 96839; 808-956-2866, fax 808-956-2858; tabata@hawaii.edu, [www.planet-hawaii.com/hea]. Responsible tourism resource network for Hawaii and the Pacific.

Himalayan High Treks, 241 Dolores St., San Francisco, CA 94103-2211; 800-455-8735; effie@himalayanhightreks.com, [www.himalayanhightreks.com]. A small trekking company that specializes in trips to Bhutan, India, Nepal, and Tibet; offers specialized programs for women; publishes newsletter.

INDECON Foundation, Jalan H. Samali No. 51, Pejaten Barat, Pasar Minggu, Jakarta 12510, Indonesia; 011-62-21-799-3955, fax 011-62-21-7947731; indecon@indosat.net.id, [www.indecon.I-2.co.id]. Center for Indonesian ecotourism research, training, and promotion; helps link ecotourists with a wide range of opportunities throughout Indonesia.

Journeys International, 107 Aprill Dr., Ann Arbor, MI 48103; 734-665-4407 or 800-255-8735; [www.journeys-intl.com]. A well-established ecotour operator. Guides are either natives or residents of the countries they visit. Part of their profits support environmental preservation. Destinations include Asia, Africa, the Middle East, Australia, the Pacific, South and Central America, Europe and the Mediterranean, and the polar regions.

Kodukant Ecotourism Initiative, SAARISOO, EE 3482 Joesuu, Parnumaa, Estonia; 011-372-446-6405. A network of small tour operators living in or near protected areas.

Lisle, Inc., 900 County Rd. 269, Leander, TX 78641-9517; 800-477-1538, fax 512-259-0392; lisle@utnet.utoledo.edu, [www.lisle.utoledo.edu]. Pioneer people-to-people program. Destinations include Costa Rica, Bali, Turkey, and India.

Oceanic Society Expeditions, Fort Mason Center, Building E, San Francisco, CA 94123; 415-441-1106, fax 415-474-3385; [www.oceanic-society.org]. Promotes environmental stewardship, education, and research through ecotourism.

Pax World Tours, 3030 Southwest 1st Ave., Portland, OR 97201; 800-292-3355 ext. 248, fax 503-796-6843; info@paxworld.org. Works for peace and justice through innovative programs

that encourage peacemaking and community-based development. Promotes people-to-people links and responsible tourism.

School for Field Studies, 16 Broadway, Beverly, MA 01915-4499; 978-927-7777. Field studies and hands-on opportunities for high school and college students concerned about the environment.

Sea Turtle Restoration Project, P.O. Box 400, Forest Knolls, CA 94933; 415-488-0370; rarauz@sol.racsa.co.cr, [www.seaturtles.org]. STRP advocates responsible fishery practices, marine reserves, and environmental regulations in world trade and pursues these goals internationally. Environmental internship available Aug 15-Jan 15 in which participants learn about sea turtles and patrol their nesting beach while working with Costa Rican conservationists and biologists.

Sierra Club, 85 2nd St., 2nd Fl., San Francisco, CA 94105; 415-977-5500. Publishes good travel guides, offers conservation focused tours.

Sikkim Biodiversity and Ecotourism Project, P.O. Tadong, Sikkim 737102, India; 011-91-3592-31046, fax 011-91-3592-31090; sce@gokulnet.com. Develops and implements regional ecotourism program with local communities in the Sikkim Himalayas.

South American Explorer's Club (SAEC), 126 Indian Creek Rd., Ithaca, NY 14850; 607-277-0488; explorer@samexplo.org, [www.samexplo.org]. Promotes ecologically responsible tourism. Has clubhouses in Quito, Ecuador and Lima and Cusco, Peru. Publishes quarterly magazine and sells books and maps.

Talamanca Association for Ecotourism and Conservation, Puerto Viejo de Talamanca, Limon, Costa Rica. Local environmental organization that offers ecotourism programs.

Toledo Ecotourism Association (TEA), San Miguel Village, Toledo District, Belize. Contact Pabzo Ack, BTB Information Center, Punta Gorda, P.O. Box 180, Belize; 011-501-72-2531, fax 011-501-72-2199; tide@btl.net. Network of indigenous farm cooperatives in pristine Mayan lands.

Tour de Cana, P.O. Box 7293, Philadelphia, PA 19101; 215-222-1253, fax 215-222-1253 then press *21; tourdecana@aol.com. An outgrowth of the organization Bikes Not Bombs, this group offers bike trekking with a social, cultural, and political emphasis.

TRAVELING RESPONSIBLY

CELEBRATE THE MILLENNIUM BY GIVING THE WORLD A BREAK

By Rick Steves

As we recognize the problems confronting the earth and humankind, more and more people are recognizing the need for the world's industries, such as tourism, to function as tools for peace. Tourism is a $2 trillion industry that employs more than 60 million people. As travelers gain a global perspective, the demand for socially, environmentally, and economically responsible ways to travel will grow. Peace is more than the absence of war, and if we are to enjoy the good things of life—such as travel—into the next century, the serious issues that confront humankind must be addressed now: through responsible travel and political action.

Transitions Abroad's publications offer many exciting opportunities for both. Here are a few of my favorite organizations.

Global Volunteers, a nonprofit organization, offers useful "travel with a purpose" trips throughout the world. The work varies by country, but if Europe's your goal, you'll likely teach conversational English in Italy, Spain, Poland, Romania, Turkey, or Ukraine. Ask about peace reconciliation programs in Northern Ireland (375 E. Little Canada Rd., St. Paul, MN 55117-1628; 800-487-1074, fax 651-407-5163 [www.globalvolunteers.org].)

Volunteers for Peace, another nonprofit, runs international workcamps to promote goodwill through friendship and community service. Options include historical preservation and conservation projects (1034 Tiffany Rd., Belmont, VT 05730; 802-259-2759, fax 802-259-2922 [www.vfp.org]).

Consume Responsibly

Whether you're working or playing, consume responsibly in your travels. Understand your power to shape the marketplace by what you decide to buy—in the grocery store, in the movie theater, or in your choice of hotels.

In my travels (and in my writing), I patronize and support small, family-run, locally-owned businesses: hotels, restaurants, shops, tour guides. I choose people who invest their creativity and resources in giving travelers simple, friendly, sustainable, and honest experiences—people with ideals. Back Door places don't rely on slick advertising and marketing gimmicks, and they don't target the created needs of people whose values are shaped by capitalism gone wild. Traveling responsibly means consuming responsibly. Your trip is a vote for the kind of world we could have.

Travel Thoughtfully

Travel like Gandhi—with simple clothes, open eyes, and an uncluttered mind. Celebrate the similarities and differences in cultures. Seek international styles of living out of a genuine interest in the people and cultures you visit. Be positive and optimistic, and don't dwell on problems or compare things to back home. Accept and try to understand differences: Paying for your Italian coffee at one counter and picking it up at another may seem inefficient until you realize it's more sanitary—the person handling the food never handles money. Be observant and sensitive: If 60 people are eating quietly with hushed conversation in a Belgian restaurant, you know it's not the place to yuck it up.

Speak the Language

Make an effort to bridge that flimsy language barrier. Rudimentary communication in any language is fun and simple, even with a few basic words. On the train to Budapest you might think that a debate with a Hungarian over the merits of a common European currency would be frustrating with a 20-word vocabulary, but you'll surprise yourself at how well you connect just by trying. Don't worry about making mistakes—communicate!

Reach out to meet the people you traveled so far to see. Lunch with a group of Palestinian college students, walk through Moscow with a diehard Communist, and learn why the Swiss aren't completely comfortable with a unified Europe. Go as an ambassador, a guest, a friend. In travel, too, you reap what you sow.

Jubilee 2000

If you want to tackle more than travel, consider political action. Jubilee 2000 is a worldwide movement of concerned people and groups—religious and secular—working to cancel the international debts of the poorest countries by the new millennium. It's inspired by the Biblical "Year of Jubilee" during which, every 50 years, social wrongs are righted and debts are canceled.

Debt keeps the poorest countries poor. Money needed for health care and education is diverted to interest payments. Mozambique, with a per capita income of $90, a life expectancy of 40, and almost no health care, spends over half its government's income on interest payments. A baby in Nicaragua is born with a debt to the rich world of $2,000 and a father who earns about $400 a year. These debts translate into real suffering among local people born long after some dictator borrowed (and squandered) that money. As interest is paid, people go hungry.

The debts are owed mostly to the U.S., Japan, Germany, Britain, and France, either directly or through the World Bank and the International Monetary Fund. Rich governments can forgive the debt owed directly to them and pay the market value (10 percent) of the debts owed to the World Bank and International Monetary Fund. The U.S.'s share is under $2 billion. We have the resources. All America needs is the political will and people power.

For the sake of peace, fragile young democracies, and countless real people, forgiving this debt is the responsible thing for us in the rich world to do. Read more, write letters, or even start a local Jubilee 2000 campaign. To learn about lobbying Congress on this issue, contact Bread for the World (800-82-BREAD; [www.bread.org]). And for more on the campaign, contact Jubilee 2000 (202-783-3566; [www.j2000usa.org]). Let's celebrate the new millennium by giving the poor world a break.

Travel Quest, 5050 Sepulveda Blvd., Sherman Oaks, CA 91430; 919-789-6080; 74732.3153@compuserve.com. Promotes greater care and understanding of the planet, people, and other beings.

The Travel Specialists, 120 Beacon St., Somerville, MA 02143-4369; 617-497-8151 or 800-370-7400, ext. 51; mj@tvlcoll.com. Evaluates travel programs, operators, and the travel industry; arranges alternative trips and programs around the world.

Tropical Science Center, Apdo 8-3870, San Jose 1000, Costa Rica; fax 011-506-253-4963; hjimenez@sol.racsa.co.cr, [www.geocities.com/rainforest/9148]. Courses on Tropical Dendrology every year, in Spanish (March) and English (June).

Turismo Ecologico y Cultural del Pueblo Maya, San Cristobal de las Casas, Chiapas, Mexico. An indigenous-owned alternative ecotour group.

Wildland Adventures, Inc., 3516 NE 155th St., Seattle, WA 98155; 800-345-4453, 206-365-0686; info@wildland.com, [www.wildland.com]. Ecotour operator offers group travel, customized trips for independent travelers and families, rainforest workshops, and responsible trips such as trail cleanups and community services. Contributes part of profits to conservation and community development at the local level.

Wildlife Conservation International, P.O. Box 68244, Nairobi, Kenya; 011-222254-221-699. Information about ecotourism projects in Kenya.

World Wildlife Fund, 1250 24th St., NW, Washington, DC 20037-1175; 202-293-4800; [www.worldwildlife.org]. Offers ecotours throughout the world.

Publications

Active Woman Vacation Guide by Evelyn Kaye. Blue Panda Publications, 3031 5th St., Boulder, CO 80304; 800-800-8147 or 303-449-8474, fax 303-449-7525. $17.95 plus $4 s/h. True stories by women travelers of yesterday and today plus complete information on 50 selected adventure companies that offer hikes, bicycle trips, rafting, and more.

Adventures in Nature (Honduras, Mexico, Guatemala, Belize, Costa Rica, Alaska, Caribbean). John Muir Publications, P.O. Box 613, Santa Fe, NM 87504-9738; 800-888-7504. (Also available from [www.greenbuilder.com/bookstore]). Update to the "Natural Destina-

tion" series, focusing on environmental travel. Mexico guide is by Transitions Abroad columnnist Ron Mader.

Adventuring In…. The Sierra Club, 85 2nd St., San Francisco, CA 94105; 415-977-5500. Adventure travel guide series for many countries. Includes Adventuring in Central America by David Rains Wallace, a must-have resource.

All Asia Guide. 1994. $23.95. Charles E. Tuttle Co., 153 Milk St., 5th Fl., Boston, MA 02109. A practical Asia guide.

Backpacking in Central America by Tim Burford. $15.95. Also Backpacking in Mexico $16.95. Available from Bradt/Globe Pequot Press, P.O. Box 480, Guilford, CT 06437; 800-243-0495, fax 800-820-2329. An excellent guide by an experienced Central American hiker.

Beyond Safaris: A Guide to Building People-to-People Ties With Africa by Kevin Danaher. Africa World Press. Global Exchange, 2017 Mission St., Suite 303, San Francisco, CA 94110; 415-255-7296. 1991. $12.95. A bit old but still one of the best resources for socially conscious travelers in Africa. Lists organizations.

E/The Environmental Magazine. The Earth Action Network, P.O. Box 5098, Westport, CT 06881; 203-854-5559, fax 203-866-0602. Bimonthly magazine with a focus on environmental issues and awareness.

Ecotourism and Sustainable Development by Martha Honey. Island Press. 1999. 800-828-1302; [www.islandpress.org]. The most thorough and up-to-date account available of the promise and pitfalls of ecotourism.

The Ecotourist's Guide to the Ecuadorian Amazon by Rolfe Wesche. The Pan-American Center for Geographical Studies and Research, 3er piso, Apdo 17-01-4273, Quito, Ecuador; 011-593-245-1200.

The Ecotraveller's Wildlife Guides by Les Beletsky. Academic Press, 525 B St., Suite 1900, San Diego, CA 92101-4495; 800-321-5068. Titles include Costa Rica (1998), Belize and Northern Guatemala (1998), Tropical Mexico (1999), Hawaii (1999), Ecuador and the Galapagos Islands (1999). $27.95 each. Each book provides information on natural history, ecology, conservation, and species identification.

The Green Holiday Guides. The 16 Green Holiday Guides provide more than 1,500 addresses of a variety of ecological farms and other environmentally friendly places to lodge or camp. $10 per guide from ECEAT International, P.O. Box 10899, 1001 EW Amsterdam, the Netherlands; 011-31-20-6681030, fax 011-31-20-4630594; eceat@antenna.nl, [www.pz.nl/eceat].

Green Travel Sourcebook by Daniel Grotta and Sally Wiener Grotta. John Wiley & Sons, 1 Wiley Dr., Somerset, NJ 08775; 800-225-5945, fax 732-302-2300. 1992. $16.95.

Green-Travel Mailing List. For green travel resources on the Internet. To subscribe contact majordomo@igc.apc.org.

Holidays That Don't Cost the Earth by John Elkington and Julia Hailes. Victor Gollancz Ltd., 14 Henrietta St., London, WC2E 8QJ, U.K. 1992. £5.99. A worldwide guide to environmental vacations.

Indigenous Peoples and Global Tourism. Project Report by Deborah McLaren. $6 postpaid. The Rethinking Tourism Project, P.O. Box 581938, Minneapolis, MN 55458-1938; Tel./fax 651-644-9984; RTProject@aol.com; [www2.planeta.com/mader/ecotravel/resources/rtp/rtp.html].

Inside Indonesia Magazine edited by Dr. Gerry Van Klinken. P.O. Box 1326, Collingwood 3066, Australia; 011-61-3-9419-4504, fax 011-61-3-9419-4774; admin@insideindonesia.org, [www.insideindonesia.org]. Fosters active links with Indonesians working for change. Includes information on ecotourism travel, environment, culture, and human rights economics.

La Mosquitia: A Guide to the Land of Savannas, Rain Forests and Turtle Hungers by Derek A. Parent. The first guidebook to Honduras.

Last Resorts by Polly Pattullo. Monthly Review Press. $19. (from Amazon.com). Excellent review of the tourism industry in the Caribbean.

Lonely Planet Guides. Lonely Planet Publications, 150 Linden St., Oakland, CA 94607; 800-275-8555, fax 510-893-8563; info@lonelyplanet.com. Books on almost every country, emphasizing low-impact travel.

Moon Travel Handbooks, 5855 Beaudry St., Emeryville, CA 94608; 800-345-5473, fax 510-595-4228; travel@moon.com, [www.moon.com]. Guides provide thorough cultural, historical, and political coverage, as well as extensive practical information.

Natour: Special edition on ecotourism. Contact editor Arturo Crosby, Viriato, 20, Madrid, Spain; 011-91-593-0831.

Nature Tourism: Managing for the Environment edited by Tensie Whelan. Island Press, 1991. $19.95. Orders: 800-828-1302. Guidelines and essays on nature tourism.

New Frontiers. Anita Pleumarom, Coordinator, Tourism Investigation and Monitoring Team, P.O. Box 51, Chorakhebua, Bangkok 10230, Thailand; fax 011-66-2-519-2821. A bimonthly newsletter for briefing on tourism, development, and envrionment issues in the southeast Asian Mekong region.

The New Key to Costa Rica by Beatrice Blake and Anne Becher. 1998. $17.95 (Ulysses Press). Good all-around guide to Costa Rica with an ecology focus. Also available: *The New Key to Cancun and the Yucatan* by Richard Harris (2nd ed., $14.95); *The New Key to Ecuador and the Galapagos* by David L. Pearson and David W. Middleton (3rd ed., $17.95); and *Hidden Belize* by Stacy Ritz ($15.95), *Hidden Guatemala* by Richard Harris ($16.95).

Planeta, [www.planeta.com], a synthesis of environmental news and travel information from the Americas. Articles range from practical field guides to academic work on ecotourism. Contact: El Planeta Platica, c/o Ron Mader, Rep. De Cuba 12, #302, Col. Centro 06010, Mexico. To subscribe to the free monthly announcement service, email ron@greenbuilder.com.

Rethinking Tourism and Ecotravel: The Paving of Paradise and How You Can Stop It by Deborah McLaren. Kumarian Press, 14 Oakwood Ave., West Hartford, CT 06110-2127; 800-289-2664, fax 860-233-6072; [www.kpbooks.com]. 1997. $21.95. Useful information about the global tourism industry and creative alternatives. Use some of the hundreds of resources listed in this book and you will never travel the same way again.

Structural Adjustment, World Trade and Third World Tourism: An Introduction to the Issues by K.T. Ramesh, Ecumenical Center on Third World Tourism, P.O. Box 35, Senanikhom, Bangkok 10902, Thailand; 011-662-939-7111; contours@ksc.net.th. *Contours,* August 1995.

Working With the Environment by Tim Ryder. Vacation Work, 9 Park End St., Oxford OX1 1HJ, England; 011-44-186-52-41-978. 1996. £10.99. Guide to careers that involve working with the environment. Includes a chapter on environmental tourism.

Responsible Tourism Organizations

Airline Ambassadors, 4925 Greenville Ave., Suite 1030, Dallas, TX 75206; 214-528-9464. Or contact Carl E. Oates at 214-361-1488, fax 214-361-1405. Group is involved in sustainable tourism discussions at the U.N., and bringing medical supplies abroad.

Asia Tourism Action Network (ANTENNA), 15 Soi Soonvijai 8, New Petchburi Rd., Bangkok 10310, Thailand. A network in Asia and the Pacific promoting locally controlled tourism; publishes a newsletter.

Badri Dev Pande, Environmental Education and Awareness, P.O. Box 3923, Kathmandu, Nepal. Developing a sustainable tourism master plan of Manaslu region of Nepal.

The Bospas Forest Farm. Piet T. Sabbe, c/o Casa Dobronski, Calle Guanhuiltagua N34-457, Quito, Ecuador; bospas@hotmail.com. Visit this agroforestry/permaculture farm and enjoy the subtropical climate in the Mira Valley in northern Ecuador. Opportunities for horse riding in the hills and hikes in the nearby Golondrinas Cloudforest Reserve.

Broken Bud, 1765-D Le Roy, Berkeley, CA 94709; 510-843-5506; CRTourism@aol.com. Formed out of the Center for Responsible Tourism (below), advocates against pornography, prostitution tourism, and child trafficking.

Burma Tourism Campaign, The Free Burma Coalition, c/o Dept. of Curriculum and Instruction, Univ. of Wisconsin, 225 N. Mills St., Madison, WI 53706; 202-777-6009 leave message, fax 608-263-9992; zni@students.wisc.edu, [http://danenet.wicip.org/fbc/sites.htm]. Before traveling to Burma check out their information.

Center for Global Education at Augsburg College, 2211 Riverside Ave., Minneapolis, MN 55454; 800-299-8889; globaled@augsburg.edu, [www.augsburg.edu/global]. Sponsors travel seminars and semester programs in which participants learn from people of diverse backgrounds about their economic, political, and social realities. Emphasis on those struggling for justice. Programming in Mexico, Central America, Southern Africa, and Cuba.

Center for Responsible Tourism, P.O. Box 827, San Anselmo, CA 94979; 415-258-6594. One of the only responsible travel networks in the U.S., CRT has helped hundreds of travelers, educa-

tors, people in other countries. Publishes newsletter highlighting innovative tourism projects around the world.

Center for the Advancement of Responsible Travel (CART), 70 Dry Hill Park Rd., Tonbridge, Kent TN10 3BX, U.K. Center of information on responsible tourism in Europe.

Center for Third World Organizing, 1218 East 21st St., Oakland, CA 94606; 510-533-7583, fax 510-533-0923; ctwo@igc.org. An excellent resource for information about progressive politics, actions, and organizations in the U.S. and abroad.

Earthwatch, 680 Mt. Auburn St., Watertown, MA 02472; 617-926-8200, [www.earthwatch.org]. Offers working vacations with scientists around the world.

Ecumenical Coalition on Third World Tourism (ECTWT), c/o CPDC, P.O. Box 284, Bridgetown, Barbados; contours@caribnet.net; or ECTWT European office: 19 Chemin des Palettes, CH-1212 Grand Lancy, Switzerland; 011-41-22-794-49-59, fax 011-41-22-794-47-50; contours@geneva-link.ch. Only international Third World NGO focusing on impact of tourism, publishes a quarterly magazine called *Contours.*

Elderhostel, 75 Federal St., Boston, MA 02110-1941; 877-426-8056; [www.elderhostel.org]. For travelers over 50. Environmentally friendly educational travel programs around the world for seniors.

EQUATIONS: Equitable Tourism Options, No. 198, II Cross, Church Rd. (behind old KEB office), New Thippasandra, Bangalore 560 075, India; 011-9180-528-2313; admin@equation.ilban.ernet.in. Responsible tourism advocate; helps travelers locate environmentally and culturally sensitive projects in India.

Global Citizens Network, 130 N. Howell St., St. Paul, MN 55104; 651-644-0960 or 800-644-9292 (Kim Regnier); gcn@mtn.org, [www.globalcitizens.org]. Sends small teams of volunteers on short "alternative vacations" to rural communities worldwide to work on projects and immerse themselves in the daily life of the local culture.

Global Exchange, 2017 Mission St., Suite 303, San Francisco, CA 94110; 415-255-7296; gx-info@globalexchange.org, [www.globalexchange.org]. Reality tours focus on social, cultural, environmental issues in South Africa, Haiti, Cuba, Mexico, India, Brazil, and elsewhere.

Global Service Corps, 300 Broadway, Suite 28, San Francisco, CA 94133; 415-788-3666 ext. 128, fax 415-788-7324; gsc@igc.apc.org, [www.globalservicecorps.org]. Service-learning and cultural immersion in Costa Rica, Kenya, or Thailand. Live with a village family while assisting grassroots organizations on community service and development projects.

Indonesia Resources and Information Program (IRIP), P.O. Box 190, Northcote 3070, Australia; 011-61-3-481-1581. Fosters active links with Indonesians working for change.

Institute for Central American Development Studies (ICADS). Dept. 826, P.O. Box 025216, Miami, FL 33102-5216, or ICADS, Apartado 3-2070, Sabanilla, San Jose, Costa Rica; 011-506-225-0508, fax 011-506-234-1337; icads@netbox.com. Field course in resource management and sustainable development and interdisciplinary semester internship programs focusing on development issues from ecological and socio-economic perspectives.

International Bicycle Fund, 4887 Columbia Dr. S, #T-9, Seattle, WA 98108; 206-767-0848; ibike@ibike.org, [www.ibike.org]. Promotes bicycle transport; links with autofree and bicycling organizations around the world; publishes essays on environmentally and culturally friendly traveling; sponsors bicycle tours throughout Africa and Cuba.

International Institute for Peace Through Tourism, 3680 rue de La Montange, Montreal, PQ, Canada H3G 2AB; 802-253-8671. Facilitates tourism initiatives that contribute to international peace and cooperation.

ISEC/Ladakh (India) Project, P.O. Box 9475, Berkeley, CA 94709; 510-548-4915. An educational program that supports innovative grassroots development efforts of the Ladakhi people who live on the western edge of the Tibetan Plateau in India. Good resource materials on counterdevelopment, books, videos. Runs a farm project in Ladakh, providing westerners with an opportunity to work on a Ladakhi farm in the summer months.

Lost Valley Educational Center, 81868 Lost Valley Ln., Dexter, OR 97431; 541-937-3351; lvec@lostvalley.org, [www.lostvalley.org]. Founder Dianne G. Brause is a well-known writer and leader in the field of responsible and sustainable travel. She offers opportunities in Central America for participants to live, learn, and work with local people.

Okologischer Tourismus in Europa (OTE), Bernd Rath, Am Michaelshof 8-10, 53177 Bonn, Germany. Responsible tourism organization; resources in German.

Our Developing World, 13004 Paseo Presada, Saratoga, CA 95070-4125; 408-379-4431; fax 408-376-0755; vic_@vval.com. Educational project bringing Third World realities to North Americans. Community programs, teacher training materials, resources library. Study tour to Central America July 2000.

Responsible Tourism Network, RTN Coordinator, P.O. Box 34, Rundle Mall, Adelaide, SA, Australia 5000; 011-618-232-2727, fax 011-618-232-2808; bwitty@ozemail.com.au. Responsible tourism by Australians. Works with tourists, travel industry and host communities. Publishes *Travel Wise* and *Travel Smart,* practical tips for responsible tourists.

Rethinking Tourism Project, P.O. Box 51938, Minneapolis, MN 55458-1938; Tel./fax 651-644-9984; Rtproject@aol.com, [www2.planeta.com/mader/ecotravel/resources/rtp/rtp.html]. An educational and networking project for indigenous people. Offers some volunteer opportunities and internships, mainly based in U.S.

Tourism Concern, Stapleton House, 277-281 Holloway Rd., London N7 8HN, U.K.; 011-44-171-753-3330, fax 011-44-171-753-3331; [www.gn.apc.org/tourismconcern], tourconcern@gn.apc.org. Excellent resource on issues related to tourism: land rights, displacement, general responsible tourism information.

Tourism With Insight (Arbeitsgemeinschaft Tourismus mit Einsicht), Hadorter Str. 9B, D-8130 Starnberg, Germany. Responsible tourism study group.

Transitions Abroad, $24.95/6 issues. P.O. Box 1300, Amherst, MA 01004-1300; 800-293-0373, fax 413-256-0373; info@TransitionsAbroad@aol.com, [www.TransitionsAbroad.com]. This bimonthly resource guide to work, living, study, and travel abroad advocates and publishes information on culturally and ecologically responsible travel.

The Travel Specialists, Co-Op America Travel Links, M.J. Kietzke, 120 Beacon St., Somerville, MA 02143; 800-648-2667 outside MA, 617-497-8151; mj@tvlcoll.com. Specializes in responsible travel for individuals and groups, custom designed to suit your special interests.

The Univ. of Kansas, Office of Study Abroad, 108 Lippincott Hall, Lawrence, KS 66045; 785-864-3742. Offers a semester at the port town of Golfito on the southern Pacific coast of Costa Rica in anthropology, ecology, biology, and Spanish.

University Research Expeditions Program, Univ. of California, Davis, CA 95616; 530-752-0692. Field research expeditions worldwide for travelers of all ages. Costs are tax deductible. Director Jean Colvin has developed codes of conduct for researchers and travelers visiting indigenous lands.

EIGHT

The following listing of responsible travel tours and programs was supplied by the organizers. Contact the program directors to confirm costs, dates, and other details. Please tell them you read about their program in this book! Programs based in more than one country or region are listed under "Worldwide."

Africa and Cuba

Bicycle Africa/Cuba. Educational, people-to-people bicycle tours to all parts of Africa and Cuba. Cycling difficulty is moderate. Each tour is unique; all focus on the diversity of the culture, social institutions, and environment, and the complexity of the history, economy, and society. Programs are led by area studies specialists.

Dates: Jan (Uganda), Feb (Tanzania/Kenya), Apr (Tunisia), Jun-Aug (Zimbabwe/Malawi), Oct-Nov (Senegal/Guinea/Mali), Nov-Dec (Burkina Faso/Togo/Benin/Ghana), Dec-Mar (Cuba). **Cost:** $990-$1,490 plus airfare for 2 weeks. Includes food, lodging, guides, and fees. **Contact:** International Bicycle Fund/Bicycle Africa, 4887 Columbia Dr. S. #T-9, Seattle, WA 98108-1919; Tel./fax 206-767-0848; ibike@bike.org; [www.ibike.org/bikeafrica], [www.ibike.org/bikecuba].

Antarctica

Ecology Safari. Ecologists Gail and Doug Cheeseman have again chartered an entire ice ship the IOFFE, with all private baths, for 26 days. They and their 14 experienced leaders and 86 passengers will make 25 Zodiac landings at remote penguin and albatross colonies at South Georgia and the Antarctic Peninsula and visit 5 islands in the Falklands. Only eligibility requirement is to agree with nonsmoking policy.

Dates: Dec 27, 2000-Jan 24, 2001. **Cost:** $10,450 plus airfare ($1,150 from Miami to Usuaia, Argentina). **Contact:** Gail and Doug Cheeseman, Cheesemans' Ecology Safaris, 20800 Kittredge Rd., Saratoga, CA 95070; 800-527-5330; cheesemans@aol.com, [www.cheesemans.com].

Argentina

Argentine Universities Program. COPA offers an integrated study opportunity in which undergraduate students live with Argentine host families and study with degree-seeking Argentine students. Three partner universities offer unique blends of location, academics, and student population. There is a research track available. Academic program includes optional program classes and a required Spanish course. A 6-week, non-integrated summer program is also available. All coursework is in Spanish.

Dates: Spring: Mar-Jul, fall: Jul-Dec, summer: Jun-Jul. **Cost:** Semester: fall $7,985; spring $8,385; year $15,000. Includes tuition, housing,

2 meals daily, orientation, excursions, support services. **Contact:** Cooperating Programs in the Americas, Institute for Study Abroad, 1100 W. 42nd St., Suite 305, Indianapolis, IN 46208-3345; 888-344-9299, fax 317-940-9704; COPA@butler.edu.

Asia

P.A.D.I. Diving (Scuba). Snorkel classes and excursions (2 days), junior open water diving certificate (4 days), open water diver certificate (4 days), advanced open water diver certificate (2 days), wreck diver (2 days), photography diver (1 day), discover scuba (1 day).
Dates: Dec-Apr. **Cost:** From $25. **Contact:** Underwater Safaris, Ltd., 25c Barnes Pl., Colombo 7, Sri Lanka; 011-94-1694012, scuba@slt.lk

Belize

Reef and Rainforest Ecology. Study and enjoy the Belize barrier reef from above and below the Caribbean. Explore the jungle at Monkey River and Jaguar Reserve and assist with the iguana raising project. Climb Maya ruins and swim in limestone caves. Includes beachfront air conditioned room, meals, and adventure.
Dates: Weekly Jul-Nov. Monday arrivals, 7 nights. **Cost:** $850 per person plus air (min. 6, max. 24) not counting group leader. **Contact:** Nautical Inn Adventure Resort; 800-688-0377, fax 011-501-623594; nautical@btl.net, [www.nauticalinnbelize.com].

Canada

Strathcona Park Lodge and Outdoor Education Center. Alpine to Ocean Adventures take you to wilderness settings where you come across few other travelers, whether it be sea kayaking, canoeing, trekking, backpacking, mountaineering, rock climbing.
Dates: Mar and Nov. **Cost:** From $50 per person per day. **Contact:** Strathcona Park Lodge C.O.L.T., P.O. Box 2160, Campbell River, BC, V9W 5C9, Canada; 250-286-3122, fax 250-286-6010; info@strathcona.bc.ca, [www.strathcona.bc.ca].

Caribbean

Jaguar Reef Lodge. Nestled on miles of golden sand beach between between the Maya Mountains and the Caribbean Sea, the Jaguar Reef Lodge provides an ideal base from which to explore the wonders of a pristine barrier reef, abundant off-shore cays, and protected rainforest. Free use of sea kayaks and mountain bikes.
Dates: Summer: May 1-Oct 31; winter: Nov 1-Apr 31. **Cost:** Summer: $100 per night; winter: $175 per night. **Contact:** Bruce Foerster, Jaguar Reef Lodge; Tel./fax 011-501-21-2041; jaguarreef@btl.net, [www.jaguarreef.com].

Tacaribe Tour Operators, Ltd. Inbound. Adventure travel, bird watching, nature trails, rainforest, hiking, cave explorations, natural history, turtle watching, scuba diving, kayaking, sightseeing, etc.
Dates: Contact organization for details. **Cost:** Contact organization for details. **Contact:** Dominic Salsary, Tacaribe Tour Operators, Ltd., LIP50 Esperanza Dr., Champ Fleurs, Trinidad and Tobago, West Indies; tacaribe@tstt.met.tt.

Central America

Travel/Study Seminars. Learn from Central Americans of diverse backgrounds about their economic, political, and social realities. Emphasis on the views of those struggling for justice. Programming in El Salvador, Guatemala, and Nicaragua. Call for a schedule or to sponsor your own program.
Dates: Ongoing. **Cost:** $1,300-$1,900 depending on length of trip. **Contact:** Center for Global Education at Augsburg College, 2211 Riverside Ave., Box 307TR, Minneapolis, MN 55454; 800-299-8889, fax 612-330-1695; globaled@augsburg.edu, [www.augsburg.edu/global].

Chile

Chilean Universities: Santiago. Based at the Instituto de Estudios Internacionales, the prestigious research institute associated with the Universidad de Chile, our program allows students to take two core classes in Spanish designed to acquaint U.S. undergrads with contemporary Chile. Participants take a wide variety of integrated university classes to complete their enrollment. Independent study/directed research projects available. Students live with host families.
Dates: Spring semester: Mar-Jul, fall semester: Jul-Dec. **Cost:** Semester: fall $7,500; spring $7,800; year $14,000. Includes tuition, housing, and 2 meals daily, orientation, excursions, support services. **Contact:** Cooperating Programs in the Americas, Institute for Study Abroad, 1100 W. 42nd St., Suite 305, Indianapolis, IN 46208-3345; 888-344-9299, fax 317-940-9704; COPA@butler.edu.

By Steve Wilson

For the latest in earth-friendly travel, look for a travel agent who plants trees. Unless you walk or cycle, every time you travel somewhere you do so in a vehicle that emits carbon dioxide—the primary cause of global warming. A roundtrip flight from New York to Rome, for example, creates about four tons of carbon dioxide per passenger. Since a tree will store about 50 pounds of carbon dioxide each year, or a ton over 40 years, that means you need the lifespan of four trees to absorb the carbon dioxide it took to get you to Europe for a two-week holiday. Buying your plane ticket from a participating Trees for Travel agency means that seven trees will be planted—enough to cover your traveling partner as well.

The program is called Trees for Travel, an offshoot of the Maryland-based Trees for The Future, a nonprofit group that helps developing countries replant deforested areas. Trees for Travel helps fund tree plantings in Asia, Africa, and Latin America and sponsors publicity campaigns to help raise public awareness about environmental damage caused by tourism.

Steve McCrea came up with the Trees for Travel idea in 1996. Here's how it works: Your travel agent pays $50 for 50 certificates, agreeing to sponsor one certificate for every airline ticket purchased through their agency. Each certificate represents seven planted trees. The money is combined with other funds raised by Trees for the Future for projects like a five-acre site in Belize that will be planted with over 3,000 seedlings this winter. If seven trees seems like a lot for only a buck, that's because the planting is done by local volunteers who have asked for aid in replanting.

The trees planted grow quickly and provide usable by-products: tannin from the bark, edible young leaves, even seeds that can be roasted and used as a coffee substitute. The trees' staggering growth rate—as much as 24 feet in its first year—and the fact that they grows back even more quickly when cut down is a huge benefit to people in developing countries that depend on firewood.

Dave Deppner, Trees for the Future founder, said that in developing countries you see results in an incredibly short time. "Normally we start planting them about five months before the rainy season begins, and one of the first benefits people see is erosion control on hillsides. We have one project in Belize where we built up 11 inches of soil around these trees in one rainy season." Deppner said that the organization plants over half a million trees each month and has already planted over 40 million trees in 89 countries. Support for the organization comes primarily from the donations of its 8,000 members.

Money raised by Trees for Travel represents a small part of that—about 21,000 trees a year. The number is growing as more agencies become involved. "What we're doing is the first step," says Deppner. "We're recreating what was there when there were forests. But it's only the first step."

To find the name of the participating travel agency nearest you, call Trees for the Future at 800-643-0001.

Chilean Universities: Valparaíso. In the twin coastal cities of Valparaíso and Viña del Mar, the home to our program, students take integrated classes with Chilean students and live with a host family. Two program classes in Spanish are available to complement UCV's course offerings.

Dates: Spring semester: Mar-Jul, fall semester: Jul-Dec. **Cost:** Spring semester $6,900; fall $7,200; year $13,000. Includes tuition, housing and 2 meals daily, orientation, excursions, support services. **Contact:** Cooperating Programs in the Americas, Institute for Study Abroad, 1100 W. 42nd St., Suite 305, Indianapolis, IN 46208-3345; 888-344-9299, fax 317-940-9704; COPA@butler.edu.

China

Ethnic Minorities of SW China. Culturally sensitive low-impact small group tours explore ethnic minority areas of Guizhou and Yunnan provinces. Emphasis on the vibrant traditional cultures of the Miao (Hmong) and other ethnic people: daily and ceremonial village life, festivals, handcrafts, music, dance, and textile arts.

Dates: Feb 12-24, May 24-Jun 9, Oct 8-22. **Cost:** From $2,000 depending on itinerary. Includes all air and land costs in China. **Contact:** Peter Nelson, Minzu Explorations, 18444 Tualata Ave., Lake Oswego, OR 97035; Tel./fax 503-684-9531; petnels@aol.com, [www.minzuexplorations.com].

Costa Rica

Costa Rica Rainforst Outward Bound. CRROBS offers everything from 15-day treks to our 85-day tri-country semester course. The courses feature such activities as white-water rafting, canopy/rock climbing, village homestays, rainforest trekking with indigenous guides, surf adventures, and cave exploring.

Dates: Year round. **Cost:** Contact sponsor. **Contact:** Costa Rica Rainforest Outward Bound School, P.O. Box 243, Quepos, Costa Rica; 011-506-777-1222; crrobs@sol.racsa.co.cr, [www.crrobs.org].

Costa Rican Language Academy. Costa Rican-owned and operated language school offers first-rate Spanish instruction in a warm and friendly environment. Teachers with university degrees. Small groups or private classes. Included free in the programs are airport transportation, coffee and natural refreshments, excursions, Latin dance, Costa Rican cooking, music, and conversation classes to provide students with complete cultural immersion.

Dates: Year round (start anytime). **Cost:** $135 per week or $220 per week for program with homestay. All other activities and services included at no additional cost. **Contact:** Costa Rican Language Academy, P.O. Box 336-2070, San José, Costa Rica; 011-506-221-1624 or 011-506-233-8914 or 011-233-8938, fax 011-506-233-8670. In the U.S.: 800-854-6057; crlang@sol.racsa.co.cr, [www.crlang.co.cr/index.html].

Learn Spanish While Volunteering. Assist with the training of Costa Rican public school teachers in ESL and computers. Assist local health clinic, social service agencies, and environmental projects. Enjoy learning Spanish in the morning, volunteer work in the afternoon/evening. Spanish classes of 2-5 students plus group learning activities; conversations with middle class homestay families (1 student per family). Homestays and most volunteer projects are within walking distance of school in small town near the capital, San José.

Dates: Year round, all levels. Classes begin every Monday (except Apr 17-21 and Dec 18-29), volunteer program is continuous. **Cost:** $345 per week for 28 hours of classes and group activities plus Costa Rican dance and cooking classes. Includes tuition, 3 meals per day, 7 days per week, homestay, laundry, all materials, weekly 3-hour cultural tour, and airport transportation. $25 one-time registration fee. **Contact:** Susan Shores, Registrar, Latin American Language Center, PMB 123, 7485 Rush River Dr., Suite 710, Sacramento, CA 95831-5260; 916-447-0938, fax 916-428-9542; lalc@madre.com.

Monteverde Studios of the Arts. "Where Craft and Culture Meet." Participate in week-long classes in ceramics, painting and drawing, textiles, stained glass, jewelry, basketry, woodworking, dance, photography, storytelling, cooking, also personality studies. Work in teachers' studios and share in the luxuriant surroundings of the rainforest. Classes available in Spanish or English.

Dates: Jan-Aug. **Cost:** Room and board, tuition; $435-$565. **Contact:** Sybil Terres Gilmar, Monteverde Studios of the Arts, P.O. Box 766, Narberth, PA 19072; 800-370-3331; mstudios@sol.racsa.co.cr, [www.mvstudios.com].

The Natural History of Costa Rica. We are a small company with a nonsmoking policy since 1980. Our focus is on the enjoyment each participant can experience on a wildlife tour and the contribution we can make to wildlife preservation through sustainable tourism. Our Costa Rica trip is for 12 participants guided by 2 experienced naturalists.

Dates: Feb 28-Mar 19. Cost: $3,890 plus airfare to San Jose, Costa Rica. Contact: Gail Cheeseman, Cheesemans' Ecology Safaris, 20800 Kittredge Rd., Saratoga, CA 95070; 800-527-5330, fax 408-741-0358; cheesemans@aol.com, [www.cheesemans.com].

Sustainable Development. The Institute for Central American Development Studies (ICADS) offers an interdisciplinary semester abroad study program focusing on development issues from ecological, socio-economic perspectives. The 14-week field course includes: 1) 4 weeks of intensive Spanish and urban issues, 2) 5 weeks in the field in different managed and natural ecosystems learning techniques of field research in social and natural sciences, 3) 5 weeks of independent study— living and working in rural or urban communities.

Dates: Fall and spring terms with academic credit. Cost: $7,600. Contact: Dr. Sandra Kinghorn, Ph.D., ICADS Director, ICADS, Dept. 826, P.O. Box 025216, Miami, FL 33102-5216; 011-506-225-0508, fax 011-506-234-1337; icads@netbox.com, [www.icadscr.com].

Two-Day Pacuare Whitewater Trip. Ride the exhilerating rapids of Costa Rica's most scenic and majestic river. Spend the night in our exotic Pacuare Jungle Lodge, hidden in the middle of an enchanting tropical rainforest. Trip includes ground transfers from San Jose, superior meals, specialist guides, and one-of-a-kind accommodations.

Dates: Call for details. Cost: $249 per person. Contact: Adventuras Naturales, SJO 745, P.O. Box 025216, Miami, FL 33102-5216; 800-514-0411, fax 011-506-253-6934; avenat@sol.racsa.co.cr, [www.toenjoynature.com].

Univ. Nacional Autónoma. Costa Rica is exceptional for its political stability and environmental sensitivity. Our undergraduate program at Universidad Nacional Autónoma allows participants to enroll in both program classes and regular university courses while living with local host families. Many extracurricular activities are available through the University. All coursework is in Spanish.

Dates: Spring semester: Feb-Jun, fall semester: Jul-Dec. Cost: Semester: fall $6,295; spring $6,695; year $12,590. Includes tuition, housing, 3 meals daily, orientation, excursions, support services. Contact: Cooperating Programs in the Americas, Institute for Study Abroad, 1100 W. 42nd St., Suite 305, Indianapolis, IN 46208-3345; 888-344-9299, fax 317-940-9704; COPA@butler.edu.

Cyprus

The Laona Project. A sustainable development project assisting the economies of small rural communities in northwestern Cyprus. Visitors stay in comfortable, carefully-renovated village houses or inns in beautiful scenery and experience the quiet rhythm of a traditional way of life.

Dates: Year round. Cost: Approx. $40 per day (low season) to $55 (high season). Contact: The Laona Project, P.O. Box 50257, 3502 Limassol, Cyprus; 011-357-5-369475, fax 011-357-5-352657; ccf@dial.cylink.com.cy.

Ecuador

Academia Latinoamericana. Proud to be the friendliest Spanish school you have ever known. Family owned and operated. The program offers language study at 9 levels, for complete beginners through advanced. Experienced staff, native Ecuadorians. Carefully selected host families within walking distance of school. Exclusive "SierrAzul Cloud Forest and Galapagos" extension program, volunteer program. U.S. college credit available.

Dates: Year round. Cost: $230 per week. Includes 20 hours of lessons, 7 days with host family, 2 meals per day, transfer, services at the school, and teaching material. Contact: Suzanne S. Bell, Admissions Director, USA/International, 640 East 3990 South, Suite E, Salt Lake City, UT, 84107; 801-268-4608, fax 801-265-9156; academia@juno.com, delco@spanish.com.ec.

Workshops in the Galápagos Islands. Specializing in comprehensive, educationally-oriented, professionally-led natural history tours of the Galápagos Islands. Each trip spends 11 days to 2 full weeks in the Galápagos, touring all the significant outer islands, and allowing for a maximum of wildlife observation. Four distinct itineraries available.

Dates: Monthly departures on 16-passenger yachts. Cost: Approx. $3,150-$3,750. Airfare not included. Contact: Galápagos Travel, 783 Rio Del Mar Blvd., Suite 47, Aptos, CA 95003; 800-

969-9014, fax 831-689-9195;
galapagostravel@compuserve.com,
[www.galapagostravel.com].

El Salvador

Ecotourism in San Carlos Lempa. This area near the Pacific Ocean was repopulated after the recent civil war, and today is an agricultural zone organized for integral socially, economically, and politically sustainable development. Enjoy the beautiful mangrove environment and the beaches while getting to know the people. You will also visit the war museum, organic cashew groves, and the farm school.
Dates: Year round. **Cost:** Call for details, approx. $10 per day. **Contact:** Maryse Brouwer, CORDES San Vicente, Apdo. 2841, San Salvador, El Salvador; Tel./fax 011-503-883-4825; cordes.sanvicente@salnet.net.

Europe

Bicycle and Walking Tours. With an emphasis on the culture of the individual countries.
Dates: Contact organization for details. **Cost:** Contact organization for details. **Contact:** Michael Sorgi, VanGogh Tours, P.O. Box 57, Winchester, MA 01890; vangogh@vangoghtours.com, www.vangoghtours.com.

Explore Europe by Bicycle. A leisurely way of seeing beautiful regions in Europe.
Dates: Mid Apr-mid Oct. **Cost:** $1,390-$1,830 **Contact:** International Bicycle Tours, P.O. Box 754, Essex, CT 06426; 860-767-7005, fax 860-767-3090; bikeibt@worldnet.att.net.

Overland. Overland offers backpacking, bicycle touring, and mountain biking to boys and girls ages 13-18. We hire 40 first-year trip leaders (ages 20-30) to lead in the U.S. and Europe. Please send a resume and cover letter.
Dates: Jun-Aug. **Cost:** Salary paid. **Contact:** Send resume and cover letter to Overland, P.O. Box 31, Williamstown, MA 02167.

Guatemala

Bio-Itza Eco-Cultural Spanish School. Located in San Jose, Péten, a small community on the shore of Lake Péten Itza, in northern Guatemala. Our unique program combines intensive Spanish language instruction with participation in projects of the Maya Itza people, including the conservation of a 36 KM2 natural reserve, a medicinal plant program, and a project to preserve Itza, the community's once dying language.

Dates: Year round, begins every Monday. Average stay 3-4 weeks. **Cost:** $195 per week (includes 20 hours of private language instruction per week, room and board with local family). **Contact:** Sabrina Vigilante, Conservation International, 2501 M St., NW, Suite 200, Washington, DC 20037; 202-973-2264, fax 202-887-5188; ecoescuela@conservation.org, [www.bioitza.com].

India

Responsible Travel Programs. Itineraries within India, Nepal, Bhutan, and Sikkim, Tibet, with emphasis on small and deluxe hotels, visiting families, meeting locals at all levels, no hotel meals. Transportation ranges from deluxe motorcoaches to cars to horse carts to camel carts to cycle rickshaws; elephant and camel rides; visiting jungles and villages; walks and visiting local market places and schools.
Dates: Various. **Cost:** $4,190-$4,390 each from West coast with hotels, sightseeing, most meals and tips, airfare. (1999). **Contact:** Suraj Zutshi, CTC, Unique Journeys, 71 Keystone Ave., Reno, NV 89503; 775-323-0110, fax 775-323-6914; unqjrnys@aol.com.

Italy

Biking and Walking Tours. Specializing in Italy for over 10 years, Ciclismo Classico distills the "Best of Italy," offering more unique Italian destinations than any other active vacation company. Educational, full-service tours for all abilities in Umbria, Tuscany, Piedmont, the Dolomites, Puglia, Sicily, the Amalfi Coast, Cinque Terre, Sardegna, Abruzzo, Campania, Corsica, and Elba. Charming accommodations, expert bilingual guides, cooking demonstrations, wine tastings, support vehicle, detailed route instructions, visits to local festivals, countryside picnics—an unforgettable cultural indulgence.
Dates: Apr-Nov (70 departures). Call for specific dates. **Cost:** $1,700-$3,500. **Contact:** Lauren Hefferon, Director, Ciclismo Classico, 30 Marathon St., Arlington, MA 02474; 800-866-7314 or 781-646-3377; info@ciclismoclassico.com, [www.ciclismoclassico.com].

Jamaica

Sonrise Beach Retreat. A unique and affordable ecotourism experience awaits visits to our secluded 18-acre tropical nature reserve, resort/sanctuary with miles of undeveloped coast to explore. Families, couples, artists, special interest groups all learn and receive the healing power of nature. Ecoadventure tours, devotional, health and yoga classes are available.

Dates: Year round with reservations. **Cost:** Approx. $300-$900 per week. Airfare not included. **Contact:** Robert Chase (Bro. Bob), Sonrise Beach Retreat, Robins Bay, St. Mary, Jamaica, WI; Tel./fax 876-999-7169; sonrise@in-site.com, [www.in-site.com/sonrise].

Japan

Japan Exchange and Teaching (JET). Sponsored by the Japanese Government, the JET Program invites over 1,000 American college graduates and young professionals to share their language and culture with Japanese youth. One-year positions are available in schools and government offices throughout Japan. Apply by early December for positions beginning in July of the following year.

Dates: One-year contracts renewable by mutual consent not more than 2 times. **Cost:** Participants receive approx. ¥3,600,000 per year in monthly payments. **Contact:** JET Program Office, Embassy of Japan, 2520 Massachusetts Ave. NW, Washington, DC 20008; 202-238-6772, fax 202-265-9484; eojjet@erols.com, [www.jet.org].

Teaching English in Japan. Two-year program to maximize linguistic and cultural integration of participants who work as teachers' assistants. Placements twice yearly in Apr and Aug. Most positions are in junior high schools in urban and rural areas. Bachelor's degree and willingness to learn Japanese required.

Dates: Hiring for positions every Apr and Aug. Applications accepted year round. **Cost:** No application fees. **Contact:** Institute for Education in Japan, Earlham College, 801 National Rd. West, D-202, Richmond, IN 47374; 888-685-2726, fax 765-983-1553; [www.earlham.edu/~aet].

Latin America

Community Development Internship. This is a credit-bearing internship where volunteers live with a family in rural Mexico and Ecuador, or semi-urban Cuba, while working side by side with community members on grassroots development projects. Project assignments are available in the areas of agriculture, construction, reforestation, animal husbandry, micro-enterprise development, data collection, public health and other fields. These projects are designed, developed and implemented by the beneficiaries themselves. While project

opportunities change as new ones come online and others are completed, every effort is made to match interns' interests with their assignment.

Dates: Year round. Two months advance needed for placement in Cuba. Six-week program (3 weeks in Cuba). **Cost:** Six credits: $3,400, no credit: $2,700, 3 credits: $2,900. **Contact:** Nicholas A. Robins, Director, Cuban Studies Institute, Center for Latin American Studies, Tulane Univ., Caroline Richardson Bldg., New Orleans, LA 70118-5698; 504-862-8629 or 504-862-8000 ext. 2601, fax 504-862-8678; nrobins@mailhost.tcs.tulane.edu, [http://cuba.tulane.edu].

Explorama Lodge Special. One night at the Iquitos Hotel plus 2 nights at each of the 3 Explorama lodges, including visits to the longest canopy walkway in the world, ethnobotanical plant garden, primary rainforest reserve of over 250,000 acres. Meals, lodging, excursions, guides, 200 miles total boat excursions on Amazon and Napo rivers.

Dates: Starts every Tuesday year round. **Cost:** 2000-2001: $899 per person in twin bedded room. **Contact:** Peter Jenson, Explorama Lodges, Box 446, Iquitos, Peru; 800-707-5275. In Peru: 011-51-94-25-2530, fax 011-51-94-25-2533; amazon@explorama.com, [www.explorama.com].

Mexico

Cemanahuac Community. Trips are highly educational, with college credit (graduate and undergraduate) available. Countries include Mexico, Belize, Costa Rica, and Guatemala. Focus areas include history, anthropology, archaeology, social issues, cooking and cuisine, and popular and folk art. Previous groups include teachers, social workers, artists, senior citizens, chefs, museum members, alumni groups, and other adult participants. Each trip individually planned.

Dates: Field study trips can be held at any time of the year. **Cost:** Dependent on requirements and length of the field study trips. **Contact:** Vivian B. Harvey, Educational Programs Coordinator, Cemanahuac Educational Community, Apartado 5-21, Cuernavaca, Morelos, Mexico; 011-52-7-3186407, fax 011-52-7-312-5418; 74052.2570@compuserve.com, [www.cemanahuac.com].

Intensive Spanish in Cuernavaca. Cuauhnahuac, founded in 1972, offers a variety of intensive and flexible programs geared to individual needs. Six hours of classes daily with no more than 4 students to a class. Housing with Mexican families who really care about you. Cultural conferences, excursions, and special classes for professionals. College credit available.

Dates: Year round. New classes begin every Monday. **Cost:** $70 registration fee; $680 for 4 weeks tuition; housing $18 per night. **Contact:** Marcia Snell, 519 Park Dr., Kenilworth, IL 60043; 800-245-9335, fax 847-256-9475; lankysam@aol.com.

Language and Culture in Guanajuato. Improve your Spanish in the most beautiful colonial city in Mexico. We teach one-on-one or in small groups for up to 8 hours daily. Spanish, Mexican history, cooking, literature, business, folk dancing, and politics. Students of all ages and many nationalities. Homestays with families, field trips, movies, hikes, theater, dance performances.

Dates: Year round. New classes begin every Monday. Semester programs begin in Jan and Aug. **Cost:** $925. Includes 4 weeks of classes and homestay with 3 meals daily. **Contact:** Director Jorge Barroso, Instituto Falcon, Mora 158, Guanajuato, Gto. 36000 Mexico; 011-52-473-1-0745; infalcon@redes.int.com.mx, [http://institutofalcon.com].

Travel/Study Seminars. Learn from Mexicans of diverse backgrounds about their economic, political, and social realities. Emphasis on the views of the poor and oppressed. Programming in Cuernavaca, Mexico City, and Chiapas. Call for a free list of upcoming programs.

Dates: Ongoing. **Cost:** $800-$1,900 depending on package, destination, and length of trip. **Contact:** Center for Global Education at Augsburg College, 2211 Riverside Ave., Box 307TR, Minneapolis, MN 55454; 800-299-8889, fax 612-330-1695; globaled@augsburg.edu, [www.augsburg.edu/global].

Way of Nature. Alternative Vacations for under 30: learning experiencing, working, playing together surfing, sailing, backpacking, kayaking, gardening, music, dance, landscaping, yoga, Tai Chi, meditation.

Dates: Nov-Jul. **Cost:** $10 per day camping plus meals approx. $5 per day. **Contact:** Way of Nature Alternative Vacations, P.O. Box 116, Todos Santos, Mexico 23300; 804-633-5106 (U.S.); wayofnature@yahoo.com, [http://members.aol.com/rhythmwood].

New Zealand

New Zealand Pedaltours. New Zealand is a cycling paradise with fantastically beautiful scenery. Cycle as much as you wish each day with a comfortable minibus and trailer to carry your luggage and you at any time. Excellent accommodations and great meals. Experienced local guides knowledgeable about local flora and history.

Dates: Nov-Mar. **Cost:** $330-$3,245. **Contact:** Allan Blackman, 522 29th Ave. S., Seattle, WA 98144; 888-696-2080, fax 206-727-6597; blackallan@aol.com.

Serious Fun New Zealand. Serious Fun has operated hiking-oriented, small-group, comfortably-lodged adventure tours of New Zealand's since 1987. The 14-day Best of the South Island Tour (Nov-Mar) is highlighted by a swim with the dolphins at Kaikoura and a 3-day tramp along the Routeburn Track.

Dates: Jan 17-30; Feb 21-Mar 5, Mar 20-Apr 2; Nov 20-Dec 3; Dec 4-17; Dec 18, 2000-Jan 1, 2001. **Cost:** $2,800. **Contact:** Stu Wilson, Serious Fun New Zealand, 3103 Whiteway Dr., Austin, TX 78757; 800-411-5724, outland@bga.com, [www.seriousfunnewzealand.com].

Papua New Guinea

Guiye/Waiye Range Environment Project. This is an environment project started by the community to achieve sustainable development at community level. The main aim is to create sustainable ecotourism in the area.

Dates: Aug-Dec. **Cost:** Contact sponsor. **Contact:** Peter Gundu, P.O. Box 463, Simbu Province, Papua New Guinea.

Peru

Tree House International (THI). THI is a clearinghouse for cultural, spiritual, and archaeological travel experiences. Live, work, and play within the communities of the Peruvian Amazon, Highlands, and the South Coast. Opportunities to travel in remote areas, visit Shamans, teach English or join an archaeological dig with the California Institute for Peruvian Studies.

Dates: Year round. Write for program listings, dates, prices, and application. **Cost:** Vary. A nonrefundable $100 application fee. **Contact:** Sandy Asmussen, Tree House International, 45 Quakie Way, Bailey, CO 80421; sandyperu@hotmail.com.

THE ROAD LESS TRAVELED

By Abigail Rome

In *Ecotourism and Sustainable Development: Who Owns Paradise?* (Island Press, 1999, $25) Martha Honey takes a long and critical look at the reality and rhetoric of ecotourism in the developing world. Through intensive study of the worldwide tourism industry and of nature-based tourism in seven countries in Latin America and Africa, Honey examines the links between tourism and sustainable development.

The author's many years of experience as a journalist served her well in researching this information-packed book. By talking to key players in the field, from international and policy strategists to local community members, Honey develops a balanced and coherent picture of the ecotourism industry and related policy and development issues. While she firmly criticizes those whom she feels are "greenwashing" their programs by promoting environmental and social benefits which may not be real, she gives credit to those organizations and individuals who indeed walk their talk.

Balanced approaches in this field are difficult to come by. The subject and even the very words "ecotourism," "sustainable tourism," "green tourism," etc. mean different things to writers and marketers, depending upon the constituencies they represent. Those who criticize often fail to give credit where it is due; those whose promote their own programs and actions are often short-sighted and self-serving. Honey scrutinizes not only business and marketing practices but also cultural and social values at all levels of society.

The bulk of the book is devoted to an examination of ecotourism in the context of economic policies and practices in seven countries: Ecuador (the Galápagos), Costa Rica, Cuba, Tanzania, Zanzibar, Kenya, and South Africa. For readers who do not want to take the time to wade through the long, though provocative, analyses, she summarizes her findings. Each chapter ends with an ecotourism scorecard—an evaluation of how the country stacks up in regard to the seven characteristics of genuine ecotourism that she spells out in her opening chapters.

Honey concludes: "Ecotourism is far from fulfilling its promise to transform the way in which modern, conventional tourism is conducted. . . . It will take much stronger grassroots movements ... to curb the power of the conventional tourism industry. Although this appears unlikely to happen soon, it is still worth the struggle. Along the way, some excellent models are being built; some local communities are being empowered and their members' lives improved ... and there is a growing awareness that we cannot continue to play in other people's lands as we have in the past. Despite the constraints, today's traveler does, as Robert Frost suggests, have a choice about which road to take."

South Africa

Travel-Study Seminars. Learn from South Africans of diverse backgrounds about their economic, political, and social realities. Emphasis on the views of those struggling for justice. Call for details.
Dates: Summer 2000. **Cost:** Approx. $3,900 depending on length of stay. **Contact:** Center for Global Education at Augsburg College, 2211 Riverside Ave., Box 307TR, Minneapolis, MN 55454; 800-299-8889, fax 612-330-1695; globaled@augsburg.edu, [www.augsburg.edu/global].

Spain

Holidays in Doñana. Nature vacations in protected area of southwestern Spain.
Dates: Year round. **Cost:** $67 per day. **Contact:** Doñatour, Centro de Naturaleza Doñana, Casa Hermandad de Rociana del Condado, C/El Real, 31, El Rocío, Almonte 21750, Huelva, Spain; Tel./fax 011-34-959-44-24-68; info@donana.com, [www.donana.com].

Señor Valcia Spanish Institute. "Explorador Programme"—a program designed for those who desire fewer hours of Spanish in the classroom and plenty of outdoor practice to get to know the true culture by partcipating in activities and excursions on the most majestic places of Andalucia.
Dates: Year round. **Contact:** Señor Valcia, Central Office, P.O. Box 358, 11540 Sanlúcar de Bda., Cadiz, Spain; Tel./fax 011-34-956-380859; club@valcia.es, [www.valcia.es]. U.S. address: 640 East, 3990 South, Suite E, Salt Lake City, UT 84107; Worldcom 800-484-5554 pin 5554; academia@juno.com.

Sri Lanka

Peace Work. Samasevaya works for development of Sri Lanka. It focuses on issues of poverty alleviation, environmental protection, women's development, childcare, human rights, and peace education.
Dates: Year round. **Cost:** $3 per day. **Contact:** Samson Jayasinghe, Samasevaya, Anuradhapura Rd., Talawa, Sri Lanka; 011-94-25-76266.

United Kingdom and Ireland

Walking/Camping Journeys. We arrange walking adventures in the U.K.s wildest parts. Camp in wild places. Crew transport camp ahead and prepare acclaimed vegetarian food. If you want to see Britain there's no finer way to go.

Dates: Easter-Oct, 4-7 nights. **Cost:** £38 per night includes all meals, equipment, and guide. (1999 dates and prices). **Contact:** Head for the Hills, Little Grove, Grove Ln., Chesham, Bucks HP5 3QQ, U.K.; 011-44-1494-794060, fax 011-44-1494-776066.

United States

Adventure Alaska Tours. Adventure Alaska offers unique small group tours and vacation travel packages from sightseeing to wildlife to wilderness trips. Five- to 16-day itineraries feature Alaska, the Yukon, Arctic, Inside Passage, as well as Denali, Glacier Bay, Kenai Fjords, and Wrangell-St. Elias National parks. Themes include natural history, hiking, canoeing, and dog sledding with tour styles from cozy small lodges to camping.
Dates: Call for details. **Cost:** Call for details. **Contact:** Todd Bureau, Adventure Alaska Tours, P.O. Box 64, Hope, AK 99605; 800-365-7057, 907-782-3730, fax 907-782-3725; info@AdventureAlaskaTours.com, [www.AdventureAlaskaTours.com].

Alaska Wilderness Rec. and Tourism Assn (AWRTA), Explore Alaska! We have contact information for more than 200 Alaskan ecotourism, wilderness, adventure, and educational tour guides and lodges. Get more out of your trip with local interpreters and guides. Visit our web site for information on responsible travel and wildlife viewing guidelines.
Dates: Year round. **Cost:** Vary. **Contact:** Steve Behnke, AWRTA, P.O. Box 22827, Juneau, AK 99802; 907-463-3038, fax 907-463-3280; awrta@alaska.net, [www.alaska.net/~awrta].

Rethinking Tourism Project. Next summer (2000) the Rethinking Tourism Project will offer 3 volunteer tours to Alaska to study Athabascan culture. Small group of approximately 10 people will spend 3-4 days working at an Indian salmon fish camp along the Yukon River, improving the site and making it handicap accessible. Each day will be an opportunity to explore one of the world's most important boreal frontier forests and meet the Koyukon Athabascan people who live along the mighty Yukon River. An additional 3-4 days will be spent learning about the culture and the environment, and traveling through northern Alaska.
Dates: Contact sponsor. **Cost:** Contact sponsor. **Contact:** The Rethinking Tourism Project, P.O. Box 581938, Minneapolis, MN

55458-1938; Tel./fax 651-644-9984; RTproject@aol.com, [www2.planeta.com/mader/ecotravel/resources.rtp/rtp.html].

Worldwide

Adventure Travel. The Northwest Passage offers unique adventures from a dogsled/ski expedition to the North Pole, ski expedition to the South Pole, sea kayaking in Crete, Patagonia, Ellemere Island, and Greenland, cycling/rafting/safari in southern Africa, mountaineering in European high Alps and Greenland.
Dates: Vary. **Cost:** Vary. **Contact:** Annie Aggens, Director, The Northwest Passage, 1130 Greenleaf Ave., Wilmette, IL 60091; 800-732-7328, 847-256-4409, fax 847-256-4476; info@nwpassage.com, [www.nwpassage.com or www.northpole-expeditions.com].

Camp Sadako. Named after the High Commissioner for Refugees, Sadako Ogata, combines hands-on relief experience with public awareness and outreach about refugees. Participants spend 6 weeks working alongside United Natios High Commissioner for Refugees (UNHCR) in refugee camps on projects such as registration, relief distribution, education, and community services. Phase two: conducting public awareness activities about their experience and refugee issues in their home countries.
Dates: Five-7 weeks (Sep-Oct), Apr 30 deadline. **Cost:** Preparation and travel arrangements. Room and board are free. **Contact:** Camp Sadako Committee, USA for UNHCR, 1775 K St., NW, Suite 300, Washington, DC 20006; 800-770-1100, 202-296-1115, fax 202-296-1081; usaforunhcr@usaforunhcr.org, [www.usaforunhcr.org].

Classic Journeys. Easy-going walking, cultural, and natural history adventures worldwide. Small groups, expert local guides, first class accommodations, and fine cuisine.
Dates: Tours offered throughout the year. **Cost:** Around $2,000 for a week. Airfare not included. **Contact:** Classic Journeys at 800-200-3887; [www.classicjourneys.com].

ExperiencePlus! Specialty Tours, Inc. Since 1972 ExperiencePlus! has offered quality bicycle and walking tours at affordable prices. Local guides help bring the culture and character of each country to life for participants. Accommodations are clean and comfortable, with a private bath, but are not luxury. Participants range in skill level from beginning to advance and in age from 20s-70s.

Dates: Year round. **Cost:** $1,675-$2,850. **Contact:** Melissa Groom, Director of Sales, ExperiencePlus! Specialty Tours, Inc., 415 Mason Court, Unit 1, Ft. Collins, CO 80524; 800-685-4565, 970-484-8489, fax 970-493-0377; tours@experienceplus.com, [www.experienceplus.com].

Global Ecology and Cities in the 21st Century. Two different academic programs to be offered by the International Honors Program in 1999-2000. "Global Ecology" is a 2-semester program of around-the-world study and travel to England, India, the Philippines, New Zealand, and Mexico with academic coursework in ecology, anthropology, economics, and environmental issues. The "Cities in the 21st Century" program is a 1-semester program of study and travel to Egypt, India, and Brazil with academic coursework in urban studies, anthropology, sociology, economics, and political science.
Dates: "Global Ecology": Sep 2000-May 2001. "Cities in 21st Century": Jan-May 2000. **Cost:** "Global Ecology": $22,950 plus airfare, includes tuition, room and board. "Cities in the 21st Century": $13,650 plus airfare, includes tuition, room and board. Estimated airfare for each program is $3,900. Financial aid is available. **Contact:** Joan Tiffany, Director, International Honors Program, 19 Braddock Pk., Boston, MA 02116; 617-267-0026, fax 617-262-9299; info@ihp.edu, [www.ihp.edu].

Global Volunteers. The nation's premier short-term service programs for people of all ages and backgrounds. Assist mutual international understanding through ongoing development projects throughout Africa, Asia, the Caribbean, Europe, the Pacific, North and South America. Programs of 1, 2, and 3 weeks range from natural resource preservation, light construction, and painting to teaching English, assisting with health care, and nurturing at-risk children. No special skills or foreign languages are required. Ask about the Millennium Service Project.
Dates: Over 150 teams year round. **Cost:** Tax-deductible program fees range from $450 to $2,395. Airfare not included. **Contact:** Global Volunteers, 375 E. Little Canada Rd., St. Paul, MN 55117; 800-487-1074, fax 651-407-5163; email@globalvolunteers.org, [www.globalvolunteers.org].

Photo Explorer Tours. Efficient and economical access to some of the world's best photo opportunities. Small groups led by 1997 travel photographer of the year, Dennis Cox.

Dates: Contact sponsor. **Cost:** Contact sponsor. **Contact:** Dennis Cox, Photo Explorer Tours, 2506 Country Village, Ann Arbor, MI 48103-6500; 800-315-4462, fax 734-996-1481; decoxphoto@aol.com, [www.denniscox.com/tours.htm].

Roads Less Traveled. Extraordinary biking, hiking, and multisport backcountry adventures for over a decade. Experience 50 adventures for all ages and abilities to 25 destinations worldwide. Small groups, local guides, cozy inns, or scenic camps. Specialty trips include singles, seniors, family and women-only, custom, charter, and self-guided tours.
Dates: Year round. **Cost:** $295 (4 days)-$3,050 (14 days) (1999). **Contact:** Mariann Van Den Elzen or Brian T. Mullis, Roads Less Traveled, 2840 Wilderness Pl., #F, Boulder, CO 80301; 800-488-8483 or 303-413-0938, fax 303-413-0926; fun@roadslesstraveled.com, [www.RoadsLessTraveled.com].

Sea Kayak/Whale Watch Camping. Explore the natural and cultural history of extraordinary places by sea kayak. San Juan/Canadian Gulf Islands, the Inside Passage, West Coast Vancouver Island, Baja, New Zealand, Hawaii, Virgin Islands. Scheduled and custom group tours.
Dates: Jun-Aug. **Cost:** Contact organization for details. **Contact:** Kathleen Grimbly, Blue Moon Explorations, 4658 Blank Rd., Sedro-Woolley, WA 98284; 800-966-8806, Tel./fax 360-856-5622; bluemoon@xpressmail.net, [www.home.cio.net/bluemoon].

Transformational Journeys. Vacations that make a difference: Brazil: service and cultural immersion experience, hands-on work with children's service project, construction opportunities in partnership projects with local faith communities, host family stays, seminars led by local professors, excursions to coral reefs, local beaches, and rainforests.
Dates: Jan, Jun-Jul. **Cost:** $1,990 (1999). **Contact:** Dan Hickey, Transformational Journeys, P.O. Box 8571, Kansas City, MO 64114-0857; 816-361-2111; journey@qni.com.

WorldTeach. WorldTeach is a nonprofit, nongovernmental organization which provides opportunities for individuals to make a meaningful contribution to international education by living and working as volunteer teachers in developing countries.
Dates: Year round. **Cost:** $4,800-$5,950. Includes international airfare, health insurance, extensive training, and in-country support.
Contact: WorldTeach, Harvard Institute for International Development, 14 Story St., Cambridge, MA 02138; 800-4-TEACH-0 or 617-495-5527, fax 617-495-1599; info@worldteach.org, [www.worldteach.org].

Worldwide Expeditionary Adventures. Zegrahm Expeditions is dedicated to offering an expeditionary adventure to the inquisitive traveler. Our programs are operated with great concern for the environment and sensitivity to fragile wildlife areas and cultures worldwide. Expeditions are accompanied by some of the world's foremost naturalists and expedition leaders.
Dates: Year round. **Cost:** From $3,690-$30,000 per person. **Contact:** Zegrahm Expeditions, 1414 Dexter Ave. N., #327, Seattle, WA 98109; 800-628-8747 or 206-285-4000, fax 206-285-5037; zoe@zeco.com, [www.zeco.com].

Youth International. An experiential education program focusing on international travel and intercultural exchange, adventure, community service, and homestays. Teams of 12, aged 18-25, travel together for 1 semester to Southeast Asia and India/Nepal, or East Africa and the Middle East. Assist refugees, hike the Himalayas, live with and help an African tribe, scuba dive, and much more.
Dates: Sep 7-Dec 18, 1999 (15 weeks); Jan 24-May 30 (18 weeks) and early Sep-mid-Dec (15 weeks), 2000. **Cost:** 1999: $6,500 (Asia), $7,000 (Africa/Middle East). 2000: $6,500 (Asia, 15 weeks), $7,500 (18 weeks); $7,000 (Africa/Middle East, 15 weeks), $8,000 (18 weeks).
Contact: Brad Gillings, Youth International, 1121 Downing St., #2, Denver, CO 80218; 303-839-5877, fax 303-839-5887; youth.international@bigfoot.com, [www.youthinternational.org].

NINE

The following listing of volunteer abroad programs was supplied by the organizers. Contact the program directors to confirm costs, dates, and other details. Please tell them you read about their program in this book! Programs based in more than one country or region are listed under "Worldwide."

Africa

Cross-Cultural Solutions in Ghana. Experience the vibrant, colorful culture of West Africa and make a difference at the same time. This unique short-term volunteer program enables volunteers to work with local social service organizations in fields as diverse as health care, education, skills training, and arts/recreation. Volunteers receive continual professional support from our U.S. and Ghana-based staff. No skills or experience required—only a desire to help and learn.

Dates: Three-week programs run year round. Longer term placements can be arranged. **Cost:** $1,850 covers all Ghana-based expenses. International airfare, insurance, and visa not included. Program fee is tax deductible for U.S. residents. **Contact:** Cross-Cultural Solutions, 47 Potter Ave., New Rochelle, NY 10801; 914-632-0022 or 800-380-4777, fax 914-632-8494; info@crossculturalsolutions.org, [www.crossculturalsolutions.org].

International Volunteering Network. Involvement Volunteers Assn., Inc. has volunteer placements in this country, all months of the year. Please see Worldwide for their main entry.

Dates: Year round. **Cost:** The volunteer meets all travel costs (including insurance). Most hosts provide accommodations and food for free, but some placements in projects or countries with limited resources can cost up to $55 per week for food. **Contact:** Involvement Volunteers Assn., Inc., P.O. Box 218, Port Melbourne, Victoria 3207, Australia; 011-61-3-9646-9392, fax 011-61-3-9646-5504; ivimel@iaccess.com.au, [www.volunteering.org.au].

Operation Crossroads Africa. A 7-week, cross-cultural immersion program with rural projects in 10 African countries and Brazil. Education, agriculture, construction, and medical programs. Six weeks in village, 1 week travel in host country, 2-day orientation beginning in New York City.

Dates: Jun 24-Aug 12. **Cost:** $3,500 includes airfare, orientation, and all in-continent expenses. **Contact:** Kate Shackford, Operation Crossroads Africa, 475 Riverside Dr., Suite 1366, New York, NY 10115; oca@igc.apc.org, [www.igc.org/oca].

Volunteer Service Program in Ghana. Volunteers assist teachers and those in authority in the smooth running of the school. Duties will be based upon what the volunteers are able to teach.
Dates: First term: Jan-Apr, 2nd term: May-Aug, 3rd term: Sep-Dec. **Cost:** Participating fee $50, plus $285 per month. **Contact:** Mr. Alfred O. Anang, Rising Star Preparation and Junior Secondary School, P.O. Box TS 148, Ghana, Africa; 011-233-21-244669, fax 011-33-21-712213.

Australia

Australian Trust for Conservation Volunteers. ATCV is a national, nonprofit, nonpolitical organization undertaking practical conservation projects including tree planting, seed collection, flora/fauna surveys, endangered species projects, coastal restoration, habitat protection, track construction, and weed eradication. Volunteers work in teams of 6-10; all training is provided.
Dates: Year round in all states and territories; choose any Friday throughout the year as starting date. **Cost:** Six-week Conservation Experience Package: AUS$840 includes all food, accommodations, and project-related transport within Australia. **Contact:** ATCV, P.O. Box 423, Ballarat, Victoria 3353, Australia (please include IRC); 011-61-3-5333-1483, fax 011-61-3-5333-2166; info@atcv.com.au, [www.atcv.com.au].

International Volunteering Network. Involvement Volunteers Assn., Inc. has volunteer placements in this country, all months of the year. Please see Worldwide for their main entry.
Dates: Year round. **Cost:** The volunteer meets all travel costs (including insurance). Most hosts provide accommodations and food for free, but some placements in projects or countries with limited resources can cost up to $55 per week for food. **Contact:** Involvement Volunteers Assn., Inc., P.O. Box 218, Port Melbourne, Victoria 3207, Australia; 011-61-3-9646-9392, fax 011-61-3-9646-5504; ivimel@iaccess.com.au, [www.iaccess.com.au/ivimel/index.html].

WWOOFING (Willing Workers on Organic Farms). Learn organic growing while living with a host family. Twelve hundred hosts in Australia or travel the world with over 600 hosts on all continent where you work in exchange for food and board.
Dates: Year round. **Cost:** AUS$40 single, AUS$45 double. **Contact:** WWOOF Australia, Buchan, Victoria 3885, Australia; 011-61-3-5155-0218, fax 011-61-3-5155-0342; wwoof@net-tech.com.au, [www.wwoof.com.au].

Canada

Mingan Island Cetacean Study's Research Expeditions. Ecoresearch tours with field biologists in the Mingan Island region of the Quebec North Shore. Observation of large baleen whales, blue, fin humpback, and minke, as well as Atlantic white-sided and harbor porpoise.
Dates: St. Lawrence Jun 15-Oct 15, Baja Feb-Mar. **Cost:** St. Lawrence CAN$1,584-CAN$1,685 per week. Baja US$1,375 per week. **Contact:** Richard Sears, MICS Inc., 285 Green St., Lambert, PQ, Canada; Tel./fax 450-465-9176 (Nov-Jun); Tel./fax 418-949-2845 (Jun-Oct).

WWOOF-Canada (Willing Workers on Organic Farms). In exchange for your help (4-6 hours per day, 5-5 1/2 days per week) you receive accommodations, meals, and an interesting and valuable experience. Host farms/homesteads in every region of Canada, East to West, with some farm hosts also in the U.S.
Dates: Year round. Most opportunities early spring- late fall. **Cost:** $30 per person includes membership plus 2 International Postal Coupons. **Contact:** WWOOF-Canada, RR 2, S. 18, C. 9 Nelson, BC, V1L 5P5, Canada; 250-354-4417; wwoofcan@uniserve.com, [www.members.tripod.com/~wwoof].

Caribbean

Historic Preservation. CVE recruits volunteers to work on historic preservation projects throughout the Caribbean. We work with local agencies: national trusts, museums, and historical societies.
Dates: One-week trips throughout year: Dominica Aug 22, Aruba Oct 17, Tobago Mar 2000, St. Croix May 2000, Grenada Sep 2000. **Cost:** $500-$700 per week plus airfare. **Contact:** CVE, Box 388, Corning, NY 14830; 607-962-7846; [www.cvexp.org].

Central America

Internship and Research Program. The Institute for Central American Development Studies (ICADS) offers a semester abroad study program, including coursework and structured internship opportunities, in Costa Rica, Nicaragua, Belize, and Cuba in the following areas: women's studies, environment/ecology, public health, education, human rights, and many others. The program is progressive and aimed at students who wish to work on social justice issues and on behalf of the poor, women, and the oppressed in Central America. Fall and spring with academic credit, summer noncredit Spanish and internship program.

Dates: Fall and spring terms with academic credit. **Cost:** $7,600. **Contact:** Sandra Kinghorn, PhD, Director, ICADS, Dept. 826, P.O. Box 025216, Miami, FL 33102-5216; 011-506-225-0508, fax 011-506-234-1337; icads@netbox.com, [www.icadscr.com].

Central Europe

Central European Teaching Program. Places teachers in Hungary, Romania, Poland, and Lithuania. Candidates must have a university degree, some experience in TEFL, and a strong interest in the region. Orientation, housing, stipend, and basic health insurance are provided.

Dates: Sep 2000-Jun 2001. **Cost:** Placement fee: $1,500. **Contact:** Alex Dunlop, CETP Director, Beloit College, 700 College St., Beloit, WI 53511; 608-363-2619, fax 608-363-2449; dunlopa@beloit.edu, [www.beloit.edu/~cetp].

Costa Rica

COSI (Costa Rica Spanish Institute). COSI offers high quality instruction at reasonable prices. We offer Spanish classes in San José and at a beautiful national park (beach and rainforest). Homestay is also available. Volunteer work opportunities and special discounts in tours.

Dates: Year round. **Cost:** Prices start at $280 per week including classes in groups of maximum 5 students, homestay, cultural activities, books, access to email, airport pickup. **Contact:** COSI, P.O. Box 1366-2050, San Pedro, San José, Costa Rica; 011-506-234-1001, fax 011-506-253-2117. From U.S. 800-771-5184; cosicr@sol.racsa.co.cr, [www.cosi.co.cr].

Intensive Spanish Training. The Institute for Central American Development Studies (ICADS) offers 4-week progressive programs in intensive Spanish language—4 1/2 hours daily, 5 days a week. Small classes (4 or fewer students). Activities and optional afternoon internships emphasize environmental issues, women's issues, development, human rights, and public health. Supportive learning environment. Homestays and field trips. Great alternative for the socially conscious.

Dates: Programs begin first Monday of each month. **Cost:** $1,400 includes airport pick-up, classes, books, homestay, meals, laundry, lectures, activities, field trips, and internship placements. **Contact:** ICADS, Dept. 826, P.O. Box 025216, Miami, FL 33102-5216; 011-506-225-0508, fax 011-506-234-1337; icads@netbox.com, [www.icadscr.com].

Learn Spanish While Volunteering. Assist with the training of Costa Rican public school teachers in ESL and computers. Assist local health clinic, social service agencies, and environmental projects. Enjoy learning Spanish in the morning, volunteer work in the afternoon/evening. Spanish classes of 2-5 students plus group learning activities; conversations with middle class homestay families (1 student per family). Homestays and most volunteer projects are within walking distance of school in small town near the capital, San José.

Dates: Year round, all levels. Classes begin every Monday (except Apr 17-21 and Dec 18-29), volunteer program is continuous. **Cost:** $345 per week for 28 hours of classes and group activities plus Costa Rican dance and cooking classes. Includes tuition, 3 meals per day, 7 days per week, homestay, laundry, all materials, weekly 3-hour cultural tour, and airport transportation. $25 one-time registration fee. **Contact:** Susan Shores, Registrar, Latin American Language Center, PMB 123, 7485 Rush River Dr., Suite 710, Sacramento, CA 95831-5260; 916-447-0938, fax 916-428-9542; lalc@madre.com.

Denmark

We Help Each Other. Organic Farming. Work 3-4 hours a day and get free food and accommodations. No money is paid. Also a home exchange club.

Dates: Year round. **Cost:** None. **Contact:** VHH-DK, Inga Nielsen, Åsenvej 35, 9881 Bindslev, Denmark.

El Salvador

CRISPAZ. Offers 3 programs: 1) Volunteer program is designed for individuals who wish to spend a minimum of 1 year living and working in a marginalized urban or rural community. Volunteers donate their time, skills, and interests as they work alongside Salvadorans in areas such as literacy, health care, community organization, education, agriculture, appropriate technology, youth work, etc. 2) El Salvador Encounters are 7 to 10 days long and offer the opportunity to explore a different reality and build relationships with people. 3) The Summer Internship Program is designed to provide an intensive learning and service experience in a poor community in El Salvador. Homestays with Salvadoran families.

Dates: Ongoing programs. Encounters are generally facilited 10-12 times per year. **Cost:** $70 per day per person includes in-country travel, accommodations, and meals. Airfare not included. Long term volunteers responsible for living expenses, generally through sponsorship by community or organization, and airfare. A small stipend is provided to volunteer upon re-entry. Health insurance included. CRISPAZ can faciliate fundraising for volunteer placement. **Contact:** CRISPAZ, Stan de Voogd or Jennifer Collins, 319 Camden, San Antonio, TX 78215; 210-222-2018, fax 210-226-9119; crispaz@igc.apc.org, [www.crispaz.org].

Melida Anaya Montes Language School. Teach small-size English classes, all levels offered. Training provided. Students are adults working in the Salvadoran opposition who need to increase their capacity for their work and/or complete their studies. CIS also seeks volunteers for their human rights work. Volunteers can receive half-price Spanish classes.

Dates: Three-month sessions beginning mid-Jan, Apr, and Aug. Mini-sessions offered Jul and Nov. **Cost:** No fee. Must pay living costs ($250-$400 per month). **Contact:** CIS MAM Language School, Boulevard Universitario, Casa #4, San Salvador, El Salvador, Central America; Tel./fax 011-503-226-2623; cis@netcomsa.com.

Europe

Cook and Ski in Val d'Isere France. YSE, the top chalet company in Europe's best ski resort, is recruiting chefs and cooks plus helpers. Wonderful job. Free 3-week training course, free skis, free lessons, skiing most days. You must hold a British passport and be over 21.

Dates: End of Nov 1999-May 2000. **Cost:** Flight to Europe. Free equipment and accom-modations. **Contact:** The Business Village, Broomhill Rd., London SW18 4JQ, U.K.; 011-44-181-871-5117, fax 011-44-181-871-5229; staff@yseski.co.uk, [www.yseski.co.uk].

International Voluntary Service. To foster peace and understanding through voluntary work, mainly international workcamps (short-term projects where groups drawn from different countries live and work together for 2 or 3 weeks for the benefit of the local community).

Dates: Summer (mainly). **Cost:** Up to $150. **Contact:** I.V.S. (in Britain); ivs@ivsgbsouth.demon.co.uk. In U.S. scitalk@sci-ivs.org.

International Volunteer Program. Volunteer for nonprofit organizations in France or England during the summer.

Dates: Summer. **Cost:** $1,500 includes roundtrip ticket (New York or San Francisco), room, meals for 6 weeks. **Contact:** Christelle Proti, Société Française de Bienfaisance Mutuelle, 210 Post St., Suite 502, San Francisco, CA 94108; 415-477-3667, fax 415-477-3669; crystal6@ix.netcom.com, [www.ivpsf.com].

France

Archaeological Excavations. Excavations, drawing, mapping in a medieval town.

Dates: Jul-Sep. **Cost:** Contact organization for details. **Contact:** Service Archaeologique de Douai, 191 rue Saint Albin, F59500 Douai, France; 011-33-3-2771-3890, fax 011-33-3-2771-383; arkeos@wanadoo.fr.

Club du Vieux. Camps, chantiers, stages. Restoration of ancient monuments. Building awareness of and conserving French cultural heritage.

Dates: See program for projects and dates. **Cost:** FF80 per day plus insurance. **Contact:** Club du Vieux Manoir, Abbaye Royale du Nouvel, 60700 Pontpoint, France; 011-33-3-44-72-33-98, 011-33-3-44-70-13-14.

Restoration of Medieval Buildings. Volunteers restore and maintain medieval buildings and sites, including 2 fortified castles at Ottrott, Alsace, destined as cultural and recreational centers. We provide participants with both cultural enrichment and physical exercise.

Dates: Jul, Aug, Aug (1999). **Cost:** Approx. FF550 (1999). **Contact:** Chantiers d'Études Médiévales, 4 rue du Tonnelet Rouge, 67000 Strasbourg, France; 011-33-88-37-17-20; castrum@wanadoo.fr, [http://peiso.wanadoo.fr/castrum].

Guatemala

Eco-Escuela de Español and Bio Itza Programs. You want to learn Spanish, we want volunteers for conservation and community development projects in El Petén, Guatemala. The town is located close to Tikal and adjacent to the Maya Biosphere Reserve (the largest protected area in Central America) so you will be surrounded by natural and archaeological wonders and immersed in Mayan culture. This is a commu-nity owned project and participation in it will support local communities.

Dates: Year round. Arrive on weekend, start classes on Monday. **Cost:** A fee of $200 covers tuition with 20 hours per week of one-on-one

Spanish language instruction, airport pick-up, transfer to the town by boat, homestay, and 3 meals per day. **Contact:** Sandra at G.A.P. Adventures, 266 Dupont St., Toronto, ON, M5R 1V7, Canada; 800-465-5600; adventure@gap.ca.

Israel

Kibbutz Volunteer. Live and work on a kibbutz for a minimum of 2 months. Meet people from all over the world.

Dates: Year round. **Contact:** Alisha Goodman, Kibbutz Aliyah Desk, 633 3rd Ave., 21st Fl., New York, NY 10017; 800-247-7852, fax 212-318-6134.

Volunteering at Archaeological Digs. A listings of digs recruiting volunteers can be found on the web site of the Israel Ministry of Foreign Affairs: [www.mfa.gov.il/mfa/go.asp?MFAH00wk0].

Dates: Spring and summer. **Cost:** Vary. **Contact:** Israel Antiquities Authority, P.O. Box 586, Jerusalem 91004, Israel.

Jamaica

Jamaica Work Project. HFH Canada organizes teams of volunteers to help build homes in partnership with low-income families in Jamaica. Experience Jamaican culture, meet the families, and work with them to help eliminate poverty housing.

Dates: Jan and Feb. **Cost:** Approx. $3,000. Volunteers arrange own transportation and pay registration fee that covers accommodations and food. **Contact:** Carolyn Bouius, Volunteer Coordinator, Habitat for Humanity Canada, 40 Albert St., Waterloo, ON, N2L 3S2, Canada; 519-885-4565, fax 519-885-5225; hfhc@sentex.net, [www.habitat.ca].

Japan

Teaching English in Japan. Two-year program to maximize linguistic and cultural integration of participants who work as teachers' assistants. Placements twice yearly in Apr and Aug. Most positions are in junior high schools in urban and rural areas. Bachelor's degree and willingness to learn Japanese required.

Dates: Hiring for positions every Apr and Aug. Applications accepted year round. **Cost:** No application fees. **Contact:** Institute for Education in Japan, Earlham College, 801 National Rd. West, D-202, Richmond, IN 47374; 888-685-2726, fax 765-983-1553; [www.earlham.edu/~aet].

Latin America

Community Development Internship. This is a credit-bearing internship where volunteers live with a family in rural Mexico and Ecuador, or semi-urban Cuba, while working side by side with community members on grassroots development projects. Project assignments are available in the areas of agriculture, construction, reforestation, animal husbandry, microenterprise development, data collection, public health and other fields. These projects are designed, developed and implemented by the beneficiaries themselves. While project opportunities change as new ones come online and others are completed, every effort is made to match interns' interests with their assignment.

Dates: Year round. Two months advance needed for placement in Cuba. Six-week program (3 weeks in Cuba). **Cost:** Six credits: $3,400, no credit: $2,700, 3 credits: $2,900. **Contact:** Nicholas A. Robins, Director, Cuban Studies Institute, Center for Latin American Studies, Tulane Univ., Caroline Richardson Bldg., New Orleans, LA 70118-5698; 504-862-8629 or 504-862-8000 ext. 2601, fax 504-862-8678; nrobins@mailhost.tcs.tulane.edu, [http://cuba.tulane.edu].

Voluntarios Solidarios. Volunteers work with grassroots peace and justice organizations. Work ranges from research, translation, administration to community workshops, teaching street kids, documenting rights abuses. Must be conventionally fluent in Spanish. **Countries:** Mexico, Puerto Rico, Nicaragua, Panama, Colombia, Ecuador, Peru, Chile, Argentina, Paraguay, Bolivia.

Dates: Rolling. Apply at least 2 months before you wish to begin service. All host organizations require a minimum of 3 months or service or more. **Cost:** Travel, $60 application fee, and living expenses, which range from $75-$1,000 per month. **Contact:** Fellowship of Reconciliation, 995 Market St., #1414, San Francisco, CA 94103; 415-495-6334; forlatam@igc.org.

Volunteer Positions. In Costa Rica, Mexico, Guatemala, Ecuador, Argentina, Peru, Dominican Republic. Various positions in the fields of health care, education, tourism, ESL, business, law, marketing, administrative, environmental, and social work. Additional customized options available. Two weeks to 6 months. Inexpensive lodging in homestays or dorms. Some positions provide free room and board.

Dates: Year round. Flexible start dates. **Cost:** $350 placement and application fee. Travel insurance and pre-departure preparation included. Lodging costs depend on location. **Contact:** AmeriSpan Unlimited, P.O. Box 40007, Philadelphia, PA 19106; 800-879-6640, fax 215-751-1100; info@amerispan.com, [www.amerispan.com].

Mexico

Annunciation House. An experience of service, accompaniment, and solidarity with the poor in the border community of El Paso, TX and Juarez, Mexico. The primary focus is responding to the undocumented, immigrants, refugees, and the internally displaced within Mexico living in the colonias of Juarez. Commitments are made for 1 year.
Dates: Jan 20, Apr 20, Aug 15, Jun 4, Nov 1.
Cost: None. **Contact:** Ruben Garcia, Annunciation House, 815 Myrtle, El Paso, TX 79901.

Bi-Cultural Programs IMAC. Spanish in Guadalajara is more than a classroom. Group sizes of 1 to 5. Guadalajara offers the conveniences of a modern city. We are a few hours drive to Puerto Vallarta. Homestays with only 1 student per family. Hotel discounts available. Free Internet and email access. Excursions and extracurricular activities.
Dates: Year round. Group classes start every Monday. Individual tutoring may begin any day. Christmas vacation Dec 18-Jan 1, 2000; Easter vacation Apr 17-30, 2000. **Cost:** Contact organizations for details. **Contact:** Leticia Orozco, Instituto Mèxico Americano de Cultura, Donata Guerra 180, Guadalajara, Jalisco, 44100 Mèxico; 011-52-3-613-1080, fax 011-52-3-613-4621; spanish-imac@imac-ac.edu.mx, [www.spanish-school.com.mx].

Cáritas. Different programs designed to decrease poor people's needs, such as: education, food, clothing, medical services, etc.
Dates: Contact organization for details. **Cost:** Contact organization for details. **Contact:** Sandra Elizondo, Cáritas de Monterrey A.C., Fco. Garza Sada #2810 Pte. Col Deportivo Obispado, Monterrey, Nuevo Leon, Mexico; 011-52-8-333-0990 or 011-52-8-346-3213 or 3331225, ext 229 and 288; bco_voluntarios@hotmail.com.

Development, Indigenous People, and Ecology. The center, located in Oaxaca in southern Mexico, offers tailor-made programs focusing on environment and indigenous people in Oaxaca, Mexico. We provide a mix of langauge training, academic classes by experts and local activists, and field trips where students become involved in our research, environmental and cultural activities.
Dates: Flexible. **Cost:** Generally around $400 per week, including room and board, local transportation, and all program activities.
Contact: Gustavo Esteva/Oliver Froehling, Centro Intercultural de Encuentros y Diálogos, m. Bravo 210-altos, Mexico; 011-52-951-4-6490; insopcion@infosel.net.mx, [http:spersaoaxaca.com.mx/clientes/icdm/cied/cied.htm].

Intensive Spanish in Yucatan. Centro de Idiomas del Sureste, A.C. (CIS), founded in 1974, offers 3-5 hours per day of intensive conversational Spanish classes with native-speaking, university-trained professors. Maximum 6 students per group, average 3. Program includes beginner courses to very advanced with related field trips and recommended optional homestay. Also special classes in business, legal, medical vocabulary, or Mayan studies.
Dates: Year round. Starts any Monday, except last 2 weeks in Dec. **Cost:** Tuition (3 hours per day program: $350 first 2 weeks, $125 each additional week); tuition 5 hours per day programs $550 first 2 weeks, $225 each additional week. **Contact:** Chloe C. Pacheco, Director, Centro de Idiomas del Sureste, A.C., Calle 14 #106 X25, col. Mexico, CP 97128, Mérida, Yucatán, Mexico; 011-52-99-26-11-55 or 011-52-99-26-94-94, 20-28-10, fax 011-52-99-26-00-20; cis@sureste.com.

Mar de Jade Ocean-Front Resort. Tropical ocean-front retreat center in a small fishing village on a beautiful half-mile beach north of Puerto Vallarta. Surrounded by lush jungle with the warm, clear sea at our door, enjoy swimming, hiking, horseback riding, massage, and meditation. Study Spanish in small groups. Gain insight into local culture by optional volunteer work in community projects, such as rural community clinic, our local library, or a model home garden. Mar de Jade also has meeting facilities and provides a serene and intimate setting for group events.
Dates: Year round. **Cost:** Twenty-one day volunteer/Spanish program May-Nov 15 $1,000 (student discount available); Nov 15-Apr $1,080. Includes room and board in a shared occupancy room and 15 hours per week of volunteer work. Vacation: May-Nov 15 room and board $50 per night; Nov 16-Apr $55 per night. Spanish $80 per week with minimum 1 week (6 nights) stay. **Contact:** In Mexico: Tel./

fax 011-52-322-2-3524; info@mardejade.com, [www.mardejade.com]. U.S. mailing address: 9051 Siempre Viva Rd., Suite 78-344, San Diego, CA 92173-3628.

Piña Palmera. A rural communitary rehabilitation center for disabled and malnourished people on the coast of the state of Oaxaca works with 300 patients in surrounding villages. Some our programs are: early stimulation for children, community based rehabilitation, sign language classes.
Dates: Volunteer year round if you speak Spanish and stay for a minimum of 6 months. **Cost:** Offers bed and food. **Contact:** Anna Johansson, C.A.I. Piña Palmera, Apdo. Postal 109, 70900 Pochutla, Oaxaca, Mexico; pinapalmera@laneta.apc.org.

QUEST. QUEST offers yearlong volunteer opportunities to women and summer opportunities to women and men. Volunteers share simple living in Christian community while daily serving the poor through various agencies and schools.
Dates: Year-long: late Aug-late Aug; summer: end of Jun-early Aug. **Cost:** Volunteers must pay own costs and transportation to site. **Contact:** Erin Hartshorn, QUEST, 3706 Rhode Island Ave., Mt. Rainier, MO 20712; 301-277-2514, fax 301-277-8656; questrjm@erols.com.

SIPAZ - Int'l. Service for Peace. The international volunteer team in Chiapas maintains communication with all actors in the conflict, serves as an objective source of information, provides an international observer presence, strengthens local peacebuilding capabilities through workshops and courses.
Dates: Ongoing. **Cost:** Volunteer. **Contact:** Robert Poen, Int'l. Office Coordinator, SIPAZ - Int'l. Service for Peace, P.O. Box 2415, Santa Cruz, CA 95063; 831-425-1257; sipaz@igc.org.

Stella Maris School of Nursing. We are a small school of nursing in need of volunteers serving as nurse instructors and clinical supervisors, a librarian, secretaries, maintenance men, or "jack-of-all-trades." Zacapu has a large market with everything you need. There are many beautiful places nearby to visit on weekends.
Dates: Six-month commitment required. School year is from late Aug-early Jul. **Cost:** Room and board, and small stipend provided. **Contact:** Sister Theresa Avila, Apdo. 28, Zacapu, Michoacan, 58670 Mexico; Tel./fax 011-52-436-31300.

Nepal

Volunteer Nepal Himalaya. Participants live near the base of Mt. Everest with a Sherpa family and teach English in a Sherpa school for 3 months. The program includes teaching training, a 10-day language and cultural orientation, and a trek to Everst base camp. Learn about the culture and customs of the Sherpa people, and give back to their community.
Dates: Fall, summer, and spring programs. **Cost:** $900 per month for land costs. **Contact:** Scott Dimetrosky, Himalayan Explorers Club, P.O. Box 3665, Boulder, CO 80307; 888-420-8822, fax 303-998-1007; info@hec.org, [www.hec.org].

Volunteer Service Work. This program is designed to meet the needs of participants who desire more than typical tourist experience. It provides volunteer service opportunities for people who are genuinely interested in learning about a new and different community and culture while contributing their time and skills to benefit worthwhile community service throughout Nepal. By partaking in the program, it is hoped that participants will experience personal growth as well as open communication channels between different countries and cultures.
Dates: Feb, Apr, Aug, and Oct. Other dates can be arranged. **Cost:** $650 includes pre-service training, language instruction, homestay, trekking, rafting, jungle safari, volunteering, food and accommodations, etc. **Contact:** Rajesh Shrestha, Director, Cultural Destination Nepal, GPO Box 11535, Kathmandu, Nepal; 011-977-1-426996, fax 011-977-1-428925 or 011-977-1-416417; cdnnepal@wlink.com.np.

New Zealand

International Volunteering Network. Involvement Volunteers Assn., Inc. has volunteer placements in this country, all months of the year. Please see Worldwide for their main entry.
Dates: Year round. **Cost:** The volunteer meets all travel costs (including insurance). Most hosts provide accommodations and food for free, but some placements in projects or countries with limited resources can cost up to $55 per week for food. **Contact:** Involvement Volunteers Assn., Inc., P.O. Box 218, Port Melbourne, Victoria 3207, Australia; 011-61-3-9646-9392, fax 011-61-3-9646-5504; ivimel@iaccess.com.au, [www.volunteering.org.au].

WHY VOLUNTEER?

OVERSEAS VOLUNTEERS RECEIVE AS MUCH AS THEY GIVE

By Peter Hodge

The fall of the Berlin Wall and the end of the Cold War led to talk of a "new world order" in which nations would work toward mutual prosperity, yet never has the chasm separating the First World from the Third appeared so great. Never has the environment been so imperiled.

Because of this, volunteers continue to travel the world, working with government or nongovernment agencies to fill gaps and build bridges for the betterment of humankind. Each year they apply in the thousands to hundreds of agencies which organize volunteer placements.

Volunteering is often expensive and should never be undertaken lightly. These are some of the questions that must be answered: Am I comfortable with the mission of the agency organizing my position? Will I tolerate the living conditions? Can I cope with the poverty and culture shock? Will I find satisfaction in my work? What will be the financial impact of my decision? Will I miss my lifestyle too much?

Why Do It?

The motivating factors that lead people to become volunteers vary from person to person and may alter dramatically as volunteers move from perception to reality. An individual's reasons for volunteering—whether selfish, altruistic, or a combination of both—aren't necessarily right or wrong, provided that they are well considered.

Some volunteer to escape what they perceive to be the rat race that defines their lives: the endless cycle of bills, the constant drone of city traffic, and the pressure to fit accepted social molds can leave us feeling numb. The perception of a simpler, more earthy lifestyle, possibly in a rural location abroad, is attractive. Indeed, liberated from the watchful eyes of their home community, many volunteers feel wonderfully alive.

Others are attracted by the challenges of a volunteer position. Leaving home for up to two years to live in a foreign culture in what may be difficult conditions is a huge and frightening step for most. The potential for personal development can be seen as reason enough to pursue a position. Indeed, most volunteers return home more confident people, having achieved things they'd never previously imagined possible.

Today's typical volunteer is not filled with the same missionary zeal as volunteers of old. We're no longer braving obstacles to "save" the natives. Nowadays, it's more often the positive impact a volunteer has on the daily lives of the local people that counts.

Many volunteers have a travel bug. By merely passing through a culture, travelers realize that their experiences lack something that actually living in the culture could remedy. The structured nature of a volunteer position can offer security, the promise of company, and the satisfaction of a desire to explore an interest or profession. Opportunities to roam come to most volunteers, allowing them to fulfill their desire both to travel and to stay in one place.

Volunteers may have other interests which they hope to pursue and develop in the course of their stint. Musicians, singers, dancers, writers, and photographers, for example, may all expect to find opportunities to express and improve on their talents.

At least as important as the labor and professional expertise which volunteers donate to the host nation are the cultural exchanges that take place between volunteers and locals. The heightened level of understanding impacts both cultures. Volunteers receive as much as they give.

Search for an organization that suits your needs, then go for it!

Short Term or Long Term?

With some overlap, volunteer placement organizations can be separated into those that facilitate long-term positions and those that facilitate short-term positions.

Short-term positions last from several weeks to several months. Organizations that sponsor such placements are many in number and usually small in size. Often independent of government funding, they rely on the fees paid by volunteers to facilitate an amazing diversity of activities, filling niches beyond the scope of larger agencies. Many such organizations welcome volunteers with a broad range of experiences and place few bars in the way of age or qualifications. Earthwatch, Habitat for Humanity, and Global Volunteers are just some of the organizations that arrange short-term positions.

Long-term positions require volunteers to commit for at least a full year. They tend to be sponsored by larger agencies that often receive some form of government funding. Volunteers usually receive a stipend and in many cases are not required to pay their own airfare. However, greater demands are usually made on volunteers in terms of their qualifications and accomplishments than those made on short-term volunteers.

Pacific

Hawaii's Kalani Oceanside Eco-Resort. Kalani Educational Eco-Resort, the only coastal lodging facility within Hawaii's largest conservation area, offers traditional culture, healthful cuisine, wellness programs, and extraordinary natural beauty: thermal springs, a naturist dolphin beach, snorkel pools, kayaking, waterfalls, crater lake, and spectacular Volcanoes National Park. Ongoing offerings in yoga, dance, hula, mythology, and massage. Or participate in an annual week-long event: men's/women's/couples conferences, dance/music/hula festivals, yoga/meditation/transformation retreats. Applications are also being accepted for our international Volunteer Scholar program.
Dates: Year round. **Cost:** Lodging $45-$120 per day. Camping $20-$30. $570-$1,240 per week for most programs, including meals and lodging choice. **Contact:** Richard Koob, Director, Kalani Educational Eco-Resort, RR2, Box 4500, Pahoa-Beach Rd., HI 96778-9724; 800-900-6886 or 808-965-7828 (call for fax info); kalani@kalani.com, [www.kalani.com].

Romania

Child Development Program. Romanian Children's Relief sponsors experienced, degreed professionals in child development (OT, Ed, MSW, etc.) fields to go to Romania and train caregivers in pediatric hospitals and orphanages. Programs are in Bucharest and Bistrita, Romania.
Dates: Vary. Minimum 2-year commitment. **Cost:** RCR pays for housing, living stipend, transportation, and health insurance. **Contact:** Eileen McHenry, Romanian Children's Relief, P.O. Box 107, Southboro, MA 01772; 508-303-6299; emmc2@aol.com.

Russia and the NIS

Citizens Democracy Corps. CDC is a nonprofit organization that matches seasoned business volunteers with small and medium sized businesses in Eastern Europe and Russia to provide business and management knowledge and develop market economies.
Dates: Two to 6-week assignments year round. **Cost:** Meals, incidental expenses, and insurance not included. **Contact:** Cameron Bushnell, Citizens Democracy Corps., 1400 I St., NW, Suite 1125, Washington, DC 20005; 800-394-1945, fax 202-872-0923; [www.cdc.org].

Russian Studies Program. Unpaid internships in journalism, government, business. Working knowledge of Russian language recommended but not required.
Dates: Early Sep-mid-Dec, early Jan-mid-May, mid-May-mid-Aug. **Cost:** $4,975 per semester, $3,450 summer. **Contact:** Dr. Patrick Lecaque, CIEA/Truman State Univ., Kirksville, MO 63501; plecaque@truman.edu.

Spain

Arid Land Recovery Trust. Aims to find and spread methods that will improve the lives and environments of people in poverty in desertified areas. It aims to seek, demonstrate, and promote more sustainable lifestyles and to raise concern about these matters.
Dates: Year round. **Cost:** £42-£90 per week depending upon season, full or part time. **Contact:** Mary Eiloart, Sunseed Trust; 011-44-1480-411784; sunseed@clara.net, [www.sunseed.clara.net].

Sweden

Camphill. Voluntary work with mentally handicapped adults.
Dates: Minimum stay of 6 months. **Cost:** Travel to Sweden. **Contact:** Per Iversen, Staffansgarden, Box 66, S-82060 Delsbo, Sweden; fax 011-46-653-10968.

Taiwan

Overseas Service Corps YMCA (OSCY). Place BAs to PhDs in ESL teaching positions in community-based YMCAs in Taiwan. No Chinese language necessary. Preference given to applicants with teaching experience, either general or ESL, or degree in teaching. This conversational English program provides an opportunity for cultural exchange. Must reside in North America and be a citizen of an English-speaking country. Twenty to 30 openings.
Dates: Call anytime for a brochure and application. Placement end Sep through following Sep, 1-year commitment. **Cost:** $50 application fee. Benefits include: Housing, health insurance, return airfare, paid vacation, bonus, orientation, sponsorship for visa, and monthly stipend. **Contact:** Jann Sterling, Program Assistant, International Group, YMCA of the USA, 101 N. Wacker Dr., Chicago, IL 60606; 800-872-9622 ext. 167, fax 312-977-0884; sterling@ymcausa.org, [www.ymca.net].

United Kingdom and Ireland

Archaeological Excavation. Volunteer and study programs in archaeological excavation techniques based on early medieval settlement in mid-Wales. No previous experience necessary, but reasonable fitness required. Must be at least 16 years old.
Dates: Inquire. 7-day minimum, Jul-Aug. **Cost:** Volunteer, food, and campsite £45 weekly. Tuition, food, and campsite £150. **Contact:** Dr. C.J. Arnold, Gwarffynnon, Bethania, Llanon, Ceredigion SY23 5NJ, U.K.; Tel./fax 011-44-1-970-272562.

Ffestiniog Railway (Wales). Get involved, meet new friends, and learn new skills helping to restore and operate the world's oldest independent railway. Areas include track work, painting, building, catering and retail, locomotive cleaning.
Dates: Year round, trains run Mar-Oct. **Cost:** £3.50 per night in Railway hostel (self-catering). **Contact:** Robert Shrives; 011-44-1766-771280, fax 011-44-1766-770260; [www.festrail.co.uk].

Full-Time Volunteer. Full-time volunteers work with homeless adults in our projects in Cork, Dundalk, Dublin, and Galway. Your contribution includes companionship with residents and arranging recreational activities with residents. Must be 18-35 years of age and committed to volunteering for a minimum period of 3 months any time.
Dates: Year round. **Cost:** No placement fee. Free accommodations, free meals, weekly pocket money, allowance provided. Airfare not included. **Contact:** Anne O'Donovan, Recruitment Coordinator, Simon Community of Ireland, 28/30 Exchequer St., Dublin 2, Ireland; 011-353-1-6711606, fax 011-353-1-6711098; simonnat@indigo.ie, [http://indigo.ie/~simonnat].

Holiday Helpers Needed. Volunteers needed at seaside holiday and respite center for physically disabled people. Help staff provide personal care and assist with outings and entertainment. Lots of fun and hard work. Friendly atmosphere. No experience necessary. Free board and accommodations.
Dates: One-2 weeks. From Jan 20. **Cost:** Travel to Lulworth Court. **Contact:** Mrs. Pat McCallion, Lulworth Court, 25 Chalkwell Esplanade, Westcliff on Sea, Essex, SS0 8JQ, U.K.; 011-44-1702-431725, fax 011-44-1702-433165.

Lakeside Activity Center. Share is a charity providing an activity center with outdoor and arts activities promoting integration between able-bodied people and persons with special needs. Working with all ages. Volunteer placements last 3-12 months. Full board accommodations and a payment of £40 per week. Volunteers work in all aspects of Share's program from caring for disabled visitors, housekeeping, maintenance and arts and outdoor programs.
Dates: Year round. **Cost:** Contact organization for details. **Contact:** Dawn Latimer, Share Holiday Village, Smiths Strand, Lisnaskea BT92 0EQ, Ireland; 011-353-13657-22122, fax 011-353-13657-21893; share@dnet.co.uk, [www.sharevillage.org].

The National Trust for Scotland Thistle Camps. Thistle Camps are practical outdoor conservation working holidays which take place on trust properties at beautiful and remote locations all over Scotland. Anyone who is reasonably fit and over 16 years can join.
Dates: Mar-Oct. **Cost:** £35-£100 for 1 to 3 weeks. All food, training, travel, and accommodations is provided. **Contact:** Julia Downes, NTS, 5 Charlotte Sq., Edinburgh EH2 4DU, Scotland; 011-44-131-243-9470, fax 011-44-131-243-9444; mhume@nts.org.uk.

School Exclusion Project. For pupils aged 8-12 who are presenting unacceptable behavior and disrupting the class. To develop the emotional intelligence of these pupils, to improve their social and intellectual skills.
Dates: Sep 1999-July 2000. **Contact:** Vince Southcott, Atlow Mill Centre, Hognaston, Nr. Ashbourne, Derbyshire DE6 1PX, U.K.; 011-44-1-335-370494, fax 011-44-1-335-370279; centre@atlowmill.ndo.co.uk.

Short-Term Volunteer Program. In 1975, The Center for Alternative Technology opened with a vision to set out to develop and prove, by a positive living example, new technologies which would provide practical solutions to the problems that worry the world's ecologists. CAT acts as a bridge between those seeking to explore a more ecological way of living and the store of practical, hands-on experience gained by working with sustainable technologies over 2 decades.
Dates: Specified weeks between Mar and Sep. **Cost:** £5/£4 per weekday and £6/£5 per weekend day. **Contact:** Rick Dance, Centre for Alternative Technology, Machynlleth, Powsy SY20 9AZ, Wales, U.K.; 011-44-1654-702400, fax 011-44-1654-702782.

Time for God. TFG provides volunteer opportunities for 9-12 months for young adults aged 18-25. Opportunities include youth work in churches, recreational work with homeless, mentally ill, assisting people with learning difficulties. TFG provides training and a spiritual development program.
Dates: Begins Sep or Jan for 9-12 months. **Cost:** £1,900 includes board, lodging and stipend. **Contact:** Tracy Phillips, TFG, Chester House, Pages Ln., London N10 1PR, U.K.; 011-44-181-883-1504; tracytfg@cs.com.

Worcestershire Lifestyle. Full-time volunteer workers are required to act as the arms and legs of people with physical disabilities who wish to live independently in their own home. Duties include personal care, household tasks, and sharing leisure interests. Free accommodations are provided in Worcestershire or Herefordshire and £55 per week.
Dates: Vacancies are on-going. **Cost:** Contact organization for details. **Contact:** Worcestershire Lifestyles, Woodside Lodge, Lark Hill Rd., Worcester WR5 2EF, U.K.; 011-44-1905-350686, fax 011-44-1905 350684.

Work on Organic Farm in Scotland. Daily help with dairy goats, friendly sheep, and in organic kitchen garden in stress-free, beautiful country-side near Sea (Dornoch Firth). Home-produced food (vegetarian), comfortable caravan, pocket money. Can take paying guests.
Dates: Any time throughout summer. **Cost:** Getting here (North of Inverness). **Contact:** Pam Shaw, The Rhanich, Edderton, Tain Rossshire, Scotland, 1V19 1LG; 011-44-1862-821-265.

United States

Masters of International and Intercultural Management. The School for International Training Masters of International and Intercultural Management offers concentrations in sustainable development, international education, and training and human resource development in 1 academic year program. This degree is designed for individuals wishing to make a career change or enter the field. A practical training component enables "on-the-job" training and an opportunity to work internationally.
Dates: Call for details. **Cost:** Call for details. **Contact:** Admissions, School for International Learning, P.O. Box 676, Kipling Rd., Brattleboro, VT 05302; 800-336-1616, 802-257-7751, fax 802-258-3500; info@sit.edu, [www.sit.edu].

Worldwide

BTCV-Conservation Holidays. Program of practical conservation holidays at locations around the U.K. and worldwide. No experience necessary, just energy and enthusiasm. You could be drystone walling in the English Lake District or trail building in Costa Rica.
Dates: Year round. **Cost:** From £45-£500 includes food and accommodations. **Contact:** BTCV, 36 St. Mary's St., Wallingford, Oxfordshire OX10 0EU, U.K.; 011-44-1491-839766, fax 011-44-1491-839646; information@btcv.org.uk, [www.btcv.org].

Catholic Network of Volunteer Service. Publishes *Response,* an annual directory of volunteer opportunities with 180 listings of international and domestic faith-based volunteer/lay missioner, full-time (long- and short-term) service programs.
Dates: Vary. Call or write for directory of programs. **Cost:** Vary. **Contact:** Catholic Network of Volunteer Service, 4121 Harewood Rd., NE, Washington, DC 20017; 800-543-5046, 202-529-1100, fax 202-526-1094; volunteer@cnvs.org, [www.cnvs.org].

Coordinating Voluntary Service Organizations. Coordinates 140 voluntary service organizations in 90 countries. Publications (lists of addresses, advices, guidebooks, studies) on voluntary service. We have an information center. Created in 1948 by UNESCO.
Dates: Year round (workcamps and long-term voluntary service). **Contact:** Coordinating Committee for International Voluntary Service (CCIVS), UNESCO House, 1 rue Miollis, 75732 Paris, Cedex 15, France; 011-33-1-45-68-27-31; ccivs@zcc.net.

Cross-Cultural Solutions. Experience the vibrant, colorful culture of India, Ghana, or Peru and make a difference at the same time. This unique short-term volunteer program enables volunteers to work with local social service organizations in fields as diverse as health care, education, skills training, and arts/recreation. Volunteers receive continual professional support from our U.S. and India-based staff. No skills or experience required—only a desire to help and learn.
Dates: Contact organization for details. **Cost:** $1,850 covers in-country transportation, accommodations, board, and support. International airfare, insurance, and visa not included. Program fee is tax deductible. **Contact:** Cross-Cultural Solutions, 47 Potter Ave., New Rochelle, NY 10801; 800-380-4777 or 914-632-

0022, fax 914-632-8494; info@crossculturalsolutions.org, [www.crossculturalsolutions.org].

Earthwatch Institute. Unique opportunities to work with leading scientists on 1- to 3-week field research projects worldwide. Earthwatch sponsors 160 expeditions in over 30 U.S. states and in 60 countries. Project disciplines include archaeology, wildlife management, ecology, ornithology and marine mammalogy. No special skills needed—all training is done in the field.

Dates: Year round. **Cost:** Tax deductible contributions ranging from $695-$3,995 support the research and cover food and lodging expenses. Airfare not included. **Contact:** Earthwatch, 680 Mt. Auburn St., P.O. Box 9104-MA, Watertown, MA 02472; 800-776-0188, 617-926.8200; info@earthwatch.org, [www.earthwatch.org].

Franciscan Mission Service. FMS prepares and sends Catholic women and men for extended assignments among oppressed and poor peoples of Africa, Asia, and Latin America. Volunteers are needed to work in the areas of health care, social service, education, agriculture and community organizing. Allow a different culture to expand your worldview.

Dates: Jan-Mar or Sep-Nov, 2000; 3-month preparation. **Contact:** Joanne Blaney, Co-director, Franciscan Mission Service, P.O. Box 29034, Washington, DC 20017; 202-832-1762, fax 202-832-1778; fms5@juno.com.

Global Service Corps. Service-learning programs in Costa Rica, Kenya, or Thailand. Live with a village family while assisting grassroots organizations on community service and development projects. Project areas: rainforest conservation, sustainable agriculture, AIDS/HIV awareness, clinical health care, women's groups, classroom teaching. Experience the challenges of developing countries from the inside out. Includes orientation, training, excursions.

Dates: Year round. Contact GSC office or check the web site for specific starting dates. **Cost:** $1,695-$1,795 for 2-4 week project trips; $495 per month for 2-6 month long-term extensions. Includes extensive pre-departure preparation and in-country expenses (hotel and homestay room and board, orientation, training, project expenses, transportation, excursions). Airfare not included, discount rates available. **Contact:** Global Service Corps., 300

Broadway, #28, San Francisco, CA 94133; 415-788-3666 ext. 128, fax 415-788-7324; gsc@igc.apc.org, [www.globalservicecorps.org].

Global Volunteers. The nation's premier short-term service programs for people of all ages and backgrounds. Assist mutual international understanding through ongoing development projects throughout Africa, Asia, the Caribbean, Europe, the Pacific, North and South America. Programs of 1, 2, and 3 weeks range from natural resource preservation, light construction, and painting to teaching English, assisting with health care, and nurturing at-risk children. No special skills or foreign languages are required. Ask about the Millennium Service Project.

Dates: Over 150 teams year round. **Cost:** Tax-deductible program fees range from $450 to $2,395. Airfare not included. **Contact:** Global Volunteers, 375 E. Little Canada Rd., St. Paul, MN 55117; 800-487-1074, fax 651-407-5163; email@globalvolunteers.org, [www.globalvolunteers.org].

IICD. The Institute for International Cooperation and Development (IICD) is a nonprofit organization dedicated to global education and assistance to developing countries. IICD sends teams of volunteers to work on educational, environmental, community health, and agricultural projects in Africa, Latin America, and India. Programs vary in length from 6-18 months.

Dates: Starting dates: Aug 1, Sep 1, Jan 5, Feb 1. **Cost:** From $3,800-$5,500. Financial aid is available. **Contact:** IICD, Promotion Director, P.O. Box 520, Williamstown, MA 01267; 413-458-9828; IICDINFO@berkshire.net, [www.iicd-volunteer.org].

International Volunteer Projects. Council offers short-term international volunteer projects in 30 plus countries, and the Teach in China program, giving semester or academic year opportunities to teach English in Chinese universities or high schools.

Dates: Year round. **Cost:** From $300-$1,200 and up. **Contact:** Council Exchanges, 205 E. 42nd St., New York, NY 10017-5706; 888-COUNCIL; [www.councilexchanges.org].

International Volunteer Projects. Concordia offers young people between the ages of 18-30 the opportunity to do 2-3 weeks voluntary work abroad. Projects include environment, renovation, manual or social work.

Dates: Jun-Sep. Applications taken from Apr onward. Send SASE for more information. **Cost:** Registration fee £75 (includes board and accommodations) plus travel costs. **Contact:** Gwyn Lewis, Concordia, 20-22 Heversham House, Boundary Rd. Hove, East Sussex BN3 4ET, U.K.; 011-44-1273-422218.

International Volunteering Network. Involvement Volunteers Association, Inc. (IVI) arranges group or individual placements for applicants of all ages of 2-4 weeks to suit the requirements, abilities and experiences of volunteers in programs which combine travel with volunteering. Countries include: Armenia, Australia, Bangladesh, Belgium, Cambodia, China, Denmark, Ecuador, England, Fiji, Finland, Germany, Ghana, Greece, India, Italy, Japan, Kenya, Korea, Lebanon, Macau, Mexico, Mongolia, Nepal, New Zealand, Papua New Guinea, Philippines, Poland, Russia, Sabah (Malaysia), Samoa, South Africa, Spain, Thailand, Turkey, Ukraine, and Vietnam. Placements can be extended for 12 months and relate to sustainable environmental conservation or community-based social service. Individual placements may be on farms, in historic gardens, animal reserves, national parks, zoological parks, bird observatories, rescue or research centers, with schools or special homes. Age is no barrier.

Dates: Year round. **Cost:** Approx. $350 for program, plus $40 per placement. The volunteer meets all travel costs (including insurance). Most hosts provide accommodations and food for free, but some placements in projects or countries with limited resources can cost up to $55 per week for food. **Contact:** Involvement Volunteers Assn., Inc., P.O. Box 218, Port Melbourne, Victoria 3207, Australia; 011-61-3-9646-9392, fax 011-61-3-9646-5504; ivimel@iaccess.com.au, [www.volunteering.org.au].

Internships International. Quality, nonpaying internships in London, Paris, Dublin, Cologne, France, Shanghai, Santiago, Budapest, Melbourne, Bangkok, Hanoi, Ho Chi Minh City, and Glasgow. Internships in all fields, from 8 weeks to 6 months. Open to college graduates and seniors requiring an internship to graduate.

Dates: Based on individual's needs. **Cost:** $700 program fee for all cities except London ($800) and Dublin ($1,000). **Contact:** Judy Tilson, Director, Internships International, 1612 Oberlin Rd., Raleigh, NC 27608; 919-832-1575, fax 919-834-7170; intintl@aol.com, [http://rtpnet.org/~intintl].

Jewish Volunteer Corps. The Jewish Volunteer Corps sends skilled Jewish men and women to provide technical assistance in the fields of health, agriculture, business, and education to the developing world. JVC volunteers work with local grassroots partner organizations throughout Latin America, Asia, and Africa from 1 to 9 months.

Dates: Year round, minimum 1 month. **Cost:** JVC covers airfare, NGO's help with housing. **Contact:** American Jewish World Service, 989 Avenue of the Americas, 10th Fl., New York, NY 10018; 212-736-2597, fax 212-736-3463; jvcvol@jws.org.

Natural History and Research Trips. Since 1972, specialists in natural history expeditions to prime wildlife habitats. Noninvasive/noncaptive wildlife research and habitat restoration projects: dolphins, humpback and blue whales, manatees, seabirds, coral reefs, primates. No prior experience necessary. Nonprofit 501.C.3 organization.

Dates: Year round. Programs range from 5-14 days; call for current schedule. **Cost:** From $995. **Contact:** Oceanic Society Expeditions, Ft. Mason Ctr., Bldg. E, Rm. 230, San Francisco, CA 94123-1394; 800-326-7491 or 415-441-1106, fax 415-474-3395; [www.oceanic-society.org].

Peace Corps Opportunities. Since 1961, more than 150,000 Americans have joined the Peace Corps. Assignments are 27 months long. Volunteers must be U.S. citizens at least 18 years old and in good health. Peace Corps has volunteer programs in education, business, agriculture, the environment, and health.

Dates: Apply 9 to 12 months prior to availability. **Cost:** Volunteers receive transportation to and from assignment, a stipend, complete health care, and $5,400 after 27 months of service. **Contact:** Peace Corps, 1111 20th St., NW, Washington, DC 20526; 800-424-8580 (mention code 824); [www.peacecorps.gov].

Professional Placement Program. CMMB recruits licensed healthcare volunteers from the U.S. and Canada, for service around the world. We have both long and short term placements in Africa, Asia, Latin America, the Caribbean, and Eastern Europe. Our greatest need right now is for primary care physicians willing to serve in developing countries.

Dates: Year round. **Cost:** All volunteers receive room and board and most receive a stipend. CMMB offers in-kind support to volunteers at their site of service. Medicines and health care supplies are hand carried or sent to them. CMMB currently provides insurance for emergency evacuation. With long-term volunteers, assistance is also given for traveling, licensing, and visas. **Contact:** Rosemary DeCostanzo, Catholic Medical Mission Board, 10 W. 17th St., New York, NY 10011; 800-678-5659, fax 212-242-0930; rdeconstanzo@cmmb.org.

Service Learning Programs. The International Partnership for Service-Learning, founded in 1982, is an incorporated not-for-profit organization serving colleges, universities, service agencies, and related organizations around the world by fostering programs that link community service and academic study. Countries include: Czech Republic, Ecuador, England, France, Jamaica, Israel, India, Mexico, Philippines, and Scotland. Students gain hands-on experience in an international community service agency. We also offer a Master's degree in International Service.

Dates: Summer, semester, year, or intersession. **Cost:** Vary. **Contact:** Coordinator of Student Programs, The International Partnership for Service-Learning, 815 2nd Ave., Suite 315, New York, NY 10017; 212-986-0989, fax 212-986-5039; pslny@aol.com, [www.studyabroad.com].

Teaching and Projects Abroad. With Teaching and Projects Abroad you can enjoy adventurous foreign travel with a chance to do a worthwhile job. You can teach conversational English or gain experience in medicine, veterinary medicine, conservation, journalism, or business.

Dates: Programs available throughout the year. **Cost:** From $1,280, includes all accommodations, food, placement insurance, and local support. **Contact:** Teaching and Projects Abroad, Gerrard House, Rustington, W. Sussex BN16 1AW, U.K.; 011-44-1903-859911, fax 011-44-1903-785779; info@teaching-abroad.co.uk.

Up With People Worldsmart™. The Worldsmart™ program accelerates education and career opportunities through the unique combination of international travel, stage-based musical performance, and community service. Every year, 700 university-aged students from a variety of countries spend 11 months traveling throughout and experiencing the world.

Dates: Programs begin in Jan and Jul. **Cost:** $13,700 includes all travel, lodging, food, and student program expenses within the 11-month program. **Contact:** Admissions Department, Up With People, 1 International Ct., Broomfield, CO 80021; 800- 596-7353 or 303-438-7373, fax 303-438-7301; admissions@upwithpeople.org, [www.upwithpeople.org].

Volunteers for Peace. Short-term voluntary service opportunities around the world. Live and work with volunteers from several countries doing community service work.

Dates: Most programs are May-Sep. **Cost:** $195 per program. **Contact:** VFP, 1034 Tiffany Rd., Belmont, VT 05730; 802-259-2759, fax 802-259-2922; vfp@vfp.org, [www.vfp.org].

WorldTeach. WorldTeach is a nonprofit, nongovernmental organization which provides opportunities for individuals to make a meaningful contribution to international education by living and working as volunteer teachers in developing countries.

Dates: Year round. **Cost:** $4,800-$5,950. Includes international airfare, health insurance, extensive training, and in-country support. **Contact:** WorldTeach, Harvard Institute for International Development, 14 Story St., Cambridge, MA 02138; 800-4-TEACH-0 or 617-495-5527, fax 617-495-1599; info@worldteach.org, [www.worldteach.org].

Worldwide Volunteers and Services. WWVS offers volunteers a global listing of supervised placements in their areas of interest; multicultural experiences emphasized. Undergraduate credit an option. Free application, free consultation to colleges to develop volunteer for credit program.

Dates: Year round. **Cost:** Varies. **Contact:** Director, WWVS, P.O. Box 3242, West End, NJ 07740; 732-571-3215; worldvol@aol.com.

Youth International. An experiential education program focusing on international travel and intercultural exchange, adventure, community service, and homestays. Teams of 12, aged 18-25, travel together for 1 semester to Southeast Asia and India/Nepal, or East Africa and the Middle East. Assist refugees, hike the Himalayas, live with and help an African tribe, scuba dive, and much more.

Dates: Sep 7-Dec 18, 1999 (15 weeks); Jan 24-May 30 (18 weeks) and early Sep-mid-Dec (15 weeks), 2000. **Cost:** 1999: $6,500 (Asia), $7,000 (Africa/Middle East). 2000: $6,500 (Asia, 15 weeks), $7,500 (18 weeks); $7,000 (Africa/Middle East, 15 weeks), $8,000 (18 weeks). **Contact:** Brad Gillings, Youth International, 1121 Downing St., #2, Denver, CO 80218; 303-839-5877, fax 303-839-5887; youth.international@bigfoot.com, [www.youthinternational.org].

STUDY ABROAD

Study abroad today is largely a buyer's bazaar–at least for students who have the financial and academic support of their parents and college and are thus free to shop widely and wisely for the program which best corresponds to their individual interests and needs. But ending up in the right program demands informed planning.

Since no two programs or participants are precisely the same, the challenge is to learn enough about the ways in which programs differ from each other to develop a short list of programs which best match individual learning styles, resources, motivations, and interests. This is best done with the assistance of campus guidance and the resources listed in this section.

Bill Hoffa, Ph.D., Education Abroad Editor

*T*EN

STUDY ABROAD
THE BEST RESOURCES

Whether you're a student or an adviser looking for the right international study program or someone who wants to combine the least expense abroad with the most rewards, you'll find the information you need in the resources described below. Asterisks indicate resources of broadest interest. Resources covering more than one country or region are listed under "Worldwide." Addresses of the publishers are listed at the end of the chapter.

Key Publishers and Organizations

Africa-American Institute, 380 Lexington Ave., New York, NY 10168; 212-949-5666, fax 212-682-6174; aainy@aaionline.org. Works closely with educational institutions and sustainable development organizations in Africa.

American-Scandinavian Foundation, Exchange Division, 725 Park Ave., New York, NY 10021; 212-879-9779, fax 212-249-3444; asf@amscan.org, [www.amscan.org]. Free publications on study/work in Scandinavia. Offers scholarships and internships in Scandinavia.

AMIDEAST, 1730 M St., NW, Washington, DC 20036-4505; 202-776-9600, fax 202-776-7019; inquiries@amideast.org, [www.amideast.org]. Assists with educational exchanges with Middle East institutions. Web site includes a directory of Middle East/North Africa study abroad program sponsors.

British Information Services, 845 3rd Ave., New York, NY 10022; 212- 752-5747, fax 212-758-5395; [www.britain-info.org]. Free fact sheets on study in Britain.

Center for Civil Society International, 2929 N.E. Blakely St., Seattle, WA 98105; 206-523-4755, fax 206-523-1974; ccsi@u.washington.edu, [www.friends-partners.org/ccsi]. CCSI's large web site offers a free email service (CivilSoc), job announcements, and news on grants, new NGOs, and other related developments in the former Soviet Union.

Council on International Education Exchange (CIEE), Publication Dept., 205 E. 42nd St., New York, NY 10017-5706; 888-COUNCIL, fax 212-822-2699; info@ciee.org, [www.ciee.org]. Publisher of materials on study, work, and travel abroad.

French Cultural Services, 972 5th Ave., New York, NY 10021; 212-439-1400, fax 212-439-1455. Free publications on French higher education and opportunities in France for U.S. students.

German Academic Exchange Service (DAAD), 950 3rd Ave., 19th Fl., New York, NY 10022; 212-758-3223, fax 212-755-5780; daadny@daad.org, [www.daad.org]. Information on studying in Germany, including scholarships.

Global Exchange, 2017 Mission St., #303, San Francisco, CA 94110; 800-497-1994; fax 415-255-7498; [www.globalexchange.org]. Publishes materials on education in and solidarity with developing countries and sponsors fact-finding programs.

Groves Dictionaries, 345 Park Ave. S., 10th Fl., New York, NY 10010-1707; 800-221-2123 or 212-689-9200, fax 212-689-9711; grove@grovereference.com, [www.grovereference.com]. Publishers of directories of universities worldwide. Formerly Stockton Press.

Institute of International Education (IIE). IIE Books, Institute of International Education, P.O. Box 371, Annapolis Junction, MD 20701-0371; 800-445-0443, fax 301-206-9789; iiebooks@pmds.com. Free catalog. Publisher of authoritative directories for study abroad and financial aid, and distributor of Central Bureau (U.K.) publications on working abroad.

Intercultural Press, P.O. Box 700, Yarmouth, ME 04096; 207-846-5168, fax 207-846-5181; books@interculturalpress.com, [www.interculturalpress.com]. Leading publisher of books dealing with cross-cultural issues. Free quarterly catalog.

Just Act - Youth Action for Global Justice, 333 Valencia St., Suite 101, San Francisco, CA 94103; 415-431-4204, fax 415-431-5953; odn@igc.org, [www.igc.apc.org/odn]. Publishes material on work and internships in international development. Formerly Overseas Development Network.

Mobility International USA (MIUSA), P.O. Box 10767, Eugene, OR 97440; 541- 343-1284 (voice and TDD), fax 541-343-6812; miusa@igc. Publications and videos on including persons with disabilities in international exchange programs.

NAFSA Publications, P.O. Box 1020, Sewickley, PA 15143; 800- 836-4994, fax 412-741-0609. Free catalog. Publishers of informational materials, geared toward its professional membership, on study, work, and travel abroad opportunities as well as advising and admissions.

National Clearinghouse on Disability and Exchange, Mobility International USA, P.O. Box 10767, Eugene, OR 97440; 541-343-1284 v/tty; clearinghouse@miusa.org, [www.miusa.org]. A joint project of Mobility International USA and the U.S. Information Agency; offers a variety of publications and videos, presents workshops and trainings, and provides consultation, information and referral about international exchange and disability issues.

Peterson's Guides, 202 Carnegie Center, P.O. Box 2123, Princeton, NJ 08543-2123; 800-338-3282, fax 609-243-9150; [www.petersons.com]. Guides to jobs and careers abroad and study abroad.

Seven Hills Book Distributors, 1531 Tremont St., Cincinnati, OH 45214; 800-545-2005; jenniferb@sevenhillsbooks.com (orders). Carries a wide range of travel books and maps from foreign publishers, including British Tourist Authority and Vacation Work publications.

Superintendent of Documents, U.S. Government Printing Office, Washington, DC 20402; fax 202-512-2250; gpoaccess@gpo.gov, [www.access.gpo.gov]. Publishes a wide range of material, including country "Background Notes" series.

Transitions Abroad Publishing, P.O. Box 1300, Amherst, MA 01004-1300; 413-256-3414, 800-293-0373, fax 413-256-0373; info@TransitionsAbroad.com, [www.TransitionsAbroad.com]. The premier publisher of resources for the learning traveler. Publishes the bimonthly magazine *Transitions Abroad,* and the books *The Alternative Travel Directory* and *Work Abroad.*

Vacation Work Publications, 9 Park End St., Oxford, OX1 1HJ, U.K.; 011-44-1865-241978, fax 011-44-1865-790885. Publisher of books on work abroad and international careers; distributed in the U.S by Peterson's Guides and Seven Hills (each has different titles).

Funding for International Activities

* * Financial Resources for International Study. Sara J. Steen, ed. 1996. IIE. $39.95 plus $6 s/h from IIE. Lists funding sources available to support undergraduate, graduate, post-doctorate, and professional learning abroad, from study and research to internships and other work experiences. Very useful indexes, including field of study, internships/work abroad.

* A Student's Guide to Scholarships, Grants, and Funding Publications in International Education and Other Disciplines. Vlada Musayelova, John Harrison, and Charles Gliozzo, eds. 1st ed., April 1997. 79 pp. Published by Michigan State Univ. International

Sex and Love Abroad

The Golden Rule Is to Do What You Normally Enjoy Doing

By Marina Wolf

You're two weeks into your summer abroad, minding your own business, when an interesting human specimen crosses your path. If you're smart, you already know enough of the other person's native tongue so that an invitation to coffee won't get you into trouble for proposing an unspeakable act with a hand trowel and an alligator. But whether it's almost as shocking just to propose a coffee date is something that you shouldn't guess about.

The fact is that sex and love are problematic in every culture, but how they are problematic varies greatly from country to country. And when you throw in linguistic challenges, the potential for disappointment or disaster goes off the charts.

Crossed Signals

Amy Kidd Raphael, Overseas Program Manager at Univ. of Pennsylvania, recalls the story of a U-Penn woman who had just started dating a Spanish man. Being from the U.S., the young woman couldn't understand why all the young Spaniards dated in groups. Three weeks later she figured it out when her boyfriend wanted to bring her home to meet the family—as his prospective wife!

In the orientation sessions Raphael facilitates for students, primarily women going abroad, she emphasizes that talking with other people in the culture is the best way to discover the norms for sexual behavior: Is sex appropriate on the first date, or is it something you do only when you're married? Is it okay to hold hands on the street? Where is it acceptable to go for dates?

Travelers shouldn't assume that dating has the same significance as it does at home. Another of Raphael's group participants talked about a relationship she was in during her six-month stay in Japan. They had never even kissed, yet both parties knew that it was a romantic involvement. "That's just the way it is in Japan," says Raphael. "They were definitely in a dating relationship, but there was nothing physical."

Safety Rules

However different the culture is, certain elementary rules of safety are always in order:

- Tell someone you trust where you are going and when you expect to return.
- Try to figure out in advance how you can get back. Take whatever contact numbers and coins you need to make a call or use public transportation in case you end up stranded somewhere.
- Go out in groups, at least until you've really gotten to know the person you're interested in.

- Be aware of how much you drink, and try to designate someone in the group to keep track of everybody.

Think about your own limitations and boundaries before you go out, so that you can enforce them in a few short words: No, we are not going back to my hotel room. Yes, let's go on a picnic. Practice saying no in several different ways. Decide what elements would have to be included in an activity for you to agree to it.

"You may end up making a mistake and embarrassing yourself, but that happens no matter what you're doing abroad," says Raphael. "If it has to do with your safety, then that should come first."

Sexual Behavior

This is no time to get shy or evasive with yourself about just how sexual you think you might be in your host country, because the truth is you just never know. Whatever method of birth control you use, bring enough to last your stay, and bring condoms as a necessary disease preventative. Bring a bagful—party-colored, ribbed, glow in the dark—and give them away if you don't use them. (You should be able to get some basic ones for free at student health centers or AIDS/HIV education centers.) Remember, in some countries a well-made condom is a rare and beautiful thing.

Marriage Proposals

In countries where conditions are such that emigrating is a legitimate career step, you won't even have to date someone to receive a proposal. My first time in Russia I was asked to marry twice; during my third visit, after I had come out as a lesbian and was living with my girlfriend, I got three proposals.

Marriages abroad are performed according to the laws of the host country, which usually involves obtaining all kinds of documentation, followed by a lengthy waiting period. Blood tests and translations of results may also be required. Our State Department has information about every country's marriage laws and can provide certain types of necessary documentation.

A word to the wise about "fake" marriages: You can get away with it. But verification interviews can be grueling—up to two weeks if there is something suspicious, says one source at the U.S. State Department—and the price is high for both parties if you get caught. If you can figure out any other way to help your "betrothed" accomplish his or her objectives, try it first.

Making Contacts

If all of this hasn't frightened you into leaving the key to your chastity belt in the hotel safe, congratulations. Getting out there and getting some companionship (or whatever) can greatly enrich your living abroad experience and lead to long-term relationships that you'll treasure.

Where to go to meet people is something to check out with your local contacts. One cliched but still valid guideline is to do what you'd enjoy doing anyway, the idea being that you'll meet other people who enjoy doing it too. Go to concerts, lectures, or performances that regular folks might attend, staying away from tourist traps, of course. Universities and cafes can also be good places to hang out.

Gay, lesbian, and bisexual travelers looking for romance are better off connecting with whatever groups they can find through the International Gay and Lesbian Human Rights Commission or through guidebooks. Local groups often host dances or parties, and these are a much easier and safer way of finding someone who shares your orientation than trusting to blind chance on the street.

And, finally, don't overlook the possibility of finding love among traveling companions from your own country. Raphael, who met her husband on a study abroad program, says pairing up between fellow citizens abroad is not uncommon. "There's certainly a heightened sense of needing to latch onto something familiar, and so people connect a lot quicker and on a much deeper level," says Raphael. "They're in a place where nobody understands them, so they want as much understanding from whoever's around them as possible."

Additional Resources

If your school doesn't have a study abroad orientation session about love and relationships or if you aren't traveling with a program that offers one, you'll have to take your enlightenment into your own hands. First, check with your local international student union and look for groups of people from the country you'll be visiting. Get to know members of this group and discreetly pump them for information. Also, the web is your friend. Following are some web sites that I have found helpful in the areas of sex and safety abroad.

Inter-Organization Task Force on Safety and Responsibility Abroad, [www.ciee.org/study/safety.htm]. This collaborative set of guidelines comes out a little dry, but the suggestions for students, parents or guardians, and program leaders are solid.

Journeywoman, [www.journeywoman.com]. This smartly designed web site is a great resource for the traveling female. Check out the "100 Female Travel Tips from Around the World."

International Gay and Lesbian Human Rights commission, [www.iglhrc.org]. If you are a gay or HIV-positive traveler, stop here to find out the latest in what's happening around the world. For a less political, but still very useful take on events and associations around the world, you can also try the International Lesbian and Gay Association at [www.ilga.org].

The U.S. State Department's official communique on marriage abroad is at [http://travel.state.gov/marriage.html]. All the facts, Jack, about issues of legality, citizenship, and documentation. Just one of the State Department's many useful web pages.

Studies and Programs in cooperation with the Michigan State Univ. Library. $5 postpaid ($4 each for 10 copies or more) from: Office of the Dean, International Studies and Programs, 209 International Ctr., Michigan State Univ., East Lansing, MI 48824. Attn: Student Guide. An annotated listing of funding sources with directions on where to go for more information, including web sites.

* **Financial Aid for Research and Creative Activities Abroad 1999-2001.** Gail Ann Schlachter and R. David Weber. 1999. 345 pp. $39.50 plus $5 s/h from: Reference Service Press, 5000 Windplay Dr., Suite 4, El Dorado Hills, CA 95762; 916-939-9620, fax 916-939-9626. Lists over 1,300 funding sources that support research, professional development, teaching assignments, and creative activities (most for graduate students, postdoctorates, professionals).

* **Financial Aid for Study Abroad: A Manual for Advisers and Administrators.** Stephen Cooper, William W. Cressey, and Nancy K. Stubbs, eds. 1989. 105 pp. $12 (nonmembers) $8 (members) plus $5 s/h from NAFSA. How to use primarily federal sources of financial aid for study abroad programs for undergraduate students and how to utilize this information to help shape institutional policies.

* **Financial Aid for Study and Training Abroad 1999-2001.** Gail Ann Schlachter and R. David Weber. 1999. 452 pp. $45 plus $5 s/h from Reference Service Press, 5000 Windplay Dr., Suite 4, Eldorado Hills, CA 95762; 916-939-9620, fax 916-939-9626. Lists more than 1,000 financial aid opportunities open to Americans at any level. Very useful indexes.

* **Rotary Foundation Ambassadorial Scholarships.** Information available from The Rotary Foundation of Rotary International, 1 Rotary Center, 1560 Sherman Ave., Evanston, IL 60201-3698; 847-866-3000, fax 847-328-8554; [www.rotary.org]. Information about Rotary scholarships for study abroad, available to undergraduates and graduates who are unrelated to a member of Rotary. Application possible only through local Rotary clubs. Deadlines range from March to mid-July.

Council Scholarships. Bailey Minority Student Scholarships cover transportation costs for undergraduate students of color to study, work, or volunteer with any Council program. Contact Council at 888-COUNCIL for applications.

Fellowships in International Affairs: A Guide to Opportunities in the U.S. and Abroad. Gale Mattox, ed. Women International Security. 1994. 195 pp. $10 plus $3.50 s/h from Lynne Rienner Publishers, 1800 30th St., Suite #314, Boulder, CO 80301; 303-444-668, fax 303-444-0824; [www.reinner.com]. Fellowships and grants for students, scholars, and practitioners (most are for graduate and postdoctoral students or professionals).

Fulbright and Related Grants for Graduate Study and Research Abroad 2000-2001. Free from IIE, U.S. Student Programs, 809 United Nations Plaza, New York, NY 10017-3580; 212-984-5330; [www.iie.org/Fulbright]. Describes grants administered by IIE for study and research abroad.

Money for International Exchange in the Arts edited by Jane Gullong and Noreen Tomassi. 1992. 126 pp. $16.95 postpaid from IIE. Lists grant sources, exchange programs, and artists residencies and colonies for individuals and organizations in the creative arts.

Africa

* **Study in Africa: New Opportunities for American Students.** 1997. $20 postpaid from the National Consortium for Study in Africa, c/o African Studies Center, Michigan State Univ., 100 International Ctr., E. Lansing, MI 48824-1035; 517-353-1700, fax 517-432-1209; NCSA@pilot.msu.edu, [www.isp.msu.edu/AfricanStudies]. Outstanding 27-minute video features onsite interviews with Americans studying in several very different countries in Africa. Oriented to parents, students, advisers; promotes Africa as an important site for study abroad.

Beyond Safaris: A Guide to Building People-to-People Ties with Africa. Kevin Danaher. Africa World Press, Inc. 1991. $14.90 postpaid from Global Exchange. Handbook on how to help build and strengthen links between U.S. citizens and grassroots development efforts in Africa. Annotated list of organizations.

Asia

Civil Society in Central Asia edited by M. Holt Ruffin and Daniel C. Waugh. 1999. 350 pp. Center for Civil Society International, Central Asia-Caucasus Institute (Washington, DC). Univ. of Washington Press. $19.95 paper plus $4 s/h. Order from CCSI or UW Press, 800-441-4115; [www.washington.edu/uwpress]. Comprehensive guide to U.S. and host-country organizations involved in institutional reform in the former USSR, many of which offer professional, academic, and volunteer exchanges. Includes an excellent guide to online resources.

Australia

Education Quality Education Excellence 1999. Free from Australian Education Office, Australian Embassy, 1601 Massachusetts Ave. NW, Washington, DC 20036; 800-245-2575 or 202-332-8285; edu@austudies.org, [www.austudies.org/aeo]. Official information on year, semester, and summer programs; undergraduate, graduate, medical, and law degrees; scholarships and financial aid information (for both U.S. and Canadian citizens); internships. Also available from AEO: *Study Abroad Advisor's Guide, Guide to Australian Short Courses* and *Predeparture Guide*.

Austria

Austria: Information for Foreign Students; Summer Language Courses for Foreign Students; Summer Courses in Austria; German Language Courses. Annual. Free from the Austrian Cultural Institute, 950 3rd Ave., 20th Fl., New York, NY 10022; 212-759-5165; desk@aci.org, [www.austriaculture.net/ScienceEduc3.html]. Information for foreign students intending to study at an Austrian institution of higher learning.

Canada

Destination Canada: Information for International Students. Free from Canadian Bureau for International Education (CBIE), 220 Laurier Ave. W., Suite 1100, Ottawa, ON K1P 5Z9, Canada; 613-237-4820. General information on Canadian education system and tuition fees.

Directory of Canadian Universities. 1999 ed. Annual. $49 U.S., $59 other countries. Association of Universities and Colleges of Canada 350 Albert St., Suite 600, Ottawa ON, K1R 1B1, Canada; 613-563-1236, fax 613-563-9745. Undergraduate and graduate program listings plus summary information on each university.

China

* **Living in China: A Guide to Teaching and Studying in China, Including Taiwan & Hong Kong.** Rebecca Weiner, Margaret Murphy, and Albert Li. China Books. 1997. 300 pp. $19.95 from China Books and Periodicals, Inc., 2929 24th St., San Francisco, CA 94110; 415-282-2994, fax 415-282-0994;

orders@chinabooks.com. Contains directories of universities in China and Taiwan that offer study abroad or teaching placement with contact names and particulars. Good for travel plnning as well as teaching and studying.

Eastern and Central Europe (See also Russia and the NIS)

International Research and Exchanges Board (IREX) Grant. Opportunities for U.S. Scholars. Annual. Free from International Research and Exchanges Board, 1616 H. St., NW, Washington, DC 20006; 202-628-8188. Descriptions of academic exchange programs and special projects administered by IREX in the Baltic States, Central and Eastern Europe, Mongolia, and the successor states of the former Soviet Union.

REESWEB: Russian and East European Studies, Univ. of Pittsburgh (home page). Free on the World Wide Web at [www.pitt.edu/~cjp/rees.html]. Karen Rondestvedt. Continuously updated. No hard copy version available. Click on "Academic Programs and Centers" for listings of language and study abroad programs. Links to other REES area studies centers and information.

France

Studies in France. Free from the French Cultural Services, 972 5th Ave., New York, NY 10021; 212-439-1400, fax 212-439-1455. Basic document outlining various possibilities for study in France, including direct enrollment at French institutions. Also, distributes *French Courses for Foreign Students* (annual list of French universities and language centers offering summer and year courses for foreigners) and *I Am Going to France* (extensive overview of university degree programs).

Studying and Working in France: A Student Guide. Russell Cousins, Ron Hallmark, and Ian Pickup. 1994. 314 pp. $17.95 from Manchester Univ. Press (distributed in the U.S by St. Martin's Press). Useful, detailed information on directly enrolling in French universities and language courses; one brief chapter on working.

Germany

CDS International, 871 United Nations Plaza, 15th Fl., New York, NY 10017-1814; 212-497-3500, fax 212-497-3535; info@cdsintl.org. Paid study/internship programs in Germany offered by CDS for high school and college students and professionals.

Discovering Germany. German language courses and other study abroad options plus work opportunities and travel information. $19.95 plus $3 s/h from NAFSA.

Information from the German Academic Exchange Service: *Scholarships and Funding for Foreign Students, Graduates, and Academics in Germany; Sommerkúrse in Bundesrepublik Deutschland (summer language and culture courses); Postgraduate Courses in Germany, Studying in Germany—Universities Study in Germany—College of Art and Music.* Each publication revised annually. Available free from the German Academic Exchange Service (DAAD), 950 3rd Ave., 19th Fl., New York, NY 10022; 212-758-3223, fax 212-755-5780; daadny@daad.org, [www.daad.org]. Complete information about studying in Germany from its official exchange office.

India

Studying in India. Published by Indian Council for Cultural Relations. Free from Indian consulates and embassies. Basic information and advice on studies or research in India's numerous educational and scientific institutions.

Universities Handbook (India). 27th ed. Published biannually. $250 airmail from: Association of Indian Universities, AIU House, 16 Kotla Marg, New Delhi 110002, India. Overview of courses of studies, faculty members, degrees, library, and research facilities.

Israel

* Complete Guide to the Israel Experience. Annual. Available from the World Zionist Organization, 110 E. 59th St., 4th Fl., New York, NY 10022; 800-27-ISRAEL, fax 212- 318-6193; info@usd.org, [www.usd.org]. Information on study and volunteer work opportunities in Israel.

Italy

* Living, Studying and Working in Italy by Travis Neighbor and Monica Larner. 1998. 340 pp. Owl Books. $14.95 from Henry Holt & Co., 115 W. 18th St., New York, NY 10011. Book by two American journalists who lived in Italy is an essential purchase for anyone interested in studying or working in Italy, containing much information available nowhere else. It has extensive coverage of study abroad options and nearly 100 pages on various means of working in Italy, from internships to professional jobs.

Anglo American Centre, Via Mameli 46, 02124 Cagliari, Sardinia, Italy; 011-39-070-654955; anglo@sol.dada.it. Needs 30 qualified EFL teachers to teach English.

Japan

Academic Year in Japan. The Japan-U.S. Educational Commission. 1995. 118 pp. $20 plus $5 s/h from NAFSA. Practical guide distilled from reports from U.S. Fulbright scholars studying in Japan.

Directory of Japan Specialists and Japanese Studies Institutions in the U.S. and Canada. Patricia G. Steinhoff, ed. The Japan Foundation. 1995. $50 plus $8 s/h ($12 non-U.S.) from Association for Asian Studies, 1021 E. Huron St., Ann Arbor, MI 48104; 734-665-2490, fax 734-665-3801; postmaster@aasianst.org, [www.aasianst.org].

Japanese Colleges and Universities, 1997-99. Association of International Education, Japan (AIEJ) and Monbusho, Ministry of Education, Science, Sports, and Culture. 1997. Biennial. 395 pp. Available to institutions from the Association of International Education Japan, Information Center, 4-5-29 Komaba, Meguro-ku, Tokyo 153-8503, Japan; fax 011-81-3-5454-5236; [www.aiej.or.jp]. A directory of degree and short-term programs (latter in English) offered by Japanese institutions and open to foreign students. Produced by AIEJ, a government-sponsored organization that assists with exchanges. Available free from AIEJ: Index of Majors; Scholarships for International Students in Japan; Student Guide to Japan.

Survey of Japanese Studies in the United States: The 1990s. $15 plus $4 s/h ($5 outside U.S.) from Association for Asian Studies, 1021 E. Huron St., Ann Arbor, MI 48104; 734-665-2490, fax 734-665-3801; postmaster@aasianst.org, [www.aasianst.org].

Latin America/Caribbean

After Latin American Studies. A Guide to Graduate Study and Fellowships, Internships, and Employment. Shirley A. Kregar and Annabelle Conroy. 1995. $10 (check payable to Univ. of Pittsburgh) postpaid from: Center for Latin American Studies, 4E04 Forbes Quad, Univ. of Pittsburgh, Pittsburgh, PA 15260; 412-648-7392, fax 412-648-2199; clas+@pitt.edu, [www.pit.edu/~clas]. Packed with useful information for anyone with career or scholarly interests in this region, though most listings are not overseas. Extensive bibliography. Also available, free: * A Guide to Financial Assistance for Graduate Study, Dissertation Research and Internships for Students in Latin American Studies, 1996.

Mediterranean

Athanassopoulos Language Schools, 6 Einstein St., 18757 Keratsini-Piraeus, Greece; 011-30-1-43-14-921. Eight-month teaching contracts in Greece.

Middle East

* Guide to Study Abroad in The Middle East. AMIDEAST. Available free from web site: www.amideast.org. Study options throughout the Middle East except Israel.

Netherlands

Study in the Netherlands. Annual. 100 pp. Free from NUFFIC, P.O. Box 29777, 2502 LT The Hague, Netherlands; fax 011-31-70-426-03-99; mknaapen@nuffic.nl; [www.nuffic.nl]. Official directory of all study abroad and degree courses (most taught in English) open to foreign students in the Netherlands. Also available from NUFFIC: *The Education System of the Netherlands* and materials on living in Holland.

Russia and the NIS

* The Post-Soviet Handbook: A Guide to Grassroots Organizations and Internet Resources by M. Holt Ruffin, et al. 1999. 418 pp. Univ. of Washington Press. $19.95 plus $4 s/h. Order from UW Press, 800-441-4115; [www.washington.edu/uwpress]. Comprehensive guide to U.S. and host-country organizations involved in institutional reform in the former Soviet Union, many of which offer professional, academic, and volunteer exchanges. Includes an excellent guide to online resources.

Scandinavia

* Study in Scandinavia. Annual. Free from the American-Scandinavian Foundation, 725 Park Ave., New York, NY 10021; [www.amscan.org]. Summer and academic year programs offered to high school and college students and anyone interested in Scandinavia. Available on web site.

Norden: Higher Education and Research in the Nordic Countries. Overview of higher education systems. Available free from the Nordic Council of Ministers, Store Strandstraede 18, DK-1255 Copenhagen K, Denmark; fax 011-45-33-96-02-02. Higher Education in Norway; Studying in Denmark; Study in Finland—University Sector; Swedish in Sweden; and Courses in English at Swedish Universities are available from consulates and embassies of each country.

Spain

Courses for Foreigners in Spain Sponsored by Spanish Institutions; American Programs in Spain; Study in Spain (entering the Spanish university system). Available from the Education Office of Spain, 150 5th Ave., Suite 918, New York, NY 10011.

United Kingdom and Ireland

* The BUTEX Guide to Undergraduate Study in the U.K.; The BUTEX Guide to Graduate Study in the U.K. British Universities Transatlantic Exchange Association (BUTEX). Biennial. Each guide approximately 90 pp. Free from BUTEX Secretariat, Int'l. Office, Univ. of Birmingham, Edgbaston, Birmingham B15 2TT, U.K.; fax 011-44-121-414-3850; butex@bham.ac.uk. Guides from a consortium of 80 U.K. universities, with complete contact information.

Graduate Study and Research in the U.K. The British Council, Education Information Service, 3100 Massachusetts Ave., NW, Washington, DC 20008-3600; 202-588-6500, fax 202-588-7918; study.uk@bc-washingtondc.sprint.com, [www.britishcouncil-usa.org]. Web site provides comprehensive information on study in Britain, funding information, and links to British universities.

Study Abroad in Ireland. Annual. Free from Irish Tourist Board, 345 Park Ave., 17th Fl., New York, NY 10154; 800-223-6470, fax 800-748-3739; [www.ireland.travel.com]. Academic programs and travel-study tours.

Study in Britain. Guide to undergraduate study and for visiting students. Free from British Information Services, 845 3rd Ave., New York, NY 10022; 212-752-5747, fax 212-758-5395; [www.britain-info.org]. Guide to study abroad and undergraduate degree study.

University Courses in Education Open to Students from Overseas 2000-2001. £7.50 surface mail from Universities Council for the Education of Teachers, 58 Gordon Square,

London WC1H ONT, England. Postgraduate courses in education open to foreigners at British universities.

Young Britain. Annual. Free from British Tourist Authority, 557 W. 57th St., New York, NY 10176-0799. Information on study, work, and accommodations.

Worldwide

* **Advisory List of International Educational Travel & Exchange Programs.** 1998-99. Annual. Council on Standards for International Educational Travel, 212 Henry St., Alexandria, VA 22314; 703-739-9050, fax 703-739-9035; exchanges@aol.com, [www.csiet.org]. $15 ($20 overseas). Lists programs for high school students which adhere to CSIET's standards. The most valuable single resource for prospective exchange students, host families, and schools.

* **Alternative Travel Directory: The Complete Guide to Travel, Study, and Living Overseas.** Annual. $23.95 postpaid from Transitions Abroad. A compilation of directories of resources and programs for educational travel, study abroad, and living abroad which appeared in the previous year's issues of *Transitions Abroad* magazine.

* **Basic Facts on Study Abroad.** CIEE, IIE, NAFSA. 1997. 28 pp. Single copies available free from any of the three joint publishers, bulk orders from NAFSA. Basic information for students interested in an educational experience abroad.

* **How to Read Study Abroad Literature.** Lily von Klemperer. Reprinted in IIE's *Academic Year Abroad and Vacation Study Abroad* and in *NAFSA's Guide to Education Abroad*. What to look for in ads for a study abroad program.

* **Peace Corps and More: 175 Ways to Work, Study, and Travel at Home and Abroad.** Medea Benjamin and Miya Rodolfo-Sioson. Global Exchange. 1997. 107 pp. $8.95. Describes nearly 200 programs that allow anyone to gain Third World experience while promoting the ideas of social justice and sustainable development.

* **Study Abroad 1999.** Peterson's Guides. 1999. Annual. 1,008 pages. $29.95 plus $6.75 s/h. Detailed information on over 1,600 programs at more than 500 accredited institutions worldwide.

* **Taking Time Off: Inspiring Stories of Students Who Enjoyed Successful Breaks from College and How You Can Plan Your Own.**

Colin Hall and Ron Lieber. 1996. 288 pp. The Noonday Press. $12 from Farrar, Strauss, and Giroux, 19 Union Square West, New York, NY 10003. Thoughtful reports of individuals who studied abroad or interned, worked, volunteered, or traveled both abroad and in the U.S. Contains useful directories to other resources.

** **Academic Year Abroad 1999/2000.** Sara J. Steen, ed. 1999. $44.95 plus $6 s/h from IIE. Authoritative directory of nearly 2,700 semester and academic year programs offered by U.S. and foreign universities and private organizations. Indexed for internships, practical training, student teaching, adult courses, volunteer work, as well as fields of study. Companion volume to *Vacation Study Abroad* (below).

** **Directory of International Internships: A World of Opportunities.** Compiled and edited by Charles A. Gliozzo and Vernieka K. Tyson. 4th ed., 1998. Available for $25 postpaid from Michigan State Univ., Attn: International Placement, Career Services & Placement, 113 Student Services Bldg., East Lansing, MI 48824. Based on a wide survey of organizations, this directory describes a variety of experiential educational opportunities—for academic credit, for pay, or simply for experience. Useful indexes. This is the only directory to internships entirely located abroad.

** **Vacation Study Abroad 1999/2000.** Sara J. Steen, ed. 1999. $42.95 plus $6 s/h from IIE. Authoritative guide to over 2,200 summer and short-term study programs sponsored by U.S. and foreign organizations and language schools in over 60 countries. Indexed for internships, practical training, student teaching, adult courses, volunteer service, as well as fields of study. Companion volume to *Academic Year Abroad.*

*dNAFSA's Guide to Education Abroad.** William Hoffa and John Pearson, eds. NAFSA. 2nd ed., 1997. 494 pp. $45 (nonmembers), $36 (members) plus $5 s/h. An indispensable reference providing both an overview of principles and practices and detailed information and advice for advisers. Includes bibliography on work, study, and travel; case histories; program evaluation guide.

A Handbook for Creating Your Own Internship in International Development. Just Act: Youth Action for Global Justice. Updated 1996. $7.95 plus $2 s/h. How to arrange a position with an international development organization;

LIVING LIKE A LOCAL

By Martine Klaassen

My greatest memories of the three years I studied in the U.K. are of the people I met. From the day of my arrival, the other international students welcomed me with open arms. Together we explored the campus and talked about life back home.

Hanging out with other international students made me feel safe. We had a lot in common. But having a safety net of international friends stopped me from completely adjusting to my new life in England. Only at Christmas, when all my friends went home for the holidays, did I decide that I no longer wanted to live like an outsider looking in. Here are some ways I learned to go about becoming part of the local culture and meeting local people:

Join a college club. The choices are endless, from language clubs to acting clubs to sports clubs. Meet people with similar interests and have fun.

Try a course outside your college. The local community center is a great place to start. Try your hand at something new or further pursue something you've been doing for years. Most community centers offer a great variety of activities like pottery, photography courses, or yoga classes.

Attend all-college activities. You're likely to be bombarded with social activities for international students, but don't forget about college activities organized for all students.

Get a job. You'll not only make extra money, you'll meet new people while gaining valuable work experience. Most student visas allow you to work on campus, but you should also try to work outside in the "real world." If your visa prevents you from working for pay, try volunteering. There are lots of interesting volunteer jobs available.

Consider living in a shared house off campus rather than in college accommodations. Sharing a household with others will teach you valuable lessons about yourself and help you make new friends for life. But never compromise your safety. Talk to your parents before making this decision.

Once you meet some local people, ask them to show you the sights and sounds. This can be a lot more interesting and fun than trips organized for international students. In return, invite your friends to dinner and cook something special from home. Chances are you will be invited back.

Becoming a part of the local culture requires some effort. Don't keep reminding yourself and others that you're a foreigner. Your nationality is only part of who you are—be yourself and before you know it you will be accepted for who you are not where you are from.

The moment will come when you realize that you are no longer an outsider but actually part of the local life. In the end, this feeling was the most rewarding part of my stay.

evaluate your skills, motivations, and learning objectives; practical advice on financing an internship, living overseas, and returning home.

A World Awaits You (Away). National Clearinghouse on Disability and Exchange. 1998. 36 pp. Free. Published by Mobility International USA and U.S. Information Agency. Order from: Mobility International USA, P.O. Box 10767, Eugene, OR 97440; clearinghouse@miusa.org. *Away* is a biannual journal with articles and interviews about people with disabilities who have successfully participated in international exchanges and organizations that are creatively including people with disabilities in all aspects of their international programs.

A World of Options: A Guide to International Exchange, Community Service and Travel for Persons with Disabilities. Christa Bucks. Mobility International USA. 3rd ed., 1996. 659 pp. $35 individuals, $45 organizations. A guide to international exchange, study, and volunteer opportunities for people with disabilities.

A Year Between. Central Bureau for Educational Visits and Exchanges. 2nd ed. 1994. 288 pp. Plus $3 s/h from IIE. Designed for young British adults who have a year between high school and college, or during college, and want to explore and learn. Volunteer work, internships service, and study options.

AIFS Advisors' Guides. Various authors and dates. AIFS. Free. Published quarterly by AIFS; 800-727-AIFS. Study abroad topics include political advocacy, nontraditional programs, promoting ethnic diversity, and reentry.

Archaeological Fieldwork Opportunities Bulletin. Annual in January. 160 pp. Archaeological Institute of America. $10 for AIA members, $12 nonmembers plus $4 s/h from Kendall/Hunt Publishing Co., Order Dept., 4050 Westmark Dr., Dubuque, IA 52002; 800-228-0810; [www.kendallhunt.com] (orders can be placed via web site). A comprehensive guide to excavations, field schools, and special programs with openings for volunteers, students, and staff worldwide.

Architecture Schools: Special Programs. Beth Young, ed. 1999. Annual. 60 pp. $12.95 including shipping from the Association of Collegiate Schools of Architecture, 1735 New York Ave., NW, Washington, DC 20006; 202-785-2324, fax 202-628-0448; [www.acsa-arch.org]. Lists more than 100 study abroad programs sponsored by U.S. collegiate schools of architecture as well as short-term programs in the U.S.

Building Bridges: A Manual on Including People with Disabilities in International Exchange Programs. MIUSA. 1998. $20. Information on accessibility, resource lists to recruit people with disabilities, and checklists to identify specific needs of participants with disabilities.

Commonwealth Universities Yearbook. Compiled by the Association of Commonwealth Universities. 1999. Two-volume set. $265 plus $15 s/h from Groves Dictionaries. Detailed profiles of universities in all 34 of the Commonwealth countries, with comprehensive guide to degree programs and a register of 230,000 academic and administrative staff. Available in major libraries.

Directory of International Organizations by Hans-Albrecht Schraepler. Georgetown Univ. Press. 1997. 456 pp. $24.95 paper. Orders: 800-246-9606 or 410-516-6995, fax 410-516-6998. Practical information about international and European governmental organizations of political, economic, social, and cultural importance in the world community.

Directory of Work and Study in Developing Countries. Toby Milner. 1997. 256 pp. Vacation Work. $16.95 from Seven Hills. A comprehensive guide to employment, voluntary work, and academic opportunities in developing countries worldwide. Intended for a British audience, it may omit some organizations of interest to Americans.

Figuring Foreigners Out. Craig Storti. 1999. $17.95 plus $3 s/h from Intercultural Press. Enjoyable and practical workbook which will help anyone going abroad "figure out" the behavior of foreigners.

Guide to Careers, Internships, and Graduate Education in Peace Studies. 1996. $6 from PAWSS, Hampshire College, Amherst, MA 01002. Includes information on internships, fellowships, and relevant organizations.

Home from Home. Central Bureau for Educational Visits and Exchanges. 3rd ed., 1994. 224 pp. $18.95 plus $3 s/h from IIE. Compiled from a comprehensive database used by U.K. government agencies, this guide contains details on homestays, home exchanges, hospitality exchanges, and school exchanges worldwide. Includes profiles of organizations by country.

InterAct Series. Intercultural Press. (Call for prices.) InterActs analyzes how Americans and nationals of other countries see and do things differently and how these differences affect relationships. Countries/areas covered include Japan, Spain, Mexico, Greece, Israel, Eastern Europe, Russia, Australia, China, Thailand, Arab World, the Philippines, and Sub-Saharan Africa.

International Handbook of Universities. 15th ed. 1998. $245 plus $15 s/h. International Association of Universities. Distributed in U.S. and Canada by Groves Dictionaries. Entries for more than 5,700 universities and other institutions of higher education in 170 countries and territories. Complements of **Commonwealth Universities Yearbook.**

Planning Guides Catalog. Transitions Abroad Publishing, Inc., P.O. Box 1300, Amherst, MA 01004-1300; www.TransitionsAbroad.com. Free descriptive listing of planning guides on international work, study, living, educational and socially responsible travel.

The Pros and Cons of the Peace Corps by Erica Chinn and Kristina Taylor. 1997. 50 pp. $7 plus $2 s/h from Just Act: Youth Action for Global Justice, 333 Valencia St., Suite 101, San Francisco, CA 94103; info@justact.org, [www.justact.org]. A compilation of articles by journalists and interviews with former Peace Corps volunteers which reflect the pros and cons of being a Peace Corps volunteer.

Student Travels Magazine. Fall and spring. Free from Council. Covers rail passes, insurance, work and study opportunities abroad, airfares, car rentals, and other services offered by CIEE and Council Travel.

Study Abroad. UNESCO. Vol. 30, 1998-99. $29.95 plus $5 s/h from Bernan Associates, 4611-F Assembly Dr., Lanham, MD 20706; 301-459-7666. Describes approximately 4,000 international study programs and sources of financial assistance in more than 100 countries.

Study Abroad: A Parent's Guide by William Hoffa. NAFSA, 1998. 112 pp. $15 ($12 members) plus $5 s/h. The first full-length book geared to what parents want and need to know about study abroad.

Studying Abroad/Learning Abroad. J. Daniel Hess. Intercultural Press, 1997. 147 pp. $13.95 plus $3 s/h. This new abridged edition of **The Whole World Guide to Culture Learning** provides a guide to cross-cultural analysis and adaptation.

Summer Study Abroad 1999. Peterson's Guides. 1998. Annual. 512 pp. $29.95 plus $6.75 s/h. Guide to over 1,400 credit and noncredit programs overseas.

Survival Kit for Overseas Living: For Americans Planning to Live and Work Abroad. L. Robert Kohls. 3rd ed., 1996. $11.95 plus $3 s/h from Intercultural Press. Practical information and insights into the process of cross-cultural adaptation combined with suggestions for getting the most from overseas experience.

What in the World is Going On? Canada's Guide to International Careers and Studies. Alan Cumyn. 6th ed. 188 pp. 1998. CAN$23 including s/h from Canadian Bureau for International Education, 220 Laurier Ave. W, Suite 1100, Ottawa, Ontario K1P 5Z9, Canada; 613-237-4820. Includes a lengthy list of study and work abroad possibilities, some restricted to Canadian citizens. Indexed by country and field. Now available with CD-ROM, add $10.

World List of Universities. 21st ed., 1997. $170 plus $15 s/h from Groves Dictionaries. Addresses of over 9,000 institutions of higher education worldwide.

The World of Learning. 46th ed. Annual. 2,025 pp. Europa Publications Ltd. $445 plus postage from International Publications Service, c/o Taylor & Francis Group, 1900 Frost Rd., Suite 101, Bristol, PA 19007; 215-625-8900, fax 215-625-2940; bkorders@tandf.pa.com. This authoritative guide lists over 26,000 institutions of higher education by country, gives names of staff and faculty, and includes information on international organizations involved in education throughout the world.

ELEVEN

STUDENT OVERSEAS PROGRAMS

The following listing of study programs was supplied by the organizers. Contact the program directors to confirm costs, dates, and other details. Please tell them you read about their programs in this book! Programs based in more than one country or region are listed under "Worldwide."

Africa

Global Education in Namibia. Earn a semester of college credit with "Multicultural Societies in Transition" (fall) or "Nation Building, Globalization, and Decolonizing the Mind" (spring). Includes homestay in rural area, seminar in South Africa, and courses in political science, history, sociology, religion, or interdisciplinary studies. Internship opportunity.

Dates: Semesters (Sep-Dec or Feb-May). **Cost:** Contact the Center for current costs. **Contact:** Academic Programs Abroad, Center for Global Education, Augsburg College, 2211 Riverside Ave., Box 307TR, Minneapolis, MN 55454; 800-299-8889, fax 612-330-1695; globaled@augsburg.edu, [www.augsburg.edu/global].

Americas

Educational Homestays. Foreign students or visitors live with host families and may also have optional ESL teaching and/or excursions. Short- or long-term homestays provided for high school or college students in universities, at langauge schools, or just visiting America or Canada.

Dates: Any time of year. **Cost:** $175 and up, depending on program and city. Includes room, meals, airport or bus transfers, plus use of all household amenities and local area supervision. **Contact:** Connections, John Shephard, 17324 185th Ave. NE, Woodinville, WA 98072; 425-788-9803, fax 425-788-2785; [www.connections-inc.com].

Argentina

Argentum, Universidad Blas Pascal. Argentum, The Institute for International Education at Universidad Blas Pascal in Córdoba, Argentina, offers Spanish language and culture courses suited for adults, who want to either learn Spanish or improve their language skills. Participants are paired up with a tutor that acts as a bridge to the Argentinean culture.

Dates: Intensive 3-week adult programs; group instruction Feb and Aug; individual or paired instruction is 1st Monday of Apr, May, June, Sep, Oct, and Nov. **Cost:** Intensive 3-week program $1,900; 5-week program $2,200. Includes tuition, room and board, organized group excursions. **Contact:** Argentum, P.O. Box 99, Medford, MA 02153; Tel./fax 781-488-3552.

Learn Spanish and Study Abroad. Study Spanish language in Buenos Aires, take credit-transferred courses in advertising, architecture, business administration, computer sciences, economics, engineering, graphic design, international relations, journalism, law, political science, psychology, radio and TV production, South American culture courses and Tango classes at the Univ. of Belgrano. Homestays or private students residences. Fifteeen week programs.

Dates: Mar-Jul; Jul-Dec. **Cost:** Tuition: 1 semester $2,652, housing $2,000. **Contact:** Dr. Victor Beker, Director, Int'l Programs, Universidad de Belgrano, Zabala 1837, Piso 17°, Buenos Aires 1426, Argentina; 011- 54-11-788-5400; jimena@ub.edu.ar, gaby@ub.edu.ar, [www.ub.edu.ar].

Australia

Academic Semester or Year Abroad. Australia's direct enrollment program offer choice of 35 universities full curriculum. Free advising and enrollment, assistance with subject selection, credit transfer, financial aid, accommodations, visa, predeparture support, on-arrival assistance, orientation. Prices for tuition and medical start at $2,900 for semester. Opportunities for additional tours and travel.

Dates: Mar 30 deadline for Ju 2000 start. **Cost:** $2,900-$4,600 includes tuition and medical or $4,900-$6,900 includes tuition, medical, accommodations, and meals. **Contact:** Jonathan Cooper, Australian Education Connection, 5722 S. Flamingo Rd., #303, Ft. Lauderdale, FL 33330; 954-680-0453, fax 954-680-0597, student hotline 800-565-9553; auststudy@aol.com.

BUNAC's Work in Australia Program. Work and travel in Australia for up to a year. Full support services, job listings, meet and greet, etc. provided in Australia by BUNAC subsidiary, IEP. For U.S. students and recent graduates up to 25 years old.

Dates: Call for details. **Cost:** $550 includes visa, admin. Australian support. **Contact:** BUNAC USA, P.O. Box 430, Southbury, CT 06488; 800-GO-BUNAC; [www.bunac.org].

Education Australia. Study abroad for a semester or a year at Australian National Univ. (Canberra), Deakin Univ. (Victoria), Univ. of Ballarat (Victoria), Univ. of Tasmania (Tasmania), Univ. of Wollongong (New South Wales), or Monash Univ. (Victoria). In New Zealand courses are offered at the Univ. of Canterbury and Lincoln Univ. (Christchurch). Liberal arts, science, business, biology, psychology, education, Australian studies, etc. Customized internships in all fields are also available.

Dates: Mid-Jul-mid-Nov, mid-Feb-late Jun. **Cost:** Tuition approx. $4,000, accommodations approx. $2,250. Airfare. **Contact:** Dr. Maurice A. Howe, Executive Director, Education Australia, P.O. Box 2233, Amherst, MA 01004; 800-344-6741, fax 413-549-0741; edaust@javanet.com, [www.javanet.com/~edaust].

Environmental Management in Australia. Univ. of Buffalo is pleased to offer the 1999 Summer Study Abroad Program in Queensland in conjunction with Griffith Univ. This 3-week program involves 1 week at each of the following sites: the campus of Griffith Univ., Numinbah Valley Environmental Education Center, and the Townsville/Cairns region, the tropical gateway to the Great Barrier Reef.

Dates: Jun 10-Jul 4. **Cost:** $2,125 program fee includes tuition for 6 credit hours, all accommodations, a meal stipend, field trips, and administrative costs. Transportation to Australia, health insurance, passport and visa fees, and miscellaneous personal expenses not included. **Contact:** SUNY at Buffalo, Study Abroad Programs, 210 Talbert Hall, Box 601604, Buffalo, NY 14260-1604; 716-645-3912, fax 716-645-6197; studyabroad@acsu.buffalo.edu, [www.buffalo.edu/studyabroad].

General Studies in Australia. Victoria offers nearly every discipline in undergraduate/ graduate levels at 5 different university campus sites: Australian studies, art, journalism, performing arts, women's studies, biology, chemistry, math, business, computing, etc. Known as the Garden State, Victoria has some of the country's most beautiful mountain and coastal areas.

Dates: First semester: Jul-Nov; second semester: Feb-Jun. **Cost:** $4,315 per semester, $7,775 for 1 year. **Contact:** University Studies Abroad Consortium (USAC), Univ. of Nevada, Reno #323, Reno, NV 89557-0093; 775-784-6569, fax 775-784-6010; usac@admin.unr.edu, [www.scsr.nevada.edu/~usac].

Marine Ecology of Temperate Australia. This course provides a general background to the major concepts of contemporary marine ecology and detailed study and analysis of temperate Australian marine systems. It includes fieldwork, laboratory practicals, lectures, tutorials, and workshops under the guidance of an international staff of outstanding scientists.

Dates: Early Jan-end Jan, 2000 (4 weeks). Cost: Call for details. Contact: Mr. Peter Millen, Study Abroad Adviser, Int'l. Office, Flinders Univ. of South Australia, GPO Box 2100, Adelaide, SA 5001, Australia; 011-61-8-8201-2727, fax 011-61-8-8201-3177; intl.office@flinders.edu.au, [http://adminwww.flinders.edu.au/intloff/home.html].

Semester in Australia. The Australian International Hotel School in Canberra offers semester-long programs focusing on international hospitality management. Students earn 12-15 credits; courses include Pacific Tourism, Multicultural Management, International Cuisine, Global Hotel Operations, and Resort Development. Students live at AIHS and participate in many travel and cultural activities. AIHS is affiliated with RMIT Univ. (Melbourne) and Cornell Univ.

Dates: Semester: Feb-May, May-Aug, Sep-Dec. Cost: $8,500 includes tuition, room and board, and course-related trips. Contact: Prof. Richard H. Penner, AIHS Semester in Australia, Cornell Univ., 182 Statler Hall, Ithaca, NY 14853-6902; 607-255-1842, 800-235-8220, fax 607-255-4179; aihs@cornell.edu, [http://hotelschool.cornell.edu/aihs].

Study in Australia. Eleven programs available in Sydney, Melbourne, Brisbane, Gold Coast, Perth, including summer opportunities in cooperation with the National Institute of Dramatic Art, the Univ. of New South Wales, and James Cook Univ. Full range of program services. Need-based scholarships available.

Dates: Fall, spring, academic year, summer. Cost: Varies. Call for current fees. Contact: Beaver College CEA, 450 S. Easton Rd., Glenside, PA 19038-3295; 888-BEAVER-9, fax 215-572-2174; cea@beaver.edu, [www.beaver.edu/cea].

Austria

Central College Abroad. In Vienna, intermediate German speakers are enrolled at the university, language, business, art, or music schools. Students live in dorms, are taught only in German, and may complete an internship. Excursions and ISIC included. Onsite director. Intensive German course prior to study offered at Goethe Institut is highly recommended.

Dates: Semester or full year. Cost: Varies. Contact: Central College Abroad, 812 University, Pella, IA 50219; 800-831-3629, fax 515-628-5375; studyabroad@central.edu, [www.studyabroad.com/central].

Deutsch in Österreich. German language courses for everybody from age 16. We teach all levels (from beginners to mastery) nearly all year round. We have organized German as a foreign language course for more than 20 years.

Dates: Jul 10-Aug 4; Aug 7-25; Aug 28-Sep 15. Cost: ATS6,000,00-ATS9,900,00 Contact: Deutsch in Österreich, Univ. of Klagenfurt, Universitaetsstrasse 65-67, A-9020 Klagenfurt, Austria; 011-43-463-24180, fax 011-43-463-24180-3; dia@uni-klu.uc.at; [www.uni-klu.ac.at/dia].

European Studies. Interdisciplinary evaluation and the interrelations of legal, economic, political, social, and cultural studies with regard to the geopolitical and cultural situation of the city of Vienna. The first 3 semesters will each have a particular emphasis. The study program will be made up of elective and compulsory subjects in interdisciplinary foundation and extension modules. Language tuition.

Dates: Oct 1999-Jun 2001 (4 semesters). Application deadline Aug 31. Cost: ATS30,000 per semester. Contact: Magister Sigrun Inmann-Trojer, Wiener Internationale Hochschulkurse, Ebendorferstrasse 10/4, A-1010 Vienna, Austria; fax 011-43-1-405-12-5410, [www.univie.ac.at/europaeistik].

German Courses at the University. German for beginners and advanced students, perfectionist courses, courses for students of the German language and teachers of German in foreign countries (6 levels). Lectures on German and Austrian literature, music, Austria—the country, people, and language. Special courses: translation, commercial German, commercial correspondence, phonetics, conversation, communication. Excursions.

Dates: Three sessions: Jul 2-29, Jul 30-Aug 26, Aug 27-Sep 16. Cost: Course fee (4 weeks): approx. ATS4,500. Accommodations: approx. ATS5,800. Contact: Magister Sigrun Inmann-Trojer, Wiener Internationale Hochschulkurse, Ebendorferstrasse 10/4, A-1010 Vienna, Austria; fax 011-43-1-405-12-5410, [www.univie.ac.at/WIHOR].

German Language and Austrian Culture. A semester or academic year in Vienna is offered via Slippery Rock Univ. at the Cultura Wien. The program is ideal for students at the beginning or intermediate level of German. Music courses can also be taken at the Vienna Conservatory. Housing options are apartments or residence halls.

Dates: Oct 4-Dec 17 (1999); Jan 10-Mar 31; Mar 6-May 26 (2000). **Cost:** $3,450 includes tuition and housing. **Contact:** Dr. Donald E. Kerchis, Director, International Initiatives, Slippery Rock Univ., Slippery Rock, PA 16057; 724-738-2057, fax 724-738-2959; donald.kerchis@sru.edu, [www.sru.edu].

Study in Vienna. Semester program with courses in politics, music, culture, and history. No knowledge of German required, study of German during program. Field study trips.
Dates: Fall, spring, academic year, and summer. **Cost:** Summer, psychology or art nouveau $2,950; both courses $3,950, fall or spring $10,990 semester, and full year $20,590. **Contact:** Stacy Johnston, Program Coordinator, Beaver College Center for Education Abroad, 450 S. Easton Rd., Glenside, PA 19038-3295; 888-BEAVER-9, fax 215-572-2174; cea@beaver.edu, [www.beaver.edu/cea].

Vienna Master Courses for Music. Master classes (2 weeks) in: singing, opera, lied, piano, violin, cello, guitar, chamber music, conducting, flute. Diploma for active participation, certificate for listeners, final concerts. Twenty lessons per week. Instructors are leading artists or renowned teachers.
Dates: Jul 5-Aug 15. **Cost:** Registration fee: AS1,500; course fee active: AS5,200; listen AS2,700. **Contact:** Vienna Master Courses, A-1030 Vienna, Reisnerstr. 3, Austria; 011-43-1-714-88-22, fax 011-43-1-714-88-21 (Elisabeth Keschmann or Monika Wildauer), [www.wiener-meisterkurse.music.at].

Belgium

Vesalius College, Liberal Arts. Vesalius College, the accredited international undergraduate English language college of the Vrije Univ. Brussels-VUB, offers American-style, liberal arts and sciences programs in coordination with Boston Univ. BA and BS in business economics, international affairs, political studies, literature, communications and computing. Exciting summer programs. About 400 students representing over 60 nationalities have access to excellent research and sports facilities. Over 90 percent of faculty hold PhDs.
Dates: Aug-Dec (fall), Jan-May (spring), Jun-Jul (summer). **Cost:** $4,500 per semester (tuition and fees). **Contact:** Admissions Dept. 64/0, Vesalius College-VUB, Pleinlaan 2, B-1050 Brussels, Belgium; 011-32-2-629-36-26, fax 011-32-2-629-36-37; vesalius@vub.ac.be, [www.vub.ac.be/VECO].

Brazil

Brazilian Ecosystems Program. This program is an intensive field study of the tropical and subtropical ecosystems of Brazil. Students learn about current research in ecology, and human impact and resource development from Brazilian scientists. The courses are conducted at program sites in the states of Amazonas, Pará, Mato Grosso, Paraná, and Santa Catarina. Portuguese language and a 4-week internship are integral parts of the program.
Dates: Sep-Dec. **Cost:** Contact office for details. **Contact:** Antioch Education Abroad, Antioch College, 795 Livermore St., Yellow Springs, OH 45387; 800-874-7986, fax 937-767-6469; aea@antioch-college.edu, [www.antioch-college.edu/aea].

Canada

Ecole de français, Montréal. For the last 50 years, the Ecole de français has offered courses in French as a second language to students from around the world. The Ecole is continually improving its programs to meet the changing needs of its students. Choose from Oral and Written Communication French (beginner to advanced), Workshop on Teaching French as a Second Language (for teachers), Contemporary Québec Culture (for advanced students), Business French (intermediate to advanced students).
Dates: Spring: May 18-Jun 10; summer: Jul 5-23, Jul 26-Aug 13; fall: Sep 13-Dec 10; winter 2000: Jan 10-Apr 7. **Cost:** Spring/summer: (3 weeks, 60 hours) CAN$495; summer: (3 weeks, 45 hours) CAN$390; fall/Winter: (12 weeks, 240 hours) CAN$1,495. Prices subject to change. **Contact:** Serge Bienvenu, Coordinator, Ecole de français, Faculté de l'education permanente, Université de Montréal, C.P. 6128, succursale Centre-ville, Montréal, PQ, H3C 3J7, Canada; 514-343-7492, fax 514-343-5984; infolang@fep.umontreal.ca, [www.fep.umontreal.ca/langues/index.html].

Central America

Sustainable Development and Social Change. Study Spanish while living with families in Guatemala (3 weeks); study the role of the church in social injustice in El Salvador (3 weeks), and examine the theory and practice of economic development and social change movements in Nicaragua (6 weeks). Courses in Spanish, religion, economics, and interdisciplinary studies.

Dates: Sep-Dec or Feb-May. **Cost:** Call for details. **Contact:** Academic Programs Abroad, Center for Global Education, Augsburg College, 2211 Riverside Ave., Box 307TR, Minneapolis, MN 55454; 800-299-8889, fax 612-330-1695; globaled@augsburg.edu, [www.augsburg.edu/global].

Chile

CWU Semester Program in Chile. Semester abroad program hosted by the Universidad Autral de Chile (Valdivia) that combines intensive language training, core electives in Latin American politics, history and literature, direct enrollment courses, and field research/independent study. Participants enjoy cross-cultural learning experience in the beautiful lake region of southern Chile.

Dates: Spring semester Mar 20-Jul 7 (approx.); fall Aug 16-Dec 10 (approx.). **Cost:** Approx. $4,000 (tuition, housing and meals). **Contact:** Study Abroad Adviser, Central Washington Univ., Office of International Studies and Programs, 400 E. 8th Ave., Ellensburg, WA 98926-7408; 509-963-3612, fax 509-963-1558; goabroad@cwu.edu.

Spanish and Latin American Studies. Santiago offers intensive language studies fulfilling up to 2 years of university Spanish requirements in 1 semester, with additional courses in literature, business, teacher ed., history, political science. Week-long, program-oriented field trips to the south and north of Chile, homestays, and many university activities at Chilean university.

Dates: Fall semester Aug-Dec, spring semester Jan-May. **Cost:** One semester $3,980; fall and spring semester $6,650. **Contact:** University Studies Abroad Consortium (USAC), Univ. of Nevada, Reno #323, Reno, NV 89557-0093; 775-784-6569, fax 775-784-6010; usac@admin.unr.edu, [www.scsr.nevada.edu/~usac].

China

BCA Program in Dalian. Earn 16-20 credits per semester at the Dalian Univ. of Foreign Languages in China, with a 1-week orientation period, field trips, and extended study tours through northern or southern China. Advanced Chinese program requires college intermediate level language; beginning program has no language prerequisite. Students from all U.S. colleges and universities accepted. All levels of Chinese language available plus Russian and Japanese, Chinese History, literature, politics, and internships.

Dates: Sep-Dec or Jan (fall), Feb-Jun or Jul (spring), Sep-Jun or Jul (year). **Cost:** $14,245 (academic year); $8,345 (semester) includes international transportation, tuition, room and board, insurance, group in-country travel. **Contact:** Cristina Garcia-Cervigon, 605 E. College Ave., North Manchester, IN 46962; 219-982-5238, fax 219-982-7755; bca@manchester.edu, [www.bcanet.org].

Beijing Capital Normal Univ. Schiller Univ. is an American-style university with all courses except language classes taught in English. Schiller's particular strengths are in international business and international relations but it offers courses in the humanities and social sciences as well. Students may take German at Schiller or intensive German at the Collegium Palatinum, a specialized language division. One semester college German or equivalent is recommended.

Dates: Fall: late Aug-late Jan; spring: mid-Feb-lateJun; academic: late Aug-late Jun. **Cost:** Fall 1999 or spring 2000 estimate: $3,940 per semester. Estimates include full-day orientation before departure, application fee, room and food allowance in residence hall, airfare, books and supplies, health and accident insurance, travel allownace, visa, administrative fees and passport. SUNY tuition not included. **Contact:** Dr. John Ogden, Director, Office of International Programs, Box 2000, SUNY Cortland, Cortland, NY 13045; 607-753-2209, fax 607-753-5989; studyabroad@cortland.edu, [www.studyabroad.com/suny/cortland].

Chinese Studies: Chengdu. The Chinese Studies Program offers intensive language study fulfilling up to 2 years of university language requirements in 1 semester. Additional courses in art history, economics, anthropology, political science, physics, chemistry, literature, history, and calligraphy are taught in English and offer a multidisciplinary approach to understanding the complexities of China and Asia.

Dates: Summer term: Jun-Aug; fall semester: Aug-Dec, spring semester: Jan-May. **Cost:** Fall or spring semester $4,260; summer term $1,680; year $6,860. **Contact:** University Studies Abroad Consortium (USAC), Univ. of Nevada, Reno #323, Reno, NV 89557-0093; 775-784-6569, fax 775-784-6010; usac@admin.unr.edu, [www.scsr.nevada.edu/~usac].

Friends World Program (Hangzhou). A semester or year program at Zhejiang Univ. in Hangzhou, including Chinese language instruction, field trips, and an extensive stay in

Yunnan Province spring semester. Classes include Chinese culture, customs, Chinese arts or calligraphy. Students also have their own research projects which may include the study of Chinese medicine, gender issues, religion, or environmental issues. Students may earn 12-18 credits per semester.

Dates: Fall: early Sep to end of Dec; or, for year to mid-May; spring semester is limited to year-long participants. **Cost:** $11,675 per semester in 1999/2000. Includes tuition, travel, room and board, fees, and books. **Contact:** Admissions, Friends World Program, 239 Montauk Highway, Southampton, NY 11968; 516-287-8474; fw@southampton.liunet.edu.

Costa Rica

Enjoy Learning Spanish Faster. Techniques developed from our ongoing research enable students to learn more, faster, in a comfortable environment. Classes of 2-5 students plus group learning activities; conversations with middle-class homestay families (1 student per family). Homestays are within walking distance of school in small town near the capital, San Jose.

Dates: Year round. Classes begin every Monday at all levels. **Cost:** $345 per week for 28 hours of classes and group activities plus Costa Rican dance and cooking classes. Includes tuition, 3 meals per day, 7 days per week, homestay, laundry, all materials, and airport transportation. $25 one-time registration fee. **Contact:** Susan Shores, Registrar, Latin American Language Center, 7485 Rush River Dr., Suite 710-123, Sacramento, CA 95831; 916-447-0938, fax 916-428-9542; lalc@madre.com.

Friends World Program (San José). A semester or year in Latin America at Friends World Center in San José, Costa Rica, incorporates seminars, field study, travel, and independent projects. Seminars to introduce students into Latin America and its culture include Central American realities today, intensive Spanish for any level student, ecology and development, women's studies in Latin America. Independent work has included: ecology, community development, peace studies, health and refugee studies. Students may earn 12-18 credits per semester.

Dates: Fall: mid-Sep-mid-Dec; spring: mid-Jan-mid-May. **Cost:** $12,285 per semester in 1999/2000. Includes tuition, travel, room and board, fees and books. **Contact:** Admissions, Friends World Program, 239 Montauk Hwy., Southampton, NY 11968; 516-287-8474; fw@southampton.liunet.edu.

Intensive Spanish and Homestay. Intercultura Costa Rica offers intensive university accredited Spanish courses. Homestays available. Volunteer programs, beach and city campuses, emphasis on individual attention. Caring, multilingual staff. Located in university town close to the capital. Daily Latin dance classes, weekly cooking, music, indigenous culture, and other classes.

Dates: Year round. **Cost:** $1,045 per month includes classes, homestay and activities (shorter stays available). In 2000, approx. a 5 percent increase expected. **Contact:** Laura Ellington, Intercultura Costa Rica, Language Center, P.O. Box 1952-3000, Heredia, Costa Rica; 011-506-260-8480, Tel./fax 011-506-260-9243; info@spanish-intercultura.com, [www.spanish-intercultura.com].

Intercultura and Language Link. Intensive Spanish language programs in peaceful Costa Rica. Choose either 4 hours daily of small classes, a combination of 4 hours group and 2 hours private, or completely private. Professional adults, college students, and all Spanish levels accommodated. Programs of 1 to 12 weeks starting on any Monday. U.S. graduate and undergraduate credit through accredited university. Free weekly activities, caring homestays, and excursions to rainforests, volcano parks. Located in Heredia, a small university town. Option of a week's stay at our beach campus.

Dates: Year round. New classes begin every Monday (summer months fill very early). **Cost:** Four hours daily of group classes and homestay: 2 weeks $625, 4 weeks $1,095. Includes registration, insurance, tuition, airport pickup, private room, and 2 meals daily. **Contact:** Kay G. Rafool, Language Link Inc., P.O. Box 3006, Peoria, IL 61612; 800-552-2051, fax 309-692-2926; info@langlink.com, [www.langlink.com].

Learn About Tropical Plants and Birds. Two-week courses on field identification of trees and shrubs (Dendrology) offered every year in Spanish (March) and in English (June-July). Please ask for opinions by former participants.

Dates: Mar 13-25 (Spanish); Jun 26-Jul 8 (English). **Cost:** Each course is $1,800. Includes fees, material, lodging and meals during 15 days, insurance, course-related local transport, farewell dinner, and certificate of attendance. **Contact:** Humberto Jiménez Saa, TSC, Apdo. 8-3870-1000, San José, Costa Rica; 011-506-253-3267, fax 011-506-253-4963; hjimenez@sol.racsa.co.cr, [www.geocities.com/RainForest/9148].

Learn Spanish While Volunteering. Assist with the training of Costa Rican public school teachers in ESL and computers. Assist local health clinic, social service agencies, and environmental projects. Enjoy learning Spanish in the morning, volunteer work in the afternoon/evening. Spanish classes of 2-5 students plus group learning activities; conversations with middle class homestay families (1 student per family). Homestays and most volunteer projects are within walking distance of school in small town near the capital, San José.

Dates: Year round, all levels. Classes begin every Monday (except Apr 17-21 and Dec 18-29), volunteer program is continuous. **Cost:** $345 per week for 28 hours of classes and group activities plus Costa Rican dance and cooking classes. Includes tuition, 3 meals per day, 7 days per week, homestay, laundry, all materials, weekly 3-hour cultural tour, and airport transportation. $25 one-time registration fee. **Contact:** Susan Shores, Registrar, Latin American Language Center, PMB 123, 7485 Rush River Dr., Suite 710, Sacramento, CA 95831-5260; 916-447-0938, fax 916-428-9542; lalc@madre.com.

Spanish and More in Heredia. Heredia offers intensive language studies which fulfills up to 2-year university Spanish requirements in a semester or 1 year in the 8-week summer program. Additional courses offered in political science, history, biology, teacher ed., business, literature, etc. Program organized week-long and weekend field trips, homestays, and many local university activities.

Dates: Fall semester: Aug-Dec (1999), spring semester: Jan-May (2000), summer sessions: May 28-Jul 2, Jun 25-Aug 1, Jul 30-Aug 29. **Cost:** Fall or spring semester $4,620; year $7,600; Jun or Jul $1,980; Aug $1,610; Jun and Jul $3,680; June/July, and Aug $3,190; Jun, Jul, and Aug $4,680. **Contact:** University Studies Abroad Consortium (USAC), Univ. of Nevada, Reno #323, Reno, NV 89557-0093; 775-784-6569, fax 775-784-6010; usac@admin.unr.edu, [www.scsr.nevada.edu/~usac].

Spanish and More in Puntarenas. Puntarenas offers intensive language studies which fulfills up to 2-year university Spanish requirements in a semester or 1 year in the 8-week summer program. Additional courses offered in political science, history, biology, teacher ed., business, literature, etc. Program organized week-long and weekend field trips, homestays, and many local university activities.

Dates: Fall semester: Aug-Dec; spring semester: Jan-May. **Cost:** Fall or spring semester $4,620; year $7,600. **Contact:** University Studies Abroad Consortium (USAC), Univ. of Nevada, Reno #323, Reno, NV 89557-0093; 775-784-6569, fax 775-784-6010; usac@admin.unr.edu, [www.scsr.nevada.edu/~usac].

Spanish Language Program. Twenty hours of small group instruction, maximum 4 students per class, Monday-Friday. All ages and all levels. Each student takes an oral and written exam and is placed at a level that matches his/her knowledge. Students live with a Costa Rican family. Organized activities are part of the program.

Dates: Courses start every Monday of the year. **Cost:** Four-week program $1,260: host family stay, language classes 4 hours per day, 5 days a week. (Also 1-week, 2-week, or 3-week program.) **Contact:** Guiselle Ballestero, Sonia Rojas, Ronny Garcia; 011-506-458-3157, fax 011-506-458-3214; [www.institutodecultura.com].

Study in San José. The oldest academic exchange in the Western Hemisphere, the Grupo de Kansas program begins with a 4-week history and culture orientation session. During the academic year participants are regularly enrolled in a full load of courses at the Univ. of Costa Rica. A full range of services from homestays to excursions are built into the program.

Dates: Fall and academic year. **Cost:** Semester $5,370; academic year $9,340 includes San José and KU orientation, room and board, tuition and fees, visa, field trips (1999). **Contact:** Pina Pereiro, Office of Study Abroad, 108 Lippincott, Univ. of Kansas, Lawrence, KS 66045; 785-864-3742, fax 785-864-5040; osa@ukans.edu, [www.ukans.edu/~osa].

Sustainable Development. The Institute for Central American Development Studies (ICADS) offers an interdisciplinary semester abroad study program focusing on development issues from ecological, socio-economic perspectives. The 14-week field course includes: 1) 4 weeks of intensive Spanish and urban issues, 2) 5 weeks in the field in different managed and natural ecosystems learning techniques of field research in social and natural sciences, 3) 5 weeks of independent study—living and working in rural or urban communities.

Dates: Fall and spring terms with academic credit. **Cost:** $7,600. **Contact:** Dr. Sandra Kinghorn, Ph.D., ICADS Director, ICADS,

Dept. 826, P.O. Box 025216, Miami, FL 33102-5216; 011-506-225-0508, fax 011-506-234-1337; icads@netbox.com, [www.icadscr.com].

Tropical Forest Workshop. Tropical Forest Ecology (400 level, 4 credit hours). Intensive study of wet tropical forest structure and function. Trips to mangrove, elfin, and cloud forests. Field experience: forest restoration, biodiversity monitoring, nursery, plantations. Environmental studies (300, 400 level, 2-4 credit hours). Field experience, independent study. Living with a Costa Rican family.

Dates: Month of July. **Cost:** $1,800 includes courses, room and board, field trips. Airfare not included. **Contact:** Dick Andrus, Binghamton Univ., Biology Dept., Binghamton, NY 13902; 607-777-2160, fax 607-777-6521; randrus@binghamton.edu.

Universidad de Costa Rica (MLSA). A graduate and undergraduate program at the Universidad de Costa Rica for students interested in studying courses in language, literature, culture and civilization, composition, and history of Costa Rica. All courses are taught by full-time faculty members from the Univ. of Costa Rica, the most prestigious university in Costa Rica. A lot of extra activities and excursions are organized for students. Students stay with Costa Rican families.

Dates: Summer: Jun-Jul; semester: fall and winter. **Cost:** Total cost $1,885 including airfare. **Contact:** Modern Language Studies Abroad, P.O. Box 623, Griffith, IN 46319; Tel./fax 219-838-9460; mlsa@sprintmail.com.

Cuba

Introduction to Contemporary Cuba. Four-credit, 3 1/2-week summer and winter program taught at the Univ. of Havana by Cuban faculty. A unique opportunity to experience the blend of African, European, and American cultures that form Cuba. Study trips to Pinar del Rio, Matanzas provinces, Varadero beach, Regla, Ernest Hemingway's home, and other sites. Orientation in Cancún.

Dates: Winter: Jan 3-23; summer: Jun 8-30. **Cost:** Winter $2,510; summer $2,825 includes tuition, lodging with 2 meals per day, study/ visits and tours, orientation meeting and night in Cancún, Mexico; hotel-airport transfers, roundtrip flight between Cancún and Havana, transcript from The Center for Cross-Cultural Study. **Contact:** Dr. Judith Ortiz, Director U.S., Center for Cross-Cultural Study, 446 Main St., Amherst, MA 01002; 800-377-2621, fax 413-256-1968; cccs@crocker.com, [www.cccs.com].

Czech Republic

NYU in Prague. NYU in Prague takes students to the crossroads of Europe with a curriculum focusing on the rich history, culture, and language of the region. The NYU Center occupies a 15th century building near the Old Town Square of this famously beautiful city. A modern dormitory houses students near Prague Castle.

Dates: Jun-Aug. **Cost:** $1,070 housing and activities; $3,350 undergraduate tuition; $550 per point, graduate tuition. **Contact:** NYU Summer Session, 7 E. 12th St., 6th Fl., New York, NY 10003; 212-998-2292, fax 212-995-4103; summer.info@nyu.edu.

Penn-in-Prague. For students interested in Czech and central European culture, this program, located amidst the fairy tale beauty of Prague and affiliated with Charles Univ., offers an insight into the rich history and urgent contemporary problems of this important region, as well as an opportunity to learn beginning and intermediate Czech.

Dates: Jul 5-Aug 13. **Cost:** Tuition $3,072; housing and activities $300. **Contact:** Penn Summer Abroad, College of General Studies, Univ. of Pennsylvania, 3440 Market St., Suite 100, Philadelphia, PA 19104-3335; 215-898-5738, fax 215-573-2053.

Denmark

Business and Economic Studies. The Copenhagen program combines academic coursework with practical learning. At Copenhagen Business School (CBS), you have the opportunity to study international business and economics, giving you an important academic foundation as well as an opportunity for cultural enrichment and making personal international business contacts.

Dates: Fall semester: Aug-Dec; spring semester: Jan-Jun. **Cost:** Fall semester $4,750; spring semester $4,750; year $7,880. **Contact:** University Studies Abroad Consortium (USAC), Univ. of Nevada, Reno #323, Reno, NV 89557-0093; 775-784-6569, fax 775-784-6010; usac@admin.unr.edu, [www.scsr.nevada.edu/~usac].

Denmark's International Study Program (DIS). Study Abroad Program in Copenhagen. Courses are taught in English at the upper division undergraduate level within the following programs: biology, international business, arts and humanities, architecture and design, engineering, medical practice and policy, and arctic biology. Program includes study tours and field work.

Dates: Fall semester: Aug-Dec.; spring semester: Jan-May. **Cost:** Call for details. **Contact:** DIS North American Office; 800-247-3477; dis@tc.umn.edu, www.disp.dk.

Ecuador

Academia de Español Quito. Intensive Spanish language programs from 4 to 7 hours daily. Private classes, one-on-one instruction for professional adults, college students, and all Spanish levels in programs of 1 to 12 weeks. U.S. graduate and undergraduate credit. Caring homestays and many additional weekly activities included. Activa program students study 4 hours in the morning in the classroom and in the afternoon explore Quito and surrounding area with their teacher. The Anaconda 1-week program located on an island in an Amazon River tributary. Group classes in the morning; explore the jungle and rainforest in the afternoon. Also discounted Galapagos trips.

Dates: Year round. New classes begin every Monday (summer months fill very early). **Cost:** Four hours daily private classes and homestay: $294 per week; 7 hours daily Activa program (includes all transportation, entry fees, etc.): $439 per week; Anaconda program $550. Includes tuition, insurance, materials, airport pickup, private room, 3 meals daily, and laundry. **Contact:** Kay G. Rafool, Language Link Inc., P.O. Box 3006, Peoria, IL 61612; 800-552-2051, fax 309-692-2926; info@langlink.com, [www.langlink.com].

Academia de Español Quito. Specially designed programs for foreign students. One-on-one instruction up to 7 hours daily. Courses based on conversation, vocabulary, and grammar at all levels. Cultural and social activities provided weekly. The system is self-paced, and it is possible to start at any time. Earn academic credits. Live with an Ecuadorian family, 1 student per family, full board.

Dates: Year round. **Cost:** $1,600 for 4 weeks includes tuition, meals, housing, fees, airport transfer. **Contact:** Edgar J. Alvarez, Director, 130 Marchena St. and 10 de Agosto Ave., P.O. Box 17-15-0039-C, Quito, Ecuador; 011-593-2-553647/554811, fax 011-593-2-506474/504330; edalvare@pi.pro.ec, [www.academiaquito.com.ec].

Academia Latinoamericana. Proud to be the friendliest Spanish school you have ever known. Family owned and operated. The program offers language study at 9 levels, for complete beginners through advanced. Experienced staff, native Ecuadorians. Carefully selected host families within walking distance of school. Exclusive "SierrAzul Cloud Forest and Galapagos" extension program, volunteer program. U.S. college credit available.

Dates: Year round. **Cost:** $230 per week. Includes 20 hours of lessons, 7 days with host family, 2 meals per day, transfer, services at the school, and teaching material. **Contact:** Suzanne S. Bell, Admissions Director, USA/International, 640 East 3990 South, Suite E, Salt Lake City, UT, 84107; 801-268-4608, fax 801-265-9156; academia@juno.com, delco@spanish.com.ec.

BCA Program in Quito. Earn 13-18 credits per semester at Universidad San Francisco de Quito, with a fall 4-week intensive language and orientation, homestay with Ecuadoran families, field trips, extended study tour to Amazon headwaters and Galápagos islands. Students from all U.S. colleges and universities accepted. Intermediate level college Spanish required. Full liberal arts curriculum available. Ecology field studies and internships.

Dates: Aug-Dec (fall), Jan-May (spring), Aug-May (year). **Cost:** $19,445 (academic year); $10,845 (semester). Includes international transportation, room and board, tuition, insurance, group travel in country. **Contact:** Cristina Garcia-Cervigon, 605 E. College Ave., North Manchester, IN 46962; 219-982-5238, fax 219-982-7755; bca@manchester.edu, [www.bcanet.org].

Community Internships in Latin America. Emphasis on community participation for social change. Students work 3 days a week in an internship, meet together for core seminar and internship seminar, and carry out independent study project. Wide range of internship opportunities in community development and related activities. Family homestay, field trips. Latin American faculty. Full semester's credit, U.S. transcript provided. All majors, 2 years Spanish language required.

Dates: Early Feb-mid-May. **Cost:** Spring $9,250 . Includes tuition, internship placement and supervision, room and board, field trips. **Contact:** Rebecca Rassier, Director of Student Services, HECUA, Mail #36, Hamline Univ., 1536 Hewitt Ave., St. Paul, MN 55104-1284; 612-646-8832 or 800-554-1089; info@hecua.org, [www.hecua.org].

Environment and Ecology in Ecuador. The program focuses on the growing conflict between the development of Ecuador's economy and the preservation of its ecological resources. Program includes course work in Spanish with Ecuadoran students at the Universidad San Francisco de Quito, field study trips to several regions of the country, and an independent research project. Minimum 2 years college Spanish and strong background in biology required. **Dates:** Jan-mid-Jun. **Cost:** (1999-2000) $16,650 includes roundtrip international transportation, tuition and fees, field study trips, room and board, and some excursions. **Contact:** Center for International Programs, Kalamazoo College, 1200 Academy St., Kalamazoo, MI 49006; 616-337-7133, fax 616-337-7400; cip@kzoo.edu, [www.kzoo.edu/cip].

Egypt

The American Univ. in Cairo. Study abroad for a semester, year, or summer with Egyptian and international students from over 50 countries at The American Univ. in Cairo. Directly enroll in liberal arts and professional program courses taught in English at an American-style university. Located in the political and cultural hub or the Arab world and the largest city in Africa, study at AUC offers exceptional educational and travel opportunities. **Dates:** Sep-Jan, Jan-Jun, Jun-Aug. **Cost:** Year $11,060, semester $5,575, summer $2,788. **Contact:** Matrans Davidson, The American Univ. in Cairo, 420 5th Ave., 3rd Fl., New York, NY 10018-2729; aucegypt@aucnyo.edu, [www.aucegypt.edu].

Europe

¿?don Quijote In-Country Spanish Language Schools. Offers Spanish language courses in our 6 schools in Spain and 5 partner schools in Latinoamerica. Our courses (standard, intensive, business, D.E.L.E., tourism, flight attendants and refresher for teachers) are all year round, from 2 weeks on. Students can combine different cities and schools. Academic credit is available. **Dates:** Year round—fall, spring, winter, and summer, 2 weeks to a full year of study. **Cost:** Email or check web site for details. **Contact:** ¿?don Quijote In-Country Spanish Language Schools, calle/Placentinos n°2, Salamanca 37008, Spain; 011-34-923-268860, fax 011-34-923-268815; amusa@donquijote.org, [www.donquijote.org].

Archaeology Summer School. Introduces participants to the theory and practice of archaeology in general and to Mediterranean and Maltese archaeology in particular. Two-week course is followed by 4 weeks of excavation and finds processing experience. Participants may register for a range of 2-6 week options. **Dates:** Jun 12-Jul 21. **Cost:** From $625-$2,000 includes accommodations. **Contact:** Jean Killick, International Office, Foundation for International Studies, Old Univ. Bldg., St. Paul St., Valletta VLT 07, Malta; 011-356-234121/2, fax 011-356-230538; jkil@um.edu.mt, [www.um.edu.mt/shortcourses/].

BGSU AYA in Salzburg. The Bowling Green State Univ. Academic Year Abroad in Salzburg program, presently in its 31st year (on the web at www.bgsu/departments/greal/AYA-Salzburg.html), is designed to help American students perfect their German skills. Participants gain first-hand knowledge of German-speaking countries while earning credit toward undergraduate and master's degrees in a variety of subjects. **Dates:** Full year program Oct-Jun. **Cost:** $10,098 (OH res.), $12,743 (non-res.) includes program costs, room and board. **Contact:** Bowling Green State Univ., Dept. of German, Russian, and EAL; 419-372-6815, fax 419-372-2571; sidors@bgnet.bgsu.edu.

Budapest Semesters in Mathematics. A rigorous mathematics program for students attending colleges and universities in North America majoring in mathematics or computer science. Classes taught in English by eminent Hungarian professors. Unlike any other program you will ever encounter. Mix it all in a world as warm and friendly as Budapest, and it's paradise. **Dates:** Spring: Feb 7-May 26, 2000; fall: Sep 11-Dec 22, 2000. **Cost:** Tuition: $3,500 plus $300 refundable housing deposit. **Contact:** Prof. Paul D. Humke, Director, Budapest Semesters in Mathematics, St. Olaf College, 1520 St. Olaf Ave., Northfield, MN 55057; 800-277-0434; budapest@stolaf.edu, [www.stolaf.edu/depts/math/budapest].

Center for University Programs Abroad (Paris, France). Assisting American undergraduates with individualized study programs at the universities, and a range of institutes, in Paris. Semester and year abroad options for highly motivated, linguistically and academically prepared students.

Dates: Fall, year: Mar 31; spring: Oct 31. **Cost:** Year $23,000 includes tuition, room and board; semester $14,000 includes tuition, room and board. **Contact:** Mary S. Cattani, Director, C.V.P.A. P.O. Box 9611, N. Amherst, MA 01059.

Comparative Women's Studies in Europe. This program is an examination and comparison of international feminist issues. Topics include women's history, current political movements, cultural expectations, and social structures. Lectures, site visits, and extensive research are conducted in Poland, the Netherlands, Germany, and Britain. Independent research is synthesized during the final weeks of the program.

Dates: Sep-Dec. **Cost:** Contact office for details. **Contact:** Antioch Education Abroad, Antioch College, 795 Livermore St., Yellow Springs, OH 45387; 800-874-7986, fax 937-767-6469; aea@antioch-college.edu, www.antioch-college.edu/aea.

Europe in Transition. An in-depth exploration of contemporary social, economic and political changes across Europe through a semester in Germany, Poland, Hungary, and England. Students examine emerging changes in political economy; growing conflicts over the autonomy of women, and ethnic and racial minorities; and the post Cold-War dynamics of European integration.

Dates: Sep-Dec. **Cost:** Contact office for details. **Contact:** Antioch Education Abroad, Antioch College, 795 Livermore St., Yellow Springs, OH 45387; 800-874-7986, fax 937-767-6469; aea@antioch-college.edu, www.antioch-college.edu/aea.

Friends World Program. A semester or year program in Europe beginning at Friends World Center in London includes an intensive introduction into European culture and history. The program offers seminars, field study, travel, and independent work anywhere in Europe after the first semester. The center serves as a base to explore all regions and cultures in the European continent. Field studies in literature, politics, arts, history, peace studies, theater, education, and community development are all available. Students may earn 12-18 credits per semester.

Dates: Fall: early Sep-mid-Dec; spring: mid-Jan-mid-May. **Cost:** $13,400 per semester in 1999/2000. Includes tuition, travel, room and board, fees and books. **Contact:** Admissions, Friends World Program, 239 Montauk Hwy., Southampton, NY 11968; 516-287-8474; fw@southampton.liunet.edu.

InterStudy. InterStudy offers integrated study abroad opportunities at selected European and South African universities.

Dates: Rolling admissions. **Cost:** Contact sponsor. **Contact:** InterStudy, 63 Edward St., Medford, MA 02155; 800-663-1999, fax 781-391-7463; InterStudy@interstudy-usa.org.

Issue-Specific Travel Courses. Visit 1 to 4 cities. Topics include International Business and Economics, Comparative Education, Historical Literature, Social Service Systems, and other crosscultural studies. Emphasis on personal interaction between students and European professionals and providing a holistic cultural experience. Two- to 5-week programs. Three to 6 credit hours—undergraduate, graduate, or audit basis—through the Univ. of Missouri-Kansas City.

Dates: Early summer. **Cost:** Approx. $2,000 (does not include airfare). **Contact:** People to People International, Collegiate and Professional Studies Abroad, 501 E. Armour Blvd., Kansas City, MO 64109-2200; 816-531-4701, fax 816-561-7502; collegiate@ptpi.org, [www.ptpi.org/studyabroad].

Middlebury College Schools Abroad. Middlebury College operates Schools Abroad in France (Paris), Germany (Mainz), Italy (Florence), Russia (Moscow, Irkutsk, Voronezh, and Yaroslavl), and Spain (Madrid, Getafe, Logroño, and Segovia) for college students who meet the language proficiency requirements. The Schools Abroad are renowned to be intellectually challenging and culturally stimulating. Undergraduate and graduate programs abroad offered.

Dates: Most schools are Sep-Dec, and Jan-May, except Mainz which is Oct-Feb and Mar-Jul. **Cost:** 1999-2000 fees: Florence, Getafe, Logroño, Madrid, Mainz, Paris, Segovia Year: $11,485 (tuition only); semester: $6,000 (tuition only). Irkutsk, Moscow year: $17,770 (tuition, room, visas, and roundtrip airfare from NYC); semester: $11,000 (tuition, room, visas, and roundtrip airfare from NYC). Voronezh, Yaroslavl Year: $16,470 (tuition, room, partial board, visas, and roundtrip airfare from NYC); semester: $8,235 (tuition, room, partial board, visas, and roundtrip airfare from NYC). **Contact:** Schools Abroad, Middlebury College, Middlebury, VT 05753; 802-443-5745, fax 802-443-3157; schoolsabroad@middlebury.edu, [www.middlebury.edu/~msa].

NYU Study Abroad (Arts and Science). NYU's Faculty of Arts and Science offers undergraduate and graduate programs in Athens, Dublin, Florence, London, Madrid, Paris, and Prague. Led by distinguished faculty, courses on the art, architecture, culture, civilization, politics, languages, and literature of the region are supplemented by excursions.

Dates: Jun-Aug. **Cost:** Call for details. **Contact:** NYU Summer Session, 7 E. 12th St., 6th Fl., New York, NY 10003; 212-998-2292, fax 212-995-4103; summer.info@nyu.edu.

Summer School-Shakespearean Acting. One of U.K.'s top drama schools offers an intensive Shakespeare course, full-time, over 4 weeks.

Dates: Jul 24-Aug 18. **Cost:** £850 (subject to increase). **Contact:** Administration, London Academy of Performing Arts, St. Matthew's Church, St. Petersburgh Pl., London W2 4LA, U.K.; 011-44-207-727-0220, fax 011-44-207-727-0330; londonacademy.performingarts @btinternet.com, [www.btinternet.com/ ~londonacademy.performingarts].

France

Academic Year Abroad Paris. Direct registration at the Sorbonne in liberal arts, fine arts, social sciences, and AYA-sponsored orientation and tutorials. Supplementary courses at Institut Catholique, intensive language at the Cours de Civilisation of the Sorbonne. Optional room and board with Parisian families and cultural activities.

Dates: Late Sep-mid-Jan; late Jan-end May. **Cost:** Term $8,850; year $15,000. Includes tuition, tutorials, room and board, and cultural activities. **Contact:** Dr. A.M. Cinquemani, Academic Year Abroad, P.O. 733, Stone Ridge, NY 12484-0733, fax 914-687-2470; aya@ulster.net, [www.studyabroad.com/aya].

BCA in Strasbourg or Nancy. Earn 14-16 credits per semester at either the Université de Nancy or the Université de Strasbourg, with a fall 4-week intensive language training and orientation plus field trips and extended study tour to Paris. Selective Honors Program offered in both universities. Internships available. Students accepted from all U.S. colleges and universities. Intermediate level college French required.

Dates: Sep-Dec or Jan (fall), Jan-May or Jun (spring), Sep-May or Jun (year). **Cost:** $19,445 (academic year), $10,845 (semester). Includes international transportation, room and board, tuition, insurance, group travel in country. **Contact:** Cristina Garcia-Cervigon, 605 E.

College Ave., North Manchester, IN 46962; 219-982-5238, fax 219-982-7755; bca@manchester.edu, [www.bcanet.org].

Center for Univ. Progs. Abroad. CUPA assists American undergraduates with individualized study programs at the universities and a range of institutes in Paris. Semester and year abroad options for highly motivated, linguistically and academically prepared students.

Dates: Fall, spring, year. **Cost:** Year $23,000 includes tuition, room and board. Semester $14,000 includes tuition, room and board. **Contact:** Mary S. Cattani, Director, C.U.P.A., P.O. Box 9611, N. Amherst, MA 01059.

Central College Abroad. In Paris, all students are enrolled at the Sorbonne and Alliance Française, and live in French dorms. Various courses, all taught in French, excursions, intensive language orientation in Nice with homestay, ISIC included. Special business track option for advanced students through Chamber of Commerce and Industry. Onsite director.

Dates: Semester or full-year. **Cost:** 1999-2000: semester $11,250; year $19,850. **Contact:** Central College Abroad, 812 University, Pella, IA 50219; 800-831-3629, fax 515-628-5375; studyabroad@central.edu, [www.studyabroad.com/central].

Columbia Univ. in Paris at Reid Hall. Courses are offered at Reid Hall as well as at 3 divisions of the Univ. of Paris. Open to students who have completed 2 or 3 years of college French or the equivalent.

Dates: Summer Jun, fall Sep-Jun, spring Jan-Jun. **Cost:** $610 credit tuition (1999). **Contact:** Columbia Univ. CE/SP, 2970 Broadway, MC 4119, New York, NY 10027-6902; 212-854-8939, fax 212-854-2400; studyaway@columbia.edu, [www.ce.columbia.edu/].

Davidson in Tours. Academic year at Univ. of Tours or semester at the Institute of Touraine in Tours. Earn 8 course credits for the year or 4 per semester. Live with families in Tours. A 2- to 4-week stay in Paris as well as numerous group activities and excursions is included. A Davidson faculty member serves as resident director and teaches one course each semester.

Dates: Sep-Jun (may attend for semester or year). **Cost:** $14,300 per semester includes all academic expenses, room, board, international airfare, excursions, international student identity card. **Contact:** Carolyn Ortmayer, Office of Study Abroad, Davidson College, P.O. Box 1719, Davidson, NC 28036; 704-892-2250, fax 704-892-2005; abroad@davidson.edu, [www.davidson.edu/administrative/ study_abroad/abroad.html].

French in France. Among the ways to learn French, total immersion is the most enjoyable and the most effective. We have been doing it for 20 years in a small historical city located in Normandy (west of Paris, close to the seaside). We welcome people at any age and any level in 1- to 10-week programs, intensive or vacation type, from mid-Mar to mid-Nov.

Dates: Spring: Mar 20-May 27; summer: Jun 12-Aug 26; fall: Sep 4-Nov 11. **Cost:** From $525 per week (tuition, room and board, and excursions). **Contact:** Dr. Alméras, Chairman, French American Study Center, 12, 14, Blvd. Carnot, B.P. 4176, 14104 Lisieux Cedex, France; 011-33-2-31-31-22-01, fax 011-33-2-31-31-22-21; centre.normandie@wanadoo.fr, [http://perso.wanadoo.fr/centre.normandie/].

French Language and Culture Cannes. A semester, academic year, or summer in Cannes is offered by Slippery Rock Univ. at the College International de Cannes. Students with no previous French language study as well as students with advanced levels can be accommodated. Student residence halls are double occupancy and the campus is ideally located adjacent to the beach.

Dates: Feb 27-May 27. **Cost:** $5,610 includes tuition, housing, and meals. **Contact:** Dr. Donald E. Kerchis, Director, International Initiatives, Slippery Rock Univ., Slippery Rock, PA 16057; 724-738-2057, fax 724-738-2959; donald.kerchis@sru.edu, [www.sru.edu].

French Studies: Pau. Pau offers intensive language studies—up to 4 semesters of university language courses in 1 semester, 1 year in the 8-week summer program, in addition to art, political science, history, literature, second language teaching methods, etc. Week-long field trips to Paris, homestay or student residence, and many activities at the French university.

Dates: Summer terms: May 27-Jun 27; Jun 27-Aug 1; Jul 31-Aug 23; fall semester: Sep-Dec; spring semester: Jan-April. **Cost:** Fall or spring semester $4,280; Jun $1,770; Jul $1,880; Aug $1,580; Jun and Jul $3,480; Jun and Aug $2,870; Jul and Aug $2,970; Jun, Jul, and Aug $4,580; year $6,980. **Contact:** University Studies Abroad Consortium (USAC), Univ. of Nevada, Reno #323, Reno, NV 89557-0093; 775-784-6569, fax 775-784-6010; usac@admin.unr.edu, [www.scsr.nevada.edu/~usac].

Immersion Course in French. Intensive 2-4 week course for professional adults in Villefranche (next to Nice) overlooking the French Riviera's most beautiful bay; 8 hours a day with 2 meals. Audiovisual classes, language lab, practice sessions, discussion-lunch. Evening film showings, evening outings with teachers, excursions to cultural landmarks. Accommodations in comfortable private apartments.

Dates: Courses start Jan, Feb, Mar, May, Jun, Aug, Sep, Oct, Nov, Dec. **Cost:** Tuition fees: Dec-Apr FF14,100/4 weeks; May-Nov FF16,700/4 weeks. Accommdations: Dec-Apr FF2,000-FF5,200/4 week; May-Nov FF2,300-FF5,800/4 weeks. **Contact:** Frédéric Latty, Institut de Francais, 23, avenue General Leclerc, 06230 Villefranche Sur Mer, France; 011-33-493-01-88-44, fax 011-33-493-76-92-17; instfran@aol.com, [www.institutdefrancais.com].

Institute for American Universities. An educational center for those with a passion for French language and culture, art historians and artists, students, and all who know that experience in another culture is essential for their future. Substantive integration in the local community and culture for every student results in broadened awareness and long-held memories.

Dates: Summer: Jun 19-Jul 28; fall semester Sep-Dec; spring semester Jan-May. **Cost:** Summer 2000: $3,385. Includes tuition, room, and daily breakfast and dinner. Semester $8,985, year $17,970. Includes tuition, room, and daily breakfast. **Contact:** Institute for American Universities, U.S. Office, 1830 Sherman Ave. at University Place, P.O. Box 592, Evanston, IL 60204; 800-221-2051, fax 847-864-6897; iauusa@univ-aix.fr, [www.iau-univ.org].

Intensive Professional Culinary Program. Over 24 weeks this new Lenotre program alternates intensive culinary training in small classes at Ecole Lenotre with hands-on experience in Lenotre kitchens, restaurants, and gourmet boutiques. By the end of the program, students earn qualification as a professional maker of fine French cuisine and pastry.

Dates: Year round, except Aug and 2 weeks during Christmas and New Year's Eve. **Cost:** FF120,000 (approx. $20,000) includes breakfast and lunch. **Contact:** Marie-Anne Dufeu, Ecole Lenotre, 40 rue Pierre Curie, B.P. 6, 78375 Plaisir Cedex, France; 011-33-1-30-81-46-34/35, fax 011-33-1-30-54-73-70.

Internships in Francophone Europe. IFE is an academic internship program—accredited at a number of schools—that places student interns in mid to high levels of French public life including government, politics, the press, social institutions, NGOs, etc. For motivated students, proficient in French, who are interested in immersion in the working life of a French institution and in today's France. The program includes intensive preparatory course work in French history, sociology, politics, language training, and the completion of a research project related to the internship. Open to undergraduates and recent graduates.

Dates: Fall semester (Aug-Dec), spring semester (Jan-May). **Cost:** $5,950 (tuition only); tuition plus housing (approx.) $7,660. Need-based scholarships available, especially for post BA's. **Contact:** Timothy Carlson, Internships in Francophone Europe, 26, rue Cmdt. Mouchotte J108, 75014 Paris, France; 011- 33-1-43-21-78-07, fax 011-33-1-42-79-94-13; ifeparis@worldnet.fr, [www.ifeparis.org].

Kalamazoo in Clermont-Ferrand. This university-integrated program begins with an intensive French course and an orientation. Participants enroll in regular courses at the Ecole Supérieure Normale de Commerce. All participants complete a local business project working with French students in small groups. Minimum of 2 years of college French is required.

Dates: Late Aug-late May (academic year); late Aug-late Feb (fall). **Cost:** Academic year: (1999-2000) $24,975; fall: $16,650. Both fees include roundtrip international transportation, tuition and fees, room and board, and some excursions. **Contact:** Center for International Programs, Kalamazoo College, 1200 Academy St., Kalamazoo, MI 49006; 616-337-7133, fax 616-337-7400; cip@kzoo.edu, [www.kzoo.edu/cip].

MA in French Cultural Studies. This MA program critically examines the many ways in which French society represents itself and the many voices that engage in discourse to produce what we call French society. A variety of required and elective courses allows students to concentrate in specific areas. Study of the francophone diaspora puts French studies in an international context. Under the direction of a faculty associate, each student writes an MA essay (in French or English) on one particular aspect of modern France. Students study in Paris, 2 semesters of residency plus a summer term at Reid Hall and at French institutions of higher learning.

Dates: Sep-Aug. **Cost:** $19,000 includes tuition and fees (1999). **Contact:** Beatrice Terrien-Somerville, Assistant Dean for Academic Affairs, Graduate School of Arts and Sciences, Columbia Univ., 109 Low Memorial Library, 535 W. 116th St., MC 4306, New York, NY 10027; 212-854-5052, fax 212-854-2863; bt3@columbia.edu, [www.columbia.edu/cu/gsas/].

Penn-in-Bordeaux. For students interested in anthropology, archaeology, and the origins of humankind. This program is located near Lascaux and Cro-Magnon, areas where anthropologists have unearthed much of our knowledge about the beginnings of modern humankind. It will center on the issue of what makes us human and how this quality evolved. Lectures will be augmented with the examination of artifacts and fossils as well as visits to important sites.

Dates: Jun 20-Jul 8. **Cost:** Tuition $1,536; housing and excursions $400. **Contact:** Penn Summer Abroad, College of General Studies, Univ. of Pennsylvania, 3440 Market St., Suite 100, Philadelphia, PA 19104-3335; 215-898-5738, fax 215-573-2053.

Penn-in-Compiegne. For students with some proficiency in French who are interested in international relations, economics, or business. The program, affiliated with The Université de Technologi de Compiegne, also offers a 2-week internship in a French enterprise. Students live with local families.

Dates: May 23-Jul 2; with internship: May 23-Jul 18. **Cost:** Tuition $3,094; room and board, and activities $960 (study only) or $1,280 (full program). **Contact:** Penn Summer Abroad, College of General Studies, Univ. of Pennsylvania, 3440 Market St., Suite 100, Philadelphia, PA 19104-3335; 215-898-5738, fax 215-573-2053.

Penn-in-Tours. For students interested in French language, literature, art, and civilization. Penn-in-Tours also offers various cultural opportunities and excursions in the beautiful Loire Valley. Students live with local families.

Dates: May 24-Jul 7. **Cost:** Tuition $3,072; family lodging $1,300; excursion and activity fee $200. **Contact:** Penn Summer Abroad, College of General Studies, Univ. of Pennsylvania, 3440 Market St., Suite 100, Philadelphia, PA 19104-3335; 215-898-5738, fax 215-573-2053.

Summer International Language Program. Six-week intermediate to advanced-level intensive French language, culture, and business at the Institut de Formation Internationale in Rouen, France. Program includes an internship with a local company. Students earn 6 semester units of credit.

Dates: May 25-Jul 2. **Cost:** $4,560 includes tuition, homestay, 2 meals per day, materials, excursions, and internship. **Contact:** International Language Programs, Monterey Institute

By Heather O'Connor

Today's college student spends an average of 4.9 hours per week on the Internet, more than any other age group, according to Jupiter Communications, a New York-based research firm. Wil Doane from TransitionsAbroad.com said he has seen an increase in traffic to their web site from approximately 1,000 visitors in May 1997 to 35,000 in September 1999.

Many study abroad program sponsors are establishing an Internet presence in hopes of attracting a few of these online hours to their programs. They understand that through a web site they can reach a large and growing audience of students, parents, and international educators without spending a fortune on brochures, envelopes, and postage.

Web sites can promote study abroad programs any time of day or night, whether the office is open or not, by showing photographs, audio clips, and virtual tours. Program information can be updated as the changes occur so that students, parents, and colleagues have the most up-to-date information available. At the same time, program sponsors can fulfill their role as educators by providing students a means to learn about any number of areas related to study abroad (legal issues, currency exchange, health and safety, tourism) through links to other web sites on the Internet.

Most study abroad program sponsors already have some form of a paper-based marketing plan that includes flyers, catalogs, mailings, recruiting visits, or study abroad fairs—all the "traditional" ways of getting the word out to potential participants. The challenge is to combine traditional and Internet marketing in a way that will make the sponsor's job of being both an educator and a marketer easier.

Internet-Based Marketing

Bentley College, a private business school outside Boston, sponsors Bentley College Business Programs Abroad (BCBPA), full-immersion study abroad programs open to non-Bentley College students. In 1997, the college began to call itself "The Business School for the Information Age." Institution funds were reallocated to departments utilizing technology in their programs and the study abroad budget for printing and mailing our annual full-color catalog of programs was eliminated. BCBPA responded to the challenge by designing a web site and an Internet-based marketing plan to promote our programs to students both on and off campus. Along the way we learned a few lessons:

1. **Create a game plan.** The first step in any marketing plan is to decide who your audience is and the best medium to reach it. Since students already spend several hours per week on the Internet, they will probably respond well to online marketing. However, their parents may not have Internet access from their homes and may respond better to letters and informational flyers.

Ideally, you should develop your Internet and print marketing plan together and tailor each to the audience you wish to reach. One should complement the other. If you have a paper catalog, have a place on your web site for visitors to request a copy. Make sure you reference your web site on everything that leaves your office.

2. **Design a good web site.** Once you have developed a plan, take a critical look at your web site. This is the first, and often only, impression visitors have of your organization and programs, so make it a good one.
- Verify that the information on your web site is correct and corresponds with print publications.
- Make sure your web site is easy to navigate; if students have to spend too much time searching for the information they want, they will move on to the next site.
- Photos, videos, and other graphics will catch the eye of casual web surfers. But these can be a problem for those with slow Internet connections or those who use older browsers that cannot display graphics.
- Indicate at the bottom of each page when it was last updated.
- Include a clear call to action on your web site. What do you want your visitors to do after visiting your site? Request a paper catalog? Complete an online application? Speak to their home institution's study abroad adviser? Tell visitors to your site what they should do next if they are interested in your programs.
- Include a brief registration form somewhere on your web site so that visitors can complete it and send it to you via email. This is useful for visitors who want to ask questions or request a catalog or application. It is also useful to you, the program sponsor, as a way to collect email and mailing addresses for future marketing.
- Finally, you should solicit visitor feedback on your web site and make changes in your site and marketing plan when necessary.

3. **Allot the necessary resources.** Equally important to having a good web site is having a plan to respond to the increase in traffic as a result of your Internet presence. Decide who is going to be responsible for managing and updating your web site and if additional staff training or technical resources are needed. Decide how you will respond to student inquiries, both the serious ones and the junk emails that you will most certainly receive. You will also have to think about a budget—both in terms of staff time and the money to market your web site. Do not attempt an Internet marketing plan if you do not have the resources to support it. You will soon find yourself drowning in unreturned emails!

4. **Submit your URL to search engines and directories.** Once your web site is up and running and your policies are in place, you can start marketing. There are several free ways to get the word out about your programs on the Internet. The first is to register your URL (web site address) with search engines and directories. Web surfers can then search the catalogs by keywords to find lists of web sites on specific topics.

Once you submit your URL to a search engine it is important to check on it. Hundreds of new web sites are added to the Internet each day, so it can take several weeks for your web site to be listed. Once it is listed, it can be bumped off by newer sites. Check up every month or so to see where you stand on the search engines and resubmit your URL(s), if necessary. You should also resubmit your URL(s) if you make any major changes to your site. See the MarketPosition Newsletter, [www.webposition.com/newsletter.htm], for advice on search engine submissions.

5. **Exchange links with other programs and directories.** You can also request that your web site be listed in commercial online directories. These topic-specific directories often will provide a link to your web site for free, or free with the purchase of an advertisement in their paper publication. Transitions Abroad is one such organization which offers a free listing in their online directory with the purchase of a classified ad or directory listing in their print publications. Program sponsors can also purchase banner advertisements (see below) on the Transitions Abroad web site without purchasing a print advertisement.

It is also worth asking other study abroad offices or program sponsors to trade links with you: You provide a link to their web site if they do the same. This can increase traffic to both sites and benefit your students by providing them with additional study abroad options to choose from.

6. **Consider banner advertising.** If you have the budget for it, you may want to look into banner advertising. Banner ads run on related web sites or search engines and provide a link to your site. They can cost from several hundred to thousands of dollars, depending on where and how often you advertise, but they can mean a huge increase in traffic to your site.

Placing banner ads, checking on search engine listings, and maintaining links with study abroad directories can easily become a full-time job. If you can afford it, you may want to consider getting an intern or hiring a consultant or an online marketing organization to assist you.

7. **Create a "virtual community."** After all this, you should see an increase in traffic to your web site. But your job is not over yet. As study abroad program sponsors, we all have a responsibility to prepare students for the experience of study abroad, not just to sell a product. The Internet gives program sponsors the opportunity to make their web site an extension of their office and an educational tool for students, parents, and the general public.

You can do this by creating a "virtual community." Pack your web site full of useful information on not only your own programs but on all aspects of international education. Provide links to the host institution or country, the U.S. State Department, student travel agencies, etc. Create chat rooms or listservs where students can exchange information on programs, travel plans, and cross-cultural issues. Send out an email newsletter to prospective students (whose names and email addresses you have collected from your registration form) to let them know about additions to your web site or to draw their attention to information they may have missed. This way students, parents, and others will return to your site again and again.

The extra effort put into creating a virtual community can have exponential benefits. You empower students and parents to do their own research and learn more about study abroad opportunities and international issues. You create a support and informational network for potential, current, and former program participants. And you identify yourself as a resource for students, parents, and your fellow international educators. This in turn can increase the visibility and reputation of your programs.

Internet Resources

Search Engines/Directories. The following search engines and directories are free and have a link from their home page to a form you can use to register your URL: [www.altavista.com], [www.excite.com], [www.hotbot.com], [www.infoseek.com], [www.webcrawler.com], [www.looksmart.com], [www.lycos.com], [www.yahoo.com].

Study Abroad Directories. These directories are specifically geared towards international education. Many will provide a link or listing on their web site for free, or free with the purchase of an advertisement in their print publication. Contact the organization directly for details and rates: [www.AllAbroad.com], [www.edunet.com], [www.iie.org/svcs/sartoc.htm], [www.istc.umn.edu/osad/], [www.petersons.com], [www.studyabroad.com], [www.TransitionsAbroad.com].

Check How You Rank. Once your web site is listed with the search engines and directories above, it is important to monitor your listings and update them, if necessary. The following web site will evaluate and report your standing in the more popular search engines/directories: [http://siteowner.linkexchange.com].

Recommended Reading. Getting Hits: The Definitive Guide to Promoting Your Web Site by Don Sellers (Peachpit Press, 1997, $19.95). Recommended for beginners only. Guerrilla Marketing On-line by Jay Conrad Levinson and Charles Rubin (Houghton Mifflin, 1997, $14). Marketing on the Internet by Jill and Matthew Ellsworth (John Wiley & Sons, 1996, $24.95). World Wide Web Marketing by Jim Sterne (John Wiley & Sons, 1999, $29.99).

For more information on search engines, directories, banner advertisements, and other methods of marketing on the Internet, you may wish to visit these web sites: [www.rankhigh.com], [www.smartbiz.com], [www.wprc.com], [http://searchenginewatch.com], [www.submit-it.com], [http://erebus.bentley.edu/empl/o/hoconnor/mktintro.htm], [www.promoteone.com].

of International Studies, 425 Van Buren St., Monterey, CA 93940; 831-647-6548, fax 831-647-6551; ilp@miis.edu.

Welcome to Burgundy. The CIEF, founded in Dijon in 1902, offers courses (16-20 hours a week) throughout the year at the Univ. of Burgundy taught by specialists in the teaching of French as a foreign language. Further recreational possibilities: winetasting sessions, cookery classes, drama of French song workshop, concerts, cinema, outings, and guided tours. Accommodations provided.
Dates: Year round. **Cost:** FF1,950-FF6,300. **Contact:** Centre International d'Études Françaises, Maison de l'Université, Esplanade Érasme, BP28, 21001 Dijon Cedex, France; 011-33-3-80-39-35-60, fax 011-33-80-39-35-61; cief@u-bourgogne.fr, [www.u-bourgogne.fr/Etranger/cief.htm].

Germany

Antioch in Germany Program. This program is the closest experience to living and studying as German students do. Orientation and intensive language study precede enrollment in Eberhard-Karls-Universität in Tübingen. Language of instruction is primarily German; 2 years of college-level German is recommended.
Dates: Fall, spring, year. **Cost:** Contact office for details. **Contact:** Antioch Education Abroad, Antioch College, 795 Livermore St., Yellow Springs, OH 45387; 800-874-7986, fax 937-767-6469; aea@antioch-college.edu, [www.antioch-college.edu/aea].

BCA Program in Marburg. Earn 14-16 credits per semester at Philipps-Universität in Marburg, with a 4-week intensive language training and orientation, field trips, and an extended study tour. Students accepted from all U.S. colleges and universities. Intermediate level college German required.
Dates: Sep-Feb (fall); Feb-Jul (spring); Sep-Jul (year). **Cost:** $19,445 (academic year), $10,845 (semester). Includes international transportation, room and board, tuition, insurance, group travel in country. **Contact:** Cristina Garcia-Cervigon, 605 E. College Ave., North Manchester, IN 46962; 219-982-5238, fax 219-982-7755; bca@manchester.edu, [www.bcanet.org].

Davidson in Würzburg. This program starts with a month-long family stay in northern Germany followed by an intensive language course in Würzburg after which students enroll at the university. Students earn 8 course credits for the year. A Davidson faculty member serves as resident director and teaches 1 course in the fall. Students live in dormitories. Numerous group activities and excursions are included.
Dates: Sep 1-late Jul. **Cost:** $25,000 includes all academic expenses, room, international airfare, insurance, excursions. **Contact:** Carolyn Ortmayer, Office of Study Abroad, Davidson College, P.O. Box 1719, Davidson, NC 28036; 704-892-2250, fax 704-892-2005; abroad@davidson.edu, [www.davidson.edu/administrative/study_abroad/abroad.html].

German Studies: Lüneburg. Intensive language study—up to 2 years of university language requirements in 1 semester. Additional courses in history, political science, culture, literature, etc. Program-organized field trips and housing. Beautiful city only 30 minutes from Hamburg.
Dates: Summer term: May 22-Jun 25 and Jun 21-Jul 24; fall semester: Aug-Dec; spring semester: Jan-May. **Cost:** One semester $3,960; fall and spring semester $5,980; summer term $1,760 per session, $2,990 both sessions. **Contact:** University Studies Abroad Consortium (USAC), Univ. of Nevada, Reno #323, Reno, NV 89557-0093; 775-784-6569, fax 775-784-6010; usac@admin.unr.edu, [www.scsr.nevada.edu/~usac].

Kalamazoo in Erlangen. This university-integrated program begins with a 5- to 6-week intensive German course. Participants then enroll in regular courses at the Univ. of Erlangen-Nuernberg. All participants complete an individualized cultural research project or internship of personal interest under the guidance of a local mentor. Minimum of 2 years of college German required.
Dates: Late Sep-late Jul (academic year); late Sep-late Feb (fall); Apr-late-Jul (spring). **Cost:** (1999-2000) Academic year: $24,975; one semester $16,650 includes roundtrip international transportation, tuition and fees, room and board, and some excursions. **Contact:** Center for International Programs, Kalamazoo College, 1200 Academy St., Kalamazoo, MI 49006; 616-337-7133, fax 616-337-7400; cip@kzoo.edu, [www.kzoo.edu/cip].

Learn German and Discover Berlin. GLS is one of the leading institutions teaching German as a foreign language in Germany. GLS offers various levels of German all year round (age 16 and up), preparation for all language certificates, business German, German for bankers, lawyers. Special feature: internships in German companies.

Dates: Year round. **Cost:** Contact school for details. **Contact:** GLS Sprachenzentrum, Barbara Jaeschke, Managing Director, Kolonnenstrasse 26, 10829 Berlin, Germany; 011-49-30-780-08-90; fax 011-49-30-787-41-92; gls.berlin@t-online.de, [www.gls-berlin.com].

Penn-in-Freiburg. For students interested in coursework in intensive intermediate German, cultural exploration of Freiburg and the Black Forest as well as the role of Germany in the European Union. Numerous field trips will complement class instruction.

Dates: Jul 14-Aug 24. **Cost:** Tuition $3,072; housing and activities $700. **Contact:** Penn Summer Abroad, College of General Studies, Univ. of Pennsylvania, 3440 Market St., Suite 100, Philadelphia, PA 19104-3335; 215-898-5738, fax 215-573-2053.

Program for Bilingual Careers. A professional program abroad for young Americans who wish additional language training, university study in Germany, and option of a paid internship under the auspices of AGABUR Foundation, Inc. Designed for undergrads, graduating seniors, and young professionals. See web site for application form and information.

Dates: Spring: Mar-Aug; summer: Jun-Aug; fall: Sep-Feb. **Cost:** Six months $7,935 (plus $500), 3 months $4,500 (plus $500). **Contact:** Prof. Gerhard Austin, AGABUR Foundation, Inc., 9 Eastwood Rd., Storrs, CT 06268-2401; 860-429-1279, fax 860-487-7709; austin@uconnvm.uconn.edu.

Schiller International Univ. at Heidelberg. Schiller Univ. is an American-style university with all courses except language classes taught in English. Schiller's particular strengths are in international business and international relations but it offers courses in the humanities and social sciences as well. Students may take German at Schiller or intensive German at the Collegium Palatinum, a specialized language division. One semester college German or equivalent is recommended.

Dates: Fall: late Aug-mid-Dec; spring: mid-Jan-mid-May. **Cost:** Fall 1999 or spring 2000 estimate: $6,905 per semester. (Prices somewhat higher for Collegium students staying in homes). Estimates include full-day orientation before departure, application fee, room and food allowance in residence hall, airfare, books and supplies, health and accident insurance, German Residence Permit, administrative fees and passport. SUNY tuition not included. **Contact:** Dr. John Ogden, Director, Office of International Programs, Box 2000, SUNY

Cortland, Cortland, NY 13045; 607-753-2209, fax 607-753-5989; studyabroad@cortland.edu, [www.studyabroad.com/suny/cortland].

Semester in Regensburg. This program combines German language courses at the beginning and intermediate levels with a range of courses in humanities, German culture, economics, and international business taught in English. Language courses are taught by Univ. of Regensburg faculty and others by Murray State Univ. faculty. No prior knowledge of German is required.

Dates: Aug 26-Dec 9. **Cost:** $2,895 program fee, MSU tuition ($1,150 for KY residents, $3,070 others in 1999), airfare. **Contact:** Dr. Fred Miller, Regensburg Program Director, Murray State Univ., P.O. Box 9, Murray, KY 42071; 502-762-6206, fax 502-762-3740; Fred.Miller@murraystate.edu, or Ms. Linda Bartnik, Institute for International Studies, P.O. Box 9, Murray State Univ., Murray, KY 42071; 502-752-4152, fax 502-762-3237; linda.bartnik@murraystate.edu, [www.mursuky.edu/qacd/cip/sirprog.htm]

Summer Study/Travel. A 4-week summer study/travel session at Constance, Germany. Lake Constance, bordered by Germany, Switzerland, and Australia, presents an ideal setting for relaxation, study, and travel. Included are trips to Munich, Neuschwanstein Castle, the Black Forest, Switzerland, and France. All age groups.

Dates: Jul-Aug. **Cost:** $1,495. **Contact:** Dr. Peter Schroeck, German Lang. School Conf, 1 Hiram Sq., New Brunswick, NJ 08901; 732-249-9785; pschroec@rvcc.raritanval.edu.

Univ. of Maryland Univ. College at Schwäbisch Gmünd. UMUC at Schwäbisch Gmünd is a 4-year residential campus located 60 km from Stuttgart in scenic southern Germany. Through classes taught in English, individualized attention, and an international student body, UMUC provides an ideal environment for academic achievement and cultural enrichment. Applications are invited from potential freshman, transfer, and semester or academic year abroad students.

Dates: Semesters run from Aug-Dec and Jan-May. **Cost:** Approx. $12,000 per year for tuition, approx. $4,800 for double room with full board. For Maryland residents, tuition is $6,200 per year. **Contact:** Assistant Director of Admissions, UMUC-Overseas Programs (SG), University Blvd. at Adelphi Rd., College Park, MD 20742-1642; 301-985-7070, fax 301-985-7075; sginfo@umuc.edu or Admissions Office,

UMUC, Universitätspark, 73525 Schwäbisch Gmünd, Germany; 011-49-7171-18070, fax 011-49-7171-180732; enroll@admin.sg.umuc.edu, [www.sg.umuc.edu].

Wayne State Univ.'s Junior Year in Munich. The full university curriculum in arts and sciences at the Univ. of Munich will be open to you, plus German studies courses through the program itself. All instruction is in German, taught by German faculty. A 6-week orientation period including intensive language preparation precedes the beginning of university classes. Juniors, seniors, and graduate students with 2 years of college German and an overall "B" average are eligible.
Dates: Sep 21-Jul 31. Includes a 2-month semester break. **Cost:** $7,600 for tuition and fees. Scholarships and financial aid available. **Contact:** Junior Year in Germany, Wayne State Univ., Detroit, MI 48202; 313-577-4605; jym@wayne.edu, [www.langlab.wayne.edu/JuniorYear/JrYrHome.html].

Greece

BCA Program in Athens. Earn 15-16 credits per semester at the Univ. of La Verne Athens, with a 1-week orientation and survival Greek training. Field trips and an extended study tour. All classes taught in English by international faculty. No foreign language prerequisite. Graduate courses in business and education. Students from all U.S. colleges and universities accepted. Full liberal arts curriculum for undergraduates.
Dates: Sep-Nov (fall), Mar-Jun (spring), Sep-Jun (year). **Cost:** $19,445 (academic year), $10,845 (semester). Includes international transportation, room and board, tuition, insurance, group travel in country, and a study tour to eastern Europe. **Contact:** Cristina Garcia-Cervigon, 605 E. College Ave., North Manchester, IN 46962; 219-982-5238, fax 219-982-7755; bca@manchester.edu, [www.bcanet.org].

Beaver College Study in Greece. An individualized opportunity to learn about Greece, its people and its heritage. Courses available in classical, Byzantine, and modern Greek studies, with required study of modern Greek language (no prior knowledge of Greek required). On-site resident director and expert specialist faculty. Field trips. Full range of program services. Scholarships available.
Dates: Fall, spring, full year, and summer. **Cost:** Summer: $3,550; full year: $17,490; fall or spring semester: $9,340. **Contact:** Susan

Plummer, Beaver College CEA, 450 S. Easton Rd., Glenside, PA 19038-3295; 888-BEAVER-9, fax 215-572-2174; cea@beaver.edu, [www.beaver.edu/cea].

Classic Theatre Study. Three weeks on a Greek island with morning workshops in voice, movement, acting, and drama and evening rehearsals of a classic tragedy or comedy. Then a week of touring sites, seeing a play at Epidauros, and performing in amphitheaters. Admission by audition. Company includes students, teachers, and professionals.
Dates: Mid-Jun to mid-Jul. **Cost:** $3,700 includes food, housing, travel, and courses/6 hours credit additional $1,000. **Contact:** Dr. Arthur J. Beer, Theatre Company, Univ. of Detroit Mercy, P.O. Box 19900, Detroit, MI 48219-0900; beeraj@udmercy.edu, [http://libarts.udmercy.edu/dep/greece.html].

College Year in Athens (CYA). One- or 2-semester programs during the academic year. The 2-track curriculum offers a focus on either Ancient Greek Civilization or Mediterranean Studies and is supplemented by at least 10 days each semester of study and travel within Greece. Instruction is in English. Credit is granted by prearrangement with the home institution.
Dates: Aug 30-Dec 17, 1999; Jan 17-May 12, 2000. **Cost:** Semester fee of $9,900 includes tuition, housing, partial board, study, travel, most course materials, $100 refundable damage deposit. **Contact:** College Year in Athens, North American Office, Dept. T, P.O. Box 390890, Cambridge, MA 02139-0010; 617-868-8200, fax 617-868-8207; cyathens@aol.com.

CYA Summer Programs. Three- and 6-week programs on Ancient Greek Civilization, Modern Greek Ethnography, Modern Greek Language (4 levels).
Dates: Jun-Jul. **Cost:** $3,450 (Jun-Jul, including study-travel); $1,750 (Jun-Jul on island of Paros); $1,550 (Jun 7-Jun 25 in Athens). Covers tuition, housing, and course materials. **Contact:** College Year in Athens, North American Office, Dept. T, P.O. Box 390890, Cambridge, MA 02139-0010; 617-868-8200, fax 617-868-8207; cyathens@aol.com.

Intensive Modern Greek Language. Beginning, intermediate, and advanced levels of modern Greek classes meet for a total of 60 hours of intensive exercises and instruction in speaking, vocabulary, role-playing, grammar, reading, and writing. Held on the island of Paros.

Dates: Jun-Jul. **Cost:** $1,750. Includes tuition, course materials, housing. **Contact:** College Year in Athens, North American Office, Dept. T, P.O. Box 390890, Cambridge, MA 02139-0010; 617-868-8200, fax 617-868-8207; cyathens@aol.com.

NYU in Athens. NYU in Athens, in the historical center of the city, combines classroom study of the language, history, and culture of Greece with extracurricular activities to introduce students to modern Hellenic culture. Includes visits to monuments, museums, dramatic and musical performances, and a half-day trip to Attica's beautiful coastline.

Dates: Jun-Aug. **Cost:** $1,430 housing and activities; $3,350 undergraduate tuition; $550 per point, graduate tuition. **Contact:** NYU Summer Session, 7 E. 12th St., 6th Fl., New York, NY 10003; 212-998-2292, fax 212- 995-4103; summer.info@nyu.edu.

Odyssey in Athens. A semester or full year program for mature and resourceful college-age students eager to explore the rich cultural and historical landscape of Greece. Sponsored by the Univ. of Indianapolis at Athens, we offer courses in language, culture, art, business, and international affairs. Accredited by the Midwest Association of Schools and Colleges. Summer program offers art, archaeology, and anthropology.

Dates: First semester mid-Sep-mid-Dec, 2nd semester mid-Feb-mid-Jun, summer term Jun 20-Jul 19. **Cost:** $6,950 for 1 semester, $13,124 for full year. Includes tuition, fees, housing, and excursions. Summer term $1,800 includes tuition, housing, excursions, and museum admissions. **Contact:** Barbara Tsairis, U.S. Director, P.O. Box 5666, Portsmouth, NH 03802-5666; odyssey@star.net, [www.star.net/People/~odyssey].

Guatemala

Bio-Itza Eco-Cultural Spanish School. Located in San Jose, Péten, a small community on the shore of Lake Péten Itza, in northern Guatemala. Our unique program combines intensive Spanish language instruction with participation in projects of the Maya Itza people, including the conservation of a 36 KM2 natural reserve, a medicinal plant program, and a project to preserve Itza, the community's once dying language.

Dates: Year round, begins every Monday. Average stay 3-4 weeks. **Cost:** $195 per week (includes 20 hours of private language instruction per week, room and board with local family). **Contact:** Sabrina Vigilante, Conservation International, 2501 M St., NW, Suite 200, Washington, DC 20037; 202-973-2264, fax 202-887-5188; ecoescuela@conservation.org, [www.bioitza.com].

Culture and Society in Latin America. Innovative approach combines classroom experience with extensive field work. Focus on issues of identity, ethnicity, power and worldviews in the Latin American context. Courses include ideologies of social change, Latin American arts and society, Latin American literature's perspectives on social change, and independent study. Based in Guatemala with field study in Cuba. Family homestay. Latin American faculty. Full semester's credit, U.S. transcript provided. All majors, 2 years Spanish language required.

Dates: Early Feb-mid-May. **Cost:** $9,250 (spring 2000). Includes tuition, room and board, field trips. **Contact:** Rebecca Rassier, Director of Student Services, HECUA, Mail #36, Hamline Univ., 1536 Hewitt Ave., St. Paul, MN 55104-1284; 651-646-8832 or 800-554-1089, fax 651-659-9421; info@hecua.org, [www.hecua.org].

P.L.F.M. of Antigua. Private Spanish instruction in the most prestigious school in beautiful Antigua. A nonprofit foundation which helps preserve Mayan languages, 7 hours daily of one-one-on classes. Family stays and excursions. Airport pickups can be arranged.

Dates: Start any Monday, year round. **Cost:** $200 per week, tuition and family stay. **Contact:** Kay G. Rafool, Language Link Inc. (U.S. Office for P.L.F.M.), P.O. Box 3006, Peoria, IL 61612; 800-552-2051, fax 309-692-2926; info@langlink.com, [www.plfm-antigua.org].

P.L.F.M. of Antigua. Private Spanish instruction in the most prestigious school in beautiful Antigua. A nonprofit foundation which helps preserve Mayan languages. Seven hours daily of one-on-one classes. Family stays and excursions. Airport pickups can be arranged.

Dates: Start any Monday, year round. **Cost:** $200 per week, tuition and family stay. **Contact:** Kay G. Rafool, U.S. Office for P.L.F.M., Language Link Inc., P.O. Box 3006, Peoria, IL 61612; 800-552-2051, fax 309-692-2926; info@langlink.com, [www.plfm-antigua.org].

South American Urban Semester. Innovative approach combines classroom experience with extensive field work. Courses include introduction to Latin America, urbanization and development in Latin America, Spanish language, and independent study. Based in Guatemala with 2 weeks field study in Ecuador.

Family homestay. Latin American faculty. Full semester's credit, U.S. transcript provided. All majors, 2 years Spanish language required.

Dates: Late Aug-early Dec. **Cost:** $9,250 (fall1999). Includes tuition, room and board, field trips. **Contact:** Rebecca Rassier, Director of Student Services, HECUA, Mail #36, Hamline Univ., 1536 Hewitt Ave., St. Paul, MN 55104-1284; 651-646-8832 or 800-554-1089, fax 651-659-9421; info@hecua.org, [www.hecua.org].

Hong Kong

Cantonese and Putonghua. Intensive Cantonese and Putonghua courses from beginning through advanced levels for foreigners, optimum 15 classroom hours per week. At advanced levels, part-time or private tutorials available. Students at any level may register for admission to any term. Center study recognized by major international universities for degree credit.

Dates: Fall term (Sep); spring term (Jan); summer term (Jun). **Cost:** HK$23,250 (fall); HK$23,250 (spring); HK$16,950 (summer). **Contact:** Director, New Asia—Yale-in-China Chinese Language Ctr., Shatin, NT, Hong Kong; 011- 852-2609-6727, fax 011-852-2603-5004; chilangctr@cuhk.edu.hk, [www.cuhk.edu.hk/lac].

Hungary

Human Origins in Hungary. A field school in the methods of paleonanthropology at the site of Rudabánya northern Hungary. Students learn to identify fossils, excavate specimens, process sediment and specimens and will acquire a basic background in paleontology, geology, and paleonanthropology.

Dates: Contact organization for details. **Cost:** CAN$2,300 fees, CAN$700 tuition (1999). **Contact:** Carol Farquhar, Dept. of Anthropology, Univ. of Toronto, Toronto, ON M5S 3G3, Canada; 416-978-6414, fax 416-978-3217; carol@artsci.utoronto.ca, [www.chass.utoronto.ca/anthropology/field.htm].

India

BCA Program in Cochin. Earn 16-18 credits per semester at the Cochin Univ. of Science and Technology, with an orientation period, field trips, and extended study tour to northern India (Delhi, Agra, Jaipur). Students from all U.S. colleges and universities accepted. No foreign language prerequisite. Liberal arts curriculum including Hindi, Gandhian Studies, and international relations.

Dates: Sep-Dec, Jan-May or Sep-May. **Cost:** $14,245 (year), $8,345 (semester). Includes international transportation, room and board, tuition, insurance, group travel in country. **Contact:** Cristina Garcia-Cervigon, 605 E. College Ave., North Manchester, IN 46962; 219-982-5238, fax 219-982-7755; bca@manchester.edu, [www.bcanet.org].

Buddhist Studies Program in India. Living and studying in Bodh Gaya, an internaitonal pilgrimage center, provides students with an opportunity to examine Buddhism and its impact on several Asian cultures. Course offerings include: history, philosophy, anthropology, a meditation practicum, Hindi, Tibetan, and an independent research component.

Dates: Sep-Dec. **Cost:** Contact office for details. **Contact:** Antioch Education Abroad, Antioch College, 795 Livermore St., Yellow Springs, OH 45387; 800-874-7986, fax 937-767-6469; aea@antioch-college.edu, [www.antioch-college.edu/aea].

Friends World Program (Bangalore). A semester or year program in India at the Friends World Center in Bangalore includes orientation, intensive seminars, field studies, travel, and independent work. The core curriculum serves as an introduction to India's complex cultures. Independent study sample topics include: Gandhian studies, sustainable development, Buddhist studies in Nepal, dance, women's studies, philosophy, and traditional medicine. Students may earn 12-18 credits per semester.

Dates: Fall: early Sep-mid-Dec; spring: mid-Jan-mid-May. **Cost:** $12,725 per semester in 1999/2000. Includes tuition, travel, room and board, fees, and books. **Contact:** Admissions, Friends World Program, 239 Montauk Hwy., Southampton, NY 11968; 516-287-8474; fw@southampton.liunet.edu.

International Communities Semester. A Geocommons College program in ecological awareness, cooperative community, and mindful living. Participants spend 3 months in Auroville (Tamil Nadu), an international community of 1,300 people working toward sustainability and "human unity," 3 weeks traveling in India, and 1 week at Green Mt. Dharma Center, a Buddhist community in Vermont. College credit through Univ. of New Hampshire.

Dates: Spring semester: approx. Jan 20-Apr 28; fall semester: approx. Aug 24-Dec 8. **Cost:** Approx. $11,500 for tuition, room and board, and travel. Current financial aid accepted, some grants. **Contact:** Colleen O'Connell, Executive Director, Geocommons College Program, P.O. Box 538, Durham, NH 03824; geo@ic.org, [www.ic.org/geo].

Penn-in-India. For students interested in South Asian studies, performing arts, religion, and traditional medicine, PSA's newest program offers students a survey of both India's rich cultural history and its burgeoning industrial life. The program is located in Pune, a cosmopolitan city of 4,000,000 which is a thriving arts center, a hub of scholarship, and a growing economic presence. Students will live with Indian families in the area and be involved in community projects.

Dates: Jun 17-Jul 30. **Cost:** Tuition $3,072; program cost $1,790. **Contact:** Penn Summer Abroad, College of General Studies, Univ. of Pennsylvania, 3440 Market St., Suite 100, Philadelphia, PA 19104-3335; 215-898-5738, fax 215-573-2053.

Israel

Bar-Ilan Univ. Junior Year. Eligible students must have completed at least 1 year of university study. Bar-Ilan Univ., a 100-acre campus, is located in Ramat Gan, a beautiful suburb of Tel Aviv. Courses offered in humanities, international relations, Israeli studies, Judaic studies, Middle Eastern studies, natural and social sciences. All courses taught in English. The only program in Israel providing university study with an emphasis on Jewish culture and heritage as a key component. Option of 1 year or semester. Program includes optional touring throughout Israel, volunteer work, and intensive Hebrew language study. Students may live in campus dorms or off-campus apartments. Financial aid available.

Dates: Sep-Jan, Feb-Jun. **Cost:** Approx. $10,000 per year ($5,000 per semester). Includes tuition, housing, and trips throughout Israel. **Contact:** Bar-Ilan Univ., Office of Academic Affairs, 235 Park Ave. S., New York, NY 10003; 212-637-4991 or 888-BIU-YEAR, fax 212-637-4056; tobiu@idt.net, [www.roxcorp.com/barilan].

Freshman Year Program. One-year study abroad for credit at an American college of university. Courses range from Israeli studies to Jewish studies to business and economics, art, archaeology, women's studies, and more.

Exciting array of internship/volunteer opportunities. Trips and cultural activities throughout the country.

Dates: Fall: Jul-Jan; spring: Jan-Jun; full year: Jul-Jun. **Cost:** Year $11,000 plus board and transportation. Semester $8,000 plus board and transportation. **Contact:** Hebrew Univ., Office of Academic Affairs, 11 E. 69th St., New York, NY 10021; 800-404-8622; hebrewu@compuserve.com, [http://atar.mscc.huji.ac.il/~rsos].

Friends World Program (Jerusalem). A semester or year program in the Middle East at Friends World Center in Jerusalem consists of intensive seminars that introduce students to the culture of the Middle East. Field work, travel, and independent research are also offered. Sample topics include: desert agriculture, archaeology, anthropology, journalism, public health, conflict resolution, religious studies. Fieldwork can be conducted in Israel, Jordan, and other countries and may earn 12-18 credits per semester.

Dates: Fall: early-Sep-mid-Dec; spring: mid-Jan-mid-May. **Cost:** $13,460 per semester (1999/2000). Includes tuition, travel, room and board, fees and books. **Contact:** Admissions, Friends World Program, 239 Montauk Hwy., Southampton, NY 11968; 516-287-8474; fw@southampton.liunet.edu.

General Studies: Beer Sheva. The program offers students the opportunity to enroll in a wide range of courses at the Ben-Gurion Univ. in a variety of disciplines. You may take courses in anthropology, archaeology, biology, engineering, environmental studies, Hebrew, history, political science, social sciences, etc. These courses are taught in English.

Dates: Aug 4-Dec 1999, Jan 4-Jun 1, 2000. **Cost:** Spring semester $5,800; year $8,800. **Contact:** University Studies Abroad Consortium (USAC), Univ. of Nevada, Reno #323, Reno, NV 89557-0093; 775-784-6569, fax 775-784-6010; usac@admin.unr.edu, [www.scsr.nevada.edu/~usac].

Graduate Year/Semester Program. One-year study abroad for credit at an American college or university. Courses range from Israeli studies to Jewish studies to business and economics, art, archaeology, women's studies, and more. Exciting array of internship/volunteer opportunities. Trips and cultural activities throughout the country.

Dates: Fall: Jul-Jan; spring: Jan-Jun; full year: Jul-Jun. **Cost:** Year $11,000 plus board and transportation. Semester $8,000 plus board and transportation. **Contact:** Hebrew Univ., Office of Academic Affairs, 11 E. 69th St., New York, NY 10021; 800-404-8622; hebrewu@compuserve.com, [http://atar.mscc.huji.ac.il/~rsos].

MA in English. Five- 2-year MA programs in English in Israeli studies, Jewish studies, religious studies, Bible studies, and Middle Eastern studies. Learn under tutelage of Hebrew Univ.'s renowned professors. Take advantage of opportunities for private tutorials, intensive language study, and internships.
Dates: Jul-Jun each academic year. **Cost:** Approx. $11,000 plus board and transportation per year. **Contact:** Hebrew Univ., Office of Academic Affairs, 11 E. 69th St., New York, NY 10021; 800-404-8622; hebrewu@compuserve.com, [http://atar.mscc.huji.ac.il/~rsos].

One Year/Semester Programs for Undergrads. One-year study abroad for credit at an American college of university. Courses range from Israeli studies to Jewish studies to business and economics, art, archaeology, women's studies, and more. Exciting array of internship/volunteer opportunities. Trips and cultural activities throughout the country.
Dates: Fall: Jul-Jan; spring: Jan-Jun; full year: Jul-Jun. **Cost:** Year $11,000 plus board and transportation. Semester $8,000 plus board and transportation. **Contact:** Hebrew Univ., Office of Academic Affairs, 11 E. 69th St., New York, NY 10021; 800-404-8622; hebrewu@compuserve.com, [http://atar.mscc.huji.ac.il/~rsos].

Summer Courses. Three, 4-, or 6-week academic courses at Hebrew Univ.'s Mount Scopus campus. Courses include Hebrew, Yiddish, and Arabic languages, archaeology, history, political science, law, film, and more.
Dates: Jul 1-21, Jul 1-27, Jul 1-Aug 15. **Cost:** Approx. $1,500 includes tuition and housing. **Contact:** Hebrew Univ., Office of Academic Affairs, 11 E. 69th St., New York, NY 10021; 800-404-8622; hebrewu@compuserve.com, [http://atar.mscc.huji.ac.il/~rsos].

Italy

Academic Programs in Florence. Spend a semester/year/summer session in the heart of the Renaissance. More than 250 courses available: Studio Art (painting, drawing, etc.), Art History, Communications, Liberal Arts, Italian Language, Sociology, International Business, etc. in an international atmosphere.

Dates: Semesters: mid-Jan-end of Apr; summer: May-Jun-Jul-Aug. Beginning Sep-mid-Dec. **Cost:** From LIT1,250,000. **Contact:** Dr. Gabriella Ganugi, The Art Institute of Florence, Lorenzo de'Medici, Via Faenza 43, 50123 Florence, Italy; 011-390-55-287360, fax 011-390-55-23989 20/287203; ldm@dada.it, [www.lorenzodemedici.It].

Art and Design in Florence. The Accademia Italiana is an international, university-level institute of art and design. The Accademia offers courses in art, fashion, interior, industrial and textile design during the autumn and spring semesters and fashion design, fashion illustration, drawing and painting, window display design and Italian language during the months of June and July.
Dates: Jan 14-May 22, Jun, Jul, Sep 9-Dec 22. **Cost:** Depends on course chosen. **Contact:** Barbara McHugh, Accademia Italiana, Piazza Pitti n. 15, 50125 Florence, Italy; 011-390-55-284616/211619, fax 011-390-55-284486; modaita@tin.it, [www accademic.italiana.com].

Art Under One Roof. One of Europe's most complete art studio programs. Over 15 areas of study, academic term or year abroad. Studies include Euro programs. Academic studies include jewelry making, interior and boutique design, furniture and industrial design, painting restoration, painting and drawing, figurative sculpture, mural and fresco painting, wood decoration, and many more.
Dates: Academic studies: Jan, May, Sep. Many courses offered monthly. Deadlines: Jun, Nov, Mar. **Cost:** Academic term studies $3,000; summer studies $1,000. **Contact:** Arte Sotto un Tetto Admissions, Florence Programs, Via Pandolfini, 46/R 50122 Florence, Italy; Tel./fax 011-390-55-247-8867; arte2@arteurope.it, [www.arteuropa.org].

Business, Economics, Italian Studies. Turin offers a diversified curriculum in English and in business and economics, plus intensive courses in Italian language and culture, literature, etc., at the foot of the majestic Alps. Program-organized housing and field trips and many Italian university activities.
Dates: Summer term: May-Jul and Jun-Jul; fall semester: Aug-Dec; spring semester: Jan-May. **Cost:** $7,320 fall and spring semesters; summer term $1,980 per session $3,680 both sessions; fall semester $4,180; spring semester $4,180. **Contact:** University Studies Abroad Consortium (USAC), Univ. of Nevada, Reno

#323, Reno, NV 89557-0093; 775-784-6569, fax 775-784-6010; usac@admin.unr.edu, [www.scsr.nevada.edu/~usac].

Fashion, Interior Design, Jewelry. L'Atelier, a school of fashion, jewelry, and interior design, in Florence, is renowned for some of the most important fashion and design exhibitions. The courses are designed to provide students with a solid knowledge of design fundamentals while the master's programs provide a more specialized educational preparation.

Dates: Two-week courses in Jun and Jul; semesters: Sep-Dec, Jan-Apr. **Cost:** From LIT700,000. **Contact:** Dr. Gabriella Ganugi, L'Atelier, via Dei Bardi 46, 50124 Firenze, Italy; 011-390-55-2657962, fax 011-390-55-27-28074; info@atelierfirenze.it, [www.atelierfirenze.it].

Italian at the Seaside. Italian summer language school at the seaside. The Giacomo Puccini Centro culture courses is in Viareggio, one of Tuscany's most beautiful beach towns. Stay in small hotels or shared apartments with use of kitchen. Enjoy the language, enjoy the beach, enjoy life.

Dates: Jun 7-Sep 26, every 2 weeks. **Cost:** LIT870,000 includes 2-week course and accommodations. **Contact:** Mr. Giovanni Poggi, Centro Culturale Giacomo Puccini, Via Ugo Foscolo, 36-55049 Viareggio, Italy; 011-390-55-290305, fax 011-390-55-290396; puccini@ats.it, [www.bwline.com/itschools/puccini].

Italian Studies in Florence. For students interested in intensive beginning and intermediate language courses and cultural studies in literature, cinema, and art history taught in one of the world's most beautiful cities. Numerous cultural opportunities and field trips offer a valuable supplement to class work.

Dates: Jun 7-Jul 16. **Cost:** Tuition $2,900; housing $1,700; travel $750. **Contact:** Penn Summer Abroad, College of General Studies, Univ. of Pennsylvania, 3440 Market St., Suite 100, Philadelphia, PA 19104-3335; 215-898-5738, fax 215-573-2053.

Semester in Florence. Scuolo Leonardo da Vinci is located in the heart of the historical centers of Florence, Rome, and Siena. Founded in 1977 it is now the leading institute in the teaching of Italian as a second language. Semester at the Scuolo Leonardo da Vinci will full credit transfer assistance. The schools also offer a wide range of quality cultural courses (cooking, wine, art, drawing) and extracurricular activities. Full range of accommodation choices provided.

Dates: Year round, starts every 2 weeks. **Cost:** Call for details. **Contact:** Mr. Giambattista Pace, Scuolo Leonardo da Vinci, via Brunelleschi 4, 50123, Firenze, Italy; 011-390-55-290305, fax 011-390-55-290396; scuolaleonardo@scuolaleonardo.com, [www.scuolaleonardo.com].

Studio Art Centers International (SACI). Located in central Florence, SACI is the largest and most comprehensive studio art program in Italy with 6 different programs of study: year/semester abroad, 2-year diploma, post-baccalaureate certificate, master of fine arts, master of art history, and late spring and summer studies. Field trips take students to Pisa, Siena, San Gimignano, Lucca, Arezzo, Assisi, Rome, Bologna, etc.

Dates: Sep-Dec; Jan-Apr; May-Jun; Jun-Jul. **Cost:** Fall/spring tuition $7,950 per term; post-baccalaureate $8,500 per term; tuition late spring/summer $3,000; fall/spring housing $2,600; late spring/summer $1,000/$800 respectively. **Contact:** SACI Coordinator, Institute of International Education, 809 UN Plaza, New York, NY 10017-3580; 800-344-9186, 212-984-5548, fax 212-984-5325; saci@iie.org, [www.saci-florence.org].

Summer Art Workshop in Tuscany. A 4-week workshop in multi-plate color etching with 2 sections: Section A covers the technique of 3 plates with 3 primary colors to obtain 100 colors using both the "additive" and "subtractive" methods. Section B is for more advanced students developing a personal iconography in the multi-plate color etching technique.

Dates: Jul 5-30. **Cost:** $1,300 (Section A: all materials included; Section B: paper, plates, and inks extra) plus $500 for accommodations. **Contact:** Swietlan N. Kraczyna, Studio for Color Etching in Tuscany, Via Colleramole 61, Tavarnuzze, Firenze 50029, Italy; fax 011-390-55-202-2468.

Tech Rome (Summer-Travel-Study). Tech Rome is a 6-week summer travel-study program of Louisiana Tech Univ. It features hotel housing, 3 meals per day, tours, and traditional classroom courses combined with field travel for college credit. Up to 13 semester hours may be earned in a choice of over 40 courses in diverse subject areas. Courses are taught by American professors.

Dates: May-Jul. **Cost:** $4,328 includes tuition, all housing for 6 weeks, 3 meals per day, tours. Group flights are available. **Contact:** Tech Rome, P.O. Box 3172, Ruston, LA 71272; 318-257-4854; [http://techrome.latech.edu].

Temple Univ. Rome. Temple Univ. in Rome, established in 1966, offers a semester or academic year and a 6-week summer program of full-time study designed primarily for 3rd year undergraduate students. The semester program is comprised of 4 academic components: Architecture, Liberal Arts and Italian Studies, Visual Arts, and International Business. Except for courses in Italian language and literature, all instruction is in English. The academic program is enriched by course field trips and a broad range of extracurricular activities.

Dates: Fall: Aug 30-Dec 12, application deadline Apr 1; summer: May 30-Jul 2, application deadline Mar 1; spring: Jan 10-Apr 24, 2000, application deadline Oct 15, 1999. **Cost:** Costs (1998-99) 1 semester: $7,454-$11,215. Includes tuition and fees, housing, meals. **Contact:** Mike Dever, Temple Univ., International Programs, Conwell Hall, 5th Fl., Philadelphia, PA 19122; 215-204-4684, fax 215-204-5735; intlprog@vm.temple.edu, [www.temple.edu/intlprog].

UGA Studies Abroad. For 29 years students of art have particpated in the Cortona experience. You too can discover this small hill town in Tuscany while earning undergraduate university credit in studio art and art history. Semesters begin early Feb, Jun, and Sep.

Dates: Feb (spring semester), Jun (summer session), Sep (fall semester). **Cost:** $8,000 spring and fall, $6,500 summer (estimates only). **Contact:** R.G. Brown, III, Director, UGA Studies Abroad-Cortona, Lamar Dodd School of Art, Athens, GA 30602-4102; 706-542-7011, 706-542-2967; cortona@arches.uga.edu, [www.uga.edu/~cortono_italy].

Jamaica

Tropical Marine Biology. Intense course studies coral reefs, turtle grass beds, tropical sandy and rocky shores, mangrove swamps. Two field trips per day, 2 or 3 hours of lectures per day. Boats leave at 9 a.m. for coral reefs and other habitats. Room and board in small campus hotel, all Jamaican staff, 3 undergraduate or graduate credits.

Dates: Jul 23-Aug 3. **Cost:** Call for details. **Contact:** Dr. Eugene Kaplan, Director, HUML, Gittelson Hall 114, Hofstra Univ., Hempstead, NY 11550; bioehk@hofstra.edu.

Japan

BCA Program in Sapporo. Earn 15-18 credits per semester at Hokusei Gakuen Univ. in Sapporo, with a 1-week orientation, homestay with Japanese families, field trips, and extended study tour through Honshu. Extensive extracurricular activities. Students accepted from all U.S. colleges and universities. No foreign language prerequisite. All levels of Japanese language study available.

Dates: Aug-Dec (fall), Mar-Jul (spring), Aug-Jul or Mar-Dec (year). **Cost:** $19,445 (academic year); $10,845 (semester). Includes international transportation, room and board, tuition, insurance, group travel in country. **Contact:** Cristina Garcia-Cervigon, 605 E. College Ave., North Manchester, IN 46962; 219-982-5238, fax 219-982-7755; bca@manchester.edu, [www.bcanet.org].

Buddhist Studies Program in Japan. Study and experience Zen, Pure Land, and Shingon Buddhist traditions in Kyoto. Course offerings include: philosophy and historical development of Buddhism in Japan, Japanese Buddhist culture, meditation traditions, Japanese language, and an independent research component. Participants live in a series of 3 monasteries; previous Japanese language study is not required.

Dates: Sep-Dec. **Cost:** Contact office for details. **Contact:** Antioch Education Abroad, Antioch College, 795 Livermore St., Yellow Springs, OH 45387; 800-874-7986, fax 937-767-6469; aea@antioch-college.edu, [www.antioch-college.edu/aea].

College of Business and Communication. Beginners to advanced in Japanese study the language, life, and culture of Japan.

Dates: Apr and Oct entrance. **Cost:** ¥790,000 (1999). **Contact:** Ms. Mutsumi Harada, College of Business and Communication, Kawasaki 20-7 Ekimae-honcho, Kawasaki-ku, Kawasaki-shi, Kanagawa-ken 210-0007, Japan; 011-81-44-244-3959, fax 011-81-44-244-2499; cbc@kw.NetLaputa.ne.jp, [www.NetLaputa.ne.jp/~cbc].

Friends World Program (Kyoto). A semester or year program at the Friends World Center in Kyoto includes intensive seminars focused on Japanese culture, language, and the arts. Writing workshops are also offered. Students design internships and independent research projects. Sample topics include: traditional medicine, education, Buddhism, gender studies, peace movements, and environmental policy. Student may earn 12-18 credits per semester. **Dates:** Fall: early-Sep-mid-Dec; spring: mid-Jan-mid-May. **Cost:** $13,750 per semester (1999/2000). Includes tuition, travel, room and board, fees, and books. **Contact:** Admissions, Friends World Program, 239 Montauk Hwy., Southampton, NY 11968; 516-287-8474; fw@southampton.liunet.edu.

Japan Exchange and Teaching (JET). Sponsored by the Japanese Government, the JET Program invites over 1,000 American college graduates and young professionals to share their language and culture with Japanese youth. One-year positions are available in schools and government offices throughout Japan. Apply by early December for positions beginning in July of the following year. **Dates:** One-year contracts renewable by mutual consent not more than 2 times. **Cost:** Participants receive approx. ¥3,600,000 per year in monthly payments. **Contact:** JET Program Office, Embassy of Japan, 2520 Massachusetts Ave. NW, Washington, DC 20008; 202-238-6772, fax 202-265-9484; eojjet@erols.com, [www.jet.org].

Minnesota State Univ.-Akita. Accredited American university campus in Japan, with classes taught in English. Campus consists of Japanese, American and other international students who live and learn together in a residential community atmosphere. No prior Japanese language required. Courses include Japanese area studies, Japanese language, computer science, speech communications, biology, music, mathematics, and others. Typical class size 10-20. Homestays encouraged. Japanese roommate for each student. Program is ideal way to live and learn Japanese culture. **Dates:** Apr and Aug start dates. Dec 15 and May 15 application deadlines (accepted late on a space available basis). One semester or 1 year. **Cost:** $5,967-$9,253 for 1 semester; $10,084-$16,656 for 1 year. Includes tuition, room and board, fees, airfare, books. **Contact:** Akita Support Office, 1450 Energy Park Dr., Suite 300, St. Paul, MN 55108-5227; 877-703-6782, fax 651-649-5762; msuakita@so.mnscu.edu, [www.msua.ac.jp].

Teaching English in Japan. Two-year program to maximize linguistic and cultural integration of participants who work as teachers' assistants. Placements twice yearly in Apr and Aug. Most positions are in junior high schools in urban and rural areas. Bachelor's degree and willingness to learn Japanese required. **Dates:** Hiring for positions every Apr and Aug. Applications accepted year round. **Cost:** No application fees. **Contact:** Institute for Education in Japan, Earlham College, 801 National Rd. West, D-202, Richmond, IN 47374; 888-685-2726, fax 765-983-1553; [www.earlham.edu/~aet].

Temple Univ. Japan. U.S. undergraduate students can study in the heart of Tokyo for a semester, academic year, or summer alongside bilingual Japanese students. The academic program is comprised of an extensive liberal arts curriculum that includes Japanese language at all levels and upper level Asian studies courses. A special engineering program is also offered in the fall semester for sophomore engineering majors. With the exception of Japanese language courses, all courses are conducted in English. **Dates:** Fall: Aug 30-Dec 9, application deadline Apr 1; summer: May 22-Jul 30, application deadline Mar 1; spring: Jan 4-Apr 9, 2000, application deadline Oct 1, 1999. **Cost:** Costs (1998-99) $9,240 per semester; $7,100 for the summer. Includes tuition, housing in shared accommodation, refundable housing deposit, and activity fee. **Contact:** Mike Dever, Temple Univ., International Programs, Conwell Hall, 5th Fl., Philadelphia, PA 19122; 215-204-4684, fax 215-204-5735; intlprog@vm.temple.edu, [www.temple.edu/intlprog].

Kenya

Friends World Program. Friends World/Kenya suspended operations for 1999-2000. The program will resume in Sep 2000. Seminars are offered in historical and contemporary East Africa and Swahili language. Field projects have been done in the area of sustainable development, education, traditional medicine, agroforestry, marine ecology, wildlife studies, and music. Students may earn 12-18 credits per semester. **Dates:** Fall: early-Sep-mid-Dec.; spring: mid-Jan-mid-May. **Cost:** $12,640 per semester in 1998/1999. Includes tuition, travel, room and board, fees, and books. **Contact:** Admissions, Friends World Program, 239 Montauk Hwy., Southampton, NY 11968; 516-287-8474; fw@southampton.liunet.edu.

Kalamazoo in Kenya (Nairobi). Program combines academics with experiential learning. Course work at Univ. of Nairobi (with local students) and excursions give participants a broad overview of Kenya. Instruction in Kiswahili as well as a field study project provides opportunity for greater understanding of host culture.

Dates: Sep-Jun. **Cost:** Academic year: (1999-2000) $24,975. Includes roundtrip international transportation, tuition and fees, room and board, and some excursions. **Contact:** Center for International Programs, Kalamazoo College, 1200 Academy St., Kalamazoo, MI 49006; 616-337-7133, fax 616-337-7400; cip@kzoo.edu, [www.kzoo.edu/cip].

Korea

Penn-in-Seoul. For students interested in East Asia, Korea, international relations and other business disciplines. This program, offered in conjunction with Kyung Hee Univ., includes courses in the area of international relations as well as internships with multinational corporations, government agencies, and think tanks. Field trips exploring Korean history and culture are integral to the program.

Dates: Jun 13-Aug 16. **Cost:** Tuition $3,094; housing $850. **Contact:** Penn Summer Abroad, College of General Studies, Univ. of Pennsylvania, 3440 Market St., Suite 100, Philadelphia, PA 19104-3335; 215-898-5738, fax 215-573-2053.

Latin America

Community Development Internship. This is a credit-bearing internship where volunteers live with a family in rural Mexico and Ecuador, or semi-urban Cuba, while working side by side with community members on grassroots development projects. Project assignments are available in the areas of agriculture, construction, reforestation, animal husbandry, micro-enterprise development, data collection, public health and other fields. These projects are designed, developed and implemented by the beneficiaries themselves. While project opportunities change as new ones come online and others are completed, every effort is made to match interns' interests with their assignment.

Dates: Year round. Two months advance needed for placement in Cuba. Six-week program (3 weeks in Cuba). **Cost:** Six credits: $3,400, no credit: $2,700, 3 credits: $2,900. **Contact:** Nicholas A. Robins, Director, Cuban Studies Institute, Center for Latin American Studies, Tulane Univ., Caroline Richardson Bldg., New Orleans, LA 70118-5698; 504-862-

8629 or 504-862-8000 ext. 2601, fax 504-862-8678; nrobins@mailhost.tcs.tulane.edu, [http://cuba.tulane.edu].

Instituto Internacional Euskalduna. Spanish language program on a beautiful Caribbean island. No passport or visa needed. We offer communicative, learner-centered classes for all language levels. Small groups and private programs, U.S. university credit, weekly cultural activities and homestay programs with or without meals. Licensed by the General Council of Education.

Dates: Classes begin every Monday. **Cost:** Programs starting at $570. **Contact:** NESOL/IIE, Edif. Euskalduna, Calle Navarro #56, Hato Rey, PR 00918; 787-281-8013, fax 787-767-1494; nesol@coqui.net, [http://home.coqui.net/nesol].

Malta

General Studies: Univ. of Malta. The Malta program offers students the opportunity to enroll in a wide range of courses at the Univ. of Malta in a variety of disciplines such as art, architecture, engineering, education, sciences, etc. The Univ. is located in Msida about four miles outside of Valletta, the capital city of Malta.

Dates: Fall semester: Sep 26, 1999-Jan 29, 2000; spring semester: Jan 28-May 31, 2000. **Cost:** Fall or spring semester $1,980, year $3,480. **Contact:** University Studies Abroad Consortium (USAC), Univ. of Nevada, Reno #323, Reno, NV 89557-0093; 775-784-6569, fax 775-784-6010; usac@admin.unr.edu, [www.scsr.nevada.edu/~usac].

Mexico

BCA Program in Xalapa. Earn 15-18 credits per semester at Univ. Veracruzana. Three to 5 weeks premester intensive language in Cuernavaca, homestay with families, field trips, and extended study tour. Beginning and intermediate Spanish students accepted. Intermediate college level Spanish required for regular university courses. Students accepted from all U.S. colleges and universities.

Dates: Sep-Dec or Jan (fall), Mar-Jun or Jul (spring), Aug-Jun or Jul (year). **Cost:** $14,245 (academic year); $8,345 (semester). Includes international transportation, room and board, tuition, insurance, group travel in country. **Contact:** Cristina Garcia-Cervigon, 605 E. College Ave., North Manchester, IN 46962; 219-982-5238, fax 219-982-7755; bca@manchester.edu, [www.bcanet.org].

Bi-Cultural Programs IMAC. Spanish in Guadalajara is more than a classroom. Group sizes of 1 to 5. Guadalajara offers the conveniences of a modern city. We are a few hours drive to Puerto Vallarta. Homestays with only 1 student per family. Hotel discounts available. Free Internet and email access. Excursions and extracurricular activities.

Dates: Year round. Group classes start every Monday. Individual tutoring may begin any day. Christmas vacation Dec 18-Jan 1, 2000; Easter vacation Apr 17-30, 2000. **Cost:** Contact organizations for details. **Contact:** Leticia Orozco, Instituto Mèxico Americano de Cultura, Donata Guerra 180, Guadalajara, Jalisco, 44100 Mèxico; 011-52-3-613-1080, fax 011-52-3-613-4621; spanish-imac@imac-ac.edu.mx, [www.spanish-school.com.mx].

El Bosque del Caribe, Cancun. Take a professional Spanish course 25 hours per week and enjoy the Caribbean beaches. Relaxed family-like atmosphere. No more than 6 students per class. Special conversation program. Mexican cooking classes and excursions to the Mayan sites. Housing with Mexican families. College credit available.

Dates: Year round. New classes begin every Monday. Group programs arranged at reduced fees. **Cost:** Enrollment fee $100, $185 per week. One week with a Mexican family $160. **Contact:** Eduardo Sotelo, Director, Calle Piña 1, S.M. 25, 77500 Cancún, Mexico; 011-52-98-84-10-38, fax 011-52-98-84-58-88; bcaribe@mail.cancun-language.com.mx.

Gender Issues in Cuernavaca. Study "Crossing Borders: Gender and Social Change" or "Gender and the Environment" in a semester-long program in Cuernavaca with travel to Central America. Program includes homestay, Spanish, political science, sociology, religion, and interdisciplinary studies. Community-based learning with meetings with a range of grassroots and civic leaders.

Dates: Sep-Dec or Feb-May. **Cost:** Call for details. **Contact:** Academic Programs Abroad, Center for Global Education, Augsburg College, 2211 Riverside Ave., Box 307TR, Minneapolis, MN 55454; 800-299-8889, fax 612-330-1695; globaled@augsburg.edu, [www.augsburg.edu/global].

Guadalajara Summer School. For the 48th year, the Univ. of Arizona Guadalajara Summer School will offer intensive Spanish in the 6-week session, intensive Spanish in the 3-week session, and upper-division Spanish and Mexico-related courses in the 5-week session. Courses may be taken for credit or audit.

Dates: Jul 3-Aug 17. **Cost:** $1,077-$2,000 includes tuition and host family housing with meals. **Contact:** Dr. Macario Saldate IV, Director, Guadalajara Summer School, The Univ. of Arizona, P.O. Box 40966, Tucson, AZ 85717; 520-621-5137; gss@u.arizona.edu, [www.coh.arizona.edu/gss].

Language and Culture in Guanajuato. Improve your Spanish in the most beautiful colonial city in Mexico. We teach one-on-one or in small groups for up to 8 hours daily. Spanish, Mexican history, cooking, literature, business, folk dancing, and politics. Students of all ages and many nationalities. Homestays with families, field trips, movies, hikes, theater, dance performances.

Dates: Year round. New classes begin every Monday. Semester programs begin in Jan and Aug. **Cost:** $925. Includes 4 weeks of classes and homestay with 3 meals daily. **Contact:** Director Jorge Barroso, Instituto Falcon, Mora 158, Guanajuato, Gto. 36000 Mexico; 011-52-473-1-0745; infalcon@redes.int.com.mx, [http://institutofalcon.com].

Latin American Studies, Spanish. Intensive Spanish language study in small groups at all language levels, taught by native speakers. Latin American studies courses in history, literature, Mexican arts and crafts, current events, Mexican cuisine, anthropology of Mexico, extensive program of field study excursions led by Cemanahuac anthropologists. Academic credit available; professional seminars arranged; family homestay highly recommended.

Dates: Classes begin each Monday year round. **Cost:** Registration, tuition, room and board with Mexican family for 2 weeks: $756. **Contact:** Vivian B. Harvey, Educational Programs Coordinator, Cemanahuac Educational Community, Apartado 5-21, Cuernavaca, Morelos, Mexico; 011-52-73-18-6407, fax 011-52-73-12-5418; 74052.2570@compuserve.com, [www.cemanahuac.com]. Call 800-247-6641 for a brochure.

Mar de Jade Ocean-Front Resort. Tropical ocean-front retreat center in a small fishing village on a beautiful half-mile beach north of Puerto Vallarta. Surrounded by lush jungle with the warm, clear sea at our door, enjoy swimming, hiking, horseback riding, massage, and meditation. Study Spanish in small groups. Gain insight into local culture by optional volunteer work in community projects, such as rural community clinic, our local library, or a model home garden. Mar de Jade also has meeting facilities and provides a serene and intimate setting for group events.

Dates: Year round. **Cost:** Twenty-one day volunteer/Spanish program May-Nov 15 $1,000 (student discount available); Nov 15-Apr $1,080. Includes room and board in a shared occupancy room and 15 hours per week of volunteer work. Vacation: May-Nov 15 room and board $50 per night; Nov 16-Apr $55 per night. Spanish $80 per week with minimum 1 week (6 nights) stay. **Contact:** In Mexico: Tel./ fax 011-52-322-2-3524; info@mardejade.com, [www.mardejade.com]. U.S. mailing address: 9051 Siempre Viva Rd., Suite 78-344, San Diego, CA 92173-3628.

Spanish Immersion Program. Founded in 1948, the center offers students of all nationalities university-level Spanish language instruction as well as all history, literature, culture, business, economics, and political science courses focused on Mexico and Latin America. All courses are taught in Spanish. Homestay program, university guest house, computer lab, multimedia language lab.

Dates: Feb 15, Mar 29, May 3, May 17, Jun 21, Jul 26, Aug 30, Oct 4, Nov 8. **Cost:** $1,238. Non-refundable registration fee, tuition (4 hours per day for 5 weeks), double occupancy homestay (35 days). **Contact:** Jocelyne Gacel-Avila, M.A. Centro de Estudios Para Extranjeros (CEPE), Univ. of Guadalajara, Apartado Postal 1-2130, Guadalajara, Jalisco 44100, Mexico; 011-52-3-616-4399, fax 011-52-3-616-4013; cepe@corp.udg.mx, [www.cepe.udg.mx].

Spanish Institute of Cuernavaca. Become a participant in Mexican culture by studying Spanish at the Spanish Language Institute in beautiful Cuernavaca on the dates of your choice. Students and professionals from ages 18 to 80 at all language levels study 6 hours daily in classes of 5 students in a small school of excellent reputation dedicated to personal attention and professionalism. U.S. graduate and undergraduate credit available. Caring family stays and full excursion program. Longer stays and additional credits also possible. Also separate teen program.

Dates: Year round, begin any Monday. **Cost:** $100 registration, $150 per week tuition, $105 (shared), $154 (private) per week for homestay, all meals, school transportation. Form a group of 12 and your trip is complimentary. Includes insurance. **Contact:** Kay G. Rafool, Language

Link Inc., P.O. Box 3006, Peoria, IL 61612; 800-552-2051, fax 309-692-2926; info@langlink.com, [www.langlink.com].

Spanish Language Institute. A program designed to provide students with ideal learning environment which is conducive to thinking, writing and speaking naturally in Spanish within the context or real-life situations. Discover the Mexican culture with a university group, organization, professionals, travelers and special program of individualized needs for executives.

Dates: Year round. Classes begin every Monday. **Cost:** $150 per week. **Contact:** María Ramos, Academic Spanish Language Institute, Bajada de la Pradera #208, Colonia Pradera, Cuernavaca, Morelos 62191, Mexico; jessram@mor1.telmex.net.mx, [http:// Cuernavaca.infosel.com.mx/sli/sli-page.htm].

Study in Mexico. Beginning to advanced level intensive Spanish language study with a special required seminar in Mexican history and the opportunity to take integrated courses at the Autonomous Univ. of Guadalajara. Students live in private households. All meals are included.

Dates: Fall, spring, summer, academic year. **Cost:** Summer session I $1,950; session I and II $3,250, fall or spring semester $6,450, full year $10,610. **Contact:** Stacy Johnston, Program Coordinator, Beaver College Center for Education Abroad, 450 S. Easton Rd., Glenside, PA 19038-3295; 888-BEAVER-9, fax 215-572-2174; cea@beaver.edu, [www.beaver.edu/cea].

WSU Puebla Summer Program. The WSU Summer Program in Puebla provides an outstanding opportunity for students, teachers, and other interested individuals to study the Spanish language, gain the invaluable experience of living in another country, and earn college credit toward a degree or teaching certification. Students in the program spend 6 weeks in Puebla, either in the Hotel Colonial or in a private home with a Mexican family or both.

Dates: Jun 19-Jul 28. **Cost:** $1,825. **Contact:** Robert Phillips, Wichita State Univ., Wichita, KS 67260-0011; 316-978-3422, fax 316-978-3293; phillips@twsu.edu.

Nepal

Cornell-Nepal Study Program. Offers undergraduate and graduate students the opportunity for academic study, independent field research, and cultural immersion in a country known for its rich ecological and cultural diversity. Courses include Nepali language, contemporary issues in Nepali studies, and research design and proposal writing taught in English by Nepalese faculty from the Tribhuvan National Univ. of Nepal. In addition, students design individual research projects in subjects such as rural sociology, anthropology, natural resources, botany, ethnobotany, Buddhist studies and culture. The program includes a 7-10 study trek. American students live and take courses with Nepalese students in residential program houses.

Dates: Fall, spring, and academic year. Application deadlines: Mar 1, 2000 for fall or academic year 2000-2001. Cost: $14,650 per semester. Contact: Cornell Abroad, 474 Uris Hall, Cornell Univ., Ithaca, NY 14853-7601; 607-255-6224, fax 607-255-8700; cuabroad@cornell.edu, [www.einaudi.cornell.edu/cuabroad/program/nepal.html].

Volunteer Service Work. This program is designed to meet the needs of participants who desire more than typical tourist experience. It provides volunteer service opportunities for people who are genuinely interested in learning about a new and different community and culture while contributing their time and skills to benefit worthwhile community service throughout Nepal. By partaking in the program, it is hoped that participants will experience personal growth as well as open communication channels between different countries and cultures.

Dates: Feb, Apr, Aug, and Oct. Other dates can be arranged. Cost: $650 includes pre-service training, language instruction, homestay, trekking, rafting, jungle safari, volunteering, food and accommodations, etc. Contact: Rajesh Shrestha, Director, Cultural Destination Nepal, GPO Box 11535, Kathmandu, Nepal; 011-977-1-426996, fax 011-977-1-428925 or 011-977-1-416417; cdnnepal@wlink.com.np.

New Zealand

General Studies in New Zealand. Located in the City of Hamilton at the Univ. of Waikato, students are able to take a variety of courses in several disciplines. The courses concerning New Zealand/Pacific Society and Culture are especially popular with international students. Students are able to enjoy excellent study facilities and participate in organized university activities.

Dates: Semester 1: Jul-Nov; semester 2: Feb-Jun. Cost: Semester 1 or 2 $4,315; year $7,775. Contact: University Studies Abroad Consortium

(USAC), Univ. of Nevada, Reno #323, Reno, NV 89557-0093; 775-784-6569, fax 775-784-6010; usac@admin.unr.edu, [www.scsr.nevada.edu/~usac].

Norway

Camp Norway. Camp Norway is an innovative summer program combining fast-paced learning with the direct experience of living in Norway. Camp Norway takes place in Skogn, about a 1-hour drive north of Trondheim on the beautiful Trondheimsfjord. Camp Norway provides top-notch language instructon, as well as field trips exploring the spectacular scenery of the area, visits to historic sights and opportunities to develop international friendships. College and high school credit are available.

Dates: Jun 20-Jul 17 (optional post-program tour Jul 17-21). Cost: $2,650 for Sons of Norway members, $2,750 for nonmembers (1999 prices). Cost includes room and board, books, field trips, activities, and transportation from Trondheim to Skogn. (Prices subject to change if significant fluctuations in the exchange rate occur.) Contact: Sons of Norway, 1455 W. Lake St., Minneapolis, MN 55408; 612-827-3611 or 800-945-8851; fratenal@sofn.com.

Oslo International Summer School. The International Summer School of the Univ. of Oslo in Norway welcomes qualified participants from all parts of the world from late Jun-early Aug. The ISS is a center for learning in an international context, offering courses in the humanities, social sciences, and environmental protection to more than 500 students from over 80 nations every summer.

Dates: Jun 26-Aug 6. Cost: Approx. $2,425 (basic fees, room and board). Contact: Torild Homstad, Administrator, Univ. of Oslo, International Summer School, North American Admissions-A, St. Olaf College, 1520 St. Olaf Ave., Northfield, MN 55057-1098; 800-639-0058 or 507-646-3269, fax 507-646-3732; iss@stolaf.edu.

Scandinavian Urban Studies Term. Courses include urbanization and development in Scandinavia, Scandinavia in the world, art and literature/perspectives on social change, independent study, and Norwegian language. Incorporates many experiential learning activities. Offered in cooperation with Univ. of Oslo. Housing in student village. Field study travel to Stockholm, Sweden and Tallin, Estonia, plus 2 weekend homestays in Norway. Full semester's credit. All majors. No language requirement.

Dates: Sep-Dec. **Cost:** $10,100 (fall 1999). Includes tuition, room and board, field trips. **Contact:** Rebecca Rassier, Director of Student Services, HECUA, Mail #36, Hamline Univ., 1536 Hewitt Ave., St. Paul, MN 55104-1284; 651-646-8832 or 800-554-1089, fax 651-659-9421; info@hecua.org, [www.hecua.org].

Peru

Amauta Language School and Language Link. Become a resident in the former capital of the Incas by studying Spanish in Cusco. Students and professionals of all ages and all language levels study 4 hours daily in one-on-one classes. Family stays or school residence hotel. Two-week stay includes a trip to incredible Machu Picchu. Also optional location in Urubamba and study-volunteer packages. Additional weeks possible, from 2-16.
Dates: Start any Monday, year round. **Cost:** Two weeks $525, includes 4 hours daily private lessons, homestay with all meals or residence hotel without meals, city tour, trip to Machu Picchu, insurance. **Contact:** Kay G. Rafool, Language Link Inc., P.O. Box 3006, Peoria, IL 61612; 800-552-2051, fax 309-692-2926; info@langlink.com, [www.langlink.com].

Poland

Penn-in-Warsaw. For students interested in Polish history and culture, as well as international relations, economics, and other business disciplines. Taught in English, this program will acquaint students with the political and economic changes occurring in Poland and provide insight into the conditions for doing business in a changing economy. Short-term internships with Polish or joint-venture institutions will complement class instruction.
Dates: Jun 26-Jul 30. **Cost:** Tuition $3,072; housing $250. **Contact:** Penn Summer Abroad, College of General Studies, Univ. of Pennsylvania, 3440 Market St., Suite 100, Philadelphia, PA 19104-3335; 215-898-5738, fax 215-573-2053.

Semester in East Central Europe. English based program at the Jagiellonian Univ. (1364) with entry tour through Germany, the Czech and Slovak Republics, Hungary, Austria. Field trips in Poland. Witness history in the making as the history of the 20th century is now being rewritten in these countries. International student dorm living. Classes in humanities, social sciences. Polish language at all levels (8-credit intensive option).

Dates: Sep 1-Dec 15 **Cost:** Approx. $5,350-$5,650 (for Wisconsin residents; tuition surcharge for out-of-staters), room and board, group travel, airfare, etc. **Contact:** International Programs, Univ. of Wisconsin-Stevens Point, 2100 Main St., Stevens Point, WI 54481; 715-346-2717, fax 715-346-3591; intlprog@uwsp.edu, [www.uwsp.edu/acad/internat].

Russia and the NIS

ACTR Russian/NIS Language Progs. ACTR's semester, academic year, and summer programs maximize linguistic and cultural immersion into the societies of the former Soviet Union. The academic programs emphasize the development of practical linguistic skills while providing participants with a structured opportunity to learn about the contemporary societies of the post-Soviet NIS. Financial aid available pending grant approval.
Dates: Summer term, academic year, fall, and spring. **Cost:** Vary according to program and length of stay. **Contact:** Karen Aguilera or Graham Hettlinger, ACTR, 1776 Massachusetts Ave., NW, Suite 700, Washington, DC 20036; 202-833-7522, fax 202-833-7523; aguilera@actr.org, hettlinger@actr.org, [www.actr.org].

Moscow Institute for Advanced Studies. A comprehensive program in Russian language, politics, and culture. The Moscow Institute, in association with the International Univ. of Moscow, offers a year round program featuring language courses at all levels, a wide range of electives in English and Russian, internships, excursions, and graduate research support, and our exclusive lecture series "A Changing Russia."
Dates: Spring: Jan 29-May 12; summer: Jun 11-Aug 6; fall: Aug 27-Dec 10. **Cost:** $6,700-$7,800. Includes full-time tuition, room and board, visa, administrative fees and registration, excursions. Books provided. Financial aid available. **Contact:** Louise White, Program Coordinator, Moscow Institute for Advanced Studies, 152 W. 57th St., 48th Fl., New York, NY 10019; 212-245-0461, fax 212-636-0502; mifas1@aol.com, [www.studyabroad.com/moscow].

Senegal

Kalamazoo in Senegal. Program combines academics with experiential learning. Course work at Universite Cheikh Anta Diop in Dakar and excursions give participants a broad overview of Senegal. Instruction in Wolof as well as a field study project provides opportunity for greater understanding of host culture. All courses taught in French. Minimum 2 years of French required.

Dates: Sep-Jun. **Cost:** Academic year: (1999-2000) $24,975. Includes roundtrip international transportation, tuition and fees, room and board, and some excursions. **Contact:** Center for International Programs, Kalamazoo College, 1200 Academy St., Kalamazoo, MI 49006; 616-337-7133, fax 616-337-7400; cip@kzoo.edu, [www.kzoo.edu/cip].

Spain

Academic Year Abroad Madrid. Direct registration at the Universidades Reunidas of the Complutense primarily in the Facultad de Filosofia y Letras but including social sciences: advanced (virtually graduate) courses possible at the Complutense. AYA-sponsored orientation and tutorials. Optional room and board with Madrileña families and cultural activities.

Dates: Early Sep-end Jan; late Jan-end May; mid-Jun. **Cost:** Term $8,050; year $14,300. Includes tuition, tutorials, room and board, cultural activities. **Contact:** Dr. A.M. Cinquemani, Academic Year Abroad, P.O. 733, Stone Ridge, NY 12484-0733, fax 914-687-2470; aya@ulster.net, [www.studyabroad.com/aya].

Arid Land Recovery Trust. Aims to find and spread methods that will improve the lives and environments of people in poverty in desertified areas. It aims to seek, demonstrate, and promote more sustainable lifestyles and to raise concern about these matters.

Dates: Year round. **Cost:** £42-£90 per week depending upon season, full or part time. **Contact:** Mary Eiloart, Sunseed Trust; 011-44-1480-411784; sunseed@clara.net, [www.sunseed.clara.net].

BCA Program in Barcelona. Earn 14-16 credits per semester at Universidad de Barcelona, with a fall 4-week intensive language training and orientation, field trips, and an extended study tour to Madrid and Toledo or Andalucia. Internships and practica available. Students from all U.S. colleges and universities accepted. Intermediate level college Spanish required. Courses in all academic disciplines taught by university professors.

Dates: Sep-Dec or Jan (fall), Jan-Jun (spring), Sep-Jun (year). **Cost:** $19,445 (academic year); $10,845 (semester). Includes international transportation, room and board, tuition, insurance, group travel in country. **Contact:** Beverly S. Eikenberry, 605 E. College Ave.,

North Manchester, IN 46962; 219-982-5238, fax 219-982-7755; bca@manchester.edu, [www.bcanet.org].

Central College Abroad. In Granada, all students are enrolled at the Center for Modern Languages (Univ. of Granada) and live with families. Orientation in Ronda, excursions, ISIC included. Various courses, all taught in Spanish, and service learning internships available. Ronda summer program, "Doing Business in Spain," combines language/business study with practicum.

Dates: Quarter, semester or full year in Granada, summer in Ronda. **Cost:** Vary by program. **Contact:** Central College Abroad, 812 University, Pella, IA 50219; 800-831-3629, fax 515-628-5375; studyabroad@central.edu, [www.studyabroad.com/central].

CLIC of Sevilla and Language Link. Your choice of intensive groups of 3-6 students or completely private classes. Professional adults, college students, and all Spanish levels accommodated in programs of 2-16 weeks. Graduate and undergraduate credit through accredited U.S. university. Earn 6 units in 5 weeks. Homestays or residence hall. Program for high school teens in Jul. Additional weekly activities included.

Dates: Year round. New classes begin every Monday. **Cost:** Four hours daily of group (3-6) classes and homestay: 2 weeks $620. Includes registration, tuition, insurance, accommodation arrangements fee, homestay with 2 meals or residence hall. **Contact:** Kay G. Rafool, Language Link Inc., P.O. Box 3006, Peoria, IL 61612; 800-552-2051, fax 309-692-2926; info@langlink.com, [www.langlink.com].

Escuela Internacional. Escuela Internacional offers quality programs in Spanish language and culture with U.S. undergraduate credits in Madrid, Salamanca, and Malaga. Qualified teachers and small classes (maximum 12 students) guarantee a successful program. Stay with a selected family or in a shared apartment. Enjoy extensive afternoon activities and weekend excursions. Our professionalism, enthusiasm, and personal touch will make your experience in Spain memorable and fun.

Dates: Year round, 2-48 weeks. **Cost:** From PTS61,000 for 2 weeks (includes 15 hours per week instruction, room and books) to PTS120,000 (includes 30 hours per week instruction, room and full board, books, activities, and excursion). **Contact:** Escuela Internacional, Midori Ishizaka, Director of Admissions, c/o Talamanca 10, 28807 Alcalá de

Henares, Madrid, Spain; 011-34-91-8831264, fax 011-34-91-8831301; escuelai@ergos.es, [www.ergos.es/escuelai].

Hispanic Studies in Malaga. Widely recognized to be one of Spain's leading language schools, Malaca Instituto offers Hispanic studies programs of 1 month to 5 months duration for students with advanced Spanish. Courses qualified by the Univ. of Alcala. EAQUALS guarantee of quality (see www.eaquals.org).

Dates: Starting dates: Jan 24; Feb 21; Mar 20; Apr 17; May 15. Cost: PTS89,500 for 4 weeks. Contact: Bob Burger, Malaca Instituto, c/ Cortada 6, 29018 Malaga, Spain; 011-34-95-229-3242, fax 011-34-95-229-6316; espanol@malacainst-ch.es, [www.malacainst-ch.es].

Hispanic Studies in Spain. Summer, year, and semester programs at the Univ. of Valencia, in collaboration with the Univ. of Virginia. A wide range of courses in language, literature, art history, and culture. Participants from over 100 colleges and universities.

Dates: Fall, spring, full academic year, summer. Cost: Summer: $3,560; fall $5,880; spring $6,685 (2000); year $10,575 includes airfare, homestay, and full-time staff. Contact: Martha Redinger, Hispanic Studies, Univ. of Virginia, 115 Wilson Hall, Charlottesville, VA 22903; 804-924-7155, 804-924-4025; aam4s@virginia.edu.

Intensive Spanish Courses, Seville. CLIC IH, one of Spain's leading language schools, is located in the heart of Seville, the vibrant capital of Andalucia. With year-round intensive Spanish language courses, business Spanish, and official exam preparation taught by highly qualified and motivated native teachers, CLIC IH combines professionalism with a friendly atmosphere. Academic credits available. Accommodations are carefully selected and we offer a varied cultural program as well as exchanges with local students.

Dates: Year round. Cost: Approx. $930 for a 4-week Spanish course and homestay, individual room, 2 meals per day. Contact: Bernhard Roters, CLIC International House Seville, Calle Albareda 19, 41001 Sevilla, Spain; 011-34-95-450-2131, fax 011-34-95-456-1696; clic@clic.es, [www.clic.es].

ISIS Bacelona Program. ISIS is an independent institution specializing in the social sciences taught within an international and cross-cultural context. Spanish language is offered at all levels and elective classes are taught in English. Transcripting is provided by Portland State Univ. Programs offered fall, winter, spring, summer.

Dates: Sep-Dec; Jan-Mar; Apr-Jul. Cost: Fall winter, spring tuition and fees $4,850; homestay and meals $1,895; summer tuition and fees $2,500, homestay and meals $750. Contact: Monya Lemery, Institute for Social and Int'l. Studies (ISIS), Portland State Univ., Int'l. Education Services, P.O. Box 751, Portland, Or 97207-0751; isis@pdx.edu, [www.isis.pdx.edu].

La Coruña Summer Program. Intensive language program providing participants with the opportunity to study Spanish language, civilization, and culture in one of the most beautiful regions in Spain. Cultural immersion is further achieved through homestays with Spanish families. Cultural excursions include Madrid and nearby Santiago de Compostela, site of the famous pilgrimage of Saint James.

Dates: Approx. mid-Jun-mid-July (5-week program). Cost: Approx. $2,200 (tuition and room and board). Contact: Study Abroad Adviser, Central Washington Univ., Office of International Studies and Programs, 400 E. 8th Ave., Ellensburg, WA 98926-7408; 509-963-3612, fax 509-963-1558; goabroad@cwu.edu.

Language and Culture in Seville. A semester or academic year in Seville is offered via Slippery Rock Univ. at the Institute of Int'l. Studies. The program is ideal for students at the beginning or intermediate level of Spanish. Those fluent may also take courses at the Univ. of Seville. Housing is with local families.

Dates: Sep 15-Dec 17, Jan 27-May 26. Cost: $6,145 includes tuition, insurance, housing, and meals. Contact: Dr. Donald E. Kerchis, Director, International Initiatives, Slippery Rock Univ., Slippery Rock, PA 16057; 724-738-2057, fax 724-738-2959; donald.kerchis@sru.edu, [www.sru.edu].

Penn-in-Alicante. For students interested in the language, literature, and culture of Spain, this program combines classroom instruction with visits to points of cultural and historical interest, including Madrid and Toledo. Students live with local families.

Dates: Jun 28-Jul 31. Cost: Tuition $3,072; room and board $1,500. Contact: Penn Summer Abroad, College of General Studies, Univ. of Pennsylvania, 3440 Market St., Suite 100, Philadelphia, PA 19104-3335; 215-898-5738, fax 215-573-2053.

Semester in Spain. Semester, year, summer, and January terms for high school graduates, college students, and adult learners. Beginning, intermediate, and advanced Spanish language studies along with Spanish literature, culture, history, and art. All courses taught in Spanish by native Spaniards. Four courses per semester, 4 credits each. Homestays are arranged for all students.

Dates: Winter: Jan; spring semester: late Jan-mid-May; summer term: Jun and/or Jun-Jul; fall semester: late Aug-mid-Dec. **Cost:** Fall or spring semester $7,950; year approx. $15,900; summer term and Jan term approx. $2,000 each term. Includes tuition, books, full room and board. **Contact:** Debra Veenstra, U.S. Coordinator, Semester in Spain, 6601 W. College Dr., Palos Heights, IL 60463; 800- 748-0087 or 708-239-4766, fax 708-239-3986.

Spanish and Basque Studies (Getxo-Bilbao). The Getxo-Bilbao area offers intensive language studies (Spanish or Basque) that fulfill up to 2 years of university language requirements in 1 semester, plus courses in history, political science, art, culture, economics, teacher education, literature, etc. Program organized field trips, housing, and many local university activities at this seaside city.

Dates: Fall semester: Aug-Dec; spring semester: Jan-May. **Cost:** Fall or spring semester $4,620; year $7,600. **Contact:** University Studies Abroad Consortium (USAC), Univ. of Nevada, Reno #323, Reno, NV 89557-0093; 775-784-6569, fax 775-784-6010; usac@admin.unr.edu, [www.scsr.nevada.edu/~usac].

Spanish and Basque Studies (San Sebastian). San Sebastian offers intensive language (Spanish or Basque) that fulfill up to 2 years of university language requirements in 1 semester, plus courses in history, literature, political science, economics, art, teacher education, etc. Program organized field trips to Madrid and elsewhere, housing, and many local university activities in this beautiful seaside resort.

Dates: Summer terms: May-Jul, Jun-Jul, Jul-Aug; fall semester: Aug-Dec, spring semester: Jan-May. **Cost:** Fall or spring semester $6,580; year $10,380; Jun or Jul $2,080; Aug $1,690; Jun and Jul $3,870; Jun/Jul and Aug $3,355; Jun, Jul, and Aug $4,910. **Contact:** University Studies Abroad Consortium (USAC), Univ. of Nevada, Reno #323, Reno, NV 89557-0093; 775-784-6569, fax 775-784-6010; usac@admin.unr.edu, [www.scsr.nevada.edu/~usac].

Spanish for Foreigners. Do you want to learn Spanish in Valencia, the city which never sleeps? Study Spanish efficiently in small classes, with PhD faculty from Univ. of Valencia? Our main goal is to combine proper academic Spanish

instruction and cultural and sports activities, with optional weekend trips, and living with Spanish families. If you want to have fun learning Spanish on the Mediterranean coast of Spain, visit our web site.

Dates: Jul 1-29. **Cost:** Through Old Westbury $3,167 for NY state residents and $4,003 for out-of-state residents, international airfares included. Independent students $1,850, international airfares and U.S. credits are not included. **Contact:** AIP Advisers for International Programs in Spain, C/Fernando el Catolico 73, pta. 9, 46008 Valencia, Spain; 011-34-6-382-22-78, fax 011-34-6-382-22-78; aip@xpress.es, [www.xpress.es/aip] or Ruben Gonzalez, Assoc. Vice President for Academic Affairs, SUNY Old Westbury, Old Westbury, NY 11568-0210; gonzalezr@soldvx.oldwestbury.edu.

Spanish Language and Civilization. IEMA is known for its excellent teachers, emphasis on practical Spanish and communicative skills. Situated in Avila, near Madrid, in a 11th century palace protected by UNESCO, in the best walled city of the world. Standard Spanish is spoken in Avila unlike in other regions of Spain and South America. Carefully selected homestays.

Dates: Year round. **Cost:** From $450. **Contact:** Dr. Rainer Rutkowski, IEMA, c/o Martín Carramolino, 6, 05001 Avila, Spain; 011-34-920222773, fax 011-34-920252955; iema@iema.com, [www.iema.com].

Spanish Language Courses in Malaga. Widely recognized to be one of Spain's leading language schools, Malaca Instituto offers language and cultural programs at all levels for adults of all ages. Qualifying American students can apply for academic credit. Courses qualified by the Univ. of Alcala. EAQUALS guarantee of quality (see www.eaquals.org).

Dates: Courses begin every 2 weeks from Jan 10. **Cost:** PTS48,000 for 2-week course. **Contact:** Bob Burger, Malaca Instituto, c/Cortada 6, 29018 Malaga, Spain; 011-34-95-229-3242, fax 011-34-95-229-6316; espanol@malacainst-ch.es, [www.malacainst-ch.es].

Study in Seville. Semester, academic year, January, and summer terms in Seville. Intensive immersion. Classes taught in Spanish by Spanish faculty. Intermediate and advanced-level courses are offered during Jan and semester programs. All levels are offered during summer. Resident director, homestays, 35-room mansion, library, computer lab, email, included

study/tours, "intercambios" with Spaniards, scholarships, internships, credits transferable, free video.
Dates: Jan term: Jan 3-Jan 27; spring: Jan 26-May 21; summer I: Jun 1-Jun 28; summer II: Jun 29-Jul 26. Fall: Call for details. **Cost:** Semester $8,175, Jan term $2,060, summer term $1,995. Includes tuition, double occupancy room and full board, laundry, study visits, orientation, health insurance, enrollment, activity and computer fees including email account. **Contact:** Dr. Judith Ortiz, Director U.S., Center for Cross-Cultural Study, 446 Main St., Amherst, MA 01002; 800-377-2621, fax 413-256-1968; cccs@crocker.com, [www.cccs.com].

Study in Spain. Administered in cooperation with the Fundación José Ortega y Gasset in Toledo and features courses in Spanish language and culture, history, literature, ethnology and politics of historical and contemporary Spain. Many courses taught in Spanish; intermediate level knowledge required. Field trips included.
Dates: Fall and spring semester programs available. **Cost:** $8,795 per semester includes tuition, housing, most meals, field trips, Beaver College services, ISIC, transcript. **Contact:** Lorna Stern, Deputy Director, Beaver College Center for Education Abroad, 450 S. Easton Rd., Glenside, PA 19038; 888-BEAVER-9, 215-572-2174; cea@beaver.edu, [www.beaver.edu/cea].

Summer Courses in Malaga. Widely recognized to be one of Spain's leading language schools, Malaca Instituto offers vacation courses in Spanish at all levels for young adults aged 16-20. Courses qualified by the Univ. of Alcala. EAQUALS guarantee of quality (see www.eaquals.org).
Dates: Starting dates: Jun 12, 26; Jul 10, 24; Aug 7, 21. Also adult courses year round, 2 weeks or longer. **Cost:** From PTS48,500 for 2-week course. **Contact:** Bob Burger, Malaca Instituto, c/Cortada 6, 29018 Malaga, Spain; 011-34-95-229-3242, fax 011-34-95-229-6316; espanol@malacainst-ch.es, [www.malacainst-ch.es].

Summer Study in Salamanca. Spend over 4 weeks in Spain studying Spanish language, literature, and culture in the beautiful city of Salamanca. The program is designed for college students, graduates, and teachers, as well as for college-bound high school students. Program options: A) Intensive undergraduate language and culture; up to 9 credits. B) Literature, language and culture, and business Spanish. Six graduate or advanced undergraduate credits.

Dates: Jul 1-30. **Cost:** Program A: $1,800. Program B: $2,000 (tentative). **Contact:** Mario F. Trubiano, Director, Univ. of Rhode Island, Summer Program in Spain, Dept. of Languages, Kingston, RI 02881-0812; 401- 874-4717 or 401-874-5911; fax 401-874-4694.

Univ. of Salamanca. Founded in the early 13th century, the Univ. of Salamanca is one of the most distinguished centers of learning in Europe. SUNY Cortland is celebrating the 33rd consecutive year in this "City of the Golden Stones." The lives of Cervantes, Lope de Vega, Santa Teresa, and Miguel de Unamuno were all linked to the Univ. of Salamanca. Fields of study include Spanish language and literature, humanities, social sciences. Upper division and some qualified sophomores may apply. Requires at least 4 semesters college-level Spanish. Homestays.
Dates: Fall: early Sep-mid-Dec; spring: early Jan-end of Mar or stay on through early May. **Cost:** Fall estimate: $6,450, spring Jan-Mar $3,455; Jan-May $5,855. Estimates include full-day orientation before departure, application fee, room and food allowance, mandatory Spanish insurance, airfare, transportation from Madrid to Salamanca, books and supplies, insurance, walking tour of Salamanca, 2 excursions, administrative fees. SUNY tuition not included. **Contact:** Liz Kopp, Assistant Directory, Office of International Programs, Box 2000, SUNY Cortland, Cortland, NY 13045; 607-753-2209, fax 607-753-5989; koppl@cortland.edu, [www.studyabroad.com/suny/cortland].

Universidad de León. Courses in Spanish as a foreign language offered since 1995 by a public higher education institution. A special atmosphere made by 17,000 Spanish students. All grades. Small groups. Accommodations options: halls of residence, host families, and self-catering. Summer and permanent courses (minimum 1 month). Cultural and touristic excursions available. Official attendance certificate and/or transcript of grades.
Dates: Summer courses: Jul, Aug. Permanent course: Oct-Jun. Spanish Teacher's Training Courses: Jul, Aug. **Cost:** Summer courses: 1-month PTS75,000, 2-month PTS100,000. Permanent course: 4-month session PTS100,000. Academic year PTS190,000. Spanish Teacher's Training Courses: PTS75,000.
Contact: Cursos de Español Lengua Extranjera, Universidad de León, Avda. Facultad 25, 24071,

Léon, Spain; 011-34-987-291650, fax 011-34-987-291693; neggeuri@isidoro.unileon.es, [www.unileon.es/veuri/cele/cursos].

Universidad de Madrid (MLSA). A graduate and undergraduate program at the Universidad (Complutense) de Madrid for students interested in studying courses in language, literature, culture and civilization, composition, art history, philosophy of Spain. Students are taught by full-time faculty members from the Universidad (Complutense) de Madrid, the most prestigious university in Spain. A lot of extra activities and excursions are organized for students.

Dates: Summer program: Jul; semester: fall, winter, spring. **Cost:** Summer: total cost from $1,985 including airfare; year: $10,250 total cost including airfare. **Contact:** Modern Language Studies Abroad, P.O. Box 623, Griffith, IN 46319; Tel./fax 219-838-9460; mlsa@sprintmail.com.

Sweden

Uppsala Int'l. Summer Session. Sweden's oldest academic summer program focuses on learning the Swedish language. All levels from beginners to advanced. Additional courses in Swedish history, social institutions, arts in Sweden, Swedish film. Excursions every Friday. Extensive evening program includes both lectures and entertainment. Single rooms in dormitories. Apartments at extra cost. Open to both students and adults. Credit possible.

Dates: Jun 18-Aug 11; Jun 18-Jul 14; Jul 16-Aug 11, Jul 2-Aug 11. **Cost:** SEK22,200 (approx. $2,620) for the 8-week session, SEK12,000 (approx. $1,420) for the 4-week session. Includes room, some meals, all classes, evening and excursion program. **Contact:** Dr. Nelleke van Oevelen-Dorrestijn, Uppsala Int'l. Summer Session, Box 1972, 751 47 Uppsala, Sweden; 011-31-13-521-23-88 or 011-46-18-10-23-70, fax 011-31-13-521-2389; nduiss@wxs.nl or nelleke.vanoevelen@uiss.org, [www.uiss.org].

Switzerland

French Language in Neuchâtel. Teaching of French as a foreign language in a Swiss university. Summer course and full-year programs (SFM). Linguistic immersion, tandem exchanges, literature and culture just some meters by the lake, in the middle of the town and of the 2001 National Exhibition. Sports, theater, and chorals.

Dates: Jul 1-Aug 4 for summer course (plus full year for the SFM—Oct-Jun). **Cost:** Summer: CHF600 includes tuition and books; CHF825 includes tuition, books, and 6 excursions; CHF350-CHF500 includes room for 4 weeks; CHF400-CHF500 includes homestay; CHF1,265 includes room with full board. Full year at the Seminaire de français moderne CHF1,550, CHF775 for a semester. **Contact:** Cours de vacances et seminaire de français moderne, Université de Neuchâtel, Ave. du ler-Mars 26, CH-2000 Neuchâtel, Switzerland; 011-41-32-718-1800, fax 011-41-32-718-1801; sfm.cv@lettres.unine.ch, [www.unine.ch/sfm/].

Univ. of Geneva Summer Courses. Three-week French language and civilization at all levels, beginners to advanced. All instructors have a university diploma. Excursions and visits to Geneva and its surroundings. Class of 15-20 students. Minimum age 17.

Dates: Jul, Aug, Sep. **Cost:** SFR470 for 3 weeks (tuition). **Contact:** Mr. G. Benz, Univ. of Geneva, Summer Courses, rue de Candolle 3, CH-1211 Geneva 4, Switzerland; 011-41-22-705-74-34, fax 011-41-22-705-74-39; elcfete@uni2a.unige.ch, [www.unige.ch/lettres/elcf/coursete/cournet.html].

Univ. of Lausanne-Summer Courses. Courses are taught in French in 4 series of 3 weeks each, for all levels from beginner to advanced. We also offer 2 intensive courses for beginners that last at least 6 weeks. One or more series may be attended. Classes are constituted according to the students' tested level of competence. Students can also practice sports at the sports center or use our multimediacenter (Macintosh, tapes, and videos).

Dates: Series I: Jul 5-23; Series II: Jul 26-Aug 13; Series III: Aug 16-Sep 3; Series IV: Sep 6-Sep 24. **Cost:** FR470 for 3 weeks; FR1,400 for beginners (6 weeks). **Contact:** Univ. of Lausanne, Cours de Vacances, BFSH2, CH-1015 Lausanne, Switzerland; 011-41-21-692-30-90, fax 011-41-21-692-30-85; CoursDeVacances@cvac.unil.ch, [www.unil.ch/cvac].

Thailand

Globalization and Development. Program combines academics with experiential education. Specially arranged course work at the Univ. of Chiang Mai and field study excursions give students overview of problems and processes of globalization and development in

Northern Thailand. Field study project with local NGO provides intensive opportunity for understanding host culture.

Dates: Sep-Jan. **Cost:** Academic year: (1999-2000) $16,650. **Contact:** Center for International Programs, Kalamazoo College, 1200 Academy St., Kalamazoo, MI 49006; 616-337-7133, fax 616-337-7400; cip@kzoo.edu, [www.kzoo.edu/cip].

Southeast Asian Studies: Bangkok. Diverse courses in culture, language, economics, business, society, and religions provide a fascinating, well-balanced approach to Southeast Asia. Program-organized field trips, student residence halls, and many university activities at one of Thailand's most modern universities.

Dates: Summer session: Jun-Aug; fall semester: Aug-Dec, spring semester: Jan-May. **Cost:** One semester $2,680; year $4,380; summer term $1,480. **Contact:** University Studies Abroad Consortium (USAC), Univ. of Nevada, Reno #323, Reno, NV 89557-0093; 775-784-6569, fax 775-784-6010; usac@admin.unr.edu, [www.scsr.nevada.edu/~usac].

Webster Univ. Thailand Campus. Our newest campus, opening in fall 1999, is situated near the Gulf of Thailand resort town of Cha-am, a few hours south of Bangkok. Students can live in on-campus apartments. Library and computer labs on campus. Undergraduate programs in management, business administration, and computer science.

Dates: Contact organization for details. **Cost:** Contact organization for details. **Contact:** Teresa Bruno, Director, Study Abroad Programs; 800-984-6857, fax 314-968-7119; worldview@webster.edu, [www.webster.edu].

United Kingdom and Ireland

American College Dublin. Study abroad in Dublin for a summer, semester, or a year to earn U.S. college credit for courses in business, psychology, sociology, history, literature, liberal arts, and tourism. Opportunities for internship and study tour to Europe are available. Accommodations are in a residence hall of Georgian architecture.

Dates: Spring: Jan 11-May 7, summer and fall: Call for details. **Cost:** Spring $8,150. Summer and fall. Call for details. **Contact:** Coordinator, American College Dublin, Study Abroad Program, 3601 N. Military Trail, Boca Raton, FL

33431; 800-453-8306, fax 561-989-4983; acdinfo@aol.com, [www.cybervillage.com/acdireland].

BCA Program in Cheltenham. Earn 15-16 credits per semester at the Cheltenham and Gloucester College of Higher Education with a 2-week orientation in country, field trips, and an extended study tour to Wales or Kent. Courses in all academic disciplines. Internships and practica available. Students accepted from all U.S. colleges and universities.

Dates: Sep-Dec (fall), Feb-May (spring), Sep-May (year). **Cost:** $19,445 (year); $10,845 (semester). Includes international transportation, room and board, tuition, insurance, group travel in country. **Contact:** Cristina Garcia-Cervigon, 605 E. College Ave., North Manchester, IN 46962; 219-982-5238, fax 219-982-7755; bca@manchester.edu, [www.bcanet.org].

British Studies at Oxford. This program of study in one of the world's most prestigious universities offers undergraduate and graduate credit in art history, business, communication, drama, education, English literature, history, and political science taught by Oxford Univ. professors. The participants live in private rooms tidied daily by the college staff, who also serve 3 bountiful and tasty meals a day in the Great Hall. Field trips are an integral part of each course as well as group trips to the theater in Stratford-upon-Avon and London.

Dates: Summer: Jul 4-Jul 24; Jul 25-Aug 14; or Jul 4-Aug 14. **Cost:** $3,100 for 3 weeks; $5,750 for 6 weeks. Includes 4 or 8 credits, travel in Britain for course related events, theater, entrance to museums, dinners in country inns, and many field trips. Overseas travel not included. **Contact:** Dr. M.B. Pigott, Director, British Studies at Oxford, 322 Wilson Hall, Oakland Univ., Rochester, MI 48309-4401; 248-652-3405 or 248-370-4131, fax 248-650-9107; pigott@oakland.edu, [www.oakland.edu/oxford].

BUNAC's Work in Britain Program. Allows full-time U.S. students and recent graduates to work for up to 6 months, in any job, any time of year in England, Scotland, Wales, or Northern Ireland. Job and accommodations listings and general support from BUNAC in London and Edinburgh. Eligibility depends on full-time student status in the U.S.

Dates: Year round. **Cost:** $225 work permit, admin., U.K. support. **Contact:** BUNAC USA, P.O. Box 430, Southbury, CT 06488; 800-GO-BUNAC; [www.bunac.org].

Central Saint Martins Short Courses. Short practical courses in all aspects of art and design suitable for professional and student artists and designers. Includes fashion, graphics, fine art, theater design, textiles, product design, computer graphics, and multimedia. All courses held in heart of London in the U.K.'s largest college of art and design.

Dates: Courses run year round in evenings and on Saturdays. Intensive week long courses in summer, Christmas, and Easter. **Cost:** Costs from £150 ($250) per week for tuition. Accommodations from £22 ($35) per night. **Contact:** Developments at Central Saint Martins, Southampton Row, London WC1B 4AP, U.K.; 011-44-171-514-7015, fax 011-44-171-514-7016; shortcourse@csm.linst.ac.uk, [www.csm.linst.ac.uk].

General Studies: Brighton. Brighton offers courses in many disciplines: art, business, sports science, engineering, computing, geography, design, education, math, etc. Organized field trips, housing in student residence halls. Only 45 minutes from London.

Dates: Fall semester: Sep-Dec; spring semester: Jan-Jun. **Cost:** Fall or spring semester $3,440; year $5,675. **Contact:** University Studies Abroad Consortium (USAC), Univ. of Nevada, Reno #323, Reno, NV 89557-0093; 775-784-6569, fax 775-784-6010; usac@admin.unr.edu, [www.scsr.nevada.edu/~usac].

General Studies: Reading. Reading offers courses in nearly every academic disciplines: art, business, literature, performing arts, engineering, computing, geography, education, agriculture, etc. Housing in student residence halls. Only 25 minutes from London.

Dates: Fall semester: Sep-Dec; winter semester: Jan-Mar; summer term: Apr-Jun. **Cost:** Summer $2,880; one-term $3,780; two terms $6,580; year long $9,360. **Contact:** University Studies Abroad Consortium (USAC), Univ. of Nevada, Reno #323, Reno, NV 89557-0093; 775-784-6569, fax 775-784-6010; usac@admin.unr.edu, [www.scsr.nevada.edu/~usac].

General Studies: St Andrews. The program at the Univ. of St Andrews offers students the opportunity to enroll in a wide range of courses such as International Relations, Scottish History, Management, Economics, Environmental Sciences, etc. St Andrews is a beautiful town situated in its own sheltered bay on the Fife coast, 45 miles north of Edinburgh.

Dates: Fall semester: Sep-Jan; spring semester: Jan-May. **Cost:** Fall semester $6,780; spring semester $6,780; year $12,980. **Contact:** University Studies Abroad Consortium (USAC), Univ. of Nevada, Reno #323, Reno, NV 89557-0093; 775-784-6569, fax 775-784-6010; usac@admin.unr.edu, [www.scsr.nevada.edu/~usac].

Graduate Study Abroad. One year taught master's programs at 5 universities in the U.K. and 1 in Australia. Programs in all academic areas. Degree is conferred by overseas university. Federal financial aid can be applied to program of study; call for information.

Dates: Twelve month programs, usually beginning in October. **Cost:** Fees vary. Call for information. **Contact:** Suzanne Fogel, Program Coordinator, Beaver College Center for Education Abroad, 450 S. Easton Rd., Glenside, PA 19038; 888-BEAVER-9, 215-572-2174; cea@beaver.edu, [www.beaver.edu/cea].

Harlaxton College. Harlaxton College is owned and operated by the Univ. of Evansville in Indiana. Therefore, all courses are U.S. accredited and usually transfer easily. Students live and study in a magnificent 19th-century Victorian manor house in the English Midlands. Assistance is available with air arrangements and airport pickup; optional field trips are available throughout England, Ireland, Scotland, Wales, and the Continent. Harlaxton is a full-service study abroad program with help every step of the way.

Dates: Fall: Aug 25-Dec 7; summer: May 12-Jun 16; spring 2001: Jan 5-Apr 19. **Cost:** $10,550 per semester. Includes tuition, room and board (1999-2000). **Contact:** Suzy Lantz, Harlaxton Coordinator, Univ. of Evansville, 1800 Lincoln Ave., Evansville, IN 47722; 800-UKMANOR or 812-488-1040; sl5@evansville.edu, [www.ueharlax.ac.uk]

The Institute of Economic and Political Studies. The Institute of Economic and Political Studies is an independent organization established in 1979 on the principle that North American undergraduates could benefit from an intensive, individualized semester study abroad experience featuring a scholarly, European perspective on economics, politics, law and international relations. The London Center focuses on politics, law, Europe, social sciences, and internships. The Cambridge Center focuses on geopolitics, political economy and economics, social sciences and the humanities, business and finance.

WHO ARE YOU?

WHERE CULTURE SHOCK ENDS AND "EGO SHOCK" BEGINS

By Marina Wolf

After months of counseling and introspective writing, I came to understand the reason for the anxiety and depression I experienced during and long after my visits to Russia: my entire sense of self—as an articulate individual, a savvy activist, a capable worker—had been blown away by the demands of living in another culture.

Before my first trip, I had not an inkling that such struggles might come, nor how to cope with them if they did. In fact, neither my university nor the first study program I traveled with offered much more than packing suggestions and safety tips. Administrators seemed to believe that talking beforehand about the psychological impact of living abroad is not effective, that the best results come from "reorientation" programs.

Unfortunately, the actual situations that trigger the traveler's questioning happen during, not after, the trip.

My friend Diane, for example, remembers vividly her summer of independent undergraduate research in the Middle East. She was as prepared as anyone could be for the intercultural experience. Most important, she thought, she wasn't like the other foreigners; she was no ugly American. In fact, Diane had long felt a distance from her peers: "The way I made myself feel better was by thinking, 'I'm not like the other kids and that's not a bad thing.' "

But Diane's carefully nourished identity began to crumble in contact with a culture in which Americans tended to be perceived as a group.

Those of us who travel for study or work share other qualities that may render us more susceptible to the blows of "ego shock."

- We often are committed to goals with specific outcomes (attaining good grades) or to general causes (alleviating world hunger). Such goals may become so integral to our self-identity that failures to accomplish them can be emotionally devastating.
- We are likely to be highly articulate in our native language and place great stock in our ability to communicate. If we are unable to retain that same facility in the new language, that too can wreak havoc on our egos.

The list goes on, with as many items as there are aspects of personality. But when we become aware—even dimly—of our egos, the selves we bring to the experience, we are much more prepared to cope with, and grow from, our travel.

Dealing with the Experience of Travel

One of the simplest tools for introspection is meditation, which Tassielli uses to start off her intercultural workshop at UC-Berkeley. She makes it clear that she is not offering a specific discipline of meditation. "I'm just trying to give this to them as a tool for whatever purpose they might want to use it," Tassielli says. "When you're hit with all kinds of new things at once, this is something that doesn't take a lot of time or space, but it's going to help you center yourself."

Another helpful self-awareness tool is journaling—that is, keeping a diary during the living-abroad experience. Tassielli gives away journals to participants in her workshops, but she says many people are resistant to the idea. Keeping a journal can be a truly adult practice that allows space and time for the traveler's self to unfold in the pages. Just moving a pen across the page can be soothing, and I have often found the results invaluable afterward as a record of where I've been and where I'm going.

Many intercultural books offer exercises and "games" that help us travelers become aware of our own biases and blind spots and teach us to suspend judgment—an important quality to cultivate during times of shifting self, says Dr. Annella Dalrymple, a psychologist in Santa Rosa, California, who specializes in transitions. "If [people] can suspend judgment of themselves and their circumstances for a while and look at it like Alice going down the rabbit hole— 'Oh, let's see what's here'—with as little judgment as possible, they are more likely to get through the journey without too much pain and wounding, and come out the other side faster."

As part of being nonjudgmental, we should remember that we aren't necessarily "bad travelers" because we feel depressed or confused in another country.

And facilitators and administrators with study abroad and travel organizations should at least consider the possibility that not every behavior and attitude that a traveler exhibits is directly related to the clash of cultures. Sometimes it's just part of who a person is. Challenges to the self can be difficult, if not outright traumatic, and to send young people out without even rudimentary self-awareness and self-care techniques is like throwing us out to sink or swim. Teach us to dog-paddle, at least, and we'll go a bit further.

Dates: Fall and spring semester, summer and supplemental spring internship programs available. **Cost:** $11,500 per semester; $5,190 for supplemental spring internship; $3,950 for summer. **Contact:** Marjorie Rotstein, Program Coordinator, Beaver College Center for Education Abroad, 450 S. Easton Rd., Glenside, PA 19038; 888-BEAVER-9, 215-572-2174; cea@beaver.edu, [www.beaver.edu/cea].

Integrated Study Program. Program allows integration of American students into the Irish Third Level Education System. They take the same lectures, tutorials, and assessments as the Kish students. Students can choose from a wide range of modules in all years and may register across faculties and departments.

Dates: Fall semester Jun, spring semester Nov. **Cost:** Contact organization for details. **Contact:** Josephine Page or Mary Hayden, Univ. of Limerick, Limerick, Ireland; 011-44-61-202338, fax 011-44-61-334859; mary.hayden@ul.ie, [www.ul.ie].

Irish Language and Culture. Irish language programs at all learning levels for adults are offered by Oideas Gael, which also offers cultural activities, learning programs in hillwalking, dances of Ireland, painting, tapestry weaving, Raku-Celtic pottery, and archaeology.

Dates: Weekly, Apr-Sep. **Cost:** $150 plus accommodations (from $90 per week). **Contact:** Liam O'Cuinneagain, Director, Oideas Gael, Gleann Cholm Cille, County Donegal, Ireland; 011-353-73-30248, fax 011-353-73-30348; oidsgael@iol.ie, [www.oideas-gael.com].

Laban Centre London. Program for students outside the U.K. to spend 1 year (2 semesters) in London studying contemporary dance, choreography, and related subjects. Courses are planned for your individual needs and credits are given for subjects taken. Please ask for a booklet.

Dates: Sep-Jul. **Cost:** Call for details. **Contact:** Admissions Officer, Laban Centre London, Laurie Grove, London SE14 6NH, U.K.; 011-44-181-692-4070, fax 011-44-181-694-8749; info@laban.co.uk, [www.laban.co.uk].

M.A. Continental Philosophy. Taught M.A. with substantial independent research component. Modules selected from a list including phenomenology, existentialism, deconstruction, feminism, post-modernism, etc. Lively but intimate and friendly department at the center of the U.K. Entry requirement: good first degree involving significant study of philosophy; cognate study considered.

Dates: Sep-Aug (12 months); apply by June. **Cost:** Approx. $10,000 tuition for full year. Area has low living costs. **Contact:** Dr. Douglas Burnham, Staffordshire Univ., Stoke-on-Trent, ST4 2XW, U.K.; 011-44-1782-294415, fax 011-44-1782-294470; h.d.burnham@staffs.ac.uk.

MPHIL/Diploma in Publishing Studies. Wide-ranging course on print (book and magazine) and electronic publishing. Strong international component. Experienced professional staff. Modern library. Excellent facilities for computing; hand-printing; excellent employment record. Beautiful campus close to Edinburgh and Glasgow.

Dates: Sep-May. **Cost:** Approx. $10,400. **Contact:** Centre for Publishing Studies, Univ. of Stirling, Stirling FK9 4LA, U.K. 011-44-1786-467496, fax 011-44-1786-466210; engl1@stir.ac.uk, [ww.stir.ac.uk/publishing].

NYU in Dublin. NYU in Dublin is located at beautiful Trinity College, Ireland's oldest university. Along with a lively review of contemporary Irish culture through courses in literature, history, politics, cinema and language, students also attend theater, poetry readings, traditional music sessions and film screenings, and visits to Belfast, Donegal, and other significant sites.

Dates: Jun-Aug. **Cost:** $1,962 housing and activities; $3,350 undergraduate tuition; $550 per point, graduate tuition. **Contact:** NYU Summer Session, 7 E. 12th St., 6th Fl., New York, NY 10003; 212-998-2292, fax 212-995-4103; summer.info@nyu.edu.

Oxford Summer Programs. A very wide range of courses including literature, art, philosophy, history, social studies, international relations, creative writing, and environmental studies.

Dates: May-Oct. Minimum stay: 2 weeks. **Cost:** £400 per week, single room and board. **Contact:** Carolyn Llewelyn, Centre for International Education, 5 Worcester St., Oxford OX1 2BX, U.K.; 011-44-1865-202238, fax 011-44-1865-202241; info@ceninted.demon.co.uk, [www.utsinternational.com/cie].

Penn-in-London. For students interested in theater and literature, this program offers first-hand opportunities to experience the best in traditional and contemporary British theater, from page to footlights.

Dates: Jun 26-Jul 30. **Cost:** Tuition $3,072; theater tickets $500; housing $875. **Contact:** Penn Summer Abroad, College of General Studies, Univ. of Pennsylvania, 3440 Market St., Suite 100, Philadelphia, PA 19104-3335; 215-898-5738, fax 215-573-2053.

Regent's College in London. Study at Regent's College gives you the overseas experience so many employers are seeking. You'll live and study in an international community on a full-service campus in the heart of London. Fully accredited courses are taught by primarily British faculty, with a variety of internships available. You'll have opportunities to explore the London area, the British Isles, the continent and beyond.

Dates: Late Aug-Dec and late Jan-May. **Cost:** Tuition $6,820, room and board (double) $3,475 (1999). **Contact:** Rockford College, Regent's Admissions, 5050 E. State St., Rockford, IL 61108-2393; 800-REGENTS, fax 815-226-2822; regents@rockford.edu, [www.rockford.edu].

Semester Abroad. Middlesex is a large university in north London. Semester abroad students study alongside U.K. students and can choose from over 4,000 credit-rated courses. Students live in halls of residence only a short train ride from central London.

Dates: Fall, spring semesters. **Cost:** Approx. $5,200 tuition (15 credits). Includes orientation, and airport pick-up. **Contact:** Valdev Chaggar, Registry Admissions, Middlesex Univ., White Hart Ln., London N17 8HR, U.K.; 011-44-181-362-5782, fax 011-181-362-5649; admissions@mdx.ac.uk.

Semester in London. Combines study in a London setting with excursions. Students live and attend classes in the Bloomsbury district. Courses include British politics, art history, theater, a seminar in British culture, and an additional course.

Dates: Sep-mid-Dec, Feb-mid-May. **Cost:** Tuition, room, 12-meal plan: $8,050. Estimated personal expenses $3,000 plus airfare (1999). **Contact:** Millie Gibbs, Office of International Education, Eckerd College, 4200 54th Ave. South, St. Petersburg, FL 33711; 800-456-9009 ext 8381, fax 727-864-7995, gibbsm@eckerd.edu, [www.eckerd.edu].

Study Abroad. The Univ. of Ulster is now the largest university on the island of Ireland with a wide range of semester to year-long study abroad programs.

Dates: May 30. **Cost:** £4,070 tuition only (1999). **Contact:** Dr. David Kitchen, Univ. of Ulster, Jordanstown, Co. Antrim, Northern Ireland BT37 OQB; dkitchen@ulst.ac.uk, [www.ulst.ac.uk].

Study Abroad at Keele Univ. Keele offers American students the chance to study for a semester or year on one of the largest campuses in England, set in beautiful countryside in the heart of Staffordshire. We offer a flexible, modular curriculum, with accessible modules from 30 different subject areas. Students are guaranteed accommodations in single-study bedrooms.

Dates: Sep-Jan, Jan-Jun. **Cost:** 1999-2000 prices: £5,590 full year; £2,990 for semester tuition only. Accommodations £1,360-£2,055 for year. **Contact:** Dr. Annette Kratz, International Office, Keele Univ., Staffordshire, ST5 5BG, U.K.; 011-44-1782-584008; fax 011-44-1782-632343; aaa29@keele.ac.uk.

Study Abroad in Ireland. Semester, academic year, or summer term. Two to 6 courses per semester taught in English. Typical class size 25. Most students are from host institution, host country, or other programs. Instruction method is lectures, seminars, and tutorials. Use of all campus student facilities.

Dates: Spring: Jan-May; summer: Jun-Sep depending on program; fall: Sep-Dec. **Cost:** Summer $1,700-$3,400, semester $7,000-$9,000, year $14,000-$16,500. Includes tuition, accommodations, and predeparture handbook. **Contact:** Amy Armstrong, North American Institute for Study Abroad, P.O. Box 279, Riverside, PA 17868; 570-275-5099, fax 570-275-1644; naisa@naisa.com, [www.naisa.com].

Study Abroad in Northern Ireland. The Queen's Univ. of Belfast offers study abroad opportunities in all subject areas except medicine. Attendance can be for 1 or 2 semesters; students usually take 3 modules per semester.

Dates: First semester Sep-Jan, second semester Feb-Jun (3 weeks vacation at Christmas and Easter). **Cost:** Call for current rates. Accommodations range from £45-£60 per week. **Contact:** Mrs. C. McEachern, Administrative Officer, International Liaison Office, The Queen's Univ. of Belfast, Belfast BT7 1NN, Northern Ireland, U.K; 011-44-28-9033-5415, fax 011- 44-28-9068-7297; ilo@qub.ac.uk.

Study Abroad-Strathclyde. Participants will integrate fully into student life at the Univ. of Strathclyde, Scotland's third largest university. Choose from a vast range of courses in engineering, business, science, education, and arts including Scottish history, literature, and politics. Full credit is normally awarded and transferred upon the completion of the course.

Dates: Oct-Jun; Oct-Dec. **Cost:** $7,400 includes tuition and accommodations for 1 semester; $14,000 includes tuition and accommodations for 2 semesters. **Contact:**

Michelle Stewart, International Office, Univ. of Strathclyde, 50 George St., Glasgow G1 1QE, Scotland, U.K.; m.stewart@mis.strath.ac.uk, [www.strath.ac.uk.]

Study in Great Britain. Thirty-one program opportunities in England, Scotland, and Wales. University study and special subject area programs, including internships, for fall, spring, academic year and summer. Program provides a full range of services including predeparture advising, orientation, homestay, and guaranteed housing. Need-based scholarships available.

Dates: Fall, spring, academic year. Summer semester and terms. **Cost:** Varies. Call for current fees. **Contact:** Beaver College Center for Education Abroad, 450 S. Easton Rd., Glenside, PA 19038-3295; 888-BEAVER-9, fax 215-572-2174; cea@beaver.edu, [www.beaver.edu/cea].

Study in Ireland. Eleven program opportunities in the Republic of Ireland and Northern Ireland. University study and special subject area programs, including fine arts and Irish parliamentary internship. Program provides a full range of services including predeparture advising, orientation, homestay and guaranteed housing. Scholarships available.

Dates: Full year, fall and spring semester, and summer programs available. **Cost:** Fees vary. Call for information. **Contact:** Jennifer Hammer, Program Coordinator, Beaver College Center for Education Abroad, 450 S. Easton Rd., Glenside, PA 19038; 888-BEAVER-9, 215-572-2174; cea@beaver.edu, [www.beaver.edu/cea].

Study in Wales. Opportunities for either year-long or semester study abroad at the Univ. of Wales Swansea (10,500 students, located by the sea) in fully integrated programs. Host family and internship programs are available. University housing, orientation, and cultural events are integral to all programs. Swansea is a lively maritime city with great social life and numerous outdoor activities.

Dates: Sep-Dec/Jan-May. **Cost:** From $5,000. Tuition and accommmodations. **Contact:** Emma Frearson, American Studies Centre, Univ. of Wales Swansea, Singleton Park, Swansea SA2 8PP, Wales, U.K.; 011-44-1-792-295135, fax 011-44-1-792-295719; e.frearson@swansea.ac.uk, [www.swan.ac.uk/sao].

Study/Work with Drexel in London. The Drexel in London program offers students the opportunity to study and work in London, England. Students can select from courses in Business and Administration, Design and Merchandising, Hotel and Restaurant Management. Students may choose to study only or pair their studies with a 3-month internship.

Dates: Fall: Sep-Dec, winter: Jan-Mar, spring Mar-Jun, summer: Jun-Sep. **Cost:** $7,800 for months, $9,900 for 6 months (1999). **Contact:** Erika Richards, Drexel Univ., 3141 Chestnut St., Philadelphia, PA 19104; 215-895-1704, fax 215-895-6184; studyabroad@drexel.edu

Summer in Dalkeith, Scotland. SUNY Cortland Summer Scotland Program is located at Newbattle Abbey in Dalkeith, a rustic town outside of Edinburgh. Classes are taught in the Abbey, an historic 12th century monastery, with housing in a newly renovated dormitory attached. Instructors for the 5-week program are from SUNY Cortland and Newbattle Abbey College. Classes may include "The Making of the European Union" and "Scotland Through Its Visual Culture." Students earn 6 undergraduate credits.

Dates: Jun 10-Jul 15 (approx.) **Cost:** Approx. $3,100 (subject to change). Estimates include full-day orientation in the U.S., application fee, accommodations, meals, books and supplies, various cultural activities, excursions, administrative fees, passport, insurance, and airfare from NY. **Contact:** Dr. Del Janik, Program Coordinator, Office of International Programs, Box 2000, SUNY Cortland, Cortland, NY 13045; 607-753-2209, fax 607-753-5989; studyabroad@cortland.edu, [www.studyabroad.com/suny/cortland].

Summer in Scotland. Housed in modern dorms at the 12th century Newbattle Abbey near Edinburgh, students earn 6 credits studying Scotland Through Its Visual Culture and The Making of the European Union. Weekly field trips to architectural and historic monuments complement classroom study.

Dates: Jun 12-Jul 17. **Cost:** $2,122 includes NY in-state tuition, housing, all meals, 5 field trips, and books. Non-NY resident cost: $2,276. **Contact:** Office of International Programs, SUNY Cortland, Box 2000, Cortland, NY 13045; 607-753-2209, fax 607-753-5989; studyabroad@snycorva.cortland.edu.

Summer Teacher Institute. Elementary and secondary teachers live in Univ. of North London residence halls and study either option (6 credits each): Cultures and Communities in London examines the history and constituent cultures of London and how to integrate them into classrooms; Arts in Education explores arts in London and their place in the English curriculum.

Dates: Jul 3-Aug 1. **Cost:** $2,583 includes SUNY tuition, orientation, airport transfer, bed and breakfast, weekly field trips, day excursion, underground pass, and materials. **Contact:** Office of International Programs, SUNY Cortland, Box 2000, Cortland, NY 13045; 607-753-2209, fax 607-753-5989; studyabroad@snycorva.cortland.edu.

Summer Teachers Institute in London. Earn 6 graduate credits in Education in a 4-week program at the Univ. of North London, sponsored by the State Univ. of New York College at Cortland. Curricular options in arts or social science are appropriate for both elementary and secondary teachers. Classes and field visits are scheduled Mondays-Thursdays, leaving 3-day weekends for study and independent travel.

Dates: Fall: mid-Sep-mid-Dec:; spring: end-Jan-mid-May. **Cost:** Approx. $4,000. Estimates include full-day orientation in the U.S., application fee, accommodations, meals, commuter ticket on underground and buses, excursions, insurance, roundtrip airfare from N.Y., transportation from airport to London upon arrival, books and supplies, various cultural activities, administrative fees. SUNY tuition and spending money not included. **Contact:** Dr. Del Janik, Program Coordinator, Office of International Programs, Box 2000, SUNY Cortland, Cortland, NY 13045; 607-753-2209, fax 607-753-5989; studyabroad@cortland.edu, [www.studyabroad.com/suny/cortland].

Temple Univ. London. A student can spend a semester or summer abroad studying communications as part of the Temple/London Fall Semester Program or the British Mass Media Seminar. For the semester program, students may choose from courses in liberal arts and British communications and theater. Students also can get practical, resume-enhancing experience in internships. Classes and housing are located in the heart of London within minutes of Bloomsbury, the British Museum, and the Univ. of London.

Dates: Fall: late Aug-Dec, application deadline Apr 1; summer: Jul-Aug. **Cost:** Fall: $10,991 (resident) to $13,486 (nonresident) per semester; summer approx.: $5,100 (resident) for 5-week program. Includes tuition, housing, computer lab fee, daily out-of-pocket expenses, flight and transfer. **Contact:** Debbie Marshall, School of Communications and Theater,

Temple Univ., 2020 N. 13th St., Philadelphia, PA 19122; 215-204-1961; augusta@astro.temple.edu.

Two Pre-Session Programs. "This Scepter 'd Isle" introduces important general aspects of British history and culture. "Changing Places: Lancaster and the Lake District" focuses on historical, geographical and cultural perspectives on Northern England. Different topics for each of 4 weeks. Each worth 4 semester credits—fits ideally with fall study at a U.K. university.

Dates: Aug 17-Sep 16. **Cost:** £1,012 includes orientation, accommodations, teaching, assessment, field trips. **Contact:** Paula Foster, Lancaster Summer Univ., Dept. of Continuing Education, Lancaster Univ., LA1 4YN U.K.; 011-44-1524-592567, fax 011-44-1524-592448; summer.university@lancaster.ac.uk, [www.lancs.ac.uk/users/conted/suindex.htm].

UNH Cambridge Summer Program. This program's outstanding reputation rests in its balance between offerings of challenging courses in literature, and history taught by primarily Cambridge Univ. professors and a wealth of activities including fine theater, excursions, lectures, readings, and socializing, all in traditional English style.

Dates: Jul 10-Aug 18, 2000. **Cost:** Call for details. **Contact:** Margaret-Love Denman, Director, UNH Cambridge Summer Program, 95 Main St., Durham, NH 03824; Tel./fax 603-862-3962; cambridge.program@unh.edu, [www.unh.edu/cambridge].

Univ. College Cork. First opened in 1849, the Univ. College Cork (UCC) is 1 of 3 constituent colleges of the National Univ. of Ireland. Direct enrollment. Eight faculties comprise the educational offerings of UCC: arts, Celtic studies, commerce, law, science, food science and technology, engineering and medicine. Enrollment in regular UCC classes with Irish students. Cortland's program specializes in language, history, and culture, but other courses may be available. Housing arranged prior to departure from U.S. in apartments near campus. Fall, spring, summer, academic year.

Dates: Fall: Early Sep-mid-Dec:; spring: mid-Jan-early Jun; summer: early Jul-end of Jul. **Cost:** Fall 1999 or spring 2000 estimate: $6,850; summer: $3,400; academic year: $13,250. Estimates include full-day orientation before departure, application fee, apartment rental (including utilities), food allowance, health and accident insurance, roundtrip airfare from NY, books and supplies, passport. SUNY tuition not included. **Contact:** Office of International Programs, Box 2000, SUNY Cortland, Cortland, NY 13045; 607-753-2209, fax 607-753-5989; studyabroad@cortland.edu, [www.studyabroad.com/suny/cortland].

Univ. of Cambridge International Summer Schools. Largest and longest established program of summer schools in the U.K. Intensive study in Cambridge as part of an international community. Term I (4 weeks) and Term II (2 weeks) of the International Summer School offer over 60 different courses. Three-week specialist programs: Art History, Medieval Studies, History, English Literature, Shakespeare, Science. Wide range of classes on all programs. U.S. and other overseas institutions grant credit. Guidelines available.

Dates: Jul-Aug. **Cost:** Tuition from £475-£690 (2 to 4 weeks), accommodations from £250-£950 (2 to 4 weeks). Six-week period of study also possible by combining 2 summer schools. **Contact:** Ali James, Development as Publicity Officer, International Division, Univ. of Cambridge, Madingley Hall, Cambridge CB3 8AQ, U.K.; 011-44-1954-280398, fax 011-44-1954-280200; acj28@cam.ac.uk, [www.cam.ac.uk/cambuniv/conted/intsummer].

Univ. of North London. SUNY Cortland celebrates its 27th consecutive year at UNL. Over 400 courses are offered. Fields of study include education, natural sciences, humanities, communications, social sciences, business, health, theater arts, and others. Direct enrollment with British students. Credits per semester: 12-16. Pre-arranged housing in flats in the Bayswater district. Full- and part-time internships available.

Dates: Spring: end-Jan-mid-May. **Cost:** Estimates: spring 2000: $7,350; academic year: $13,000. Estimates include full-day orientation in the U.S., application fee, apartment rental, meals, commuter ticket on underground, London tour and Thames cruise, insurance, roundtrip airfare from N.Y., transportation from airport to downtown London upon arrival, passport, books and supplies, various cultural activities, administrative fees. SUNY tuition and spending money not included. **Contact:** Dr. Del Janik, Program Coordinator, Office of International Programs, Box 2000, SUNY Cortland, Cortland, NY 13045; 607-753-2209, fax 607-753-5989; studyabroad@cortland.edu, [www.studyabroad.com/suny/cortland].

Univ. of Northumbria. Semester or year abroad at the Univ. of Northumbria at Newcastle. Special orientation program for U.S. students, including course in British Heritage. Opportunity to tutor in local schools.

Dates: Fall semester: mid-Sep-3rd week in Jan; spring semester: mid-Jan-early Jun. **Cost:** $5,560 (depending on exchange rage). Includes tuition, room and board (14-meal plan), airfare, and study abroad fee. **Contact:** Dr. Amy C. Simes, Director, Ctr. for Int'l. Education, Frostburg State Univ., 101 Braddock Rd., Frostburg, MD 21532; 301-687-3091; asimes@frostburg.edu.

Univ. of Warwick Study Abroad. Warwick, among the U.K.'s top 10 universities, offers the choice of a wide range of subjects to juniors spending a year or semester abroad. Attractive campus, with guaranteed accommodations integrated with British students, and excellent study and social facilities. In the heart of England but only 75 minutes to London.

Dates: Spring: Jan-Jul, fall: Oct-Dec, year: Oct-Jul. **Cost:** $12,400 year (part year pro-rata), living $8,800 per year. **Contact:** Ms. Caroline Pack, International Office, Univ. of Warwick, Coventry CV4 7AL, U.K.; 011-44-1203-523705, fax 011-44-1203-461606; c.m.pack@warwick.ac.uk, [www.warwick.ac.uk].

Vacation with College Credits. First 4 days in London, balance at Univ. of Bath; 3-credit courses in literature, history, fine arts, political science, international business. Single room housing. Excursions to historical and archaeological sites, 3 1/2 day weekends, morning classes with British faculty. Ideal location for American students.

Dates: Contact organization for details. **Cost:** $2,620 tuition (6 credits), housing excursions, ground travel, some meals, computer access; low-cost airfare available (1999). **Contact:** College Consortium for Study Abroad, P.O. Box 562, Paramus, NJ 07653-0562; 201-261-8753, fax 201-261-6389; toccsa@juno.com.

Visual Arts and Crafts Courses. Week and weekend courses. Summer schools in art, ceramics, woodworking, textiles, sculpture, silversmithing, music, and art appreciation. One-, 2-, and 3-year full-time diploma courses in conservation and restoration of antique furniture, clocks, ceramics, and fine metalwork; tapestry weaving (also 6-week modules); making early stringed instruments. Validation at postgraduate level is by the Univ. of Sussex.

Dates: Diploma courses start each year and end in July. Short courses are year round. **Cost:** Diploma courses £7,500 per annum; residential accommodations £3,750 per annum; short courses (residential) £388, weekends £162, 6 days £457. **Contact:** Victoria Stentiford, West Dean College, West Dean, Chichester, West Sussex, PO18 0QZ U.K.; 011-44-1243-811301, fax 011-44-1243-811343; westdean@pavilion.co.uk, [www.westdean.org.uk].

WISC Oxford Program. Qualified students (3.2 GPA) may study in one-on-one tutorials for 1, 2, or 3 terms or in the summer, as associate students of a medieval Oxford college. Students are not degree candidates in O.U. Almost any subject may be studied. Housing is with British students in the center of Oxford.

Dates: One year (Oct-Jul) or 3 terms. Also summer (May-Aug). **Cost:** $12,200 1 term; $26,800 year (1999). **Contact:** Virginia Thompson, WISC, 214 Mass. Ave., NE, Rm. 370, Washington, DC 20016; 800-323-WISC, 202-547-3275; wisc@erols.com, [www.studyabroad.com/wisc].

Work in Britain. Santa Rosa Junior College offers college credits (up to 8 semester units) for students working in London for a semester. Students obtain their work permit through BUNAC, attend an in-person or online orientation through Santa Rosa Junior College, and work and live in London independently while remaining in contact with college faculty.

Dates: Spring and fall 2000. **Cost:** Approx. $3,500. **Contact:** Kathleen Simmons, Program Coordiantor, Work and Earn College Credit in Britain, Work Experience Dept., Santa Rosa Junior College,1501 Mendocino Ave., Santa Rosa, CA 95401; kathleen_simmons@garfiield.santarosa.edu, [www.santarosa.edu/workexp/brit-].

York Visiting Student Program. York's well-respected program offers the opportunity of studying at one of U.K.'s top-ranked universities. A wide range of courses is available in arts, sciences, and social sciences. Students are fully integrated into the academic and social life of the university, located on a beautiful parkland campus on the edge of one of Britain's most historic cities.

Dates: Oct-Dec, Jan-Jun. **Cost:** Approx. $13,000 including tuition and room. **Contact:** International Office, Univ. of York, York YO10 5DD, U.K.; 011-44-1904-433534, fax 011-44-1904-433538; international@york.ac.uk, [www.york.ac.uk/admin/intnat/visiting].

United States

English Language Instruction. Dates: Thirty start dates each year. **Cost:** $1,325 per 4-week session. **Contact:** ELS Language Centers, 400 Alexander Park, Suite 100-TA, Princeton, NJ 08540-6306; 609-750-3500, fax 309-750-3597; info@els.com, [www.els.com].

Venezuela

Study Abroad in Venezuela. Students are fully immersed in the language and culture of Venezuela. The program is offered in several cities (Caracas, Valencia, Barquisimeto, Maturin, Merida, and Maracay) at local universities. Students attend classes with students from Venezuela and live with host families.

Dates: Fall: Sep-Dec; spring: Jan-Apr; summer: May-Jun, Jul-Aug. **Cost:** Semester $5,000, summer (6 weeks), $3,000. (1999). **Contact:** Beatriz G. Silva, Director, Office of International Programs,10211 Pines Blvd., PMB#217, Pembroke Pines, FL 33026; 954-432-2355; culture@interpoint.net

Venusa Institute of Int'l. Studies and Modern Languages. Students enroll at the Venusa Institute of International Studies and Modern Languages in Mérida, located in the heart of the Venezuelan Andes. Fields of study include Spanish language, Latin American history and culture, international business, cross-cultural communications, teaching of English as a second language (TESOL), int'l. agriculture, ecology and botany, anthropology and sociology, and more. Most classes taught in Spanish, with a limited number being offered in English. Homestays. One semester college-level Spanish recommended and overall GPA of 2.5 required. **Global Professional Internship Program** available to students having sufficient preparation in Spanish language.

Dates: Fall: late Aug-mid-Dec; spring: early Jan-end of Apr; summer: 2 sessions, mid-May-late Jun and late Jun-mid-Aug. For the Global Internship program: fall and spring: same as above; summer: late-May-Aug. **Cost:** Fall/spring estimate $6,450 per semester; summer 2000 $3,700. Estimates include SUNY tuition, full day orientation in the U.S., orientation in Venezuela, application fee, room and 2 meals daily with local family, airfare from Miami to Mérida roundtrip, 2 full day field trips, insurance, books and supplies, program administration costs. For the Global Internship program: fall or spring 2000 $5,825; summer 2000 $4,300. **Contact:** Office of International Programs, Box

2000, SUNY Cortland, Cortland, NY 13045; 607-753-2209, fax 607-753-5989; koppl@cortland.edu, [www.studyabroad.com/suny/cortland].

Worldwide

American Int'l. Youth Student Exchange Program (AIYSEP). Nonprofit AIYSEP offers high school foreign exchange program for students in Europe, Australia, New Zealand, America, and many other countries. Area counselors are located in Europe, U.S., Australia, New Zealand, South America, Peru, Canada, and Japan. AIYSEP believes a greater international understanding is achieved among people and countries through cultural homestay programs.

Dates: Year, semester, and summer programs. **Cost:** Year $3,995-$6,000, semester $3,495-$4,200, summer $1,900-$3,500. **Contact:** American International Youth Student Exchange, 200 Round Hill Rd., Tiburon, CA 94920; 800-347-7575 or 415-435-4049, 415-499-7669, fax 415-499-5651; AIYSEP@aol.com, [www.aiysep.org].

ASPECT Outbound Program. The ASPECT Foundation offers semester and academic year programs in Brazil, Denmark, England, Ireland, France, Japan, Spain, Germany, Uruguay, and a summer program in Australia. Students aged 15-18 experience another culture first-hand by living as a member of a host family, attending local school, and making new friends.

Dates: Call for details. **Cost:** Summer term $2,700; semester and year $3,300 and up. **Contact:** Eileen O'Neill, Outbound Program Coordinator, ASPECT Foundation, 350 Sansome St. #900, San Francisco, CA 94104; 800-879-6884, fax 415-228-8051; eileen.o'neill@educate.com.

Boston Univ. International Programs. Offering internship and language/liberal arts programs in 16 cities on 6 continents and in 9 different languages. Course offerings range from intermediate-level language and liberal arts study through advanced-level, direct enrollment in local universities. Internship programs combine coursework with participation in local work life. Application materials: 2 references, transcript, essays, and academic approval.

Dates: Fall, spring, and summer (length varies). **Cost:** $4,350-$16,000; application fee: $40. **Contact:** Boston Univ., International Programs, 232 Bay State Rd., 5th Fl., Boston, MA 02215; 617-353-9888, fax 617-353-5402; abroad@bu.edu, [www.bu.edu/abroad].

CCIS. The College Consortium for International Studies (CCIS) is a nonprofit organization made up of over 150 2-year and 4-year U.S. colleges and universities. Member institutions collaborate to offer study abroad opportunities for U.S. undergraduate students in over 25 countries around the world.

Dates: Call for details. **Cost:** Call for details. **Contact:** College Consortium for International Studies, 2000 P St., NW, Suite 503, Washington, DC 20036; 800-453-6956, fax 202-223-0999; info@ccisabroad.org, [www.ccisabroad.org].

Central College Abroad. English language study abroad programs in: Carmarthen, Wales; Colchester and London, England; Leiden, Netherlands; and Mérida, Mexico. Internship and/or service learning projects are also available at all sites. Excursions/cultural activities and ISIC included. Onsite directors.

Dates: Semester or full year available. Exact dates vary by program. **Cost:** Vary by program. **Contact:** Central College Abroad, 812 University, Pella, IA 50219; 800-831-3629, fax 515-628-5375; studyabroad@central.edu, [www.studyabroad.com/central].

CHI World Travel/Study Programs for All Ages. CHI was established in 1980 as a nonprofit organization to encourage people to reach out and explore the world. Call us or visit our website. We have worldwide highschool academic programs, cultural and/or language immersions with homestays; group tours personalized for schools or for the general public. Internships, au pair and teaching positions also available.

Dates: Vary. **Cost:** Vary according to destination and length of program. **Contact:** Cultural Homestay International, 2455 Bennett Valley Rd., #210B, Santa Rosa, CA 95404; 800-395-2726, fax 707-523-3704; chigaylep@msn.com, [www.chinet.org/outbound.html].

The Cooperative Center for Study Abroad. CCSA is a consortium of American colleges and universities with study abroad programs in Australia, Canada, Ireland, England, New Zealand, Scotland, and South Africa. Classes are taught by faculty from consortium member schools. In addition, internships are also available in London, England.

Dates: Contact sponsor. **Cost:** Contact sponsor. **Contact:** Dr. Michael A. Klembara, CCSA, BEP 301, Northern Kentucky Univ., Highland Heights, KY 41099; 800-319-6015; ccsa@nku.edu, [www.nku.edu/ccsa].

ERDT/SHARE! Exchange Program. ERDT/
SHARE! Provides American students, ages 16 to
18, opportunities for summer, semester, or
academic year homestays/study abroad.
Language proficiency, academic standing,
maturity are criteria for selection. Students live
with host families and, depending on program
selected, attend local school or language school.
ERDT/SHARE! also provides opportunities for
American families to host international
exchange students.
Dates: Vary with type of program selected
and academic year dates. Students and host
family applications are accepted year round.
Cost: $1,500-$7,000 (depending on program),
excluding transportation and personal
expenses. **Contact:** Roger Riske, President, 475
Washington Blvd., Suite 220, Marina del Rey,
CA 90292; 800-321-3738, 310-821-9977, fax
310-821-9282; info@erdtshare.org,
[www.erdtshare.org].

Flinders Univ. Study Abroad. Students may
attend classes at Flinders Univ. in Adelaide,
Australia for 1 term or the full academic year.
Organized excursions to Cleland Wildlife Park,
Aboriginal cultural tour of Adelaide, subsidized
optional trips to Kangaroo Island and Flinders
Ranges. On-campus accommodations available.
Open to undergraduates (2.5 GPA), adults.
Dates: Semester 1: Feb-Jul, semester 2: Jul-
Nov. **Cost:** AUS$5,125 per semester. Includes
tuition, fees, orientation. **Contact:** Mr. Peter
Millen, Study Abroad Adviser, Int'l. Office,
Flinders Univ. of South Australia, GPO Box
2100, Adelaide, SA 5001, Australia; 011-61-8-
8201-2727, fax 011-61-8-8201-3177;
intl.office@flinders.edu.au, [http://
adminwww.flinders.edu.au/intloff/home.html].

Friends World Program-Comparative Religion.
A 9-month program in comparative religion
and culture. Students will study for three 10-
week terms in Taiwan, India, and Israel. The
field course will be based on experiential
approaches, emphasizing participation,
observation, and involvement in local religious
life. Culture's relation to religion and social
change will be emphasized.
Dates: Early Sep-mid-May. **Cost:** $28,050 for
year (1999/2000). Includes tuition, travel, room
and board, fees and books. **Contact:** Admissions, Friends World Program, 239 Montauk
Hwy., Southampton, NY 11968; 516-287-8474;
fw@southampton.liunet.edu.

Global Ecology and Cities in the 21st Century.
Two different academic programs to be offered
by the International Honors Program in 1999-
2000. "Global Ecology" is a 2-semester program
of around-the-world study and travel to
England, India, the Philippines, New Zealand,
and Mexico with academic coursework in
ecology, anthropology, economics, and
environmental issues. The "Cities in the 21st
Century" program is a 1-semester program of
study and travel to Egypt, India, and Brazil with
academic coursework in urban studies,
anthropology, sociology, economics, and
political science.
Dates: "Global Ecology": Sep 2000-May 2001.
"Cities in 21st Century": Jan-May 2000. **Cost:**
"Global Ecology": $22,950 plus airfare, includes
tuition, room and board. "Cities in the 21st
Century": $13,650 plus airfare, includes tuition,
room and board. Estimated airfare for each
program is $3,900. Financial aid is available.
Contact: Joan Tiffany, Director, International
Honors Program, 19 Braddock Pk., Boston, MA
02116; 617-267-0026, fax 617-262-9299;
info@ihp.edu, [www.ihp.edu].

Global Service Corps. Service-learning
programs in Costa Rica, Kenya, or Thailand.
Individualized community service and
development projects assignments with
grassroots organizations. Project areas:
rainforest conservation, sustainable agriculture,
HIV/AIDS awareness, clinical health care,
women's groups, classroom teaching. Experience the challenges of developing countries
from the inside out. Includes orientation,
training, excursions, and homestays. Academic
credit available.
Dates: Year round. Contact GSC office or
check the web site for specific starting dates.
Cost: $1,695-$1,795 for 2-4 week project trips;
$2,520-$2,820 for 10-12 week internships; $250-
$495 per month for extensions. Includes
extensive pre-departure preparation and in-
country expenses (hotel and homestay room
and board, orientation, training, project
expenses, transportation, excursions). Airfare
not included, discount rates available. **Contact:**
Global Service Corps., 300 Broadway, #28, San
Francisco, CA 94133; 415-788-3666 ext. 128, fax
415-788-7324; gsc@igc.apc.org,
[www.globalservicecorps.org].

I.A.B. One-year multidisciplinary postgraduate
program in the arts and sciences of radio and
television.
Dates: One term starts Sep 25. **Cost:**
CHF26,000 tuition fee, CHF19,000 accommodations and board. **Contact:** Aleksandar
Todorovic, IAB, 11 Av. Florimont, 1820

Montreux, Switzerland; 011-4121-961-1660, fax 011-4121-961-1665; secretariat@izb.ch, [www.iab.ch].

Illinois Programs Abroad. Brazil, Cuba, Ecuador, Great Britain, Mexico, Turkey, and Russia. Summer: language, literature, culture, social sciences. Brazil: business. Semester/year: Ecuador—full curriculum. Great Britain: art and design. Mexico (spring only) social sciences and humanities. Russia (spring only) language, literature, and social sciences.

Dates: Summer, fall, spring, and year. **Cost:** Varies by program. **Contact:** Illinois Programs Abroad, Univ. of Illinois, 115 International Studies Bldg., 910 S. 5th St., Champaign, IL 61820; 800-531-4404, fax 217-244-0249; ipa@uiuc.edu, [www.uiuc.edu/providers/ips/sao].

International Cooperative Education. Paid internship/employment for college and university students for a period of 8-12 weeks in 4 European (Belgium, Finland, Germany, and Switzerland) and two Asian (Japan and Singapore) countries. Employment depends on foreign language knowledge, major, and previous work experience. Work permits and housing are provided.

Dates: From Jun-Sep. **Cost:** Students must pay for air transportation and have a reserve of at least $800 for initial expenses. Program fee $800. **Contact:** Günter Seefeldt, PhD, Director, International Cooperative Education Program, 15 Spiros Way, Menlo Park, CA 94025; 650-323-4944, fax 650-323-1104, ICEMenlo@aol.com, [http://members.aol.com/ICEMenlo].

Italian Courses, Language, Art, and Culture. Intensive and non-intensive, individual and or group, beginning throughout the year. General Italian plus optional courses (Italian cooking, Roman archaeology and others). From beginner to advanced level. Free access to self study center. Social activities.

Dates: Contact organization for details. **Cost:** Contact organization for details. **Contact:** Giorgio Piva, Dilit International House, Via Marghera 22, I-00815 Rome, Italy; 011-39-06-4462592, fax 011-39-06-4440888; information@dilit.it, [www.dilit.it].

Language Immersion Programs. Learn a language in the country where it's spoken. Intensive foreign language training offered in Costa Rica, Russia, Spain, France, Italy, Germany, and Ecuador for students aged 16 and older. Classes are taught in up to 8 different proficiency levels and are suitable for beginners as well as people with advanced linguistic skills.

All courses include accommodations and meals. Lots of extracurricular activities available. Students can earn college credit through Providence College.

Dates: Courses start every second Monday year round. Year programs commence in Sep, semester programs in Jan, May, and Sep. **Cost:** Varies with program, approx. $950 per 2-week course. **Contact:** Stephanie Greco, Director of Admissions, EF International Language Schools, EF Center, 1 Education St., Cambridge, MA 02142; 800-992-1892, fax 617-619-1701; ils@ef.com.

Linguistic Stay/Au Pair Stay. Learn various languages in different countries and improve your language level. We offer a variety of courses and accommodations. If you choose an au pair stay and have to look after children during 25 or 30 hours per week, you receive pocket money that will allow you to take courses and improve your language skills.

Dates: Year round. **Cost:** Depends on the program and country. **Contact:** Mrs. Pierrot, Inter-Sejours, 179 rue de Courcelles, 75017 Paris, France; 011-33-1-47-63-06-81, fax 011-33-1-40-54-89-41; intersejours@europost.org.

Marist International Internships. Internship and study abroad programs in Sydney, Australia; Leeds, England; Dublin, Ireland; Florence, Italy; Madrid, Spain; Quito, Ecuador; and Monterrey, Mexico. Programs combine internships, homestays, and course work at host institutions.

Dates: Fall and spring semesters and full academic year. **Cost:** Average program fee is $10,500. **Contact:** Brian Whalen, Marist College, 290 North Rd., Poughkeepsie, NY 12601; 914-575-3330, fax 914-575-3294; international@marist.edu, [www.marist.edu/international].

NYU Study Abroad. Fall/spring/summer study abroad programs in Florence, Madrid, Paris, Prague, London, and Buenos Aires (many additional locations in summer). Courses in English or in native language of host country. Scholarships available to NYU and visiting students based on financial need and merit.

Dates: Vary by site. **Cost:** Fall or spring semester $11,728 for tuition, fees, and numerous excursions and local events. Room and board charges vary by site and type of housing selected. Summer fees vary by site and program. **Contact:** Study Abroad Admissions, New York Univ., 7 E. 12th St., 6th Fl., New York, NY

10003-4475; 212-998-4433, fax 212-995-4103; studyabroad@nyu.edu, [www.nyu.edu/abroad/go].

Overseas Studies at Univ. of Haifa. The Dept. of Overseas Studies at the Univ. of Haifa, Israel offers a wide variety of fully accredited courses for a year, semester, or summer in the humanities, arts and social sciences. The program features a kibbutz-university program, a psychology honors program, internships, the Summer Hebrew Ulpan and other summer courses.

Dates: Call for details. **Cost:** $4,600 per semester, $7,700 per year. Includes tuition fee, housing, and activities. **Contact:** Dept. of Overseas Studies, Univ. of Haifa, Haifa 31905, Israel; 011-972-4-8240766, fax 011-972-4-8240391; overseas@research.haifa.ac.il, [www.haifa.ac.il].

Penn Summer Abroad. Academic programs granting Univ. of Pennsylvania credits. Courses focusing on language, culture, economics, theater, anthropology, cinema, art history, traditional folk medicine, performing arts, and religion. Several programs offer homestays, some offer internships.

Dates: Mid-May-late Aug (2-8 weeks). **Cost:** Tuition: $1,536 per course. Living costs vary. **Contact:** Elizabeth Sachs, Penn Summer Abroad, College of General Studies, Univ. of Pennsylvania, 3440 Market St., Suite 100, Philadelphia, PA 19104-3335; 215-898-5738, fax 215-573-2053.

School for International Training. A pioneer in study abroad, the School for International Training (SIT) offers 56 programs in over 40 countries worldwide. For over 40 years SIT has been a leader in offering field-based study abroad programs to U.S. college and university students.

Dates: Fall and spring semester. **Cost:** $9,300-$12,600 depending on location. Includes airfare, tuition, room and board, excursions, and insurance. **Contact:** School for International Training, P.O. Box AA1TA, Kipling Rd., Brattleboro, VT 05302; 800-336-1616, 802-257-7751, fax 802-258-3500; csa@sit.edu, [www.sit.edu].

Study Abroad, Adelaide. The Univ. of Adelaide is in the top rank of Australian universities. The University's study abroad program actively encourages you to study subjects which provide you with an insight into the Australian culture and environment. Adelaide is the gateway to the Australian Outback.

Dates: Call for details. **Cost:** AUS$6,000 tuition per semester. **Contact:** Study Abroad Office, International Programs, Univ. of Adelaide, Adelaide, South Australia 5005; 011-61-8-8303-4379, fax 011-61-8-8303-3988; pritchie@registry.adelaide.edu.au, [www.ipo.adelaide.edu.au/].

Study Europe in Maastricht. The Center for European Studies, Maastricht Univ. offers semester and year programs. Students compose their own "package of courses"—all taught in English (16 credits per semester). Students will be fully integrated with European students in classes and in housing.

Dates: Spring: mid-Jan-end of May; fall: mid-Aug-end of Dec. **Cost:** Tuition $7,200 per semester. Other $700 per month (housing, food, miscellaneous). **Contact:** Karin Quanten, Coordinator Undergraduate Programs, Center for European Studies, Witmakersstraat 10, 6211 JB Maastricht, the Netherlands; 011-31-43-3212627, fax 011-31-43-3257324; K.Quanten@ccs.unimass.nl.

Summer Program European Studies. The Center for European Studies, Maastricht Univ. offers a 6-week summer program. Courses focus on European Union, European culture and history. Students take 2 courses—all taught in English (6 credits total).

Dates: Jul 1-Aug 15. **Cost:** Tuition $300 per credit. Expenses $700 per month (housing, food, miscellaneous). **Contact:** Karin Quanten, Coordinator Undergraduate Programs, Center for European Studies, Witmakersstraat 10, 6211 JB Maastricht, the Netherlands; 011-31-43-3212627, fax 011-31-43-3257324; K.Quanten@ccs.unimass.nl.

Summer Study Abroad. Summer opportunities in Australia, Austria, England, Ireland, Mexico, and Scotland, including internships, fine arts, drama, history, literature, environmental studies, psychology, and languages. Full range of program services. Guaranteed housing.

Dates: Vary. Call for tentative dates. **Cost:** Varies. Call for fees. **Contact:** Beaver College Center for Education Abroad, 450 S. Easton Rd., Glenside, PA 19038-3295; 888-BEAVER-9, fax 215-572-2174; cea@beaver.edu, [www.beaver.edu/cea].

Teaching Internship Program. Global Routes interns are assigned in pairs to remote villages where they teach in local schools and complete at least 1 community service project. Each intern lives separately with a local family in a simple, traditional home. Training, support, and adventure travel are an integral part of the programs. Programs offered in Costa Rica, Ecuador, Kenya, Thailand, Zimbabwe, Navajo Nation, Dharamsala, India.

Dates: Year round in 3-month session. **Cost:** $3,950 summer, $4,250 during year. Includes all expenses (room, board, adventure travel) except airfare to and from country. Scholarships and fundraising information available. **Contact:** Global Routes, 1814 7th St., Suite A, Berkeley, CA 94710; 510-848-4800, fax 510-848-4801; mail@globalroutes.org, [www.globalroutes.org].

Thunderbird. Thunderbird, The American Graduate School of International Management offers students an opportunity to gain knowledge and experience in the global business environment through various programs located around the globe, including North and South America, Europe, Africa, and Asia. Programs also emphasize exposure to other cultures, political and economic systems and language.

Dates: Spring, summer, fall, and winter programs, in addition to 2-week mini-terms (interims) held throughout the year. **Cost:** Dependent upon the number of courses taken. **Contact:** Thunderbird, The American Graduate School of International Management, 15249 North 59th Ave., Glendale, AZ 85306; 602-978-7252, fax 602-978-7419; overseasprograms@t-bird.edu, [www.t-bird.edu].

Trent International. Trent Univ.'s international study and exchange programs provides students with an opportunity to spend an academic study year abroad. Students take regular courses and examinations and credits are counted toward their undergraduate degree. Available in most disciplines. Orientation and special services for visiting students.

Dates: Full academic year, some semester programs available. Sep-Oct and May-Jun. **Cost:** Differs according to program but generally includes Trent's tuition and often residence. **Contact:** Cynthia Bennett Awe, Int'l. Programs and Services Manager, Trent Univ., Peterborough, ON, K9J 7B8, Canada; fax 705-748-1626; cawe@trentu.ca.

Univ. of Nebraska-Lincoln World Campus. Offers a variety of study abroad programs worldwide for an academic year, semester, or summer. Many programs open to nonUNL students. To explore the unique opportunities available, visit our web site: [www.iaffairs.unl.edu].

Dates: Contact organization for details. **Cost:** Contact organization for details. **Contact:** International Affairs at the Univ. of Nebraska-Lincoln, 1237 R St., Lincoln, NE 68588-0221; 402-472-5358, fax 402-472-5383; iaffairs@unl.edu.

Univ. of Sydney. The Univ. of Sydney (Australia's first university) hosts study abroad programs for university students who would like to undertake a semester (or more) of their studies overseas. The program covers a broad range of units of study including: agriculture, architecture, economics, education, engineering, health sciences, law, liberal arts, music, nursing, pharmacy, and science.

Dates: Semesters begin in Jul and Mar. **Cost:** Base rate AUS$6,000. Additional loading $300 per 8-credit point unit. **Contact:** Study Abroad Advisor, Int'l. Office, Univ. of Sydney, Sydney NSW, 2006, Australia; 011- 61-2-9351-5841, fax 011-61-2-9351-4013; s.tropiano@io.usyd.edu.au, [www.usyd.edu.au].

Up With People Worldsmart™. The Worldsmart™ program accelerates education and career opportunities through the unique combination of international travel, stage-based musical performance, and community service. Every year, 700 university-aged students from a variety of countries spend 11 months traveling throughout and experiencing the world.

Dates: Programs begin in Jan and Jul. **Cost:** $13,700 includes all travel, lodging, food, and student program expenses within the 11-month program. **Contact:** Admissions Department, Up With People, 1 International Ct., Broomfield, CO 80021; 800- 596-7353 or 303-438-7373, fax 303-438-7301; admissions@upwithpeople.org, [www.upwithpeople.org].

Visions. VISIONS community service summer programs for teenagers combine community service, outdoor adventure and exploration, intercultural activities at sites in Peru, Alaska, Montana, South Carolina Sea Islands, and 5 Caribbean islands. Co-ed groups of 24 students and 6 staff live in cross-cultural host communities for up to 4 weeks.

Dates: Late Jun-late Jul, first weeks of Aug; 4-week or 3-week sessions. **Cost:** $2,400-$3,500 depending on program site and length. **Contact:** Joanne Pinaire, Visions, P.O. Box 220, Newport, PA 17074; 717-567-7313, 800-813-9283, fax 717-567-7853; visions@pa.net, [www.visions-adventure.org].

Webster Univ. in Europe. Webster Univ. in Europe has more than 250 students at each campus in Leiden, Geneva, London, and Vienna. Students may pursue a degree program leading to a BA, MA, or MBA. In addition, students may enroll for a study abroad semester or year (summer session and other short-term options also available). All courses are taught in English and are fully accredited. Major areas of study include: business, international relations, management, marketing and psychology. A complete range of electives is also offered.

Dates: Five entry terms: late Aug-mid-Oct, mid-Jan, mid-Mar, late May. **Cost:** $20,000 (1998-99 academic year), $10,000 (semester 1998-99). Estimate includes tuition, room and board, books, local transportation, social activities. **Contact:** Study Abroad Office, Webster Univ., 470 E. Lockwood Ave., St. Louis, MO 63119-3194; 314-968-6988 or 800-984-6857, fax 314-968-7119; worldview@websteruniv.edu, [www.webster.edu].

World Experience Student Exchange. Have the experience of a lifetime. Learn another language and culture. Live as a member of a family and attend a local school. Choose from 30 countries. One- or 2-semester programs. Add a new dimension to your life. Eligibility: 15-18 years, 3.0 GPA.

Dates: Aug or Jan departure for 1 to 2 semesters. **Cost:** $2,640 plus individual country fees for 1 year; $2,265 plus individual country fees for 1 semester. Travel expenses not included. **Contact:** World Experience, 2440 Hacienda Blvd #116, Hacienda Heights, CA 91745; 800-633-6653, fax 626-333-4914; weworld@worldexperience.org, [www.worldexperience.org].

WorldTeach. WorldTeach is a nonprofit, nongovernmental organization which provides opportunities for individuals to make a meaningful contribution to international education by living and working as volunteer teachers in developing countries.

Dates: Year round. **Cost:** $4,800-$5,950. Includes international airfare, health insurance, extensive training, and in-country support. **Contact:** WorldTeach, Harvard Institute for International Development, 14 Story St., Cambridge, MA 02138; 800-4-TEACH-0 or 617-495-5527, fax 617-495-1599; info@worldteach.org, [www.worldteach.org].

TWELVE

ADULT STUDY & TRAVEL PROGRAMS

The following listing of adult study/travel programs was supplied by the organizers. Contact the program directors to confirm costs, dates, and other details. Please tell them you read about their programs in this book! Programs based in more than one country or region are listed under "Worldwide."

Africa and Cuba

Bicycle Africa/Cuba. Educational, people-to-people bicycle tours to all parts of Africa and Cuba. Cycling difficulty is moderate. Each tour is unique; all focus on the diversity of the culture, social institutions, and environment, and the complexity of the history, economy, and society. Programs are led by area studies specialists.

   Dates: Jan (Uganda), Feb (Tanzania/Kenya), Apr (Tunisia), Jun-Aug (Zimbabwe/Malawi), Oct-Nov (Senegal/Guinea/Mali), Nov-Dec (Burkina Faso/Togo/Benin/Ghana), Dec-Mar (Cuba). **Cost:** $990-$1,490 plus airfare for 2 weeks. Includes food, lodging, guides, and fees. **Contact:** International Bicycle Fund/Bicycle Africa, 4887 Columbia Dr. S. #T-9, Seattle, WA 98108-1919; Tel./fax 206-767-0848; ibike@bike.org; [www.ibike.org/bikeafrica], [www.ibike.org/bikecuba].

Argentina

Argentum. Argentum is a Spanish language and culture program for undergraduate, graduate, and high school students. It is part of Universidad Blas Pascal in Córdoba. We offer the total immersion experience. Students can take other classes in literature, Latin American politics, international relations, art, music, economics, and more.

   Dates: Fall: Aug 8-Nov 26; Intensive: Feb-Mar, mid Jun-Jul, Jul-Aug; Spring: Mar 12-Jun 30, 2000. **Cost:** $6,100 for 1 semester, $10,100 for entire year, $2,200 for intensive program, includes tuition and fees, room and board, cultural activities, and field trips. **Contact:** Prof. Marta Rosso-O'Laughlin, Argentum, P.O. Box 99, Medford, MA 02153-0099; Tel./fax 781-488-3552, mrosso@aol.com.

Instituto de Lengua Española (ILEE). Located downtown. Dedicated exclusively to teaching Spanish to foreigners. Small groups and private classes year round. All teachers hold a university degree. Method is intensive, conversation-based. Student body is international, mostly European. Highly recommended worldwide. Ask for individual recommendations in U.S.

   Dates: Year round. **Cost:** Four-week intensive program (20 hours a week) including homestay $1,400; 2 weeks $700. Individual classes: $19 per hour. Registration fee (includes books) $100. **Contact:** ILEE, Daniel Korman, Director, Av. Callao 339, 3 Fl., (1048) Buenos Aires, Argentina; Tel./fax 011-54-11-47827173; ilee@overnet.com.ar, [www.studyabroad.com/ilee].

Asia

Summer Homestays in Japan and Korea. Lex exchange programs are homestays in which participants live as members of a Japanese or Korean host family. Participants of all ages absorb the customs of their host culture by taking part in every day life. Go beyond being a tourist, immerse yourself in another culture and language. Semeser and year-long high school program also available.

Dates: Four-week programs mid-Jul to mid-Aug; 2-week program to Japan in spring and summer. **Cost:** Four weeks $3,350, 2 weeks (summer) $3,050; spring $2,450 (1999). **Contact:** Lex America, 68 Leonard St., Belmont, MA 02478-2566; 617-489-5800, fax 617- 489-5898; exchange@lexlrf.com, [www.lexlrf.org].

Australia

The Adventure Company. The Adventure Company, Australia specializes in top quality adventure and nature tours for individuals and groups. We run a variety of scheduled trips, all of which involve a strong nature element. Many of the tours take place in World Heritage Listed National Parks. Dive with marine researchers, hike the ancient rainforest of far North Queensland, study flora and fauna, or visit Aboriginal art sites dating back 40,000 years.

Dates: Call program for information. Join 1- to 12-day trips. **Cost:** $50-$1,500, including all trips departing from Cairns. **Contact:** Gary Hill, The Adventure Company, Australia, P.O. Box 5740, Cairns, Queensland 4870, Australia; 011-61-7-4051-4777, fax 011-61-7-4051-4888; adventures@adventures.com.au, [www.adventures.com.au]. In U.S.: 800-388-7333.

Belgium

Masters in Business Administration. Open to graduates in economics and commercial engineers. Students who have graduated in another discipline can first follow the "Complementary Studies in Management" program (both 1 academic year).

Dates: Contact sponsor. **Cost:** BEF18,000 plus course material (1999). **Contact:** Simone DeMaeyer, UFSAI, Center for Business Administration, Prinsstraat 13, 2000 Antwerpen, Belgium; simone.demaeyer@ufsia.ac.be; [www.ufsia.ac.be/mba/].

Canada

Classical Pursuits. Classical Pursuits offers week-long summer seminars in Great Books and Opera on the campus of the University of Toronto. Join adults of all ages for conversation and reflection about a book or opera. Summer 2000 options: St. Augustine's Confessions, Dante's Purgatorio, Cervantes' Don Quixote, Shakespeare's Hamlet, Mozart's Don Giovanni, and 3 treatments of Death in Venice.

Dates: July. (TBA in December) **Cost:** $1000. Commuter rates available. **Contact:** Classical Pursuits, St. Michael's College, University of Toronto, Continuing Education Division, 81 St. Mary Street, Toronto, ON, M5S 1J4 CANADA; 877-633-2555; continuinged.stmikes@utoronto.ca, [www.utoronto.ca/stmikes].

English Dramatic Literature. Attendance at 5-7 plays at the Stratford Festival in Ontario, plus a week of classes at Ball State Univ.

Dates: May. **Cost:** $830 plus housing for week at Ball State Univ. (1999). **Contact:** William T. Liston, Dept. of English, Ball State Univ., Muncie, IN 47306-0460; 765-285-8473, fax 765-285-3765; 00wtliston@bsu.edu.

French Studies in Montréal. Intensive French programs offered in historic Old Montreal. Grammar, lots of conversation and weekly monitored outings to French cultural and social events. Also weekly language exchange lounge with local French Canadians.

Dates: Year round. Start dates every second Monday. Complete beginners start every 4 weeks. Minimum 2-week program. Small classes with max. 10 students in a roundtable setting. **Cost:** $360 for 2 weeks, 44 hours, includes access to CD Rom language lab, 24-hour voice messaging service, free email and Internet. Also available homestay with French or bilingual families. Special: Register for 4 weeks and get 1 week free tuition by mentioning this listing. **Contact:** Y&N - Language and Cultural Studies, 404 Saint Pierre, Suite 201, Montréal, PQ, H2Y 2M2, Canada; 514-840-7228, fax 514-840-7111; info@languageco.com, [www.languageco.com].

Central America

Internship and Research Program. The Institute for Central American Development Studies (ICADS) offers a semester abroad study program, including coursework and structured internship opportunities, in Costa Rica, Nicaragua, Belize, and Cuba in the following areas: women's studies, environment/ecology, public health, education, human rights, and many others. The program is progressive and aimed at students who wish to work on social justice issues and on behalf of the poor, women, and the oppressed in Central America. Fall and spring with academic credit, summer noncredit Spanish and internship program.

Dates: Fall and spring terms with academic credit. Cost: $7,600. Contact: Sandra Kinghorn, PhD, Director, ICADS, Dept. 826, P.O. Box 025216, Miami, FL 33102-5216; 011-506-225-0508, fax 011-506-234-1337; icads@netbox.com, [www.icadscr.com].

Travel/Study Seminars. Learn from Central Americans of diverse backgrounds about their economic, political, and social realities. Emphasis on the views of those struggling for justice. Programming in El Salvador, Guatemala, and Nicaragua. Call for a free listing of upcoming programs.

Dates: Ongoing. Cost: $1,500-$2,500 depending on length of trip. Contact: Center for Global Education, Augsburg College, 2211 Riverside Ave., Box 307TR, Minneapolis, MN 55454; 800-299-8889, fax 612-330-1695; globaled@augsburg.edu, [www.augsburg.edu/global].

China

Excavation Practicum in Xi'an. In collaboration with Xi'an Jiastong Univ. and the Archaeological Institute in Xi'an, Chian the Sino-American Field School of Archaeology offers credit. Archaeological Practicum (field work) and Chinese Art and Culture. In English.

Dates: Jul 4-Aug 3. Cost: Deposit $200; participation fee $3,595. Contact: Dr. Alfonz Lengyel, Fudan Museum Foundation, 4206 73rd Terr. E., Sarasota, FL 34243; Tel./fax 941-351-8208; fmfsafsa@juno.com.

Costa Rica

COSI (Costa Rica Spanish Institute). COSI offers high quality instruction at reasonable prices. We offer Spanish classes in San José and at a beautiful national park (beach and rainforest). Homestay is also available. Volunteer work opportunities and special discounts in tours.

Dates: Year round. Cost: Prices start at $280 per week including classes in groups of maximum 5 students, homestay, cultural activities, books, access to email, airport pickup. Contact: COSI, P.O. Box 1366-2050, San Pedro, San José, Costa Rica; 011-506-234-1001, fax 011-506-253-2117. From U.S. 800-771-5184; cosicr@sol.racsa.co.cr, [www.cosi.co.cr].

Costa Rican Language Academy. Costa Rican-owned and operated language school offers first-rate Spanish instruction in a warm and friendly environment. Teachers with university degrees. Small groups or private classes. Included free in the programs are airport transportation, coffee and natural refreshments, excursions, Latin dance, Costa Rican cooking, music, and conversation classes to provide students with complete cultural immersion.

Dates: Year round (start anytime). Cost: $135 per week or $220 per week for program with homestay. All other activities and services included at no additional cost. Contact: Costa Rican Language Academy, P.O. Box 336-2070, San José, Costa Rica; 011-506-221-1624 or 011-506-233-8914 or 011-233-8938, fax 011-506-233-8670. In the U.S.: 800-854-6057; crlang@sol.racsa.co.cr, [www.crlang.co.cr/index.html].

Ecological Health Gardens. Classes on tropical medicinal plants and ecological health gardens. Also Spanish classes. Study with us on a tropical farm.

Dates: Classes begin first Monday of each month. Cost: $350 per course, work exchange for room and board. Contact: Ed Bernhardt, The New Dawn Center, A.P. 372-8000, San Isidro, P.Z., Costa Rica; fax 011-506-771-7771; minevpz@racsa.co.cr.

Intensive Spanish and Homestay. Intercultura Costa Rica offers intensive university accredited Spanish courses. Homestays available. Volunteer programs, beach and city campuses, emphasis on individual attention. Caring, multilingual staff. Located in university town close to the capital. Daily Latin dance classes, weekly cooking, music, indigenous culture, and other classes.

Dates: Year round. Cost: $1,045 per month includes classes, homestay and activities (shorter stays available). In 2000, approx. a 5 percent increase expected. Contact: Laura Ellington, Intercultura Costa Rica, Language Center, P.O. Box 1952-3000, Heredia, Costa Rica; 011-506-260-8480, Tel./fax 011-506-260-9243; info@spanish-intercultura.com, [www.spanish-intercultura.com].

Intensive Spanish Training. The Institute for Central American Development Studies (ICADS) offers 4-week progressive programs in intensive Spanish language—4 1/2 hours daily, 5 days a week. Small classes (4 or fewer students). Activities and optional afternoon internships emphasize environmental issues, women's issues, development, human rights, and public health. Supportive learning environment. Homestays and field trips. Great alternative for the socially conscious.

Dates: Programs begin first Monday of each month. **Cost:** $1,400 includes airport pick-up, classes, books, homestay, meals, laundry, lectures, activities, field trips, and internship placements. **Contact:** ICADS, Dept. 826, P.O. Box 025216, Miami, FL 33102-5216; 011-506-225-0508, fax 011-506-234-1337; icads@netbox.com, [www.icadscr.com].

Learn About Tropical Plants and Birds. Two-week courses on field identification of trees and shrubs (Dendrology) offered every year in Spanish (March) and in English (June-July). Please ask for opinions by former participants.

Dates: Mar 13-25 (Spanish); Jun 26-Jul 8 (English). **Cost:** Each course is $1,800. Includes fees, material, lodging and meals during 15 days, insurance, course-related local transport, farewell dinner, and certificate of attendance. **Contact:** Humberto Jiménez Saa, TSC, Apdo. 8-3870-1000, San José, Costa Rica; 011-506-253-3267, fax 011-506-253-4963; hjimenez@sol.racsa.co.cr, [www.geocities.com/RainForest/9148].

Learn Spanish While Volunteering. Assist with the training of Costa Rican public school teachers in ESL and computers. Assist local health clinic, social service agencies, and environmental projects. Enjoy learning Spanish in the morning, volunteer work in the afternoon/evening. Spanish classes of 2-5 students plus group learning activities; conversations with middle class homestay families (1 student per family). Homestays and most volunteer projects are within walking distance of school in small town near the capital, San José.

Dates: Year round, all levels. Classes begin every Monday (except Apr 17-21 and Dec 18-29), volunteer program is continuous. **Cost:** $345 per week for 28 hours of classes and group activities plus Costa Rican dance and cooking classes. Includes tuition, 3 meals per day, 7 days per week, homestay, laundry, all materials, weekly 3-hour cultural tour, and airport transportation. $25 one-time registration fee. **Contact:** Susan Shores, Registrar, Latin American Language Center, PMB 123, 7485 Rush River Dr., Suite 710, Sacramento, CA 95831-5260; 916-447-0938, fax 916-428-9542; lalc@madre.com.

Multi Media Landscape Painting. Enjoy extensive on-location painting. Course content suitable for beginners and more advanced

painters. Students may use medium of choice. Individual expression encouraged. Instructor: John Leonard.

Dates: Feb 2-9, 1997. **Cost:** $1,315 from San Jose. **Contact:** Haliburton School of Fine Art, Box 839, Haliburton, ON, Canada K0M 1S0; 705-457-1680, fax 705-457-2255.

Sustainable Development. The Institute for Central American Development Studies (ICADS) offers an interdisciplinary semester abroad study program focusing on development issues from ecological, socio-economic perspectives. The 14-week field course includes: 1) 4 weeks of intensive Spanish and urban issues, 2) 5 weeks in the field in different managed and natural ecosystems learning techniques of field research in social and natural sciences, 3) 5 weeks of independent study—living and working in rural or urban communities.

Dates: Fall and spring terms with academic credit. **Cost:** $7,600. **Contact:** Dr. Sandra Kinghorn, Ph.D., ICADS Director, ICADS, Dept. 826, P.O. Box 025216, Miami, FL 33102-5216; 011-506-225-0508, fax 011-506-234-1337; icads@netbox.com, [www.icadscr.com].

Watercolor Painting-Floral. Enjoy creativity and impressionism in flower painting. Learn wet-in-wet techniques, bold use of colors and how to solve background problems. Capture the spirit of a floral painting. Instructor: Pauline Holancin.

Dates: Feb. **Cost:** $1,315 from San Jose. **Contact:** Haliburton School of Fine Art, Box 839, Haliburton, ON, K0M 1S0, Canada; 705-457-1680, fax 705-457-2255.

Ecuador

Academia Latinoamericana. Proud to be the friendliest Spanish school you have ever known. Family owned and operated. The program offers language study at 9 levels, for complete beginners through advanced. Experienced staff, native Ecuadorians. Carefully selected host families within walking distance of school. Exclusive "SierrAzul Cloud Forest and Galapagos" extension program, volunteer program. U.S. college credit available.

Dates: Year round. **Cost:** $230 per week. Includes 20 hours of lessons, 7 days with host family, 2 meals per day, transfer, services at the school, and teaching material. **Contact:** Suzanne S. Bell, Admissions Director, USA/International, 640 East 3990 South, Suite E, Salt Lake City, UT, 84107; 801-268-4608, fax 801-265-9156; academia@juno.com, delco@spanish.com.ec.

Spanish in the Middle of the World. Spanish Institute offers the opportunity of learning the language and culture while enjoying the wonderful weather and landscape of 0 degrees latitude. One-on-one and group courses to fit all needs. Accommodation facilities in Ecuadorian homes or dormitories. English teachers may have a job while learning a second language.

Dates: Classes start on Monday year round (except holidays). **Cost:** $5 per hour includes texts, workbook, language lab, teaching aids, completion diploma. **Contact:** Benedict Schools of Languages, Edmundo Chiriboga, N47-133y Jorge Paez, Quito, Ecuador; fax 011-593-2-432729, 011-593-2-462972; benedict@accessinter.net, info@quitospanish.com, [www.quitospanish.com].

Europe

¿?don Quijote In-Country Spanish Language Schools. Offers Spanish language courses in our 6 schools in Spain and 5 partner schools in Latinoamerica. Our courses (standard, intensive, business, D.E.L.E., tourism, flight attendants and refresher for teachers) are all year round, from 2 weeks on. Students can combine different cities and schools. Academic credit is available.

Dates: Year round—fall, spring, winter, and summer, 2 weeks to a full year of study. **Cost:** Email or check web site for details. **Contact:** ¿?don Quijote In-Country Spanish Language Schools, calle/Placentinos n°2, Salamanca 37008, Spain; 011-34-923-268860, fax 011-34-923-268815; amusa@donquijote.org, [www.donquijote.org].

Atelier des Artes. The Atelier de Artes, a unique workshop in art, dance, and jazz in the beautiful Jura mountains of French Switzerland. Art courses include painting and drawing, photography, watercolor, printmaking, art history, and bookarts. Innovative dance program centered on choreographic process, also technique and improvisation. Jazz courses include repertoire, ensembles, masterclasses and performances. Numerous trips to cities and natural attractions.

Dates: Jul 18-Aug 9. **Cost:** $2,275 plus airfare and some additional expenses. **Contact:** Atelier des Artes, Francia Tobacman, 55 Bethune St., B645, New York, NY 10014; 212-727-1756; bruce.smith@pobox.com.

En Famille Overseas. Homestays in friendly families in France, Spain, Germany, and Italy. All ages. Language courses or one-to-one tuition.

Dates: One week or more year round. **Cost:** £58 fees. One week full board approx. £175-£250 plus tuition and fees (1999). **Contact:** En Famille Overseas, 60B Maltravers St., Arundel, BN18 9BG, U.K.; 011-44-1903-883266, fax 011-44-1903-883582.

ICCE Educational Travel Programs. Learn the language, study the culture. French Riviera, Paris, Aix-en-Provence, Italian Riviera della Versilia, Spanish Costa del Sol. Also summers in Tokyo and Beijing. For credit or just for pleasure. More program—less cost. For students of all ages.

Dates: Call for details. **Cost:** From $2,479 and up (2 weeks). Includes airfare, tuition, room and board. **Contact:** Dr. Stanley I. Gochman, ICCE, 5 Bellport Ln., Bellport, NY 11713; 516-286-5228.

Language, Arts, and Sports. Active learning vacations: French, Spanish, Italian, Portuguese; cooking, painting, drawing, photography workshops. Combine eduVacational interests. French and sailing or skiing; Spanish and golf; bicycle tours—more countries, more ideas. We match individual needs and interests with programs and options: family stay, apartment, hotel; intensive to total immersion; small groups or study and live in your teacher's home.

Dates: Programs run from 1 week to months. **Cost:** Includes room and board, tuition. **Contact:** Mary Ann Puglisi, eduVacations^sm, 1431 21st St. NW, Suite 302, Washington, DC 20036; 202-857-8384, fax 202-463-8091.

Learn French in France, Monaco, or Switzerland. Language immersion courses in France (Paris, Nice, Aix-en-Provence, Antibes, Bordeaux, Cannes, Monaco, Montpellier, Tours); Monaco (Monte Carlo); or Switzerland (Lausanne). Private language schools with programs for adults, senior citizens, and teenagers. Centrally located, convenient to interesting places, cultural events, sports activities. Programs feature qualified teachers, small classes, attractive surroundings and facilities. Affordable prices for instruction. Accommodations with French, Monegasque or Swiss families with meals, student residences, apartments, and nearby hotels.

Dates: Year round. Two weeks or more. **Cost:** Two-week courses with or without accommodations range from $605 to $2,260. **Contact:** Ms. Lorraine Haber, Study Abroad Coordinator, Embassy CES Study Abroad Programs, The Center for English Studies, 330 7th Ave., 6th Fl., New York, NY 10001; 212-629-7300, fax 212-736-7950; cesnewyork@cescorp.com.

Learn German in Germany, Austria, or Switzerland. Language immersion courses in Germany (Berlin, Freiburg, Stuttgart, Munich, Hamburg, Wiesbaden, Frankfurt); Austria (Vienna); or Switzerland (Zurich). Private language schools with programs for adults, senior citizens, and teenagers. Centrally located, convenient to interesting places, cultural events, sports activities. Programs feature qualified teachers, small classes, attractive surroundings and facilities. Affordable prices for instruction. Accommodations with German, Austrian, or Swiss families with meals, student residences, apartments, and nearby hotels.

Dates: Year round. Two weeks or more. **Cost:** Two-week courses with or without accommodations range from $465-$1,355. **Contact:** Ms. Lorraine Haber, Study Abroad Coordinator, Embassy CES Study Abroad Programs, The Center for English Studies, 330 7th Ave., 6th Fl., New York, NY 10001; 212-629-7300, fax 212-736-7950; cesnewyork@cescorp.com.

Plantagenet Tours. Historical and cultural themes like: Eleanor, Arthur, John of Gaunt, Medicis, Templars, Vikings, Henry the Navigator, Troubadours, and Cathars, Umbrian hilltowns, Provence in spring or fall. Price includes complete land arrangement except lunches and beverages, experienced multilingual guide throughout, small groups, three-star hotels. We offer you a moveable feast for your mind.

Dates: Spring, summer, fall. **Cost:** $2,195-$3,295. **Contact:** Peter Gravgaard, Plantagenet Tours, 85 The Grove, Bournemouth BH9 2TY, U.K.; Tel./fax 011-44-1202-521-895; sue@plantagenet-tours.freeserve.co.uk, [www.plantagenet-tours.freeserve.co.uk].

Skyros Holistic Holidays. We offer over 200 courses on the beautiful Greek island of Skyros. Courses range from yoga, Tai Chi, massage, personal development, art, creative writing, dance to drumming, voicework, drama and bodywork. Delicious food and spectacular surroundings.

Dates: Jan-Dec. **Cost:** $1,150. **Contact:** Helen Akif, Skyros, 92 Prince of Wales Rd., London NW5 3NE, U.K.; 011-171-267-4424; fax 011-171-284-3063; skyros@easynet.co.uk, [www.skyros.com].

Travel with Scholars. Educational and cultural programs for the sophisticated adult traveler feature distinguished instructors and custom-made itineraries. Programs are available in Oxford, Paris, London, Ireland, Florence, Sicily, South of France, Prague, and Turkey.

Dates: Two- to 3-week programs in Jun and Jul. **Cost:** Prague $2,150; Turkey $2,800; Ireland $3,200; London $3,250; Paris $3,500; Oxford $3,550; South of France $3,700; Florence $3,750; Sicily $3,850 (land costs only, 1999). **Contact:** Shirley Beller or Elizabeth Newton, UC Berkeley Extension, Travel/Study, 55 Laguna St., San Francisco, CA 94102; 888-209-7344, 415-252-5229/30; [www.berkeley.edu/unex/travel].

France

Aromatherapy Summer School. Run by the prestigious Australasian College USA and held in the heart of Provence at the height of the lavender harvest. Includes organic French cuisine, 4 days of instruction, 4 days of instructional tours, accommodations and transfers. Sixty-four credit hours toward the Diploma in Aromatherapy. State licensed.

Dates: Aug 14-23. **Cost:** $1,800. **Contact:** Erika Petersen, Australasian College USA, 530 1st St., P.O. Box 57, Lake Oswego, OR 97034; 800-487-8839, fax 503-636-0706; achs@herbed.com, [www.herbed.com].

Cuisine et Tradition. Hands-on, personalized Provençale Cuisine workshops in Arles, the heart of Provence. Featured: dishes cooked in olive oil, regional wines, trips to local markets, winery visits, and the history, personages and myths behind the recipes.

Dates: Mar-Jul; Sep-Oct. **Cost:** From FF500 ($85) meal, mid-day or evening to FF6,300 ($1,000) per week. Loding not included. **Contact:** Madeleine Vedel, Association Cuisine et Tradition, 30 rue Pierre Euzeby, 13200 Arles, France; Tel./fax 011-33-4-9049-6920; actvedel@provnet.fr, [www.provnet.fr/users/cuisine-tradition].

France Langue Paris and Nice. Close to the Champs Elysées, Paris, or the Mediterranean. The Ecole France Langue in Paris and Nice offers you both the language and culture of France. There are classes for all ages and levels, specialty classes (business, tourism, etc.), and custom designed classes for teachers and students offered. Language certification and university credit available as are free weekly cultural activities. Accommodations arranged by the school.

Dates: Year round. Enrollment every Monday. **Cost:** Contact for information. **Contact:** Mr. De Poly, France Langue, 22 ave. Notre Dame, 06000 Nice, France; frlang_n@club-internet.fr.

French Language Learning Vacations. Learn French while discovering the chateaux of the Loire Valley, the secrets of Provence, or the sandy beaches of the Mediterranean. Our programs are designed for independent travelers sharing a passion for the French culture and lifestyle. We offer a choice of locations in Tours, Aix-en-Provence, Montpellier, Paris, or Nice.

Dates: Two or more weeks year round. **Cost:** Two-week packages range from $825-$1,265. Includes classes, housing and fees. **Contact:** Jim Pondolfino, French-American Exchange, 111 Roberts Court, Box 7, Alexandria, VA 22314; 800-995-5087, fax 703-549-2865; faetours@erols.com, [www.faetours.com].

Horizons in Provence: Artistic Travel. Provence evokes images of vineyards, olives, sun-filled landscapes, and a profusion of antique monuments. It is all this and more. A week in the stunning hilltop village of Venasque, ringed by Roman monuments, sleepy wine villages, red ocher cliffs and mountains. Lodging in a charming bed and breakfast. Workshops include Painting, Photography, Fabric Printing, Language Arts: Conversational French.

Dates: Apr 7-14; Sep 9-16. **Cost:** $1,455 (lodging, all meals except 1 lunch, tuition, and field trips). **Contact:** Karen Totman-Gale, Horizons, 108 N. Main St.-T, Sunderland, MA 01375; 413-665-0300, fax 413-665-4141; horizons@horizons-art.org, [www.horizons-art.org].

Immersion Course in French. Intensive 2-4 week course for professional adults in Villefranche (next to Nice) overlooking the French Riviera's most beautiful bay; 8 hours a day with 2 meals. Audiovisual classes, language lab, practice sessions, discussion-lunch. Evening film showings, evening outings with teachers, excursions to cultural landmarks. Accommodations in comfortable private apartments.

Dates: Courses start Jan, Feb, Mar, May, Jun, Aug, Sep, Oct, Nov, Dec. **Cost:** Tuition fees: Dec-Apr FF14,100/4 weeks; May-Nov FF16,700/4 weeks. Accommdations: Dec-Apr FF2,000-FF5,200/4 week; May-Nov FF2,300-FF5,800/4 week. **Contact:** Frédéric Latty, Institut de Francais, 23, avenue General Leclerc, 06230 Villefranche Sur Mer, France; 011-33-493-01-88-44, fax 011-33-493-76-92-17; instfran@aol.com, [www.institutdefrancais.com].

Language Programs and Cooking Classes. Dr. Janice Ovadiah offers a menu of French study programs for many needs, budgets, and durations. Accommodations include homestays, hotels, college campuses, or chateau lodgings. Participants may choose to study in accredited schools in Paris, on the French Riviera, or in other attractive French cities. French-language programs and 1-week courses in French cuisine are available during the summer and throughout the year. Programs cater to both general students and business professionals for leisure or intensive study.

Dates: Year round. **Cost:** Rates vary according to length of program. **Contact:** Dr. Janice E. Ovadiah, 303 W. 66 St., New York, NY 10023; 212-724-5823, fax 212-496-2264; jovadiah@aol.com.

Latitude Cultural Center. Latitude, a cultural retreat on the Lot River near Cahors in southwest France, offers week-long summer courses, in French and English, in topics ranging from modern French philosophers and U.S.-French poetry to McDonaldization. Instruction by U.S. and French college professors. Also, time to relax and explore the beautiful Lot Valley.

Dates: Jun-Aug. **Cost:** $985 includes instruction, lodging, breakfasts, most lunches, welcome dinner, swimming pool, excursions (1999). **Contact:** E. Barbara Phillips, Latitude Cultural Center, 1043 Oxford St., Berkeley, CA 94707; E_Barbara_Phillips@slip.net, [www.latitude.org].

Stage Intensif Langue/Culture. The French Traveler offers 2-week workshops for French teachers in France each July. Theme courses about French life and society in mornings, related cultural excursions in the afternoon; optional homestay available. Change of city in each workshop. Graduate credit. French only spoken.

Dates: July 2000. **Cost:** $1,850. Airfare and 1 meal per day not included. **Contact:** Valerie Sutter, The French Traveler, 206 Claflin St., Belmont, MA 02478; 800-251-3464; frenchtraveler@juno.com.

Germany

Industrial Mathematics. Industrial mathematics consists of mathematical modeling and scientific computing in connection with problems posed by industry. The program teachs how to stimulate, to optimize, and to control technical and organization.

Dates: Start in Aug. **Cost:** No tuition fees. Living costs about $7,000 per year (1999). **Contact:** Dr. Falk Triebsch; fax 011-49-631-205-3052; indmath@mathematik.uni-kl.de, [www.mathematik.uni-kl.de/Studium/aufbau_e.html].

Learn German and Discover Berlin. GLS is one of the leading institutions teaching German as a foreign language in Germany. GLS offers various levels of German all year round (age 16 and up), preparation for all language certificates, business German, German for bankers, lawyers. Special feature: internships in German companies.
Dates: Year round. **Cost:** Contact school for details. **Contact:** GLS Sprachenzentrum, Barbara Jaeschke, Managing Director, Kolonnenstrasse 26, 10829 Berlin, Germany; 011-49-30-780-08-90; fax 011-49-30-787-41-92; gls.berlin@t-online.de, [www.gls-berlin.com].

Greece

Goddess Tour Crete/Lesbos. Educational tours for women led by well-known author and feminist theologian Carol P. Christ. Goddess pilgrimage to Crete and Women's Quest in Lesbos. Academic credit available. Walk on ancient stones; nourish your soul with healing images.
Dates: Crete: May 27-Jun 10, Sep 30-Oct 14; Lesbos: Jun 25-Jul 9. **Cost:** Crete $2,275 includes airfare from NYC; Lesbos $2,150 includes airfare from NYC. **Contact:** Ariadne Institute, 1306 Crestview Dr., Blacksburg, VA 24060; Tel./fax 540-951-3070.

Greek Folk Dances and Culture. Workshops on Greek dance (traditional and ancient) including general courses on Greek culture (music, costume, language, etc.).
Dates: Summer 1998. **Cost:** $200 a week. **Contact:** Alkis Raftis, Greek Dances Theatre, 8 Schoiou St., GR-10558, Plaka, Athens, Greece; 011-30-1-3244395.

Guatemala

Art Workshops in Guatemala. We provide 10-day art classes in a wide variety of arts including backstrap weaving; photography; beading; papermaking; creative writing; visual, fiber, book arts, and much more. All classes are held in Antigua, Guatemala.
Dates: Classes held during Jan, Feb, Mar, Apr, and Nov. **Cost:** Approx. $1,700 including airfare from U.S., lodging, tuition, field trips, and all ground transportation. **Contact:** Liza Fourre, Director, Art Workshops in Guatemala, 4758 Lyndale Ave. S, Minneapolis, MN 55409-2304; 612-825-0747, fax 612-825-6637; info@artguat.org, [www.artguat.org].

Eco-Escuela de Español and Bio Itza Programs. You want to learn Spanish, we want volunteers for conservation and community development projects in El Petén, Guatemala. The town is located close to Tikal and adjacent to the Maya Biosphere Reserve (the largest protected area in Central America) so you will be surrounded by natural and archaeological wonders and immersed in Mayan culture. This is a community owned project and participation in it will support local communities.
Dates: Year round. Arrive on weekend, start classes on Monday. **Cost:** A fee of $200 covers tuition with 20 hours per week of one-on-one Spanish language instruction, airport pick-up, transfer to the town by boat, homestay, and 3 meals per day. **Contact:** Sandra at G.A.P. Adventures, 266 Dupont St., Toronto, ON, M5R 1V7, Canada; 800-465-5600; adventure@gap.ca.

India

Spiritual Origins of India. This journey to North India is an exploration of the great spiritual traditions of the region. With daily meditation practice as the ground, local teachers will examine the ancient world wisdom traditions of India—Buddhism, Hinduism, Zoroastrianism, and Jainism. Through discussion and lectures, we will study karma, reincarnation and the various approaches to meditation, prayer, and yoga.
Dates: Oct 29-Nov 14. **Cost:** $2,450 plus airfare. **Contact:** Peter S. Volz, The Naropa Institute, Study Abroad Programs, 2130 Arapahoe Ave., Boulder, CO 80302; 303-546-3594, fax 303-444-0410; peter@naropa.edu, [www.naropa.edu].

Israel

Pardes Institute of Jewish Studies. Teaches text study to women and men of all backgrounds in an open and intellectually stimulating environment. Students come from all over the world and can learn for 1 year, 1 semester, or summer sessions.
Dates: Year program: Sep-Jun; summer program: Jun-Jul. **Cost:** Vary. Substantial scholarships and grants available. **Contact:** American Pardes Foundation, 136 E. 39th St., New York, NY 10016; 212-447-4333, fax 212-447-4315; pardesusa@aol.com, [www.pardes.org.il].

Italy

Arts, Culture, Language in Florence, Rome, and Siena. Scuolo Leonardo da Vinci is located in the heart of the historical centers of Florence, Rome, and Siena. Founded in 1977 it is now the leading institute in the teaching of Italian as a second language. The group courses (12 students per class) are offered from 2 weeks to a semester. The schools offer a wide range of quality cultural courses (cooking, wine, art, drawing) and extracurricular activities. Full range of accommodation choices provided. **Dates:** Year round, starts every 2 weeks. **Cost:** Call for details. **Contact:** Mr. Giambattista Pace, Scuolo Leonardo da Vinci, via Brunelleschi 4, 50123, Firenze, Italy; 011-390-55-290305, fax 011-390-55-290396; scuolaleonardo@ scuolaleonardo.com, www.scuolaleonardo.com.

Biking and Walking Tours. Specializing in Italy for over 10 years, Ciclismo Classico distills the "Best of Italy," offering more unique Italian destinations than any other active vacation company. Educational, full-service tours for all abilities in Umbria, Tuscany, Piedmont, the Dolomites, Puglia, Sicily, the Amalfi Coast, Cinque Terre, Sardegna, Abruzzo, Campania, Corsica, and Elba. Charming accommodations, expert bilingual guides, cooking demonstrations, wine tastings, support vehicle, detailed route instructions, visits to local festivals, countryside picnics—an unforgettable cultural indulgence. **Dates:** Apr-Nov (70 departures). Call for specific dates. **Cost:** $1,700-$3,500. **Contact:** Lauren Hefferon, Director, Ciclismo Classico, 30 Marathon St., Arlington, MA 02474; 800-866-7314 or 781-646-3377; info@ciclismoclassico.com, [www.ciclismoclassico.com].

Glorious Tuscany: Artistic Travel. Tuscany is studded with panoramic landscapes, ancient walled villages, olive groves, and vineyards...and capped by the gorgeous cities of Florence and Siena. Lodging in a charming country inn/villa in the heart of Chianti country, perfectly situated to see the sites of the region. Workshops include Painting, Lampworking/Glass Beads, Mosaics, Silversmithing and Jewelry, Photography, Cooking, Conversational Italian. **Dates:** Apr 20-May 6; Oct 14-21. **Cost:** $1,455 (lodging, all meals except 1 lunch, tuition, and field trips). **Contact:** Karen Totman-Gale, Horizons, 108 N. Main St.-T, Sunderland, MA 01375; 413-665-0300, fax 413-665-4141; horizons@horizons-art.org, [www.horizons-art.org].

Humanities Seminar in Italy. The course, team-taught by a literature professor and art historian, explores the literature and art of the Renaissance from multiple perspectives—the cultural and historical contexts from which

their works of art and literature emerged with special attention to such issues as gender, class, politics, and religion. **Dates:** Jun 5-25 or 3 weeks in Jun. **Cost:** Approx. $3,000 (includes 4 credits). **Contact:** Bella Mirabella, Patty Noonan, New York Univ., Gallatin School, New York, NY 10003

Italiaidea. We offer every level and format of Italian study from intensive short-term "survival Italian" courses to advanced, semester-long courses; on-site lectures and visits to historic sites in Italy, conversation, and flexible scheduling. For over 10 years we have been offering college credit courses at numerous U.S. college and university programs in Italy; we now offer both academic assistance and travel/ study assistance to our client institutions. Homestays are offered as well as accommodations in shared apartments. **Dates:** Year round. **Cost:** Sixty-hour group course LIT780,000; 25-hour one-on-one program LIT1,200,000; 15 hour-specific purposes or culture LIT1,330,000 (taxes not included). **Contact:** Carolina Ciampaglia, Co-Director, Piazza della Cancelleria 5, 00186 Roma, Italy; 011- 390-6-68307620, fax 011-390-6-6892997; italiaidea@italiaidea.com, [www.italiaidea.com].

Italian for Foreigners. The Bergamo Univ. organizes the following courses: non-intensive course (4 hours per week); writing courses (2 hours per week); business Italian courses (2 hours per week); History of Italian Cinema (1 week, 15 hours); Italian Contemporary Literature and Linguistics; summer intensive course (5 hours per day) with cultural trips. **Dates:** Year round. **Cost:** LIT300,000-LIT 850,000. **Contact:** Universita di Bergamo, Segreteria dei Corsi di Italiano per Stranieri, Via Salvecchio 19, Bergamo 24129, Italy; Tel./fax 011-39-035-220557; citastra@ibguniv.uni.it.

Italian in Florence or by the Sea. Study Italian in a 16th century Renaissance palace in the center of Florence, or in a classic Tuscan town just 30 minutes from the sea. Koiné Center's professional language teachers and small class sizes encourage active participation by each student. Cultural program, guided excursions, choice of accommodations including host families. **Dates:** Year round; starting dates each month. **Cost:** Two-week intensive program from $350; 3 weeks from $455; 4 weeks from $570. Call for prices of longer stays. **Contact:** In Italy: Dr.

Andrea Moradei, Koiné Center, Via Pandolfini 27, 50122 Firenze, Italy; 011-390-55-213881. In North America: 800-274-6007; homestay@teleport.com, koine@firenze.net, [www.koinecenter.com].

Italian Language for Foreigners. Small courses: (2 hours a day); main mini-groups (4 hours a day); intensive (main course plus 6 private lessons); two-on-one (1 teacher plus 2 students); indvidual tuition. Special courses: Tourist Industry, Business Italian. Small groups (max. 6 students). Sports (sailing, catamaran, surfing), excursions (Calabria, Sicily). Accommodations in apartments.
Dates: Mar 1-Nov 26. **Cost:** Two-week course includes single room LIT885,000. **Contact:** Caffè Italiano Club, Largo A. Pandullo 5, 89861 Tropea (VV), Italy; 011-390-963-60-32-84, fax 011-390-963-61786; caffeitaliano@tin.it, [www.paginegialle.it/caffeital].

Jewelry-Textile Design School. Jewelry-making courses all levels, from basic fabrication to advanced, including stone setting, engraving, wax modeling, granulation, and jewelry design. Textile design courses all levels includes batik, shibori, silk painting, silkscreen, printing, weaving, textile sculpture, sewing, quilting. All teachers speak at least Italian and English.
Dates: Monthly semester (Jan-Sep), 1- and 2-year programs. **Cost:** Varies according to chosen course and time. **Contact:** Art Studio Fuji, Kathleen Knippel, Via Guelfa 79/A-85, Florence 50129, Italy; 011-390-55-216877, 219914, fax 011-390-55-214500; art.fuji@fol.it.

Learn Italian in Italy. Language immersion courses in Italy (Rome, Florence, Siena, Viareggio, Rimini, Bologna, Venice, Portico, Milan). Private language schools with programs for adults, senior citizens, and teenagers. Centrally located, convenient to interesting places, cultural events, sports activities. Programs feature qualified teachers, small classes, attractive surroundings and facilities. Affordable prices for instruction. Accommodations with Italian families with meals, student residences, apartments, and nearby hotels.
Dates: Year round. Two weeks or more. **Cost:** Two-week courses with or without accommodations range from $305-$1,105. **Contact:** Ms. Lorraine Haber, Study Abroad Coordinator, Embassy CES Study Abroad Programs, The Center for English Studies, 330 7th Ave., 6th Fl., New York, NY 10001; 212-629-7300, fax 212-736-7950; cesnewyork@cescorp.com.

Studio Art Centers International (SACI). Located in central Florence, SACI is the largest and most comprehensive studio art program in Italy with 6 different programs of study: year/semester abroad, 2-year diploma, post-baccalaureate certificate, master of fine arts, master of art history, and late spring and summer studies. Field trips take students to Pisa, Siena, San Gimignano, Lucca, Arezzo, Assisi, Rome, Bologna, etc.
Dates: Sep-Dec; Jan-Apr; May-Jun; Jun-Jul. **Cost:** Fall/spring tuition $7,950 per term; post-baccalaureate $8,500 per term; tuition late spring/summer $3,000; fall/spring housing $2,600; late spring/summer $1,000/$800 respectively. **Contact:** SACI Coordinator, Institute of International Education, 809 UN Plaza, New York, NY 10017-3580; 800-344-9186, 212-984-5548, fax 212-984-5325; saci@iie.org, [www.saci-florence.org].

Tech Rome (Summer-Travel-Study). Tech Rome is a 6-week summer travel-study program of Louisiana Tech Univ. It features hotel housing, 3 meals per day, tours, and traditional classroom courses combined with field travel for college credit. Up to 13 semester hours may be earned in a choice of over 40 courses in diverse subject areas. Courses are taught by American professors.
Dates: May-Jul. **Cost:** $4,328 includes tuition, all housing for 6 weeks, 3 meals per day, tours. Group flights are available. **Contact:** Tech Rome, P.O. Box 3172, Ruston, LA 71272; 318-257-4854; [http://techrome.latech.edu].

Japan

Japan Exchange and Teaching (JET). Sponsored by the Japanese Government, the JET Program invites over 1,000 American college graduates and young professionals to share their language and culture with Japanese youth. One-year positions are available in schools and government offices throughout Japan. Apply by early December for positions beginning in July of the following year.
Dates: One-year contracts renewable by mutual consent not more than 2 times. **Cost:** Participants receive approx. ¥3,600,000 per year in monthly payments. **Contact:** JET Program Office, Embassy of Japan, 2520 Massachusetts Ave. NW, Washington, DC 20008; 202-238-6772, fax 202-265-9484; eojjet@erols.com, [www.jet.org].

Latin America

Community Development Internship. This is a credit-bearing internship where volunteers live with a family in rural Mexico and Ecuador, or semi-urban Cuba, while working side by side with community members on grassroots development projects. Project assignments are available in the areas of agriculture, construction, reforestation, animal husbandry, micro-enterprise development, data collection, public health and other fields. These projects are designed, developed and implemented by the beneficiaries themselves. While project opportunities change as new ones come online and others are completed, every effort is made to match interns' interests with their assignment.

Dates: Year round. Two months advance needed for placement in Cuba. Six-week program (3 weeks in Cuba). **Cost:** Six credits: $3,400, no credit: $2,700, 3 credits: $2,900. **Contact:** Nicholas A. Robins, Director, Cuban Studies Institute, Center for Latin American Studies, Tulane Univ., Caroline Richardson Bldg., New Orleans, LA 70118-5698; 504-862-8629 or 504-862-8000 ext. 2601, fax 504-862-8678; nrobins@mailhost.tcs.tulane.edu, [http://cuba.tulane.edu].

Explorama Lodge Special. One night at the Iquitos Hotel plus 2 nights at each of the 3 Explorama lodges, including visits to the longest canopy walkway in the world, ethnobotanical plant garden, primary rainforest reserve of over 250,000 acres. Meals, lodging, excursions, guides, 200 miles total boat excursions on Amazon and Napo rivers.

Dates: Starts every Tuesday year round. **Cost:** 2000-2001: $899 per person in twin bedded room. **Contact:** Peter Jenson, Explorama Lodges, Box 446, Iquitos, Peru; 800-707-5275. In Peru: 011-51-94-25-2530, fax 011-51-94-25-2533; amazon@explorama.com, [www.explorama.com].

Mexico

"Arte de Mexico" in Puerto Vallarta. Experience the magic of Mexico, its history, culture, and unique art. Study the cultural traditions, mythology, and art techniques of the pre-Hispanic, colonial, and contemporary eras. The course is held in a garden patio, on the beach, or in the tropical rainforest. Enjoy optional ocean and jungle ecotours.

Dates: Jan 3-10; Feb 5-12; May 6-13; Oct 23-Nov 4. **Cost:** $1,175. 2 CEUS. Includes bed and breakfast, double occupancy, lunches, materials, land travel, fiesta, galleries, fun. **Contact:** Rebecca Ratekin, Artforms Int'l., P.O. Box 716, Carlsbad, CA 92008; [www.artformsinternational.com].

Bi-Cultural Programs IMAC. Spanish in Guadalajara is more than a classroom. Group sizes of 1 to 5. Guadalajara offers the conveniences of a modern city. We are a few hours drive to Puerto Vallarta. Homestays with only 1 student per family. Hotel discounts available. Free Internet and email access. Excursions and extracurricular activities.

Dates: Year round. Group classes start every Monday. Individual tutoring may begin any day. Christmas vacation Dec 18-Jan 1, 2000; Easter vacation Apr 17-30, 2000. **Cost:** Contact organizations for details. **Contact:** Leticia Orozco, Instituto Mèxico Americano de Cultura, Donata Guerra 180, Guadalajara, Jalisco, 44100 Mèxico; 011-52-3-613-1080, fax 011-52-3-613-4621; spanish-imac@imac-ac.edu.mx, [www.spanish-school.com.mx].

Cemanahuac Community. Trips are highly educational, with college credit (graduate and undergraduate) available. Countries include Mexico, Belize, Costa Rica, and Guatemala. Focus areas include history, anthropology, archaeology, social issues, cooking and cuisine, and popular and folk art. Previous groups include teachers, social workers, artists, senior citizens, chefs, museum members, alumni groups, and other adult participants. Each trip individually planned.

Dates: Field study trips can be held at any time of the year. **Cost:** Dependent on requirements and length of the field study trips. **Contact:** Vivian B. Harvey, Educational Programs Coordinator, Cemanahuac Educational Community, Apartado 5-21, Cuernavaca, Morelos, Mexico; 011-52-7-3186407, fax 011-52-7-312-5418; 74052.2570@compuserve.com, [www.cemanahuac.com].

El Bosque del Caribe, Cancun. Take a professional Spanish course 25 hours per week and enjoy the Caribbean beaches. Relaxed family-like atmosphere. No more than 6 students per class. Special conversation program. Mexican cooking classes and excursions to the Mayan sites. Housing with Mexican families. College credit available.

Dates: Year round. New classes begin every Monday. Group programs arranged at reduced fees. **Cost:** Enrollment fee $100, $185 per week. One week with a Mexican family $160. **Contact:** Eduardo Sotelo, Director, Calle Piña 1, S.M. 25, 77500 Cancún, Mexico; 011-52-98-84-10-38, fax 011-52-98-84-58-88; bcaribe@mail.cancun-language.com.mx.

Intensive Spanish in Cuernavaca. Cuauhnahuac, founded in 1972, offers a variety of intensive and flexible programs geared to individual needs. Six hours of classes daily with no more than 4 students to a class. Housing with Mexican families who really care about you. Cultural conferences, excursions, and special classes for professionals. College credit available.

Dates: Year round. New classes begin every Monday. **Cost:** $70 registration fee; $680 for 4 weeks tuition; housing $18 per night. **Contact:** Marcia Snell, 519 Park Dr., Kenilworth, IL 60043; 800-245-9335, fax 847-256-9475; lankysam@aol.com.

Intensive Spanish in Yucatan. Centro de Idiomas del Sureste, A.C. (CIS), founded in 1974, offers 3-5 hours per day of intensive conversational Spanish classes with native-speaking, university-trained professors. Maximum 6 students per group, average 3. Program includes beginner courses to very advanced with related field trips and recommended optional homestay. Also special classes in business, legal, medical vocabulary, or Mayan studies.

Dates: Year round. Starts any Monday, except last 2 weeks in Dec. **Cost:** Tuition (3 hours per day program: $350 first 2 weeks, $125 each additional week); tuition 5 hours per day programs $550 first 2 weeks, $225 each additional week. **Contact:** Chloe C. Pacheco, Director, Centro de Idiomas del Sureste, A.C., Calle 14 #106 X25, col. Mexico, CP 97128, Mérida, Yucatán, Mexico; 011-52-99-26-11-55 or 011-52-99-26-94-94, 20-28-10, fax 011-52-99-26-00-20; cis@sureste.com.

Language and Culture in Guanajuato. Improve your Spanish in the most beautiful colonial city in Mexico. We teach one-on-one or in small groups for up to 8 hours daily. Spanish, Mexican history, cooking, literature, business, folk dancing, and politics. Students of all ages and many nationalities. Homestays with families, field trips, movies, hikes, theater, dance performances.

Dates: Year round. New classes begin every Monday. Semester programs begin in Jan and Aug. **Cost:** $925. Includes 4 weeks of classes and homestay with 3 meals daily. **Contact:** Director Jorge Barroso, Instituto Falcon, Mora 158, Guanajuato, Gto. 36000 Mexico; 011-52-473-1-0745; infalcon@redes.int.com.mx, [http://institutofalcon.com].

Mar de Jade Ocean-Front Resort. Tropical ocean-front retreat center in a small fishing village on a beautiful half-mile beach north of Puerto Vallarta. Surrounded by lush jungle with the warm, clear sea at our door, enjoy swimming, hiking, horseback riding, massage, and meditation. Study Spanish in small groups. Gain insight into local culture by optional volunteer work in community projects, such as rural community clinic, our local library, or a model home garden. Mar de Jade also has meeting facilities and provides a serene and intimate setting for group events.

Dates: Year round. **Cost:** Twenty-one day volunteer/Spanish program May-Nov 15 $1,000 (student discount available); Nov 15-Apr $1,080. Includes room and board in a shared occupancy room and 15 hours per week of volunteer work. Vacation: May-Nov 15 room and board $50 per night; Nov 16-Apr $55 per night. Spanish $80 per week with minimum 1 week (6 nights) stay. **Contact:** In Mexico: Tel./fax 011-52-322-2-3524; info@mardejade.com, [www.mardejade.com]. U.S. mailing address: 9051 Siempre Viva Rd., Suite 78-344, San Diego, CA 92173-3628.

Spanish in Ensenada. Univ. of California, San Diego Extension, offers an exciting and affordable way to learn Spanish through weekend and week-long programs in Ensenada. Study with experienced Mexican instructors in an immersion setting. Small class sizes maximize participation and enhance the language learning experience.

Dates: Year round weekend and week-long programs. **Cost:** $150 per weekend; $315 per week. Includes tuition UCSD ext. credit and homestay (3 meals per day). **Contact:** Univ. of California, San Diego Extension, Liberal Arts and International Programs, 9500 Gilman Dr., La Jolla, CA 92093-0176; 858-822-2747, fax 858-534-7385; travelstudy@ucsd.edu, [www-esps.ucsd.edu].

Spanish in Guadalajara. Live the Spanish language through UCSD Extension's Spanish immersion program in Guadalajara, "The City of Roses." Study at the Univ. of Guadalajara, the 2nd largest institution of higher learning in

By Ralph Shaffer

So you're retired now. And you, or you and your spouse, have pretty well worked out the domestic routines of the new leisure life. Now it's your time to plan a vacation. The question is where. And with whom. If you haven't already done so, maybe it's time to investigate Elderhostel.

This 22-year-old Boston-based nonprofit organization offers much more to the over 55s than just low-cost study-travel in the U.S. It arranges group study-travel tours almost everywhere in the world. Their programs feature clean, low-cost accommodations plus academic and cultural experiences found in few other travel plans. More than 300,000 Elderhostelers journey to more than 70 countries every year. The success of the organization's concept is attested to by a 75 percent repeater rate.

So what makes Elderhostel so attractive?

A typical total for a seven-day program in Britain comes to about $1,500 per person. A longer trip—say a month in Australia—comes to about $7,000. This includes everything: accommodations, meals, field trips, tips, transfers, and instruction.

Elderhostel treks are selected by participants for their academic and cultural aspects as well as for the areas to be visited.

There are no exams and no grades. The you-don't-really-have-to-study-up courses include art classes and history, folk remedies, archaeology, weaving, photography, animal legends...you name it.

To back up these casual study groups, Elderhostelers visit related places in the region—museums, farms, castles, schools, seats of government, libraries—as adjuncts to learning that are not usually a part of group tourist activities.

Elderhostel was founded in 1974 by Marty Knowlton, a former Boston educator, and Donald Bianco, a Univ. of New Hampshire administrator. Knowlton expanded on the youth hostel idea he found during a four-year walking tour of Europe and embellished it by adding instructional components similar to those he found in folk schools (adult "schools for life") in Scandinavia.

For information on the Elderhostel overseas programs contact: Elderhostel, 75 Federal St., Boston, MA 02110-1941; 877-426-8056; [www.elderhostel.org].

Mexico, and participate in a program that has been helping thousands of people to learn Spanish for nearly 50 years.

Dates: Year round 2-week and 5-week programs. **Cost:** $654 for 2-week program. Includes tuition, UCSD Ext. credit, and 14 days of homestay (3 meals per day); $1,403 for 5-week program. Includes tuition, UCSD Ext. credit, and 35 days of homestay (3 meals per day). **Contact:** Univ. of California, San Diego Extension, Liberal Arts and International Programs, 9500 Gilman Dr., La Jolla, CA 92093-0176; 858-822-2747, fax 858-534-7385; travelstudy@ucsd.edu, [www-esps.ucsd.edu].

Spanish Language Institute. A program designed to provide students with ideal learning environment which is conducive to thinking, writing and speaking naturally in Spanish within the context or real-life situations. Discover the Mexican culture with a university group, organization, professionals, travelers and special program of individualized needs for executives.

Dates: Year round. Classes begin every Monday. **Cost:** $150 per week. **Contact:** María Ramos, Academic Spanish Language Institute, Bajada de la Pradera #208, Colonia Pradera, Cuernavaca, Morelos 62191, Mexico; jessram@mor1.telmex.net.mx, [http://Cuernavaca.infosel.com.mx/sli/sli-page.htm].

Nepal

Sojourn Nepal. Sojourn Nepal is a 12-week program comprised of homestay, language study, lectures, village stay, trekking, and opportunities for apprenticeships in a vast variety of areas. Cultural immersion at its finest.

Dates: Fall and spring semesters. **Cost:** $5,500 all inclusive. Airfare not included. **Contact:** Jennifer Warren, Sojourn Nepal, 2440 N. 56th St., Phoenix, AZ 85008; Tel./fax 602-840-9197; snepal@aol.com.

Portugal

Portuguese in Portugal or Brazil. Language immersion courses in Portugal (Lisbon, Faro) or Brazil (Salvador da Bahia). Private language schools with programs for adults, senior citizens, and teenagers. Centrally located, convenient to interesting places, cultural events, sports activities. Programs feature qualified teachers, small classes, attractive surroundings and facilities. Affordable prices for instruction. Accommodations with Portuguese or Brazilian families with meals, student residences, apartments, and nearby hotels.

Dates: Year round. Two weeks or more. **Cost:** Two-week courses with or without accommodations range from $795-$1,020. **Contact:** Ms. Lorraine Haber, Study Abroad Coordinator, Embassy CES Study Abroad Programs, The Center for English Studies, 330 7th Ave., 6th Fl., New York, NY 10001; 212-629-7300, fax 212-736-7950; cesnewyork@cescorp.com.

Russia and the NIS

Moscow Study Trips. Since 1980 the program has probed political, economic, and social realities of the USSR, then of Russia's historic transition. Participants, aged 19-70, have come from various backgrounds and countries. No Russian language knowledge needed. Sample schedule and anecdotal accounts of past trips on web site.

Dates: Jun and Jul, 3 or 4 weeks, or on sufficient demand. **Cost:** Approx. $1,600-$1,800. **Contact:** Eric Fenster, Moscow Study Trips, 27150 Zeman Ave., Euclid, OH 44132; efenster@igc.org, [http://ourworld.compuserve.com/homepages/efenster].

The Tver InterContact Group. Study Russian in Russia's friendliest city. The Tver InterContact Group offers a variety of Russian language programs and internships for students and professionals. Language programs last from 2 weeks to an academic year. Ask about our special Summer and Winter Schools and professional programs for journalists, lawyers, and translators.

Dates: Year round. **Cost:** From $255 for 2 weeks. Includes tuition, room and board. **Contact:** Monica White, The Tver InterContact Group, P.O. Box 0565, Central Post Office, Tver 170000, Russia; 011-7-822-425-419, fax 011-7-822-426-210; infodesk@postman.ru, [www.volga.net].

Spain

=elemadrid= Spanish in Madrid. Our school provides a wide variety of Spanish immersion programs, Spain today classes, leisure activity courses and weekend excursions in small groups/and or individually tailored private lessons for adults. Accommodations include homestay, apartments, apartment sharing, and hotels.

Dates: Two-week courses start every other Monday year round. **Cost:** Courses $220-$760 per week; accommodations $80-$1,300 per week; leisure activity courses and weekend excursions vary. **Contact:** =elemadrid=, Calle

Serrano 4, 28001 Madrid, Spain; Tel./fax 011-34-91-432-4540/41; hola@elemadrid.com, [www.elemadrid.com].

Intensive Spanish Courses, Seville. CLIC IH, one of Spain's leading language schools, is located in the heart of Seville, the vibrant capital of Andalucia. With year-round intensive Spanish language courses, business Spanish, and official exam preparation taught by highly qualified and motivated native teachers, CLIC IH combines professionalism with a friendly atmosphere. Academic credits available. Accommodations are carefully selected and we offer a varied cultural program as well as exchanges with local students.
Dates: Year round. **Cost:** Approx. $930 for a 4-week Spanish course and homestay, individual room, 2 meals per day. **Contact:** Bernhard Roters, CLIC International House Seville, Calle Albareda 19, 41001 Sevilla, Spain; 011-34-95-450-2131, fax 011-34-95-456-1696; clic@clic.es, [www.clic.es].

Learn Spanish in Spain. Language immersion courses in Spain (Barcelona, Canary Islands, Granada, Madrid, Malaga, Salamanca, San Sebastian, Seville, and Valencia). Private language schools with programs for adults, senior citizens, and teenagers. Centrally located, convenient to interesting places, cultural events, sports activities. Programs feature qualified teachers, small classes, attractive surroundings and facilities. Affordable prices for instruction. Accommodations with Spanish families with meals, student residences, apartments, and nearby hotels.
Dates: Year round. Two weeks or more. **Cost:** Two-week courses with or without accommodations range from $275-$905. **Contact:** Ms. Lorraine Haber, Study Abroad Coordinator, Embassy CES Study Abroad Programs, The Center for English Studies, 330 7th Ave., 6th Fl., New York, NY 10001; 212-629-7300, fax 212-736-7950; cesnewyork@cescorp.com.

Señor Valcia Spanish Institute. Señor Valcia Spanish Institute welcomes you to sunny Andalusia. Year round intensive courses, D.E.L.E. certification, exclusive "Explorer" program with Doñana National Park, U.S. university credit available, academic year abroad for high school students. Optional Manzanilla Sherry Tours, flamenco, horseback riding, guitar lessons, day trips to Sevilla and more.
Dates: Year round. **Cost:** Vary. **Contact:** Señor Valcia Central Office, P.O. Box 358, Sanlúcar de Bda., Cadiz, 11540, Spain; Tel./fax 011-34-956-380859; club@valcia.es, [www.valcia.es]. U.S. address: 640 East 3990 South, Salt Lake City, UT 84107; 800-484-5554 pin 5554; academia@juno.com.

Seville and Andalusia: Artistic Travel. Andalusia—Moorish poets called it an earthly paradise. From the grandeur of the Alhambra, Seville's Alcazar and the great mosque of Cordoba . . . to mazes of white-washed streets, orange trees and flower-bedecked courtyards—a unique week in Southern Spain. Lodging in a charming Seville hotel. Workshops include Tile Making and Ceramics, Painting, Language Arts—beginning and intermediate converstional Spanish.
Dates: Mar 4-11. **Cost:** $1,465 (lodging, all meals except 2 dinners, tuition, and field trips). **Contact:** Karen Totman-Gale, Horizons, 108 N. Main St.-T, Sunderland, MA 01375; 413-665-0300, fax 413-665-4141; horizons@horizons-art.org, [www.horizons-art.org].

Sociedad Hispano Mundial. The quality of our programs is guaranteed by OCR and the Univ. of Alcala (Spain). Year round intensive Spanish courses, specialized courses (business Spanish, literature, politics, history, art, civilization, DELE exams), and one-to-one. All levels and ages. Communicative approach. Highly qualified and motivated native teachers. Extensive extracurricular social and cultural program. Great location and facilities.
Dates: Begin any Monday. **Cost:** Varies by program and length of stay. **Contact:** Jose Ruiz Cantero, Director, Sociedad Hispano Mundial, Palacio de Congresos, Paseo del Violón s/n, Granada 18006, Spain; 011-34-958-24-68-92, fax 011-34-958-24-68-93; shm@moebius.es, [http://tuspain.com/shm/shm.htm].

Spanish Courses in Malaga. Spanish courses in Malaga, Spain. All grades, small groups, 4 hours daily, courses commencing each month. Living with Spanish families (or in small apartment in town center).
Contact: F. Marin Fernandez, Director, Centro de Estudios de Castellano, Ave. Juan Sebastian Elcano 120, Málaga, 29017 Spain; Tel./fax 011-34-95-2290-551; ryoga@arrakis.es, [www.arrakis.es/~ryoga].

Spanish in Madrid. Live the Spanish language through UCSD Extension's Spanish immersion program in the vibrant capital of Madrid. Participate in a language program that has been helping thousands of people to learn languages for over 35 years. Small class sizes and experienced instructors enhance the language learning experience.

Dates: Year round programs, 2 weeks or more. **Cost:** Fees include tuition, course materials, testing, placement, and UCSD Extension credit. There is an additional $125 registration fee. Housing fees are paid directly to Eurocentres upon arrival in Madrid. Two weeks $575, 3 weeks $795, 4 weeks $995. **Contact:** Univ. of California, San Diego Extension, Liberal Arts and International Programs, 9500 Gilman Dr., La Jolla, CA 92093-0176; 858-822-2747, fax 858-534-7385; travelstudy@ucsd.edu, [www-esps.ucsd.edu].

Spanish Language Courses in Malaga. Widely recognized to be one of Spain's leading language schools, Malaca Instituto offers language and cultural programs at all levels for adults of all ages. Qualifying American students can apply for academic credit. Courses qualified by the Univ. of Alcala. EAQUALS guarantee of quality (see www.eaquals.org).

Dates: Courses begin every 2 weeks from Jan 10. **Cost:** PTS48,000 for 2-week course. **Contact:** Bob Burger, Malaca Instituto, c/Cortada 6, 29018 Malaga, Spain; 011-34-95-229-3242, fax 011-34-95-229-6316; espanol@malacainst-ch.es, [www.malacainst-ch.es].

Thailand

AUA Thai Language Program. Learn Thai using the (ALG) Automatic Language Growth method as designed by Dr. J. Marvin Brown. Gain the best results in ability to communicate of any program in the world.

Dates: Year round. **Cost:** 82 baht per hour with discounts offered for larger number of hours. **Contact:** David Long, Asst. Director, AUA Language Center, 179 Rajadamri Rd., Bangkok 10330, Thailand; 011-66-2-252-8170, ext 3201; fax 011-66-2-252-8398; info@auatd.org, [www.auatd.org].

United Kingdom and Ireland

"Ireland in Europe" Summer School. Irish culture and its place in a wider Europe is the focus of this 2-week summer school at Trinity College Dublin. The program consists of a series of seminars together with field trips and cultural activities offering a comprehensive view of contemporary Ireland.

Dates: Jul 16-29, 2000. **Cost:** From IR£850. **Contact:** USIT Now, 19 Aston Quay, Dublin 2, Ireland; 011-353-1-6021740, fax 011-353-1-6778843; 1yclarke@usit.ie.

An Irish Idyll—From Dublin to Bantry Bay: Artistic Travel. From historic Dublin to mountain landscapes, fields of green to quaint villages and dramatic ocean views...this evocative country has a beauty all its own. Lodging in a charming bed and breakfast in the gorgeous seaside village of Kinsale—perfectly situated to see the diversity of the Irish panorama. Workshops include Painting, Silversmithing and Jewelry Design, Photography, Flameworking/Glass Beads.

Dates: May 6-13, Sep 16-23. **Cost:** $1,465 (lodging, meals, tuition, and field trips). **Contact:** Karen Totman-Gale, Horizons, 108 N. Main St.-T, Sunderland, MA 01375; 413-665-0300, fax 413-665-4141; horizons@horizons-art.org, [www.horizons-art.org].

Celtic Journeys. Cultural archaeological tours of Ireland or Scotland for small groups or individuals. Guides are degreed archaeologists and historians, take you into sites known only to locals and professionals. Some well-known sites also covered. No class credit available.

Dates: Vary. **Cost:** Contact sponsor. **Contact:** Laurie or Diane, Celtic Journeys, 4017 Case St., Houston, TX 77005; Tel./fax 800-379-2482; westisle@tgn.net.

Edinburgh Univ. Summer Courses. Scotland past and present: art, architecture, history, literature, archaeology, geology presentation skills, railways, Gaelic, music, drama, creative writing, film, ecology, the Edinburgh Festival. Courses last 1-4 weeks each. Instruction by university professors: highest academic standards. Integral field trips; theatre/concert/cinema tickets provided. Social program. Choice of accommodations.

Dates: Jun-Sep. **Cost:** Inquire. **Contact:** Ursula Michels, Univ. of Edinburgh, Centre for Continuing Education, 11 Buccleuch Pl., Edinburgh EH8 9LW, U.K.; 011-44-131-650-4400, fax 011-44-131-667-6097; CCE@ed.ac.uk, [www.cce.ed.ac.uk/summer].

The Heatherley School of Fine Art. Fine art courses. Painting, drawing, sculpture, printing, watercolor, pastels. Open studio. Foundation/portfolio. Diploma in portraiture. Continuing studies.

Dates: Contact organization for details. **Cost:** Contact organization for details. **Contact:** The School Office, The Heatherley School of Fine Art, 80 Upcerne Rd., Chelsea, London SW10 0SH, U.K.; 011-44-171-351-4190, fax 011-44-171-351-6945; heatherleys@hotmail.com.

Ireland: Light and Landscape. Join acclaimed artist and faculty member Pat Traub and a local guide for a landscape drawing/painting class in old Ireland's magic light. We'll stay in our own private residence located in western Ireland with Croagh Patrick, the sacred mountain, and gorgeous seascapes nearby.

Dates: Jun, 2 weeks. **Cost:** $2,595 plus tuition and airfare (1999). **Contact:** Neil di Sabato, PAFA, Continuing Education Programs, 1301 Cherry St., Philadelphia, PA 19103; 215-972-7632, fax 215-569-0153; continuinged@pafa.org, [www.pafa.org].

Irish Way Program. The Irish Way is a 5-week travel-study program for American high school students. Participants take classes in Irish culture, history, dance, sports, Gaelic, and go on field trips and stay with an Irish host family for 1 week. The Irish Way has sent over 2,500 students to Ireland since 1976.

Dates: Jul. **Cost:** $2,995 includes roundtrip, transatlantic airfare. **Contact:** Trish Connolly, Irish American Cultural Institute, 1 Lackawanna Pl., Morristown, NJ 07960; 973-605-1991; irishwaynj@aol.com, [www.irishaci.org].

Residential Courses. Residential courses from 1 day to 1 week. A wide range of liberal adult education programs available, including music, arts and crafts.

Dates: Year round. **Cost:** From £120 **Contact:** Teresa Denning, Dillington House, Ilminster, Somerset TA19 9DT, U.K.; 011-44-1460-52427, fax 011-44-1460-52433; dillington@somerset.gov.uk.

Summer Academy. Summer Academy offers study holidays at 15 British and Irish universities. The course fee includes full accommodations for 6 to 7 nights, tuition fees, and course-related excursions. Study topics include: heritage, the arts, countryside, and creative writing. Accommodations are in single rooms in university residence halls. Locations include: Aberystwyth, Canterbury, Cork (Ireland), Durham, Exeter, Glasgow, Manchester, Norwich, Oxford, Sheffield, Southampton, Stirling, Swansea, and York.

Dates: Jun-Aug. **Cost:** £380-£475 (1999). **Contact:** Andrea McDonnell, Marketing and Reservations Coordinator, Summer Academy, Keynes College, The Univ., Canterbury, Kent CT2 7NP, U.K.; 011-44-1227-470402/823473, fax 011-44-1227-784338; summeracademy@ukc.ac.uk, [www.ukc.ac.uk/sa/index.html].

Summer Music School. Solo and choral singers, chamber music, accompanists, wrtiers. Twenty-two top class tutors, 15 house pianists. Beautiful setting in Ardingly College, Sussex.

Dates: Aug. **Cost:** £300 (1999) includes accommodations and tuition. **Contact:** Summer Music, 70 Surrenden Crescent, Brighton BN1 GWF, U.K.; Tel./fax 011-44-1273-884186; summermusicschool@yahoo.com.

Worldwide

Cross-Cultural Solutions. Experience the vibrant, colorful culture of India, Ghana, or Peru and make a difference at the same time. This unique short-term volunteer program enables volunteers to work with local social service organizations in fields as diverse as health care, education, skills training, and arts/recreation. Volunteers receive continual professional support from our U.S. and India-based staff. No skills or experience required—only a desire to help and learn.

Dates: Contact organization for details. **Cost:** $1,850 covers in-country transportation, accommodations, board, and support. International airfare, insurance, and visa not included. Program fee is tax deductible. **Contact:** Cross-Cultural Solutions, 47 Potter Ave., New Rochelle, NY 10801; 800-380-4777 or 914-632-0022, fax 914-632-8494; info@crossculturalsolutions.org, [www.crossculturalsolutions.org].

Discovery Tours. Worldwide educational travel programs of the American Museum of Natural History (53 in 2000) are accompanied by curatorial and its scientific staff.

Dates: Year round. **Cost:** $2,995-$27,950. **Contact:** Richard Houghton, Discovery Tours, American Museum of Natural History, CPW at 79th St., New York, NY 10024-5192; discovery@amnh.org, [www.amnh.org].

Earn College Credit for Travel and Study. Travel USA or abroad anytime during the year. Contact S. Tash, instructor. Undergraduate language credit and post-graduate credit for teachers.

Dates: Year round. **Cost:** Varies. **Contact:** Steve Tash, instructor; 800-484-1081 ext 7775, 9 a.m.-9 p.m. PST or email travelstudy@yahoo.com, [www.studyabroadandwork.com].

Earthwatch Institute. Unique opportunities to work with leading scientists on 1- to 3-week field research projects worldwide. Earthwatch sponsors 160 expeditions in over 30 U.S. states and in 60 countries. Project disciplines include archaeology, wildlife management, ecology, ornithology and marine mammalogy. No special skills needed—all training is done in the field.

Dates: Year round. **Cost:** Tax deductible contributions ranging from $695-$3,995 support the research and cover food and lodging expenses. Airfare not included. **Contact:** Earthwatch, 680 Mt. Auburn St., P.O. Box 9104-MA, Watertown, MA 02472; 800-776-0188, 617-926.8200; info@earthwatch.org, [www.earthwatch.org].

Educational Travel Adventures (ETA).
Fascinating programs to spectacular destinations in Latin America, Europe, Africa, Asia, South Pacific, and North America. Some involve physical (hiking, biking, etc.) or health-oriented activities. Different age groups, duration 4 days-4 weeks. Nonprofit discounts, free group leaders/organizers. Special interest custom design.
Dates: Call for details. **Cost:** From $375.
Contact: Mrs. Jeannie Graves, Forum Travel International, 91 Gregory Ln., #21, Pleasant Hill, CA 94523; 800-225-4475, 925-671-2900; fti@foruminternational.com, [www.foruminternational.com], [www.fieu.edu].

ERDT/SHARE! Exchange Program. ERDT/SHARE! Provides American students, ages 16 to 18, opportunities for summer, semester, or academic year homestays/study abroad. Language proficiency, academic standing, maturity are criteria for selection. Students live with host families and, depending on program selected, attend local school or language school. ERDT/SHARE! also provides opportunities for American families to host international exchange students.
Dates: Vary with type of program selected and academic year dates. Students and host family applications are accepted year round.
Cost: $1,500-$7,000 (depending on program), excluding transportation and personal expenses. **Contact:** Roger Riske, President, 475 Washington Blvd., Suite 220, Marina del Rey, CA 90292; 800-321-3738, 310-821-9977, fax 310-821-9282; info@erdtshare.org, [www.erdtshare.org].

Global Awareness Through Experience (GATE).
GATE offers alternative tourism through programs in Central America (Guatemala, El Salvador), Mexico, and Central Europe. Participants connect with Third World people in face-to-face dialogue to explore social, political, economic, religious, and cultural issues. Mutual learning happens between GATE participants and the indigenous people.

Dates: Various open groups. Special groups also welcome. **Cost:** $850 (Latin America) to $1,800 (Europe) plus airfare. **Contact:** Bernadette Nehl, GATE, 912 Market St., La Crosse, WI 54601; 608-791-5283, fax 608-782-6301; gate@fspa.org, [www.fspa.org] (choose Missions, then GATE).

Global Ecology and Cities in the 21st Century.
Two different academic programs to be offered by the International Honors Program in 1999-2000. "Global Ecology" is a 2-semester program of around-the-world study and travel to England, India, the Philippines, New Zealand, and Mexico with academic coursework in ecology, anthropology, economics, and environmental issues. The "Cities in the 21st Century" program is a 1-semester program of study and travel to Egypt, India, and Brazil with academic coursework in urban studies, anthropology, sociology, economics, and political science.
Dates: "Global Ecology": Sep 2000-May 2001. "Cities in 21st Century": Jan-May 2000. **Cost:** "Global Ecology": $22,950 plus airfare, includes tuition, room and board. "Cities in the 21st Century": $13,650 plus airfare, includes tuition, room and board. Estimated airfare for each program is $3,900. Financial aid is available. **Contact:** Joan Tiffany, Director, International Honors Program, 19 Braddock Pk., Boston, MA 02116; 617-267-0026, fax 617-262-9299; info@ihp.edu, [www.ihp.edu].

Global Service Corps. Service-learning, cultural immersion in Costa Rica, Kenya, or Thailand. Live with a village family while assisting grassroots organizations on community service and development projects. Project areas: rainforest conservation, sustainable agriculture, AIDS/HIV awareness, clinical health care, women's groups, classroom teaching. Experience the challenges of developing countries from the inside out. Includes orientation, training, and excursions.
Dates: Year round. Contact GSC office or check the web site for specific starting dates.
Cost: $1,695-$1,795 for 2-4 week project trips; $495 per month for 2-6-month long-term extensions. Includes extensive pre-departure preparation and in-country expenses (hotel and homestay room and board, orientation, training, project expenses, transportation, excursions). Airfare not included, discount rates available. **Contact:** Global Service Corps., 300 Broadway, #28, San Francisco, CA 94133; 415-788-3666 ext. 128, fax 415-788-7324; gsc@igc.apc.org, [www.globalservicecorps.org].

Global Volunteers. The nation's premier short-term service programs for people of all ages and backgrounds. Assist mutual international understanding through ongoing development projects throughout Africa, Asia, the Caribbean, Europe, the Pacific, North and South America. Programs of 1, 2, and 3 weeks range from natural resource preservation, light construction, and painting to teaching English, assisting with health care, and nurturing at-risk children. No special skills or foreign languages required. Ask about the Millennium Service Project.

Dates: Over 150 teams year round. **Cost:** Tax-deductible program fees range from $450 to $2,395. Airfare not included. **Contact:** Global Volunteers, 375 E. Little Canada Rd., St. Paul, MN 55117; 800-487-1074, fax 651-407-5163; email@globalvolunteers.org, [www.globalvolunteers.org].

Homestays for Peace. Servas is an international network of hosts and travelers building peace by providing opportunities for mutually arranged individual visits—typically for 2 nights—between people of diverse cultures and backgrounds. Servas encompasses more than 14,000 homes and institutions in more than 130 countries on 6 continents.

Dates: Year round. **Cost:** $65 per adult to travel for 1 year; $10 for internaton students in the U.S. **Contact:** Carole Wagner, Program Assistant, U.S. Servas, 11 John St., Room 407, New York, NY 10038-4009; 212-267-0252, fax 212-267-0292; usservas@servas.org, [http://servas.org].

IICD. The Institute for International Cooperation and Development (IICD) is a nonprofit organization dedicated to global education and assistance to developing countries. IICD sends teams of volunteers to work on educational, environmental, community health, and agricultural projects in Africa, Latin America, and India. Programs vary from 6-18 months.

Dates: Starting dates: Aug 1, Sep 1, Jan 5, Feb 1. **Cost:** From $3,800-$5,500. Financial aid is available. **Contact:** IICD, Promotion Director, P.O. Box 520, Williamstown, MA 01267; 413-458-9828; IICDINFO@berkshire.net, [www.iicd-volunteer.org].

Interhostel/Familyhostel. Interhostel (for adults 50 years and older) and Familyhostel (for families—grandparents and/or parents and school-aged children) offer study/travel programs to locations in the U.S. and all over the world. One- and 2-week programs include presentations, field trips, sightseeing, cultural and social activities, recreation. Call for a free catalog or visit our web site.

Dates: Over 75 programs throughout the year. **Cost:** U.S. programs: $600-$800; foreign programs: $2,000-$3,500. Includes meals, accommodations, activities, and foreign airfare. **Contact:** Interhostel, Univ. of New Hampshire Continuing Education, 6 Garrison Ave., Durham, NH 03824; 800-733-9753, fax 603-862-1113; learn.dce@unh.edu, [www.learn.unh.edu/interhostel].

Leisure Language Learning. Language Liaison sends people all over the world! This is the best in leisure language learning. Programs for seniors, families, executives, teens, leisure travelers and connoisseurs. Combine activities and cultural excursions with language learning and special interests. Learn something meaningful on your vacation and come back with more than just pictures.

Dates: Every week year round. **Cost:** Varies with program. **Contact:** Nancy Forman, Language Liaison Inc., 1610 Woodstead Ct., Suite 130, The Woodlands, TX 77380; 800-284-4448 or 281-367-7302, fax 281-367-4498, learn@languageliaison.com, [www.languageliaison.com].

School for International Training. A pioneer in study abroad, the School for International Training (SIT) offers 56 programs in over 40 countries worldwide. For over 40 years SIT has been a leader in offering field-based study abroad programs to U.S. college and university students.

Dates: Fall and spring semester. **Cost:** $9,300-$12,600 depending on location. Includes airfare, tuition, room and board, excursions, and insurance. **Contact:** School for International Training, P.O. Box AA1TA, Kipling Rd., Brattleboro, VT 05302; 800-336-1616, 802-257-7751, fax 802-258-3500; csa@sit.edu, [www.sit.edu].

Sugarcraft Tuition. Professional Sugarcraft tuition. All levels from beginners to advanced. Royal icing, sugarpaste, floral, modeling, novelty, pastillage, and many others aspects of Sugarcraft. One-, 2- or 5-day courses or individual tuition. Top tutors and friendly environment.

Dates: One- and 2-day tuition year round. Five-day schools in Mar and end of Jul. **Cost:** £50 per day or £275 for 5-day schools. **Contact:** Course Coordinator, Squires Kitchen School, 3 Waverley Ln., Farnham, Surrey GU9 8BB, U.K. 011-44-1252-711749, fax 011-44-1252-714714; school@squires-group.co.uk, [www.squires-group.co.uk].

TEFL and On-the-Job Tuition. Student exchange, business and language tuition, computer training, multimedia courses, translations on and offline, interpreting, hostess training, secretarial courses. Over 80 schools in Europe: Germany, Italy, Spain, Czech Republic, Poland, Russia, Switzerland, Albania; Africa: Morocco; Americas: Ecuador.

Dates: Call for details. **Cost:** Call for details. **Contact:** International Benedict Schools, P.O. Box 270, CH 1000, Lausanne 9, Switzerland; 011- 41-21-323-66-55, fax 011-41-21-323-67-77; benedict@worldcom.ch, [www.benedict.ch].

UC Research Expeditions (UREP). Adventure with a purpose. Join research expeditions in archaeology, anthropology, environmental studies, and more. Get off the beaten track, help in research that benefits local communities. No special experience necessary. Free brochure.

Dates: May-Sep (2 weeks). **Cost:** From $700-$1,700 (tax deductible). **Contact:** Univ. of California Research Expeditions Program (UREP); 530-752-0692, fax 530-752-0681; urep@ucdavis.edu, [http://urep.ucdavis.edu].

Up With People Worldsmart™. The Worldsmart™ program accelerates education and career opportunities through the unique combination of international travel, stage-based musical performance, and community service. Every year, 700 university-aged students from a variety of countries spend 11 months traveling throughout and experiencing the world.

Dates: Programs begin in Jan and Jul. **Cost:** $13,700 includes all travel, lodging, food, and student program expenses within the 11-month program. **Contact:** Admissions Department, Up With People, 1 International Ct., Broomfield, CO 80021; 800- 596-7353 or 303-438-7373, fax 303-438-7301; admissions@upwithpeople.org, [www.upwithpeople.org].

Various Educational Tours. Voyageur is a group travel company specializing in fully-escorted cultural and educational travel programs to Europe and other overseas destinations. We offer an exciting world of travel opportunities for groups of all ages and interests: high school students, college students, senior citizens, church and social organizations, etc.

Dates: Various. **Cost:** Call for free brochure. **Contact:** Voyageur, 120 Stafford St., Worcester, MA 01603-1435; 800-767-7667; info@govoyageur.com, [www.govoyageur.com].

Wildlands Studies. Students join backcountry team searching for answers to important environmental problems affecting wildlife populations and pristine wildlands in Nepal, Thailand, Canada, New Zealand, Belize, or Fiji. Each program grants 6-9 upper division credits. You do not need previous field study experience. All skills are taught onsite.

Dates: Year round 4-9 week programs. **Cost:** $1,000-$1,900 (depending on program). **Contact:** Wildlands Studies, 3 Mosswood Cir., Cazadero, CA 95421; 707-632-5665; wildlnds@sonic.net, [www.wildlandsstudies.com/ws].

World Affairs Council Travel Program. All the highlights of touring plus access to political leaders and local experts who give special briefings and behind-the-scenes views. Europe, Cuba, Asia, South American, Middle East, and North America as well as a once-in-a-lifetime private jet trip to the host cities of history.

Dates: 2000 and beyond. **Cost:** From $2,500-$29,500. **Contact:** Joan Russell, World Affairs Council, 1314 Chestnut St., Philadelphia, PA 19010; 800-942-5004; [www.libertynet.org/~wac].

WorldTeach. WorldTeach is a nonprofit, nongovernmental organization which provides opportunities for individuals to make a meaningful contribution to international education by living and working as volunteer teachers in developing countries.

Dates: Year round. **Cost:** $4,800-$5,950. Includes international airfare, health insurance, extensive training, and in-country support. **Contact:** WorldTeach, Harvard Institute for International Development, 14 Story St., Cambridge, MA 02138; 800-4-TEACH-0 or 617-495-5527, fax 617-495-1599; info@worldteach.org, [www.worldteach.org].

Youth International. An experiential education program focusing on international travel and intercultural exchange, adventure, community service, and homestays. Teams of 12, aged 18-25, travel together for 1 semester to Southeast Asia and India/Nepal, or East Africa and the Middle East. Assist refugees, hike the Himalayas, live with and help an African tribe, scuba dive, and much more.

Dates: Sep 7-Dec 18, 1999 (15 weeks); Jan 24-May 30 (18 weeks) and early Sep-mid-Dec (15 weeks), 2000. **Cost:** 1999: $6,500 (Asia), $7,000 (Africa/Middle East). 2000: $6,500 (Asia, 15 weeks), $7,500 (18 weeks); $7,000 (Africa/Middle East, 15 weeks), $8,000 (18 weeks). **Contact:** Brad Gillings, Youth International, 1121 Downing St., #2, Denver, CO 80218; 303-839-5877, fax 303-839-5887; youth.international@bigfoot.com, [www.youthinternational.org].

Interested in Working Overseas?

THIRTEEN

LANGUAGE
SCHOOLS

The following listing of language schools was supplied by the organizers. Contact the program directors to confirm costs, dates, and other details. Please tell them you read about their programs in this book! Programs based in more than one country or region are listed under "Worldwide."

Argentina

Argentine Spanish Learning Centre. CEDIC offers a completely integrated program in Spanish language with courses for different levels. Intensive language studies, immersion living in Spanish-speaking community. Private, and small group lessons with flexible schedules to meet the student's requirements. Social activities with Argentine families and students can also be arranged.
   Dates: Year round. **Cost:** Two weeks intensive program (40 hours) $370. Tutor classes $18. Ask about accommodations. **Contact:** CEDIC, Martin Duh or Susana Bernardi, Reconquista 715, Apt. 11, E., 1003 Buenos Aires, Argentina; Tel./fax 011-54-11-4315-1156; cedic@tarcos.com, [www.tarcos.com/cedic].

Argentine Universities Program. COPA offers an integrated study opportunity in which undergraduate students live with Argentine host families and study with degree-seeking Argentine students. Three partner universities offer unique blends of location, academics, and student population. There is a research track available. Academic program includes optional program classes and a required Spanish course. A 6-week, non-integrated summer program is also available. All coursework is in Spanish.
   Dates: Spring: Mar-Jul, fall: Jul-Dec, summer: Jun-Jul. **Cost:** Semester: fall $7,985; spring $8,385; year $15,000. Includes tuition, housing, 2 meals daily, orientation, excursions, support services. **Contact:** Cooperating Programs in the Americas, Institute for Study Abroad, 1100 W. 42nd St., Suite 305, Indianapolis, IN 46208-3345; 888-344-9299, fax 317-940-9704; COPA@butler.edu.

Argentum. Argentum is a Spanish language and culture program for undergraduate, graduate, and high school students. It is part of Universidad Blas Pascal in Córdoba. We offer the total immersion experience. Students can take other classes in literature, Latin American politics, international relations, art, music, economics, and more.
   Dates: Fall: Aug 8-Nov 26; Intensive: Feb-Mar, mid Jun-Jul, Jul-Aug; Spring: Mar 12-Jun 30, 2000. **Cost:** $6,100 for 1 semester, $10,100 for entire year, $2,200 for intensive program, includes tuition and fees, room and board, cultural activities, and field trips. **Contact:** Prof.

Marta Rosso-O'Laughlin, Argentum, P.O. Box 99, Medford, MA 02153-0099; Tel./fax 781-488-3552, mrosso@aol.com.

Del Sur. Intensive: This course is designed for those people who have little time available; small groups, maximum 6 people. One to One: This course is based on the student's linguistic skills, her or his professional or social needs and personal expectation. We design a tailor-made course to fit your specific needs.
Dates: Year round. Cost: Four weeks intensive (80 hours, 4 hours each day for 20 hours per week): $800 (including all materials). One to one (40 hours, 2 hours each day for 10 hours per week): $680 (including all materials). Contact: "Del Sur" Spanish School, Bernardo de Irigoyen, 668 Piso 1° (1072), Buenos Aires, Argentina; 011-54-11-4334-1487, fax 011-54-11-4334-0107; info@delsur.com.ar, [www.delsur.com.ar].

Instituto de Lengua Española (ILEE). Located downtown in the most European-like city in Latin America, Buenos Aires. Dedicated exclusively to teaching Spanish to foreigners. Small groups and private classes year round. All teachers hold Master's degrees in Education or Literature and have been full-time Spanish professors for years. Method is intensive, conversation-based. Student body is international. Highly recommended worldwide. Ask for individual references in U.S.
Dates: Year round. Cost: Four-week intensive program (20 hours per week) including homestay $1,400; 2 weeks $700. Private classes $19 per hour. Registration fee (includes books) $100. Contact: Daniel Korman, I.L.E.E., Director, Av. Callao 339, 3 fl. (1048), Buenos Aires, Argentina; Tel./fax 011-54-1-375-0730. In U.S.: David Babbitz; 415-431-8219, fax 415-431-5306; ilee@overnet.com.ar, [www.studyabroad.com/ilee].

Spanish for Foreigners. Spanish as a foreign langauge. Communication classes, friendly and relaxed atmosphere, one-on-one or small groups. Intensive and vacation courses for children, teens, or adults (all levels). Tailor-made programs for school classes and student groups. Accommodations arranged.
Dates: Year round. Cost: Hourly fees range $10-$20. Matriculation fee $50. Contact: "Albert Schweitzer" Studio of Education and Culture, Gral. Alvear 69, 2nd Fl., Martínez 1640, Buenos Aires, Argentina; 011-54-1-4792-6322/4790-6245, fax 011-54-1-4793-6888.

Austria

Campus Austria. Austria is the perfect place to learn German. An ideal holiday destination, Austria excels in the quality of language instruction offered throughout the country. Campus Austria comprises 20 language schools committed to providing state-of-the-art teaching.
Dates: Year round. Cost: Average ATS9,000 for 3-week course. Contact: Campus Austria, Prof. Kaserer, Weg 333, A-3491 Strass, Austria; 011-43-2735-5535-0, fax 011-43-2735-5535-14; campus.austria@telecom.at, [http://austria-tourism.at/campusaustria/campus.e.html].

German Courses at the University. German for beginners and advanced students, perfectionist courses, courses for students of the German language and teachers of German in foreign countries (6 levels). Lectures on German and Austrian literature, music, Austria—the country, people, and language. Special courses: translation, commercial German, commercial correspondence, phonetics, conversation, communication. Excursions.
Dates: Three sessions: Jul 2-29, Jul 30-Aug 26, Aug 27-Sep 16. Cost: Course fee (4 weeks): approx. ATS4,500. Accommodations: approx. ATS5,800. Contact: Magister Sigrun Inmann-Trojer, Wiener Internationale Hochschulkurse, Ebendorferstrasse 10/4, A-1010 Vienna, Austria; fax 011-43-1-405-12-5410, [www.univie.ac.at/WIHOR].

German Language Courses. German courses for adults with cultural activities in Vienna (age 16 and over). Junior programs in Austria (ages 9-16).
Dates: Jul and Aug. Cost: Contact sponsor. Contact: Oekista, Garnisongasse 7, 1090 Vienna, Austria; 011-43-1-401-488820, fax 011-43-1-401-488800; german.course@oekista.co.at, [www.oekista.co.at].

International German Language Courses. German language classes at all levels and for all ages. Phonetics, cultural and touristic events, all kinds of sports.
Dates: Summer courses. Cost: ATS5,700. Includes daily lessons, accommodations, and half board with host family. Contact: Helmut Lerch, Director, Interschool, Deutsch in Innsbruck, A-6020 Innsbruck, Kohlstattgasse 3, Austria; Tel./fax 011-43-0512-58-89-57.

Internationale Ferienkurse. Sixty hours in 3-week summer courses. Instruction by highly qualified university professors and experienced grammar school teachers. Small classes (7 to 15) at all levels. Austrian studies. (Compatibility with the American education system: 60 hours equals 4 credits.) The schoolbuilding is centrally located in a quiet, exclusive area of Salzburg; the school-owned grounds (16,000 square meters) are park-like. Friendly and safe setting.

Dates: Contact organization for details. **Cost:** Contact organization for details. **Contact:** Collegium Austriacum und IFK-Deutschkurse, Postfach 120, 5010 Salzburg, Austria; 011-43-662-849611.

Benelux

ISOK. Homestays with language courses in Holland and, in cooperation with St. Peter's School in Cangerbury, in England.

Dates: Holland: year; England: year, not at Christmas. **Cost:** England: summer £234, other DFL184 per week; Holland: homestay DFL385 per week; lessons DFL27 1/2 per hour. **Contact:** ISOK, Mr. J.F.H. de Zeeuw, Jan-Tooropastraat 4, 2225 XT, Katwijk, Holland; 011-31-71-4013533.

Canada

A.L.I. - Intensive Language Studies. Académie Linguistique Internationale is a private language school located in the heart of Montréal. We offer: year-round courses for intensive English and French, interactive methods and conversational approach to teaching, 8 study levels, 9 students maximum per class, 4-5 weeks each level, 100-125 hours per session, activities program, homestay and other accommodations.

Dates: Intensive courses begin every Monday for intermediate and advanced groups, and at regular intervals for beginners. Semi-intensive, private instruction, TOEFL preparation, and business English also offered throughout the year. **Cost:** For 4-week intensive: $620 for 100 hours plus access to email and Internet; $700 for full board and homestay accommodations (minimum 2 weeks). Costs of other services available upon request. **Contact:** Ms. Kimiko Hawkes, l'Académie Linguistique Internationale, 5115 deGaspé #300, Montréal, PQ, H2T 3B7, Canada; 514-270-3886, fax 514-270-6363; info@alint.com, [www.alint.com].

College Platon English or French. Full time or part time we teach over 28 languages. Since 1957. In-house cafeteria, computer labs, audio visual equipment in all class rooms. Winners of the Consumer Choice award 10 years in a row.

Dates: Year round. **Cost:** Four weeks full time CAN$675; 12 weeks CAN$1,800; 24 weeks CAN$3,200. **Contact:** College Platon, Chris Kavathas, 4521 Park Ave., Montreal, PQ, H2V

4E4; 514-281-1016, fax 514-281-6275; infos@platocollege.com, [www.platocollege.com].

École de langue française de Trois-Pistoles. The oldest university-sponsored French immersion school in Canada, our school offers two 5-week sessions each year and a French Intensive session for busy adults (7-10 days). Courses are offered in the areas of French language, culture, theater, and political science. Guided by dynamic monitors, students participate in an afternoon workshop and a varied sociocultural program. Accommodations and meals, as well as an opportunity to practice French in an informal setting, provided by families in Trois-Pistoles.

Dates: May 10-Jun 11; Jul 5-Aug 6. **Cost:** CAN$1,700 plus CAN$250 program deposit ($100 refundable) (1999). **Contact:** Annie Morin, Administrative Assistant, The Univ. of Western Ontario, École de langue française de Trois-Pistoles, Univ. College 219, London, ON, N6A 3K7, Canada; 519-661-3637, fax 519-661-3799; tpistole@julian.uwo.ca, [www.cstudies.uwo.ca/trp].

French Studies in Montréal. Intensive French programs offered in historic Old Montreal. Grammar, lots of conversation and weekly monitored outings to French cultural and social events. Also weekly language exchange lounge with local French Canadians.

Dates: Year round. Start dates every second Monday. Complete beginners start every 4 weeks. Minimum 2-week program. Small classes with max. 10 students in a roundtable setting. **Cost:** $360 for 2 weeks, 44 hours, includes access to CD Rom language lab, 24-hour voice messaging service, free email and Internet. Also available homestay with French or bilingual families. Special: Register for 4 weeks and get 1 week free tuition by mentioning this listing. **Contact:** Y&N - Language and Cultural Studies, 404 Saint Pierre, Suite 201, Montréal, PQ, H2Y 2M2, Canada; 514-840-7228, fax 514-840-7111; info@languageco.com, [www.languageco.com].

Learn English or French. English in Monteral and Toronto and French in Montreal. Transfer between 2 cities. All levels are offered from beginner to advanced. Conversation and grammer every day. Small classes, 5-12 students per class. Homestay and activities available. Central downtown location. Friendly environment and excellent highly qualified teachers.

Dates: Classes begin every Monday. **Cost:** One-month course and homestay $1,270. **Contact:** Paul Keefe, President, Centre Linguista, 500 boul. Rene-Levesque O, Suite #802, Montreal, PQ, H2Z 1W7, Canada; 514-397-1736, fax 514-397-9007; mlscl@generation.net, [www.centrelinguista.com].

Univ. of New Brunswick ELP. Established in 1953 in eastern Canada, tradition of expertise with international clientele. Language contract base; courses designed for client needs; experienced staff; residential approach. Participants live and learn English nonstop weekdays and weekends. Classes extend into the community. Extensive diagnosis, ongoing assessment, constant quality control.

Dates: Three-week format (monthly Sep-Apr) in homestay; 5-week format (May-Jun, Jul-Aug) in university residence. **Cost:** Three weeks CAN$3,579; 5 weeks CAN$1,920. Includes tuition, materials, meals, accommodations, and weekend socio-cultural activities. **Contact:** Mrs. Mary E. Murray, Director, Univ. of New Brunswick, English Language Programme, P.O. Box 4400, Fredericton, NB, E3B 5A3, Canada; 506-453-3564, fax 506-453-3578; elp@unb.ca.

Chile

Chilean Universities: Santiago. Based at the Instituto de Estudios Internacionales, the prestigious research institute associated with the Universidad de Chile, our program allows students to take two core classes in Spanish designed to acquaint U.S. undergrads with contemporary Chile. Participants take a wide variety of integrated university classes to complete their enrollment. Independent study/directed research projects available. Students live with host families.

Dates: Spring semester: Mar-Jul, fall semester: Jul-Dec. **Cost:** Semester: fall $7,500; spring $7,800; year $14,000. Includes tuition, housing, and 2 meals daily, orientation, excursions, support services. **Contact:** Cooperating Programs in the Americas, Institute for Study Abroad, 1100 W. 42nd St., Suite 305, Indianapolis, IN 46208-3345; 888-344-9299, fax 317-940-9704; COPA@butler.edu.

Chilean Universities: Valparaíso. In the twin coastal cities of Valparaíso and Viña del Mar, the home to our program, students take integrated classes with Chilean students and live with a host family. Two program classes in Spanish are available to complement UCV's course offerings.

Dates: Spring semester: Mar-Jul, fall semester: Jul-Dec. **Cost:** Spring semester $6,900; fall $7,200; year $13,000. Includes tuition, housing and 2 meals daily, orientation, excursions, support services. **Contact:** Cooperating Programs in the Americas, Institute for Study Abroad, 1100 W. 42nd St., Suite 305, Indianapolis, IN 46208-3345; 888-344-9299, fax 317-940-9704; COPA@butler.edu.

Learn Spanish in Chile. Linguatec offers intensive Spanish language programs for executives, visitors, and international students. Our highly educated and experienced instructors use Linguatec's easy conversational approach to language instruction with groups limited to 4 students, or private classes of up to 7 1/2 hours a day. Biweekly excursions are included and homestays are available.

Dates: Classes begin every Monday, year round. **Cost:** $300 per week for 20 hours of group classes. **Contact:** Bill Arnold, Linguatec Language Center, Los Leones 439, Providencia, Santiago, Chile; 011-56-2-233-4356, fax 011-56-2-234-1380; barnold@linguatec.cl, [www.linguatec.cl].

Spanish and Latin American Studies. Santiago offers intensive language studies fulfilling up to 2 years of university Spanish requirements in 1 semester, with additional courses in literature, business, teacher ed., history, political science. Week-long, program-oriented field trips to the south and north of Chile, homestays, and many university activities at Chilean university.

Dates: Fall semester Aug-Dec, spring semester Jan-May. **Cost:** One semester $3,980; fall and spring semester $6,650. **Contact:** University Studies Abroad Consortium (USAC), Univ. of Nevada, Reno #323, Reno, NV 89557-0093; 775-784-6569, fax 775-784-6010; usac@admin.unr.edu, [www.scsr.nevada.edu/~usac].

China

Chinese Studies (Chengdu). The Chinese Studies Program offers intensive language study fulfilling up to 2 years of university language requirements in 1 semester. Additional courses in art history, economics, anthropology, political science, physics, chemistry, literature, history, and calligraphy are taught in English and offer a multidisciplinary approach to understanding the complexities of China and Asia.

Dates: Summer term: Jun-Aug; fall semester: Aug-Dec, spring semester: Jan-May. **Cost:** Fall or spring semester $4,260; summer term $1,680;

year $6,860. **Contact:** University Studies Abroad Consortium (USAC), Univ. of Nevada, Reno #323, Reno, NV 89557-0093; 775-784-6569, fax 775-784-6010; usac@admin.unr.edu, [www.scsr.nevada.edu/~usac].

Mandarin Program. Elementary, intermediate, and advanced classes are offered for periods ranging from half a year to 2 years. The elementary class offers such major courses as Basic Chinese, Elementary Spoken Chinese, and Listening Comprehension. The intermediate class offers such courses as Intensive Reading, Extensive Reading, Speaking and Listening. A series of selective courses are also offered. **Dates:** Spring semester: late Feb-Jun; fall semester: Sep-Dec. **Cost:** Tuition only: $2,100 per academic year; $1,050 per semester. **Contact:** Zhong Yongqiang, External Affairs Office, Zhongshan Univ., Guangzhou, China; 011- 86-20-84036465, fax 011-86-20-84036860; adeao01@zsulink.zsu.edu.cn, [www.zsu.edu.cn].

Short-Term Chinese Language Program. The short-term Chinese language program requires at least 10 participants. Age limit is from 17 to 60. The length of the program varies from 2-4 weeks. In addition to the study of the Chinese language, the program may also offer lectures on Chinese culture, teach Taijiquan, and offer activities such as visits to the scenic spots, cultural infrastructure, factories, or neighborhoods. **Dates:** Jul 1-30 every summer or contact the External Affairs Office of Zhongshan Univ. to arrange the exact date. **Cost:** Tuition only: $330 for 4 weeks; $195 for 2 weeks; $285 for 3 weeks. **Contact:** Zhong Yongqiang, External Affairs Office, Zhongshan Univ., Guangzhou, China; 011-86-20-84036465, fax 011-86-20-84036860; adeao01@zsulink.zsu.edu.cn, [www.zsu.edu.cn].

Study and Homestay in Central Beijing. Study Mandarin Chinese this summer at Beijing Polytechnic Univ.-Mandarin Training Center. Small classes from beginning to advanced levels and daily tutor. Live with a Chinese family where you will have the opportunity to learn more about authentic Chinese culture. Weekly field trips to Beijing's cultural sites also held. **Dates:** Summer program Jun 20-Aug 20, long-term programs also offered. Autumn term Sep 1-Jan 10; spring term Feb 25-Jul 5. **Cost:** $2,400. Includes tuition, room and board subsidy, and tours. **Contact:** Mr. Jeffrey Hu, Long Tan Bei Li 5-1-1-6, Chong Wen Qu, Beijing 100061, China; 011-8610-6711-5546; jeffreyh@public.fhnet.cn.net.

Colombia

Spanish for Foreigners. Intensive and regular courses at 9 levels for foreigners of all nationalities. We have designed our own textbooks for teaching Spanish in the Colombian context. Cultural activities are included in each course. **Dates:** Year round. **Cost:** $500 each course (120 academic hours). **Contact:** Centro Latinoamericano, Univ. Javeriana, Cr. 10 #65-48, Bogotá, Colombia; dl-clam@javercol.javeriana.edu.co.

Costa Rica

COSI (Costa Rica Spanish Institute). COSI offers high quality instruction at reasonable prices. We offer Spanish classes in San José and at a beautiful national park (beach and rainforest). Homestay is also available. Volunteer work opportunities and special discounts in tours. **Dates:** Year round. **Cost:** Prices start at $280 per week including classes in groups of maximum 5 students, homestay, cultural activities, books, access to email, airport pickup. **Contact:** COSI, P.O. Box 1366-2050, San Pedro, San José, Costa Rica; 011-506-234-1001, fax 011-506-253-2117. From U.S. 800-771-5184; cosicr@sol.racsa.co.cr, [www.cosi.co.cr].

Costa Rican Language Academy. Costa Rican-owned and operated language school offers first-rate Spanish instruction in a warm and friendly environment. Teachers with university degrees. Small groups or private classes. Included free in the programs are airport transportation, coffee and natural refreshments, excursions, Latin dance, Costa Rican cooking, music, and conversation classes to provide students with complete cultural immersion. **Dates:** Year round (start anytime). **Cost:** $135 per week or $220 per week for program with homestay. All other activities and services included at no additional cost. **Contact:** Costa Rican Language Academy, P.O. Box 336-2070, San José, Costa Rica; 011-506-221-1624 or 011-506-233-8914 or 011-233-8938, fax 011-506-233-8670. In the U.S.: 800-854-6057; crlang@sol.racsa.co.cr, [www.crlang.co.cr/index.html].

Enjoy Learning Spanish Faster. Techniques developed from our ongoing research enable students at Centro Linguistico Latinoamericano to learn more, faster, in a comfortable environment. Classes are 2-5 students plus group learning activities; conversations with middle-class homestay families (1 student per family).

Homestays are within walking distance of school in small town (14,000 population) near the capital, San Jose.

Dates: Year round. Classes begin every Monday, at all levels (except Apr 17-21 and Dec 18-29). **Cost:** $345 per week for 28 hours of classes. Includes tuition, all meals (7 days a week), homestay, laundry, all materials, Costa Rican dance and cooking classes, weekly 3-hour cultural tours, and airport transportation. $25 one-time registration. **Contact:** Susan Shores, Registrar, Latin American Language Center, PMB 123, 7485 Rush River Dr., Suite 710, Sacramento, CA 95831; 916-447-0938, fax 916-428-9542; lalc@madre.com.

Immerse Yourself in Spanish. La Escuela De Idiomas D'Amore offers intensive immersion programs and homestay to students from over 30 countries. Founded in 1992, we are the original beach school and campus in Costa Rica. While our experience sets us apart from the rest, your experience is most important to us.

Dates: Year round. **Cost:** $805-$1,540. **Contact:** La Escuela De Idiomas D'Amore, P.O. Box 67, Quepos, Costa Rica; 011-506-777-1143; damore@sol.racsa.co.cr, [www.escueladamore.com]. In U.S. 323-912-0600.

Instituto de Lenguaje "Pura Vida." Only minutes from the capital in the fresh mountain air of Heredia. Intense total immersion methods of teaching. Morning classes and daily cultural activities all conducted in Spanish, maximum 5 students per class. Teachers hold university degrees. Latin music and dance lessons, tours, trips, parties. Learn Spanish fast.

Dates: Classes for all levels start every Monday year round. **Cost:** Language only, 20 hours per week $230; total immersion, 35 hours per week with homestay $370; children's classes with homestay $370 per week, daycare available. **Contact:** Instituto de Lenguaje "Pura Vida," P.O. Box 730, Garden Grove, CA 92842; 714-534-0125, fax 714-534-1201; BS7324@aol.com, [www.costaricaspanish.com].

Intensive Spanish and Homestay. Intercultura Costa Rica offers intensive university accredited Spanish courses. Homestays available. Volunteer programs, beach and city campuses, emphasis on individual attention. Caring, multilingual staff. Located in university town close to the capital. Daily Latin dance classes, weekly cooking, music, indigenous culture, and other classes.

Dates: Year round. **Cost:** $1,045 per month includes classes, homestay and activities (shorter stays available). In 2000, approx. a 5 percent increase expected. **Contact:** Laura Ellington, Intercultura Costa Rica, Language Center, P.O. Box 1952-3000, Heredia, Costa Rica; 011-506-260-8480, Tel./fax 011-506-260-9243; info@spanish-intercultura.com, [www.spanish-intercultura.com].

Intensive Spanish Training. The Institute for Central American Development Studies (ICADS) offers 4-week progressive programs in intensive Spanish language—4 1/2 hours daily, 5 days a week. Small classes (4 or fewer students). Activities and optional afternoon internships emphasize environmental issues, women's issues, development, human rights, and public health. Supportive learning environment. Homestays and field trips. Great alternative for the socially conscious.

Dates: Programs begin first Monday of each month. **Cost:** $1,400 includes airport pick-up, classes, books, homestay, meals, laundry, lectures, activities, field trips, and internship placements. **Contact:** ICADS, Dept. 826, P.O. Box 025216, Miami, FL 33102-5216; 011-506-225-0508, fax 011-506-234-1337; icads@netbox.com, [www.icadscr.com].

Spanish and More in Heredia. Heredia offers intensive language studies which fulfills up to 2-year university Spanish requirements in a semester or 1 year in the 8-week summer program. Additional courses offered in political science, history, biology, teacher ed., business, literature, etc. Program organized week-long and weekend field trips, homestays, and many local university activities.

Dates: Fall semester: Aug-Dec (1999), spring semester: Jan-May (2000), summer sessions: May 28-Jul 2, Jun 25-Aug 1, Jul 30-Aug 29. **Cost:** Fall or spring semester $4,620; year $7,600; Jun or Jul $1,980; Aug $1,610; Jun and Jul $3,680; June/July, and Aug $3,190; Jun, Jul, and Aug $4,680. **Contact:** University Studies Abroad Consortium (USAC), Univ. of Nevada, Reno #323, Reno, NV 89557-0093; 775-784-6569, fax 775-784-6010; usac@admin.unr.edu, [www.scsr.nevada.edu/~usac].

Spanish and More in Puntarenas. Puntarenas offers intensive language studies which fulfills up to 2-year university Spanish requirements in a semester or 1 year in the 8-week summer program. Additional courses offered in political science, history, biology, teacher ed., business, literature, etc. Program organized week-long and weekend field trips, homestays, and many local university activities.

Dates: Fall semester: Aug-Dec; spring semester: Jan-May. **Cost:** Fall or spring semester $4,620; year $7,600. **Contact:** University Studies Abroad Consortium (USAC), Univ. of Nevada, Reno #323, Reno, NV 89557-0093; 775-784-6569, fax 775-784-6010; usac@admin.unr.edu, [www.scsr.nevada.edu/~usac].

Spanish Immersion Program. Nestled in colonial Barva, equidistant from Heredia's National Univ. and surrounding mountains, Escuela Latina offers an intensive, experience-based Spanish language and culture program. Students live in nearby homestays. Classes (max. 6 students) are taught entirely in Spanish. Dance, music, and cooking classes included in tuition. Volunteer opportunities offered.

Dates: Classes begin every Monday. **Cost:** $1,095 for 4 weeks including homestay. **Contact:** Jill Dewey, Apdo. 203-3000, Heredia, Costa Rica; 011-506-237-5709, fax 011-506-261-5233; eslatina@amerisol.cr. In the U.S.: Roger Dewey, 970-242-6960, fax 970-242-6967.

Spanish Intensive Courses. We offer highly qualified and professional Spanish courses with tours to fascinating sites (optional) and family homestay. Our total immersion programs are possible for all knowledge levels. In addition, we offer professional practical works (internships) to all our Spanish course graduates. The Instituto de Español "Costa Rica" awaits you.

Dates: New courses start every Monday year round. **Cost:** From $242 with homestay. **Contact:** Ms. Sabina de Serrano, Instituto de Español "Costa Rica," P. O. Box 1405-2100 Guadalupe, San José, Costa Rica; Tel./fax 011-506-2834733; iespcr@sol.racsa.co.cr, [www.intensivespanish.com].

Spanish Language Program. Twenty hours of small group instruction, maximum 4 students per class, Monday-Friday. All ages and all levels. Each student takes an oral and written exam and is placed at a level that matches his/her knowledge. Students live with a Costa Rican family. Organized activities are part of the program.

Dates: Courses start every Monday of the year. **Cost:** Four-week program $1,260: host family stay, language classes 4 hours per day, 5 days a week. (Also 1-week, 2-week, or 3-week program.) **Contact:** Guiselle Ballestero, Sonia Rojas, Ronny Garcia; 011-506-458-3157, fax 011-506-458-3214; [www.institutodecultura.com].

Univ. Nacional Autónoma. Costa Rica is exceptional for its political stability and environmental sensitivity. Our undergraduate program at Universidad Nacional Autónoma allows participants to enroll in both program classes and regular university courses while living with local host families. Many extracurricular activities are available through the University. All coursework is in Spanish.

Dates: Spring semester: Feb-Jun, fall semester: Jul-Dec. **Cost:** Semester: fall $6,295; spring $6,695; year $12,590. Includes tuition, housing, 3 meals daily, orientation, excursions, support services. **Contact:** Cooperating Programs in the Americas, Institute for Study Abroad, 1100 W. 42nd St., Suite 305, Indianapolis, IN 46208-3345; 888-344-9299, fax 317-940-9704; COPA@butler.edu.

Denmark

Intensive Danish Language Courses. Danish study at 11 levels, 9 hours per week.

Dates: Year round. **Cost:** Residents free; visitors $10 per hour. **Contact:** K.I.S.S. Danish Language School, Norrebrogade 32, DK-2200 Copenhagen N, Denmark; 011-45-35362555; kiss.sprogskole@get2net.dk

The Kalo School of Languages. Danish folk high school where foreigners learn Danish and Danes learn foreign languages. No exams but a lot of learning—about language, culture, history, etc. Full room and board.

Dates: Feb 27-Jul 1. **Cost:** $875 per week. Additional costs: materials DKR1,700, excursions DKR650, trip DKR2,000. **Contact:** The Kalo School of Languages, Skouridervej 1, DK 8410 Ronde, DK; adm@kalo-adm.dk, [www.kalo.dk].

Ecuador

Academia de Español Mitad del Mundo. A simple, modern, and efficient teaching method in which students are encouraged to use commonly used written and spoken expressions. We cater both for a broad range of interests—including society, culture, politics, history, and the economy—as well as particular specializations for all ages and all levels.

Dates: Year round. **Cost:** One-to-one classes: $6 per hour. Accommodations with families: $15 per day. Incription: $20. **Contact:** Sylvia Paucar, Academia de Español "Mitad del Mundo," Gustavo Darquea Terán 0e2-58 y Versalles, Ecuador; 011-593 2-567875/546827/ 567875; mitmund1@mitadmundo.com.ec, [www.pub.ecua.net.ec/mitadmundo].

Academia de Español Quito. Specially designed programs for foreign students. One-on-one instruction up to 7 hours daily. Courses based on conversation, vocabulary, and grammar at all levels. Cultural and social activities provided weekly. The system is self-paced, and it is possible to start at any time. Earn academic credits. Live with an Ecuadorian family, 1 student per family, full board.

Dates: Year round. **Cost:** $1,600 for 4 weeks includes tuition, meals, housing, fees, airport transfer. **Contact:** Edgar J. Alvarez, Director, 130 Marchena St. and 10 de Agosto Ave., P.O. Box 17-15-0039-C, Quito, Ecuador; 011-593-2-553647/554811, fax 011-593-2-506474/504330; edalvare@pi.pro.ec, [www.academiaquito.com.ec].

Academia Latinoamericana. Proud to be the friendliest Spanish school you have ever known. Family owned and operated. The program offers language study at 9 levels, for complete beginners through advanced. Experienced staff, native Ecuadorians. Carefully selected host families within walking distance of school. Exclusive "SierrAzul Cloud Forest and Galapagos" extension program, volunteer program. U.S. college credit available.

Dates: Year round. **Cost:** $230 per week. Includes 20 hours of lessons, 7 days with host family, 2 meals per day, transfer, services at the school, and teaching material. **Contact:** Suzanne S. Bell, Admissions Director, USA/International, 640 East 3990 South, Suite E, Salt Lake City, UT, 84107; 801-268-4608, fax 801-265-9156; academia@juno.com, delco@spanish.com.ec.

Individual Spanish Lessons. Study at Simon Bolivar Spanish school, rated one of the top schools in Ecuador by members of the South American Explorers Club. We offer courses at the coast and in Quito. In addition we have group lessons.

Dates: Year round. **Cost:** From $120 per week for individual lessons. **Contact:** Escuela de Espanol, Simon Bolivar, Calle Leonidas Plaza 353 y Roca, Quito, Ecuador; 011-593-2-236688; info@simon-bolivar.com, [www.simon-bolivar.com].

Spanish in the Middle of the World. Spanish Institute offers the opportunity of learning the language and culture while enjoying the wonderful weather and landscape of 0 degrees latitude. One-on-one and group courses to fit all needs. Accommodation facilities in Ecuadorian homes or dormitories. English teachers may have a job while learning a second language.

Dates: Classes start on Monday year round (except holidays). **Cost:** $5 per hour includes texts, workbook, language lab, teaching aids, completion diploma. **Contact:** Benedict Schools of Languages, Edmundo Chiriboga, N47-133y Jorge Paez, Quito, Ecuador; fax 011-593-2-432729, 011-593-2-462972; benedict@accessinter.net, info@quitospanish.com, [www.quitospanish.com].

Egypt

The American Univ. in Cairo. Intensive Arabic study of modern standard and Egyptian colloquial for a year, semester, and summer. All levels from elementary to advanced are given in this intensive, full-time program. Course-related travel is included.

Dates: Sep-Jan; Jan-Jun; Jun-Jul. **Cost:** Year $11,005, semester $5,520, summer $2,733. Tuition and fees only. **Contact:** Matrans Davidson, The American Univ. in Cairo, 420 5th Ave., 3rd Fl., New York, NY 10018-2729; aucegypt@aucnyo.edu, [www.aucegypt.edu].

Arabic as a Second Language. Egyptian colloquial and modern standard Arabic, semi-intensive (4 days per week), intensive summer school (5 days per week). Study 1 or both disciplines. Full details on web site or brochure by mail.

Dates: Monthly, Jan-Dec. **Cost:** ECA $185 per month, MSA $230 per month; both $410 per month. **Contact:** Tina Holdrup, ILI, P.O. Box 13, 12411 Embaba, Cairo, Egypt; 011-202-3463087, fax 011-202-3035624; ili@starnet.com.eg, [www.ili.com.eg].

El Salvador

Melida Anaya Montes Spanish School. The MAM Spanish School offers intensive courses at all levels, utilizing popular education techniques and participatory methodology. An integral part of the program includes participation in afternoon meetings with popular organizations, excursions to developing communities and other places of interest, and housing with Salvadoran families with diverse interests. Volunteer opportunities also available.

Dates: Classes begin the 1st and 3rd Monday of every month, except on national holidays (Easter week, May 1, Jun 22, 1st week of Aug, Sep 15, Nov 2, and Christmas and New Year's week). **Cost:** Weekly costs: Spanish classes $100, administrative fee $12.50, political-cultural program $25, room and board $60. **Contact:** CIS MAM Language School, Boulevard Universitario, Casa #4, San Salvador, El Salvador, Centro America; Tel./fax 011-503-226-2623; cis@netcomsa.com.

Europe

¿?don Quijote In-Country Spanish Language Schools. Offers Spanish language courses in our 6 schools in Spain and 5 partner schools in Latinoamerica. Our courses (standard, intensive, business, D.E.L.E., tourism, flight attendants and refresher for teachers) are all year round, from 2 weeks on. Students can combine different cities and schools. Academic credit is available.
Dates: Year round—fall, spring, winter, and summer, 2 weeks to a full year of study. **Cost:** Email or check web site for details. **Contact:** ¿?don Quijote In-Country Spanish Language Schools, calle/Placentinos n°2, Salamanca 37008, Spain; 011-34-923-268860, fax 011-34-923-268815; amusa@donquijote.org, [www.donquijote.org].

Language and Cultural Immersion. Language programs including a choice of accommodations, meal options, and a full schedule of cultural activities.
Dates: Year round start dates (short- or long-term programs available). **Cost:** Prices start at $500 for a 2-week program. **Contact:** Margot Haldenby, Languages Plus International Education, Alderly House, 317 Adelaide St. W., Suite 900, Toronto, ON, H5V 1P9; 416-925-7117 or (U.S./Canada) 888-526-4758; langplus@inforamp.net, [www.languagesplus.com].

Language, Arts, and Sports. Active learning vacations: French, Spanish, Italian, Portuguese; cooking, painting, drawing, photography workshops. Combine eduVacational interests. French and sailing or skiing; Spanish and golf; bicycle tours—more countries, more ideas. We match individual needs and interests with programs and options: family stay, apartment, hotel; intensive to total immersion; small groups or study and live in your teacher's home.
Dates: Programs run from 1 week to months. **Cost:** Includes room and board, tuition. **Contact:** Mary Ann Puglisi, eduVacations[sm], 1431 21st St. NW, Suite 302, Washington, DC 20036; 202-857-8384, fax 202-463-8091.

Learn French in France, Monaco, or Switzerland. Language immersion courses in France (Paris, Nice, Aix-en-Provence, Antibes, Bordeaux, Cannes, Monaco, Montpellier, Tours); Monaco (Monte Carlo); or Switzerland (Lausanne). Private language schools with programs for adults, senior citizens, and teenagers. Centrally located, convenient to interesting places, cultural events, sports activities. Programs feature qualified teachers, small classes, attractive surroundings and facilities. Affordable prices for instruction. Accommodations with French, Monegasque or Swiss families with meals, student residences, apartments, and nearby hotels.
Dates: Year round. Two weeks or more. **Cost:** Two-week courses with or without accommodations range from $605 to $2,260. **Contact:** Ms. Lorraine Haber, Study Abroad Coordinator, Embassy CES Study Abroad Programs, The Center for English Studies, 330 7th Ave., 6th Fl., New York, NY 10001; 212-629-7300, fax 212-736-7950; cesnewyork@cescorp.com.

Learn German in Germany, Austria, or Switzerland. Language immersion courses in Germany (Berlin, Freiburg, Stuttgart, Munich, Hamburg, Wiesbaden, Frankfurt); Austria (Vienna); or Switzerland (Zurich). Private language schools with programs for adults, senior citizens, and teenagers. Centrally located, convenient to interesting places, cultural events, sports activities. Programs feature qualified teachers, small classes, attractive surroundings and facilities. Affordable prices for instruction. Accommodations with German, Austrian, or Swiss families with meals, student residences, apartments, and nearby hotels.
Dates: Year round. Two weeks or more. **Cost:** Two-week courses with or without accommodations range from $465-$1,355. **Contact:** Ms. Lorraine Haber, Study Abroad Coordinator, Embassy CES Study Abroad Programs, The Center for English Studies, 330 7th Ave., 6th Fl., New York, NY 10001; 212-629-7300, fax 212-736-7950; cesnewyork@cescorp.com.

Learn on Location. Language courses for revision, business, or leisure in France, Germany, Italy, Portugal, and Spain. All ages, all levels.
Dates: Year round from 1 or 2 weeks or longer. **Cost:** Contact sponsor. **Contact:** Euro-Academy Ltd., 77A George St., Croydon CR0 1LD, England; 011-44-181-680-4618, fax 011-44-181-681-850; euroacademy@brinternet.com.

France

Academic Excellence in Intimate Groups. Study and live in the Loire Valley, at CLE, a leading private institute for French studies since 1985. Short- and long-term intensive courses in a restored 18th century building in historic Tours. Maximum of 7 students per class. Professionally trained teachers. Top-quality homestay, hotels, apartments. Minimum age 18.

Dates: Year round. **Cost:** Tuition FF1,700 per week. Family stay FF950 per week. **Contact:** Isabelle or Hervé Aubert, Owners and Managers, CLE, 7-9 place de Châteauneuf, 37000 Tours, France; 011-33-247-64-06-19, fax 011-33-247-05-84-61; info@cle.fr, [www.cle.fr].

College Cevenol International. College Cevenol, a French Lyceé in the Cevennes mountains (Le Chambon), offers a summer International Work Camp (students 18-25) and an intensive course in French Language and Culture (14-18) with field trips and recreational opportunities. Two years French required U.S. students may also attend the academic year (1-3 trimesters) enrolling in special French and courses leading to the Baccalaureate.

Dates: Work camp and summer school: Aug 2-21, Academic year: Sep-Jun. **Cost:** Work camp $150; summer school $1,200; academic year $9,500. **Contact:** Meg Warren, U.S. Representative, American Friends of College Cevenol, 41 Longfellow Ave., Brunswick, ME 04011; meg_warren@hotmail.com.

Français General et de Specialité. Courses for adults who need to express themselves with the greatest possible fluency, whether for leisure or professional purposes. General French, commercial and business French, language and culture courses are available. One to 14 weeks, 4 lessons or more per day in small groups. Extracurricular activities: cooking, wine tasting, painting, golf, tennis, excursions.

Dates: Every second Monday from Jan 3. **Cost:** From FF3,500 for 2 weeks. **Contact:** Astrid Giorgetta, IS, Aix-en-Provence, 9 Cours des Arts et Mètiers, Aix-en-Provence 13100, France; 011-33-4-42-93-47-90, fax 011-33-4-42-26-31-80; is.aix@pacwan.fr, [www.is-aix.com].

France Langue Paris and Nice. Close to the Champs Elysées, Paris, or the Mediterranean. The Ecole France Langue in Paris and Nice offers you both the language and culture of France. There are classes for all ages and levels, specialty classes (business, tourism, etc.), and custom designed classes for teachers and students offered. Language certification and university credit available as are free weekly cultural activities. Accommodations arranged by the school.

Dates: Year round. Enrollment every Monday. **Cost:** Contact for information. **Contact:** Mr. De Poly, France Langue, 22 ave. Notre Dame, 06000 Nice, France; frlang_n@club-internet.fr.

French Courses. Inlingua Rouen can offer you the French language program that you need. From business and specific language courses to French and cookery and holiday courses. Groups and individual bookings.

Dates: Year round. **Cost:** From FF2,800 per week (1999). **Contact:** Mrs. Eleri Maitland, Inlingua Rouen, BP 156, 76144 Le Petit Quevilly, Cedex, France; rouen@inlingua.fr, [www.inlingua.fr/rouen].

French Courses for Foreigners. The Institute has more than 20 years of experience in teaching French as a foreign language. Students of any age over 16 are accepted. The courses combine practical French language learning with interesting social activities and excursions. The Institute arranges accommodations with families, in a student residence, or in apartments or hotels.

Dates: Year round. **Cost:** $210 per week **Contact:** Actilangue, Ecole Privée de Langue Française, 2, rue Alexis Mossa, 06000 Nice, France; 011-33-493-96-33-84, fax 011-33-493-44-37-16; actilang@imaginet.fr.

French Courses in Montpellier. Summer Courses in French language, literature, and culture, all levels, 21 hours per week. Cultural activities. Three options for accommodations. Year round courses. General French, homestay, and half-board. Teacher-training sessions Jul-Aug. Other dates on request. Language, tourism, and culture for groups of youngsters (ages 13-18).

Dates: Summer courses: Jun 2- Sep 30, 2-16 weeks. Year round courses: Oct 1-May 31, 2 weeks plus. **Cost:** Please ask for our brochure as costs vary depending on length of stay, choice of program, and type of accommodations. **Contact:** Gérard Ribot, Director of Studies, or Sophie Favre-Gilly, Assistant, Espace Universitaire Albert Camus, 21 ave. du Professeur Grasset, 34093 Montpellier Cedex 5, France; 011-33-467-91-70-00, fax 011-33-467-91-70-01; imef@fle.fr, [www.fle.fr/imef].

French in France. Among the ways to learn French, total immersion is the most enjoyable and the most effective. We have been doing it for 20 years in a small historical city located in Normandy (west of Paris, close to the seaside).

We welcome people at any age and any level in 1- to 10-week programs, intensive or vacation type, from mid-Mar to mid-Nov.

Dates: Spring: Mar 20-May 27; summer: Jun 12-Aug 26; fall: Sep 4-Nov 11. **Cost:** From $525 per week (tuition, room and board, and excursions). **Contact:** Dr. Alméras, Chairman, French American Study Center, 12, 14, Blvd. Carnot, B.P. 4176, 14104 Lisieux Cedex, France; 011-33-2-31-31-22-01, fax 011-33-2-31-31-22-21; centre.normandie@wanadoo.fr, [http://perso.wanadoo.fr/centre.normandie/].

French in the Mediterranean. Standard course, intensive course, DEFL exam preparation, business French, one-to-one tuition. Workshops. Small classes of 3-8 students. All levels from beginner to advanced. Carefully chosen accommodation options (host families, student residences, apartments, hotels). Cultural activities. Beautiful location in 18th century private mansion in historic center.

Dates: Year round. Start every Monday. **Cost:** From FF1,400 per week. **Contact:** Institut Linguistique Adenet (I.L.A.), 33, Grand Rue Jean Moulin, 34000 Montpellier, France; 011-33-4-67-60-67-83, fax 011-33-4-67-60-67-81; ila.france@mnet.fr, [www.ila-france.com].

French Language and Cooking. Live and study in 18th century Château de Mâtel. Adult residential courses in French language and French country cooking in a relaxed, convivial atmosphere. Small classes and quality teaching. Reasonable prices. Comfortable single, twin rooms. Good food and wine taken with teachers. Heart of Burgundy, Beaujolais, and Lyons area. Access to the world via Internet and computer.

Dates: Every Sunday May-Nov. **Cost:** From $820 full board and classes in château. **Contact:** Michael Giammarella in U.S.: 800-484-1234 ext 0096 or Ecole des Trois Ponts, Château de Mâtel, 42300 Roanne, France; 011-33-477-70-80-01, fax 011-33-477-71-5300; info@3ponts.edu, [www.3ponts.edu].

French Language Learning Vacations. Learn French while discovering the chateaux of the Loire Valley, the secrets of Provence, or the sandy beaches of the Mediterranean. Our programs are designed for independent travelers sharing a passion for the French culture and lifestyle. We offer a choice of locations in Tours, Aix-en-Provence, Montpellier, Paris, or Nice.

Dates: Two or more weeks year round. **Cost:** Two-week packages range from $825-$1,265. Includes classes, housing and fees. **Contact:** Jim Pondolfino, French-American Exchange, 111 Roberts Court, Box 7, Alexandria, VA 22314; 800-995-5087, fax 703-549-2865; faetours@erols.com, [www.faetours.com].

French Studies (Pau). Pau offers intensive language studies—up to 4 semesters of university language courses in 1 semester, 1 year in the 8-week summer program, in addition to art, political science, history, literature, second language teaching methods, etc. Week-long field trips to Paris, homestay or student residence, and many activities at the French university.

Dates: Summer terms: May 27-Jun 27; Jun 27-Aug 1; Jul 31-Aug 23; fall semester: Sep-Dec; spring semester: Jan-April. **Cost:** Fall or spring semester $4,280; Jun $1,770; Jul $1,880; Aug $1,580; Jun and Jul $3,480; Jun and Aug $2,870; Jul and Aug $2,970; Jun, Jul, and Aug $4,580; year $6,980. **Contact:** University Studies Abroad Consortium (USAC), Univ. of Nevada, Reno #323, Reno, NV 89557-0093; 775-784-6569, fax 775-784-6010; usac@admin.unr.edu, [www.scsr.nevada.edu/~usac].

Immersion Course in French. Intensive 2-4 week course for professional adults in Villefranche (next to Nice) overlooking the French Riviera's most beautiful bay; 8 hours a day with 2 meals. Audiovisual classes, language lab, practice sessions, discussion-lunch. Evening film showings, evening outings with teachers, excursions to cultural landmarks. Accommodations in comfortable private apartments.

Dates: Courses start Jan, Feb, Mar, May, Jun, Aug, Sep, Oct, Nov, Dec. **Cost:** Tuition fees: Dec-Apr FF14,100/4 weeks; May-Nov FF16,700/4 weeks. Accommdations: Dec-Apr FF2,000-FF5,200/4 week; May-Nov FF2,300-FF5,800/4 weeks. **Contact:** Frédéric Latty, Institut de Francais, 23, avenue General Leclerc, 06230 Villefranche Sur Mer, France; 011-33-493-01-88-44, fax 011-33-493-76-92-17; instfran@aol.com, [www.institutdefrancais.com].

Live and Learn French. Live with a carefully selected, welcoming French family in the Paris region. Learn from a family member/teacher who has a university degree and will tailor a private course to suit your needs. Share in a cultural and learning experience that will develop both your understanding of the language and the people who speak it. Minimum of 1 week stay. We also offer touristic stays in English or French.

Dates: Year round. **Cost:** Fifteen hours of study per week $1,190; 20 hours of study per week $1,350. Two people $1,730 per week.

Prices include room, 3 meals a day, and instruction. **Contact:** Sara S. Monick, Live & Learn, 4215 Poplar Dr., Minneapolis, MN 55422; 612-374-2444, fax 612-333-3554; DHILLI608@aol.com.

Perpignan Summer Language School. Located in sunny Perpignan, summer language school allows students to enjoy the Mediterranean Sea and Pyrenees mountains. All levels. Fifteen students per group, minimum age 16, 24 hours a week, choice of 2-, 3-, 4-, 8-, 10-week courses. Specialized French for diplomacy, exam center for Delf and Delf, Paris Chamber of Comerce exam center: Tourrs and Coulece and Ecouduey.

Dates: Jun, Jul, Aug, Sep, all year. **Cost:** Tuition and room, 3 weeks, FF5,350. **Contact:** Patrick Bellegarde, Université d'été de Perpignan, 52 ave. de Villeneuve, 66860 Perpignan cedex; 011-33-468-666050, fax 011-33-468-660376; ue@univ_perp.fr.

Sejours Linguistiques en France. Intensive French course on the Univ. campus of Montpellier-Mediterranean (literature, civilization, grammar, conversation, drama) plus activities with French natives (beach excursions, guided tours, wine tasting, conferences).

Dates: Jul-Aug. **Cost:** $333 per week inclusive (classes, activities, room and board). **Contact:** A.P.R.E.-Institut Cultural Francais, BP 5032, 34032 Montpellier, France; 011-33-4-6772-2277, fax 011-33-4-6779-1528; etudesfr@aol.com.

Stage Intensif Langue/Culture. The French Traveler offers 2-week workshops for French teachers in France each July. Theme courses about French life and society in mornings, related cultural excursions in the afternoon; optional homestay available. Change of city in each workshop. Graduate credit. French only spoken.

Dates: July 2000. **Cost:** $1,850. Airfare and 1 meal per day not included. **Contact:** Valerie Sutter, The French Traveler, 206 Claflin St., Belmont, MA 02478; 800-251-3464; frenchtraveler@juno.com.

Germany

Collegium Palatinum Heidelberg. A German language institute located in downtown Heidelberg offering German at all levels from beginner to advanced. Forty years of language teaching experience. Two-, 4-, and 8-week courses year round. Combination courses, one-on-one tuition, and customized courses for groups. Recreational and cultural program. Accommodations: residential, guest-family, private arrangement, or hotel.

Dates: Year round. **Cost:** Twenty-four hours tuition and accommodations in double rooms in student residence: DM465/EUR236 per week. **Contact:** Mrs. Martine Berthet-Richter, Adenauerplatz 8, D-69115 Heidelberg, Germany; 011-49-6221-436289, fax 011-49-6221-182023; schillerUS@aol.com.

Europa-Kolleg Kassel. Language, culture, life in the heart of Germany. Study with efficient, experienced, dynamic teachers. Stay with a carefully selected, friendly family. Participate in our varied and extensive extracurricular program. Enjoy the city of Kassel: Large enough to be fun, small enough to be safe—where people speak standard German.

Dates: Year round. Summer courses: Jun-Sep. **Cost:** $410 per week includes tuition and materials, extracurricular program, room and partial board (30 meals per week). Inquire about fees for college credit. **Contact:** Prof. K.E. Kuhn-Osius, 238 W. 106 St., Apt. 4A, New York, NY 10025; Tel./fax 212-865-7332; ekuhnos@shiva.hunter.cuny.edu.

Germalingua - Study German. Study German in Munich at the Germalingua language school. In our courses you will have fun in learning with young and professional teachers.

Dates: Courses begin every Monday (for beginners every 4 weeks). **Cost:** The longer you stay, the cheaper it is. Prices include registration fee, course book, arrangement of accommodations, and a course certificate. **Contact:** Germalingua-Meierhofer, Rablstr. 48, D-81669, Muenchen, Germany; 011-49-17-28-54-15-12, fax 011-49-89-48-99-79-15; germalingua@t-online.de, [www.germalingua.com].

German Courses in Freiburg. German language courses for 4 types of clients: university students, adults and business people, juniors. German teachers. Short- and long-term courses, various levels, courses throughout the year, accommodations in host families, private rooms, or residences.

Dates: Starting dates for courses for adults and business people twice a month, starting dates for university students vary. **Cost:** Adults and business people 2 weeks DM995; university students 12 weeks DM2,050 (shorter courses vary); teacher training course 4 weeks DM2,160. **Contact:** International House Freiburg, Esther Muschelknautz, Werderring 18, Freiburg, 79098

Germany; 011-49-761-34751, fax 011-49-761-382476; ihfreiburg@ihfreiburg.toplink.de, [www.ihfreiburg.toplink.de].

German Language Course in Hamburg. Colón Language Center, founded in 1952, is an excellent institute in the city center of Hamburg. An average of approx. 500 students learn German at any given time. Tuition can be combined with accommodations in Hamburg. Additional leisure program. Learn German and discover Hamburg.

Dates: Students with prior knowledge can start any Monday, real beginners start once per month (please ask for details). **Cost:** Intensive course (25 lessons per week) DM805 per month. **Contact:** Ms. Monika Tibes, Ms. Karen Pfeiffer, Colón Language Center, Colonnaden 96, 20354 Hamburg, Germany; 011-49-40-345850, fax 011-49-40-346854; colon@csi.com, [www.colon-language-center.de].

German Studies: Lüneburg. Intensive language study—up to 2 years of university language requirements in 1 semester. Additional courses in history, political science, culture, literature, etc. Program-organized field trips and housing. Beautiful city only 30 minutes from Hamburg.

Dates: Summer term: May 22-Jun 25 and Jun 21-Jul 24; fall semester: Aug-Dec; spring semester: Jan-May. **Cost:** One semester $3,960; fall and spring semester $5,980; summer term $1,760 per session, $2,990 both sessions. **Contact:** University Studies Abroad Consortium (USAC), Univ. of Nevada, Reno #323, Reno, NV 89557-0093; 775-784-6569, fax 775-784-6010; usac@admin.unr.edu, [www.scsr.nevada.edu/~usac].

Learn German and Discover Berlin. GLS is one of the leading institutions teaching German as a foreign language in Germany. GLS offers various levels of German all year round (age 16 and up), preparation for all language certificates, business German, German for bankers, lawyers. Special feature: internships in German companies.

Dates: Year round. **Cost:** Contact school for details. **Contact:** GLS Sprachenzentrum, Barbara Jaeschke, Managing Director, Kolonnenstrasse 26, 10829 Berlin, Germany; 011-49-30-780-08-90; fax 011-49-30-787-41-92; gls.berlin@t-online.de, [www.gls-berlin.com].

Semesters in Munich or Magdeburg. Fall semester in the heart of the Bavarian capital. Germans teach humanities and social science classes in English. Extended tour of Germany, Austria, and the Czech Republic. Language intensive. Spring term at the Universität in Magdeburg. Participants must come with equivalent of four college-level German classes. Housing in dorms. Classes offered *Deutsch als Fremdsprache.* Tour to Berlin, Eisenach, the Harz, etc.

Dates: Sep 1-Dec 15 for Munich; Feb 5-May 12 for Magdeburg. **Cost:** Approx. $5,350-$5,650 (for Wisconsin residents; tuition surcharge for out-of-staters), room and board, group travel, airfare, etc. **Contact:** International Programs, Univ. of Wisconsin-Stevens Point, 2100 Main St., Stevens Point, WI 54481; 715-346-2717, fax 715-346-3591; intlprog@uwsp.edu, [www.uwsp.edu/acad/internat].

Greece

Greek Language. Program of Greek language and culture courses. Ten or 20 hours per week.

Dates: Year round. **Cost:** DR 140,000. **Contact:** Aristoteleio, Univ. of Thessaloniki, School of Modern Greek Language, GR 54006, Thessaloniki, Greece; 011-3031-997571/997572, fax 011-3031-997573; thkaldi@ccf.auth.gr.

Intensive Modern Greek Language. Beginning, intermediate, and advanced levels of modern Greek classes meet for a total of 60 hours of intensive exercises and instruction in speaking, vocabulary, role-playing, grammar, reading, and writing. Held on the island of Paros.

Dates: Jun-Jul. **Cost:** $1,750. Includes tuition, course materials, housing. **Contact:** College Year in Athens, North American Office, Dept. T, P.O. Box 390890, Cambridge, MA 02139-0010; 617-868-8200, fax 617-868-8207; cyathens@aol.com.

Modern Greek Language. The modern Greek language program is a comprehensive, integrated approach to learning modern Greek. Courses are year round, and include beginning through advanced proficiency levels. The syllabus has been created to teach the language to adults of all nationalities, using textbooks developed at the Center. Classes are small, with an average of 8-12 participants in each course. Three-week summer courses in July on the island of Spetses.

Dates: Year round, new courses begin every month. **Cost:** $600 per 60-hour course. **Contact:** Rosemary Donnelly, Program Director, 48 Archimidous St., Athens 116 36, Greece; 011-301-701-5242, fax 011-30-1701-8603; athenscr@compulink.gr.

Guatemala

Academia de Español San José el Viejo. We offer one-on-one Spanish instruction in one of Guatemala's most respected, professional, and beautiful schools. Our "manos abiertas" policy is to open our hands and hearts to people of the world interested in our culture, history, and the Spanish language.

Dates: Every Monday (or Tue-Sat) year round. **Cost:** $185 per week. Includes private tutor, homestay, and meals in a Guatemalan home. School only: (full day 6 1/2 hours) $100 per week; 4 hours a.m. or p.m. $75; 2 hours p.m. $45. Casitas and rooms $210-$320 (sleeps 1-4) set in beautiful gardens with swimming pool, tennis court. **Contact:** Joan Ashton, P.O. Box 1218, Crystal Bay, NV 89402-1218; 800-JOANASH (562-6274), Tel./fax 775-832-5678; joanash@aol.com or (allow 6 weeks if writing to Guatemala): Academia San José el Viejo, 5a Avenida Sur 34, Antigua, Guatemala, Central America; 011-502-8323-028, fax 011-502-8323-029; spanish@guate.net, [www.guate.net/spanish].

Bio-Itza Eco-Cultural Spanish School. Located in San Jose, Péten, a small community on the shore of Lake Péten Itza, in northern Guatemala. Our unique program combines intensive Spanish language instruction with participation in projects of the Maya Itza people, including the conservation of a 36 KM2 natural reserve, a medicinal plant program, and a project to preserve Itza, the community's once dying language.

Dates: Year round, begins every Monday. Average stay 3-4 weeks. **Cost:** $195 per week (includes 20 hours of private language instruction per week, room and board with local family). **Contact:** Sabrina Vigilante, Conservation International, 2501 M St., NW, Suite 200, Washington, DC 20037; 202-973-2264, fax 202-887-5188; ecoescuela@conservation.org, [www.bioitza.com].

Casa Xelajú. Casa Xelajú, a socially responsible institute in Quetzaltenango, offers Spanish and Quiché language instruction, internships, Spanish/internship combination, voluntary work, semester abroad, and educational and cultural tours. One-on-one instruction 5 hours a day. Graduate/undergraduate credit in Spanish available, transferable nationwide. Homestay, daily activities, excursions, reforestation/community projects, and lectures on women, development, cultural issues.

Dates: Year round. Classes begin every Monday. **Cost:** Spanish program and homestay: $150 per week from Sep-May; $180 per week Jun-Aug. Internships: $75; Volunteer work $55 per week including homesay, 3 meals a day, 7 days a week and one-on-one instruction. $40 registration for both programs. **Contact:** Julio E. Batres, Director General, Casa Xelajú, P.O. Box 3275, Austin, TX 78764; 888-796-CASA, 512-416-6991, fax 512-416-8965; info@casaxelaju.com, [www.casaxelaju.com]. In Guatemala: Casa Xelajú, Callejon 15, Diagonal 13-02, Zona 1, Quetzaltenango, Guatemala; 011-502-761-5954, fax 011-502-761-5953; office@casaxelaju.com.

Centro de Estudios de Español Pop Wuj. This school is a teacher-owned cooperative that donates its profits to projects which alleviate poverty and environmental degradation in Guatemala. Students receive 4 1/2 hours of one-on-one instruction daily, generally live with a Guatemalan family, and participate in service projects, conferences, films, and excursions if they so choose.

Dates: Year round. Classes begin each Monday. **Cost:** $140 per week Jun, Jul, Aug, and Jan; $125 per week off season. Includes homestay. Registration fee $40 additional. **Contact:** Centro de Estudios, Pop Wuj, P.O. Box 11127, Santa Rosa, CA 95406; Tel./fax 707-869-1116; popwuj@juno.com, [http://members.aol.com/popwuj/index.html].

Juan Sisay Spanish School. Five hours per day, one-on-one total immersion Spanish classes. Student stays with host family. Not-for-profit collective.

Dates: Year round. **Cost:** $135 per week. **Contact:** JuanSisay@aol.com, jsisayxela@c.gt.net.

Proyecto Lingüístico Quetzalteco de Español. Proyecto Lingüístico Quetzalteco de Español offers affordable, quality, one-on-one Spanish language instruction to foreign visitors and generates decent-paying jobs and income to support projects that benefit the people of Guatemala. Weekly seminars, activities, and films acquaint the student with Guatemalan culture, history, and social reality.

Dates: Year round, weekly courses. **Cost:** $120-$150 per week includes 5 hours per day of individual Spanish class and homestay with local family with 3 meals a day. **Contact:** Dane Johnson, La Hermandad Educativa, P.O. Box 452, Manson, WA 98831; 800-963-9889; johnsond@televar.com, www.hermandad.com.

Spanish Immersion Program. Probigua is dedicated to two goals: 1) providing the beginning, intermediate, and advanced Spanish student with an intensive, total immersion experience with one-on-one instruction, trips, daily group activities and homestays; 2) helping the children of Guatemala by donating the school's profits to establish and maintain libraries in many rural villages.

Dates: Year round. Cost: Homestay $55 per week; 4 hours of daily classes $80 per week; 5 hours $90 per week; 6 hours $100 per week; 7 hours $110 per week. (Prices subject to change without notice in 2000.) Contact: Rigoberto Zamora Charuc, General Manager, Academia de Español Probigua, 6a. Avenida Norte #41-B, La Antigua 03001, Guatemala; Tel./fax 011-502-8320-860, alternative fax 011-502-8320-082; probigua@conexion.com.gt, [http://probigua.conexion.com].

Honduras

Ixbalanque Escuela de Español. Study just 1 km from the Mayan Ruins of Copan in Honduras. We offer one-to-one student to teacher ratio, a library with games, and study areas. All teachers are Honduran and are trained and certified to teach. Inquire about our new volunteer program.

Dates: Year round. Cost: $185 per week for 4 hours of class, 5 days per week, 7 nights of room and board with local family; $125 for classes only. Contact: Darla Brown or René Hernández, Ixbalanque Escuela de Español, Copán Ruinas, Honduras, C.A.; Tel./fax 011-504-651-4432. In U.S.: Tel./fax 512-376-5020; ixbalan@hn2.com.

Indonesia

Indonesian and Javanese Lanugage. Private course (1-4 students), survival/basic, intermediate, advance, specific purposes. Teach no words—only create situations in which you learn and enjoy communicating in the language—using communicative approach, direct method, and eclectic techniques.

Dates: Three-week course approx. 90 hours. Cost: $6.73-$12.41 per hour excluding VAT. Contact: Ms. Phoebe, Wisma Bahasa J1, Rajawali, Gg. Nuri 6, Yogyakarta, Indonesia; Tel./fax 011-62-274-588409; wisba@yogya.wasantara.net.id, [http://yogya.wasantara.net.id/~wisba/wisba].

Israel

General Studies: Beer Sheva. The program offers students the opportunity to enroll in a wide range of courses at the Ben-Gurion Univ. in a variety of disciplines. You may take courses in anthropology, archaeology, biology, engineering, environmental studies, Hebrew, history, political science, social sciences, etc. These courses are taught in English.

Dates: Aug 4-Dec 1999, Jan 4-Jun 1, 2000. Cost: Spring semester $5,800; year $8,800. Contact: University Studies Abroad Consortium (USAC), Univ. of Nevada, Reno #323, Reno, NV 89557-0093; 775-784-6569, fax 775-784-6010; usac@admin.unr.edu, [www.scsr.nevada.edu/~usac].

Italy

Babilonia Italian Language School. Study Italian, stroll through historic monuments, climb a volcano, swim aqua-blue waters. Babilonia, the only Italian language school in Sicily recognized by ASILS, offers a communicative approach, 6 levels (4 weeks each), courses from 2 weeks to 6 months length, special courses, extracurricular activities, excursions, accommodations, and much more.

Dates: Year round. Cost: Two-week standard course (4 hours per day) LIT605,000 per week. Includes extracurricular activities. Contact: Alessandro Adorno, Director, Babilonia, Centro di Lingua e Cultura Italiana, Via Ginnasio, 20, 98039 Taormina, Italy; Tel./fax 011-390-942-23441; babilonia@nti.it, www.babilonia.it.

Business, Economics, Italian Studies. Turin offers a diversified curriculum in English and in business and economics, plus intensive courses in Italian language and culture, literature, etc., at the foot of the majestic Alps. Program-organized housing and field trips and many Italian university activities.

Dates: Summer term: May-Jul and Jun-Jul; fall semester: Aug-Dec; spring semester: Jan-May. Cost: $7,320 fall and spring semesters; summer term $1,980 per session $3,680 both sessions; fall semester $4,180; spring semester $4,180. Contact: University Studies Abroad Consortium (USAC), Univ. of Nevada, Reno #323, Reno, NV 89557-0093; 775-784-6569, fax 775-784-6010; usac@admin.unr.edu, [www.scsr.nevada.edu/~usac].

Italiaidea. We offer every level and format of Italian study from intensive short-term "survival Italian" courses to advanced, semester-long courses; on-site lectures and visits to historic sites in Italy, conversation, and flexible scheduling. For over 10 years we have been offering college credit courses at numerous U.S. college and university programs in Italy; we now offer both academic assistance and travel/study assistance to our client institutions. Homestays are offered as well as accommodations in shared apartments.

Dates: Year round. **Cost:** Sixty-hour group course LIT780,000; 25-hour one-on-one program LIT1,200,000; 15 hour-specific purposes or culture LIT1,330,000 (taxes not included). **Contact:** Carolina Ciampaglia, Co-Director, Piazza della Cancelleria 5, 00186 Roma, Italy; 011- 390-6-68307620, fax 011-390-6-6892997; italiaidea@italiaidea.com, [www.italiaidea.com].

Italian at the Seaside. Italian summer language school at the seaside. The Giacomo Puccini Centro culture courses is in Viareggio, one of Tuscany's most beautiful beach towns. Stay in small hotels or shared apartments with use of kitchen. Enjoy the language, enjoy the beach, enjoy life.

Dates: Jun 7-Sep 26, every 2 weeks. **Cost:** LIT870,000 includes 2-week course and accommodations. **Contact:** Mr. Giovanni Poggi, Centro Culturale Giacomo Puccini, Via Ugo Foscolo, 36-55049 Viareggio, Italy; 011-390-55-290305, fax 011-390-55-290396; puccini@ats.it, [www.bwline.com/itschools/puccini].

Italian Courses. Institute Galilei specializes in personalized full immersion courses especially designed for excutives, business people, professionals, and students. Courses are held in Florence, in the near countryside (Chianti), and at the seaside. Training in specific vocabulary (economics, law, commercial, art history). Courses are divided in 10 levels.

Dates: One-to-one courses start and finish on any day requested. Small group courses start every 2 weeks. **Cost:** Starting from $180 per week. **Contact:** Alexandra Schmitz, Institute Galilei, Via degli Alfani 68, 50121 Florence, Italy; 011-39-055-294680, fax 011-39-055-283481; info@galilei.it, [www.galilei.it].

Italian in Florence or by the Sea. Study Italian in a 16th century Renaissance palace in the center of Florence, or in a classic Tuscan town just 30 minutes from the sea. Koiné Center's professional language teachers and small class sizes encourage active participation by each student. Cultural program, guided excursions, choice of accommodations including host families.

Dates: Year round; starting dates each month. **Cost:** Two-week intensive program from $350; 3 weeks from $455; 4 weeks from $570. Call for prices of longer stays. **Contact:** In Italy: Dr. Andrea Moradei, Koiné Center, Via Pandolfini 27, 50122 Firenze, Italy; 011-390-55-213881. In North America: 800-274-6007; homestay@teleport.com, koine@firenze.net, [www.koinecenter.com].

Italian Language and Culture. Il Sillabo is a small family-run school in San Giovanni, the heart of Tuscany, a small town connected by rail and autoroute to Florence. We offer Italian language and complementary courses: cooking, drawing, painting, ceramics, history of art, etc. Small classes. Personalized, friendly atmosphere. Well trained and experienced teachers.

Dates: Every 2 weeks. **Cost:** $1,100 (LIT1,810,000) 4-week stay in host family and half board and 4-week, 80-hour Italian course. **Contact:** Ms. Anna Paola Bosi, via Alberti, 31-52027 San Giovanni V. No (Ar), Italy; 011-390-55-9123-238, fax 011-390-55-9424-39; sillabo@tin.it, [web.tin.it/sillabo].

Italian Language Courses. Scuolo Leonardo da Vinci is located in the heart of the historical centers of Florence, Rome, and Siena. Founded in 1977 it is now the leading institute in the teaching of Italian as a second language. The group courses (12 students per class) are offered from 2 weeks to a semester. Credit transfer assistance. The schools offer a wide range of quality cultural courses (cooking, wine, art, drawing) and extracurricular activities. Full range of accommodations choices provided.

Dates: Year round, starts every 2 weeks. **Cost:** Call for details. **Contact:** Mr. Giambattista Pace, Scuolo Leonardo da Vinci, via Brunelleschi 4, 50123, Firenze, Italy; 011-390-55-290305, fax 011-390-55-290396; scuolaleonardo@scuolaleonardo.com, [www.scuolaleonardo.com].

Italian Language Courses. Two-, 3-, and 4-week courses in the undiscovered heart of Tuscany, in Arezzo (population 100,000). School approved by Education Ministry. Modern communicative methods, qualified teachers, excellent standards, friendly amtosphere, social and cultural programs. A pleasant, satisfying experience. Stay in a family and meet real Italians in historical, artistic Arezzo.

Dates: Year round. Courses begin every Monday. **Cost:** LIT895,000 for 2 weeks' tuition and accommodations. **Contact:** Gloria Convertito, Accademia Britannica Toscana, v.P.da.Cortona 10, 52100 Arezzo, Italy; 011-390-575-21366, fax 011-390-575-300426; italcors@ats.it, [www.etr.it/accademia_britannica].

LANGUAGE STUDY VACATIONS: WHAT TO EXPECT

By Jim Baird

Between 1994 and 1998 I attended four language schools with homestays in Central and South America. I found that almost everyone taking such trips goes alone. Once you're there, you'll have plenty of company. If you feel the need for more initial support, use one of the language study companies that coordinates school enrollment, housing, and transportation. Their commissions are reasonable and can be worth the peace of mind. You can use the Internet, however, to make all the arrangements for your second trip.

The highlight of your trip will probably be your homestay, so bring modest gifts for your host family. Photos of your family will be of interest, but not as much as those of your home and car—especially your car. Gifts for the children will automatically endear you to their parents. (By the way, make an effort to stay with a family with children. The kids will be fun and help to fill those awkward moments of silence sitting around the house after classes struggling to communicate.)

You'll be delivered to your new home by school staff, or your hosts will come to the school to escort you. Don't be surprised that no one speaks English. Prepare to be welcomed as an honored guest, shown to your private room, and given a key to the front door.

The family bathroom is down the hall. Don't forget to bring your own soap, towel and wash cloth, and a small mirror. You'll also need a flashlight to find your way around at night and when electricity is rationed. The water also may be turned off for several hours at a time, so it's a good idea to know the schedule.

Americans do not always enjoy good reputations either as considerate house guests or as serious students. My host mother in Honduras, for example, said she was taking a chance on me— her friends in the homestay business had warned her about American men. Some are apparently prone to stay out drinking all night, and when they finally stagger home, drunk and rowdy, they wake everyone up. (German students, incidentally, are considered very orderly and disciplined and some language schools in Guatemala cater exclusively to them.)

Your classes will likely be held in a converted residence with several small rooms for one-on-one instruction. There you will be confined to a wooden chair and table for four or five hours with an instructor who understands or speaks little English. Surprisingly, the language barrier will not get in your way of learning Spanish as much as your egocentric concern that your teacher or host family learn English.

As you are paying primarily for your teacher's time, try spending some of it outside the classroom. You both will appreciate the change. I spent several afternoons practicing my Spanish in the local shops and interviewing for teaching positions at nearby English language schools. My teacher remained at my side, critiquing my performance after each encounter. You will of course be expected to cover any expenses incurred during out-of-school excursions. If you are lucky, your teacher will include you in some aspect of his or her home life, such as a birthday party or a home-cooked meal.

All the schools I attended used the grammar-translation teaching method. There appeared to be little interest in more modern approaches. Teacher quality varies. The more advanced your Spanish language skills, the better chance you will have to get one of the school's senior and most skilled teachers. Many schools take on charitable activities in their neighborhoods, and you may find yourself volunteering to teach deprived kids or helping on a construction project after classes.

Except for the roundtrip airfare, the language study vacation is extremely economical. Use the weekends to see other parts of the country and, if it seems worthwhile, skip some classes to see more. Your instructor gets paid anyway and may offer to go with you if you pay travel expenses. If so, you will have a willing local guide.

Italian Language Courses. Dedicated to the study of the basic linguistic structures of Italian and to the progressive building of communication skills. Students eligible for admission to universities in their home country may apply.

Dates: Apr-Jun; Jul-Sep; Oct-Dec. **Cost:** LIT1,100,000-LIT1,430,000 (1999). **Contact:** Università per Stranieri di Siena, Via Pantaneto 45, 53100 Siena, Italy; 011-390-577-240161, fax 011-390-577-281030; info@unistrasi.it, [www.unistrasi.it].

Italian Language Courses. Italian Language Institute offers the possibility of studying the Italian language (2-, 3-, or 4-week courses) in the beautiful Italian hill country of central Italy. Housing available in private apartment, with families, hotel. Courses offered year round at 6 language levels. Special summer session on the Amalfi coast.

Dates: Twelve 4-week sessions starting in mid-Jan and ending in mid-Dec. **Cost:** From 250 Euros, housing from 197 Euros. **Contact:** Atrium, P.za Papa Giovanni XXIII, 3-61043 Cagli (PS), Italy; Tel./fax 011-390-721-790321; atrium@info-net.it, [www.info-net.it/atrium].

Italian Language Courses. A study holiday in the undiscovered heart of Tuscany, in Arezzo (population 100,000). School approved by education ministry. Modern communicative methods, qualified teachers, excellent standards, friendly atmosphere, social and cultural program. Italian cooking courses. A pleasant, satisfying experience. Stay with a family and meet real Italians in historical, artistic Arezzo.

Dates: Courses begin every Monday. **Cost:** LIT895,000 2 weeks' tuition/accommodations. **Contact:** Italian Language Courses-ILC, Accademia Toscana, Via Pietro da Cortona 10, 52100 Arezzo, Italy; 011-39-575-21366, fax 011-39-575-300426; italcors@ats.it, [www.etr.it/accademia_britannica].

Italian Language Courses in Perugia. Founded in 1986, Comitato Linguistico has gained an international reputation for its high quality Italian language courses year round. Member of ASILS, the association of the most renowned Italian teaching institutes, with strict quality criteria. Situated in the old city center. Friendly environment with professional approach. Personal relationship between staff and students.

Dates: Every month from Jan-Dec. Beginners courses in 2000 start every month. **Cost:** Enrollment fee: LIT100,000. Standard courses (20 lessons per week): LIT800,000; intensive courses (30 lessons per week): LIT1,190,000.

Contact: Sabatino Durante, Comitato Linguistico, Via del Conventuccio n. 13, 06121 Perugia, Italy; 011-390-75-5721471/5734258; ctlingua@edisons.it; [www.edisons.it/homepages/ctlingua/].

Italian Language Courses in Sorrento. Attending a language course means improving one's linguistic knowledge and plunging into the usages and customs of the host country. Practical and stimulating teaching method to ensure tangible results. Five levels. Every lesson lasts 60 minutes; different types of courses to fully meet the objective according to time, availability and attendance frequency. Optional excursions to Capri, Pompei, Amalfi, etc.

Dates: Year round. **Cost:** LIT570,000 (294.38 Euros), 2 weeks, 40 hours; LIT980,000 (506.13 Euros), 2 weeks, 40 hours plus 10 cultural themes; LIT1,100,000 (568.10 Euros), 2 weeks, 40 hours plus 10 individual; LIT1,530,000 (790.18 Euros), 2 weeks, 40 hours plus 20 individual. **Contact:** Dottoressa Cristiana Panicco, Centro Linguistico Internazionale Dante Alighieri, Via San Francesco n°8-80067 Sorrento, Italy; 011-390-81-807-55-99, fax 011-390-81-532-41-40; info@clidas.it, [www.clidas.it].

Italian Language for Foreigners. Small courses: (2 hours a day); main mini-groups (4 hours a day); intensive (main course plus 6 private lessons); two-on-one (1 teacher plus 2 students); individual tuition. Special courses: Tourist Industry, Business Italian. Small groups (max. 6 students). Sports (sailing, catamaran, surfing), excursions (Calabria, Sicily). Accommodations in apartments.

Dates: Mar 1-Nov 26. **Cost:** Two-week course includes single room LIT885,000. **Contact:** Caffè Italiano Club, Largo A. Pandullo 5, 89861 Tropea (VV), Italy; 011-390-963-60-32-84, fax 011-390-963-61786; caffeitaliano@tin.it, [www.paginegialle.it/caffeital].

Italian Language, Art and Culture. Accademia del Giglio is a private school, specifically aimed at helping international students gain proficiency in the Italian language and understand many aspects of Italian culture. At Accademia del Giglio every effort is made to satisfy student needs and to provide an enjoyable educational experience in a friendly atmosphere.

Dates: Year round. Contact for details. **Cost:** Two weeks, 4 hours per day LIT470,000 (245 Euros); 4 weeks, 2 hours per day LIT470,000 (245 Euros); 4 weeks, 4 hours per day LIT770,000 (400 Euros). Enrollment fee: LIT80,000 (41 Euros). Includes course material, guided visits, assessment test. A certificate at the end of the course. **Contact:** Mr. Lorenzo Capanni, c/o, Accademia del Giglio, Via Ghibellina 116, 50122 Firenze, Italy; Tel./fax 011-390-55-2302467; giglio@cosmos.it, [www.cosmos.it/bol/accademiadelgiglio].

Language and Culture. Courses in Italian language and culture at all levels, 25 hours per week. Small classes. Special courses in Italian for business and Italian musical culture for opera singers. Accommodations with host families or in furnished apartments. Situated in a small town in central Italy where you can live "All' Italiana" with Italians.
Dates: Mid-Mar-Oct. **Cost:** LIT990,000 for 4-week course (1999). **Contact:** Centro Studi Italiani, Via Boscarini, 1, 61049 Urbania (PS), Italy; 011-39-0722-318-950, fax 011-39-0722-317-286; urbania1@pesaro.com, [www.pesaro.com/urbaniastudy].

Learn Italian in Italy. Language immersion courses in Italy (Rome, Florence, Siena, Viareggio, Rimini, Bologna, Venice, Portico, Milan). Private language schools with programs for adults, senior citizens, and teenagers. Centrally located, convenient to interesting places, cultural events, sports activities. Programs feature qualified teachers, small classes, attractive surroundings and facilities. Affordable prices for instruction. Accommodations with Italian families with meals, student residences, apartments, and nearby hotels.
Dates: Year round. Two weeks or more. **Cost:** Two-week courses with or without accommodations range from $305-$1,105. **Contact:** Ms. Lorraine Haber, Study Abroad Coordinator, Embassy CES Study Abroad Programs, The Center for English Studies, 330 7th Ave., 6th Fl., New York, NY 10001; 212-629-7300, fax 212-736-7950; cesnewyork@cescorp.com.

Learn Italian in Rome. Located a few minutes walk from the Colosseum, the school occupies a 4-story building with its own terrace and garden. The school specializes in teaching Italian, offering courses on all levels, and a rich and interesting extracurricular program. Upon request, the school will provide accommodations for student in private homes or student apartments.
Dates: Year round. **Cost:** Two-week intensive course: LIT540,000; 4-week intensive course: LIT1,000,000. **Contact:** Pier Luigi Arri, Director, Torre di Babele, via Bixio, 74-00185 Rome, Italy; 011-390-6700-8434, fax 011-390-67049-7150; info@torredibabele.it, [www.torredibabele.it].

Studio Art Centers International. Combine beginning, intermediate, or advanced Italian language studies with courses in studio arts, art history, art conservation, or cultural studies at SACI's central Florence location. Students are partnered with Italian university students for language and cultural exchange. Programs include year/semester abroad, late spring and summer studies.
Dates: Sep-Dec; Jan-Apr; May-Jun; Jun-Jul. **Cost:** Fall/spring tuition $7,725 per term; late spring/summer $3,000. **Contact:** SACI Coordinator, U.S. Student Programs, Institute of International Education, 809 UN Plaza, New York, NY 10017-3580; 800-344-9186, 212-984-5548, fax 212-984-5325; saci@iie.org, [www.saci-florence.org].

Japan

Intensive Language and Culture. Japan is one of the most dynamic countries in the world, with the world's second largest economy. The Western Washington Univ., Univ. of Idaho, Lincoln Univ., and KCP offer a unique opportunity to learn more about this country and its language, people, and culture. Programs are open to all English speaking students in good class standing as well as recent college graduates. Our carefully integrated language and culture program offers the student a unique opportunity to develop Japanese language proficiency while gaining an understanding of the Japanese culture and modern society.
Dates: Jan-Mar; Apr-Jun; Jul-Sep; Jul-Aug; Oct-Dec. **Cost:** $5,150 for dorm option and $5,500 for homestay option. Includes registration fee's at sponsor university, tuition, textbooks, local transportation in Tokyo, numerous excursions in and around Tokyo, homestay or private dormitory. Summer short-term is $3,950 and includes all above. **Contact:** Mike Anderson, KCP International, P.O. Box 28028-0028, Bellingham, WA 98228-0028; 888-KCP-7020 or 360-647-0072, fax 360-647-0736; kcp@kcp-usa.com, [ww.kcp-usa.com].

Japanese Language and Culture Program. The program features courses in intensive Japanese language and Japanese studies. The Japan Center for Michigan Univ.'s is located on the shore of Lake Biwa, in Hikone, Japan, within 1 hour of Kyoto.
Dates: Sep-Dec, Jan-Apr. (Also summer intensive, Jul-Aug.) **Cost:** $5,100 per semester (1999). **Contact:** John Hazewinkel, Program Coordinator, Japan Center for Michigan Univ.'s, 108 International Center, E. Lansing, MI 48824-1035; 517-355-4654; [www.isp.msu.edu/JCMU].

Learn Japanese at Affordable Prices. Immerse yourself in Japanese language and culture in a township near Okayama that is rich in activities and cultural experiences. Happy Talk-Japanese Language Solutions offers individualized instruction and flexible length of stay. Apart-hotel accommodations are within walking distance of the school. Tuition includes Ikebana class, tea ceremony, and cultural excursions.

Dates: Year round. Classes begin every month for students wishing to study for less than 90 days or in Apr and Oct for full semester. Special arrangements can be made for groups of 5 or more. **Cost:** $924 per month for 5 hours per day (5 days per week) of instruction, including tuition, all materials, apart-hotel accommodations, cultural classes and special tours. $25 one-time registration fee. **Contact:** Linda Frisbey, Registrar, Happy Talk-Japanese Language Solutions, 119 Tidewater Dr., Hercules, CA 94547; 510-287-9283; happytalk2@aol.com.

Teach English in Japan. Teach conversational English up to 35 hours per week. Fixed 5-day work week, schedule, and location, with a maximum of 4 students per class. Guaranteed monthly salary. Paid training and promotional opportunities. Assistance given for securing health insurance, house, visa, travel arrangements.

Dates: Year round. **Cost:** None. (No application fee or deposits). **Contact:** Trevor Phillips, NOVA, 2 Oliver St., 7th Fl., Boston, MA 02109; 74507.3070@compuserve.com, [www.teachinjapan.com].

Waseda/Oregon Japanese Program. A Japanese language immersion program at Waseda Univ. in Tokyo.

Dates: Jun 19-Aug 11, 2000. **Cost:** $4,775. **Contact:** Sally Strand, Waseda/Oregon Programs, 921 SW Morrison, #548, Portland, OR 97205; 800-823-7938, [www.opie.org].

Waseda/Oregon Transnational Program. A Japanese language and comparative U.S.-Japan societies program in Tokyo, Japan, and Portland, Oregon.

Dates: Spring: Jan 10-Jun 23, 2000; fall: Sep 12, 2000. **Cost:** $7,000 for spring in Tokyo; $3,500 for fall in Portland. **Contact:** Sally Strand, Waseda/Oregon Programs, 921 SW Morrison, #548, Portland, OR 97205; 800-823-7938, [www.opie.org].

Latin America

Instituto Internacional Euskalduna. Spanish language program on a beautiful Caribbean island. No passport or visa needed. We offer communicative, learner-centered classes for all language levels. Small groups and private programs, U.S. university credit, weekly cultural activities and homestay programs with or without meals. Licensed by the General Council of Education.

Dates: Classes begin every Monday. **Cost:** Programs starting at $570. **Contact:** NESOL/IIE, Edif. Euskalduna, Calle Navarro #56, Hato Rey, PR 00918; 787-281-8013, fax 787-767-1494; nesol@coqui.net, [http://home.coqui.net/nesol].

Language and Cultural Studies. Which school is best for you? Let us help you choose the Spanish language school in Mexico or Costa Rica that best suits your needs. Whether you want college credit, special vocabulary for your job, or just a fabulous language learning vacation, we can guide you in your selection because we've been there ourselves.

Dates: Flexible starting dates throughout the year. **Cost:** Depends on location, options, length of stay. Tuition prices start at $125 per week. **Contact:** Talking Traveler, 620 SW 5th, #400, Portland, OR 97204; 800-274-6007, fax 503-274-9004; homestay@teleport.com, [www.talkingtraveler.org].

Study and Live in Buenos Aires. Universidad de San Andrés, an internationally recognized university, offers 2 programs in Spanish language: Beginners and intermediate take an intensive course in Spanish and Latin American Culture during summer recess; intermediate students spend a semester taking language and regular courses. Both options include homestay with families, tuition, and extracurricular activities.

Dates: Jun 28-Aug 7 (summer); Aug 2-Dec 4 or May 1-Jun 30 (regular term intermediate only). **Cost:** $2,500 (summer), $7,000 (regular term). Both include tuition, room and board, and cultural activities. **Contact:** Ana Garat, Foreign Studies Office, Universidad de San Andrés, V. Dumas 284, 1644 Victoria, P. de Buenos Aires, Argentina; 011-541-4746-2608, fax 011-541-4746-5090; fso@udesa.edu.ar, [www.udesa.edu.ar].

Mexico

Baja California Language College. This Spanish immersion program offered in Ensenada has been the site of Spanish language education for thousands of students from throughout the world. Contemporary new campus 1 mile from the Pacific and 1 hour south of the U.S. border. Homestay program. Groups and children welcome. Well-appointed cafeteria offers free coffee, soda, teas, beer, and purified water. **Dates:** Classes begin every Monday all year. Orientation each Sunday at 2 p.m. Weekend sessions are also available. **Cost:** No registration fees. Weekly rate $240 M-F classes, 30-33 hours; weekend rate $120 Sat and Sun, 13 hours. Twenty percent discount for 5 pre-paid weeks, 25 percent for 10 pre-paid weeks. Homestay is $25 per night, 3 meals included. **Contact:** Keith Rolle, Baja California Language College, P.O. Box 7556, San Diego, CA 92167; 877-444-2252 (toll free from U.S.); college@bajacal.com, [www.bajacal.com].

Bi-Cultural Programs IMAC. Spanish in Guadalajara is more than a classroom. Group sizes of 1 to 5. Guadalajara offers the conveniences of a modern city. We are a few hours drive to Puerto Vallarta. Homestays with only 1 student per family. Hotel discounts available. Free Internet and email access. Excursions and extracurricular activities. **Dates:** Year round. Group classes start every Monday. Individual tutoring may begin any day. Christmas vacation Dec 18-Jan 1, 2000; Easter vacation Apr 17-30, 2000. **Cost:** Contact organizations for details. **Contact:** Leticia Orozco, Instituto Mèxico Americano de Cultura, Donata Guerra 180, Guadalajara, Jalisco, 44100 Mèxico; 011-52-3-613-1080, fax 011-52-3-613-4621; spanish-imac@imac-ac.edu.mx, [www.spanish-school.com.mx].

Cuauhnahuac Intensive Spanish Language Instutite. Intensive Spanish language program since 1972 in Cuernavaca, Mexico. Four students per Spanish grammar class, flexible hours, own teaching Spanish language method. Excursions, activities, and workshops. Conferences dealing with Mexican culture, economy, and society. Internship programs in law, medicine, business, and education. Homestays with caring Mexican families. **Dates:** Every Monday, year round. **Cost:** From $200 per week ($650 4 weeks), $2,160 per semester (12 weeks) **Contact:** David M. Cano, Cuauhnahuac Esc. C.I.C.L.C., Av. Morelos Sur 123 Col. Chipitlan, Cuernavaca, Morelos 62070, Mexico; 011-52-73-12-36-73, 18-92-75 or 12-47-82, fax 011-52-73-18-26-93; inform@cuauhnahuac.edu.mx, [www.cuauhnahuac.edu.mx].

El Bosque del Caribe, Cancun. Take a professional Spanish course 25 hours per week and enjoy the Caribbean beaches. Relaxed family-like atmosphere. No more than 6 students per class. Special conversation program. Mexican cooking classes and excursions to the Mayan sites. Housing with Mexican families. College credit available. **Dates:** Year round. New classes begin every Monday. Group programs arranged at reduced fees. **Cost:** Enrollment fee $100, $185 per week. One week with a Mexican family $160. **Contact:** Eduardo Sotelo, Director, Calle Piña 1, S.M. 25, 77500 Cancún, Mexico; 011-52-98-84-10-38, fax 011-52-98-84-58-88; bcaribe@mail.cancun-language.com.mx.

Encuentros. Spanish immersion program in Cuernavaca, Morelos that focuses on adults who need the language for professional purposes or other specific reasons such as travel in Spanish-speaking countries. Fun and effective communicative approach. **Dates:** New classes begin every Monday year round. Flexible scheduling upon request. **Cost:** $50 registration fee. Regular program $150 per week, private tutorials $15 per hour. Homestays $15 per night shared room, $25 per night single room including meals. **Contact:** Jeannie K. Andersen, Encuentros, Calle Morelos 36, Colonia Acapantzingo, CP 62440 Cuernavaca, Morelos, Mexico; 011-52-73-12-50-88, messages 011-52-73-12-98-00; [http://cuernavaca.infosel.com.mx/encuentros/spanish.htm].

Experiencia: Cuernavaca. Experiencia has offered intensive Spanish language courses and homestay programs since 1977. Groups of no more than 5 students, study for as short as 1 week. Extracurricular activities, such as bilingual exchanges, lectures, cultural events, and Saturday excursions are included. Sunday and 3-day excursions offered for a small fee. **Dates:** Year round. Group classes begin every Monday. **Cost:** Group studies: 1 week $135, 4 weeks $500, 8 weeks $900. Further discounts for extended study. (Double the amounts for one-on-one instruction.) Plus $100 one-time registration fee. Books $16. Accommodations with a Mexican family or in dorm begin at $9 per night. **Contact:** Sherry Howell, Experiencia Representative, 1303 Candelero Court, Placerville, CA 95667; 888-397-8363 or 530-622-4262, fax 530-626-4272; study@experiencia.com, [www.experiencia.com].

Guadalajara Summer School. For the 48th year, the Univ. of Arizona Guadalajara Summer School will offer intensive Spanish in the 6-week session, intensive Spanish in the 3-week session, and upper-division Spanish and Mexico-related courses in the 5-week session. Courses may be taken for credit or audit.

Dates: Jul 3-Aug 17. **Cost:** $1,077-$2,000 includes tuition and host family housing with meals. **Contact:** Dr. Macario Saldate IV, Director, Guadalajara Summer School, The Univ. of Arizona, P.O. Box 40966, Tucson, AZ 85717; 520-621-5137; gss@u.arizona.edu, [www.coh.arizona.edu/gss].

Have Fun While You Learn Spanish!. O.L.E. is a specialized school in Spanish for foreign students. We have 9 practical and dynamic programs which are open to students on all levels and ages. We offer a wide variety of cultural and extracurricular activities, also accommodations with carefully chosen Mexican families.

Dates: Year round. Courses start every Monday. **Cost:** Prices start at $140 per week. **Contact:** Dulce Wirz and Karina Ayala, O.L.E., Organización Lingüística de Español, Av. Universidad Pte. #1-D, Col-Centro, Querétaro, Qro. 76000, México; 011-52-4-224-1628; olemex@queretaro.podernet.com.mx, [www.bapqro-mex.com/ole].

Institute of Modern Spanish. Spanish language and Mexican/Mayan culture studies immersion programs. Daily spanish language, conversation and culture classes in small groups. Mexican family homestays and excursions to the famous Mayan ruins in Mérida, Yucatán. Child care available.

Dates: Study for 1 to 15 weeks. Start any Monday year round with special inclusive packages in Apr and Oct. Four-week summer programs Jun-Aug. **Cost:** $300-$370 per week. Includes classes and full room and board in homestay housing. Major credit cards accepted. **Contact:** U.S. Office, Institute of Modern Spanish, 106 Holiday Circle, West Des Moines, IA 50265-4224; 1-877-4MERIDA 877-463-7432, toll free from U.S. 515-226-0419, fax 515-224-6511; 4merida@modernspanish.com, [www.modernspanish.com].

Instituto Cultural Oaxaca. Spanish Language and Mexican Culture Immersion Program on lovely Oaxacan estate. Grammar, literature, and conversation classes offered at all levels. Cultural workshops in cooking, pottery, dancing, weaving, music, culture, and education. Local conversation partner. Weekly lectures and cultural activities. Seven contact hours daily. Optional tours to archaeological sites and artisan villages. Homestays available. Special group programs.

Dates: Year-round monthly sessions. May begin any Monday. Write, call, or fax for specific dates and informative brochure. **Cost:** $50 registration fee and $400 per 4-week session or $105 per week. **Contact:** Lic Lucero Topete, Director, Instituto Cultural Oaxaca, Apartado Postal #340, Oaxaca, Oaxaca, C.P. 68000, Mexico; 011- 52-951-53404/51323, fax 011-52-951-53728; inscuoax@antequera.com, [http://antequera.com/inscuoax].

Intensive Spanish Course. The Academia Hispano Americana, the oldest full-time specialized Spanish language program in Mexico, offers students 35 hours per week of activities in the Spanish language. Courses are held year round and start almost every 4 weeks. San Miguel is a pleasant mountain community with clear air and many cultural opportunities.

Dates: Jan 3 and 31, Feb 28, Mar 27, Apr 3, May 2 and 29, Jun 26, Jul 4, Aug 21, Sep 18, Oct 16, Nov 13. Dates in 2001 will be slightly different. **Cost:** Tuition $450 per session, discounts after first full session. Room and board from $17 per day. **Contact:** Gary De Mirjyn, Director, Academia Hispano Americana, Mesones 4, San Miguel de Allende, Gto., Mexico; 011-52-415-2-0349 or 2-4349, fax 011-52-415-2-2333; academia@unisono.net.mx.

Intensive Spanish in Cuernavaca. Cuauhnahuac, founded in 1972, offers a variety of intensive and flexible programs geared to individual needs. Six hours of classes daily with no more than 4 students to a class. Housing with Mexican families who really care about you. Cultural conferences, excursions, and special classes for professionals. College credit available.

Dates: Year round. New classes begin every Monday. **Cost:** $70 registration fee; $680 for 4 weeks tuition; housing $18 per night. **Contact:** Marcia Snell, 519 Park Dr., Kenilworth, IL 60043; 800-245-9335, fax 847-256-9475; lankysam@aol.com.

Intensive Spanish in Yucatan. Centro de Idiomas del Sureste, A.C. (CIS), founded in 1974, offers 3-5 hours per day of intensive conversational Spanish classes with native-speaking, university-trained professors. Maximum 6 students per group, average 3. Program includes beginner courses to very advanced with related field trips and recommended optional homestay. Also special classes in business, legal, medical vocabulary, or Mayan studies.

Dates: Year round. Starts any Monday, except last 2 weeks in Dec. **Cost:** Tuition (3 hours per day program: $350 first 2 weeks, $125 each additional week); tuition 5 hours per day programs $550 first 2 weeks, $225 each additional week. **Contact:** Chloe C. Pacheco, Director, Centro de Idiomas del Sureste, A.C., Calle 14 #106 X25, col. Mexico, CP 97128, Mérida, Yucatán, Mexico; 011-52-99-26-11-55 or 011-52-99-26-94-94, 20-28-10, fax 011-52-99-26-00-20; cis@sureste.com.

Intensive Spanish Language Program. Five 6-week programs each year, 3 hours daily of Spanish, all levels.

Dates: Jan, Apr, Jun, Aug, Oct (request school calendar). **Cost:** Registration $25, tuition $275 per person. **Contact:** Lic. Marta Basave, Head Info. Dept. School for Foreign Students, Apartado Postal 70-391, Ciudad Universitaria, Delegación Coyoacán, 04510 México, D.F.; 011-525-622-24-70, fax 011-525-616-26-72; [http://serpiente.dgsca.unam.mx/rectoria/htm/cepecu.html].

Interactive Spanish. Spanish from A to Z in 40 hours. Groups of 3 maximum.

Dates: Open **Cost:** $220 for 40 hours in group of 3 (1999). **Contact:** Inter/Idiomas, 20 de Enero Sur 42, Colonia San Antonio, San Miguel Allende, Guanajuato, Mexico; 011-52-415-2-41-15; [http://unisono.net.mx/inter].

Language and Culture in Guanajuato. Improve your Spanish in the most beautiful colonial city in Mexico. We teach one-on-one or in small groups for up to 8 hours daily. Spanish, Mexican history, cooking, literature, business, folk dancing, and politics. Students of all ages and many nationalities. Homestays with families, field trips, movies, hikes, theater, dance performances.

Dates: Year round. New classes begin every Monday. Semester programs begin in Jan and Aug. **Cost:** $925. Includes 4 weeks of classes and homestay with 3 meals daily. **Contact:** Director Jorge Barroso, Instituto Falcon, Mora 158, Guanajuato, Gto. 36000 Mexico; 011-52-473-1-0745; infalcon@redes.int.com.mx, [http://institutofalcon.com].

Mar de Jade Ocean-Front Resort. Tropical ocean-front retreat center in a small fishing village on a beautiful half-mile beach north of Puerto Vallarta. Surrounded by lush jungle with the warm, clear sea at our door, enjoy swimming, hiking, horseback riding, massage, and meditation. Study Spanish in small groups. Gain insight into local culture by optional volunteer work in community projects, such as rural community clinic, our local library, or a model home garden. Mar de Jade also has meeting facilities and provides a serene and intimate setting for group events.

Dates: Year round. **Cost:** Twenty-one day volunteer/Spanish program May-Nov 15 $1,000 (student discount available); Nov 15-Apr $1,080. Includes room and board in a shared occupancy room and 15 hours per week of volunteer work. Vacation: May-Nov 15 room and board $50 per night; Nov 16-Apr $55 per night. Spanish $80 per week with minimum 1 week (6 nights) stay. **Contact:** In Mexico: Tel./fax 011-52-322-2-3524; info@mardejade.com, [www.mardejade.com]. U.S. mailing address: 9051 Siempre Viva Rd., Suite 78-344, San Diego, CA 92173-3628.

Romance Language Institute. Private language school, established in 1967, offers an immersion Spanish program with homestay: language, literature and culture, emphasis on speaking Spanish; M.A. in Spanish program; grants for teachers who bring students; reasonable costs. Durango is a beautiful colonial city.

Dates: Year round. **Cost:** Two weeks $520, 3 weeks $760, 4 weeks $1,020, 5 weeks $1,250, 6 weeks $1,500. **Contact:** Romance Language Institute, P.O. Box 527, Durango, Dgo. Mexico; Tel./fax 011-52-12-41-58; cintidio@logicnet.com.mx, [www.logicnet.com.mx./romlanginst].

Spanish Language Institute. A program designed to provide students with ideal learning environment which is conducive to thinking, writing and speaking naturally in Spanish within the context or real-life situations. Discover the Mexican culture with a university group, organization, professionals, travelers and special program of individualized needs for executives.

Dates: Year round. Classes begin every Monday. **Cost:** $150 per week. **Contact:** María Ramos, Academic Spanish Language Institute, Bajada de la Pradera #208, Colonia Pradera, Cuernavaca, Morelos 62191, Mexico; jessram@mor1.telmex.net.mx, [http://Cuernavaca.infosel.com.mx/sli/sli-page.htm].

Summer Study Program in Mexico. Three-week study program in Cuernavaca, language and culture classes. Excursions to Mexico City, Taxco, and areas around these cities. Room and board with Mexican family. Can earn $600 while in Mexico. Final excursion to Yucatán and Cáncun.

Dates: Jun 1-27. **Cost:** $1,795. **Contact:** Compton Community College, 1111 E. Artesia Blvd., Compton, CA 90221-5393; 310-900-1600 ext. 2545, fax 310-900-1696; hart2163@juno.com.

Universal, Centro de Lengua. Universal offers Spanish language programs specifically tailored to meet the needs of each student. Spanish courses are offered at all levels, individually or in groups, and are complemented by diverse lectures. Classes range from 2 to 5 students and meet 5 hours daily with hourly breaks of 10 minutes.

Dates: Year round. **Cost:** Normal $150 per week, advanced $200, professional $230. **Contact:** Ramiro Cuéllar Hernández, Universal, Centro de Lengua, J.H. Preciado #171, Col. San Antón, Cuernavaca, Morelos, C.P. 62020, Mexico; 011-52-73-18-29-04/12-49-02, fax 011-52-73-18-29-10; students@universal-spanish.com, [www.universal-spanish.com].

Nicaragua

Casa Xalteva Language Center. Casa Xalteva offers high-quality intensive Spanish language courses at beginning, intermediate, and advanced levels with Nicaraguan teachers. Classes have a maximum of 4 students and meet 4 hours per day Monday-Friday. We also offer homestays with families, volunteer work opportunities, and cultural programs.

Dates: Classes begin each Monday year round. **Cost:** Instruction - $125 per week, $425 per month; homestays $70 per week. **Contact:** Casa Xalteva, Calle Real Xalteva #103, Granada, Nicaragua; 011-505-552-2436; casaxal@ibw.com.ni. In U.S.: P.O. Box 4542, Albuquerque, NM 87196; 505-254-7535; communit@nmia.com.

Nicaragua Spanish Schools. Learn Español in one of Latin America's most hospitable countries where you can choose to study consecutively at 2, 3, or all 4 of our diverse Nicaraguan-run Spanish schools for the same price as our single school program. Program includes 4 hours individualized instruction daily. Nicaraguan teachers, Nicaraguan family homestay, cultural activities, volunteer opportunities, eco-excursions, and mucho más! Transferable university credit is available.

Dates: Year round. Start any weekend. **Cost:** One week $210, 2 weeks $400, 3 weeks $570, 4 weeks or more $185 per week. **Contact:** Nicaragua Spanish Schools, P.O. Box 20042, Santa Barbara, CA 93120; 800-211-7393, 805-687-9941; nss-pmc@prodigy.net, [http://pages.prodigy.net/nss-pmc/].

Portugal

Portuguese in Portugal or Brazil. Language immersion courses in Portugal (Lisbon, Faro) or Brazil (Salvador da Bahia). Private language schools with programs for adults, senior citizens, and teenagers. Centrally located, convenient to interesting places, cultural events, sports activities. Programs feature qualified teachers, small classes, attractive surroundings and facilities. Affordable prices for instruction. Accommodations with Portuguese or Brazilian families with meals, student residences, apartments, and nearby hotels.

Dates: Year round. Two weeks or more. **Cost:** Two-week courses with or without accommodations range from $795-$1,020. **Contact:** Ms. Lorraine Haber, Study Abroad Coordinator, Embassy CES Study Abroad Programs, The Center for English Studies, 330 7th Ave., 6th Fl., New York, NY 10001; 212-629-7300, fax 212-736-7950; cesnewyork@cescorp.com.

Russia and the NIS

Liden & Denz Language Center. Liden & Denz is a full-service year-round language school for Russian, located in the historical center of St. Petersburg. The school is run by Swiss and offers intensive group courses and various one-to-one and closed group programs. With 15 classrooms, its own library and Internet for all students, and 7 years of operation, Liden & Denz is a prime address for Russian language studies in Russia.

Dates: Two-week group courses: spring, summer, fall. Individual courses start any Monday. Dates open for total beginners. **Cost:** Two weeks spring and fall $680; additional week $285 per week. Two weeks summer $790; additional week $335 per week. Fees include family accommodations. One-to-one rates on demand (on our web page). **Contact:** Liden &

Denz Language Center St. Petersburg (Russia), P.O. Box 8, FIN 53501 Lappeenranta, Suomi-Finland. School address: Transportny pereulok 11, St. Petersburg, Russia; 011-7-812-325-22-41, fax 011-7-812-325-12-84; lidenz@lidenz.ru, [www.lidenz.ru].

Moscow Institute for Advanced Studies. A comprehensive program in Russian language, politics, and culture. The Moscow Institute, in association with the International Univ. of Moscow, offers a year round program featuring language courses at all levels, a wide range of electives in English and Russian, internships, excursions, and graduate research support, and our exclusive lecture series "A Changing Russia."
Dates: Spring: Jan 29-May 12; summer: Jun 11-Aug 6; fall: Aug 27-Dec 10. **Cost:** $6,700-$7,800. Includes full-time tuition, room and board, visa, administrative fees and registration, excursions. Books provided. Financial aid available. **Contact:** Louise White, Program Coordinator, Moscow Institute for Advanced Studies, 152 W. 57th St., 48th Fl., New York, NY 10019; 212-245-0461, fax 212-636-0502; mifas1@aol.com, [www.studyabroad.com/moscow].

Russian as a Foreign Language. General Russian, Business Russian, TORFL (Teaching of Russian as a Foreign Language), individual and group courses, semester and part-time courses, crash courses for businessmen, labor service, unique cultural program. Accommodations with a Russian host-family included in the total course fee, a hotel, or student hostel (on request).
Dates: Courses start any Monday throughout the year. **Cost:** From $1,220 per month, all but airfare. **Contact:** Vyatcheslav Oguretchnikov, ProBa Language Centre, street address: Russia, 197376, St. Petersburg, Professora Popova str. 5; mailing addres: P.O. Box 109, Lappeenranta, Fin-53101, Finland; 011-7-812-234-50-24, fax 011-7-812-3462758; sp@mail.nevalink.ru, olp@aura.ru, [www.studyrussian.spb.ru].

Spain

=elemadrid= Spanish in Madrid. Our school provides a wide variety of Spanish immersion programs, Spain today classes, leisure activity courses and weekend excursions in small groups/and or individually tailored private lessons for adults. Accommodations include homestay, apartments, apartment sharing, and hotels.

Dates: Two-week courses start every other Monday year round. **Cost:** Courses $220-$760 per week; accommodations $80-$1,300 per week; leisure activity courses and weekend excursions vary. **Contact:** =elemadrid=, Calle Serrano 4, 28001 Madrid, Spain; Tel./fax 011-34-91-432-4540/41; hola@elemadrid.com, [www.elemadrid.com].

Alicante - Proyecto Español. Language school in the center of Alicante on the Costa Blanca. Intensive language courses in small groups of 4-8 students. Besides the courses we offer (at no additional cost) a cultural and lingual exchange with Spaniards who are interested in meeting foreigners and learning about foreign cultures.
Dates: Courses start every Monday from May-Oct. **Cost:** Intensive course 25 hours per week: 2 weeks including accommodations PTS38,000 ($250); 4 weeks including accommodations PTS69,000 ($450). **Contact:** Steffen Schmid; Proyecto Español, Urb. Carabasí 159, 03130 Santa Pola (Alicante), Spain; 011-34-966-69-78-47, 011-34-639-92-62-10, fax 011-34-966-69-78-91; proyespa@aol.com, [http://members.aol.com/proyespa/indexe].

CP Madrid. Located in the town center of Madrid. Two- to 8-week standard and intensive courses, 4 hours per day. One-on-one instruction, customized courses for groups and combination courses. All levels available. Classes are small and thus offer a great deal of attention to the student. Cultural activities are an integral part of the program. Accommodations with selected guest families.
Dates: Year round (except Aug). **Cost:** PTS23,750/EUR142 per week, 20 hours tuition; PTS23,000/EUR138 (approx.) half-board accommodations with guest family. **Contact:** Mrs. Maria Dolores Romero, CP Language Institute, c/o Schiller International Univ., Calle San Bernardo 97/99, 28015 Madrid, Spain; 011-34-9-1448-2488, fax 011-34-9-1445-2110; cp@schillermadrid.edu.

DELE Exam Courses in Malaga. Widely recognized to be one of Spain's leading language schools, Malaca Instituto offers preparation courses for the internationally recognized DELE exams. Courses qualified by the Univ. of Alcala. EAQUALS guarantee of quality (see www.eaquals.org).
Dates: Starting dates: Apr 17 and Oct 16.
Cost: From PTS91,000 for 4-week course.
Contact: Bob Burger, Malaca Instituto, c/

Cortada 6, 29018 Malaga, Spain; 011-34-95-229-3242, fax 011-34-95-229-6316; espanol@malacainst-ch.es, [www.malacainst-ch.es].

ENFOREX Language School. Enforex Spanish School was 4 schools in Spain (Madrid, Barcelona, Salamanca, Marbella) open all year round and one in Quito, Ecuador. Small groups and more than 15 different intensive programs.
   Dates: Start every Monday. **Cost:** One month $1,000 includes accommodations and tuition. **Contact:** ENFOREX, Calle Alberto Aguilera 26, 28015 Madrid, Spain; fax 011-34-91-5945-159; spanish@enforex.es, [www.enforex.es].

Introduction to Spain. This is an intensive two week course in Spanish language and culture. It combines language classes with activities including art, wine, dance, cinema, history and theatre. Accommodation can be provided.
   Dates: Year round. **Cost:** $320-$390. **Contact:** Madrazo Language School Calle Los Madrazo, 16 - 3º 28014 Madrid Spain; tel/fax 011-34-91-369-04-73; pynches@teleline.es, [http://members.tripod.co.uk/madrazo/index.htm].

Institute of Spanish Studies. Founded in 1950, ISS offers courses in Valencia (Spain) in Spanish language, literature, art, history, geography, civilization, and culture. In collaboration with Longwood College, the Institute offers 2 summer sessions as well as fall and spring semesters with over 40 different courses of instruction from beginners to graduate level.
   Dates: Fall and spring semesters, summer 1 (May-Jun, 4 weeks), summer 2 (Jul, 4 weeks). **Cost:** Semester $6,500, summer $2,600. **Contact:** Institute of Spanish Studies, 17303 SW 80 Pl., Miami, FL 33157; 888-454-6777, fax 305-971-5354; institut@spanish-studies.com.

Institutos Internacionales Hispalingua. Year-round Spanish language schools for adults in Barcelona and Palma de Mallorca. Instituto Barcelona is located near the famous shopping boulevard Paseo de Gracia; Instituto Palma de Mallorca has direct access to a swimming pool overlooking Palma. Both schools offer small classes for all levels and a large variety of social and cultural activities. Choice of accommodations: homestay, residence (in Barcelona), and apartments (Palma de Mallorca).
   Dates: Year round. **Cost:** Two-week standard course (20 lessons per week) PTS44,000; 2-week host family accommodations (half board) PTS41,600. **Contact:** Instituto Barcelona, Consejo de Ciento, 314 pral, 080007 Barcelona, Spain; 011-34-932155452, fax 011-34-934873146; bcn@lalschool.org. Instituto Palma

de Mallorca, Corb Mari, 22, 07014 Palma de Mallorca, Spain; 011-34-971702430, fax 011-34-971701684; pmi@lalschool.org.

Intensive Spanish Courses, Seville. CLIC IH, one of Spain's leading language schools, is located in the heart of Seville, the vibrant capital of Andalucia. With year-round intensive Spanish language courses, business Spanish, and official exam preparation taught by highly qualified and motivated native teachers, CLIC IH combines professionalism with a friendly atmosphere. Academic credits available. Accommodations are carefully selected and we offer a varied cultural program as well as exchanges with local students.
   Dates: Year round. **Cost:** Approx. $930 for a 4-week Spanish course and homestay, individual room, 2 meals per day. **Contact:** Bernhard Roters, CLIC International House Seville, Calle Albareda 19, 41001 Sevilla, Spain; 011-34-95-450-2131, fax 011-34-95-456-1696; clic@clic.es, [www.clic.es].

Intensive Spanish Language Courses. Four hours tuition per day Monday-Friday. All levels. Students can enroll for as many weeks as they like. Average 8 students per class. A social program is included in the price. Wide range of accommodations options.
   Dates: Year round, starting every 2 weeks. **Cost:** $605 for a 2-week course (accommodations included). **Contact:** Carmen Sanchez, International House Barcelona, Trafalgar, 14, 08010 Barcelona, Spain; 011-34-93-268-4511, fax 011-34-93-268-0239; spanish@bcn.ihes.com, [www.ihes.com/ben].

Learn Spanish in Northern Spain. All levels: oral exercises in grammar and vocabulary, guided conversation according to the student's level. From intermediate level: commentaries on newspaper articles and literary or other texts; prepared discussions on current affairs.
   Dates: Year round, 2 weeks or more. **Cost:** PTAS50,625-PTAS26,950 per week with or without half-board family accommodations. Fifteen (summer courses) or 20 (winter courses) lessons per week of 55 minutes each. **Contact:** Ingrid Antons, Inlingua Santander S.L., Avenida de Pontejos 5, E-39005 Santander, Spain; 011-34-942-278465, fax 011-34-942-274402; inlingua-sdr@nexo.es, [www.inlingua.com/santander.htm].

Learn Spanish in Spain. Language immersion courses in Spain (Barcelona, Canary Islands, Granada, Madrid, Malaga, Salamanca, San Sebastian, Seville, and Valencia). Private language schools with programs for adults, senior citizens, and teenagers. Centrally located, convenient to interesting places, cultural events, sports activities. Programs feature qualified teachers, small classes, attractive surroundings and facilities. Affordable prices for instruction. Accommodations with Spanish families with meals, student residences, apartments, and nearby hotels.

Dates: Year round. Two weeks or more. **Cost:** Two-week courses with or without accommodations range from $275-$905. **Contact:** Ms. Lorraine Haber, Study Abroad Coordinator, Embassy CES Study Abroad Programs, The Center for English Studies, 330 7th Ave., 6th Fl., New York, NY 10001; 212-629-7300, fax 212-736-7950; cesnewyork@cescorp.com.

Refresher Courses for Teachers. Widely recognized to be one of Spain's leading language schools, Malaca Instituto offers courses for practicing teachers of Spanish. Methodology, culture, and advanced language. Courses qualified by the Univ. of Alcala. EAQUALS guarantee of quality (see www.eaquals.org).

Dates: Starting dates: Jan 24; Apr 17, Oct 16. **Cost:** PTS66,200 for 2-week course. **Contact:** Bob Burger, Malaca Instituto, c/Cortada 6, 29018 Malaga, Spain; 011-34-95-229-3242, fax 011-34-95-229-6316; espanol@malacainst-ch.es, [www.malacainst-ch.es].

Semester in Spain. Semester, year, summer, and January terms for high school graduates, college students, and adult learners. Beginning, intermediate, and advanced Spanish language studies along with Spanish literature, culture, history, and art. All courses taught in Spanish by native Spaniards. Four courses per semester, 4 credits each. Homestays are arranged for all students.

Dates: Winter: Jan; spring semester: late Jan-mid-May; summer term: Jun and/or Jun-Jul; fall semester: late Aug-mid-Dec. **Cost:** Fall or spring semester $7,950; year approx. $15,900; summer term and Jan term approx. $2,000 each term. Includes tuition, books, full room and board. **Contact:** Debra Veenstra, U.S. Coordinator, Semester in Spain, 6601 W. College Dr., Palos Heights, IL 60463; 800-748-0087 or 708-239-4766, fax 708-239-3986.

Sociedad Hispano Mundial. The quality of our programs is guaranteed by OCR and the Univ. of Alcala (Spain). Year round intensive Spanish courses, specialized courses (business Spanish, literature, politics, history, art, civilization, DELE exams), and one-to-one. All levels and ages. Communicative approach. Highly qualified and motivated native teachers. Extensive extracurricular social and cultural program. Great location and facilities.

Dates: Begin any Monday. **Cost:** Varies by program and length of stay. **Contact:** Jose Ruiz Cantero, Director, Sociedad Hispano Mundial, Palacio de Congresos, Paseo del Violón s/n, Granada 18006, Spain; 011-34-958-24-68-92, fax 011-34-958-24-68-93; shm@moebius.es, [http://tuspain.com/shm/shm.htm].

Spanish and Basque Studies (Getxo-Bilbao). The Getxo-Bilbao area offers intensive language studies (Spanish or Basque) that fulfill up to 2 years of university language requirements in 1 semester, plus courses in history, political science, art, culture, economics, teacher education, literature, etc. Program organized field trips, housing, and many local university activities at this seaside city.

Dates: Fall semester: Aug-Dec; spring semester: Jan-May. **Cost:** Fall or spring semester $4,620; year $7,600. **Contact:** University Studies Abroad Consortium (USAC), Univ. of Nevada, Reno #323, Reno, NV 89557-0093; 775-784-6569, fax 775-784-6010; usac@admin.unr.edu, [www.scsr.nevada.edu/~usac].

Spanish and Basque Studies (San Sebastian). San Sebastian offers intensive language (Spanish or Basque) that fulfill up to 2 years of university language requirements in 1 semester, plus courses in history, literature, political science, economics, art, teacher education, etc. Program organized field trips to Madrid and elsewhere, housing, and many local university activities in this beautiful seaside resort.

Dates: Summer terms: May-Jul, Jun-Jul, Jul-Aug; fall semester: Aug-Dec, spring semester: Jan-May. **Cost:** Fall or spring semester $6,580; year $10,380; Jun or Jul $2,080; Aug $1,690; Jun and Jul $3,870; Jun/Jul and Aug $3,355; Jun, Jul, and Aug $4,910. **Contact:** University Studies Abroad Consortium (USAC), Univ. of Nevada, Reno #323, Reno, NV 89557-0093; 775-784-6569, fax 775-784-6010; usac@admin.unr.edu, [www.scsr.nevada.edu/~usac].

Spanish Courses in Malaga. Spanish courses in Malaga, Spain. All grades, small groups, 4 hours daily, courses commencing each month. Living with Spanish families (or in small apartment in town center).

Contact: F. Marin Fernandez, Director, Centro de Estudios de Castellano, Ave. Juan Sebastian Elcano 120, Málaga, 29017 Spain; Tel./fax 011-34-95-2290-551; ryoga@arrakis.es, [www.arrakis.es/~ryoga].

Spanish Language and Civilization. IEMA is known for its excellent teachers, emphasis on practical Spanish and communicative skills. Situated in Avila, near Madrid, in a 11th century palace protected by UNESCO, in the best walled city of the world. Standard Spanish is spoken in Avila unlike in other regions of Spain and South America. Carefully selected homestays.

Dates: Year round. **Cost:** From $450. **Contact:** Dr. Rainer Rutkowski, IEMA, c/o Martín Carramolino, 6, 05001 Avila, Spain; 011-34-920222773, fax 011-34-920252955; iema@iema.com, [www.iema.com].

Spanish Language Courses in Malaga. Widely recognized to be one of Spain's leading language schools, Malaca Instituto offers language and cultural programs at all levels for adults of all ages. Qualifying American students can apply for academic credit. Courses qualified by the Univ. of Alcala. EAQUALS guarantee of quality (see www.eaquals.org).

Dates: Courses begin every 2 weeks from Jan 10. **Cost:** PTS48,000 for 2-week course. **Contact:** Bob Burger, Malaca Instituto, c/Cortada 6, 29018 Malaga, Spain; 011-34-95-229-3242, fax 011-34-95-229-6316; espanol@malacainst-ch.es, [www.malacainst-ch.es].

Spanish Langue and Culture Courses. The best program to learn the Spanish language, to know the Spanish culture, and at the same time to spend unfortettable holidays with a full program of complementary activities: parties, films, workshops, cooking course, dancing course, sports activities. Come with us to enjoy your time.

Dates: Year round. **Cost:** PTS18,000 per week. **Contact:** C.E.V.A., Guesta del Aljibetrillo, 4-18010 Granada, Spain; 011-34-958-80-60-77, fax 011-34-958-80-60-81.

Summer Intensive in Segovia. Duration: 4 weeks; Contents: 4 hours of class daily, 5 days a week; Options: A) 2 hours of grammar, 1 hour of conversation, 1 hour of culture and civilization; b) 1 hour of grammar, 2 hours of conversation, 1 hour of culture and civilization.

Dates: Jul 1-Aug 15. **Cost:** $1,500 includes 80 hours of class plus 32 hours of cultural activities and homestay or student dorm (meeting and transportation). **Contact:** Aula Magna Castellana, Santo Tomás 1, 3° D, 40002 Segovia, Spain; 011-34-607-78-11-57; amagnac@arrakis.es.

Summer Study in Salamanca. Spend over 4 weeks in Spain studying Spanish language, literature, and culture in the beautiful city of Salamanca. The program is designed for college

students, graduates, and teachers, as well as for college-bound high school students. Program options: A) Intensive undergraduate language and culture; up to 9 credits. B) Literature, language and culture, and business Spanish. Six graduate or advanced undergraduate credits.

Dates: Jul 1-30. **Cost:** Program A: $1,800. Program B: $2,000 (tentative). **Contact:** Mario F. Trubiano, Director, Univ. of Rhode Island, Summer Program in Spain, Dept. of Languages, Kingston, RI 02881-0812; 401- 874-4717 or 401-874-5911; fax 401-874-4694.

Sweden

Uppsala Int'l. Summer Session. Sweden's oldest academic summer program focuses on learning the Swedish language. All levels from beginners to advanced. Additional courses in Swedish history, social institutions, arts in Sweden, Swedish film. Excursions every Friday. Extensive evening program includes both lectures and entertainment. Single rooms in dormitories. Apartments at extra cost. Open to both students and adults. Credit possible.

Dates: Jun 18-Aug 11; Jun 18-Jul 14; Jul 16-Aug 11, Jul 2-Aug 11. **Cost:** SEK22,200 (approx. $2,620) for the 8-week session, SEK12,000 (approx. $1,420) for the 4-week session. Includes room, some meals, all classes, evening and excursion program. **Contact:** Dr. Nelleke van Oevelen-Dorrestijn, Uppsala Int'l. Summer Session, Box 1972, 751 47 Uppsala, Sweden; 011-31-13-521-23-88 or 011-46-18-10-23-70, fax 011-31-13-521-2389; nduiss@wxs.nl or nelleke.vanoevelen@uiss.org, [www.uiss.org].

Switzerland

CP Leysin. Located in Leysin, a beautiful mountain resort above Lake Geneva in a former Grand Hotel. Two- to 32-week intensive French language courses at all levels. International student body, highly experienced teachers, and a unique atmosphere. Classes are small and thus offer a great deal of attention to the student. Activity and recreational program offered. Courses can be taken in conjunction with university courses at the American College of Switzerland.

Dates: Year round. **Cost:** SFR747 per week including 24 hours tuition and full board accommodations. **Contact:** Mrs. Francoise Bailey, CP Language Institutes, c/o American College of Switzerland, CH 1854, Leysin, Switzerland; 011-41-24-494-2223, fax 011-41-24-494-13-46; schillerUS@aol.com.

Study Italian in Lugano. FORMAT is located in Lugano, a city famous for its Italian architecture, its Italian ambiance, and the mildest and sunniest climate in the country, situated on the shores of one of the most romantic lakes in the foothills of the Alps. Standard intensive courses (M-F 4 hours a day); one-to-one course; diploma courses (CILS and CELI); small groups (max. 6 students). A variety of accommodations available (family, inn, youth hostels).

Dates: Courses start every Monday. **Cost:** CHF2,480 for 4-week intensive course. Includes accommodations, enrollment, and placement fees. **Contact:** Giuseppe Rauseo, Director, FORMAT Scuola di lingue, Via Marco da Carona 1, 6900 Lugano, Switzerland; 011-41-91-9212600, fax 011-41-91-9212666; format@swissonline.ch, [www.linkstudy.ch/format].

Univ. of Geneva Summer Courses. Three-week French language and civilization at all levels, beginners to advanced. All instructors have a university diploma. Excursions and visits to Geneva and its surroundings. Class of 15-20 students. Minimum age 17.

Dates: Jul, Aug, Sep. **Cost:** SFR470 for 3 weeks (tuition). **Contact:** Mr. G. Benz, Univ. of Geneva, Summer Courses, rue de Candolle 3, CH-1211 Geneva 4, Switzerland; 011-41-22-705-74-34, fax 011-41-22-705-74-39; elcfete@uni2a.unige.ch, [www.unige.ch/lettres/elcf/coursete/cournet.html].

Thailand

AUA Thai Language Program. Learn Thai using the (ALG) Automatic Language Growth method as designed by Dr. J. Marvin Brown. Gain the best results in ability to communicate of any program in the world.

Dates: Year round. **Cost:** 82 baht per hour with discounts offered for larger number of hours. **Contact:** David Long, Asst. Director, AUA Language Center, 179 Rajadamri Rd., Bangkok 10330, Thailand; 011-66-2-252-8170, ext 3201; fax 011-66-2-252-8398; info@auatd.org, [www.auatd.org].

United States

English Language Instruction. Dates: Thirty start dates each year. **Cost:** $1,325 per 4-week session. **Contact:** ELS Language Centers, 400 Alexander Park, Suite 100-TA, Princeton, NJ 08540-6306; 609-750-3500, fax 309-750-3597; info@els.com, [www.els.com].

Intensive English Program. Intensive English Program has over 20 years of experience providing English instruction to students. Our international students progress toward their academic, professional, or personal language goals using our up-to-date computer/media lab. We organize activities for international students, including trips, volleyball, rafting, skiing, and dinners. We provide homestays, and conversation partners.

Dates: Aug, Oct, Jan, Mar, May, Jul. **Cost:** Call for details. **Contact:** Paulette Rudolf, Administrative Assistant, Intensive English Program, 101 Co-Op Units Building, Colorado State Univ., Ft. Collins, CO 80523-1788; 970-491-6616, fax 970-491-5399; iep@vines.colorado.edu, [www.colostate.edu/Depts/IEP].

Live and Learn English. Offers group activities in a lovely language institute outside New York City. Courses are offered on all levels by an experienced ESL teacher with an MA from NYU. Program offers a complete cultural experience.

Dates: Fall and spring. **Cost:** $250 per week for full room and board, language lessons, and activities. **Contact:** Modern English, Inc., P.O. Box 761, Dumfries, VA 22026; ModernEnglish@prodigy.net.

Middlebury Summer Courses. Middlebury College's Summer Language Schools in Vermont offer language immersion in a unique, controlled linguistic environment. Since 1915, Middlebury has provided students with unlimited opportunities to speak in their target language with native and near-native language professionals and with each other in Arabic, Chinese, French, German, Italian, Japanese, Russian, and Spanish. Undergraduate and graduate credit awarded. Programs range from beginner to advanced. MA and DML (Doctor of Modern Languages) degree programs also available. Linkage with Middlebury's Schools Abroad. Summer sessions range from 3 to 9 weeks in duration, depending upon the school. Student to faculty ratio is less than 6 to 1.

Dates: Nine-week sessions (Arabic, Chinese, Japanese, and Russian) Jun 11-Aug 13; 7-week sessions (French, German, Italian, and Spanish) Jun 25-Aug 13; 6-week graduate sessions (French, German, Italian, Russian, and Spanish) Jun 28-Aug 13. **Cost:** Tuition varies from $975 for a 3-week session to $3,800 for 9 weeks. Room and board additional. **Contact:** The Language Schools, Middlebury College, Middlebury, VT 05753; 802-443-5510, fax 802-443-2075; languages@middlebury.edu, [www.middlebury.edu/~ls].

St Giles Language Teaching Center. Earn the Certificate in English Language Teaching to Adults (CELTA) in San Francisco, approved by the Royal Society of Arts/Univ. of Cambridge Examination Syndicate. The course on practical training and teaching methodology includes access to international job postings, graduate contacts, and teaching opportunities abroad. EFL school on site for observation and practice teaching. Part of a group of schools in England, Switzerland, and the U.S. with over 40 years of teaching and training experience, led by highly-qualified instructors with extensive overseas teaching experience. CELTA courses also offered in Brighton and London, England.

Dates: Jan 10-Feb 21, Mar 27, May 1, Jun 5, Jul 10, Aug 7, Sep 11, Oct 16, Nov 20. Cost: $2,695 ($2,495 in Jan and Feb). Contact: St Giles Language Teaching Center, 1 Hallidie Plaza, Suite 350, San Francisco, CA 94102; 415-788-3552, fax 415-788-1923; sfstgile@slip.net, [www.stgiles-usa.com].

Venezuela

Spanish as a Second Language. Beginners, intermediate, advanced, and conversation. Grammar-based program encourages the 4 skills: reading, writing, speaking, and listening. Lead students toward communicative competence in Spanish, 20 hours per level.

Dates: Start any Monday. Cost: $175.50 per level (group up to 4 students). Includes placement examination, registration fee, material 20 hours tuition, certificate. Family lodging: week $118. Contact: Carmen H. Montilla, Instituto Latinoamericano de Idiomas, Av. Las AmTricas, C.C. Mamayeya, 4to piso, ofc. 26, Vene, Venezuela; 011-58-74-445463, fax 011-58-74-447808; ildi@bolivar.funmrd.gov.ve, [www.worldwide.edu/venezeula/ili/index.html].

Venusa Institute of Int'l. Studies and Modern Languages. Students enroll at the Venusa Institute of International Studies and Modern Languages in Mérida, located in the heart of the Venezuelan Andes. Fields of study include Spanish language, Latin American history and culture, international business, cross-cultural communications, teaching of English as a second language (TESOL), int'l. agriculture, ecology and botany, anthropology and sociology, and more. Most classes taught in Spanish, with a limited number being offered in English. Homestays. One semester college-level Spanish recommended and overall GPA of 2.5

required. Global Professional Internship Program available to students having sufficient preparation in Spanish language.

Dates: Fall: late Aug-mid-Dec; spring: early Jan-end of Apr; summer: 2 sessions, mid-May-late Jun and late Jun-mid-Aug. For the Global Internship program: fall and spring: same as above; summer: late-May-Aug. Cost: Fall/spring estimate $6,450 per semester; summer 2000 $3,700. Estimates include SUNY tuition, full day orientation in the U.S., orientation in Venezuela, application fee, room and 2 meals daily with local family, airfare from Miami to Mérida roundtrip, 2 full day field trips, insurance, books and supplies, program administration costs. For the Global Internship program: fall or spring 2000 $5,825; summer 2000 $4,300. Contact: Office of International Programs, Box 2000, SUNY Cortland, Cortland, NY 13045; 607-753-2209, fax 607-753-5989; koppl@cortland.edu, [www.studyabroad.com/suny/cortland].

Worldwide

CHI World Travel/Study Programs for All Ages. CHI was established in 1980 as a nonprofit organization to encourage people to reach out and explore the world. Call us or visit our website. We have worldwide highschool academic programs, cultural and/or language immersions with homestays; group tours personalized for schools or for the general public. Internships, au pair and teaching positions also available.

Dates: Vary. Cost: Vary according to destination and length of program. Contact: Cultural Homestay International, 2455 Bennett Valley Rd., #210B, Santa Rosa, CA 95404; 800-395-2726, fax 707-523-3704; chigaylep@msn.com, [www.chinet.org/outbound.html].

Cultural and Language Immersion Courses. Over 90 programs and courses around the world, offering over 25 languages.

Dates: Year round start dates (from 2-week to 36-week programs available). Cost: $450 and up. Contact: Carina Attwood, Program Manager, Abroad Languages, 502-99 Avenue Rd., Toronto, ON, M5R 2G5, Canada; U.S./Canada: 800-219-9924, 416-925-2112; info@LanguagesAbroad.com, [www.LanguagesAbroad.com].

Dutch Language Study. Dutch language instruction (one-to-one or group lessons) to people of all ages interested in language and culture of Holland. Students stay with carefully chosen host families.

Dates: Year round. **Cost:** Homestay DFL385 per week. Group lessons DFL15 per day, private lessons DFL27.50 per hour. **Contact:** ISOK, Mr.J.F.H. de Zeeuw, Principal, Jan-Tooropstraat 4, 2225 XT, Katwijk, Zh, Holland; 011-31-71-40-13533.

Intensive Immersion/Langue et Didactique. 1. Intensive 3- and 5-week programs are offered May-Jun and Jul-Aug for 18-year-olds and older. Open to students, teachers, business people, retired people, or anyone wishing to improve his or her proficiency in French. 2. Designed for teachers of French as a second or foreign language, the "Langue et didactique" program will bring you up to date on newer techniques and pedagogical material for the teaching of French.

Dates: 1. May-Jun, Jul-Aug. 2. Jul. **Cost:** 1. CDN$1,495 and CDN$1,995. 2. CDN$1,575. **Contact:** Mr. Damien Ferland, Director, Ecole de langue française et de culture québécoise, Université de Québec à Chicoutimi, 555 blvd. de l'université, Chicoutimi, PQ, G7H 2B1, Canada; 418-545-5036, fax 418-545-5012; ecolanfr@uqac.uquebec.ca, [www.d4m.com/ecoledelangue].

International Schools Services. Learn about teaching opportunities in private American and international schools around the world and discover how you can carry your education career overseas. The Educational Staffing program of International Schools Services has placed over 15,000 K-12 teachers and administrators in overseas schools since 1955. Most candidates obtain their overseas teaching positions by attending our U.S.-based International Recruitment Centers (IRCs) where ISS candidates interview with overseas school heads seeking new staff. Applicants must have a bachelor's degree and 2 years of current K-12 teaching experience. The experience may be waived for those who have overseas living or working experience, teaching certification, and a motivation to work in the developing world. IRC registration materials are provided upon approval of your completed ISS application. See web site for more information or to fill out an application.

Dates: International Recruitment Centers in Feb and Jun. **Cost:** Application: $150; International Recruitment Center registration: $150. There are no placement fees charged to candidates who are placed through the work of ISS. **Contact:** Erika Fitzsimmons, ISS, P.O. Box 5910, Princeton, NJ 08543; 609-452-0990 or 609-452-2690; edustaffing@iss.edu, [www.iss.edu].

Language and Business Courses. Language business studies for young people and adults. Long- and short-term vacation courses. Recognized examinations. Vocational language courses. Located in "Castel Les Chênes" in Montreux on Lake Geneva. Accommodations on the premises.

Dates: Jan 3-Apr 25. **Cost:** $516-$577 per week tuition, full board, lodging, extras (through Jun 2000). **Contact:** Hermann and Ulla Schusterbauer, Study Centre "C & L," Av. deNaye 15, CH-1820 Montreux, Switzerland; 011-41-963-08-80, fax 011-41-963-73-34; studycl@studycentrecl.ch, [www.studycentre.ch].

Language Immersion Programs. Learn a language in the country where it's spoken. Intensive foreign language training offered in Costa Rica, Russia, Spain, France, Italy, Germany, and Ecuador for students aged 16 and older. Classes are taught in up to 8 different proficiency levels and are suitable for beginners as well as people with advanced linguistic skills. All courses include accommodations and meals. Lots of extracurricular activities available. Students can earn college credit through Providence College.

Dates: Courses start every second Monday year round. Year programs commence in Sep, semester programs in Jan, May, and Sep. **Cost:** Varies with program, approx. $950 per 2-week course. **Contact:** Stephanie Greco, Director of, Admissions, EF International Language Schools, EF Center, 1 Education St., Cambridge, MA 02142; 800-992-1892, fax 617-619-1701; ils@ef.com.

Language School Programs. Language School Programs emphasize language study in small classes and the opportunity to participate in planned cultural activities while sharing in the daily life of a host family. Programs available for teens and adults in many countries including Spain, France, Germany, and Mexico.

Dates: Year round, some summer only. Available for 3, 4, or 6 weeks. **Cost:** Approx. $2,000 for 3 weeks, $2,300 for 4 weeks, $2,800 for 6 weeks. **Contact:** Outbound Department, Center for Cultural Interchange, 17 N. 2nd Ave., St. Charles, IL 60174; 888-ABROAD1, fax 630-377-2307; karen@cci-exchange.com, [www.cci-exchange.com].

Language Study Abroad/College Credit for Travel. Language homestay programs worldwide. College credit course options for students and teachers who travel, learn language, work-intern-volunteer abroad or in U.S. Language credit includes Spanish, Italian, French, Portuguese, German, Japanese, Chinese, and English. Short- and long-term travel credit available year round.

Dates: Year round. **Cost:** Undergraduate credit options $250 for 3 semester credit; postgraduate credit for educators $225 plus for 2 semesters. Languge immersion programs vary in cost depending on location—Europe, Asia, Africa, Australia, South America, Central America, and North America. **Contact:** Professor Steve Tash, Travel Study, P.O. Box 16501, Irvine, CA 92623-6501; 800-484-1081 ext 7775 (9 a.m.-9 p.m. PST), fax 949- 552-0740; travelstudy@yahoo.com, [www.studyabroadandwork.com].

Language Study in 30 Countries. We offer intercultural and foreign langauge immersion programs around the world. All ages are welcome and programs vary in length from 1 week to several months.

Dates: Year round. **Cost:** Vary according to program and program length. **Contact:** Mary E.Croy, NRCSA, Box 1393, Milwaukee, WI 53201; 414-278-0631, fax 414-271-8884; inquire@nrcsa, [www.nrcsa.com].

Linguistic Stay/Au Pair Stay. Learn various languages in different countries and improve your language level. We offer a variety of courses and accommodations. If you choose an au pair stay and have to look after children during 25 or 30 hours per week, you receive pocket money that will allow you to take courses and improve your language skills.

Dates: Year round. **Cost:** Depends on the program and country. **Contact:** Mrs. Pierrot, Inter-Sejours, 179 rue de Courcelles, 75017 Paris, France; 011-33-1-47-63-06-81, fax 011-33-1-40-54-89-41; intersejours@europost.org.

Spanish Immersion Programs. Study with small groups or private tutor. Live with local host families or in hotels. One-week to 6 months. All ages and levels. Various settings: beaches, mountains, small towns, large cities, etc. Country options: Costa Rica, Guatemala, Honduras, Panamá, El Salvador, Argentina, Chile, Ecuador, Peru, Uruguay, Venezuela, Puerto Rico, Dominican Republic, Bolivia, and Spain.

Dates: Rolling admission. Programs start every week or every month. **Cost:** Depends on location. Prices start at $175 per week and include classes, homestay, travel insurance, most meals, some cultural activities. **Contact:** AmeriSpan Unlimited, P.O. Box 40007, Philadelphia, PA 19106; 800-879-6640, fax 215-751-1100; info@amerispan.com, [www.amerispan.com].

TEFL and On-the-Job Tuition. Student exchange, business and language tuition, computer training, multimedia courses, translations on and offline, interpreting, hostess training, secretarial courses. Over 80 schools in Europe: Germany, Italy, Spain, Czech Republic, Poland, Russia, Switzerland, Albania; Africa: Morocco; Americas: Ecuador.

Dates: Call for details. **Cost:** Call for details. **Contact:** International Benedict Schools, P.O. Box 270, CH 1000, Lausanne 9, Switzerland; 011- 41-21-323-66-55, fax 011-41-21-323-67-77; benedict@worldcom.ch, [www.benedict.ch].

WorldTeach. WorldTeach is a nonprofit, nongovernmental organization which provides opportunities for individuals to make a meaningful contribution to international education by living and working as volunteer teachers in developing countries.

Dates: Year round. **Cost:** $4,800-$5,950. Includes international airfare, health insurance, extensive training, and in-country support. **Contact:** WorldTeach, Harvard Institute for International Development, 14 Story St., Cambridge, MA 02138; 800-4-TEACH-0 or 617-495-5527, fax 617-495-1599; info@worldteach.org, [www.worldteach.org].

FOURTEEN

The following listing of internship programs was supplied by the organizers. Contact the program directors to confirm costs, dates, and other details. Please tell them you read about their programs in this book! Programs based in more than one country or region are listed under "Worldwide."

Australia

Australian Internships. Interns are placed with research teams, Australian employers, political administrations, etc., for periods ranging from 6 weeks to a year. The positions are unpaid. Homestay (or other) accommodations are included. Placement is arranged to suit the individual provided 4 months notice is given. Most placements are in Queensland or New South Wales. Fields: marine and wildlife biology, business, etc. No academic credit offered. Unlimited internships. Prerequisites: a) High School Graduates, b) Professional Development for Graduates and Junior/Senior college students.
Dates: Year round. Application deadline: Four months before start date. **Cost:** $2,455 (includes room and board) for 6-week program. Application fee: $500. **Contact:** Dr. Maurice A. Howe, Education Australia, P.O. Box 2233, Amherst, MA 01004; 800-344-6741, fax 413-549-0741; edaust@javanet.com.

Austria

Univ. of Salzburg. If fluent in German, students can be placed in business administration internsihps. These are particularly timely as the European Union develops and former eastern bloc states forge new identities. Austria's cultural and economic ties are in both eastern and western Europe. The Univ. of Salzburg's interdisciplinary Dept. of International Relations and Political Science draws students from around the world.
Dates: Sep-Jan; Feb-Jun. **Cost:** $11,000 includes orientation, tuition, housing, meal allowance for breakfast and lunch, one way flight from any of 28 U.S. cities, ongoing cultural activities and excursions. **Contact:** AIFS, 102 Greenwich Ave., Greenwich, CT 06830; 800-727-2437; collegeinfo@aifs.com, [www.aifs.com/java/us/aifsay_s/austria/salz.htm].

Belize

CHAA Creek Natural History Center. CHAA offers a unique inter-active learning experience in a variety of fields. On-going program and research include neo-tropical migratory birds, reforestation, mammal re-introduction, tropical butterflies, Maya archaeology, natural resources management, environmental education and ecotourism.

Dates: Year round. **Cost:** Vary depending on program and expertise. **Contact:** Mike Green, CHAA Creek Natural History Center, P.O. Box 53, San Ignacio, Belize; 011-501-91-2010; frontdesk@btl.net.

Central America

Internship and Research Program. The Institute for Central American Development Studies (ICADS) offers a semester abroad study program, including coursework and structured internship opportunities, in Costa Rica, Nicaragua, Belize, and Cuba in the following areas: women's studies, environment/ecology, public health, education, human rights, and many others. The program is progressive and aimed at students who wish to work on social justice issues and on behalf of the poor, women, and the oppressed in Central America. Fall and spring with academic credit, summer noncredit Spanish and internship program.

Dates: Fall and spring terms with academic credit. **Cost:** $7,600. **Contact:** Sandra Kinghorn, PhD, Director, ICADS, Dept. 826, P.O. Box 025216, Miami, FL 33102-5216; 011-506-225-0508, fax 011-506-234-1337; icads@netbox.com, [www.icadscr.com].

Internships. ICAS offers a limited number of unpaid 6-month internships on a minimum half-time basis for qualified university students and graduates. As researchers and writers for *Mesoamerica*, the interns gain valuable experience in journalism and Central American studies while living in a Spanish-speaking culture. Interns must have a good command of the English language and a working knowledge of Spanish. Please send your resume, 2 letters of recommendation, a short writing sample, and indicate times available.

Dates: Open. **Cost:** Housing and food $400 per month, miscellaneous $150 per month. **Contact:** Linda Holland, Apdo 1524-2050, San Pedro, Costa Rica; 011-506-253-3195, fax 011-506-234-7682; mesoamer@sol.racsa.co.cr.

Chile

SUNY Southern Cone Programs. Since 1990 the Southern Cone Programs have offered internships in 6 Chilean cities: La Serena, Santiago, Valparaiso, Concepcion, Temuco, and Valdivia. Administered through the program office in Santiago, 30 student interns per semester participate in government offices, business and industry, social agencies, advocacy groups, Congress, medical clinics, schools, and communication media.

Dates: First Southern Hemisphere semester Mar 1-Jun 30, second semester Jul 27-Dec 15. **Cost:** Tuition $4,150. Program fee $1,685. Transportation to Chile (approx.) $1,600. Housing (approx.) $1,600. **Contact:** Carmen Madariaga Culver, Academic Director, Latin American Southern Cone Programs, Plattsburgh State Univ., Plattsburgh, NY 12901-2681; 518-564-2395, fax 518-564-2300; socone@plattsburgh.edu, [www.plattsburgh.edu/socone].

Dominican Republic

Internship and Study Program. English-speaking program exposes students to career opportunities in business, human services, and government agencies in conjunction with academic program featuring intensive Spanish, Latin American studies, African-American studies. Direct enrollment in host universities for fluent Spanish speakers. Host families. Field trips.

Dates: Aug-Dec, Jan-May, Jul-Aug. **Cost:** $4,662 per semester (fall, spring) for in-state tuition and fees, housing, meals, internship arrangements, and excursions (English program). Surcharge possible for direct enrollment students. **Contact:** Office of International Programs, Univ. at Albany-SUNY, LI 66, Albany, NY 12222; 518-442-3525, fax 518-442-3338; oipua@csc.albany.edu, [www.albany.edu/~oipwebua].

Ecuador

Academia Latinoamericana. Proud to be the friendliest Spanish school you have ever known. Family owned and operated. The program offers language study at 9 levels, for complete beginners through advanced. Experienced staff, native Ecuadorians. Carefully selected host families within walking distance of school. Exclusive "SierrAzul Cloud Forest and Galapagos" extension program, volunteer program. U.S. college credit available.

Dates: Year round. **Cost:** $230 per week. Includes 20 hours of lessons, 7 days with host family, 2 meals per day, transfer, services at the school, and teaching material. **Contact:** Suzanne S. Bell, Admissions Director, USA/International, 640 East 3990 South, Suite E, Salt Lake City, UT, 84107; 801-268-4608, fax 801-265-9156; academia@juno.com, delco@spanish.com.ec.

The Bospas Forest Farm. You are invited to bring your practical skills to the deforested subtropical Andean valley of Mira. Those with experience of permaculture and/or agroforestry are sought to assist in the further development of a demonstration fruit forest farm. Costs cover full board and lodging. Detailed application and/or subject of study requested 3 months in advance.

Dates: Year round, minimum 3 months stay. **Cost:** $200 per month (negotiable for longer stay). **Contact:** Piet T. Sabbe, c/o Casa Dobronski, Calle Guanhuiltagua N34-457, Quito, Ecuador; bospas@hotmail.com.

Community Internships in Latin America. Emphasis on community participation for social change. Students work 3 days a week in an internship, meet together for core seminar and internship seminar, and carry out independent study project. Wide range of internship opportunities in community development and related activities. Family homestay, field trips. Latin American faculty. Full semester's credit, U.S. transcript provided. All majors, 2 years Spanish language required.

Dates: Early Feb-mid-May. **Cost:** Spring $9,250 . Includes tuition, internship placement and supervision, room and board, field trips. **Contact:** Rebecca Rassier, Director of Student Services, HECUA, Mail #36, Hamline Univ., 1536 Hewitt Ave., St. Paul, MN 55104-1284; 612-646-8832 or 800-554-1089; info@hecua.org, [www.hecua.org].

Europe

¿?don Quijote In-Country Spanish Language Schools. Offers Spanish language courses in our 6 schools in Spain and 5 partner schools in Latinoamerica. Our courses (standard, intensive, business, D.E.L.E., tourism, flight attendants and refresher for teachers) are all year round, from 2 weeks on. Students can combine different cities and schools. Academic credit is available.

Dates: Year round—fall, spring, winter, and summer, 2 weeks to a full year of study. **Cost:** Email or check web site for details. **Contact:** ¿?don Quijote In-Country Spanish Language Schools, calle/Placentinos n°2, Salamanca 37008, Spain; 011-34-923-268860, fax 011-34-923-268815; amusa@donquijote.org, [www.donquijote.org].

Internship Program. CCI's Discovery Abroad Internship Program gives students (18-28) the opportunity to participate in a volunteer internship in one of 7 countries. Internships provide exciting opportunities for language and cross-cultural immersion and valuable work experience. Participants live with a host family for the duration of the program and will be placed in an internship related to their course of study.

Dates: Year round. **Cost:** One month approx. $1,800, 2 months approx. $2,500, 3 months approx. $3,200. **Contact:** Outbound Department, Center for Cultural Interchange, 17 N. 2nd Ave., St. Charles, IL 60174; 888-ABROAD1, fax 630-377-2307; karen@cci-exchange.com, [www.cci-exchange.com].

Internships in Europe/E.P.A. The Univ. of Rochester and Educational Programs Abroad sponsor programs in London, Bonn, Brussels, Madrid, and Paris that combine coursework with unpaid internships for academic credit. Fields include politics, law, business, health science, and the arts. Available to juniors, seniors, and recent graduates. Requirements: 3.0 GPA or better, and at least 2 years of college-level language study where appropriate.

Dates: Sep-Dec, Jan-Apr; 2 summer terms of 8 weeks each. **Cost:** Semester programs range from $6,700-$9,390; summer $5,150. **Contact:** Jacqueline Levine, Director, Center for Study Abroad, Univ. of Rochester, Rochester, NY 14627; 716-275-7532, fax 716-461-5131; csaip@cc.rochester.edu, [www.rochester.edu/College/study-abroad/europe.html].

Prehistoric and Tribal Art. Apprenticeship in prehistoric and tribal art: research, editing, international relations, museums, and exhibitions planning, evaluation and definition of rock art and of art objects. Minimum stay: 3 months; stage 6 months.

Dates: Year round. **Cost:** Contact sponsor. **Contact:** Prof. Emmanuel Anati, Centro Camuno di Studi Preistorici (CCSP), 25044 Capo di Ponte, BS, Italy; 011-390-364-42091, fax 011-390-364-42572; ccsp@globalnet.it, [www.globalnet.it/ccsp/ccsp.htm].

France

Internships in Francophone Europe. IFE is an academic internship program—accredited at a number of schools—that places student interns in mid to high levels of French public life including government, politics, the press, social institutions, NGOs, etc. For motivated students, proficient in French, who are interested in immersion in the working life of a French institution and in today's France. The program includes intensive preparatory course work in French history, sociology, politics, language training, and the completion of a research project related to the internship. Open to undergraduates and recent graduates.

Dates: Fall semester (Aug-Dec), spring semester (Jan-May). **Cost:** $5,950 (tuition only); tuition plus housing (approx.) $7,660. Need-based scholarships available, especially for post BA's. **Contact:** Timothy Carlson, Internships in Francophone Europe, 26, rue Cmdt. Mouchotte J108, 75014 Paris, France; 011- 33-1-43-21-78-07, fax 011-33-1-42-79-94-13; ifeparis@worldnet.fr, [www.ifeparis.org].

Penn-in-Compiegne. For students with some proficiency in French who are interested in international relations, economics, or business. The program, affiliated with The Université de Technologi de Compiegne, also offers a 2-week internship in a French enterprise. Students live with local families.
Dates: May 23-Jul 2; with internship: May 23-Jul 18. **Cost:** Tuition $3,094; room and board, and activities $960 (study only) or $1,280 (full program). **Contact:** Penn Summer Abroad, College of General Studies, Univ. of Pennsylvania, 3440 Market St., Suite 100, Philadelphia, PA 19104-3335; 215-898-5738, fax 215-573-2053.

Germany

Internship Programs. This program is designed for American college seniors or recent graduates in business, hotel management, engineering, or technical fields who want 6-12 months of practical on-the-job training in an international environment. Individuals are placed in paid internships with companies that match their professional interests.
Dates: Programs begin the first day of each month. **Cost:** Application fee: $400. Participants responsible for airfare, housing, and living expenses. **Contact:** Beate Witzler, CDS International, Inc., 871 United Nations Plaza, 15th Fl., New York, NY 10017; 212-497-3500; info@cdsintl.org; [www.cdsintl.org].

Learn German and Discover Berlin. GLS is one of the leading institutions teaching German as a foreign language in Germany. GLS offers various levels of German all year round (age 16 and up), preparation for all language certificates, business German, German for bankers, lawyers. Special feature: internships in German companies.
Dates: Year round. **Cost:** Contact school for details. **Contact:** GLS Sprachenzentrum, Barbara Jaeschke, Managing Director, Kolonnenstrasse 26, 10829 Berlin, Germany; 011-49-30-780-08-90; fax 011-49-30-787-41-92; gls.berlin@t-online.de, [www.gls-berlin.com].

Germany, Switzerland, Austria

First Choice/Ski Bound. First Choice leases and runs 30 hotels and 75 chalets in European ski resorts. Recruits over 850 staff to work in resorts each year. Positions include hotel managers, chefs (all grades), kitchen porters/night porters, bar staff, waiting/cleaning staff and maintenance staff. A job with First Choice provides the opportunity to travel, meet many new friends, improve language skills, and learn to ski while gaining valuable job experience. Training is carried out in house either prior to departure or while in resort. Offers attractive package that includes travel to and from resort, medical insurance, personal belonging insurance, food, accommodations, and either a free or subsidized lift pass (dependent on position).
Dates: Contact organization for details. **Cost:** Contact organization for details. **Contact:** Applications should be made in writing with a resume: First Choice Ski Lakes and Mountains Division, Olivier House, 18 Marine Parade, Brighton BN2 1TL, U.K.; 011-44-1273-677777, fax 011-44-1273-600486.

India

Penn-in-India. For students interested in South Asian studies, performing arts, religion, and traditional medicine, PSA's newest program offers students a survey of both India's rich cultural history and its burgeoning industrial life. The program is located in Pune, a cosmopolitan city of 4,000,000 which is a thriving arts center, a hub of scholarship, and a growing economic presence. Students will live with Indian families in the area and be involved in community projects.
Dates: Jun 17-Jul 30. **Cost:** Tuition $3,072; program cost $1,790. **Contact:** Penn Summer Abroad, College of General Studies, Univ. of Pennsylvania, 3440 Market St., Suite 100, Philadelphia, PA 19104-3335; 215-898-5738, fax 215-573-2053.

Italy

Au Pair: At Home in the World. Euro Au Pair places young people who wish to learn the Italian language and culture in selected Italian families in Florence or its suburbs.
Dates: Year round. **Cost:** LIT180,000 (1999). Includes all personal services. **Contact:** Laura Pini or Lynda Kuhlke, Euro Au Pair, Di Elleal Quadrato S.N.C., Borgo Santa Croce 4, 50122 Florence, Italy; 011-39-055-242181, fax 011-39-055-241722.

Japan

Richmond in Shizuoka, Japan. Last 4 weeks of a semester in Shizuoka, located between Tokyo and Kyoto. Typical placements are with Mitsubishi, Toshiba, Tamiya Toy Factor and local banks. Early part of semester is a program of Japanese language and art history at Prospera Institute, a 2-year professional school where the majority of the students are Japanese. Courses are offered in English and Japanese. AIFS students are housed with carefully selected families for cultural immersion.

Dates: Sep-Dec; Jan-Apr. **Cost:** $10,400 includes orientation, tuition, housing, most meals and roundtrip flight from any of 28 U.S. cities, ongoing cultural activities and excursions. **Contact:** AIFS, 102 Greenwich Ave., Greenwich, CT 06830; 800-727-2437; collegeinfo@aifs.com, [www.aifs.com/java/us/aifsay_s/japan/japan.htm].

Teaching English in Japan. Two-year program to maximize linguistic and cultural integration of participants who work as teachers' assistants. Placements twice yearly in Apr and Aug. Most positions are in junior high schools in urban and rural areas. Bachelor's degree and willingness to learn Japanese required.

Dates: Hiring for positions every Apr and Aug. Applications accepted year round. **Cost:** No application fees. **Contact:** Institute for Education in Japan, Earlham College, 801 National Rd. West, D-202, Richmond, IN 47374; 888-685-2726, fax 765-983-1553; [www.earlham.edu/~aet].

Korea

Penn-in-Seoul. For students interested in East Asia, Korea, international relations and other business disciplines. This program, offered in conjunction with Kyung Hee Univ., includes courses in the area of international relations as well as internships with multinational corporations, government agencies, and think tanks. Field trips exploring Korean history and culture are integral to the program.

Dates: Jun 13-Aug 16. **Cost:** Tuition $3,094; housing $850. **Contact:** Penn Summer Abroad, College of General Studies, Univ. of Pennsylvania, 3440 Market St., Suite 100, Philadelphia, PA 19104-3335; 215-898-5738, fax 215-573-2053.

Latin America

Community Development Internship. This is a credit-bearing internship where volunteers live with a family in rural Mexico and Ecuador, or semi-urban Cuba, while working side by side with community members on grassroots development projects. Project assignments are available in the areas of agriculture, construction, reforestation, animal husbandry, micro-enterprise development, data collection, public health and other fields. Projects are designed, developed and implemented by the beneficiaries themselves. While project opportunities change as new ones come online and others are completed, every effort is made to match interns' interests with their assignment.

Dates: Year round. Two months advance needed for placement in Cuba. Six-week program (3 weeks in Cuba). **Cost:** Six credits: $3,400, no credit: $2,700, 3 credits: $2,900. **Contact:** Nicholas A. Robins, Director, Cuban Studies Institute, Center for Latin American Studies, Tulane Univ., Caroline Richardson Bldg., New Orleans, LA 70118-5698; 504-862-8629 or 504-862-8000 ext. 2601, fax 504-862-8678; nrobins@mailhost.tcs.tulane.edu, [http://cuba.tulane.edu].

Internship Positions. In Costa Rica, Mexico, Guatemala, Ecuador, Argentina, Peru, Dominican Republic. Various positions in the fields of health care, education, tourism, ESL, business, law, marketing, administrative, environmental, and social work. Additional customized options available. Two weeks to 6 months. Inexpensive lodging in homestays or dorms. Some positions provide free room and board.

Dates: Year round. Flexible start dates. **Cost:** $350 placement and application fee. Travel insurance and pre-departure preparation included. Lodging costs depend on location. **Contact:** AmeriSpan Unlimited, P.O. Box 40007, Philadelphia, PA 19106; 800-879-6640, fax 215-751-1100; info@amerispan.com, [www.amerispan.com].

Mexico

El Bosque del Caribe, Cancun. Take a professional Spanish course 25 hours per week and enjoy the Caribbean beaches. Relaxed family-like atmosphere. No more than 6 students per class. Special conversation program. Mexican cooking classes and excursions to the Mayan sites. Housing with Mexican families. College credit available.

Dates: Year round. New classes begin every Monday. Group programs at reduced fees. **Cost:** Enrollment fee $100, $185 per week. One week with a Mexican family $160. **Contact:** Eduardo Sotelo, Director, Calle Piña 1, S.M. 25, 77500 Cancún, Mexico; 011-52-98-84-10-38, fax 011-52-98-84-58-88; bcaribe@mail.cancun-language.com.mx.

CHEAP AIRLINE TICKETS

AN INDEPENDENT TRAVELER'S GUIDE TO CONSOLIDATORS

By Kent St. John

With the cost of airline tickets rising like the stock market, all options for finding low-priced tickets should be considered, including consolidators. A consolidator contracts with an airline for bulk tickets and sells them at a discount to the public. From the first "bucket shops" in London in the early '60s several types of consolidators have evolved, each with its own specialty and function.

The first place to start looking for a consolidator ticket is with a travel agent with whom you have a good working relationship. You may end up paying a bit more than if you booked on your own, but your agent's access to some of the largest consolidators can pay off. (Consolidators are not always necessary; sometimes, during fare wars, cheaper seats can be found through regular ticketing.)

If you are shopping on your own with discount agencies (who provide cheaper tickets by connecting you to a consolidator) or retail consolidators (who sell tickets both to the public at cost and to agencies at a "net fare"), make sure you have all dates and destinations set before calling: Consolidators work on volume and are not trip planners.

A consolidator is generally a good choice when traveling during high season; when demand for tickets is high, the consolidators' negotiated prices are usually lower than current fares. A consolidator may also be a good choice for travel to more offbeat destinations such as Eastern Europe. Many consolidator tickets come from smaller foreign airlines which specialize in marketing to those areas.

Another instance when a consolidator can be very useful is when super saver deadlines on airlines have passed and you are flying on short notice. Consolidators' tickets often have better minimum/maximum stay requirements, allowing more days to complete travel than many super saver fares.

Most horror stories about using consolidator tickets date from the early days of "bucket shops." There are, however, some things about these tickets a traveler should be aware of: Many consolidator tickets are issued on foreign airlines which offer no frequent flyer miles. Another concern may be connections—see how many stops and changes are involved and make sure the savings are worth it. Most consolidator tickets are good only for the airline ticketed; if a delay occurs you will not be switched to another. Refunds usually are only available through the consolidator, not the airline. This may make travel insurance a worthwhile consideration.

The most frequent question that arises with consolidators is how to pay for your ticket. I either pay by credit card or buy my ticket through a travel agent. While not all consolidators accept credit cards, many now will. Those that do usually add 3 percent to 5 percent to the price to cover the extra cost to them. Your ability to stop payment if you receive an incorrect ticket makes the extra fee worth it. The benefit of booking a consolidator ticket with a travel agent one knows is that the agent will correct the mistakes of consolidators. It also gives you someone locally to deal with in case of problems.

Ask to receive your tickets as soon as possible; this will give you time to check them and deal with possible problems. Be wary of tickets tied to a frequent flyer coupon. Call the airline ticketed by the consolidator to make sure your name is in their system; if not, contact the consolidator immediately, then check again. Your reservation must be shown by the carrier's computer system!

Consolidators can be found in several ways. Many advertise in the Sunday travel sections of major newspapers. The Internet also can be a great source to find consolidators. Many now only conduct business that way. The book Fly Cheap by Kelly Monaghan ($17.95 from The Intrepid Traveler, 800-356-9315) lists 200 consolidators and their phone numbers. But the best source of information is always friends who travel. Chances are good that in the never-ending search for low-priced tickets, some have used consolidators.

To get you started, here is a list of retail consolidators I have found reliable:

- DER Travel Service's, Inc. 888-337-7350; [www.dertravel.com/der_air.htm]. For travel to Europe, the Middle East, Africa, Asia, Australia, and Latin America.
- Far Deal Ltd., 800-347-7006. [www.faredeal.com]. For travel worldwide.
- Fly Wise Travel, 800-359-4386. For travel worldwide. Good for last-minute tickets.
- Intl. Travel Exchange, 800-727-7830. For travel to Europe, Africa, and Middle East.
- MT&T, 800-832-2668. For travel to Asia, South Pacific, Australia, and New Zealand.
- Viktor Weyand Travel Service, 800-800-8891; [www.vwts.com]. For travel to East and Central Europe.
- All Destinations, 800-228-1510. For travel to the Caribbean, Central and South America.
- Glavs Travel, 800-336-5727; [www.glavs.com]. For travel to Russia.
- ITS Tours, 800-533-8688. For travel to Eastern Europe and Russia.
- Sundance Travel, 800-235-3253. For travel worldwide, specializes in student travel.

Poland

Penn-in-Warsaw. For students interested in Polish history and culture, as well as international relations, economics, and other business disciplines. Taught in English, this program will acquaint students with the political and economic changes occurring in Poland and provide insight into the conditions for doing business in a changing economy. Short-term internships with Polish or joint-venture institutions will complement class instruction.

Dates: Jun 26-Jul 30. Cost: Tuition $3,072; housing $250. Contact: Penn Summer Abroad, College of General Studies, Univ. of Pennsylvania, 3440 Market St., Suite 100, Philadelphia, PA 19104-3335; 215-898-5738, fax 215-573-2053.

Russia and the NIS

ACTR Business Russian Language and Internship Program. This program combines a curriculum focusing on the language of Russian business communication with a 20-hour per week internship in a U.S. or Russian business, NGO, or government agency. The program emphasizes speaking and reading skills for business communications, commercial document preparation, and reading the Russian business press.

Dates: Summer term, academic year, fall and spring. Cost: Summer $5,000, fall/spring terms $7,250, academic year $12,450. Contact: Karen Aguilera or Graham Hettlinger, ACTR, 1776 Massachusetts Ave., NW, Suite 700, Washington, DC 20036; 202-833-7522, fax 202-833-7523; aguilera@actr.org, hettlinger@actr.org, [www.actr.org].

St. Petersburg Polytechnic Univ. If fluent in Russian or have completed Russian 201, students may take an internship of 3-5 hours a week in a local business; 800-727-2437 ext. 6089 for internship possibilities. Housing may be residence halls or homestays.

Dates: Sep-Dec; Feb-May. Cost: $6,200 includes orientation, tuition, housing, roundtrip flights from any of 28 U.S. cities, ongoing cultural activities and excursions, public transport pass, field trip to Moscow, and the services of an on-site Resident Director. Contact: AIFS, 102 Greenwich Ave., Greenwich, CT 06830; 800-727-2437; collegeinfo@aifs.com, [www.aifs.com/java/us/aifsay_s/russia/russia.htm].

Scandinavia

Training Program. Two- to 6-month positions in engineering, chemistry, computer science, agriculture, business, TEFOL. Most positions are in Finland and Sweden.

Dates: Contact organization for details. Cost: $50 application fee. Contact: Tommi Makila, The American-Scandinavian Foundation, 725 Park Ave., New York, NY 10021; 212-879-9779, fax 212-879-3444; tommi@amscan.org, [www.amscan.org].

Spain

International Program in Toledo. Great location with its historical and artist heritage. Participants with 2 years of Spanish select from a wide variety of Spanish language, Latin American, and European studies courses taught in Spanish. New internship options also available for credit. Summer term requires only 1 year Spanish. Monday-Thursday classes are enhanced by excursions. Housing available in an historic residence or with Spanish families. Univ. of Minnesota accredited.

Dates: Fall and/or spring semester, summer term. Cost: $8,450 (fall or spring), $3,665 (summer). Includes tuition, study abroad and registration fees, room and board, and 1-day excursions. Contact: Global Campus, Study Abroad, Univ. of Minnesota, 102 Nicholson Hall, 216 Pillsbury Dr. SE, Minneapolis, MN 55455-0138; 612-626-9000, fax 612-626-8009; UMabroad@umn.edu, [www.UMabroad.umn.edu].

Seville Internship Option. A 3- or 6-credit internship may be requested by students attending the CC-CS academic program during the Fall or Spring semester. Applicants must have completed 1 advanced college-level Spanish course. Internships are unpaid and not guaranteed. Many potential areas available. An internship application must be requested in addition to the program application.

Dates: Spring: Jan 26-May 21. Fall: Call for details. Cost: Semester $8,175. Includes tuition, double occupancy room and full board, laundry, study visits, orientation, health insurance, enrollment, activity and computer fees including email account. Contact: Dr. Judith Ortiz, Director U.S., Center for Cross-Cultural Study, 446 Main St., Amherst, MA 01002; 800-377-2621, fax 413-256-1968; cccs@crocker.com, [www.cccs.com].

Switzerland

Caux Scholars Program (CSP). The CSP, held in Caux, Switzerland, is an academic program in conflict transformation with an internship component. It is open to college and graduate students from around the world who are interested in learning about the moral and spiritual dimensions of peacemaking and the relationship between individual transformation and change in the world.

Dates: Mid-Jul to mid-Aug every year. **Cost:** $2,000 includes tuition, room and board. **Contact:** Program Director, 1156 15th St., NW, #910, Washington, DC 20005; 202-872-9077, fax 202-872-9137; cauxsp@aol.com, [http://members.aol.com/causxp/web/cspweb.htm].

Taiwan

Overseas Service Corps YMCA (OSCY). Place BAs to PhDs in ESL teaching positions in community-based YMCAs in Taiwan. No Chinese language necessary. Preference given to applicants with teaching experience, either general or ESL, or degree in teaching. This conversational English program provides an opportunity for cultural exchange. Must reside in North America and be a citizen of an English-speaking country. Twenty to 30 openings.

Dates: Call anytime for a brochure and application. Placement end Sep through following Sep, 1-year commitment. **Cost:** $50 application fee. Benefits include: Housing, health insurance, return airfare, paid vacation, bonus, orientation, sponsorship for visa, and monthly stipend. **Contact:** Jann Sterling, Program Assistant, International Group, YMCA of the USA, 101 N. Wacker Dr., Chicago, IL 60606; 800-872-9622 ext. 167, fax 312-977-0884; sterling@ymcausa.org, [www.ymca.net].

United Kingdom and Ireland

AIFS International Internship Program in London. A 1-semester program awarding 12 to 18 credits for an unpaid internship in London. Placements are in international business, finance, marketing, international relations, education, media, museums and galleries, art and design firms, theater and entertainment. Individual attention given to clarify and set goals, support during placement.

Dates: Sep-Dec; Jan-May. **Cost:** $11,000 includes tuition, housing, most meals and one way flight to London from any of 28 U.S. cities. **Contact:** AIFS, 102 Greenwich Ave., Greenwich,

CT 06830; 800-727-2437; collegeinfo@aifs.com, [www.aifs.com/java/us/aifsay_s/ukintem/int.htm].

Archaeological Excavation Techniques. A training excavation at Degrton Street Roman villa (near Faversham, Kent) aimed at those who have little or no archaeological practical experience. Experts give tuition in surveying, "digging," recording stratigraphy, recording and care of finds and the site archive.

Dates: Jul 31-Aug 4, Aug 7-11. **Cost:** $250 per week plus accommodations (camping free). **Contact:** James Black, Int'l. Academic Projects, 6 Fitzroy Sq., London W1P 6DX, England; 011-44-20-7380-0800, fax 011-44-20-7380-0500; jb@archetype.co.uk

Hansard Scholars Programme. An opportunity for students to become involved in the workings of the British government and British politics, accompanied by a comprehensive study of British politics and British public policy. Students are mainly assigned internships with Members of Parliament, but also to political parties, think tanks, and pressure groups.

Prerequisites: 2 or more years of college. Application materials: transcript, 2 letters of recommendation, an essay, and a personal statement.

Dates: Spring: mid-Jan-early Apr; summer: mid-May-late Jul; fall: late-Sep-mid-Dec 18. **Cost:** £4,600 per semester (includes housing and London travel costs). (1999). **Contact:** Melanie Rimmer, Programme Coordinator, The Hansard Society, St. Philips, Building North, Sheffield St., London WC2A 2EX, U.K.; 011-44-171-955-7478, fax 011-44-171-955-7492; hansard@lse.ac.uk.

Internship Program. We personally design internship packages, both in New York and London to suit individual needs and career interests. Internships are available year round in just about any field imaginable.

Dates: Year round. **Cost:** From $995 year round internship to $4,995 London summer internship packages (4 weeks). Includes program, theater, trips, room and partial board. **Contact:** Janet Kollek Evans, Director, American Assn. of Overseas Studies, 51 Drayton Gardens, Suite 4, London SW10 9RX, U.K.; 800-EDU-BRIT, aaos2000@hotmail.com, [www.worldwide.edu/uk/aaos].

London Internships. This program offers a wide range of internship options including business, politics, environment, community, and media. All internships are project based, supervised by

University faculty and carrying University credit. They can be taken alongside other university study. Semester, year, and summer school programs available.

Dates: Fall and spring semester. **Cost:** Approx. $1,760 includes induction, internship, tuition, and credit. **Contact:** Maggie Paddon-Smith, Internship Program Coordinator, Middlesex Univ., Enfield Campus, Queensway, London EN3 4SF, U.K.; 011-44-181-362-5459; m.paddon-smith@mdx.ac.uk.

New House Organic Farm. Working organic farm with a range of animals, vegetables, and tree crops. Opportunities for work experience, accommodations, and pocket money provided. Opportunity for archaeological/historical research. Regular B and B £8-£15 per person.

Dates: Contact organization for details. **Cost:** Contact organization for details. **Contact:** Mary Smail, New House Organic Farm, Kniveton, Ashbourne, Derbyshire DE6 1JL, U.K.; 011-44-1335-342429.

The Nottingham Trent Univ. Internship. Gain a valuable U.K. work experience in vibrant and exciting Nottingham. A flexible program where you tell us what type of internship you would like to undertake and when. Internship can be combined with study. Each student has access to a designated internship coordinator, orientation, ongoing support, and accommodations.

Dates: Full-time internship 6-12 weeks any time of year; combined internship with study semester Sep-Feb or Feb-Jun. **Cost:** Full-time £800; combined £2,200 per semester. Halls of residence £1,124 per semester; homestay £87 per week. **Contact:** Yvonne Wroughton, International Office, The Nottingham Trent Univ., Burton St., Nottingham NG1 4BU, United Kingdom; 011-44-115-848-6194, fax 011-44-115-848-6528; yvonne.wroughton@ntu.ac.uk.

Study in Great Britain. Thirty-one program opportunities in England, Scotland, and Wales. University study and special subject area programs, including internships, for fall, spring, academic year and summer. Program provides a full range of services including predeparture advising, orientation, homestay, and guaranteed housing. Need-based scholarships available.

Dates: Fall, spring, academic year. Summer semester and terms. **Cost:** Varies. Call for current fees. **Contact:** Beaver College Center for Education Abroad, 450 S. Easton Rd., Glenside, PA 19038-3295; 888-BEAVER-9, fax 215-572-2174; cea@beaver.edu, [www.beaver.edu/cea].

Univ. of North London. SUNY Cortland celebrates its 27th consecutive year at UNL. Over 400 courses are offered. Fields of study include education, natural sciences, humanities, communications, social sciences, business, health, theater arts, and others. Direct enrollment with British students. Credits per semester: 12-16. Pre-arranged housing in flats in the Bayswater district. Full- and part-time internships available.

Dates: Spring: end-Jan-mid-May. **Cost:** Estimates: spring 2000: $7,350; academic year: $13,000. Estimates include full-day orientation in the U.S., application fee, apartment rental, meals, commuter ticket on underground, London tour and Thames cruise, insurance, roundtrip airfare from N.Y., transportation from airport to downtown London upon arrival, passport, books and supplies, various cultural activities, administrative fees. SUNY tuition and spending money not included. **Contact:** Dr. Del Janik, Program Coordinator, Office of International Programs, Box 2000, SUNY Cortland, Cortland, NY 13045; 607-753-2209, fax 607-753-5989; studyabroad@cortland.edu, [www.studyabroad.com/suny/cortland].

Univ. of North London. SUNY Cortland celebrates its 27th consecutive year at UNL. Over 400 courses are offered. Fields of study include education, natural sciences, humanities, communications, social sciences, business, health, theater arts, and others. Direct enrollment with British students. Credits per semester: 12-16. Pre-arranged housing in flats in the Bayswater district. Full- and part-time internships available.

Dates: Fall: mid-Sep-mid-Dec:, spring: end-Jan-mid-May. **Cost:** Fall 1999 estimates: $6,650; spring 2000: $7,350; academic year: $13,000. Estimates include full-day orientation in the U.S., application fee, apartment rental, meals, commuter ticket on underground, London tour and Thames cruise, insurance, roundtrip airfare from N.Y., transportation from airport to downtown London upon arrival, passport, books and supplies, various cultural activities, administrative fees. SUNY tuition and spending money not included. **Contact:** Dr. Del Janik, Program Coordinator, Office of International Programs, Box 2000, SUNY Cortland, Cortland, NY 13045; 607-753-2209, fax 607-753-5989; studyabroad@cortland.edu, [www.studyabroad.com/suny/cortland].

United States

Masters of International and Intercultural Management. The School for International Training Masters of International and Intercultural Management offers concentrations in sustainable development, international education, and training and human resource development in 1 academic year program. This degree is designed for individuals wishing to make a career change or enter the field. A practical training component enables "on-the-job" training and an opportunity to work internationally.
Dates: Call for details. **Cost:** Call for details. **Contact:** Admissions, School for International Learning, P.O. Box 676, Kipling Rd., Brattleboro, VT 05302; 800-336-1616, 802-257-7751, fax 802-258-3500; info@sit.edu, [www.sit.edu].

Venezuela

Venusa Institute of Int'l. Studies and Modern Languages. Students enroll at the Venusa Institute of International Studies and Modern Languages in Mérida, located in the heart of the Venezuelan Andes. Fields of study include Spanish language, Latin American history and culture, international business, cross-cultural communications, teaching of English as a second language (TESOL), int'l. agriculture, ecology and botany, anthropology and sociology, and more. Most classes taught in Spanish, with a limited number being offered in English. Homestays. One semester college-level Spanish recommended and overall GPA of 2.5 required. **Global Professional Internship Program** available to students having sufficient preparation in Spanish language.
Dates: Fall: late Aug-mid-Dec; spring: early Jan-end of Apr; summer: 2 sessions, mid-May-late Jun and late Jun-mid-Aug. For the Global Internship program: fall and spring: same as above; summer: late-May-Aug. **Cost:** Fall/spring estimate $6,450 per semester; summer 2000 $3,700. Estimates include SUNY tuition, full day orientation in the U.S., orientation in Venezuela, application fee, room and 2 meals daily with local family, airfare from Miami to Mérida roundtrip, 2 full day field trips, insurance, books and supplies, program administration costs. For the Global Internship program: fall or spring 2000 $5,825; summer 2000 $4,300. **Contact:** Office of International Programs, Box 2000, SUNY Cortland, Cortland, NY 13045; 607-753-2209, fax 607-753-5989; koppl@cortland.edu, [www.studyabroad.com/suny/cortland].

Worldwide

AIPT Exchanges. AIPT is a nonprofit international educational exchange organization that facilitates on-the-job practical training exchanges for students and professionals between the U.S. and other countries in a variety of fields. AIPT is also the U.S. affiliate of the International Association for the Exchange of Students for Technical Experience (IAESTE), which provides international training opportunities for university students in technical fields.
Dates: Year round. **Cost:** A nonrefundable application fee must be submitted with each application. Cooperating organizations in some countries require additional application and/or program fees. Please contact AIPT for details. **Contact:** Jessica Saltzman, Customer Service Representative, Association for International Practical Training, 10400 Little Patuxent Pkwy., Suite 250, Columbia, MD 21044-3510; 410-997-2200, fax 410-992-3924; aipt@aipt.org, [www.aipt.org].

Boston Univ. International Programs. Students enroll in 3 academic courses in conjunction with a professional internship experience. Students choose from internships in advertising and public relations, the arts, business and economics, health and human service, hospitality administration, the media (journalism, film, and television), politics, and prelaw. The internship experience allows students to explore organizations from multi-national corporations to local businesses, from hospitals to community service centers, from major magazine publishers or film production studios to local radio or advertising agencies. Academic credit offered. Prerequisites: good academic standing, 3.0 GPA; language depending on site. Application materials: 2 references, transcript, essays, academic approval, interview for upper-level language programs.
Dates: Fall, spring, and summer (length varies). Application deadline: Mar 15 (fall); Oct 15 (spring); Mar 1 (summer). **Cost:** $4,800-$9,240. Application fee: $40. **Contact:** Boston Univ., International Programs, 232 Bay State Rd., 5th Fl., Boston, MA 02215; 617-353-9888, fax 617-353-5402; abroad@bu.edu, [www.bu.edu/abroad].

CHI World Travel/Study Programs for All Ages. CHI was established in 1980 as a nonprofit organization to encourage people to reach out and explore the world. Call us or visit our website. We have worldwide highschool academic programs, cultural and/or language immersions with homestays; group tours personalized for schools or for the general public. Internships, au pair and teaching positions also available.

Dates: Vary. **Cost:** Vary according to destination and length of program. **Contact:** Cultural Homestay International, 2455 Bennett Valley Rd., #210B, Santa Rosa, CA 95404; 800-395-2726, fax 707-523-3704; chigaylep@msn.com, [www.chinet.org/outbound.html].

Directory of International Internships. The Directory is a comprehensive guide to international internships sponsored by educational institutions, government agencies, and private organizations. The Directory consists of 170 pages which includes subject and location indexes, international internship opportunities, and a bibliography.

Dates: Up-to-date, 4th ed., revised in late 1998. **Cost:** $25 includes s/h. **Contact:** Charles Gliozzo, Michigan State Univ., Rm. 209, International Center, E. Lansing, MI 48824; 517-353-5589, fax 517-353-7254; gliozzo@pilot.msu.edu, [www.isp.msu.edu].

Fine Arts Intern. Unpaid internship at a nonprofit organization that supports alternative artists, fights censorship by providing censored artists with legal counsel and by educating the public on freedom of special issues. Interns participate in fundraising, supporting artists, data entry, general office work. Also places interns with artists and organizations overseas.

Dates: Ongoing, no deadline. **Cost:** None. **Contact:** Institute for Unpopular Culture, Internship Coordinator, 1850 Union St., #1523, San Francisco, CA 94123; 415-986-4382, fax 415-986-4354.

Global Campus-Study Abroad. Select from a growing list of programs in Costa Rica, Ecuador, England, France, India, Kenya, Mexico, Senegal, and Venezuela. Curriculum may include language, culture, area studies, international development, and much more with integrated classroom options. Internships are available for credit at many sites. Open to all students and professionals.

Dates: Academic year, semester, quarter, and summer options. **Cost:** From $2,900-$16,900. Includes tuition, study abroad, and registration fees, room and board, and excursions. **Contact:** The Global Campus, Univ. of Minnesota, 102 Nicholson Hall, 216 Pillsbury Dr. SE, Minneapolis, MN 55455-0138; 612-626-9000, fax 612-626-8009; UMabroad@umn.edu, [www.UMabroad.umn.edu].

Global Service Corps. Service-learning programs in Costa Rica, Kenya, or Thailand. Individualized community service and development projects assignments with grassroots organizations. Project areas: rainforest conservation, sustainable agriculture, HIV/AIDS awareness, clinical health care, women's groups, classroom teaching. Experience the challenges of developing countries from the inside out. Includes orientation, training, excursions, and homestays. Academic credit available.

Dates: Year round. Contact GSC office or check the web site for specific starting dates. **Cost:** $1,695-$1,795 for 2-4 week project trips; $2,520-$2,820 for 10-12 week internships; $250-$495 per month for extensions. Includes extensive pre-departure preparation and in-country expenses (hotel and homestay room and board, orientation, training, project expenses, transportation, excursions). Airfare not included, discount rates available. **Contact:** Global Service Corps., 300 Broadway, #28, San Francisco, CA 94133; 415-788-3666 ext. 128, fax 415-788-7324; gsc@igc.apc.org, [www.globalservicecorps.org].

IES Internships. If you're looking for a study abroad program that's serious about internships for credit—consider IES. IES internships are designed by local IES staff and professionals to complement course work while pursuing personal and career goals. Internship categories include: business, communications, education, fine arts, international relations, science and politics.

Dates: Year, semester, and summer programs. **Cost:** Contact organization for details. **Contact:** Institute for the International Education of Students (IES), 223 W. Ohio St., Chicago, IL 60610; 800-995-2300, fax 312-944-1448; info@iesabroad.org, [www.iesabroad.org].

Internships International. Quality, nonpaying internships in London, Paris, Dublin, Cologne, France, Shanghai, Santiago, Budapest, Melbourne, Bangkok, Hanoi, Ho Chi Minh City, and Glasgow. Internships in all fields, from 8 weeks to 6 months. Open to college graduates and seniors requiring an internship to graduate.

Dates: Based on individual's needs. **Cost:** $700 program fee for all cities except London ($800) and Dublin ($1,000). **Contact:** Judy Tilson, Director, Internships International, 1612 Oberlin Rd., Raleigh, NC 27608; 919-832-1575, fax 919-834-7170; intintl@aol.com, [http://rtpnet.org/~intintl].

Marist International Internships. Internship and study abroad programs in Sydney, Australia; Leeds, England; Dublin, Ireland; Florence, Italy; Madrid, Spain; Quito, Ecuador; and Monterrey, Mexico. Programs combine internships, homestays, and course work at host institutions.

Dates: Fall and spring semesters and full academic year. **Cost:** Average program fee is $10,500. **Contact:** Brian Whalen, Marist College, 290 North Rd., Poughkeepsie, NY 12601; 914-575-3330, fax 914-575-3294; international@marist.edu, [www.marist.edu/international].

MAST Experience Abroad. A chance to learn first-hand under the guidance of innovative and successful farmers, agribusiness operators, and horticulturists around the world. Spend 2 to 12 months training on a farm or agricultural, horticultural, or forestry business in one of 15 countries. Develop lifelong friendships with your host family and colleagues. Gain a personal and professional learning experience that will shape your life. Single men and women between the ages of 18 and 30.

Dates: Jan, Mar, Jun, Sep. Other dates available. **Cost:** $400 program fee. **Contact:** Susan VonBank, MAST International, Univ. of Minnesota, 1954 Buford Ave., #240, St. Paul, MN 55108; 800-346-6278, 612-624-3740; mast@coa1.agoff.umn.edu, [www.mast.agri.umn.edu].

FIFTEEN

TEEN STUDY & TRAVEL
PROGRAMS & RESOURCES

The following listing of teen programs was supplied by the organizers. Contact the program directors to confirm costs, dates, and other details. Please tell them you read about their programs in this book! Programs based in more than one country or region are listed under "Worldwide."

Asia

Youth For Understanding (YFU). YFU, established in 1951, prepares young people, aged 15-18 years, for their responsibilities and opportunities in a changing, interdependent world through homestay exchange programs. YFU offers year, semester, and summer study abroad and scholarship opportunities in Japan, the Philippines, and South Korea.
Dates: Year: Mar-Dec, semester: Mar-Aug and Aug-Dec, summer: 4, 6, 8 weeks (Jun, Jul, Aug). **Cost:** $2,975-$6,575. **Contact:** Program Information Office, Youth For Understanding (YFU) International Exchange, 3501 Newark St., NW, Washington, DC 20016; 800-TEENAGE or 202-966-6800, fax 202-895-1104; pio@yfu.org, [www.youthforunderstanding.org].

Australasia

Youth For Understanding (YFU). YFU, established in 1951, prepares young people, aged 15-18 years, for their responsibilities and opportunities in a changing, interdependent world through homestay exchange programs.

YFU offers year, semester, and summer study abroad and scholarship opportunities in Australia and New Zealand.
Dates: Year: Jan-Dec and Aug-Jun, Semester: Jan-Jul and Jul-Dec, summer: 4, 6, 8 weeks (Jun, Jul, Aug). **Cost:** $3,475-$6,175. **Contact:** Program Information Office, Youth For Understanding (YFU) International Exchange, 3501 Newark St., NW, Washington, DC 20016; 800-TEENAGE or 202-966-6800, fax 202-895-1104; pio@yfu.org, [www.youthforunderstanding.org].

Australia

The Adventure Company. The Adventure Company, Australia specializes in top quality adventure and nature tours for individuals and groups. We run a variety of scheduled trips, all of which involve a strong nature element. Many of the tours take place in World Heritage Listed National Parks. Assist marine scientists with their research, explore the ecology of the ancient rainforest of far North Queensland, study flora and fauna, or examine Aboriginal art sites dating back 40,000 years, with highly experienced specialist guides.

Dates: Call program for information. Join 1- to 12-day trips. Cost: $50-$1,500, including all trips departing from Cairns. Contact: Gary Hill, The Adventure Company, Australia, P.O. Box 5740, Cairns, Queensland 4870, Australia; 011-61-7-4051-4777, fax 011-61-7-4051-4888; adventures@adventures.com.au, [www.adventures.com.au]. In U.S.: 800-388-7333.

Austria

German Courses at the University. German for beginners and advanced students, perfectionist courses, courses for students of the German language and teachers of German in foreign countries (6 levels). Lectures on German and Austrian literature, music, Austria—the country, people, and language. Special courses: translation, commercial German, commercial correspondence, phonetics, conversation, communication. Excursions.

Dates: Three sessions: Jul 2-29, Jul 30-Aug 26, Aug 27-Sep 16. Cost: Course fee (4 weeks): approx. ATS4,500. Accommodations: approx. ATS5,800. Contact: Magister Sigrun Inmann-Trojer, Wiener Internationale Hochschulkurse, Ebendorferstrasse 10/4, A-1010 Vienna, Austria; fax 011-43-1-405-12-5410, [www.univie.ac.at/WIHOR].

Belize

Reef and Rainforest Ecology. Study and enjoy the Belize barrier reef from above and below the Caribbean. Explore the jungle at Monkey River and Jaguar Reserve and assist with the iguana raising project. Climb Maya ruins and swim in limestone caves. Includes beachfront air conditioned room, meals, and adventure.

Dates: Weekly Jul-Nov. Monday arrivals, 7 nights. Cost: $850 per person plus air (min. 6, max. 24) not counting group leader. Contact: Nautical Inn Adventure Resort; 800-688-0377, fax 011-501-623594; nautical@btl.net, [www.nauticalinnbelize.com].

Canada

Canadian Adventure Camp. Beautiful island camp offering 4 main programs for boys and girls 6-16. Daily choice of over 30 exciting activities. L.I.T. program for 17-18 year olds. Color brochure and video available.

Dates: Jun-Sep. Cost: $1,500 includes transportation to camp from Toronto, water transportation to island, tuck shop deposit, t-shirt, all taxes. Contact: Canadian Adventure Camp, F.B. (Skip) Connett, Director, 15

Idleswift Dr., Thornhill, ON, L4J 1K9, Canada; 905-886-1406, fax 905-889-8983; cacamp@hotmail.com.

Summer Camp. Wilvaken is a bilingual summer camp situated in the eastern townships of Quebec. We have children from many parts of the world coming to enjoy our traditional camp setting as well as learning or improving their second language (English/French).

Dates: Two-, 4-, 6-, 8-week from Jun-Aug. Cost: CAN$1,010 for 2 weeks, CAN$3,775 for 8 weeks (1999). Contact: Camp Wilvaken (Sep 1-Jun 15), Maya and Dave Willis, P.O. Box 141, Hudson Heights, QC, J0P 1J0, Canada; 450-458-5051, fax 450-458-2581; wilvaken@wilvaken.com, [www.wilvaken.com]. Summer address: 241 ch. Willis, Magog, QC, J1X 3W2, Canada; 819-843-5353, fax 819-843-3024.

Central Europe

Youth For Understanding (YFU). YFU, established in 1951, prepares young people, aged 15-18 years, for their responsibilities and opportunities in a changing, interdependent world through homestay exchange programs. YFU offers year, semester, and summer study abroad and scholarship opportunities in Czech/Slovak Republics, Estonia, Hungary, Latvia, Poland, Russia, and Ukraine.

Dates: Year: Aug-Jun, semester: Aug-Jan, summer: 4, 6, 8 weeks (Jun, Jul, Aug). Cost: $2,775-$4,975. Contact: Program Information Office, Youth For Understanding (YFU) International Exchange, 3501 Newark St., NW, Washington, DC 20016; 800-TEENAGE or 202-966-6800, fax 202-895-1104; pio@yfu.org, [www.youthforunderstanding.org].

Costa Rica

Enjoy Learning Spanish Faster. Techniques developed from our ongoing research enable students to learn more, faster, in a comfortable environment. Classes of 2-5 students plus group learning activities; conversations with middle-class homestay families (1 student per family). Homestays are within walking distance of school in small town near the capital, San Jose.

Dates: Year round. Classes begin every Monday at all levels. Cost: $345 per week for 28 hours of classes and group activities plus Costa Rican dance and cooking classes. Includes tuition, 3 meals per day, 7 days per week, homestay, laundry, all materials, and airport transportation. $25 one-time registration fee. Contact: Susan Shores, Registrar, Latin American Language Center, 7485 Rush River Dr., Suite 710-123, Sacramento, CA 95831; 916-447-0938, fax 916-428-9542; lalc@madre.com.

Ecuador

Academia Latinoamericana. Proud to be the friendliest Spanish school you have ever known. Family owned and operated. The program offers language study at 9 levels, for complete beginners through advanced. Experienced staff, native Ecuadorians. Carefully selected host families within walking distance of school. Exclusive "SierrAzul Cloud Forest and Galapagos" extension program, volunteer program. U.S. college credit available.
  Dates: Year round. **Cost:** $230 per week. Includes 20 hours of lessons, 7 days with host family, 2 meals per day, transfer, services at the school, and teaching material. **Contact:** Suzanne S. Bell, Admissions Director, USA/International, 640 East 3990 South, Suite E, Salt Lake City, UT, 84107; 801-268-4608, fax 801-265-9156; academia@juno.com, delco@spanish.com.ec.

Europe

AIFS, Pre-College Summer Study Abroad Program. For 35 years, the American Institute For Foreign Study (AIFS) has been a leader in the field of international education. Each year AIFS organizes cultural exchange programs throughout the world for more than 50,000 students. Programs are offered on college campuses throughout Europe to students who have completed their junior or senior year of high school. All students are issued transcripts from the host institution.
  Dates: Jun-Aug, varying by location. **Cost:** $3,000-$6,000 includes tuition, meals, and airfare (cost varies by location). **Contact:** stacy-miller@acis.com.

Anglo Adventure Tours. Adventure Holidays, taking in the finest of England, Ireland, Scotland, Wales, France, and Greece. From 1-week sailing to 4-week tours that include hiking, climbing, scuba diving, canoeing, and mountaineering. With time out to visit London, Paris, Dublin, and Edinburgh, what more could you want?
  Dates: Jun, Jul, Aug, Oct 2000. **Cost:** $450 to $5,000. **Contact:** Matt Walster, Anglo Adventure Tours, 60 Cromwell St., Nottingham NG7 4GJ, U.K.; 011-44-115-942-7471, fax 011-44-7070-712801; [www.anglo-adventure.co.uk].

The Biking Expedition. The ultimate in road touring and mountain biking programs for students ages 11-18. Trips for all ability levels, 2-8 weeks.
  Dates: Jul and Aug. **Cost:** $1,700 and up. **Contact:** The Biking Expedition, P.O. Box 547, Henniker, NH 03242; 800-245-4649, fax 603-428-3414; info@bikingx.com, [www.bikingx.com].

Youth For Understanding (YFU). YFU, established in 1951, prepares young people, aged 15-18 years, for their responsibilities and opportunities in a changing, interdependent world through homestay exchange programs. YFU offers year, semester, and summer study abroad and scholarship opportunities in Belgium, France, Germany, Greece, Ireland, Italy, Netherlands, Spain, and Switzerland.
  Dates: Year: Aug-Jun and Jan-Dec, semester: Aug-Jan and Jan-Jul, summer: 4, 6, 8 weeks (Jun, Jul, Aug). **Cost:** $2,975-$6,175. **Contact:** Program Information Office, Youth For Understanding (YFU) International Exchange, 3501 Newark St., NW, Washington, DC 20016; 800-TEENAGE or 202-966-6800, fax 202-895-1104; pio@yfu.org, [www.youthforunderstanding.org].

France

Academic Year Program. For students 16-18 years of age, full academic program follows the French national curriculum, including French as a foreign language courses and some courses in English. Residential, full board accommodations. Family at the weekends, tutoring, support. Also summer courses open to all.
  Dates: Sep-Jun. **Cost:** $10,480 (1999). **Contact:** Ph. Minereau, Saint-Denis European School, BP 146, 37600 Loches, France; 011-33-267-94-0450; euroschool@saint-denis.net.

Educational Programs for Juniors. French courses with host families or in residential accommodations. Cultural, sports and social programs in the afternoon. Summer camps offer sports activities and French lessons. Participate in a high school or internship experience in a French company. Tours and short-stays; educational and tourism visits for groups.
  Dates: Linguistic stays for individuals: Jun, Jul, Aug. Groups: all year round. **Cost:** From FF5,200 (2 weeks). Includes full board, accommodations, French courses (30 hours) activities and excursions (fees included).

Contact: C.E.I./Club des 4 Vents, José Luis Ponti, BP 5, 75660 Paris, Cedex 14, France; 011-33-1-45-65-95-21, fax 011-33-1-45-65-95-30; france@cei4vents.com, [www.cei4vents.com].

Encore! Summer Theatre Program. Encore! draws participants from around the world. Living in intensive 4-week program, they study all facets of theatre arts and write and perform original work. Located in the south of France, participants have a better chance to explore that area and attend the International Theatre Festival in Avignon.
Dates: Jun 30-Jul 28. Cost: Contact organization for details. Contact: Susan Burke, Learning Theatre, 5912 Alexa Rd., Charlotte, NC 28777.

Germany

Learn German and Discover Berlin. GLS is one of the leading institutions teaching German as a foreign language in Germany. GLS offers various levels of German all year round (age 16 and up), preparation for all language certificates, business German, German for bankers, lawyers. Special feature: internships in German companies.
Dates: Year round. Cost: Contact school for details. Contact: GLS Sprachenzentrum, Barbara Jaeschke, Managing Director, Kolonnenstrasse 26, 10829 Berlin, Germany; 011-49-30-780-08-90; fax 011-49-30-787-41-92; gls.berlin@t-online.de, [www.gls-berlin.com].

Greece

Greek Summer. A 5-week work and travel program for high school students from America and Europe. Participants live with families in a village in northern Greece while they complete a service project. Includes travel all across Greece to most major sites, the islands, and a climb to the peak of Mt. Olympus. A once-in-a-lifetime adventure.
Dates: Late Jun-Jul. Cost: $2,600 plus a $500 tax deductible donation (1999). Airfare not included. Contact: Nicholas Apostal, Program Coordinator, American Farm School, 1133 Broadway, New York, NY 10023; 212-463-8434, fax 212-463-8208; nyoffice@amerfarm.org, [www.afs.edu.gr].

Latin America

Youth for Understanding (YFU). YFU, established in 1951, prepares young people, aged 15-18 years, for their responsibilities and opportunities in a changing, interdependent world through homestay exchange programs. YFU offers year, semester, and summer study abroad and scholarship opportunities in Argentina, Brazil, Chile, Ecuador, Mexico, Uruguay, and Venezuela.
Dates: Year: Aug-Jun and Jan-Dec, semester: Aug-Jan, Jan-Jul, summer: 4, 6, 8 weeks (Jun, Jul, Aug). Cost: $2,975-$5,775. Contact: Program Information Office, Youth For Understanding (YFU) International Exchange, 3501 Newark St., NW, Washington, DC 20016; 800-TEENAGE or 202-966-6800, fax 202-895-1104; pio@yfu.org, [www.youthforunderstanding.org].

Mexico

Bi-Cultural Programs IMAC. Spanish in Guadalajara is more than a classroom. Group sizes of 1 to 5. Guadalajara offers the conveniences of a modern city. We are a few hours drive to Puerto Vallarta. Homestays with only 1 student per family. Hotel discounts available. Free Internet and email access. Excursions and extracurricular activities.
Dates: Year round. Group classes start every Monday. Individual tutoring may begin any day. Christmas vacation Dec 18-Jan 1, 2000; Easter vacation Apr 17-30, 2000. Cost: Contact organizations for details. Contact: Leticia Orozco, Instituto Mèxico Americano de Cultura, Donata Guerra 180, Guadalajara, Jalisco, 44100 Mèxico; 011-52-3-613-1080, fax 011-52-3-613-4621; spanish-imac@imac-ac.edu.mx, [www.spanish-school.com.mx].

Intensive Spanish (Cuernavaca). The Cemanahuac Educational Community offers intensive Spanish language study taught by native speakers. Special classes on history, literature, art, and anthropology of Mexico and Latin America, with field study excursions led by Cemanahuac anthropologists. Group programs with special fees. College credit available for juniors and seniors. Family homestay highly recommended.
Dates: Classes begin each Monday, year round. Advanced placement (AP) classes available. Cost: Registration, tuition, room and board with Mexican family for 2 weeks: $776. Contact: Vivian B. Harvey, Educational Programs Coordinator, Cemanahuac Educational Community, Apartado 5-21, Cuernavaca, Morelos, Mexico; 011-52-7-3186407, fax 011-52-7-312-5418; 74052-2570@compuserve.com, [www.cemanahuac.com].

Language and Culture in Guanajuato. Improve your Spanish in the most beautiful colonial city in Mexico. We teach one-on-one or in small groups for up to 8 hours daily. Spanish,

By Rick Steves

Travelers in Europe have a choice between using a railpass or buying point-to-point tickets at European train stations as they travel. To help you decide whether to buy a pass or tickets, first come up with a rough itinerary, then use the map at right to add up the cost of your journey in point-to-point second-class fares (for first class, add 50 percent). Compare the cost of tickets with the price of the railpass that best fits your trip. If the costs are close, it makes sense to buy the pass—unless you enjoy standing in lines at ticket windows.

Here's a brief rundown of the types of railpasses available: Eurailpasses cover train travel in 17 West European countries (except Britain). The cheaper Europasses are more focused, covering France, Germany, Switzerland, Italy, and Spain. Country passes, which focus on a single country, are offered by virtually every nation in Europe; this is often your best bet if you're limiting your trip to one country.

While the major railpasses are first class only (if you're age 26 or over), travelers of any age save 33 percent over first class prices by purchasing second class point-to-point tickets.

Class Differences. Wrestling with the difference between first and second class? Obviously, the cars of any train go at precisely the same speed and arrive at the same time. First class cars offer three seats across (whether in a compartment or open-style seating) and second class cars offer four seats across. First class is pricier, comfortable, and isolating. Second class is cheaper and crowded, offering more possibilities for meeting people. Most Europeans travel second class.

If you're buying a Eurail or Europass, the choice is made for you. If you're 26 or over, you have to buy a first class pass. (Those under age 26 have the choice of buying either a second or a first class pass.) People with first class passes may travel in second class compartments, although the conductor may give you a puzzled look. Most country passes are available in second class versions for travelers of any age.

Youth Passes. If you're under 26, you'll get discounts on most point-to-point tickets and railpasses. To be eligible for a discounted second class railpass, you must be under 26 (according to your passport) the day you validate the pass in Europe. Children aged four to 11 generally get passes for half the cost of the adult first class pass; those under four travel free.

Railpasses. Most passes are offered in flexipass and consecutive-day versions. The major exception is the Europass, which comes only in a flexipass version.

The flexipass, designed for travelers who like to linger at destinations, offers a specified number of travel days within a longer period of time (e.g., any 10 days within two months). Sprinkle these days throughout your trip, and take as many trips as you like on a travel day. (A travel day runs from midnight to midnight; as a bonus, an overnight journey that starts after 7 p.m. on the preceding night is included.)

The consecutive-day pass, ideal for whirlwind travelers, offers unlimited travel for a solid block of days (e.g., an eight-day pass covers your travel for eight days in a row).

Sample Costs. The most popular passes are Eurail and Europasses. Eurailpasses, which cover 17 European countries (except Britain), range in cost from a 10-day flexipass for $654 to a three-month consecutive-day pass for $1,558 (15-day flexi: $862; 15 consecutive days: $554; 21 consecutive days: $718; one consecutive month: $890; two consecutive months: $1,260). Europasses—which cover France, Germany, Italy, Spain, and Switzerland—range in cost from a five-day flexipass for $348 to a 15-day flexipass for $728 (six-day: $368; eight-day: $448; 10-day: $528). You can add adjacent countries at an additional cost. Groups of two or more companions who plan to travel together will save 15 percent per person by buying a Eurail or Euro Saverpass.

My free Rail Guide lists the costs of all the passes, including country passes. Find it online at [www.ricksteves.com] or call us at 425-771-8303.

Tips on Buying Passes

Both consecutive day and flexi railpasses offer a varying number of travel days. Once you've planned a route for your trip, your next step in choosing a railpass should be to figure out how many travel days you'll need to cover everything.

You can stretch a flexipass by paying out of pocket for short trips and using your valuable railpass days only for long hauls. To determine if a particular trip is a good use of a travel day, first divide the cost of your pass by the number of travel days. For example, a 15-day Europass for $728 costs about $50 per travel day. If a particular trip costs a lot less than $50, pay out of pocket.

A shorter consecutive day pass can cover a longer trip. For example, you can take a one-month trip with a 21-day Eurailpass ($172 cheaper than a one-month pass) by starting and/or ending your trip in a city where you'd like to stay for several days or more. For example, on a Paris-Rome trip, spend a few days in Paris, validate your pass upon departure, and arrive in Rome as your pass expires. Or you can stretch your railpass by starting and/or ending your trip in a country not covered by your pass. For example, a Eurailpass does not cover Britain. On a London-Vienna trip, start with a couple of days in London, pay for the train trip from the border of France to Paris (to save your railpass), sightsee in Paris for several days, and validate your consecutive day pass when you leave Paris.

One overall pass is cheaper than several country passes. To cover a multiple-country trip, it's usually cheaper to buy one Eurailpass or Europass than to buy several country passes.

Validating Your Pass

You must get your pass validated at a European train station before you use it. Eurail and Europasses must be validated within three months of the issue date (usually the day you bought it) and all others within six months of the issue date. For example, if May 24 is stamped on your Eurailpass as the issue date, you must validate—or start—the pass by August 23. Never write anything on your pass before it's been validated.

To validate your railpass, present your pass and passport at a ticket window to a railway official who will write in the first and last dates of your travel period. If you have a Saverpass, all group members must be present when the pass is validated.

You may validate your country pass before arriving in that country or en route. Let's say you're in Amsterdam with a French railpass, you're heading to Paris, and you want the French portion of your route to be covered by your French railpass. At the Amsterdam train station, buy a ticket to the French border. Validate your French pass either at the Amsterdam station for free or on the train for a small cost ($5 to $12 in local currency).

Making Reservations

A railpass doesn't cover train reservations, required on Europe's high-speed trains (and any train marked with an "R" in the schedule). For most trains, reservations are not necessary and not worth the trouble and expense unless you're traveling during a busy holiday period.

Reservations, which cost from $3 to $10, can be made as long as two months up to a few hours in advance. You can reserve in Europe at train stations or travel agencies or, if you prefer to pay more, in the U.S. through the company who issued your pass (RailEurope at 800-438-7245; DER at 800-549-3737).

Train Tips

Learn to use the 24-hour clock used in European train timetables. After 12 noon, the Europeans keep going—1300, 1400, and so on. To convert to the 12-hour clock, subtract 12 and add p.m. (1600 is 4 p.m.).

European train schedules are available through the Forsyth Travel Library (Thomas Cook Timetable, 800-FORSYTH, $33 postpaid), free with your railpass, free at most European train stations, cheap at some newsstands (in Italy, ask for the orario ferroviario, $5), and online at [http://bahn.hafas.de/] and [http://mercurio.iet.unipi.it].

Confirm your plans in writing with the train station's information desk (for example, write "Torino → à Milano 8:50-10:40; Milano → à Verona 13:05-14:27)." Written communication shrinks the language barrier.

Ask from which station your train will leave. Many cities have more than one train station. Paris has six, Brussels has three, and even Switzerland's little Interlaken has two.

Never assume the whole train is going where you are. Each car is labeled separately because cars are often added and dropped along the journey. Be sure that the city on your car's nameplate is your destination. The nameplate lists the final stop and some (but not all) of the stops in between.

Clip your luggage to the overhead rack to foil thieves.

For safety and comfort on overnight trains, get a couchette—a berth in a sleeping compartment monitored by an attendant. Reserve a couchette at least a day or two in advance from a local travel agency, any train station, or, depending on availability, from the conductor on the train. For about $20, you'll get a pillow, sheet, blanket, a berth in a compartment with three to five other people, and a decent night's sleep.

Mexican history, cooking, literature, business, folk dancing, and politics. Students of all ages and many nationalities. Homestays with families, field trips, movies, hikes, theater, dance performances.

Dates: Year round. New classes begin every Monday. Semester programs begin in Jan and Aug. **Cost:** $925. Includes 4 weeks of classes and homestay with 3 meals daily. **Contact:** Director Jorge Barroso, Instituto Falcon, Mora 158, Guanajuato, Gto. 36000 Mexico; 011-52-473-1-0745; infalcon@redes.int.com.mx, [http://institutofalcon.com].

Spanish Language Institute. A program designed to provide students with ideal learning environment which is conducive to thinking, writing and speaking naturally in Spanish within the context or real-life situations. Discover the Mexican culture with a university group, organization, professionals, travelers and special program of individualized needs for executives.

Dates: Year round. Classes begin every Monday. **Cost:** $150 per week. **Contact:** María Ramos, Academic Spanish Language Institute, Bajada de la Pradera #208, Colonia Pradera, Cuernavaca, Morelos 62191, Mexico; jessram@mor1.telmex.net.mx, [http://Cuernavaca.infosel.com.mx/sli/sli-page.htm].

Scandinavia

Youth For Understanding (YFU). YFU, established in 1951, prepares young people, aged 15-18 years, for their responsibilities and opportunities in a changing, interdependent world through homestay exchange programs. YFU offers year, semester, and summer study abroad and scholarship opportunities in Denmark, Finland, Norway, and Sweden.

Dates: Year: Aug-Jun, Jan-Dec, semester: Aug-Jan, Jan-Jul, summer: 4, 6, 8 weeks (Jun, Jul, Aug). **Cost:** $2,875-$5,775. **Contact:** Program Information Office, Youth For Understanding (YFU) International Exchange, 3501 Newark St., NW, Washington, DC 20016; 800-TEENAGE or 202-966-6800, fax 202-895-1104; pio@yfu.org, [www.youthforunderstanding.org].

South Africa

Youth For Understanding (YFU). YFU, established in 1951, prepares young people, ages 15-18 years, for their responsibilities and opportunities in a changing, interdependent

world through homestay exchange programs. YFU offers year study abroad and scholarship opportunities in South Africa.

Dates: Year: Jul-Jun. **Cost:** $5,975. **Contact:** Program Information Office, Youth For Understanding (YFU) International Exchange, 3501 Newark St., NW, Washington, DC 20016; 800-TEENAGE or 202-966-6800, fax 202-895-1104; pio@yfu.org, [www.youthforunderstanding.org].

Spain

Sociedad Hispano Mundial. The quality of our programs is guaranteed by OCR and the Univ. of Alcala (Spain). Year round intensive Spanish courses, specialized courses (business Spanish, literature, politics, history, art, civilization, DELE exams), and one-to-one. All levels and ages. Communicative approach. Highly qualified and motivated native teachers. Extensive extracurricular social and cultural program. Great location and facilities.

Dates: Begin any Monday. **Cost:** Varies by program and length of stay. **Contact:** Jose Ruiz Cantero, Director, Sociedad Hispano Mundial, Palacio de Congresos, Paseo del Violón s/n, Granada 18006, Spain; 011-34-958-24-68-92, fax 011-34-958-24-68-93; shm@moebius.es, [http://tuspain.com/shm/shm.htm].

Switzerland

International Finishing and Language School for Girls. French and English obligatory basic program. Optional courses: cookery, etiquette, dressmaking, design/painting, ceramics, photography, history of art, computer. Bachelor of Science in business administration, German, Italian, Spanish. Television studies, graphic design, sports. Summer holiday courses.

Dates: Sept, Jan, Apr, Jul, Aug. **Cost:** $9,000 per term includes full board, lodging. French and English. **Contact:** Mr. F. Sidler, Surval Mont-Fleuri, Route de Glion 56, 1820 Montreux, Switzerland; 011-41-21-966-16-16, fax 011-41-21-963-70-13; surval@surval.ch.

Turkey

International Teenage Workcamp. Teenage camp consists of 10 Turkish and 10 international teenage participants. Group leader is an experienced person. We meet the participants at the airport. Work: Painting buildings and gardening. Accommodations are in the dormitory. Language is English.

Dates: Last 2 weeks in July every year. **Cost:** Inscription fee £35. **Contact:** Gençtur Travel Agency, Mr. Zafer Yilmaz, Istiklal Cad. Zambak Sok. 15/5, 80080 Istanbul, Turkey; 011-90-212-249-25-15, fax 011-90-212-249-25-54; workcamps@genctur.com.tr, [www.genctur.com].

United Kingdom and Ireland

Anglia Summer Schools. Residential 1 week theater performance holidays for 12- to 19-year olds; beautiful school campus only 45 minutes from London. Immersed in every aspect of theater—acting, singing, dancing, and more, whatever your ability we will develop your enthusiasm in creating a show.

Dates: Aug. **Cost:** £295 (inclusive of a theater trip). **Contact:** Jeremy Lucas, Anglia Summer Schools, 15 Inglis Rd., Colchester, Essex CO3 3HU, England; 011-44-1206-540111, fax 011-44-1206-766944; anglia.summer.schools@inglis-house.demon.co.uk.

Burklyn Youth Ballet. BYB travels to Edinburgh to perform for 2 weeks at the Edinburgh Festival Fringe. Dancers are at an advanced level and must audition for acceptance. A 4-week workshop and rehearsal period is in Vermont at Burklyn Ballet Theatre.

Dates: VT: Jul-Aug, Scotland: Aug. **Cost:** VT $2,700, Scotland $2,600 (1999). **Contact:** Angela Whitehill, Burklyn Ballet Theatre, Inc., P.O. Box 907, Island Heights, NJ 08732; burkly@aol.com.

Worldwide

AAVE Teen Adventures. Since 1976 we have offered summer teen adventure travel in Hawaii, Alaska, Europe, Colorado, etc., 3-6 week programs with small groups. Includes backpacking, white water, rock climbing, kayaking, sailing, biking, French and Spanish language.

Dates: Eighteen-40 days, Jun 26-Aug 20. **Cost:** $2,000-$4,000. **Contact:** AAVE Teen Adventures, 2245 Stonecrop Way, Golden, CO 80401; 800-222-3595, fax 303-526-0885; adventur76@aol.com, [www.aave.com].

AIFS Foundation—AYA. For over 30 years, the American Institute For Foreign Study (AIFS) has been a leader in the field of international education. We offer academic year and semester homestay programs in Spain, Germany, France, and Holland to high school students 15-19 years old, with an overall GPA of at least a C, who have studied 2 years of a foreign language. Summer programs to Chile, Brazil, France, Spain, and Austria. Winter program to Germany.

Dates: Varies by program. **Cost:** Academic year: from $4,995-$7,795; summer: from $2,675-$5,395; winter: $2,999. Includes roundtrip airfare to and from NY, orientation (for some programs), insurance, homestay/accommodations, and school enrollment. **Contact:** Andrea Baskinger, AIFS Foundation-AYA, Greenwich Office Park, 51 Weaver St., Greenwich, CT 06851; 800-322-4678 ext. 6078; [www.academicyear.org].

American Int'l. Youth Student Exchange Program (AIYSEP). Nonprofit AIYSEP offers high school foreign exchange program for students in Europe, Australia, New Zealand, America, and many other countries. Area counselors are located in Europe, U.S., Australia, New Zealand, South America, Peru, Canada, and Japan. AIYSEP believes a greater international understanding is achieved among people and countries through cultural homestay programs.

Dates: Year, semester, and summer programs. **Cost:** Year $3,995-$6,000, semester $3,495-$4,200, summer $1,900-$3,500. **Contact:** American International Youth Student Exchange, 200 Round Hill Rd., Tiburon, CA 94920; 800-347-7575 or 415-435-4049, 415-499-7669, fax 415-499-5651; AIYSEP@aol.com, [www.aiysep.org].

American International Youth Student Exchange Program, 200 Round Hill Rd., Tiburon, CA 94920; 415-499-7669, 415-435-4049, fax 415-499-5651; AIYSEP@aol.com. Nonprofit AIYSEP offers high school foreign exchange program for students in Europe, Australia, New Zealand, South America, Peru, Canada, Japan. AIYSEP believes a greater international understanding is achieved among people and countries through cultural and homestay programs.

Broadreach Summer Adventures. International scuba, sailing, marine biology, and wilderness programs for teenagers ages 13-19. Locations include the Caribbean, Australia, the Red Sea, Costa Rica, Honduras, Fiji, the Solomon Islands, Ecuador, and the Galapagos islands. Activities include whitewater rafting, sea kayaking, waterskiing, rainforest trekking, community service, and leadership training. No experience required.

Dates: Programs of 17-31 days in Jun, Jul, and Aug. Most trips are 3 weeks long. **Cost:** $2,900-$4,900. Airfare not included. **Contact:** Carlton Goldthwaite, Broadreach, P.O. Box 27076, Raleigh, NC 27611; 888-833-1907, 919-833-1907, fax 919-833-2129; info@gobroadreach.com, [www.gobroadreach.com].

CHI World Travel/Study Programs for All Ages. CHI was established in 1980 as a nonprofit organization to encourage people to reach out and explore the world. Call us or visit our website. We have worldwide highschool academic programs, cultural and/or language immersions with homestays; group tours personalized for schools or for the general public. Internships, au pair and teaching positions also available.

Dates: Vary. **Cost:** Vary according to destination and length of program. **Contact:** Cultural Homestay International, 2455 Bennett Valley Rd., #210B, Santa Rosa, CA 95404; 800-395-2726, fax 707-523-3704; chigaylep@msn.com, [www.chinet.org/outbound.html].

ERDT/SHARE! Exchange Program. ERDT/SHARE! Provides American students, ages 16 to 18, opportunities for summer, semester, or academic year homestays/study abroad. Language proficiency, academic standing, maturity are criteria for selection. Students live with host families and, depending on program selected, attend local school or language school. ERDT/SHARE! also provides opportunities for American families to host international exchange students.

Dates: Vary with type of program selected and academic year dates. Students and host family applications are accepted year round. **Cost:** $1,500-$7,000 (depending on program), excluding transportation and personal expenses. **Contact:** Roger Riske, President, 475 Washington Blvd., Suite 220, Marina del Rey, CA 90292; 800-321-3738, 310-821-9977, fax 310-821-9282; info@erdtshare.org, [www.erdtshare.org].

The Experiment in International Living. Challenging and exciting 3- to 5-week international cross-cultural summer programs for high school students. Choose from over 30 programs in Africa, Asia, the Americas, Europe, and Oceania. All programs include homestays and choice of language study, community service, ecological adventure, and travel.

Dates: Jun 29-Aug 5. **Cost:** $1,800-$4,900. Financial aid available. **Contact:** Spencer Moser, EIL, Kipling Rd., P.O. Box 676, Brattleboro, VT 05302-0676; 800-345-2929, fax 802-258-3428; eil@worldlearning.org, [www.usexperiment.org].

High School Abroad. CCI's High School Abroad program focuses on the importance of complete linguistic and cultural immersion. Students live with host families for 3, 5, or 10 months while attending high school in 1 of 7 countries including Spain, France, Germany, Australia, or Ireland.

Dates: Approx. Aug-May or Aug-Jan or Jan-May. **Cost:** Approx. $4,000 for 5 months, approx. $5,000 for 10 months. Varies. **Contact:** Outbound Department, Center for Cultural Interchange, 17 N. 2nd Ave., St. Charles, IL 60174; 888-ABROAD1, fax 630-377-2307; karen@cci-exchange.com, [www.cci-exchange.com].

Interlocken Adventure Travel. Small group adventures for high school age students in North America, Europe, Latin America, Africa, Asia, and the Caribbean. Programs focus on performing arts, wilderness, cycling, leadership development, and community service.

Dates: Jul and Aug, 3-6 weeks. **Cost:** $2,400-$4,300. Scholarship available. **Contact:** Interlocken Center for Experiential Learning, RR2, Box 165, Hillsboro, NH 03244; 603-478-3166; mail@interlocken.org, [www.interlocken.org].

Musiker Tours. Student travel and adventure programs throughout the U.S., Canada, and Europe. Camping, hotel, and college dorm stays available. Activities include: biking, hiking, visits to national parks and monuments, whitewater rafting, and visits to movie studios and theme parks, to name a few. An action-packed summer for 3-6 weeks for students ages 12-17, in compatible coed groupings.

Dates: Jun-Aug (variable dates). **Cost:** $3,599-$6,699. **Contact:** Musiker Tours, 1326 Old Northern Blvd., Roslyn, NY 11576; 888-878-6637 or 516-621-0718 in NY, fax 516-625-3438; [www.summerfun.com].

Pax Abroad. Offers opportunities for high school, homestay programs in Ecuador, France, Germany, and Spain. Some custom academic programs available. Summer adventures to Australia, Brazil, China, and Ecuador.

Dates: Semester or full year. Summer. **Cost:** Varies. **Contact:** Pax Abroad, Pax-Program of Academic Exchange, 71 Arch St., Greenwich, CT 06830; 800-555-6211, fax 203-629-0486; academicexchange@pax.org, [www.pax.org].

School Year Abroad. College-preparatory education in China, France, and Spain. Nine-month homestay and intensive language training combined with full academic credit, college counseling and standardized testing. Up to 6 classes are taught exclusively in Mandarin, French, and Spanish by native instructors, yet English and math are also offered. Financial aid is available.

Dates: Aug/Sep to May 31 (academic year). **Cost:** $24,000 for 1999-2000. Includes tuition, room and board, travel, activities fund, and health insurance. **Contact:** Woodruff W. Halsey II, Executive Director, School Year Abroad, Phillips Academy, Andover, MA 01810; 978-725-6828, fax 978-725-6833; mail@sya.org, [www.sya.org].

Spanish Programs Abroad for Teens. For teens traveling alone, with family, or school group. Various supervision levels available. Homestay or dorm. Cultural activities. Summer camp options. Spain, the Caribbean, Mexico, Central and South America. Beaches, mountains, small towns, large cities. One week to 6 months. **Dates:** Programs start every week or month. **Cost:** Depends on location. Prices begin at $175 per week and include classes, homestay, travel insurance, most meals, some cultural activities. **Contact:** AmericaSpan Unlimited, P.O. Box 40007, Philadelphia, PA 19106; 800-879-6640, fax 215-751-1100; info@amerispan.com, [www.amerispan.com].

Summer Discovery Pre-College Programs. Summer Discovery Pre-College Enrichment Programs at UCLA, Univ. of Michigan, Univ. of Vermont, Georgetown Univ., and Cambridge Univ., England. Helping to prepare students from high school to college and beyond. Students learn to balance their academic, social, and recreational activities for 3-6 weeks during the summer. Appropriate for students completing grades 9-12. Courses offered: college-credit, enrichment courses, SAT preparation, driver education, ESL/TOEFL, community service, etc. Trips, sports, and excursions offered daily. **Dates:** Jun-Aug (variable dates). **Cost:** $2,900-$5,400. **Contact:** Summer Discovery, 1326 Old Northern Blvd., Roslyn, NY 11576; 888-878-6637 or 516-621-0718 in NY, fax 516-625-3438; [www.summerfun.com].

Supercamp. Supercamp, held on prominent college campuses worldwide, is a fun 8-10 day residential program that balances an academic environment with everyday life skills. A learning experience, for grades 4 through college, which raises grades, self-confidence, and motivation. Call for free brochure and video. **Dates:** Jun, Jul, Aug. **Cost:** $1,495-$1,995 (1999). **Contact:** Learning Forum, 1725 South Coast Hwy., Oceanside, CA 92054; 800-285-3276, fax 760-722-3507; info@supercamp.com, [www.supercamp.com].

Traveling Seminars Abroad, Inc. This program is for young people who are concerned about poverty and malnutrition in Africa and Asia, and want to do something about it. We work with Habitat for Humanity projects building homes and also assist programs that are helping people provide more food and income for themselves. **Dates:** Thailand Dec 14-Jan 10; Ghana 6 weeks summer 2000; Ethiopia 6 weeks summer 2000. **Cost:** $2,450-$2,600. Scholarship aid available. **Contact:** Rich Hiler, Traveling Seminars Abroad, 1037 Society Hill, Cherry Hill, NJ 08003-2419.

Visions. VISIONS community service summer programs for teenagers combine community service, outdoor adventure and exploration, intercultural activities at sites in Peru, Alaska, Montana, South Carolina Sea Islands, and 5 Caribbean islands. Co-ed groups of 24 students and 6 staff live in cross-cultural host communities for up to 4 weeks. **Dates:** Late Jun-late Jul, first weeks of Aug; 4-week or 3-week sessions. **Cost:** $2,400-$3,500 depending on program site and length. **Contact:** Joanne Pinaire, Visions, P.O. Box 220, Newport, PA 17074; 717-567-7313, 800-813-9283, fax 717-567-7853; visions@pa.net, [www.visions-adventure.org].

Youth International. An experiential education program focusing on international travel and intercultural exchange, adventure, community service, and homestays. Teams of 12, aged 18-25, travel together for 1 semester to Southeast Asia and India/Nepal, or East Africa and the Middle East. Assist refugees, hike the Himalayas, live with and help an African tribe, scuba dive, and much more. **Dates:** Sep 7-Dec 18, 1999 (15 weeks); Jan 24-May 30 (18 weeks) and early Sep-mid-Dec (15 weeks), 2000. **Cost:** 1999: $6,500 (Asia), $7,000 (Africa/Middle East). 2000: $6,500 (Asia, 15 weeks), $7,500 (18 weeks); $7,000 (Africa/Middle East, 15 weeks), $8,000 (18 weeks). **Contact:** Brad Gillings, Youth International, 1121 Downing St., #2, Denver, CO 80218; 303-839-5877, fax 303-839-5887; youth.international@bigfoot.com, [www.youthinternational.org].

Teen Study and Travel Organizations

Alliance for International Educational and Cultural Exchange, 1776 Massachusetts Ave., Suite 620, Washington, DC 20036; 202-293-6141, fax 202-293-6144; infoalliance-exchange.org, [www.alliance-exchange.org]. Publishes the *International Exchange Locator: A Guide to U.S. Organizations, Federal Agencies,* *and Congressional Committees Active in International Exchange.* Annual. $11.95 plus $4 s/h. Lists high school and college exchange organizations and others involved in international exchange at all levels.

Council on International Educational Exchange (Council), Council-Pubs Dept., 205 E. 42nd St., New York, NY 10017-5706; 888-COUNCIL, fax 212-822-2699; info@ciee.org, [www.ciee.org]. Publishers of materials on work, study, and travel abroad, especially for students; also administers the Council Work Abroad Program and Council Workcamps.

Council on Standards for International Education Travel (CSIET), 212 S Henry St., Alexandria, VA 22314; 703-739-9050, fax 703-739-9035; exchanges@aol.co, [www.csiet.org]. CSIET is a nonprofit organization committed to quality international educational travel and exchange. It establishes standards for organizations operating international educational travel and exchange programs at the high school level and monitors compliance with those standards by annually reviewing those programs that submit themselves for evaluation. It also disseminates information on international educational travel organizations. *Advisory List of International Educational Travel & Exchange Programs,* published annually ($15 postpaid, $20 overseas), lists programs for high school students which adhere to CSIET's standards and provides valuable information for prospective exchange students, host families, and schools.

EF Foundation for Foreign Study (known internationally as EF High School Year), 1 Education St., Cambridge, MA 02141; 617-619-1400, fax 617-619-1001; [www.ef.com]. Nonprofit organization dedicated to encouraging cultural awareness and mutual respect between nations through cultural exchange. Over 40,000 students from 25 countries since 1979.

Institute of International Education (IIE). IIE Books, Institute of International Education, P.O. Box 371, Annapolis Junction, MD 20701-0371; 800-445-0443, fax 301-206-9789; info@iie.org, [www.iie.org]. Free catalog. Publisher of authoritative directories for study abroad and financial aid and distributor of Central Bureau (U.K.) publications on working abroad.

Intercultural Press, P.O. Box 700, Yarmouth, ME 04096; 800-370-2665, or 207-846-5168, fax 207-846-5181; books@interculturalpress.com, [www.interculturalpress.com]. Publishes numerous books on international living, travel,

study, and cross-cultural experiences. Titles include: *Host Family Survival Kit: A Guide for American Host Families, Survival Kit for Overseas Living, Exchange Student Survival Kit.*

International Student Travel Confederation, Herengracht 479, 1017 BS Amsterdam, the Netherlands, 011-31-20-421-28-00, fax 011-31-20-421-28-10; [www.istc.org]. The International Student Travel Confederation is a nonprofit confederation of student travel organizations around the world whose focus is to develop, promote and facilitate travel among young people and students. ISTC members provide student flights, other forms of transportation, student and youth cards, travel insurance, work exchange programs and lots more.

International Youth Exchange Staff (USIA), 301 4th St., SW, Room 568, Washington, DC 20547; 202-619-6299. The International Youth Exchange Staff of USIA offers activities initiated under the President's International Youth Exchange Initiative and works closely with other organizations involved in international educational exchange activities.

Mobility International USA (MIUSA). Available from MIUSA, P.O. Box 10767, Eugene, OR 97440; 541-343-1284, fax 541-343-6812; miusa@igc, [www.miusa.org]. A national, nonprofit organization dedicated to expanding equal opportunities for people with disabilities in international exchange, leadership development, disability rights training, and community service. The National Clearinghouse on Disability and Exchange (NCDE), a joint venture by MIUSA and United States Information Agency, strives to increase the participation of people with disabilities in the full range of international exchange opportunities by providing free information and referrals to individuals, disability organizations and exchange.

NAFSA: Association of International Educators. Essential publications for advisers and administrators in international educational exchange. For membership information, contact NAFSA: Association of International Educators, 1307 New York Avenue, NW, 8th Fl., Washington, DC 20005-4701; 202-737-3699, fax 202-737-3657; inbox@nafsa.org, [www.nafsa.org].

U.S. Information Agency (USIA), Exchange Visitor Program Services, 301 4th St., Room 734, SW, Washington, DC 20547; 202-401-9810. The USIA evaluates not-for-profit organizations to determine whether they meet criteria for Teenage Visitor Programs. It designates sponsors to issue Form IAP-66 for securing J-1 visas to enter the U.S.

Youth Programs Division, USIA, 301 4th St., SW, Rm. 568, Washington, DC 20547; 202-619-6299. A federal grants program in support of secondary school exchanges involving the New Independent States of the former Soviet Union and Germany. The staff works closely with private organizations involved in international educational exchange activities.

LIVING ABROAD

Are you excitedly looking forward to leaving home for greener and more exotic pastures? Or are you feeling trepidation over the prospect of moving to a new place? Most of us fall somewhere in between, excited about the adventure, but a bit apprehensive about the challenge.

Gina Doggett, Living Abroad Editor

SIXTEEN

LIVING ABROAD
THE BEST RESOURCES

As more Americans choose to work, live, and retire overseas, the resources and support organizations for expatriates have become better and better. A selection of the best resources follows to help you make your own transitions abroad.

Americans Abroad Organizations

American Citizens Abroad (ACA), 5 bis, rue Liotard, CH-1202, Geneva, Switzerland; Tel./fax 011-41-22-3400233 or 3400448; acage@aca.ch. In the U.S. fax 703-527-3269. A nonprofit association dedicated to serving and defending the interests of individual U.S. citizens worldwide.

Association of American Residents Overseas, BP 127, 92154 Suresnes Cedex, France. 011-33-1-42040938; fax 011-33-1-42020912; aaroparis@aol.com; [http://members.aol.com/aaroparis/aarohome.htm]. An organization founded in 1974 to fight for legislation affecting the interests of U.S. citizens overseas. Offers 2 group insurance plans, a quarterly newsletter, seminars. At same address: **Association of American Wives of Europeans.**

Democrats Abroad, 7900 Rebecca Dr., Alexandria, VA 22307; 703-768-3174. A political organization with affiliates around the world dedicated to getting out the vote for the Democratic party and promoting the party's causes.

Federation of American Women's Clubs Overseas. Ruetistrasse 30, 8906 Bonstettem, Switzerland; [www.fawco.org].

Republicans Abroad, 310 1st St., SE, Washington, DC 20003; 202-608-1423; [www.republicansabroad.org]. An organization with affiliates around the world dedicated to getting out the vote for the Republican party and promoting the party's causes.

World Federation of Americans Abroad, 49 rue Pierre Charron, 75008 Paris, France.

Best Web Sites

American Citizens Abroad, [www.aca.ch]. Web site for a nonprofit association dedicated to serving and defending the interests of U.S. citizens worldwide. Features their newsletter.

The Embassy Page Newsletter, [www.embassyweb.com], is a quarterly featuring articles on diplomatic news and events and other helpful topics to anyone involved in international trade and diplomacy. Each issue includes an in-depth profile of an outstanding web site, and other useful information.

Escape Artist, [www.escapeartist.com]. Expatriate resources include an impressive collection of web links, immigration resources, general expat resources, expatriate taxpayer resources, printed resources, worldwide moving companies, overseas jobs, Index of World Wide

Embassy and Consulate Resources, and a bulletin board. Almost a glut of information here.

Expat Exchange, [www.expatexchange.com]. Extensive site with chat rooms, tax assistance, links, information on international careers, plus the Overseas Digest, a free newsletter.

Global Nomad Virtual Village (GNVV), [www.gnvv.org]. Nonprofit organization dedicated to the support and understanding of Third Culture Kids (TCKs), providing a virtual village for anyone who shares the common bond of growing up in a foreign land). A repository for global nomad-related information and resources.

Living Abroad, [www.livingabroad.com]. Web site of Living Abroad Publishing, publishers of Living Abroad magazine. The "Relocation Services" section provides resource information on relocating to about 40 different countries.

Living in Indonesia, [www.expat.or.id]. Loads of information covering all aspects of relocating to Indonesia, from preparing before you go to where to buy groceries in Jakarta.

On the Move, The Military Brat Newsletter, [www.military-brats.com/onthemove.html]. An e-zine written by military brats for military brats. News, stories, articles and photographs, announcements and classifieds. There is also a Military-Brats Registry run by Marc Curtis at newsletter@military-brats.com, [www.military-brats.com].

Overseas Digest, [http://overseasdigest.com]. Sister site to Expat Exchange, monthly newsletter with travel warnings, financial news, and other features of interest to expats. Chat room, bookstore offering many titles on working abroad.

Spouses Underground Newsletter, [www.thesun.org]. Lively online quarterly aimed at overseas spouses.

Taxi's Newspaper List, [http://users.deltanet.com/users/taxicat/e_papers.html]. What better way to keep yourself informed than by reading the local newspaper? This site has links to the web sites of hundreds of newspapers, inside the U.S. and abroad.

U.S. Department of State, [www.state.gov]. U.S. foreign policy, outreach, hot issues; links to online embassies and other missions, business, living, travel nitty-gritty, employment.

Country Specific Publications

Background Notes Series. Published irregularly throughout year. Available from Superintendent of Documents, U.S. Government Printing Office, Washington, DC 20402; fax 202-512-2250; [www.access.gpo.gov/su_docs]. $2.50 per copy, $19 per year in U.S. More than 150 pamphlets by country about the people, land, history, foreign relations, etc., from Afghanistan to Zambia.

Bloom Where You're Planted (in Paris). $25 includes s/h from The American Church in Paris, 65 quai d'Orsay, 75007 Paris; 011-33-1-40620500. The definitive resource for expats coming to France. Updated each year to accompany an annual orientation program in October, it's full of practical information on living in Paris.

Choose Costa Rica by John Howells (Gateway Books). Wintering and retirement in Costa Rica (includes Guatemala).

Choose Mexico by J. Howells and D. Merwin (Gateway Books). Guide for those interested in retiring or living in Mexico.

Craighead Publications Inc., P.O. Box 1253, Darien, CT 06820; [www.craighead.com]. Country intelligence reports on 84 countries including living information, financial and economic data, cultural information, and business practices. *Craighead's International Business, Travel, and Relocation Guide to 81 Countries* (Gale Research Inc.) is available in large libraries.

Culturgrams. David M. Kennedy Center for International Studies. Brigham Young Univ., Publication Services, P.O. Box 24538, Provo, UT 84602; 800-528-6279. Four-page summaries of the basic features of over 160 cultures worldwide.

Finding a Job in New Zealand by Joy Muirhead. £9.99 plus £4 s/h from How to Books (above). Unique information source on finding work in New Zealand.

Getting a Job in Australia by Nick Vandome. £9.90 plus £4 s/h from How to Books (above). Discover well paid work and a great new lifestyle.

Gulf Publishing Company, P.O. Box 2608, Houston, TX 75252; 713- 529-4301, fax 713-525-5647 has supplements to the book *Managing Cultural Differences* for Asia, Europe and Latin America—at $20 each.

How to Live and Work in Germany by Christine Hall (2nd ed.). £9.99 plus £4 s/h from How To Books (above).

How to Live and Work in Greece by Peter Reynolds. £9.99 plus £4 s/h from How To Books (above).

How to Live and Work in Italy by Amanda Hinton. (2nd ed.) £9.99 plus £4 s/h from How To Books (above).

How to Live and Work in the Gulf by Hamid Atiyyah. Country-by-country expert advice. £9.99 plus £4 s/h from How To Books (above).

Intercultural Press, P.O. Box 700, Yarmouth, ME 04096; 800-370-2665; [www.bookmasters.com/interclt.htm]. Publishes numerous books on international living, travel, study, and cross-cultural experiences. Titles include: *Survival Kit for Overseas Living, Moving Your Family Overseas, The Art of Crossing Cultures, The Art of Coming Home, Cross-Cultural Adaptability Inventory, Cross-Cultural Dialogues, Transcultural Odysseys, Women's Guide to Living Overseas, The Third Culture Kid Experience: Growing Up Among Worlds.* Country specific publications include: *Understanding the Arabs; Understanding Cultural Differences: Germans, French, and Americans; Encountering the Chinese, From Nyet to Da: Understanding the Russians.*

Live and Work in... (Vacation Work). A series of guides written with the British reader in mind covering Europe and beyond. Most of the practical information also applies to North Americans considering work or retirement abroad. Titles to date: France, Spain and Portugal, Italy, Germany, Belgium, the Netherlands, and Luxembourg, U.S. and Canada, Scandinavia, Australia, and New Zealand. Available for $16.95 plus $3.50 s/h from Seven Hills Book Distributors, 49 Central Ave., Cincinatti, OH 45202; 800-545-2005.

Live Well in Honduras by Frank Ford (John Muir Publications). Relocation, retirement, employment, and information.

Living and Making Money in Mexico. 1998. $15 plus $2.50 s/h from Living Overseas Books, P.O. Box 2062, Vashon Island, WA 98070; 800-341-2510, ext. 27; sales@livingoverseas.com, [www.livingoverseas.com]. Created by overseas entrepreneur Robert Lawrence Johston III who also publishes *Living and Making Money in Costa Rica* and *The Official Guide to Living and Making Money in Central America.*

Living and Working Abroad. Over 40 books offering country-specific information on immigration formalities, education, housing, health, law, economy, and leisure. All books are regularly updated and some are into their 6th edition. Prices from $15 to $20, excluding shipping charges. How to Books Ltd., Customer Services, Plymbridge Distributors Ltd., Estover Rd., Plymouth PL6 7PZ; 011-44-1-752-202301, fax 011-44-1-752-202331; [www.howtobooks.co.uk].

Living and Working in Australia by Laura Veltman (6th ed. 1998). £12.99 plus £4 s/h from How To Books (above).

Living and Working in Britain by Christine Hall. £9.99 plus £4 s/h from How To Books (above).

Living and Working in Britain by David Hampshire (Survival Books, 1999, $21.95). The most comprehensive source of practical information about everyday life in Britain. Similar titles by same author on France, Spain, Australia, Switzerland; also, *Buying a Home Abroad,* $21, and similar titles for France, Ireland, Italy, Portugal, Spain. Order from Seven Hills Book Distributors, above, 800-545-2005.

Living and Working in China by Christine Hall. £9.99 plus £4 s/h from How To Books (above).

Living and Working in France by Alan Hart. £9.99 plus £4 s/h from How To Books (above).

Living and Working in Hong Kong by Jeremy Gough. £10.99 plus £4 s/h from How To Books (above).

Living and Working in Israel by Ahron Bregman. £10.99 plus £4 s/h from How To Books (above).

Living and Working in New Zealand by Joy Muirhead. £9.99 plus £4 s/h from How To Books (above).

Living and Working in Saudi Arabia by Rosalie Rayburn and Kate Bush. 2nd ed. £12.99 from How To Books (above).

Living and Working in Spain. 2nd. ed. £9.99 plus £4 s/h from How To Books (above).

Living and Working in the Netherlands by Pat Rush. £9.99 plus £4 s/h from How To Books (above).

Living, Studying, and Working in Italy: Everything You Need to Know to Fulfill Your Dream of Living Abroad by Travis Neighbor and Monica Larner. 1998. $14.95. From Henry Holt and Co.; 212-886-9268, fax 212-647-1874;

LIFE IN THE FOREIGN SERVICE
IT'S A GREAT PLACE TO VISIT BUT WHAT'S IT LIKE TO LIVE THERE?

By Kelly Bembry Midura

In our 10 years in the Foreign Service, we have experienced some of the best that life abroad has to offer. Bolivia and El Salvador were good places to live, and Guatemala was truly exceptional. On weekends we drove to remote villages that we never would have seen on any guided tour and bargained in the local markets for textiles, paintings, and crafts. We often ate a *tipica* lunch at some hole-in-the-wall place, then drove home for a hot shower and a carry-out pizza, with a view of erupting volcanoes from our windows.

I spent two years among the people of Guatemala, and I could have spent many more. Sure, there was a crime problem, but we took reasonable precautions. There was an occasional earthquake and blackouts that lasted for months, but, like most Guatemalans, we took to eating at open-air grills and playing cards by candlelight.

To really connect with the local people in a developing country, have a baby. Motherhood is a universally understood experience, and I received fascinating advice. During a full solar eclipse in my last trimester, everyone advised me that I must dress in red, wear a crucifix, and hide under the bed during the eclipse. Otherwise, my baby would certainly be born blind. On local TV a panel of experts, including two astronomers and one obstetrician, vainly attempted to debunk this myth.

After my blonde blue-eyed daughter was born in the local hospital and provided with a Guatemalan birth certificate as a souvenir, we continued our travels. I got the lowdown on breastfeeding and baby care from every woman in the country, or so it seemed. We were constantly surrounded by people wanting to hold my daughter, touch her hair, or even "borrow" her for a minute to show to a friend! I am sure that Rachel thought her name was *qué linda* (how pretty) until we left the country.

The Tour from Hell

On the other hand, there are posts that can only be described as "learning experiences." We spent two long years in Zambia, a country bypassed by most travelers for good reason. We expected to find the vibrant African art and culture I had seen in *National Geographic* magazine. Instead we saw soul-deadening poverty, disease, and cheap mass-produced souvenirs.

The local cuisine was "mealy-meal" (a.k.a. grits, a non-native staple introduced by the former socialist government) and a range of centipedes, grasshoppers, and termites consumed by the protein-starved population. I am all for sampling the native dishes, but I draw the line at bugs.

Any Zambian who stumbled into some small material gain and refused to share it with his extended family risked being poisoned or stoned on account of being a "witch." This had a predictable effect on personal incentive and contributed to the general air of hopelessness. There was no infrastructure or medical care to speak of, and AIDS was rapidly killing off anyone with youth, energy, or talent. My husband attended the funerals of three of his employees during our stay—all AIDS victims.

Most career diplomats have a story like this. Getting to know the people of a country can be a hard lesson when you are powerless to change the unjust circumstances of their lives.

Has all of this been worth it? Oh yes! I am currently living in the Washington D.C. suburbs surrounded by every material convenience known to man, and I can't wait to get back overseas, this time to the Czech Republic. Sometimes, you end up landing that European tour after all!

Foreign Service Careers

Joining the diplomatic corps offers an unbeatable opportunity to learn about foreign cultures. But there are drawbacks. It is occasionally annoying that the U.S. government controls so much of your life. Simple requests can take weeks or even months to process, and the bureaucracy of the State Department and other foreign affairs agencies has a logic all its own.

Another drawback is that professional level jobs for spouses of foreign service officers are rare; most available jobs are clerical and poorly paid. I have taught quilting to Spanish aristocrats and Andean Indians in Bolivia, taken intensive, language classes in downtown Guatemala City, and worked as a part-time editor and writer in El Salvador. However, in the digital age, the possibilities for freelancing and telecommuting are limited only by local telephone service.

For the official line on careers with the United States Department of State, check out their recruitment page at [www.state.gov/www/careers/index.html]. To learn about the Foreign Service exam, the first step to entry into the diplomatic corps, click on "Foreign Service." This section of the site also contains some generic information about the impact of a Foreign Service career on the officer's family.

To get the unofficial lowdown on life in the Foreign Service, check out two web sites created by Foreign Service "trailing" spouses:

Foreign Service Lifelines [www.kreative.net/fslifelines] is sponsored by the American Association of Foreign Service Women and features "Tips from the Trenches" and "Perspectives" on current issues written by experienced Foreign Service spouses. "The Cyberspouse," a column on Internet-based employment opportunities (written by yours truly) is a regular feature of the site. Foreign Service Lifelines also details the services provided by the AAFSW, including the Foreign-Born Spouses Network and the Evacuee Support Network, the very existence of which tell you something about life in the Foreign Service.

The Spouses Underground Network [www.thesun.org] is an "edgier" site, which advertises itself as "definitely *not* endorsed by the U.S. government." It features a small-but-growing collection of "Real Post Reports" on various countries, chat forums on topics relevant to Foreign Service families, and excerpts from its parent publication, the *Spouses Underground Newsletter*. Subscriptions and back issues can be ordered online as well.

academic@hholt.com. Essential new step-by-step guide through all phases of finding work, planning the move, and settling in.

The New Golden Door to Retirement and Living in Costa Rica. 10th ed. By Christopher Howard (Costa Rica Books, Suite 1 SJO 981, P.O. Box 025216, Miami, FL 33102-5216; 800-365-2342, www.costaricabooks.com). A guide to living in a peaceful tropical paradise.

The Newcomer: An Introduction to Life in Belgium. Available free from the Belgian National Tourist Office, 780 3rd Ave., #1501, New York, NY 10017-2024; 212-758-8130, fax 212-355-7675; info@visitbelgium.com; [www.visitbelgium.com]. Valuable information for people who are preparing to move to Belgium.

Cross-Cultural Adjustment

A Career in Your Suitcase: Finding the Portable Career That Works for You by Joanna Parfitt. 1998. £10 plus £2.50 s/h from Summertime Publishing, 55 Easton on the Hill, Stamford, Lincolnshire, England PE9 3LL; Tel./fax 011-44-1780-480304; summertime@lineone.net. Information and innovative ideas based on interviews with spouses who have learned to "tilt" their hats, rather than change or discard them completely. From the same publisher: *Forced to Fly: Your Handbook for an Effective and Happy Life on the Move* by Joanna Parfitt. 1998. £10 plus £2.50 s/h.

The Adventures of Working Abroad by Joyce Sautters Osland. 1995. Author draws from 14 years of living abroad to help current and potential expatriates adjust. $25 from Jossey-Bass, Inc. (a division of Simon & Schuster), 350 Sansome St., 5th Fl., San Francisco, CA 94104; 415-433-1740; [www.josseybass.com].

Aletheia Publications, 46 Bell Hollow Rd., Putnam Valley, NY 10579; 914-526-2873, fax 914-526-2905; alethpub@aol.com, [http://members.aol.com/alethpub]. Publishes a number of useful books on cross-cultural adjustment and living abroad including *The Accidental Diplomat: Dilemmas of a Trailing Spouse, Managing Cross-Cultural Transitions, Military Brats: Legacies of Childhood Inside the Fortress, Strangers at Home, the Absentee American, Welcome Home: Who Are You?*

Consultants for International Living, 200 W. 57th St., Suite 1310, New York, NY 10019; 212-265-6722. Independent consulting firm serving multinational corporations, their employees,

and families at all stages of the international assignment process, from selection through repatriation.

Do's and Taboos Around the World: A Guide to International Behavior by Roger Axtell (John Wiley & Sons, $15.95). Advice for travelers on what to do and not to do in other cultures.

Employee Relocation Council, 1720 N St., NW, Washington, DC 20036; [www.erc.org]. Professional membership organization addressing domestic and international corporate relocation by providing information on policies, trends, tax and legal issues, and professional development and networking. Publishes *Mobility* magazine.

Global Nomad Resources provides programs, services, and publications for and about global nomads (those who have ever lived abroad due to a parent's career choice). Contact: 703-758-7766, fax 703-758-7766; nmccaig@gmu.edu.

Global Nomads International (GNI) assists the internationally mobile family. Publishes *Global Nomad Perspectives,* a journal for this population and the professionals who work with them. GNI's annual conference, titled "The Global Village—A Global Nomad's Home Town," will be held at the Virginia Beach Sheraton October 13-15. Global Nomads International, P.O. Box 9584, Washington, DC 20016-9584; 202-466-2244; gni@igc.org; [www.globalnomads.association.com].

Living Overseas: A Book of Preparations by Ted Ward. 1984. $19.95. Simon & Schuster. A sophisticated and readable study of cultural differences and how to cope with them.

Managing Cultural Differences (4th ed.), Philip R. Harris and Robert T. Moran. $39.95 from Gulf Publishing Company (see above). How to develop the cross-cultural expertise essential for succeeding in a world of rapid economic, political, and cultural changes.

New Relocating Spouse's Guide to Employment: Options and Strategies in the U.S. and Abroad by Frances Bastress. 1993. Addresses the unique career challenges of the men and women who accompany relocating employees. $14.95 plus $5 s/h from Impact Publications, 9104-N Manassas Dr., Manassas Park, VA 20111; 703-361-7300, fax 703-335-9486; [www.impactpublications.com]. (Impact Publications carries the largest number of books on overseas careers.)

Put Your Best Foot Forward by Mary Murray Bosrack (International Education Systems). South America (1997), Europe (1997), Asia (1996), Russia (1995), Mexico/Canada (1995). Basic guides to behavior and communication designed for businesspeople.

Society for Intercultural Education, Training, and Research (SIETAR), 808 17th St. NW, Washington DC 20006; [http://208.215.167.139]. Research and publications on transnational awareness.

Transcultural Study Guide. Volunteers in Asia. 1987. $7.95 plus $1.70 postage from VIA Press, P.O. Box 4543, Stanford, CA 93409; 650-725-1803; [www.volasia.org]. Hundreds of questions that lead a traveler toward an understanding of a new culture.

Travel That Can Change Your Life: How to Create a Transformative Experience by Jeffrey A. Kottler (Jossey-Bass Publishers). $22. Practical tips for life-changing travel.

Health and Safety

Staying Healthy in Asia, Africa, and Latin America by Dirk Schroeder. $11.95 plus $2.16 s/h from VIA Press, P.O. Box 4543, Stanford, CA 94309; 650-725-1803, fax 650-725-1805; [www.volasia.org]. Provides an overview of health problems common to Asia, Africa, and Latin America. Sections on prevention of illness as well as guidelines in case of illness.

Where There Is No Doctor: A Village Health Care Handbook by David Werner. 1992, rev. ed. This simply written, comprehensive health manual is particularly useful for those working or living in a semi-isolated or isolated location. Other Hesperian books include *Where Women Have No Doctor* ($20) and *A Book for Midwives* ($22). $17 plus s/h from the Hesperian Foundation, 1919 Addison St., Suite 304, Berkeley, CA 94704; 510-845-4507, fax 510-845-0539; bookorders@hesperian.org, [www.hesperian.org].

Language Learning

Audio Forum, 96 Broad St., Guilford, CT 06437; 800- 243-1234, 203-453-9794; fax 888-453-4329, 203-453-9774; info@audioforum.com, [www.audioforum.com]. The world's largest selection of self-instructional language courses: 280 courses in 101 languages. Publishes How to Learn a Foreign Language by Graham Fuller (1999, $11.95) and Surf's Up! A Website Workbook for Basic Language Learning, available in French, German, and Spanish.

Audio-Magazines from Champs-Elysées, Inc., 2000 Glen Echo Rd., Suite 205, Nashville, TN 37215-8067; 615-383-8534; usorders@champs-elysees.com, [www.champs-elysees.com]. Lively audio-cassette or CD magazine with transcript and glossary, in Spanish, French, German, and Italian at annual subscriptions ranging from $79 to $167.50.

Center for Applied Linguistics. 4646 40th St., NW, Washington, DC 20016-1859; 800-276-9834; [www.cal.org]. Research, data bases, encouragement—lots of resources for language learning.

How to Master Languages by Roger Jones. £8.99 plus £4 s/h from How to Books (above).

How to Study and Live in Britain by Jane Woolfenden. £8.99 plus £4 s/h from How to Books (above).

Whole World Guide to Language Learning by Terry Marshall, 1990. How to learn a language while abroad. $16.95 plus $3 s/h from Intercultural Press (above).

Living Abroad Publications

Campfollowers: A History of the Military Wife by Betty Alt and Betty Stone. 1991. $13.95 paperback plus $4 s/h from Greenwood Publishing Group, Inc., 88 Post Rd. W., Westport, CT 06881; 203-226-3571; [http://info.greenwood.com]. Comprehensive history of the military wife from the Revolutionary War through the post-Vietnam years, based on memoirs, diaries, letters, and interviews.

Doing Voluntary Work Abroad by Mark Hempshell. £19.99 from How to Books (above). Combine foreign travel with valuable work experience.

Europe the European Way: A Traveler's Guide to Living Affordably in the World's Great Cities by James F. Gollattscheck. Globe Pequot Press. 1996. $13.95.

The Expat Club Newsletter, 12427 Hedges Run Dr., #107, Woodbridge, VA 22192; $32 for 6 issues. Bimonthly newsletter by, for, and about expatriate family members living abroad.

Fact Sheets. Free from Office of Overseas Schools, U.S. Department of State, Washington, DC 20522-2902; [www.state.gov/www.about_state/school]. Fact sheets on overseas elementary and secondary schools assisted by the Department of State.

Getting a Job Abroad by Roger Jones. £12.99 from How to Books (above). The handbook for the international job seeker.

Guide to Living Abroad by Louise M. Guido. Annual. Published in 11 volumes, each containing practical information of interest to expatriates, such as health, buying a house, immigration matters, personal security, and education. The guides also have a section on regional travel. $42 plus s/h from Living Abroad Publishing, 32 Nassau St., Princeton, NJ 08542; 609-924-9302, fax 609-924-7844.

Handbook for Citizens Living Abroad. 1990. $10. Practical information on moving and living abroad in question and answer format. American Citizens Abroad, 1051 North George Mason Dr., Arlington, VA 22205; jacabr@aol.com, acage@aca.ch.

Hidden Immigrants: Legacies of Growing up Abroad by Linda Bell. 1997. Cross Cultural Publications, Cross Roads Books, P.O. Box 506, Notre Dame, IN 46556; fax 219- 273-5973.

The Insiders' Guide to Relocation by Beverly Roman. Order by calling 800-582-2665 or sending a check for $14.95 plus $4 s/h to: Falcon Publishing, P.O. Box 1718, Helena, MT 59624. Whether moving across town or across the globe.

International Living Magazine. $89 per year. St. Catherine's Hall, Catherine St., Waterford, Ireland; 011-353-51-304-556, fax 011-353-51-304-561; 102503.353@compuserve.com. Brief articles about expatriates around the world, jobs overseas, housing, travel, books, investments.

The ISS Directory of Overseas Schools (International Schools Services). American-style elementary and secondary schools overseas.

Let's Move Overseas by Beverly D. Roman. 1999. $8.45 from BR Anchor Publishing, 2044 Montrose Ln., Wilmington, NC 28405; 910-256-9598, fax 910-256-9579; branchor@aol.com, [www.branchor.com]. A book full of activities, safety advice, and positive thoughts for children moving internationally.

Letter from Washington, 7400 Rebecca Dr., Alexandria, VA 22307; 703-768-3174. $35 per year. Monthly newsletter with views of national political situation as seen by independent liberal Democrats.

Notes from a Traveling Childhood: Readings for Internationally Mobile Parents and Children by Karen Curnow McCluskey (ed.). 1994. $5.95 including s/h from the Foreign Service Youth Foundation, P.O. Box 39185, Washington, DC 20016. An anthology of writings by parents, children, educators, researchers, and mental health professionals

about the effects of international mobility on families. From same publisher: *Of Many Lands* by Sara Mansfield Taber. 1997. $10.50 plus $3 s/h. A journal for people brought up in foreign lands and to assist them in putting together their life studies.

Paper Airplanes in the Himalayas: Following the Unfinished Path Home by Paul Seaman (Cross Cultural Publications, Inc.). Moving autobiography of a missionary chld growing up in a boarding school in Pakistan.

Scaling the Dragon by Janice Moulton and George Robinson (Cross Cultural Publications, Inc.). Enlightening experience of a couple living and teaching in China.

Schools Abroad of Interest to Americans (Porter Sargent Publishers). Lists 800 elementary and secondary schools in 130 countries for young Americans.

Spending a Year Abroad by Nick Vandome (3rd ed.) Sets out the numerous options. £9.99 plus £4 s/h from How To Books (above).

Survival Kit for Overseas Living by L. Robert Kohls. 3rd ed., 1996. Best-selling guide to adaptation to living abroad. $11.95 plus $3 s/h from Intercultural Press (above).

Terra Cognita's Live Abroad! Workbook by Terra Cognita. 1997. $15.95 from Terra Cognita, Inc., 300 W. 49 St., Suite 314, New, NY 10019; 888-262-2099, 212-262-4529, fax 212-262-5789; info@terracognita.com, [www.terracognita.com]. For orders only 888-262-2099, order@terra.cognita.com. Spiral-bound workbook for potential and future corporate expatriates with 9 exercises, administrative plans, and excellent check lists. Meant for use with video (same title) but stands on its own.

The Unknown Ambassadors by Phyllis Michaux. 1996. Traces the history of efforts to establish and improve the rights of Americans living abroad, including citizenship rights of children of dual-national couples, Social Security and Medicare benefits for Americans living or traveling overseas, equitable tax treatment and voting rights. $15.95 plus $4 s/h from Aletheia Publications (above).

Worldwide Volunteering for Young People by Youth for Britain. £15.95 from How to Books (above). This directory focuses exclusively on volunteering projects.

Reentry Publications

Cross-Cultural Re-entry: Readings by Clyde Austin. 1986. $14.95 plus s/h from Abilene Christian Univ. Press, Abilene Christian Univ., ACU Station Box 29138, Abilene, TX 79699; 800-444-4228; 914-674-2720, fax 914-674-6471; lemmonst@acupres.acu.edu, [www.acu.edu/campusoffices/acupress]. From the same publisher: *Cross-Cultural Re-entry: Bibliography* by Clyde Austin. 1983. $13.95 plus s/h.

Foreign Service Youth Foundation, P.O. Box 39185, Washington DC 20016. Provides repatriation support services for children returning from overseas posts.

NFATC/Overseas Briefing Center, 4000 Arlington Blvd., Arlington VA 22204; 703-302-7268; [www.kreative.net/fslifelines/obc/htm]. Support services for U.S. government employees and their families anticipating a return or returning from overseas posts. Seminars, workshops, orientation exercises, publications.

Overseas Brats, P.O. Box 29805, San Antonio TX 78229; 210-349-1394; [www.vni.net/~mcl/osb/osbmain/htm]. Centralized registry of international high school graduates designed to facilitate communication among peers.

Overseas Schools Combined Alumni Registry (OSCAR), P.O. Box 7763, Washington, DC 20044. Registry of graduate information for overseas schools.

JIM BAIRD is a community mental health director who travels each year to Central or South America. He can be reached at ghc@ocsonline.com. Photos of his trips can be found at [www.mikebaird.com]. He writes from Dalton, GA.

MARIAN BEHAN HAMMER writes from Camas, WA.

KELLY BEMBRY MIDURA writes from Springfield, VA.

GINA DOGGETT was a Foreign Service brat, spent some years as a closet foreigner in Washington, and is now a journalist in Paris.

SUSAN GRIFFITH is the author of Work Your Way Around the World and Teaching English Abroad: Talking Your Way Around the World, both available from Peterson's Guides, 800-338-3282.

CYNTHIA HARRIMAN is the author of Take Your Kids to Europe and a passionate advocate of family travel. She welcomes readers' input at charriman@masongrant.com.

PETER HODGE, a volunteer for two years in Zimbabwe with Australian Volunteers Abroad, is the author of Volunteer Work Overseas for Australians and New Zealanders.

KATHY HOKE writes about history and business and lives in Columbus, OH. She has traveled solo in seven continents.

MARTINE KLAASSEN is from the Netherlands. After studying for her BA in journalism at Southampton Institute in England she moved to California. She now works as a freelance writer in Vancouver, Canada.

JON KOHL is the coordinator in Honduras for the Ecotourism and Community Development Program of the RARE Center for Tropical Conservation. The program trains bilingual nature guides, conducts ecotourism vision workshops, and plans public use for protected areas. You can learn more about nature guides in Honduras at [www2.planeta.com/mader/planeta/0898/0898hondurare.html].

DEBORAH McLAREN, director of the Rethinking Tourism Project, works with communities designing alternative tourism projects worldwide. Send information about your environmental travel experiences, tips, and recommended educational programs and ecotour operators to: Deborah McLaren, RTP, P.O. Box 581938, Minneapolis, MN 55458; RTProject@aol.com.

WILLIAM NOLTING is Director of International Opportunities, Univ. of Michigan International Center, 603 E. Madison St., Ann Arbor MI 48109-1370; 734-647-2299, fax 734-647-2181; icoverseas@umich.edu, [www.umich.edu/~icenter/overseas]. He welcomes new information about other work abroad programs but regretfully cannot offer individual advice.

HEATHER O'CONNOR is the Study Abroad Adviser at Bentley College in Waltham, MA [bnet.bentley.edu/dept/sa]. She maintains a web site on marketing international programs on the Internet [erebus.bentley.edu/empl/o/hoconnor/mkintro.htm] and welcomes additional suggestions at hoconnor@bentley.edu.

ABIGAIL ROME, a freelance writer and consultant in conservation and ecotourism, lives near Washington, DC. She focuses on strategies for supporting natural areas and community development in Latin America.

KENT ST. JOHN is the owner of Under the Palms Travel Services, Inc. in Scottsdale, AZ, a company that specializes in educational group travel. If you have questions, he can be reached at kents61837@aol.com.

RALPH SHAFFER is a widely published travel writer who lives in San Francisco. Before retirement, he lived abroad for 10 years.

RICK STEVES (425-771-8303 or [www.ricksteves.com]) is the host of the PBS series Travels in Europe and the author of 21 European travel guidebooks, including Europe Through the Back Door, all published by John Muir.

SUSAN SYGALL is the Director of Mobility International USA. MIUSA also serves as the National Clearinghouse on Disability and Exchange (NCDE), a joint venture by MIUSA and United States Information Agency which strives to increase the participation of people with disabilities in the full range of international exchange opportunities by providing free information and referrals to individuals and exchange organizations.

KATHY WIDING is author of Cycling the Netherlands, Belgium & Luxembourg, and is part owner of Wide World Books & Maps in Seattle, WA.

ARLINE K. WILLS is the Seniors Travel Editor for Transitions Abroad. Since her first flight to Cuba in 1958 she has made dozens of trips abroad. She lives in Lynnfield, MA.

STEVE WILSON's writing credits include Soundings, Multihulls, Big World, and regular contributions to Transitions Abroad.

MARINA WOLF received her BA in Russian language and literature and lived in Russia for 14 months. She now lives in Northern California.